Archibald MacLeish ❖

Books by Scott Donaldson

The Suburban Myth

Poet in America: Winfield Townley Scott

*By Force of Will: The Life
and Art of Ernest Hemingway*

*American Literature: Nineteenth
and Early Twentieth Centuries* (with Ann Massa)

Fool for Love, F. Scott Fitzgerald

John Cheever: A Biography

Archibald MacLeish: An American Life

Archibald MacLeish

AN AMERICAN LIFE ❖

Scott Donaldson

In collaboration
with R. H. Winnick

A Peter Davison Book

HOUGHTON MIFFLIN COMPANY

BOSTON · NEW YORK · LONDON

1992

For information about permission to reproduce selections
from this book, write to Permissions, Houghton Mifflin Company,
215 Park Avenue South, New York, New York 10003.

Library of Congress Cataloging-in-Publication Data

Donaldson, Scott.
  Archibald MacLeish : an American life / Scott Donaldson.
    p.   cm.
  "A Peter Davison book."
  Includes bibliographical references and index.
  ISBN 0-395-49326-9
    1. MacLeish, Archibald, 1892–1982 — Biography.   2. Poets,
American — 20th century — Biography.   3. Statesmen — United
States — Biography.   I. Title.
PS3525.A27763   1992
811'.52 — dc20   91-41401
[B]   CIP

Printed in the United States of America

HAD 10 9 8 7 6 5 4 3 2 1

The author is grateful for permission to quote from the following works:
    Excerpts from *A Serious Character,* by Humphrey Carpenter, reprinted by permission of
Houghton Mifflin Company.
    Excerpt from "The Waste Land," in *Collected Poems 1909–1962* by T. S. Eliot, copyright
1936 by Harcourt Brace Jovanovich, Inc. and copyright © 1963, 1964 by T. S. Eliot; reprinted
by permission of the publisher.
    Excerpts from the following works of Archibald MacLeish reprinted by permission of
Houghton Mifflin Company and the Estate of Archibald MacLeish, represented by Richard
McAdoo: *The Happy Marriage and Other Poems; Poems, 1924–1933; The Eleanor Roosevelt
Story; Herakles; Scratch; A Time to Speak; A Time to Act; Poetry and Experience; The Human
Season; Six Plays; Collected Poems, 1917–1982; The Fall of the City; J.B.; A Continuing
Journey; Riders on the Earth; Letters of Archibald MacLeish, 1907–1982.*
    Excerpt from "Open Letter to the Poet Archibald MacLeish Who Has Forsaken His Mas-
sachusetts Farm to Make Propaganda for Freedom," from *Complete Poems of Carl Sandburg,*
copyright 1950 by Carl Sandburg and renewed 1978 by Margaret Sandburg, Helga Sandburg
Crile, and Janet Sandburg; reprinted by permission of Harcourt Brace Jovanovich, Inc.
    Excerpt from "Do Not Go Gentle into That Good Night," by Dylan Thomas, in *Poems
of Dylan Thomas,* copyright 1952 by Dylan Thomas; reprinted by permission of New Directions Publishing Corporation.
    Excerpt from "To Archie, at 75," by Mark Van Doren, reprinted by permission of Dorothy
Van Doren.
    Excerpt from "The Omelet of A. MacLeish," by Edmund Wilson, copyright © 1939 and
renewal copyright © 1966 by Edmund Wilson. First appeared in *The New Yorker,* vol. XIV,
January 14, 1939. A slightly different version of this poem appeared in *Night Thoughts* by
Edmund Wilson. Reprinted by permission of Farrar, Straus & Giroux, Inc.
    Excerpt from "Politics" reprinted with permission of Macmillan Publishing Company from
The Poems of W. B. Yeats: A New Edition, edited by Richard J. Finneran. Copyright 1940 by
Georgie Yeats, renewed 1968 by Bertha Georgie Yeats, Michael Butler Yeats, and Anne Yeats.
    All photographs not otherwise credited are courtesy of A. Bruce MacLeish.

To Janet and Britton

Contents ❖

Preface ❖

ARCHIBALD MACLEISH (1892–1982) was one of the most remarkable Americans of his time. The essence of the man was his multiplicity. Even in this heyday of second and third careers, it is daunting to consider that MacLeish undertook, and mastered, half a dozen: lawyer, journalist, librarian of Congress, assistant secretary of state and spokesman for the republic, teacher, playwright, and above all poet. MacLeish won three Pulitzer Prizes, and is the only American to have been awarded both the National Medal for Literature and the Presidential Medal of Freedom. His life was driven by two powerful and sometimes competing goals: he wanted to write great poetry, and he wanted to advance great causes. The dichotomy was exemplified in MacLeish's two longest friendships — with Ernest Hemingway, arguably the nation's preeminent literary stylist of the twentieth century, and with Dean Acheson, arguably the leading contributor to American foreign policy in the same period.

"From the beginning of my more or less adult life," MacLeish wrote Felix Frankfurter in May 1939, "I have been plagued by the fact that I seem to be able to do more or less well things which don't commonly go together." At Yale, for example, he played on the football team and edited the *Yale Lit*. Whatever he set his mind to, he succeeded at. He graduated Phi Beta Kappa. He led his class at Harvard Law. "Archie didn't know how to do anything poorly," historian John Conway said.

Behind his accomplishments lay the genetic and environmental influence of MacLeish's heritage. His remote and forbidding father, Andrew, was a native Scotsman who fashioned a highly successful career in merchandising. Andrew MacLeish was in his mid-fifties when Archie, the second child of his third marriage, was born. He did not pay much attention to the lad. Like his siblings, Archie was brought up by his mother, Martha Hillard MacLeish, an educator who had been president of Rockford Seminary before her marriage, and a woman of principle whose American roots stretched back to Puritan times. At his mother's knee, the boy learned that it was his duty to make a difference, to serve the public good. If he had followed his inclinations, he might have become a poet only. Instead he rushed to confront life's challenges in order to present another glittering prize to his father's notice and to fulfill the sense of responsibility his mother instilled in him. Among the assets Archie brought to his endeavors were a quick mind, an extraordinary felicity of language, and a forward-looking turn-of-the-century middle-western optimism.

With his characteristic buoyancy, it did not seem right to MacLeish that a man's reach should exceed his grasp. There was plenty of good to be done on this earth, never mind heaven. In his notebooks for 1923, the year in which he gave up the law and sailed to Paris to make himself a poet, he recorded George Santayana's observation that the mainspring of human activity lay in the discrepancy between the ideal and the real. Since the discrepancy could not be obliterated, Santayana felt, the ideal itself was nothing and the process of trying to reach it everything. "This," MacLeish commented, "is to attach supreme importance to the precipitate of action in the nature of man and to make the fulfillment of the individual life infinitely superior to the reform of evil, the conquest of nature, or the salvation of society." MacLeish did not share Santayana's philosophical pessimism, but he believed with all his heart in the life of action he espoused. In fact he was determined to be both a poet and a man of action, and this joint ambition sometimes rubbed against the grain of public opinion.

One problem was that in the United States there was no traditional career path combining literature with the commonweal. There were a few precedents, of course, but among those who practiced letters first and statecraft second, only James Russell Lowell, who was ambassador to Great Britain, comes immediately to mind as succeeding in both fields. Certainly no other well-known American writer rose as high in service to his country as did MacLeish. In other countries such writer-statesmen were far more common. Among them were some of the poets MacLeish most admired: William Butler Yeats, St.-John Perse, and George Seferis.

Sitting on the beach of Bermuda's south shore in 1979, MacLeish came across a passage in book 11 of Robert Fitzgerald's translation of the *Odyssey* — the description of Homer as "a poet, a man who knows the world" — which summed up his objectives as a poet and public man.

He had been everywhere: Europe, Persia, Mexico, Japan, South America. He had fought in one war, prepared the nation for the next, and assisted in making the peace. He numbered among his friends such men as Hemingway, Acheson, Frankfurter, Henry Luce, Franklin Delano Roosevelt, Adlai Stevenson, Mark Van Doren. Who else knew the world as well as he?

From the 1930s on, MacLeish's career led him to make public pronouncements on the principal issues of the time. Invariably, and often stridently, he spoke out on the side of human liberty, and he made enemies into the bargain. From the right, Senator Joseph McCarthy attacked him on nationwide television, and his FBI file ran to over six hundred pages. From the left, literary critics attacked him for selling out to the establishment. In the most honorable way possible, it was true. During 1939–1945, while he was in Washington, MacLeish invested almost all of his energies in public causes — restructuring the Library of Congress, making the case for a war against fascism, directing the flow of information during the conflict, and building a consensus for the United Nations and for UNESCO, all of these tasks assigned to him by President Roosevelt. Often in those years he felt himself to be speaking for the nation, never more so than when he composed the brief and eloquent message to the American people after Roosevelt's death.

Fifty years ago, so renowned a critic as Cleanth Brooks included MacLeish in a triumvirate of poets — Frost, MacLeish, and Auden — whose work in the modern tradition promised to last. Some, at the time, thought him *the* most important American poet alive. That has changed, drastically. Now he is remembered only for a few widely anthologized poems and as the author of *J.B.*, his reworking of the story of Job for the Broadway stage. In the laudable effort to widen and diversify the canon of American literature, the fact is sometimes overlooked that anthologies still tend to have the same number of pages and courses in literature the same number of weeks, so that for each writer admitted to the canon, another is liable to be dismissed. MacLeish is conspicuous among those who have been decanonized, often for the wrong reasons. His ease of movement in the corridors of power has worked against him, as has his position as fortune's darling, spoiled by the accidental good luck of birth and education and connections. The critic William Barrett began his 1947 article on MacLeish with these words: " 'It is a difficult thing to be an American,' said Archibald MacLeish, somewhere around 1929 if I remember rightly, a good while before he had discovered how easy it is to be an Under-Secretary of State." Barrett did not remember rightly, except about the date of "American Letter," the 1929

poem dedicated to Gerald Murphy, in which MacLeish utters his am-
bivalent farewell to Europe. But what the poem says is, "It is a strange
thing to be an American," not a "difficult" one. The change of adjective
conveniently enables the critic to belittle MacLeish's service in the Department of State — though not as undersecretary — as "easy." The
sentence reeks with the odor of sour grapes, as do many of the diatribes
against his work during and after World War II.

Another handicap MacLeish labored under was that he did not at all
fit the conventional image of the poet. Poets in our society are supposed
to be poor, lonely, and alienated. MacLeish was none of these. Even
when he most bitterly fought the forces of repression — and he was
never loath to fight — he did so not as an outsider but from within the
context of the nation's guiding principles. He proved that a poet did not
have to be wild, and that discipline was as efficacious in that career as
in any other. He showed that a poet could participate in the world's
work, and even write about it.

Moreover, in a field notorious for backbiting, MacLeish was generous
to other poets, whether established or in the early stages of their development. More than anyone else, he was responsible for securing the
release of Ezra Pound from confinement in Saint Elizabeths Hospital,
despite the fact that Pound regularly denigrated both him and his poetry.
As instructor of Harvard's English S class for the best and brightest of
its young writers, he was instrumental in launching, and later in advancing, the careers of many talented aftercomers. Nor did rivalrous
feelings prevent him from forming close friendships with poets such as
Carl Sandburg, Mark Van Doren, and Richard Wilbur. It was not that
Archie was untouched by the lust for fame. He yearned for recognition
and enjoyed his share of it during his ninety years. Yet in the long run
he knew that personal fame was fleeting. "What will our reputations
be?" he asks rhetorically in "Poetical Remains," and a few lines later
answers the question:

> We leave behind
> An anthological rubble:
> Mind mingled with mind,
> Odd and even coupled.

With Frost, he was willing to rest content in the hope that some of his
poems might prove "hard to get rid of" and so take their place in the
company — the "rubble" — of what other writers had left behind. Joining that company was what mattered, and the judgment would be long
in coming. Meanwhile, why begrudge anyone else an opportunity to
submit his or her best to the bar?

MacLeish did not lead his life with an eye cocked on posterity, however. He was too busily involved with his own time for that. As he declared in "Sentiments for a Dedication," "I speak to my own time, / To no time after." It is in this sense that his life takes on a significance beyond the scope of his accomplishments, for MacLeish was not only an extraordinary but also a representative man, who repeatedly emerged at history's crisis points. It is supposed to be true that simply showing up is at least half of success. Archie showed up. He was in Paris in the twenties, during the artistic ferment of that decade. He was in New York in the thirties on the front lines of political discontent, a star at Luce's *Fortune* while deploring the greed and incompetence of capitalists in his poetry. He was in Washington in the forties, working long and hard in the battle for the survival and spread of democracy. He was at Harvard in the fifties, defending the academy against the witch-hunting of demagogues. As his daughter, Mimi, observed, much of her father's success could be traced to his knack for turning up in the right place at the right time.

Along the way he was assailed for changing his coloration to suit the climate of the period. "Archibald MacLeish is our poetic weathercock," Hyatt Waggoner wrote of him. "A glance at his work in any decade will tell us which way the wind of thought and feeling and poetic fashion was blowing." He was an Aeolian harp, a friend remarked, sounding enchanting notes but with a melody ever changing. There was much truth in these metaphors. MacLeish's poetry did change tremendously over time, from the early musical lyricism he is best known for to the polemical verse of the thirties to the postwar philosophical considerations on to the moving simplicity of the badly undervalued late poems. Similarly, his political position shifted from the far left to a more conventional liberalism, so that he came under fire both from the communists, who had once courted him as a potential figurehead, and from the communist-hunters, who thought they detected in his associations the telltale signs of disloyalty to, or at least disagreement with, the American way as they conceived of it. Yet Archie's underlying convictions never altered. He held to the end his faith in the individual human being and his insistence that freedom of thought and expression should not be compromised for any purpose.

In a letter to Iris Origo, MacLeish summarized the challenge of all biographers. "We can set down," he wrote, "a record of happenings which seem to have a shape or meaning: expectation, achievement, defeat, death; a drama with a beginning, a middle and an end; a drama often interesting, fascinating, moving; but is that a life or only a *Life*?"

Trying to capture MacLeish's life has proved especially difficult, for several reasons. He pursued so many different activities that an ideal chronicler should understand in depth the law, literary modernism, magazine journalism, librarianship, presidential politics, foreign policy, the theater, and higher education. Furthermore, to write of MacLeish's career, one should possess a solid comprehension of twentieth-century American history, for he reflected the current of history as he ran his course. He came out of a world whose attitudes about what amounted to a good and useful life and how children should be raised, for example, sound overly rigorous and demanding a hundred years later. He grew up with the prejudices of his class, and fought them down with the aid of the counterinfluence exerted by a mother far in advance of her time. A consummate biographer should also have command of the ambience of those places that meant most to MacLeish: not only the public Paris and Washington and New York and Boston but the manor house above Lake Michigan in the Glencoe of his childhood and Uphill Farm in the beloved Conway of his mature years. To do justice to MacLeish, one would have to be as much a polymath as the man himself. Obviously no such creature exists. You do the best you can.

Then, too, MacLeish was a circumspect man, reluctant to discuss the dynamics of his family life, other than to celebrate in general terms his sixty-five-year marriage to Ada Hitchcock, and careful to paper over his occasional love affairs. Some things were not to be spoken of. Two of his friends at Harvard, W. Jackson Bate and John Finley, both characterized him as having an unusually *rounded* personality, hard to get hold of. He was genial "Archie" to almost everyone who knew him, yet revealing of himself to almost no one.

And yet MacLeish left behind a wealth of material. The paper trail is so deep, in fact, that the major decisions in writing this book have had to do with what to keep *in* among the many scraps of evidence that had to be left out. R. H. Winnick, who completed Lawrance Thompson's biography of Robert Frost in 1976 and worked on an authorized MacLeish biography from 1978 into the mid-1980s (when growing professional responsibilities forced him to put it aside), recorded more than a hundred hours of taped interviews with Archie, members of his family, friends, and associates. Several of the people he interviewed are no longer alive. Winnick also located more than a thousand letters, the best of them collected in his 1983 book, *Letters of Archibald MacLeish, 1907–1982*. Independently, Bernard A. Drabeck and Helen E. Ellis of Greenfield Community College interviewed MacLeish over a period of five years, from 1976 to 1981, and published the results in *Archibald MacLeish: Reflections* (1986). In 1987 I contracted with Houghton Mifflin to put these fragments in order and reconstruct a life as best I could. Naturally I continued to conduct interviews and to unearth letters and other writings of MacLeish, but without the Winnick archive to build upon, this book would not have been possible, and his advice has been invaluable during my five-year labor of research and writing.

The single greatest resource, of course, consisted of MacLeish's writing, published and unpublished. The kernel of his emotional life lies embedded in his poems, which is why this biography is both a life story and a selective anthology. Facts any diligent biographer can assemble and present; but the poems give coherence to those facts. And in his unpublished poems, particularly, Archie makes revelations and confessions that as a gentleman of the old school he could not bring himself to speak of publicly. These poems, though unpublished, were preserved in notebooks, as if Archie wanted to be found out in those moments of love and anger and resentment when he was most nakedly himself. The poetry, in short, puts flesh on the skeleton of an otherwise routine *Life*.

SCOTT DONALDSON
Williamsburg, Virginia

Archibald MacLeish ❖

BEGINNINGS

A Foreign Potentate

THE BOY ARCHIE idled the summer day away. Drifting between daydream and sensation, he lay on his back for hours of the morning, staring up into the stillness of the tall oak trees until it seemed that everything — the little white butterflies, the insects in the grass — was drawn into and subsumed by that stillness. The boy did not think; he remembered nothing. He felt at the beginning of things, at the center of the universe. He felt, almost, as if he did not exist. With the afternoon came the hot west wind, parching the lawn, parching the glistening metallic oak leaves, plunging over the clay bluff to Lake Michigan below, dragging its green and purple shadows out to the deep blue of the horizon. The wind came from thousands of miles away, Archie's father had told him; over the prairies, over the grass and the corn and the deserts where the skulls of buffalo shone white by the dry creeks. The boy — he must have been six, and so it was 1898 — watched from the bluff as a high-shouldered congregation of sandpipers huddled to scavenge what washed ashore. He chewed the tender spears of the stiff grass. He climbed out on the tree the Indians had bent low a hundred years before. Then the jays began to riot in anticipation of the thunderstorm, and he went inside.

The great house — his father had named it Craigie Lea, after a Scottish ballad — was a mansion by the standards of Glencoe, but Archie knew nothing of that yet. What he did know was that the couch cover from Persia smelled of strange smoke and that the leather seat of his chair had a bitter smell at prayers and the table knives were silver with smooth handles and that he could easily turn the brass knob of the side door. On the wall was a picture of an empty boat pulled up on the beach of a lake among birch trees. The oars were in the boat, and it seemed to the boy that the people no longer in the boat were far away and sad like the old letters in the drawer of the cedar room desk.

And then it was evening, for the storm had come and gone and his father had come home from the store in Chicago on the 5:15 train and the coachman had picked him up and Archie could hear the carriage with its two bouncing bays coming down the road and — he did not know why — he went out the side door and his father put his head out of the window of the carriage, beamed down at the boy, the second son of his third marriage, and said, "Hello, Brownie," for Archie had his mother's deep brown eyes.

It was not much of a memory, but Archie — Archibald MacLeish, for that is who he was to become — carried it with him all his days. "Brownie," he recalled in his eighties. "I'll never forget being called that." It was the one time, the first and last and only time, that he got from his father a really spontaneous gesture of affection. At that moment, as never else, he felt sure of his father's love.

A native Scotsman, Andrew MacLeish was sixty on that summer evening, and in part it was his age that kept a barrier between father and son. "My father came from a very old country in the north and far away," Archie remembered, "and he belonged to an old strange race, the race older than any other. He did not talk of his country but he sang bits of songs with words he said no one could understand any more. When he spoke to his collies they crawled with bellies on the ground." Andrew was a vigorous sixty-year-old; he was to live, like his son, into his ninetieth year. He was impressive, too: six feet tall, well built, and handsome, with a full but neatly trimmed beard that made kissing him at Christmas — according to one grandchild — like kissing shredded wheat. Such ceremonial displays were infrequent, for the most distinctive thing about Andrew MacLeish was his extraordinary reserve. "Scots don't come shouting at you," as Archie observed, but even among the Scottish, Andrew MacLeish must have been a special case.

When he spoke, it was softly with a pronounced Scottish burr. But he spoke very little, and kept himself and his emotions under severe control. "I fear a man of frugal speech," Emily Dickinson writes, and his children did fear Andrew MacLeish. Archie's older brother Norman, a sensitive and artistically talented lad, was terrified by his father. Norman developed a stammer, which was exacerbated by his father's conviction that it would go away if only the boy would try harder. Archie regarded his father more with awe than with terror. In the long run he came to admire his hard-won success as a businessman and to respect him for his self-discipline. "Father was more of a man than I am or ever have been," he allowed half a century after his father's death in 1928. Yet in his youth and young manhood Archie resented and rebelled against the distance between them. Some of these feelings are articulated in a rare confessional poem of 1923 which Archie, with his own characteristic reserve, declined to publish in his lifetime.

> My father was a solid man
> And he was made of flesh and bone.
> I have the planet in my span
> And in my veins the stars are sown.
>
> My father walked upon the earth
> And with him would his shadow pass.
> I was rebellious at my birth.
> The sun strikes through me like a glass.
>
> My father knew Jehovah's face
> And would converse with him apart.
> I think he fears me for his place
> Is empty when I search my heart.

"God was father's father," as Archie put it in his notes, and he called Andrew "sir" whenever they conversed. His father left for the Chicago & North Western train into the city before the children were up, and in the evening he had dinner — the adult dinner, for the children were fed apart — and immediately retired to his den on the landing between the first and second stories. That den was inviolate territory, as the youngsters of the neighborhood discovered one antic weekend when they marched the family goat inside the house and on up the stairs, only to retreat hurriedly before Andrew's disapproving glare as he emerged from his den to investigate the uproar. Invited to a family picnic on the beach, Andrew declined with an aphorism: "I prefer my chop on a plate." As that remark suggests, he had a certain laconic wit. One steamy day he initiated a conversation in Yankee dialect with Norman. "T'weren't for one thing we'd have a thaw," he said. "What's that, father?" Norman asked. "T'ain't nothin' frizz."

That humor was a saving grace, or nearly so. And no one could deny Andrew MacLeish's generosity where his children's education and future were concerned. He was openhanded where it must have pained him most as a constitutionally closefisted Scot: in the pocketbook. This was small consolation, though, for his absence even when present: he simply was not *there* for the children of Craigie Lea. To Archie, looking back across the decades, Andrew MacLeish seemed more like "a foreign potentate" than a father.

Andrew and Patty

Born in Glasgow in June 1838, Andrew MacLeish was the second son of an Archibald MacLeish who was the third son of another Archibald MacLeish driven from his trade as a hand-loom weaver in Lochwinnoch, Scotland, by the introduction of steam power. Of the four sons of Archibald the elder, two eventually became educators, a third a minister in the Free Church of Scotland, and the fourth, Andrew's father, a draper — dry-goods merchant — in Glasgow. Andrew's older brother, yet another Archibald, first sought his fortune in the gold mines of Australia, and failing there, returned to become a partner in his father's business. Although the family was far from prosperous, they determined that Andrew should be educated for the ministry, to "wag his paw in the pu'pit." Andrew, who had other ideas, left school at fourteen and persuaded his father to apprentice him to Robert Webster and Sons, a retail drapery house in Argyle Street, Glasgow. While he was so employed, his mother died, a victim of illness compounded by financial and family stress.

It was assumed that at the end of his two-year apprenticeship in the fall of 1855, Andrew would join his father's firm, but again the boy disappointed expectations. In the company of Edward Couper, a youth who had earlier completed his apprenticeship at Webster's, Andrew set out for London to seek his fortune. Times were hard even in London, the drapery capital of the world, though less so than Archie later made them sound. Perhaps his father did sleep under the counter like Tiny Tim in *A Christmas Carol*, but at least he found employment. Before long he wrote home asking his father's forgiveness. That was kindly granted, and Andrew was once more encouraged to return to work at his father's side.

When Andrew did return to Glasgow in August 1856, though, it was only long enough to pack and set sail for America. Couper had told him tales of the prosperous new land across the ocean, and Andrew decided to pursue his opportunities there. Still more important, he decided to pursue Lilias Young, another former Webster's employee to whom he had lost his heart. Lilias had emigrated with her family to a rude frontier town called Chicago, and in September 1856 Andrew embarked on the *City of New York* to follow her there, his friend Couper accompanying him. Andrew was still a youth, only eighteen, and it must have taken courage to strike out for an unknown country. His departure effectively cut him off from family ties. He never saw his father again.

The land of milk and honey did not immediately live up to its notices. Luckily it was the season when you could get out of the train and pick apples, and so the two young Scotsmen had enough to eat on the three-day trip from New York to Chicago. Although bustling with growth, Chicago in 1856 was far from prepossessing. Wooden planks in the streets often gave way to deep mud holes. In one a wag had stuck a long pole with a hat on top and a sign reading "No Bottom." Still, that first evening Andrew and his friend Couper located the Youngs, he and Lilias went walking "out to the boundless prairie at Union Park," and that made the long journey worthwhile.

Andrew worked for one Chicago dry-goods store and another without much success. In the spring of 1858, on the mend after a bout of tuberculosis, he accepted an invitation from the Young family to stay on the farm they had just bought in Golconda, Illinois, in Pope County. That summer the local farmers prevailed on him to serve a six-month appointment as schoolmaster. Andrew knew he was ill prepared for the work, but he needed the job. On Christmas Day he and Lilias were married, and then — with his health restored and his teaching completed — he and his bride moved back to Chicago.

The twenty years of marriage allotted to Andrew and Lilias MacLeish were happy and prosperous ones, by and large. They had two daughters: Lily, born in 1860, and Blanche, two years later. They moved to a pleasant apartment on the city's North Side and joined the North Baptist Church, where Andrew, raised a Presbyterian but converted to his wife's faith, soon became the leading layman. He resumed his dry-goods career, and in 1867 found what was to be his life's work when Samuel Carson, a fellow Scot, invited him to join Carson and Pirie, dry-goods wholesalers, as a junior partner. Specifically, Andrew's job was to open and develop a retail store in Chicago. A shrewd, honest, and hardworking businessman, Andrew carried out his assignment with notable success, aided by the city's rapid growth in population. Even the disastrous Chicago fire of 1871 barely slowed the store's progress. By the mid-1870s Carson Pirie Scott and Company (as it was by then named) had become one of Chicago's leading department stores, and Andrew MacLeish — as founder and manager — one of its leading merchants.

Unfortunately, Lilias then fell ill, and after several years of invalidism she died, in September 1878. Shortly before her death, she asked her husband to send their two daughters to Vassar, one of the first American colleges for women. In this way the dying wish of Andrew MacLeish's first wife led to his marriage to his third.

In the interim, Andrew was married a second time, in March 1881, to M. (for Martha) Louise Little, the daughter of a Union general in the Civil War. In February of the following year she gave birth to a son, Bruce (who was eventually to follow his father's trade and become president of Carson Pirie Scott). Then Louise MacLeish too was carried off by an illness. In January 1883, at forty-four, Andrew was left a widower for a second time.

It fell to Lily MacLeish, as the elder daughter, to leave Vassar, come home, and take care of the family. After her father's first bereavement, she had briefly fulfilled a similar function while at home on vacations, but by 1883 hers was a full-time occupation. She had to manage the rather large house on Chicago's West Side that the family now occupied, to serve as her father's companion and sometime hostess, and — most important of all — to act as surrogate mother to young Bruce, who was not yet one year old when his own mother died. According to Archie, his half-sister Lily — thirty-two years his senior — was a congenital spinster (though eventually she did marry). In any event, she grew accustomed to her role and was reluctant to give it up when, five years later, her father married for a third time.

Ironically, Andrew MacLeish would not have met Martha Hillard at all but for the agency of his daughter Lily. While at Vassar she and her sister, Blanche, had grown particularly fond of Miss Hillard, who functioned both as an instructor of mathematics and as a "corridor teacher": resident adviser, friend, chaperone, and slightly older role model for Vassar students. An 1878 graduate of Vassar herself, she had taught public school for three years in Plymouth, Connecticut, before returning to her alma mater in 1881. Energetic, good-natured, pragmatic in her idealism, Martha Hillard was called away from Vassar in 1884 to become — at only twenty-eight years of age — principal of Rockford (Illinois) Seminary, and to oversee its transformation into a full-fledged women's college.

Fund raising was part of her job, and family legend has it that on one occasion she called on John D. Rockefeller to seek his support for the school. The meeting went well, and at its conclusion Rockefeller asked what train she was leaving on. That night she had just finished brushing her hair, secreting her purse beneath her pillow, and saying her prayers, when a male hand stole into the privacy of her sleeper. When she called the porter, the intruder turned out to be not the burglar she had feared but a most apologetic Mr. Rockefeller, who maintained that he had, somehow, mistaken her berth for his.

It was at the end of another trip, in the spring of 1887, that Martha Hillard decided to accept Lily MacLeish's often-extended invitation to stop and spend a night with her family in Chicago. Blanche was now married, to Cornelius Kingsley Garrison ("Ben") Billings, scion of one of Chicago's wealthiest and most distinguished families, and a dinner party was arranged. Martha Hillard was then thirty, a tiny woman with the small dark eyes, high cheekbones, and strikingly mellifluous voice she was to bequeath to her son Archie. Warm and witty, she was obviously a person of unusual energy, sharp intelligence, and deep convictions. Andrew MacLeish was immediately smitten. "My father saw the light when he saw her," as Archie later put it. After dinner he took her aside and showed her some photographs from the trip to Europe he and Lily had recently completed. Reticent though he may have been, Andrew was not a man to let the grass grow under his feet. A few days later he wrote Martha Hillard at Rockford and asked her to consider becoming his wife.

The young principal of Rockford Seminary hardly knew what to think. She had very nearly concluded that marriage was not for her. Andrew MacLeish was obviously much older than she — eighteen years older, in fact — and his proposal had come after the shortest possible acquaintance. Yet she felt an initial attraction as well — Andrew was "such a manly man," she thought — and did not reject him lightly. Instead she wrote that his letter had come as a total surprise, that she appreciated the honor he had paid her, and that she would write further when she'd given the matter the serious thought it deserved. Her second letter contained the rejection the first one had prepared him for, but it was made on the grounds of her calling and with no prejudice to Andrew.

Providence had guided her into the life of an educator, she explained. She was happy in her work and felt it her duty to continue. Besides, she pointed out by way of opening the door a crack, she hardly knew him, whereas he had the advantage of having heard a good deal about her from his daughters. Andrew's letter of response was so understanding and so generous that she "came dangerously near beginning to fall in love with him." So she carried on her tasks at Rockford during the spring term with Mr. MacLeish very much on her mind, and finally found a pretext to write him. Back came a reply that he was going to Block Island in August and would like to call on her at her home in Plymouth at that time.

The August visit sealed the bargain, though not without difficulty. The Hillards were a sizable clan, and in residence when Andrew came to call on August 26 were Martha's father, her grandmother, and siblings Helen, Emily, Fanny, and John. According to Emily's letter of that date, Andrew arrived "on the evening train and we have all lost our hearts to him." But she did not see how Patty (Martha's invariable nickname) would manage to see her caller alone, for her father and grandmother were dominating his time and conversation. Patty found a way. After fixing a fine breakfast of bacon and popovers, she remembered an errand she had to run in Thomaston, and took Andrew with her. Then, as she wrote in her memoirs, "we came home by a back road through the woods, and the matter was settled."

Since it was then the end of August, Martha Hillard could not in good conscience abandon her post at Rockford. Under a veil of secrecy about her impending marriage, she got through the 1887–88 school year before tendering her resignation. She left knowing that she had fulfilled her mission. During her time at Rockford, she installed an honor system, broadened student opportunities for physical exercise and social life, strengthened the curriculum, and brought in outstanding teachers from Vassar, Smith, Wellesley, and Radcliffe. The student body grew from fifty to one hundred, and by 1888 the institution was ready to become the full-fledged college the trustees had hoped for when they hired her four years before. Meanwhile, Andrew let Lily know that she was to be supplanted after five years as woman of the house. He took her out for a carriage ride and presented her with a nice piece of jewelry, whereupon Lily burst into tears. Without a word spoken, she knew what that meant, for once before he had taken her out riding, given her a bauble, and announced that he was going to marry Louise Little. On August 22, 1888, Martha Hillard and Andrew MacLeish were married in the old Plymouth church by its pastor, her father, Elias Brewster Hillard.

Half Puritan, Half Scot

Archibald MacLeish was proud of his mother, and of the Puritan heritage that came down to him from her side of the family. All four of her grandparents — Hillard, Brewster, Whittlesey, and Burrell — were descendants of early American settlers. The most notable among these ancestors was undoubtedly Elder William Brewster (1567–1644), the English separatist who came across on the *Mayflower* and served as spiritual adviser to the Plymouth (Massachusetts) Colony. Yet it was the Hillards who most interested Archie, and particularly his grandfather, Elias, and great-grandfather, Moses Hillard.

Most of the Hillards were carpenters and wheelwrights and farmers, and Moses himself spent many years wresting a living from "a hundred and thirty of the most ungrateful acres on earth." But in the vigor of early manhood he lived a remarkably adventurous life. Born at Preston, Connecticut, in 1780, Moses went to sea at eighteen, became a sea captain at twenty-two and one of the foremost shipmasters of his day before he was thirty. Captain Moses hated governments — all governments — and he had reasons. In June 1800 he was aboard the brig *Caroline* on a trip to the West Indies when a French privateer captured and scuttled the ship, robbed the crew of their money and their clothes, put them in irons, and set them "naked and helpless ashore" in Basseterre. It took months for the young sailor to get away from his French prison and work his way home to his father's farm in Preston. Ill served as he was by the French, the British treated Moses Hillard still worse. On three different occasions — in 1804, 1808, and 1812 — British seamen boarded and plundered vessels under his command. As for his own government, Moses detested the administrations of Thomas Jefferson and James Madison, whose embargoes kept him at home for fear of risking disaster at sea.

For all his misfortunes, Moses was an unusually successful sea captain whose expertise at business and ability to converse with equal skill in the galley of his ship and the salons of Europe made shipowners eager to employ him. In January 1813, racing back from Archangel, he brought to the United States the first news of Napoleon's retreat from Moscow. And on yet another occasion, just before Napoleon's defeat at Waterloo, he was approached with a proposition to bring the emperor himself to the United States should the battle go against him. Hating the British still more than the French, he agreed to the proposal and prepared to hide Napoleon in a false-bottomed water tank on deck. It was no fault of his that the emperor lingered too long and did not escape. The greatest sorrow of Moses's seagoing days occurred in February 1817, when he lost his ship *Oneida,* one of the queens of the Atlantic, in a dreadful storm at sea. He vowed then never to sail again, and, though the vow was broken a time or two, retired soon thereafter to work his hardscrabble farm in Preston.

Moses was a man "of iron will and fixed convictions," traits that descended to his great-grandson Archie. In Preston he was accused of assault and battery by a busybody named John Starkweather, who so infuriated Moses with his prying and troublemaking that the sea captain bloodied him with "two violent blows . . . on the right side of his nose," as Starkweather alleged, or merely told Starkweather to mind his own business, at which point he scratched his own nose and produced blood from a pimple thereon, as Hillard argued in defense. It was said of Captain Moses that when he returned from his voyages he "immediately took off his coat, rolled up his shirt sleeves, and gave his sons a sound thrashing each, because he 'knew they deserved it.' "

Among those sons was Elias Brewster Hillard, born September 6,

1825. The boy suffered no ill effects from paternal thrashings, but did rebel against the religion of fear preached by his mother, Martha Brewster Hillard. She taught her children that they, like all mortals, were wicked, that God was always angry with the wicked, and that he might take his vengeance at any hour. As a lad Elias often went to bed in terror that he might die before morning, since he was certain that however much he wanted to do right, he committed sins every day. Those Puritan beliefs he repudiated when, after graduating from Yale, teaching for a time, and studying for the ministry, he was ordained in March 1855. That September Elias married Julia Whittlesey, who had been his pupil at Southington (Connecticut) Academy. In August 1856 the first of their nine children was born: Archie's mother, Martha ("Patty") Hillard. Nearly a century later, Archie summed up his mother's heritage this way: "If Martha MacLeish inherited courage and force of character from Captain Moses, and a deeply religious nature from her father Elias and his mother, Martha Brewster, it was from Julia Whittlesey Hillard that she had the sweet selflessness which was the peculiar genius of her being." Daughter of a Cleveland lawyer and granddaughter of a judge, both of whom were Phi Beta Kappa graduates of Yale, Julia was the sort of person who made others happy to be near her. "Even now," Archie wrote in 1949, "it is impossible to read my grandmother's letters without loving her."

Elias Brewster Hillard ministered to a series of four different Congregational churches in Connecticut and a last one in Conway, Massachusetts, the picturesque farming community in the Hoosac Hills of western Massachusetts, where his grandson was eventually to settle. Successively, Elias was pastor at Hadlyme (1855–60), Berlin (1860–67), South Glastonbury (1867–69), for twenty years in Plymouth (1869–89), and finally Conway (1889–93). As a pastor he repudiated the Calvinism of his ancestors and adopted a liberal progressive outlook. Influenced by the writing of men such as Oliver Wendell Holmes and John Greenleaf Whittier, he offered his children and his congregation a concept of God that inspired confidence, not dread. But he was no Pollyanna. Elias understood that this world was not nearly as good a place as it could be, and always stood in the "forefront of any move to make [his community] a better place in which to live." The business of the church, he believed, was to dedicate itself just as zealously to the improvement of this life as to salvation in the next.

Like his father before him, Elias Hillard had a charismatic nature. When he entered a room, one of his relatives observed, it set off a small electric shock: everyone brightened up and became alert. And, like Captain Moses on the quarterdeck, Reverend Elias in the pulpit did not hesitate to speak his mind. Usually he moved from one pastorate to another to improve his financial standing and support his growing family, but at South Glastonbury that was not the case. The community's principal business involved some large woolen mills. During the Civil War the mill owners had reaped a bonanza by manufacturing and selling uniforms made of shoddy cloth. For Elias Hillard, who had encouraged young men to enlist and otherwise done everything he could to aid the cause of the North, that behavior was morally reprehensible, and he said so from the pulpit, even though his deacon was one of the profiteers. In the summer of 1869, while the Hillards were vacationing, the church board called a meeting to consider dismissing the pastor. Word reached Elias in time for him to return the following Sunday, tender his resignation, and at his farewell sermon preach to the text "And now do they thrust us out privily? Nay, verily; but let them come themselves and fetch us out." As they were leaving the church, a parishioner took his wife, Julia, aside and said, "Mrs. Hillard, whatever happens to you, know that you've got a *man* for a husband."

Elias Hillard also possessed some literary skill. In 1864 he brought out a small book called *The Last Men of the Revolution*. As research he located six men who had fought in the Revolutionary War, then visited, photographed, and interviewed each of them. The spryest of the survivors was Sam Downing, 102, who lived in the first frame house in Edinburg, New York, in the valley of the Sacandaga. Downing characterized Benedict Arnold as a "fighting general" who wasn't given due recognition and remarked that the men would "sell their lives" for George Washington. When peace was declared, he recalled, "we burnt thirteen candles in every hut, one for each State." But Downing did not understand — Elias interviewed him in 1864 — how able-bodied men could stay at home and so aid the enemy in the great ongoing Civil War. Apparently, Elias's only other surviving written document is a twenty-eight-page temperance pamphlet of 1883, "Drunkenness a Curse, Not a Blessing," which he published anonymously as the work of "a Connecticut pastor."

Misfortune sometimes invaded the felicity of the Hillard family. Elias and Julia lost two of their nine children in infancy, and a third, their son John, died just as he was about to embark on a promising career in the law. In their later years they brought into their home Elias's half-sister Ann, who was afflicted with depression and mental illness. Caring for her was difficult, and added one more onerous task to Julia Hillard's burden of cooking and cleaning and raising children and attending to the social and spiritual work of a pastor's wife. Small and delicately made, Julia became ill in the mid-1880s. She recovered after the move to Conway in 1889, however, and attributed her improvement to the community's "hill-town air, its hill-town sun, and its northwest wind out of Vermont and the Adirondacks." For her, Conway and their parsonage were Arcadia. Come there along with me, Julia invited a friend in a letter, "in at the large gateway and up the rising, slightly winding path to the little house with its porches and vines and flowers — past that and past the garden on its high terrace to your right, and past the dull red barn on your left, and up a grassy path through a shady orchard with all the time such lovely views opening before and around you that you pay no heed to the way by which you came but feel, when here, that you have been translated and know a new heaven and a new earth." Unhappily, as her health improved, her husband's began to fail: Elias had to resign his pastorate in 1893, and he died in 1895. Yet they were never happier than in this hill town among earnest, intelligent, warm-hearted neighbors. "Our life and work here are more a labor of love than in any of the homes yet," Julia wrote. "And I do believe we were never loved as we are here."

More than thirty years later, when Archibald and Ada MacLeish and their young family moved into their house up Conway's Church Hill, not far from his grandparents' old parsonage, Archie went to introduce himself to the Boydens, who occupied the only other house on their road. As he was about to knock on the door, it was opened by a big, tall, gray old man. His wife came up behind him and stuck her head out around his arm. "You're not a stranger to me," she told Archie. "Your grandfather married us." He felt at home then, a Yankee among his kind.

But of course Archie MacLeish was a Yankee on his mother's side alone. His very name, given him in honor of his father's brother, father, and grandfather, bespoke his Scottish origins. The alloy had its effects, good and bad. In his youth Archie was beset by feelings of guilt. "If you're one half pure Puritan and the other half very dour Scot," he drily remarked, "you've got a pretty good chance to feel sin." It was not a combination he'd recommend for pleasure. Both strains regarded life as a serious matter, to be undertaken with all the vigor and ability at one's command, an expectation that Archie eternally strove to live up to. In later years he came to venerate his Scottish ancestry as much as the Yankee heritage constantly on view in Conway. On special occasions he and his sons would wear the kilts of Clan Macpherson, and the boys learned to play the bagpipe. He was proud of the contributions that leading Americans of Scottish descent had made to the "strength, character, and well-being" of the United States.

It was an observation that his Hillard grandparents, and his mother,

Patty, would certainly have endorsed, because for them accomplishment meant service to one's fellow man and one's country. In a 1948 memorial to his mother, Archie wrote that there was no greater tribute he could pay her than to say "that she was her mother's daughter and her father's daughter and worthy of them both." Her children and grandchildren, he added, might do well to "consider, earnestly and humbly, whether we are worthy, in any sense, of her." Perhaps the comment, given its context, exaggerated his attempts to live up to her standard, but perhaps not, for Patty Hillard MacLeish did not give up her dedication to good works after marrying her husband. Far from it: she became active in advancing religious and educational causes on a local, national, and even international basis, and forcefully advocated a liberalism on issues of racial and religious tolerance that ran far ahead of her time. "My mother was one of the great North American women, no question about that," Archie said of her.

Born on May 7, 1892, Archibald MacLeish was the product of parents of unusual and very different attainments. His father was an extremely successful man of business, his mother a woman devoted to public service. In his childhood, his mother was everything to him, his father merely a shadowy figure who slept in the same house at night. Yet both shaped their son: the father he wanted terribly to please, since it was so hard to attract his attention, the mother who instilled in him the conviction that he must leave the world a better place than he found it.

Archibald MacLeish's true vocation, surely, was that of a poet, and yet he was called away time and again to other careers, and particularly to the fields of government and education toward which his mother's example beckoned him. Each of his parents would have had him pursue a career he rejected. Yet if he could not or would not follow the ministry, as his mother initially wished, at least he could satisfy her by working for the benefit of others. And if he could not or would not become a businessman like his father, at least he could bring home a series of straight-A report cards from school and college and law school, and place in his hands copies of his first books, in quest of one more expansive smile, one more "Hello, Brownie."

GROWING UP

A Difficult Child

ANDREW AND PATTY MACLEISH got a late start on building a family (he was fifty and she thirty-two when they were married), but within nine years they produced five children. The first was blue-eyed, golden-haired Martha Louise, named for Andrew's departed second wife. Born in July 1889, she died of meningitis the following summer. Then came Norman Hillard in August 1890, Archibald in May 1892, Kenneth in September 1894, and Ishbel in March 1897. The children were very different from one another, and it soon became clear that among them was a prodigy. This was Norman.

Patty MacLeish took her child-rearing duties every bit as seriously as one might have anticipated from a woman who had spent the previous decade as an educator. To prepare herself, she attended Elizabeth Harrison's Kindergarten Training School once a week for two years. There she was introduced to Friedrich Froebel's philosophy of child education. According to the teachings of Froebel (1782–1852), the child was assumed to be inherently good, and human evil the product of the wrong educational methods. The inventor of the term *kindergarten,* Froebel believed that play was central to learning in the early years and to helping each child develop his or her innate potential. He was strongly opposed to the use of force in disciplining children. His ideas worked beautifully with Norman, who in his mother's words "was from the first a little philosopher, a gentle soul, very sensitive to beauty, full of imagination and keen interest": all the qualities one associates with an artist in the making. The German philosopher's methods were much less effective with Archie, a boy (as his mother described him) of "tremendous force and will power, a high-strung nervous system, easily disturbed, a sensitivity and imagination more inhibited than Norman's." When Archie's temper flared up, as it often did, she found that he could normally be restored to equanimity through "quiet and seclusion." But at least once she was driven in despair to administer a good old-fashioned spanking. "The effect," she recalled, "was magical." Archie's yells of rage turned suddenly to a sharp cry of surprise, and when the spanking was over, he threw his arms around her neck and cried, "Oh, Mama, I do love you."

As the family dynamics worked out, Norman and Archie — born barely twenty months apart — were co-beneficiaries of their mother's course of home instruction, while Kenny and Ishbel formed another slightly younger pair of students. It was clear to everyone that Norman was gifted. With his beautiful dark-gold hair, he was trotted out to show off his precocity for his mother's friends, many of them educators. He wrote stories and even a little operetta for the children of Glencoe to perform. He demonstrated an early knack for the visual arts, and some musical ability as well. Ethel de Lang, a neighbor born in 1891 who attended Glencoe School in Archie's class, remembered Norman well and Archie almost not at all. Archie was "very quiet," she said, while Norman was always stirring things up. Norman acted out Narcissus in the pool between their houses. Norman made up plays using characters from the advertising world: he was the Quaker Oats man, for example, while Ethel and her sister were the Golddust Twins. Archie did not participate in those plays, she recalled. He was, however, included in the mock funeral of an unfortunate bird who flew into a window of the MacLeishes' house and was killed. Norman led the funeral march, playing a mouth organ. Archie carried the bier.

Locked in unequal competition with his talented older brother, Archie asserted himself through misbehavior. He was "a difficult child," in the language of popular psychology, or "a thoroughly nasty little boy," as he later described himself. "If you could get into a scrape," he observed with some pride, "I got into it!" Sometimes these scrapes involved physical violence. In this respect Archie, who was wiry, tough, and athletic, more than held his own. As a fighter, at least, he was clearly superior to the docile, gentle Norman. Such combativeness earned him no rewards at home — quite the contrary — but it did enable him to work off his frustration. More important, it established a habit that was to remain with him all his life. Whatever the field of endeavor, Archibald MacLeish was always a fierce competitor, one who did not shy away from conflict and often seemed to court it. It may even be that he turned to poetry, at least in part, as a form of rivalry with the precocious Norman.

For all his initial promise, Norman did not achieve the successful career expected of him. He became in due course a professional architect and an amateur painter of considerable ability but limited accomplishment. Somehow he seemed to lack drive and self-confidence. Norman's greatest gift, according to his son Rod, the writer and PBS commentator, was for painting, but he used to refer to himself disparagingly, when drinking, as "a near-great," and he produced much less than he might have. His father's troubles began, Rod is convinced, with his grandfather Andrew, who sometimes ridiculed the boy's stuttering. (Escaped to the realm of childhood play, Ethel de Lang remembers, Norman hardly stuttered at all.) Families have a way of developing catchphrases or euphemisms, Rod believes. The MacLeish family expression for his dour Scottish grandfather was that he was "stern but fair." That phrase, in Rod's view, could best be translated as "a son of a bitch."

In a long 1924 letter to his mother, Archie proposed a different view. Norman was going through an unproductive period, and Patty MacLeish — in a rare critical comment about her husband — wrote Archie that perhaps Andrew's "lack of sympathy" for Norman was at fault. Although he agreed about his father's lack of sympathy — "which of us in childhood has his sympathy?" — Archie maintained in reply that his brother's real handicap was that he had been singled out as a child prodigy, "his powers of expression with words or paint or music facile and marked." Norman was so much the artist, in fact, that until Archie began to have a reputation as a writer, he "was not seriously considered as an artist at home. (This is *not* complaint. I thank God for it.)" What happened, Archie concluded, was that Norman's artistic mechanism developed rapidly while he himself did not, and so he "became a misfit." The result was almost inevitable: "Once in a million times the talented child arrives. The rest of the time his talents remain unrooted because they devour his life as fast as he lives it. The very fact that he can express himself as he goes along prevents his having a life rich enough to express importantly."

Here Archie clearly argues against too much recognition too soon, and in favor of a certain benign neglect. But the context counts. When he wrote these words Archie was in his middle thirties, with a pattern of success behind him to give him confidence for the future as he philosophized on the relative failure of the promising older brother. In childhood he must have felt very differently. And of course he was not neglected, at least not by his mother. For it was her nightly reading to Norman and Archie, begun when they were five and three, that opened up the world of literature to him. At Elizabeth Harrison's school she had heard a series of lectures by Denton J. Snyder on the "Literary Bibles" of the world — Homer's *Odyssey*, Dante's *Divine Comedy*,

Goethe's *Faust,* Shakespeare's plays — and she was inspired to expose her two boys to such works as early as possible. Most children's books, she felt, were mawkishly sentimental and entirely too easy to read. "To do its full part in the training of a child," she was convinced, literature must make demands on the mind and serve as a moral touchstone.

Following these standards, she began a custom of reading to the boys for half an hour every day, just after their supper. The first book she read them, in her deeply resonant voice, was Charles Kingsley's *Water Babies.* Kingsley's didactic purposes were manifest in such characters as the Do-as-you-likes, who lived under the flap-doodle tree and gradually sank back into apedom from a lack of never having to do anything hard, and the central figure, poor little Tom, with his selfishness sticking out in sharp spines all over his body so that it was impossible for anyone to cuddle him or to play with him. Next Martha MacLeish introduced her boys to exemplary figures in the legends of Greek and Norse heroes. Then she went on to Kipling's *Jungle Book,* a volume of *Wagner Opera Stories,* Howard Pyle's version of *The Merry Adventures of Robin Hood,* Uncle Remus, and Ernest Thompson Seton's *Wild Animals,* followed by the *Odyssey* (hard going at first), Sidney Lanier's *Boys' King Arthur, Ivanhoe,* and a little Chaucer. Sundays were reserved for Bible stories, and then — at Archie's insistence, for he was drawn to the Gustave Doré illustrations in the book — for Dante's *Inferno.* Dante was a difficult text, their mother acknowledged, but her sons probably got from it "a clearer conception of the character of sin than anything else could have given them." Particularly effective, she thought, were depictions of "the sullen ones, smothered in the ooze of the swamp" and "the violent standing in the river of blood . . . , showing so plainly how violence begets violence." These lessons, Patty MacLeish must have believed, would be of particular benefit to her fractious Archie.

She read the boys other books as well, including *Huckleberry Finn, Treasure Island,* and *The Swiss Family Robinson,* and eventually both of them became voracious readers on their own, just as she had hoped, and so the evening sessions were no longer required. (Besides, she was by then reading to Kenny and Ishbel.) By the time he was twelve or so, Archie estimated, he had read more than most college undergraduates. In addition, both he and Norman were inspired to attempts at literary creation. Under the influence of Dante, Norman wrote fantasies about the Ice King of Lake Michigan. His mother liked them, but Archie thought they were nonsense, and said so. That did not stop him, however, from producing his own "flagrant imitation" of the Italian master. If it accomplished nothing else, his mother's nightly reading set his imagination free to roam. As he put it in his poem "Autobiography,"

There was a landscape in my childhood
over opposite — against:
another world than this one, wild
and hence.

There was another time, an earliness:
the sun came up out of Eden, out of the Odyssey —
freshness like the fragrance of a girl
or god.

"like a leaf, a stem . . ."

Enchanted by this world of "earliness," Archie was less at ease in the round of everyday existence. As a child he felt himself separate from others, and sought peace in a sense of communion with nature. Luckily, nature was everywhere around him at Craigie Lea. His parents first moved to Glencoe, eighteen miles north of Chicago, in the spring of 1889. Patty MacLeish wanted more fresh air and open space for her young family than the city could provide. They rented for a few months, then in August, General C. H. Howard drove them out to look at a piece of property he owned. The buggy ride took them down a deserted lane and past a small cottage where a woman was watering a heifer at a wooden trough. The rest of the way they traversed on foot through the woods and dense undergrowth, down a ravine and up again. Suddenly, they were standing atop a high clay bluff. Below them, as far as they could see, was Lake Michigan. "Well!" Patty MacLeish exclaimed, "I don't believe there's much doubt about our wanting this." Canny Scot that he was, Andrew MacLeish talked instead of how expensive it would be to clear the woods and build piers to prevent erosion of the bluff.

The purchase was soon concluded, though, and building plans commenced. The site was so remote that they had to put in their own sewage system, their own lighting plant, their own water supply. Flanders and Zimmerman, a Chicago architectural firm, was hired to design a house, but the first building the MacLeishes erected on their seventeen-acre site was a stable. By the spring of 1890, they had moved into the stable, cheerful with its woodwork of Georgia pine, its yellow silk curtains, and its big Franklin stove. The family slept on the second floor, and the stalls below served as a pantry and extra bedrooms. With the horses and Crummie, the family cow, installed in a byre, the stable served as headquarters while construction of their home went forward. Andrew came up with the name Craigie Lea from a Scottish song, and arranged

to have one of its verses carved in the beam above the fireplace in the
entrance hall:

The broom, the briar, the birken bush
Bloom bonny o'er thy flowery lea,
And a' the sweets that ain can wish
Fra' Nature's hand are strewn on thee.

Bonny was the site indeed, with its twelve acres of oak grove, its bluff
and beach, its ravines. But labor troubles held up completion of the
house until the fall of 1891. The MacLeishes celebrated Thanksgiving
in Craigie Lea that year, with Norman now a year old and Patty three-
months pregnant with Archie. In style the house was what might be
called Chicago Romanesque, influenced by H. H. Richardson and rather
too much like a French chateau for Patty's taste. Inside the rooms were
high-ceilinged, and most commanded a view of the lake. Downstairs
there was a library, a living room, a double hall, a dining room, and a
large staircase where a rather voluptuous Pan (the architects' idea) leered
out from the newel post. At the first landing, halfway up, was the den
where Andrew MacLeish repaired immediately after dinner, not to
emerge until after the children had gone to bed. Andrew and Patty each
had a bedroom on the second floor, which also held a guest room, a
sewing room, and bedrooms for the children. With as many as five
children in residence, sometimes two of the boys had to double up in
one bedroom: first Norman and Archie, then Archie and Kenneth. Neighbors thought of the place as the MacLeish estate, "like some of the big
shore houses you encounter in New England," complete with outbuild-
ings — the stable, the byre, the greenhouse, the toolshed, the icehouse.
Children were especially attracted to the windmill, and to the water
storage tank on the third floor of the house.

Wind and water figured prominently in Archie's memories of Craigie
Lea. In his poem "Cook County" he remembers the different winds: the
northeast wind blowing "the oak-leaves pale side out," blowing "the
lake smell in"; the southwest wind like "thunder in the afternoon" when
"the doors slammed all together"; the dry west wind "Burning the grass,
turning the leaves brown, filling / Noon with the bronze of cicadas"; the
north wind at night bringing "snow in the sand where in summer the
water was." Curiously the poem does not mention the east winds that
drove forest fires across upper Michigan, though they were so vivid in
Archie's memory that all great disasters smelled to him "like oak trees
burning in an east wind."

All summer long, as soon as they were old enough, the MacLeish
children spent much of their time in the waters of Lake Michigan and

on the beach below the bluff. They were living, Archie later realized, on the edge of a vanishing America, a place where "geese slept on the lake in the day, then flew back into the marshes to feed at night, making the wooden bell sound that they make, and there were foxes everywhere." Memories of that setting exerted a powerful hold over him that "no beauty of oceans of hills or mountains" could match, he wrote in 1923. And the next year, on a trip from Paris to Florence that took him to the Mediterranean, he confessed again the strength of childhood associations: "Nothing — nothing — not the Grand Corniche Road, not the sun on the sea — can ever be as beautiful as those ill painted oils at Craigie Lea of storms at night with a driven ship and an old man."

Sometimes, as his poetry and notebooks reveal, he linked his happiest memories of the natural world with his feelings for his mother. In a note of the mid-1920s, for example, he paints a tableau of blissful communion with the coming of night. His mother is allied with the joy, while his father interrupts it.

> The hot summer night on the terrace — the large soft sky — the stars — the palpable blue air — his mother lying on her back on the lawn under the oak tree — his father sitting near her — others — perhaps his brother — the warm, terrible, breathless happiness of all of them doing nothing — sitting there — the moment of having no differences, of being continuous with the earth, transparent to the light, the trembling moment of evening. And then in the oak trees over the lake an owl — an eternal sound? And his father starting to his feet, oppressed again suddenly with time — hurried — the moment broken.

In "Ancestral," a poem of the same period, he brings a similar, still more tender memory to life.

> *I was small. I lay*
> *Beside my mother on the grass, and sleep*
> *Came —*
>
> . . . .
>
> *And I was not afraid.*
> *Her hand lay over mine. Her fingers knew*
> *Darkness, — and sleep — the silent lands, the far*
> *Far off of morning where I should awake.*

Like most middle-class families of the time, the MacLeishes had help: a maid, a cook, a coachman, a gardener. But there was no governess, for Patty MacLeish was determined to raise her children herself. In

Archie's memory it was his mother who quieted his fears and listened to his troubles. In a September 1924 letter he recalled the childhood terror of being halfway across the ravine bridge on a dark winter's night (half past five) and hearing — or imagining — the crunch of unknown boots on the wooden planking behind him. But then he saw the warm light from the sewing room window, where his mother was waiting for him, and knew he would be safe. "As it is," he wrote her then, at thirty-two, "I still rest in your arms. I still feel not quite grown up, not quite responsible, not quite alone." In his boyhood she was the one person Archie could talk to about anything and everything, including his early sexual experiences. From middle age on, he could not speak of his mother without his eyes misting over.

Yet even the mother he adored could not keep young Archie out of trouble. He erred, he sinned, and then he sought refuge alone in the toolshed, where there were earthenware pots with a little dried earth in the bottom, envelopes of dry seed smelling of dust, onionlike bulbs, and an old, stale pipe on the windowsill. From inside he could see the gardener bent over the rosebushes and hear the spinning of pigeons above. For the moment, this was the center of his world, and it all came floating back to him in "Eleven":

> And summer mornings the mute child, rebellious,
> Stupid, hating the words, the meanings, hating
> The Think now, Think, the Oh but Think! would leave
> On tiptoe the three chairs on the verandah
> And crossing tree by tree the empty lawn
> Push back the shed door and upon the sill
> Stand pressing out the sunlight from his eyes
> And enter and with outstretched fingers feel
> The grindstone and behind it the bare wall
> And turn and in the corner on the cool
> Hard earth sit listening. And one by one,
> Out of the dazzled shadow in the room,
> The shapes would gather, the brown plowshare, spades,
> Mattocks, the polished helves of picks, a scythe
> Hung from the rafters, shovels, slender tines
> Glinting across the curve of sickles — shapes
> Older than men were, the wise tools, the iron
> Friendly with earth. And sit there, quiet, breathing
> The harsh dry smell of withered bulbs, the faint
> Odor of dung, the silence. And outside
> Beyond the half-shut door the blind leaves
> And the corn moving. And at noon would come,

Up from the garden, his hard crooked hands
Gentle with earth, his knees still earth-stained, smelling
Of sun, of summer, the old gardener, like
A priest, like an interpreter, and bend
Over his baskets.
                    And they would not speak:
They would say nothing. And the child would sit there
Happy as though he had no name, as though
He had been no one: like a leaf, a stem,
Like a root growing —

Childhood is happy, Archie wrote in his notes of the mid-1920s, because in childhood we are part of the earth; we feel no divorce from "the mute, unlanguaged actual." Yet church and school and the cautions to "Think now, Think" led him inevitably toward awareness of his difference, his distinctness from the vegetable kingdom.

Patty Hillard's Boy

As early as the Christmas he was six, his mother divined intimations of a religious sensibility in Archie. She took Norman and Archie on Christmas Eve to visit Aunty Waters, the family laundress. Aunty Waters, who lived alone, had fallen ill, and to cheer her up the boys strung popcorn and cranberries and made paper chains, their mother found a nice little tree, and together they wrapped some small, useful presents. When they arrived at her house, the boys put on the decorations and lighted the candles while Patty went ahead to talk to Aunty Waters. Then they brought in the tree and the presents, and Aunty Waters burst into tears of joy. As Patty MacLeish recounted the story, on the walk home through the cold, clear night there was a glorious star. And Archie, his hand in hers, looked up at her and said, "And you know, Mother, it might be — the Star!" Archie's own recollection of the night visit was somewhat hazy. He remembered certain details — the crunchy snow and the deep stars of the walk home — but could not quite summon up "something his mother said, one of the true things of his life."

Archie's baptism, by way of contrast, was not to be forgotten. Although Andrew MacLeish maintained his connection with the Fourth Baptist Church in Chicago, as a matter of convenience the family attended services in the Baptist Church of Evanston nearby. Evanston's was an unusually liberal Baptist church, with none of the hellfire and brimstone often associated with that faith. But baptism itself remained a serious sacrament. When he was twelve, Archie decided he wanted to be baptized. He was fully immersed, and the sanctity of the occasion quite overwhelmed him. In a late poem called "Photograph Album," he summons up the experience in a whimsical tone:

> When God received me in the Baptist Church
> in Evanston, Illinois, the reverend
> dry in his trout-fisher's pants, the soprano
> aching as the waters closed,
> I saw my life go on before me
> pure and singing as a bird
> and all the way home on the C and NW
> washed sins, washed sins.

But at the time he had a feeling of being terribly good, very pure, and his mother took that to be a sign of awakening religious fervor.

Both of Archie's parents were heavily committed to the support of educational institutions. Given her background and interest, it was to be expected that when Glencoe formed its first school district in 1893, Patty MacLeish would be one of three founding board members. The following year a $5,000 bond issue was approved for purchase of a school site within walking distance of the MacLeish home. By the time Norman and Archie were ready for first grade, there was a Glencoe School for them to attend. In its early years the school remained small; in Archie's class, Ethel de Lang recalls, there were ten to twelve boys and only three girls.

Strong supporter of public schooling as she was, Archie's mother held even stronger opinions about the duties of parents in educating their young. In a 1904 *Kindergarten Review* article, obviously influenced by social Darwinism and its belief in evolutionary progress, she maintained that the very future of the republic depended on raising "each succeeding generation to higher levels of patriotism, to a loftier sense of honor and a more unselfish devotion to duty. The ignorant must be made intelligent; the helpless, capable; the criminal classes, virtuous." And this could be accomplished only through "education in its modern, scientific sense." Far too often parents neglected their responsibilities in this process. In order to bring their children to full manhood and womanhood, she wrote, parents needed to do three things: first, acquire enough practical knowledge to ensure the physical and material well-being of the child; second, understand the psychology of the child mind in its various stages of development; third (and here she cited Froebel's distinctive contribution), comprehend the spiritual needs of the child's soul. If thus prepared to assist in the development of their children's bodies, minds, and souls, parents might make a contribution to "the great object of life and of education, growth in goodness as well as effectiveness, in moral power and spiritual understanding" — in short, to character formation. This high-minded view of "the great object of life" naturally communicated itself to her son Archie.

It was a measure of Andrew MacLeish's respect for higher education and of his status as leading citizen that this lower-middle-class Scotsman who did not himself complete secondary school became a member of the first board of trustees of the modern University of Chicago and served in that capacity from 1890 to 1924, for twenty-eight of those years as first vice president. Actually, his ties to the university went back still further. Andrew was a member of the board of the original university from 1878 to 1886, and a trustee both of the Baptist Union Theological Seminary (later the divinity school of the university) and of Rush Medical College (later the university's medical school). The future of that initial University of Chicago looked very dark indeed when, in 1888, the American Baptist Education Society launched a fund-raising drive to take over "all the privileges and endowments" of the existing university and to establish a larger, more comprehensive one. John D. Rockefeller was persuaded to give $600,000 for this purpose, on condition that his gift be matched by $400,000 from Chicago supporters. The newly-wed MacLeishes donated $100, a large enough sum at the time, Patty MacLeish recalled, that it had to be divided into two annual payments of $50 each. As his prosperity increased, so did Andrew's contributions to the university. Perhaps because his cousin was a missionary in China, he supported a succession of Chinese students through their studies. A great reader himself, with a particular fondness for the poetry of Robert Burns, he took a substantial interest in the University of Chicago Press and, according to Archie, actually read in their entirety the scholarly books sent him. He established a fellowship in the divinity school, contributed to the building of Harper Memorial Library, and finally, in 1918, made his great gift of $100,000, enough to endow two distinguished professorships.

Rockefeller's $600,000 in 1888 was not his last contribution to the university, either. As a boy, Archie was summoned to his father's study to see with his own eyes a check for $1 million, signed by John D. Rockefeller. He was too young to grasp the significance of such a sum, but it was clear that his father expected him to be impressed. In person the tycoon, who was given to fondling the womenfolk, was somewhat less inspiring. In fact, his name became associated with a kind of family joke. In his frugal way, Andrew invariably turned down the gas in the living room when they went in to dinner. "Mr. Rockefeller always turns the gas down when he goes in to dinner," he explained.

A young professor from Yale named William Rainey Harper was

recruited in 1889 to be president of the new University of Chicago. The Harpers became close friends of the MacLeishes, and Patty also formed friendships with other educators, and with Jane Addams (the first student to have received a bachelor's degree from Rockford Seminary, and probably the most famous social worker of the day) and Julia Lathrop of Hull House. Archie's parents never belonged to a social elite, but his mother was a naturally gregarious person, and if she had had her way, Craigie Lea would often have been filled with company. But Andrew, as retiring as his wife was sociable, generally preferred to be left alone. This difference in their natures, along with the eighteen-year gap in their ages, must have led to tensions in the marriage. Only once, however, did these tensions flare up into a quarrel of such magnitude that it remained in Archie's memory.

Patty MacLeish, it seemed, was eager to attend an outdoor concert of the Chicago Symphony Orchestra at Ravinia Park, located but one stop north of Glencoe on the new rapid transit Chicago & Milwaukee Electric Railroad. (Ravinia, opened in the summer of 1904, was designed — according to a contemporary account — as "an ideal summer pleasure resort built with the intention of attracting people of taste and fashion.") Andrew declined to go along and, when Patty proposed that she make the excursion on her own, forbade her to do so. It would mean that she would have to walk home from the electric line in the dark, alone: that he could not permit. Born in the year of Queen Victoria's coronation, Andrew had acquired his full share of Victorian values — among them the belief that a husband and father was master of his house. Patriarchal pride of place was deeply ingrained in the culture. His daughter Lily, for example, held a gathering of the MacLeish clan each New Year's Day at her house in Winnetka. Following the Scottish tradition, she let no one in the front door until her father arrived. He had to be the first to cross the threshold in the new year.

Andrew MacLeish, in short, belonged to a generation in which husbands could and did command wives to do or not to do certain things. And yet Patty MacLeish in her independence was exactly the sort of person no one would think of giving a command to. So the children were hushed, almost in a state of awe, as they listened to their parents quarreling. Nothing like this had ever happened before. In the end, Patty did not go to Ravinia. She did assert herself, however, by walking upstairs to the guest room and locking herself in. Andrew went up to talk to her through the door, then came storming downstairs while the children pretended to read. Glaring at them, he strode around the room for a time. Then, without uttering a word, he retreated to his den. And that was the end of that.

In every real sense, of course, Patty MacLeish was head of the family, founder and creator of the little kingdom above the ravines and the lake that was Craigie Lea. In the summer of 1903, she took her children back east to explore yet another world — the one she'd come from. One reason for the trip was her twenty-fifth reunion at Vassar, so they began the journey with a few days in Poughkeepsie before proceeding to Plymouth for two weeks with her relatives. There Archie, who was eleven, attached himself to a neighbor boy who had a newspaper route. He was helping deliver papers one day when an elderly spinster, detecting familiar lineaments, called out to him, "Be you Millie Hillard's gal?" "No," Archie replied, "I'm Patty Hillard's boy." There followed a tour of historical sites in Cambridge and Boston, Salem and Marblehead, Concord and Lexington. To finish the summer the family went to Cape Cod, where Norman and Archie delighted in the saltwater swimming. Having gone east in 1903, Archie was dispatched west the following year. He spent most of the summer on a ranch in the Little Big Horn of Wyoming, and forever remembered the smells of the high plains and the beauty of the Crow villages.

Breaking Away

Until her two older sons were of high school age, Patty MacLeish continued to rear her children as sets of two: Norman and Archie, Kenny and Ishbel. The younger pair of siblings proved easier to raise than the elder. Kenny especially was a happy child, with a sunny disposition and an uncanny ability to reduce people to tears of laughter. According to Ishbel, Kenny was his mother's favorite, and practically everyone else's as well. "I thought the sun rose and set on Kenny," his three-years-younger nephew Andrew Day remarked. So did Archie, who spoke of his younger brother as "one of the loveliest people" he'd ever known.

Ishbel was Andrew and Patty MacLeish's last child and only surviving daughter. She arrived at her name in an unusual way. Lady Aberdeen came to speak at the March 1897 convocation at the University of Chicago, a few days after Ishbel's birth. In the course of conversation following the convocation, Andrew MacLeish mentioned that the baby was prospering but that they had not yet settled on a name for her. They were looking for a Scottish name, he said: perhaps Lady Aberdeen could suggest one. "I can suggest nothing better than my own," her ladyship replied, and presented her card, Ishbel Marjoribanks Aberdeen. Ishbel it was, then, though several years were to pass before the MacLeishes realized that the name was not pronounced phonetically: the initial *I* is silent, and a short vowel sound follows the *sh*. Thereafter "Ishbel" became, properly, "Sh'bel."

Patty MacLeish observed the growth of her last born with particular care, and in July 1898 published her "Observations on the Development of a Child during the First Year." Included was a table of the "Scotch-American lassie's" weights and measurements for each month, along with comments on her evolving mastery of sight and sound. As early as the beginning of her tenth month, Ishbel made her first attempts at speech: "papa" and "mamma" and then — her third word — "Ah-tie" for Archie. Later, in her young girlhood, Ishbel looked upon Archie with something like hero worship.

Twinned though they were in their upbringing, Norman and Archie never achieved a strong brotherly bond. For one thing, they were nearly opposite in temperament. "There couldn't possibly be two more different brothers," Ishbel said of them — Archie aggressive and forceful, Norman sweet and docile. They might have been fetched from two different wells, as Emily Dickinson said of herself and her sister Lavinia. Besides, Archie felt too rivalrous toward Norman to befriend him. This rivalry was never so clearly demonstrated as during the 1906–7 school year, which Archie spent at the recently opened New Trier High School while Norman was sent away to prepare for college — and, presumably, get better treatment for his stammering — at the Hill School in Pottstown, Pennsylvania. New Trier, which served Winnetka, Wilmette, and Kenilworth as well as Glencoe, eventually grew into one of the nation's best public high schools, but in its early years it was not nearly so well regarded.

From the beginning of the fall term of 1906, Archie was bored and restless at New Trier. Besides, it was for him a lame-duck year; he did not expect to be returning there. In May 1906 Patty MacLeish had enrolled him, to start in September 1907, not at the Hill School but at Hotchkiss in Lakeville, Connecticut. Originally, she had planned to send Norman to Hotchkiss. The school was recommended by her sister Mary Hillard, who as headmistress of Westover, the girls' preparatory school, was in a position to advise on such matters. Then it was decided that Hill, a somewhat smaller school, would be better for Norman, and in withdrawing Norman from consideration at Hotchkiss in 1906, Patty MacLeish asked the school to hold a place for Archie instead. Resentful that Norman had been sent east ahead of him and lacking motivation to do well at a school he would soon be leaving, Archie went through a period of adolescent rebellion.

His last year at public school, Archie said, "was a horror." He got into almost daily fights with the town's bad boys at the Glencoe railroad tracks, and returned from these encounters bloody and defiant. Finally

one day he played truant — skipped school entirely — then came home
and told his mother. At fourteen he was too old to spank, but something
had to be done. She took him up to the cedar room in the attic, located
the device used for beating stuffed furniture, and applied it to his back-
side. When she was through, however, Archie merely whistled, and she
began to cry. It was clear that he needed sterner discipline than hers,
the kind of discipline that a rigorous prep school like Hotchkiss might
provide.

The redeeming feature of the 1906–7 year, from his parents' point
of view, was Archie's venture into free enterprise. In a copy of *Country
Gentleman* he read about the brand-new idea of using an incubator and
a brooder in raising chickens. He then secured a loan from his father
and went into the chicken-and-egg business. He worked hard at his
duties, which occupied a great deal of his time, and other family members
were called into service as well. Ishbel delivered eggs, for example, and
his mother often had to get up in the night to make sure that the light
for the incubator, kept in the front cellar with heat from a kerosene
lamp, hadn't gone out. Occasionally something went wrong, as when
the shoveling of winter coal into the cellar bins destroyed a whole incubator full of eggs about to hatch. But there were many successful
hatchings as well, with the little chicks transferred to the brooder to
mature. A henhouse was built on the edge of the ravine, with plenty of
exposure to sunlight. Daytimes, the grown chickens had free range of
Craigie Lea. When Archie returned from school to feed them, his Plymouth Rocks came running from all over the place to alight on his arms,
his shoulders, even his head.

As the year wore on, the market grew for eggs and for the occasional
broiler. Andrew MacLeish must have been pleased with his son's display
of capitalist enterprise, though he sometimes grumbled about paying to
feed the chickens Archie sold. As sales increased, Archie was able to
begin paying back his loan. For his part, Archie had the satisfaction of
knowing that this once, anyway, he and not Norman was embarked on
a project his parents approved of.

He did not always find the work congenial, however, especially the
killing and dressing of chickens for sale. One day Ishbel sneaked around
behind the icehouse to discover Archie at a tree stump with a chicken
in one hand and an ax in the other. He kept raising the ax and trying
to bring it down, but he couldn't bring himself to behead the chicken.
Archie spied his sister spying on him, and, embarrassed to be caught in
such sentimentality, started running after her with the ax still in hand.
Having duly terrified his little sister, he returned to complete the job.

The chicken business was going so well by spring that Patty MacLeish was reluctant to make Archie give it up to attend Hotchkiss. She wrote the school early in June 1907, asking if admission could be delayed until September 1908. Headmaster Huber Gray Buehler must have been annoyed by the repeated delays: first Norman, then not Norman, then Archie, then Archie next year. Hotchkiss had been turning down applicants every day since March in order to hold a room for Archie, he replied. Would Mrs. MacLeish please wire him immediately about her intentions? At this stage she capitulated. Archie would indeed be coming to Hotchkiss in the fall of 1907, she replied, adding that some of the vacillation had to do with Archie's chicken business and some with her husband's lack of enthusiasm for sending his boys east to preparatory school. As a Connecticut Yankee, she was sure that Archie would profit from the experience, and that Mr. MacLeish too would be "very glad" he'd sent his son to Hotchkiss, once he'd seen the results.

At what level Archie should begin his Hotchkiss education still remained uncertain. The school consisted of four grades: Senior, Upper Middle, Lower Middle, and Junior. Archie decided to try for Lower Middle, or sophomore year, but failed the examinations Hotchkiss mailed him. His grade in algebra was 32. In Latin, the master who read his exam said he was not prepared for the Junior class, much less the Lower Middle, and should work on his Latin over the summer. This meant that, academically, the two years he had spent at New Trier were a dead loss. In September 1907 he began secondary school again, this time at Hotchkiss.

3 ❖

PREP SCHOOL

Homesickness

BY THE TIME Archie MacLeish graduated from Hotchkiss in the spring of 1911, he had emerged as one of the school's leaders in athletics, in scholarship, and — particularly — in writing and speaking the English language. He was the best swimmer in his class. He played center on a varsity football team that beat Yale's freshmen but lost to Penn's. His name appeared regularly on the honor roll. He edited the school newspaper and was one of the editors of the yearbook. He belonged to the boys' religious group, the German club, the glee club, the musical art society. He won all the prizes the school had to award for debating and orating and composing essays. He was chosen to be class poet. Yet when he went back in 1934 to deliver the commencement address, it was to tell "the young Hotchkissers" just how bitterly he felt about the school. Hotchkiss "massacred" him for four years, he insisted; he was still afraid of the place. Forty-seven years later, in an interview six months before he died, his feelings had not changed. "God, how I did not like Hotchkiss!" he exclaimed.

For such abiding animosity, there had to be good reasons. One was that Hotchkiss wrenched him away from his mother and his childhood home, and he suffered transports of homesickness in his first year. At Hotchkiss, too, he went through the agonies and doubts of puberty. Seeking peace and reassurance, he turned toward religion and then away from it — or at least from religion as practiced at the school. And he became aware at Hotchkiss of a strong class consciousness and snobbery that he partly absorbed even while it disgusted him.

The Hotchkiss School, endowed by the widow of the inventor of the Hotchkiss machine gun, was the same age as young MacLeish. Founded in 1891, the school opened its doors for instruction in October 1892. By the time Archie enrolled, it had grown to accommodate two hundred boarding students and fifteen to twenty day boys from neighboring communities. One of the school's attractions was its unspoiled natural setting among the Litchfield Hills — low mountains, actually — just outside Lakeville in northwestern Connecticut. Lake Wononscopomuc, covering 350 acres and surrounded by woods, adjoined the school grounds. The countryside, Archie acknowledged, was lovely. Another selling point was Hotchkiss's close connection to Yale. By 1911, when Archie graduated, about two-thirds of each senior class went from Hotchkiss to Yale. Former Yale president Timothy Dwight, along with a dean and a professor from the university, sat on the twelve-member Hotchkiss board.

The student body was made up of the sons of the wealthy and successful who could afford the annual charge of $850 for tuition, room, and board. In the 1908–9 school year, Hotchkiss's 223 pupils came from twenty-nine different states. New York, Connecticut, and Massachusetts accounted for about half, but a substantial number were drawn from midwestern states such as Illinois, Minnesota, Ohio, and Michigan. In fact, the school was "more national in its constituency" than either Yale or Harvard, as the headmaster pointed out in his June 1909 report. Twelve religious denominations were represented among the student body, with Episcopalians, Presbyterians, and Congregationalists the largest by far. Nine Roman Catholics were enrolled, and no Jews.

The school offered three different tracks during Archie's years: Academic with Greek, Academic without Greek, and Scientific. He took the Academic-without-Greek arrangement, with a heavy emphasis on languages — four years of English, Latin, and French, and three of German, along with three years of mathematics and one of ancient history. No sciences were included. This schedule would prepare him, the catalogue pointed out, for Yale, Columbia, Cornell, and Williams, or for Harvard by substituting physics for one language in the fourth year. The required reading for English courses took Archie over some of the ground he had covered at his mother's knee, including the *Odyssey, Treasure Island,* and Shakespearean plays such as *Julius Caesar, The Merchant of Venice,* and *Macbeth.*

What impressed Patty MacLeish more than the curriculum, however, was the high moral tone the school adopted. *Moniti Meliora Sequamur* was the Hotchkiss motto: "Having been warned, we follow a better course." It was up to the school to warn, to admonish, to advise the boys who attended, so as to ensure their development into useful and upright young men of "moral character, mental ability, earnest purpose, and bodily vigor." This exactly suited the conviction of Archie's mother that he should devote himself to a life of public service. Of those who have been given so much, she felt, much should be expected.

Though nondenominational (on Sundays both Congregational and Episcopal services were conducted), the school was "strongly religious in its teachings and spirit." There was daily chapel, and boys were encouraged, even expected, to join the St. Luke's Society, which held devotional meetings on Wednesday and Sunday evenings. Presiding over the institution was the mustachioed Reverend Huber Gray Buehler, A.M., Litt.D., who had risen from English teacher to headmaster and whose textbooks in English grammar were assigned to students in Junior and Lower Middle classes. No hint of levity, or even of good humor, is evident in the photograph of Buehler in the 1911 *Mischianza,* the Hotchkiss yearbook. He is pictured solemnly reading the last page of a slim volume, eyes hooded downward in concentration. To his pupils he was known as "the King."

Fifteen-year-old Archie MacLeish arrived at Hotchkiss in September 1907, passed his entrance examinations, and immediately contracted a virulent case of homesickness, in the most literal sense of the word. He longed for his mother, and for the enchanted place she'd made of Craigie Lea. The two were inseparable in his mind. "I used to cry for my mother but when I thought of my mother I could only think of her there working in the borders among her flowers." He wanted to run away, to go back where he belonged, to escape from this new country of hills with a lake and a long valley. "The rocky hillsides excluded me. I was shut out."

Personally, too, he felt terribly alone and vulnerable. He had difficulty making friends among his classmates, and the old boys subjected him to a terrifying period of hazing. New boys were expected to bow and scrape before seniors, and those who did not courted at least the threat of violence. Archie was assigned to a room in the main building, where several of the tormenting seniors lived, and when, within a few weeks, he heard of an opening in Meeker Cottage, a small student residence run by Latin master James J. Robinson, he applied to Headmaster Buehler for a transfer. Archie's note to Buehler showed a measure of calculation. It said nothing of hazing or of homesickness, instead stressing that in Meeker he "could study a great deal better . . . because it would be so much quieter" and would also "have a chance to read a little from my Bible in the morning." Buehler must have encountered disingenuousness in pupils before, but after an exchange of telegrams with Mrs. MacLeish, he approved the transfer. By October 10, Archie was installed in his new room with "two windows, two glims, a big closet and a dandy wall paper." He'd made friends, he wrote his father, with a boy who was the grandson of the last Earl of Douglas and the son of one of his mother's Vassar classmates. And he was doing well in his school-work, too.

His letters to his mother were considerably less upbeat. To her he confessed all his troubles; from her he sought not merely sympathy but a release from his trials. The hazing did not stop with his move to Meeker, he told her, nor did his homesickness. In a letter to his mother, he described how one new boy, naked, had been tormented by a group of "bullying seniors" snapping wet towels at him. And he himself had been threatened for failing to hold a door open for one of them. "I simply hate it here," he wrote. "I hope you will consider sending me to some other school next year."

This was not at all what Patty MacLeish wanted to hear, and in rapid order Archie received visits from Aunt Mary, who came over from West-over to cheer him up, and from his mother, who made a point of stopping at the school on her way back to Chicago from an eastern trip. His father, apparently, did not come, but he did make it clear to Archie that his expressions of misery caused his mother considerable distress. In a back-channel letter to the headmaster, she revealed some of that distress, as well as her determination that her son should stick it out at Hotchkiss. "I am sorry to see him show the white feather," she wrote, "but I know he is having a hard time of it." Enclosing with her letter a copy of the towel-snapping communication, she cautioned Buehler not to take too seriously what Archie said about the school. Right now was "a desperate moment," but she was sure that he "really appreciates the school, and will be as loyal as anyone could wish, when he gets adjusted."

In response a few weeks later — he had been doing some investigating and had talked confidentially with some of the masters and with Ar-chie — the headmaster wrote that he had not discovered "a single in-stance in which your son has been molested by upper classmen" and that his tales of other victims contained "much distortion and wrong emphasis." The whole problem, in short, could be "summed up in the word 'homesickness.' " In his talk with Archie that morning, the boy had said he liked Hotchkiss better and felt less homesick, "although he did not seem very cheerful." He was not being harassed now, Archie told Buehler, but "on the other hand, he does not seem to be making friends very fast." The fact was that Archie "shrinks from the kind of contact with other boys that accompanies life in a large school, and since this contact is similar to what must be expected in life it seems to me that it is exactly what he needs." Joe Garner Estill, another master, felt it would have been better to let Archie stay in the main dormitory "and fight it out," and Buehler was inclined to agree. Implicit in Buehler's argument was the Darwinian belief that survival necessarily involved struggle, that one must be strong to survive, and that Hotchkiss, if it put boys to the test, was only preparing them for the larger battles ahead.

Patty MacLeish shared these views and took Buehler entirely into her confidence. The one thing that bothered her most about Archie, she wrote the headmaster, was his self-centeredness. His letters, his talk, and presumably his thoughts were too much concerned with himself. He needed to get out of this fixation on himself and into the life of the school. That he had not as yet done so was, however, not entirely his fault. In his physical examination Archie was discovered to have a varicocele, or a twisted, expanded vein in the spermatic cord, and as a result the school's athletic director had forbidden him to exercise. This was doubly unfortunate, since Archie "especially needs vigorous exercise and plenty of it, for his general nervous well being," and since athletics provided one of the best ways of getting acquainted. Archie was beginning to make a few friends even without athletics — notably with Norman Donaldson, who shared his literary interests, and with the musically inclined Douglas Moore — but there was no one at Hotchkiss he felt he could confide in. Over the Christmas vacation he had long talks with his mother about the first term at school, and he returned to Hotchkiss in January with "good courage, and a much firmer grip on himself." As for the varicocele, she arranged for an examination by a Chicago specialist, who pronounced him fit for athletics.

Sex, God, and Snobbery

Yet if the swelling around his testicle represented no serious physical danger, it may have contributed to Archie's psychological vexation about his developing masculinity. The trials of puberty he elaborated on in his notes of the mid-1920s. His self-consciousness had begun at Craigie Lea, first inside ("He sees himself in the guest-room mirror — alone, separated, suddenly different. He sees himself small, awkward, clumsily clothed and his face pimpled and blotched. He is ashamed as though he were naked.") and then outside ("He lies at noon under the gooseberry bushes in the hot sun. His body feels the hot sun, presses against the hot earth. His body seems to know. But he is miserable, ashamed, giddy with the sun, sick with wanting something he does not want, does not know. His body must touch, touch, touch. He cannot.") He was only happy swimming under the clear water, wading half asleep on the ribbed sand.

At school the misery continued, now complicated by the conviction that everyone else knew more about the mysteries of sex than he did. One boy gave him a postcard of a naked woman that he stared at inside the cover of his book. The picture made him want to go to that body so different from his own, to belong to that body. At the same time it made him lonely for his mother. He heard three other classmates talking together in a room and using *the words*. "Do they know?" he wondered. "These others — when they use the names, the words — do they know? And only I not?" The pretty young wife of the French master stopped him in the corridor, spoke to him, smiled at him. But he was unhappy and afraid, ashamed of his pimples, ashamed of his body. "I walked by myself to Bird Peak. There were hawks circling in the gulf below. I could look down on them. I seemed to be looking down on myself alone on the iron shelf of rocks. I could feel the rasping of my fingers against the rocks but I could not feel the rocks. My body felt hot and sick. I did not know my body. My hands went over my body, fumbling. Suddenly I was convulsed by an ecstasy of pain. Going back down the cliff I was sick."

Deeply troubled by his physical urges, Archie repudiated his body and sought expiation from God. At morning chapel he heard Buehler speak of the evils of giving in to "the flesh, the body." His body, Archie decided, was not himself. "Before, my body had been myself and there had been no difference between me and the soil, the trees. Now I was driven out of my body. My body did dark things, horrible things. This was not I. God would help me to defeat my body." *Lead us not into temptation,* the prayer asked. But it was only through temptation that he was led to God, who "lived beyond sin, through sin." Archie went to him in tears, dizzy with remorse. "O Jesus! Jesus!" he called out, "O forgive me!" He made this entreaty both privately and publicly, through the meetings of the student-run St. Luke's Society. On Sunday and Wednesday evenings the boys assembled in the wooden chapel that invariably smelled of floor wax. They sang a few hymns, and then one by one they stood up and talked about their secret lives. Archie talked about sin with tears streaming down his face.

But the drugged dreams of women and the vague desires continued, until Archie finally came to accept his sexuality. At Glencoe School he had dipped Ethel de Lang's pigtails in his inkwell, and at New Trier he had admired a few of the girls, but he had no real girlfriends until after he went east to Hotchkiss. Thereafter he came back to Craigie Lea to fall half in love with one girl or another every summer. One night at the foot of the bluff he touched by accident the breast of "Miss H.," who let herself go in his arms so that he felt the sudden weight of her body, the heady scent of her skin. Miss H. was different from the ethereal Julia, whose cool dresses "seemed not to have her under them." Together they stood on the deck of a boat, looked out over Lake Michigan, and said, "Yes — Yes." When it was time to go back to school, she came to see him off with flowers. Then, too, he was smitten with Nan Hendrix, the mother's helper at Craigie Lea, who took care of his chickens while he was away: she was "older," and therefore particularly desirable. Once his acne faded, Archie MacLeish became an extremely attractive youth: well built, with distinctive high eyebrows and a full, rather sensual mouth. According to his sister Ishbel, he was "death to women" from late adolescence on, and throughout his life took pleasure in exercising his appeal on women who attracted him.

Another thing that bothered Archie about Hotchkiss was its atmosphere of noblesse oblige, its casual assumption that its pupils were or ought to be superior. The boys who attended were the sons of the powerful and prominent, and it was expected of them that they would make some contribution to the betterment of lesser beings. To some extent this attitude was implicit in Archie's prizewinning oration on John Keats, at least as the talk was reported in the school newspaper. "The wonderful genius and ability of this poet is all the more incomprehensible," the *Hotchkiss Record* observed, "when it is known that he is the son of an English coachman." In retrospect, Archie came to regard the headmaster as particularly guilty of class consciousness. Buehler was, he decided, "a quite loathsome man, hypocritical, smug, a terrific snob." Among the boys the snobbery found its most virulent expression in invidious distinctions between those whose social backgrounds were impeccable and those whose families had acquired their wealth and status more recently or in a less socially acceptable way.

The occasional poor boy was barely tolerated, as Archie's future employer Henry Luce was to find when he attended Hotchkiss in the class of 1915. Luce, who worked his way through the school in the dining room, was forever embittered by the class consciousness he encountered among his schoolmates. But Archie MacLeish himself must also have begun to become aware at Hotchkiss (the education continued at Yale) that his origins were not entirely correct. His father had made his own money, for one thing, and he had done so in trade rather than in banking or one of the professions. And his mother's family, despite its early American roots and its devotion to public service, was not a wealthy one. Even more significant, perhaps, his parents lived in Glencoe, and Glencoe was decidedly not one of the fashionable Chicago suburbs.

The string of communities that grew up along the North Shore — Evanston, Winnetka, Glencoe, Highland Park, Lake Forest, to name some of the stops coming out from Chicago on the railroad line — could all be classified as "enduring affluent suburbs," according to a recent study. And to "an uninitiated eye," local historian Arthur Meeker commented early in the century, "these attractive villages stretching along the lake from the city limits . . . look very much alike. But, oh, the differences really." The Chicago Social Register for 1910 underscored these differences. Among 466 persons along the North Shore who were listed therein, 9 of 10 lived in one of four places: Evanston (142), Lake Forest (109), Winnetka (103), or Highland Park (67). Kenilworth, recently founded, placed 26 people on the register, and then came Glencoe with 14. Evanston, the site of Northwestern University, was by far the largest of these suburbs — really almost a city in its own right by 1910 — and its very size helped to account for its representation on the list. But this was not at all true of Lake Forest and Winnetka, much smaller towns regarded in Archie MacLeish's formative years — and to some extent still — as the most socially desirable suburbs. Lake Forest especially, with its exclusive Onwentsia Country Club, epitomized the zenith of upper-class society. The Swifts and the Armours and the McCormicks built their country mansions there. F. Scott Fitzgerald fell in love with Ginevra King from Lake Forest and visited her in the summer of 1916. In 1940, the year he died, Fitzgerald wrote his daughter that he "once thought that Lake Forest was the most glamorous place in the world. Maybe it was."

By way of contrast Glencoe was, in Archie's words, "much the simplest of the villages," much more middle class. The MacLeish children grew up at Craigie Lea, which resembled the manor house of the community. Their telephone number was 10, but — Ishbel points out — the butcher's number was 9. Still, there was no question that they were thought of as better off than most of their Glencoe neighbors, and it must have come as something of a shock to realize that they did not stack up socially with the cream of North Shore society. When they reached the proper age, the children attended the Saturday night dances at the Skokie Country Club just beyond the Glencoe city limits, but these were a far cry from the more socially select gatherings of young people in Winnetka and Lake Forest. The distinction was vividly brought home to Ishbel when, as a young woman, she was invited to a dinner party in Winnetka. Over dessert one of the men turned to her and said, "How do you possibly come from Glencoe?" Snobbish as it was, the remark made her feel inferior, and she thinks that the social snobs of these communities, and others like them whom Archie met at Hotchkiss and Yale, must have infected him with the virus. At least he must have felt a compulsion to prove that he belonged to a social elite, never mind Glencoe, never mind his father's humble origins.

Even as a lad, Archie had acquired some of the prevailing racial and

ethnic biases of the time. Glencoe was well known, and somewhat stig-
matized, among the North Shore suburbs for its African-American population, and all the MacLeish youngsters went to grade school with
black children. In kindergarten Ishbel became fond of a black child
named Johnny and asked him to lunch. He would have to ask his mother,
Johnny replied, so Ishbel asked *her* mother if it would be all right. The
invitation met with Patty MacLeish's enthusiastic approval, but Archie,
then eleven or twelve years old, objected violently when he heard about
it. His reaction bothered his sister, and it surely troubled his mother,
who was far in advance of the community in her insistence on tolerance
for others. The crisis passed, after a fashion, when Johnny's mother
would not allow him to come to lunch. Anti-Semitism was also widespread in Glencoe, as elsewhere among middle-class white Anglo-Saxon
Protestants of Archie's generation. Traces of this anti-Semitism appear
in his correspondence and in his poetry up to the mid-1930s, just as
they did in the work of such contemporaries as T. S. Eliot, a native of
St. Louis, and Ernest Hemingway, whose boyhood home of Oak Park
was on the other side of Chicago.

Triumphs, Near-Disaster

Once the worst of his homesickness had passed, Archie participated
fully in the activities of Hotchkiss. In the middle of his first year, he was
chosen for the Olympian, one of the two athletic societies, and for the
Forum, one of the two literary and debating societies. In the fall of his
second year, he made the varsity football team as a substitute end, at
sixteen years old and 138 pounds the youngest and lightest boy on the
squad. In a notebook entry he commemorates a gridiron incident that
illustrates his determination to be tough: "I turned sharply. The ball
came slanting sidewise into my arms. The fat boy crouching in front of
me suddenly disappeared. There was an open space of green. I ran
without knowing I was running. Suddenly a hand in black leather across
my hips, the shock of a fall, and the crushing weight of a body across
my back. My mouth was driven into the lime. I heard Butch say *Jesus!*
I laughed."

In the 1908–9 school year also he demonstrated his precocious facility
with the English language. His mother worried that Archie might need
extra instruction in English at Hotchkiss, so easily had he sailed through
his grammar and composition classes at New Trier. She clearly did not
suspect him of any outstanding talent as a writer, and the validation of
this talent did not occur until midway through his second year at Hotchkiss. His initial brush with literary inspiration, with "that sort of warmth

above the heart that Keats talks of," produced not verse but prose and was stimulated by his reading Thomas Carlyle's account of the French Revolution. Carlyle "started resonances going," and he began writing scenes from the Terror. One of these, "The Storming of the Bastille," was published in the January 1909 literary supplement of the school newspaper, and shared a five-dollar prize for the best contribution. According to a faculty reviewer, MacLeish's "Storming of the Bastille" was "a remarkable paragraph, showing the great imaginative power of the writer, and . . . a certain rhythmic swing which is well adapted to the description."

Soon thereafter Archie gained another triumph as winner of the first Helen Yale Ellsworth Prize, awarded for the best composition of three hundred to eight hundred words on "The Lesson of Lincoln's Life." The donors singled out MacLeish's essay for its individuality and originality and for the beauty of its style, though they detected in the prefatory paragraph "a little too much of what might be called 'fine writing.' " Nonetheless, they concluded that "when he gets over the desire to write prose as if it could be scanned in blank verse he will be a writer." In fact, Archie's beginning paragraph was marred by an indulgence in the ornate and overelegant, while at the same time it disclosed an unusual rhetorical virtuosity:

> A strangely varied land is life — a land of sunshine and of shadow, a land of rippling brooks and of black, slowly moving rivers, of wooded hills and of stark, rugged peaks. And thru this land we journey differently, some few beside the rippling brooks, and some across the summer hills, but the multitude of the great majority must wend its slow and tortuous way between the black-browed Mountain of Despair and the voiceless, winding river that neither ends nor yet begins, — the river of the Changeless Future.

In February 1909 young MacLeish read an essay to the Forum Society on "The Call of Brazil." The lure of South America was strong in his mind. The previous summer he and a young English lad named James ("Cho") Close who was visiting Glencoe had concocted a scheme to go to South America and seek adventure. Andrew MacLeish vetoed the plan, but apparently Cho managed at least the beginnings of a solo journey before returning broke, tail between his legs. Archie's early fascination with the idea of travel continued throughout his life, and impelled him on journeys covering most of his own country, much of Europe, substantial sections of South and Central America, and even such infrequently visited countries as Persia and Japan.

Archie's prep school career peaked in his third year, which was so replete with accomplishments as to make the successes of his fourth and final year pale in comparison. Oddly, for one whose own cup was about to spill over, his writing — still in prose, and in essay form — dwelled on the theme of sacrifice. In November 1909 he addressed the St. Luke's Society on "True Self-Denial," taking as his text John 12:24: "Verily, verily, I say unto you, Except a corn of wheat fall into the ground and die, it abideth alone: but if it die, it bringeth forth more fruit." Two of his three contributions to the January 1910 literary supplement addressed similar issues. In "A Chapter from a Man's Life," he placed his protagonist in a conflict between the land he loves and the woman he loves. A westerner who feels as peaceful and contented riding his pony as the herds they watch over receives a letter from a woman he'd fallen in love with while studying at Harvard. She had not seemed to care for him then; now she confesses that she loves him too, and so he speeds to her side in the East. "Youth and love urged their claims. What was greater than to love and be loved!" But a cold wind awaits him amid the "throbbing roar of the great city," and he realizes that he must give her up. He "felt the call of the mighty west, his soul answered, and he knew himself the willing slave of all that might mean, the freedom, the strength, the reliance of a man upon himself, the making of history and the moulding of a perfect nation." In the essay the lure of the West is not merely environmental. It calls on the man to perform his duty, realize his potential, subordinate himself to the service of the nation. Against such a didactic siren song no woman could compete.

MacLeish's second essay, "John Milton," raises precisely the dilemma that was to confront him time and again in his career: how to reconcile the demands of private poetry with those of public service. Using the kind of concrete detail notably missing from his Lincoln essay and from the fable of the westerner, MacLeish focuses on the choice the great English poet had to make between his art and his country, "between the dream which had become himself, and the duty which was calling him from off the road." Milton chose to do his duty, to give up the artistic career that had already produced such brilliant work as "Il Penseroso," in order to become a pamphleteer and treatise writer for the Puritan cause and Oliver Cromwell's government. "His pen, which once had traced the sweetest poetry, was turned to work that any scribbler could have done." In the process "his sight was taken — his sword was fallen from his hand." When the Stuart kings returned to the throne, Milton was left "sightless, friendless, and alone." Yet Milton made the right choice, the essay maintains, for not only did he serve when needed, but *Paradise Lost* lay ahead. As Archie expressed it in a flight of rhetoric,

"Now there gathered in his brain the threads of the great realities of life and death, and exalted by the scenes of noble beauty in his sightless eyes, he wrote his epic through the hand of one who did not know the greatness of the thing he wrote."

At the annual literary contest between the Forum and its rival society the Agora, in December 1909, Archie read his "John Milton," which won the best-essay award and contributed to the Forum's victory. A few months later he was once again triumphant when he captained the Forum to victory in the annual debate with the Agora. The question at issue was whether Theodore Roosevelt should be the nominee of the Republican party in the next presidential election. MacLeish, for the affirmative, acknowledged Roosevelt's previous history of concentrating power in the central government, but held that this had been necessary to combat the abuse of economic concentration. If Roosevelt disregarded precedent, it was only when it was his patriotic duty to do so, as when he had withdrawn wilderness lands from development in the interests of conservation. Not only did the Forum win the debate, but the judges decided unanimously to award Archie the gold medal for best debater. In the same March 22, 1910, issue of the *Hotchkiss Record* that reported the debate, it was announced that "A. MacLeish" had been elected editor-in-chief of the newspaper for the coming year. "We feel no hesitancy in placing the editorship" in his hands, the outgoing editor commented, for "he has shown marked executive ability and talent." Less than a month later, in the afterglow of these achievements, Archie very nearly got himself kicked out of school.

On Sunday April 17, the usual morning services were called off because a strong east wind and the unfinished state of the new organ chamber made it impossible to heat the chapel. With time on their hands, MacLeish and four of his classmates contrived to get into trouble. A boy named George Blossom was the ringleader. Wouldn't it be fun, he proposed, to hire an automobile and ride to the Great Barrington Ridge, forty miles north of Lakeville and just visible from the Hotchkiss campus? So five Upper Middlers — Blossom, MacLeish, Lewis Carr, Phil Lindenberg, and Wallace Whittaker — pooled their money and ventured off on this drive that they knew was against the school rule forbidding pupils to leave the area without permission. They also knew that if they had sought permission, it would not have been granted. Moreover, this was a starred rule, violation of which, the regulations declared in boldface, "may in itself result in suspension or dismissal." Presumably the boys hoped that their absence would go undetected, but they were missed at lunch. When they returned from what had turned out to be a disappointingly unexciting journey, Buehler's right-hand man, Joe Estill,

was waiting for them. "Where have you been?" he demanded. The boys
remained silent for a long moment. Then Archie, who by his own admission was "never a good public liar," firmly answered, "Great Barrington," and as he did so watched the jaws of the others drop. Estill
reminded the boys of the dire consequences possible, and sent them back
to their rooms in fear and trepidation to await the headmaster's verdict.

It "was perfect folly" for the boys to take their unauthorized trip,
Buehler wrote Andrew MacLeish the next week, for by doing so they
risked dismissal or suspension. But his decision was more lenient,
since — note the kingly "we" — "we are not disposed to say that we
want no further dealings with them." So the five sinners were sequestered
instead: confined to their rooms and classes, with no participation in
sports or other school activities except for study, chapel, St. Luke's, and
appointments with masters. Buehler thought that the boys must be made
to see "that it matters not what the forbidden thing is; the fact that it
is forbidden by the school is enough." Archie had been "thoroughly
scared by the possibility of being expelled and was thoroughly ashamed
of himself," his father wrote in reply. He and Mrs. MacLeish understood
that rules were rules and thought the penalty appropriate to the crime.
"We are very thankful," he reflected in closing, "that Archie's honor
and integrity were not involved in this affair and that it was only the
thoughtlessness and impulsiveness of youth that produced his misconduct."

The sequestering did not last very long, for Archie recalls playing
baseball on a trip to the Hill School later that spring. (Norman by then
had transferred from Hill to the Asheville School in North Carolina.)
At commencement time all was obviously forgiven, for Archie was recognized there for the accomplishments of his third year, and added still
more triumphs to the list. Prizes were awarded him for winning the
annual literary contest and the annual debate as part of the Forum team;
he also received the gold medal for best debater. In addition, he was
awarded the Converse Cup as class of 1911 swimming champion and
a book prize for excellence in English. His most notable success, however,
came June 17, 1910, in the fourteenth annual Alumni Oratorical Competition. In a field of four contestants, Archie spoke on John Keats and
was given first prize of twenty-five dollars in gold for writing and delivering "an English oration in the best manner."

Flush with his conquests at commencement, Archie and his brother
Norman, who had been taking College Board examinations for Williams,
sailed for England, where the rest of the family awaited them. On the
voyage across the Atlantic, Norman lost his money and Archie lost his
heart. In the confusion of changing into his first dinner jacket, Norman

left his wallet on the dresser. It was not there when he returned. Archie, according to his mother's account, "succumbed to the wiles of a very pretty, over-developed girl from Portland, Oregon, daughter of a self-made, ambitious man who kept himself in the public eye by pushing forward his fourteen-year-old daughter." On the return crossing two months later, Archie once again "had an affair of the heart," this time with a girl from the South his mother approved of. During the interim the MacLeish family devotedly toured the British Isles.

Their itinerary took them from the old half-timbered town of Chester down through Wales to Devon, then back up to London, Oxford, and Stratford, and finally to Scotland to see the land of their father. Their very first outing together, a day trip to the Duke of Westminster's estate on the river Dee, ended in a family disagreement. When the rest of the family was leaving to return to Chester, Norman asked his mother if he could stay to take pictures of the gardens and return by a later boat. She consented, but Andrew MacLeish was not pleased. "Have we come all this distance only to be separate and each go his own individual way?" he asked. "I'm afraid that is the case," his wife responded, "for we are of different ages and interests." The travelers might be corporeally together, as Archie recalled in a 1921 letter, but their souls were "variously wandering — mother's in a groined cathedral, father's in a stretch of heather, Norman's in a questionable adventure, Kenny's and mine in the nearest swimming hole."

Despite their differing inclinations, the MacLeishes managed to see many of the most famous sights: Stonehenge, Salisbury and Winchester cathedrals, in London Westminster Abbey, the Tower of London, the Inns of Court (where a trial was in progress), Madame Tussaud's Wax Works, the British Museum, and Saint Paul's (where they went to church on Sunday and Patty MacLeish was horrified to encounter a crowd of tourists chattering down the aisles), Hampton Court on a day trip, the Bodleian Library and Magdalen Tower at Oxford, a production of *All's Well That Ends Well* at Stratford. In Shakespeare's town Archie went adventuring alone, renting a canoe and paddling on the Avon. Showing off a bit for the people on the park benches — or so his mother speculated — he overturned the canoe. When he righted it and climbed inside, he discovered that one of the medals he had won at commencement was missing, so he dived time and again to the bottom of the river until he finally found it.

The Scottish portion of the trip took the family to Edinburgh, Glasgow, Loch Lomond, and eventually up to Oban and out to the Isle of Iona, where they saw the graves of early kings, including that of Macbeth. It was in Iona that the name MacLeish originated. The first Culdee bishop who came from Ireland to preach Christianity to the natives called himself the Servant of Jesus, or Gillie Iosa. In common parlance this became Iliosa, the son MacIliosa, and eventually MacIliosa was transformed into MacLeish. It was, the minister's daughter Patty MacLeish believed, "a name to be honored and lived up to." Characteristically, it was in connection with her own calling that she undertook to arrange the family's summer in the British Isles. Before her children were in school, she had been too occupied at home to devote much time to public service. When Ishbel was five or six, however, Patty MacLeish joined the board of the Woman's American Baptist Foreign Mission Society, an organization to which she devoted "more than twenty years of absorbingly interesting work," many of them as president. In mid-June 1910 a world missionary conference assembled in Edinburgh, and she combined attendance at that conference with the trip abroad for the children she had long wished for.

Stirrings: Love and Poetry

While still in England Archie wrote Headmaster Buehler a contrite letter about the joyride. "I'd give anything to have the ability to undo what I did that day and regain your confidence," he declared. "I'm afraid I've made quite a bungle of the three years that I've had at school and I can tell you I am thankful that I have a fourth left to me." He was especially troubled by something one of the masters had told him: that he "had a reputation for being very irresponsible and 'kiddish,' and even for not being straightforward." That made him "feel kind of shaky for a while," and he was determined to live down this reputation. "I love the school as much, I believe, as my own people," he observed in conclusion, "and I am very thankful that I shall have one more chance."

Considered closely, Archie's letter rings somewhat false. To begin with, he clearly overstates the case against himself. By no objective standpoint could he be regarded as having made a "bungle" of his three years at Hotchkiss, as both he and the headmaster would surely have known. Yet he generally tended to overwrite, to paint the lily, in almost all of his adolescent writing. In this case, however, the manifest self-criticism warred against the egotism implicit in Archie's repeated use of the first person "I" — what his friend-to-be Ernest Hemingway was to call "the perpendicular pronoun." "I'm afraid," he writes by way of self-conscious parenthetical comment, and "I believe." Whatever affection he felt for Hotchkiss, in fact, may well have been undermined by what he perceived as its expectation that he must humble himself before Buehler as its symbol of authority. Archie's self-abasement in this letter closely parallels the public confession anticipated from the members of St. Luke's Society in their evening sessions, usually with a master or two listening in the pews. Midway through his third year Archie had stopped attending these meetings, for they offended his sense of reticence where personal matters were concerned. It might be good for boys to confess themselves in public, he thought, but it was not necessarily good for anyone else to hear them.

Whatever his feelings about the school, his parents were more than satisfied with his progress there. On September 27 he arrived at Lakeville to begin his final year, accompanied by his brother Kenneth, who was enrolled in the class of 1914. Archie played first-string center on the football team that fall, and in December he once more contributed to the Forum's victory in the annual literary contest with "Impressions of an English Summer," a richly descriptive essay drawn from the experiences of his trip abroad. The essay ends with an account of his journey to Oxford. There he fulfilled his "heart's desire of dreaming, and walking, where, for centuries, statesmen and poets have dreamed and walked." In the evening, he "floated in a slim canoe across the shadows of the Charwell, and watched the long gray lines of Madeline [sic] tower fade into the pale yellow of the sunset sky. Aye, a perfect day. They come like precious jewels from God's hands and, falling in the calm sea of the past, leave only ever widening, ever vanishing ripples of remembrance."

In the spring of 1911, Archie succumbed like many another last-semester student to a mild case of senioritis. Yet again he represented the Forum, upholding the negative in debating "Resolved, that throughout the United States proper, full suffrage should be extended to women equal to that now enjoyed by men." This time, however, the Agora debaters carried the day. "MacLeish had won more literary distinctions than any boy in the school," the school newspaper explained, "and the other Forum speakers undoubtedly relied too much on his prowess." In March also he was censured by the faculty for some unspecified "misconduct in the dining room." Word of that offense prompted Patty MacLeish to write Buehler an extended analysis of her son's shortcomings.

What primarily concerned her was his religious development. "He is at sea in the matter of faith, and his spiritual life does not mean to him what it once did," she wrote. Though he was still nominally a member of St. Luke's, for example, he no longer entered into its activities with enthusiasm. The trouble was that Archie tried to discover spiritual truth through the same logical processes used to unearth intellectual truth. Besides, he was "selfish, with the selfishness of a strong nature." This could lead him to achievement and power, but his life would remain empty, she felt, "unless he makes something far bigger than himself the object of his living." In this connection, she was not at all sure that her son's success in writing was "altogether good for him in point of character." He needed to realize that his ability was a gift, and that he was "responsible for the use he makes of it."

In response Buehler agreed with her that Archie's literary success was not entirely good for him. Lately, in fact, he'd noticed a tendency in Archie toward "smarty writing." Yet he felt sure that the boy could not go very far astray with Mrs. MacLeish behind him and Yale ahead of him. Buehler knew that Archie had been considering Harvard, but "this present phase in his development" persuaded the headmaster that he ought not to go there. "He needs the democracy of Yale," he asserted.

The two great life-shaping developments of his senior year at Hotchkiss involved neither religion nor education. He met and fell in love with the girl who was, five years later, to become his wife for the succeeding sixty-five. And he began for the first time to express himself in poetry.

Aunt Mary Hillard introduced him to Ada Taylor Hitchcock during his visit to Westover School late in 1910, though she hadn't planned to. Ostensibly the occasion for the visit was a Hillard family christening. Actually Aunt Mary was interested in her young nephew's meeting some socially prominent Westover girls she thought might make him a proper match. Like her sister, Patty, Mary Hillard was concerned with the moral development of young people, but her idealism in this direction was tempered by a frank admiration for the rich and powerful. Some of this attitude rubbed off on her nephew. At first she had hoped to interest him in Esther Cleveland, the daughter of President Grover Cleveland, but Archie found her quite unattractive. There were still other girls Aunt Mary wanted him to meet, however, and so she invited him to dinner at Westover after the christening. As honored guest Archie was seated next to his aunt at the head table. One by one the girls assigned to join them took their places. One seat remained empty — the seat directly opposite Archie's. As Miss Hillard's displeasure grew more obvious, the girl she'd designated to be in charge of seating arrangements reached back, caught the skirt of a passing student, and guided her to the vacant place. The girl so commandeered to sit opposite him turned out to be the small, vivacious, and very pretty Ada Hitchcock of Farmington, Connecticut, and Archie was immediately attracted to her. After dinner, Ada took him on a brief tour of the school, and by the end of the day he was completely smitten. Then as later Archie was susceptible to infatuations, but with Ada it was different. When he returned to Hotchkiss, there was already an understanding between them. For the time being they exchanged letters almost daily.

Aunt Mary did not approve, and since in her willful Hillard way she took a very strong interest in guiding her nephew's life, she did her best to discourage the relationship. She was receiving entirely too much mail from Lakeville, she told Ada. Then she drove over to Hotchkiss specifically to warn Archie that "the Greeks have a saying: 'Nothing too much.'" But her disapproval and cautionary messages could make no headway against the tide of young love.

The girl who bewitched young Archie MacLeish was the only child of William A. and Dinah Boyle Hitchcock. Her father was a self-made man who had started out as a hardware merchant and expanded into real estate. A roly-poly man invariably seen with a cigar in his mouth, he was a popular figure in Farmington, Connecticut, where nearly everyone called him Uncle Billy. Ada's mother, in contrast, was an ineffectual woman who was often ill with asthma. In her childhood Ada played the roles of son and daughter alike for her father. He called her Jimmy. He took her to ball games, where she learned to keep score, and afterwards to the bars she was not to tell her mother about. She learned how to keep him smiling with her natural wit and gaiety. She grew up, in other words, accustomed to having a special relationship with one man, and in time she more or less naturally transferred her childhood devotion to her father to a lifelong commitment to Archie. She also grew up believing, from the example of her father's success, that by sheer force of will you could control your world and make your life come out the way you wanted it to. As a girl, Ada demonstrated considerable musical talent. In her senior year at Westover, Aunt Mary let her go into New York for advanced piano lessons. Her father encouraged her piano playing, since one day she might be able to support herself by giving lessons. Her still greater gift, as a singer, she did not develop until after she was married, and five long years lay ahead between her graduation from Westover and Archie's from Hotchkiss in June 1911 and their marriage in June 1916. There was no question of marriage while Archie was in college; his parents would not have considered it. And during the long interim they had to combat the continuing opposition of Aunt Mary, who considered Ada to be rather frivolous and not of appropriate social background.

The best teacher at Hotchkiss, Archie thought, was James J. Robinson, Latin master and one of two Ph.D.'s on the staff. But it was A. M. Stevens, master of French and sometimes of English and German as well, who stimulated Archie's interest in poetry. A giant of a man at six feet, four inches, Stevens graduated from Yale in 1905, and was a Rhodes scholar at Oxford for the three years thereafter. Hotchkiss was his first teaching appointment, and he brought to the classroom his own passionate admiration for Swinburne. In his senior year, Archie became a devotee also. "Mr. Stevens would read me Swinburne; I read Swinburne to Mr. Stevens, and Mr. Stevens would get fake Swinburne from me."

The Swinburne influence was one he looked back on with disdain. "Algernon Charles was my boyhood idol," he wrote Amy Lowell in January 1924. "What I wanted was mellifluousness — unbroken curves. . . . I was adverbial as Hell — which I believe to be mosaiced with adverbs." It took him a long time, he acknowledged, to stop writing "musical" verse. Mellifluousness and a certain fashionable melancholy are pervasive in the first of two poems he published in the *Hotchkiss Record*'s *Literary Supplement* during the spring of his senior year. The first of these — hence the first poem MacLeish published — was "The Song of the Canoe":

> *The pale moon's wake on a silver lake,*
> *A silver song from afar,*
> *The silver laugh of a rippling wave,*
> *The path of a silver star.*

> *The dip and drip of the paddle's tip,*
> *The kiss of the lake on the sand.*
> *The stately lines of the soughing pines,*
> *The clover's breath from the land.*

> *All this and thy face 'gainst the moonbeam's lace,*
> *All this and thy dreaming eyes,*
> *Thy eyes that dream in the pale moon's gleam.*
> *That dream of a dream that dies.*

The verse speaks to the ear alone, and the implied drama of the last stanza is obviously tacked on, but as a basically rhythmic descriptive poem, this is quite appealing.

The second poem attempts to capture "The Brook" of its title in three different moods as it descends from the hills. Heavily adverbial and wildly participial, it is a more obvious and less successful example of "fake Swinburne" than its predecessor.

> *Leaping, laughing, gleaming, swirling,*
> *Sun flecked foam on thy bosom whirling,*
> *Mad through the hush of the forest hurling,*
> *Merrily out of the hills.*

> *Sobbing, mourning, sadly calling,*
> *White through the night of the canon falling*
> *Black through the sedge of the marsh lake crawling,*
> *Somberly out of the hills.*

> *Smoothly, gently, tunefully flowing,*
> *Murmuring trees, and breezes blowing,*

Sun and shade and cattle lowing,
Pleasantly out of the hills.

On the basis of these and his other literary efforts, MacLeish was chosen as class poet. What he produced to read at commencement was, however, modeled not on Swinburne but on Kipling. As with the two earlier poems, his class poem dealt with the water, but this time it was the sea, and the elegant artificial language was replaced by a rugged conversational tone. The poem celebrated the call of the sea, an obvious metaphor for the Hotchkiss graduates launched into the future. "And now we've slipped our anchor, and we've flung our canvas out, / And our hearts are beatin' madly for the sea." This, presumably, was the sort of rollicking upbeat message Archie thought fitting for the occasion.

In the class pictures of the 1911 *Mischianza,* the Hotchkiss yearbook, Archie clearly stands out. Fifty-seven of the fifty-eight seniors are pictured in the conventional high collars and sober neckwear of the time. The fifty-eighth is Archie, who looks rather like a dandy by way of contrast, in his radical wing collar and what appears, even in black and white, to be an unusually colorful cravat. In addition, the section on "How the Class Voted" reveals how he was regarded by others in his class. He received a smattering of votes in a number of categories, including Wittiest, Brightest, Most Original, Most Energetic, and Most Likely to Succeed. He finished second for Most Pessimistic, behind the musically inclined Douglas Moore, and third in Done Most for Hotchkiss, behind class president James T. Bryan and star athlete Harold A. Pumpelly. He ran neck and neck with Pumpelly for Most Versatile. Finally, in two categories he led the voting by a wide margin. MacLeish received twenty-eight votes for Most Sentimental, suggesting what was then and forever true — that his emotions lay close to the surface and were easily aroused. And he got twenty votes for Windiest, indicating that he was better known at Hotchkiss for his oratorical inclinations than for his writing.

Although no such category was included in the class voting, there is a strong hint elsewhere in the yearbook that Archie was thought to be conceited. He had accused himself of that schoolboy vice in his letter to Buehler the previous summer, and promised to reform. Apparently he had not succeeded, at least as far as his classmates were concerned. At the bottom of page 143, the *Mischianza* reprinted in its entirety the following item from an advice-to-the-lovelorn column:

Chicago Tribune, Feb. 20th, 1911.
"HANDSOME, RICH, AND DISTINGUISHED"
"Dear Miss Libbey: I am a young man, 20 years of age, handsome rich and distinguished. I am simply wild about

a beautiful young girl whom I met at a dance recently. Shortly after our meeting I declared my love, but she and her parents raised some causes for delay, and I am led to think her affections have grown cold. Please, if it is in any way possible, tell me, Miss Libbey, how I can retain her affections.

ARCHIE."

No, Archie, no way except being as nice as you know how to the girl and by not forcing your affections on her. Try also not to be so self-satisfied. That will help.

Printed without exact identification, the reference was obviously to MacLeish, the only "Archie" in the graduating class.

Of the fifty-four members of the class who had settled on a choice of college, forty-two were bound either for Yale College or Yale's Sheffield Scientific School. Only three opted for Harvard, and in the end MacLeish was not among them. He had been enthusiastically recruited for Harvard by the English instructor Nathaniel Horton Batchelder, who had taken his own B.A. and M.A. there. Batchelder arranged for Archie to visit the campus in the spring of 1911, and to stay overnight in one of the Gold Coast dormitories along the Charles River. That visit backfired, for Archie was so disturbed by the opulence of the Gold Coast rooms and the snobbishness of their inhabitants that he decided on the spot in favor of Yale. Although Yale would be populated entirely by prep school boys like himself, including many of his classmates, it was at the time at least marginally less patrician and more democratic than Harvard, just as Headmaster Buehler had maintained. Besides, Archie knew that his choice would please his mother and his Aunt Mary, who naturally hoped he would follow the precedent of his Hillard forebears, including grandfather Elias Brewster Hillard, by going to Yale.

4

BIG MAN ON CAMPUS

The Blue-Sweater Era

FRESH-FACED and eager for the adventure ahead, the 380 members of Yale's class of 1915 assembled in Dwight Hall on the evening of Friday, September 29, 1911, to hear the welcoming address of President Arthur Twining Hadley. Coming at the end of a week of orientation, the gathering was clearly aimed at launching the freshmen on the right trajectory. The glee club sang. The heads of social and athletic organizations spoke briefly about the opportunities they offered. Then Hadley, every inch a man of affairs, strode to the rostrum. "There are as many lines of activity in the University as there are men," he began. Studies were important, but so were extracurricular ventures. He advised his listeners to "discover as soon as possible some serious interest" and then to work at it. "This is a place for many kinds of men but not for very many kinds of life," he pointed out. At Yale, in short, students were expected to *do*. And it was "a democratic place, for here everyone gets an equal chance and is fairly rewarded for what he does."

President Hadley's words were hardly necessary to motivate Archibald MacLeish, who soon distinguished himself in not one but two fields of "serious interest": football and literature. On the football field, despite his unimpressive five feet, ten inches, and 165 pounds, his quickness and enthusiasm won him a place as starting center on the freshman team. And at his first opportunity he dropped off a selection of poems for consideration by the editors of the *Yale Literary Magazine,* the oldest college periodical in the country. Three days after President Hadley's address, he went to the *Lit* office and found to his delight that they had taken his poem "Gifts" for the initial issue.

So commenced the college career of Arch MacLeish (as he was known at Yale), a career that was by any standard spectacular. By the time he graduated, he was widely perceived by classmates and faculty alike as the most outstanding man in Yale '15, a class that included among others Dean Acheson, the future secretary of state, and MacLeish's Hotchkiss friend Douglas Moore, two-time winner of the Pulitzer Prize for musical composition. At graduation Arch's classmates voted him Most Brilliant by an overwhelming margin, and Most Versatile by a still wider count, 233 votes to the second place man's 13. What was most remarkable was the range of his achievements. He was a star not only as an athlete and a writer but as a scholar, an orator, and a social lion. It was almost as if the same demons that had wiggled out of the bottle at Hotchkiss were still driving him forward in the competition at Yale. Eventually even Arch's father could not avoid noticing his late-begotten son's collegiate accomplishments.

The Yale MacLeish entered in the fall of 1911 was still anchored in the complacency of the nineteenth century. Students competed for grades but were not encouraged to think for themselves. Teachers dispensed received wisdom, which was returned, slightly repackaged, in examinations. Here is a classroom as MacLeish depicted it: "In the large square room the bent heads, the heads bowed together . . . and the voice speaking, stopping, speaking, stopping, running on ahead, waiting, running on ahead. Backward through the mind. The truth lies backward. The truth has been known to Plato — to Georg Wilhelm Friedrich Hegel — to Professor Pollard reading the notes in the margin of his Jowett. The truth is something-that-has-been-known." No one thought to object to professors who made Shakespeare dull, or to a curriculum that ignored Karl Marx. Conformity was the watchword among these favored young men who, with few exceptions, believed in the gospel of success and their own social, intellectual, racial, and moral superiority.

In the spring of Arch's sophomore year, the chairman of the *Yale Daily News* scathingly described this "Yale type." It wore the right clothes, had perfect manners, and did not think at all. "Sometimes it has tremendous dumb energy," the editorialist observed. "And it has nearly the mental power of the original Yale Bull Dog." The college itself, plunked down in the middle of New Haven, gave off an air of fallow mustiness. On the Old Campus, the trees, old and tame, grew out of holes in the sidewalks. There was pavement everywhere, except for a few square yards of open earth in the center of the oblong of buildings. MacLeish and his classmate Henry Woodruff walked around and around the outside of the rectangle one evening. "This is a walled

town," Arch said, "with the walls under it to keep something *down*."
"Perhaps to keep something *up*," Woodruff replied.

However it was, Arch apparently accepted Yale's values and played its games with surpassing skill. Football, for example, was "much more important" to him than his course work. At commencement time, in a class questionnaire that asked students to rank their choices among the honors the college could bestow, he ranked his "Y" letter first, his *Lit* triangle second, his Phi Beta Kappa key third and last. In freshman football his performance as center drew favorable notices in the *News* accounts. Reviewing the all-important Harvard game, the *News* described him as "probably the most efficient player in the line. He is not up to the weight of many centers but has the agility of a back combined with quick perception of a play. His passing has been uniformly accurate." Most often he snapped the ball to left halfback and team captain Thomas H. Cornell, who was to become his Yale roommate from sophomore year on. The Harvard game, on November 18, was played in a driving rainstorm at Soldiers Field in Cambridge and ended in a 0–0 tie. Arch's football career peaked in that game — the *News* account called him "an excellent center" for his exceptional head work, good passing, and strong tackling — and provided him with an anecdote he would tell all his days.

The Harvard team was heavily favored that rainy Saturday. The 1911 Crimson freshmen, "the best in a generation," featured players who would go on to defeat the Yale varsity soundly in each of the next three years. So the Yale freshmen were more or less celebrating their tie at the bar of the Tremont Hotel after the game when the Harvard coach came over, focused on MacLeish, "and announced in the voice of an indignant beagle sighting a fox that he was, without question, the dirtiest little sonofabitch of a center ever to visit Cambridge, Massachusetts." That was heady praise, Archie admitted, but he didn't really deserve the honor. He "was little but not *that* little."

MacLeish never repented his youthful enthusiasm for football. "The taste of blood and lime on an autumn afternoon," he felt, "was as much a part of the delight of being alive as anything else on earth." At least part of the reason had something to do with a group of men engaged together in playing a "wild, extravagant, difficult and often dangerous game," engaged in a common undertaking that involved a common risk. Part of it, too, lay in his own fiercely competitive nature. Characteristically, his collegiate career as an athlete took him directly from football to water polo, another sometimes violent sport — "you have to like contact sports to like water polo," he said — and one at which he excelled. Even as a freshman, he immediately became a regular on the varsity water polo team. Although the season ended in March with a loss to a physically superior Princeton team, MacLeish was among those who received votes for the All-Collegiate team. By that time he had already tried out for catcher, the most demanding and unpopular position on the baseball team, and for once failed to make the squad.

All this athletic activity fit neatly into the pattern of "the blue-sweater era," when football was valued above all other undergraduate activities. And Arch's simultaneous accomplishments in the classroom — he made the honor list his first semester and every one thereafter — were acceptable as well. But his writing, and especially his poetry, was something else. "The theory then was that a man ought to know what he was going to be," MacLeish said in a backward look on his Yale experience. "He shouldn't be doing two things as different as football and the writing of quite vague little lovelies." In fact a certain vagueness did hover about his first undergraduate poems, and he was to contribute more prose than poetry to the *Lit* during his undergraduate career. In his first year he published two poems and two essays, thereby setting a freshman record for *Lit* publications.

A historian of Yale has characterized the period 1909–1920 as the college's "Literary Renaissance." Perhaps it was because he was so much a leader of that renaissance that MacLeish seemed, even in retrospect, to have been unaware that it was going on. In the same fall he matriculated, for example, the new *Yale Review* was reborn as a national quarterly covering "literature, science, history, and public affairs" under the editorship of Professor Wilbur L. Cross, and the Elizabethan Club was founded as a meeting ground where undergraduates, graduate students, and faculty members might pursue literary interests and establish cordial relations. As for undergraduate literary lights, most of them were to shine after MacLeish's tenure — Phelps Putnam and Donald Ogden Stewart in the class of 1916, Philip Barry in 1918, Stephen Vincent Benét in 1919, Thornton Wilder in 1920.

Yale was changing in other ways, too. The rumblings of an impending overseas conflict were heard even in New Haven, and grew louder as the class of 1915 moved toward commencement. "Yours was the last class," classics professor Clarence Mendell told a reunion of Yale '15 thirty-five years later, "with whom I read Petronius and Euripides and Horace with a sense of permanence and security that made possible for us a leisurely sympathy with them, ignoring the storms and wreckage of the centuries and the continent that lay between." Meanwhile, on campus, the class of 1915 took arms against two of the college's oldest traditions. In MacLeish's sophomore year, he and his classmates managed to do away with the annual Fence Rush. That same year some class leaders challenged the procedures and intentions of the long-revered senior societies. MacLeish was conspicuously *not* among them.

The Fence and the "Daughters of Dink"

The annual Fence Rush, held each Washington's Birthday, pitted the freshman and sophomore classes against each other in a violent but generally bloodless free-for-all. In this combat the sophomores, who were supposed to be defending the Yale Fence against the freshman rush, were allowed to lay about them with light bamboo canes. The freshmen were permitted no weapons other than snowballs, yet custom required them to succeed after a fifteen- or twenty-minute melee in securing the Fence, until the following Washington's Birthday bash. Outlining the rules for the event, the *News* stipulated that the rush was to begin immediately after chapel (a daily requirement throughout MacLeish's years at Yale), that the "Y" men of the senior class would act as marshals, and that after a signal from the head marshal, the freshmen would try to take the Fence from the sophomores. In MacLeish's first year, however, the rush was something of a travesty, since few freshmen and still fewer sophomores took part. The following year saw a full-scale campaign to do away with the tradition.

Arch struck one of the heaviest blows against the rush in a bitingly satirical letter to the *Yale Daily News*. He wrote in response to a letter from "1914" favoring continuation of the tradition on the grounds of "manly strength." Those who opposed the rush, this letter maintained, did so because of a "shrinking feeling" that accompanied the prospect of "a fist fight or some strenuous extremity," but that was precisely why the rush was valuable. Certain disputes in life were decided not by arbitration but "by ounces of muscle and ability to fight." The rush provided a taste of such a fight, "which lasted but fifteen minutes and in which a genial spirit soften[ed] the force of the blow." Besides, it was "a mighty satisfactory thing" to know that one could take care of oneself in a fight.

The opening was too wide to be resisted, and MacLeish immediately filled it. "The charge that the Sophomore Class desires the abolition of the Rush because of cowardice is, of course, too true for rebuttal," he wrote in reply. But it was odd, wasn't it, that the previous year's rush failed because the then sophomores, with the apparent exception of "1914," neglected to put in an appearance. In time past, a real spirit of enmity may have existed between the freshman and sophomore classes, but "that enmity has now passed and with it the excuse for the combat. . . . As for its value in preparing the participants for fist fights in after life we can only express the belief that no member of the present Sophomore Class has pugilistic ambitions." The prospect "of smiting and being smitten" by members of the class of 1916 held no charm for him, since he could summon no wrath whatever against them.

A flurry of letters and editorials followed in the *News* and *Lit*. Although most of these supported MacLeish's position, a campuswide referendum on the subject opted for continuation of the rush under less violent guidelines, and it was duly scheduled for Washington's Birthday 1913. At this stage, however, both the sophomore and freshman classes assembled and decided to boycott the event. And that was the end of the Fence Rush.

The still more sacrosanct customs surrounding election to senior societies resisted such change, despite the efforts of a sizable group from the class of 1915. There were then three senior societies: Wolf's Head, Scroll and Key, and at the pinnacle Skull and Bones. On a Saturday afternoon in May, the junior class, or at least those of its members who thought they might have a chance of election, assembled on the campus for the Tap Day ceremony. Each society tapped fifteen men for membership, so that forty-five men out of 380, or about one in eight, were elected. The chosen elite then retreated behind the haze of mystery that surrounded the operation of the senior societies. Each of them was said to own a "tomb," or a forbiddingly dark building, somewhere near campus. Each was supposed to ensure the future success of its members by lobbying on their behalf for jobs and advancement. But no outsider knew for sure what they did, or what took place at their secret meetings. The shroud of mystery lay most conspicuously over Skull and Bones, to the extent that it became widely if erroneously believed that a Bonesman must immediately absent himself from any room in which the very name of the society was uttered.

This, then, was the institution that came under attack in mid-April 1913, a month in advance of Tap Day. According to the *Yale Daily News*, about 150 sophomores banded together to raise three objections, not to the existence of the senior societies but to the way they were organized. The first and strongest objection was to their excessive secrecy, which the ringleaders of the reform movement regarded as responsible for suppressing individuality, stifling spontaneity, engendering hypocrisy, creating unnatural relationships, and undermining existing friendships. Second, and in defiance of logic, the class of 1915 opposed the "extreme publicity" associated with Tap Day. This "unnecessary and sensational display" not only gave "undue advertisement to the societies themselves but also overemphasize[d] the distinction between those who [were] chosen and those who [were] not." Third, the reformers criticized the societies for "inadvisable choice of members," by which they meant that merit should be the determining basis of choice and that men should be elected "without undue regard to family influence or personal interests." To make their point more effectively, a significant number of sophomores bound themselves to refuse membership in senior societies until secrecy was "reduced to a reasonable privacy," Tap Day was abolished, and the choice of members was conducted more equitably.

Undoubtedly the anti–senior-society movement was largely inspired by Owen Johnson's popular novel *Stover at Yale,* published in the spring of 1912. Dink Stover, the hero of that book, spends most of his college career working toward possible election to Skull and Bones. Dink has no objection to Skull and Bones's standards of selection; in fact, he admires its seeking out of men who have had "to contend with poverty, its desire to reward ambition and industry and character." But a few weeks before Tap Day he boldly takes issue with the organization's overemphasis on secrecy and ceremony. "I've come to the point," he tells his wife-to-be, "where I believe secrecy is un-American, undemocratic and stultifying." So he speaks out against it, but in Owen Johnson's fictional universe that selfless action merely makes him more attractive to Bones. Dink is not only tapped for membership but tapped fifteenth and last, which by tradition meant that he was the society's first choice.

Arch MacLeish was not unsympathetic to the objectives of his reform-minded classmates, but he adamantly refused to bind himself not to accept election to a senior society. That seemed to him a preposterous position to take. In print he scornfully described its adherents as "the Daughters of Dink," and predicted that when Tap Day loomed for the class of 1915 the following year, many of those who had pledged themselves against joining a society would be fighting to get themselves released from their commitment. As it turned out, that is exactly what happened. One classmate who had no chance himself of being elected made it difficult for the others, refusing to release them from their vows until the last possible moment. In the end, only three members of the class of 1915 stuck to their pledge and refused election. No one turned down Skull and Bones.

Shortly after five P.M. on May 14, 1914, Herman Livingston Rogers, a senior member of Skull and Bones, wearing a black derby hat, came up behind MacLeish on the Berkeley oval, clapped him on the shoulder, and commanded him to go to his room in Vanderbilt Hall. Thus was Arch MacLeish chosen for the Bones club of 1915, along with his roommate the football star Tommy Cornell and the all-around athlete Harold Pumpelly he'd prepped with at Hotchkiss. Also tapped was Ranald H. Macdonald, chairman of the *News* and the only member of his Bones class to become MacLeish's lifelong friend. Arch himself qualified for election in a number of ways: he played football, captained the water polo team, made Phi Beta Kappa in his junior year, and was going to edit the *Lit* in his senior year. Not all of the selections, though, involved big men on campus. A notable exception was Edwin A. Burtt, a future president of the American Philosophical Society, who ranked second in the class in grade point average but did not otherwise distinguish himself.

In his own comments about Skull and Bones, MacLeish tended to downplay the organization's mystique. "As nearly as I can make out," he said in an interview, "the Bones was started in the early part of the nineteenth century by some southern Yale men who had read Walter Scott and also Laurence Sterne's *Tristram Shandy*. The whole vocabulary of the institution derives from these writers and is very humorous. The alarming discovery of any newly elected member is that the Bones is full of humor and warmth and humanity, all of which has quite a good, sound literary background." Structurally, the society was organized horizontally rather than vertically, so that loyalties were normally associated with one's own club: the fourteen other members chosen in the same year. Since MacLeish had few close connections within his own club, Bones meant less to him than to many others. He did, however, take a particular interest in two subsequent elections. In 1917 his brother Kenny was not chosen for Bones, "a brutal business" that just about demolished his feelings for the institution. Thirty-two years later he was delighted when his son Bill was tapped for membership.

The Young Aesthete

MacLeish widened the scope of his accomplishments as his career at Yale progressed. In October of his sophomore year, for example, he was elected chairman of the five-member 1915 German committee. In this role he was responsible for arranging the class dance to be held in conjunction with the junior prom. Ada Hitchcock, his once and forever girl, was his date for that occasion, and her mother came along to chaperone. Meanwhile, the transition from freshman to varsity football proved a difficult one. After watching him during a disastrous practice session, Johnny Mack, the Yale trainer, nudged MacLeish on the trolley car ride back to the old gym on Elm Street and remarked sadly in his Irish brogue, "You'll be lucky to make the training table." That was about right: Arch played on the scrub team all fall, providing cannon fodder in scrimmages and never participating in a game. When winter came, though, he returned to the pool as center forward and a leading scorer on the water polo team, which once again beat almost every opponent except Princeton.

In the spring Arch was, rather ironically, chosen as Fence Orator by his classmates. Now that the rush had been dispensed with, this marked the official presentation of the Fence from the sophomores to the freshmen, with no blows struck. MacLeish's talk, delivered on June 5, 1913, began with a barrage of puns: "Men of Yale . . . I am chosen to rail at you fiercely; and, at the same time, generously present you with a railing; to give you a fence for your pleasure and offense for your discipline." Then he laid "The Late Lamented Rush" to rest in doggerel addressed to the alumni:

> And ye who, in a younger time,
> Were wont to drink of cask and tun,
> And spend the morning's early prime
> And all the long hours of the sun
> In fistic fights ye called fair fun,
> What had ye save the battle's stain?
> Behold, the Freshies always won.
> Were not your Rushes then in vain?

Yet in conclusion he reminded his listeners that Yale's venerable tradition distinguished it from other institutions. On April 1, former President William Howard Taft, a Yale man himself, had bowed out of the presidency with a moving speech in Woolsey Hall. Such inspiring events could not happen at "that little mushroom college back home with its twentieth century Gothic chapel and its monumental endowment."

Arch came back to campus early in his junior year for football practice, and earned a spot as an all-purpose substitute at the backfield positions and at end. During the Harvard game, won by the Crimson 15 to 5, injuries propelled him into action, and he made a memorable flying tackle of Crimson star Eddie Mahan, driving him out of bounds and saving a touchdown. At the close of the season, he was one of the three members of the class to earn his football "Y." In the pool, he served as captain of another winning water polo team. Early in February 1914 he escorted Clara Whittlesey, a distant cousin, to the junior prom. Ada could not come. Her parents had sent her to Paris for the year in order to further her musical education and, quite possibly, put an ocean between her and her beau.

The remainder of the spring term was busy and triumphant. On February 25 Phi Beta Kappa elected twenty-eight juniors to membership, MacLeish among them. On March 4 he was one of five men chosen to edit the *Lit* the following year. As the leading contributor to the magazine, he assumed the post of chairman. On Saint Patrick's Day, appropriately, William Butler Yeats came to campus to lecture on the glory of Dublin's Abbey Theatre. During his stay in New Haven, Yeats was persuaded to visit the Elizabethan Club and take a glass of whisky. There he intoned some poetry with a pronounced lilting beat emphasized by rhythmic hand gestures. For a time thereafter MacLeish sought to emulate the great man by intoning his own verse, though he left out the swaying of the hand. Ten days later Arch invited a dozen classmates to a dance at Tryon Hall on Riverside Drive in New York, the palatial residence of his half-sister Blanche and her husband, Ben Billings. A half dozen Rolls-Royces met the Elis at Grand Central Station and carried them to the estate overlooking the Hudson. There they mingled with some of the city's elite, including a young actress, Elaine Hammerstein, who arrived, with fanfare, about midnight. The dancing — and the swimming in the indoor pool — continued until dawn, when the Billings' son, the host of the party, spied his parents' yacht coming up the river and encouraged his guests to disperse into the city before it arrived.

At the annual *Lit* banquet three nights later, various toasts were offered, the British poet Alfred Noyes delivered a panegyric on Tennyson, and MacLeish accepted his chairmanship with an idealistic speech. "Where other publications supply the college world with news, we supply it with literature," he said. "The *Lit* by its position is somewhat of a 'beautiful ineffectual angel,' but we can't help believing that 'there's a good time coming.' . . . Youth dreams, has visions, discovers, takes, and touches. These true sentiments and experiences make up the *Lit*."

His own dreams and visions were increasingly fixed on a life in literature, under the encouragement of a charismatic professor named Lawrence ("Larry") Mason and an admiring classmate, Frank Bangs. At the time the established stars of Yale's English department were Professors William Lyon ("Billy") Phelps, a dramatic performer in the lecture hall, and Chauncey Brewster ("Tink") Tinker, an eighteenth-century scholar of wide renown. As an English major, Arch encountered both of these men. Tinker was his instructor in freshman English — the only instructor he remembered from that year — and in his Age of Johnson course senior year. Arch respected Tinker but found his emphasis on serious scholarship arid and forbidding. Billy Phelps, by contrast, was a gregarious man who went out of his way to befriend students and participate in campus organizations. He was toastmaster at the *Lit* banquet, he read from Shakespeare's sonnets on the bard's birthday, and he assembled his own band of talented students, known as the Pundits, for literary dinners.

Arch, who was selected as one of the Pundits, regarded Phelps as "a terribly nice man" but an intellectual lightweight. He later dismissed him in verse as "Professor Phlip in Doctor Phlap's goatee." He dropped Phelps's course in English literature of the seventeenth century in the middle of his senior year. That course "almost destroyed John Donne" for him, he later said, for the poetry of Donne was beyond Billy Phelps's capacities. By senior year Arch was inclined to judge his teachers severely. Sometimes, as in Professor John Berdan's course on English literature of the sixteenth century, he admitted to tuning out the instructor in order to scribble page after page of "some of the worst verses ever perpetrated."

In Larry Mason young MacLeish found his mentor. A Phi Beta Kappa graduate of Yale in the class of 1904, Mason taught for three years at Hotchkiss before returning to his alma mater as an English instructor in the fall of 1907 (at the same time Archie was enrolling at Hotchkiss). He pursued his graduate studies while teaching, earning his doctorate in 1913. Thereafter he became "Dr. Mason" in the college course listings, but he remained a lowly instructor throughout his fifteen years on the faculty. Mason's failing was a common one in the academy. He did not publish, and scornfully sniffed at his colleagues who did. In particular, he feuded with Tinker, whose research he characterized, to the delight of his students, as "scholarshit." He also competed with Tink for Yale's best and brightest, and was interested only in those students. "If Larry didn't like you, he flunked you," as one of the survivors put it, "so that his class was always a small and congenial group." Sartorially impeccable with a flower in his buttonhole, he was "a Cellini of words": brilliant, eccentric, and to some "a genius as a teacher."

In junior year Arch took Mason's course in minor prose writers of the nineteenth century. The class met late Wednesday afternoons, and in preparation for the meetings, Mason wrote questions on the blackboards and then drew maps down over them. When the students had arrived and the bell had rung, Mason locked the door and raised the map from the blackboard to the right. The class wrote furiously on the question there revealed for fifteen minutes, when the map was lowered and the papers collected. Then Mason would lecture for twenty minutes of concentrated brilliance before raising the map from the blackboard on the left. The question there was more open-ended, and students might write for ten minutes or ten times ten minutes, as they individually chose. Remarkably, some of MacLeish's answers to these quizzes survive, and in them he displays the kind of witty erudition that Mason must have encouraged. Whatever the readings, the subject matter invariably seemed to touch on aesthetics and Platonic idealism. Mason was a brassbound idealist, convinced that the only life that mattered took place inside the mind and that the only subject the mind need concern itself with was art. Occasionally MacLeish would challenge his instructor's dogmatism on the subject. He was unwilling, then as later, to write off the outside world and live for art alone. "If all our thoughts are thoughts and there is no red fruit of action," he objected, "shall we not throw gay flags to the autumn winds and add joyousness to the 'eddies of purposeless dust'?" To which Mason replied in the margin: "But is the life of 'action' really so dust-proof, so fruitful?"

This sort of heady discussion of crucial questions did not usually take place at Yale, or at least it did not take place in so congenial and convivial an atmosphere as Mason created. During his semiannual two-hour examinations, for example, students spent the first hour on the reading they had done in the course. Then there was a fifteen-minute intermission at the bar of the Hotel Taft across the street, followed by the second half of the exam, "which was purely inspirational and for which no preparation, other than alcohol, would equip you." His coterie of students undoubtedly enjoyed this cavalier approach to the college's requirements, but Mason's fellow faculty members did not. Besides, there was the question of his sexual orientation; at the time, no overt indication of homosexuality was to be tolerated. Arch himself may have interrupted some sort of assignation when, one day, he stopped by to see Mason in his apartment at 18 Elm Street. To his amazement, Mason became furious, angrily informed him that he did not want students bothering him at home, and unceremoniously threw him out. Soon thereafter, apparently as a gesture of apology, Mason called on MacLeish at *his* room.

Still, Larry Mason exerted a considerable influence on MacLeish, both at Yale and for some years thereafter. Serving in France in World War I, Arch returned in memory to Mason's classroom with twilight coming on

> *And you in that small room with windows high*
>   *Where yearly falls Jerusalem to Greece,*
> *You with that burning reticence of eye,*
>   *Sworn enemy to unbelieving peace,*
>
> *Will summon there the hidden beautiful,*
>   *And make the poppy shine across the corn,*
> *And on the wind the silver of the gull,*
>   *And in the wood the silver of the horn . . .*

And in 1921 he again invoked "that golden, golden time" at Yale and Mason's part in it. "We judged rightly," he wrote a classmate, "when we judged that he offered us more than books and men."

In junior and senior year, Arch became something of a young aesthete himself, never mind football. He spent an increasing amount of his time on his own writing, and many of his free hours at the Elizabethan Club. MacLeish was the first member of the class of 1915 elected to the Elizabethan, late in his sophomore year. In the following year a number of his classmates joined him there, including Francis Hyde ("Frank") Bangs.

A tall, slender lad of strong cultural interests, Bangs was the son of the humorist John Kendrick Bangs. Frank Bangs admired MacLeish's rather waspish satirical thrusts in the conversational give-and-take at the tea tables and on the lawns of the Elizabethan, and he admired his poetry as well. He was, in his own ironic phrase, the classmate "most gifted in the appreciation of [MacLeish's] budding genius." Playing Boswell to his Johnson, Bangs made an annotated record of their meetings — and of all communications from MacLeish, including letters and poems — in the interests of posterity.

Like MacLeish, Bangs was a disciple of Larry Mason's, and in long talks the two students debated issues of philosophy and religion. Frank maintained the likelihood that personal identity would be obliterated in the cosmic processes; Arch was reluctant to give up the notion of individual immortality. Jerusalem might fall to Greece in Mason's classroom, but he was not yet ready to abandon Christianity in favor of a thoroughgoing Platonism. In his notes of the mid-1920s, MacLeish recorded Bangs's side of the debate by way of a vignette: "Bangs, the lean head, the blue pale eye, the pipe stem between smooth fingers. The rain dripped in the chimney. The black glass of the windows crawled with rain. 'Words, words — the arithmetic of words. Add a name to a name and the sum is still a name. Divide the word and what have you — the word still. And who has told you that the word for god is God?' Time dripping from the roof, from the black elms."

At one stage, in the spring of his junior year, Arch considered a career in the ministry. He wrote Ada to that effect in Paris, and she was so alarmed, as family legend has it, that on a trip to North Africa, her unease communicated itself to the camel she was riding and the beast ran away with her. Arch's own enthusiasm cooled after a searching discussion with Sidney Lovett, a fellow Bonesman who had graduated in 1913 and was studying at Union Theological Seminary. MacLeish and Lovett took a long walk out to West Rock, climbed five hundred feet to the top, gazed out at the dwindling lights of the city, and talked about the religious life. A lovable and sympathetic man, Lovett quietly heard MacLeish out. When they climbed down West Rock, well past midnight, he gently suggested that whatever else Arch might be destined for, he did not seem to have the makings of a minister of the gospel.

The principal difficulty, of course, was the shaky foundation of Arch's faith. Indeed, he seems to have turned toward religion in an attempt to bring his doubts to heel. His undergraduate writing is full of these doubts — of the conflict between religion and art, cynicism and altruism. He published in all fourteen prose pieces in the *Lit* and nine poems. Seven of the prose publications were short stories, and while these are flawed in a number of ways, including overingenious plotting and lack of character development, they demonstrate MacLeish's early attempts to find answers to the riddles of human experience. In "The Charity of Love" (March 1913), for example, he constructs a romantic hero who probably represented his ideal at the time. John Claverhill is a romantic youth, sensitive to the wonders of nature and skeptical about conventional religion. "I believe in a religion that speaks to the heart, not the head," he declares, and when the girl who hopes to convert him to the higher altruism remonstrates that that is paganism, he defiantly agrees. Yes, he is pagan, but so are all youths. "Our gods are the laughing brooks, the winds in the treetops, the flowing seas of grain." Yet two months later, in "The Virtues of Vice," MacLeish pulled the rug out from under yet another religiously radical hero. For Will Target, happiness is the only thing worth seeking. With *carpe diem* as his motto, he pursues his hedonistic goal. In the end, however, he discovers happiness not through the pleasures of the flesh, but by committing — almost despite himself — an act of Christian love.

The quest for something to believe in, whether it be beauty or art or God, is even more prevalent in Arch's undergraduate poetry. His "Wanderlust" (April 1913) reveals a Byronic romanticism at once adventurous and sensitive:

> I ride to the snarling hounds of the storm in the mane of the typhoon's wrath,
> I drift on the hyacinth echo of song down the new moon's opal path;
> I sleep in the perfume of sandal wood and under the lulling pines,
> I drink of the flow of the sun-kissed snow, and the ruby of Eastern wines.

Two years later, in "The Grail" (June 1915), that self-assured paganism gives way to soul-searching questionings.

> Yes, I have sought for Truth,
> And flung against the ready-rending tooth
> Of doubt, and beat with bleeding blows
> The bars invisible of Heaven.
> I have cried out to Christ who loves and knows,
> And knowing still can love,
> That my night may be riven
> With lightning of His truth and might thereof:
>
> . . . .
>
> Shall be no answer made?

The answer, or at least the one Archie espoused in a June 1916 letter to his father, he found in Ralph Waldo Emerson, "the great figure of his century . . . and one of the great figures of history." Emerson he thought of as "a later Plato who has known Christianity." By combining the two, he had arrived at a persuasive conception of divinity. Emerson's belief in the Oversoul, his conviction "that we are all, in essence, god-head, that there is in each one of us that common soul which eternally IS": that was an idea MacLeish could accept. It did not end his quest for assurance of individual immortality, but it did give him a measure of faith in a God that existed in and through all mankind.

"A Lad of Parts"

As he headed into his senior year at Yale, Arch was confronted with two crucial and interrelated questions: When could he marry Ada? What career was he going to pursue? And on a trip to England in the summer of 1914, he was made vividly aware of the ways the international conflict looming on the horizon could affect him. He traveled with classmate Douglas Moore, who had already demonstrated his talent for musical composition by writing the still popular Yale football song "Goodnight, Harvard." On the journey across, they encountered Arch's Aunt Mary Hillard and a traveling companion. Aunt Mary, true to form, took charge of their itinerary. Together they went out to Wrexham to lay a wreath on the tomb of Eli Yale; together they motored through the Cotswolds.

On Saturday July 30, Arch and Doug escaped to London on their own. Immediately things went wrong. They were short of ready cash, but thought that on Monday they could cash an American Express check. Monday, though, was a Bank Holiday, and the holiday continued through the first part of the week. On Tuesday the famished Yalies went into a restaurant, ate a big meal, and paid for it with a ten-dollar American Express check, from which they got no change. Ten dollars for one meal was more than their resources could stand. On Thursday August 4, Great Britain declared war against Germany, and all of a sudden a great many people who did not have to stay in England were eager to get away. Arch and Doug at once took the train to Liverpool and managed to secure steerage accommodations on the *Lusitania*. Conditions in steerage were miserable, and the food worse. After a few days, however, an older gentleman traveling in first class discovered that a fellow Bonesman was in distress, and saw that Arch and his friend were moved to his stateroom and the pleasures of first-cabin table.

Safely back in New Haven, MacLeish resumed his football career as a second-string back. He ran back a kickoff against Lehigh, intercepted a pass against Colgate, and was hurt — not seriously — in a 28–0 victory over Notre Dame. The season ended in yet another defeat by Harvard, the first Yale-Harvard game played in the vast expanse of the new Yale Bowl. Although Arch did not go out for water polo senior year, the family was still represented. Younger brother Kenny, a freshman, replaced him as a regular forward.

In November, Arch came to the defense of Yale's heritage in the pages of the *Yale Daily News*. The *Yale Record*, the campus humor magazine, had made a slighting reference to "Nathan's strangulation." Nathan Hale's statue, with his memorable statement — "I only regret that I have but one life to lose for my country" — was a prominent fixture on campus, and MacLeish objected to making fun of him. "Hale is our chiefest hero. To mock his supreme sacrifice is to mock what most of us hold worthy of reverence." In reply, Charles A. ("Doc") Merz, editor of the *Record* (and editorial-page editor-to-be of the *New York Times*), accused MacLeish of "rearing an Himalaya out of an ant-hill," for no good purpose. Whatever the merits of the case, the exchange illustrated MacLeish's lifelong propensity to feel a deep emotional tie to certain heroes from the early days of the republic. Should anyone make light of Hale (or Jefferson, or Adams), he took the insult personally.

Somewhere during his years at Yale MacLeish discovered sex. First there was Mrs. Lanahan with the full breasts during a summer picnic. The voices of the others faded away, and they were alone under the willow tree, her dark eyes full of wisdom, she the interpreter. "Her hand over his hand, over his ———, the suffocation of thick blood . . . the warm soft shaft, the agitation of her raised legs, her fingers showing, her wet mouth, all." And later, on the boat coming back, an "unutterable sadness" overtook him, "a sadness *for* nothing, of *nothing,* but as though I still wept for a dream I had forgotten."

At the studio tea there was Marjory, the tall dark girl who came up beside him looking out at the rain against the streetlights. "It will rain all night, and perhaps for days," she said. "When you sail south towards the cape the skies change and people stand for hours staring at the stars — even those who never look at the stars at home." Afterwards they walked the dark streets, their hands clinging, their mouths pressing together but never quite meeting. Later she received him, giving the gift of "herself and the moment of selflessness." At night in New Haven, desire sometimes drove MacLeish along the dark pavement to her room under the flat tin roof, where the smell of asphalt competed with the smell of lilacs. "Suddenly she called my name and we clung to each other, alone, we two alone, each, each alone and the rain beat upon our naked flesh."

Yet he was aware, once the transport passed, of the "ridiculous momentary agitation of the male . . . the elaborate, complicated preparation of the elephant for the minute act . . . the unlaughing flesh working like a root in the ground, grave, dumb." Nor did he think that these sexual experiences, trivial as they were, compromised his feeling for Ada. More dangerous in that sense was his brief infatuation with Sally McGill, another of the mother's helpers Patty MacLeish employed. Arch met Sally during Ada's long absence in Europe and asked her to "wait for him," though she was a college graduate and some years older. That romance, like many others to come, faded away. Archie and Ada's lasted.

After their year of forced separation, Archie and Ada came together with renewed passion. Impatiently they planned for their marriage. Ada came to Craigie Lea over the 1914 Christmas holiday to receive the blessing of his parents — Patty MacLeish recalled the look of trepidation she wore upon her arrival — and once that had been granted, Archie bought her a $200 engagement ring. As far as Archie's father was concerned, however, the engagement was likely to be a long one. Andrew MacLeish, who at eighteen had followed his true love across an ocean, was not yet prepared to permit his twenty-two-year-old son to marry: not until he had established himself. This attitude became abundantly clear in an exchange of letters between father and son, shortly after Ada's visit to Craigie Lea.

Prior to that time, Andrew's letters to his son at Yale had been primarily concerned with budgetary matters. Arch was expected to supply meticulous monthly accounts of his expenditures against his $100-a-month allowance. Everything was to be accounted for, with no catchall "miscellaneous" category permitted. Andrew was sometimes displeased with his son's reports, as his letter of October 10, 1913, shows:

> A statement purporting to represent your September account arrived in an envelope addressed to me here and without any superscription and signed by you. I wish to ask you if you think this way of communicating is entirely respectful to me, not to mention any other considerations?
>
> In respect to the account, however, as it does not include or refer to the balance on hand of the $100.00 deposit you induced me to grant for emergencies, and as that was impaired according to your verbal statement to me of August 27 by $26.00, your account should show $74.00 more on hand than is shown in the statement forwarded.
>
> Please correct this and forward to me.
>
> Affectionately, your father

Despite the forbidding tone of correspondence such as this, Archie, in the afterglow of Ada's Christmas visit, wrote his father an optimistic letter about his forthcoming marriage. "You were kind enough to say during our short interview of this vacation that you were interested even in the things I dream of," he began. He was to graduate in June, and his fondest dream would be satisfied if he and Ada could be married in the fall of 1915. That could be managed if his father continued his allowance, since Ada had an income of her own of about $500 to $700 annually. Archie could then add to that total whatever he earned "in his first year," though he did not specify his probable occupation.

His father's response was anything but reassuring. "I am unable to think it wise or best for you to marry next fall," he wrote. He was shocked to hear "as coming from you" his son's proposal to subsist on Ada's income and his allowance. The "desire for possession," he concluded, must have been so urgent as to make Archie overlook "the prerequisite" of being able to support a family. Besides, Archie would be beginning a new vocation in the fall, and should be prepared to devote all of his time and energy to his work. Andrew (like his father before him) clearly hoped that his son Archie would follow him into the business, just as his son Bruce had already done. He had spoken to S. C. Pirie about the possibility and been assured that Carson Pirie Scott would welcome "young blood of promise" into the firm. For the first year, Andrew suggested, Archie would save money by living at home and commuting to the store with him.

At this stage Archie beat a strategic retreat. He was sorry that his father found the proposal unworthy, but reiterated his hope that the marriage might take place as soon as possible, if not as soon as the coming fall. "It is something more than the desire to possess," he assured Andrew. "It is complete inability to live at my fullest and best without the help and love of the woman I intend to marry." Privately he had no intention of entering his father's business, but in this letter of January 9 he sounded very much as if he planned to do so. "I must confess that one reason which has influenced me more than any other in my choice of an occupation has been the knowledge that my entering the store would please you and would be a step toward meeting my very great obligation to you, and I would not willingly do anything now to color your pleasure in that choice." At best, he was not entirely straightforward with his father, but he was after all determined to marry as soon as possible — he and Ada had been courting for more than four years — and prepared to do anything that might secure that end. "I was dead without her," he explained.

Although a marriage date could not be set, the engagement was enough to bring Aunt Mary around. In March, she held a dance for Ada and Archie, along with a number of his friends from Yale and hers from Westover. Archie had been attending eastern schools for eight years, always within a short train trip from Farmington and this aunt who took a proprietary interest in his welfare. "She and I were closer to each other when I was young than any aunt and nephew I have known," Archie was later to observe. That closeness was only intensified when, as in 1914–15, Aunt Mary also played surrogate mother to his siblings: Kenny as a Yale freshman, Ishbel as a Westover junior. Yet Archie was not content to let his dominating aunt "mould and control" his life. Both of them had strong wills, and it must have caused her some pain to capitulate to his choice of Ada. "She'll never be able to handle Archie," Aunt Mary declared of Ada, quite wrongly, but with absolute conviction. When she gave them a party, it was probably not so much to validate the marriage as to reassert her position of authority.

The spring of Arch's senior year confirmed his turn away from prose and toward poetry. For the first time, his poems gained recognition beyond the pages of the *Lit*. In April the widely circulated *Yale Review* ran his elegiac "Grief," in which the speaker laments the death of a loved one and, still more, of the "silver dreams" they dreamed together. Never before had the *Review* printed a poem by an undergraduate. In response Lawrence Mason designated MacLeish "the most remarkably promising" of Yale writers. Huber Gray Buehler, at Hotchkiss, declared a holiday for the boys in his honor. Early in June, Arch won the seventeenth Albert Stanburrough Cook Prize, given annually for the best unpublished verse by a Yale undergraduate. By that time he was already mulling over possible approaches to the Class Poem he had been chosen to deliver at commencement.

In the back row of Johnny Berdan's class, Arch passed fragments of the poem as it developed to Frank Bangs, sitting next to him. His first attempt to stitch these together led only to doggerel. "I tried to write a poem, / An epic of the Class, / An Iliad of Greatness, / A Dunciad of Mass," he confessed, but the image of Ada confounded his attempts. "I tried — but oh what would you! / My inspiration *lived!* / She moved, she breathed, she — could you / Conceive a poet wived?" The final version came quickly, once he decided on a theme. What he and his classmates had learned in the college's classrooms would soon be forgotten, while other "magic things" persisted in memory:

> *The fog that creeps in wanly from the sea,*
> *The rotten harbor smell, the mystery*
> *Of moonlit elms, the flash of pigeon wings,*
> *The sunny Green, the old-world peace that clings*
> *About the college yard where endlessly*
> *The dead go up and down.*

But this was not all, for elsewhere

The people of the earth go down,
Each with his wealth of dream,
To barter in the market town
A star for a torch's gleam . . .

Too easily did they sell "their treasuries of dreams" for a "shimmering reality" that would soon fade away. Despite its evocation of the genteel tradition in moonlight mysteries and gleams, as a class poem MacLeish's is first-rate, and he never disavowed it. "I'm not dead sure it's a poem," he commented in his eighties, "but I think it's awfully close."

His poetic success in senior year fueled Archie's literary ambitions. He would be a poet if he could, but he knew that he could not pay his own way, much less anyone else's, by a life in poetry. Meanwhile, he hoped that the awards he was accumulating would impress his father, and tried for still others. On May 2, for example, he wrote Andrew that he was preparing to compete for the De Forest Prize, for writing and speaking an essay. (He did not win.) Winding up the letter, he paid hyperbolic tribute to his father's influence. "You have been not only the opportunity for my education and happiness but the figure I have most respected and admired in life." Nothing he had accomplished could begin to repay his debt. And yet, he added, "I *do* wish . . . that you knew more of this university and more of the relative importance of things here because I feel that I have been a little more worthy of your hopes for me than you realize." In short, Archie wanted his father to recognize what he had accomplished, and to grant him the permission — and the wherewithal — that would enable him to marry Ada, without going to work for Carson Pirie Scott. Over the commencement weekend, with the connivance of his mother, this goal was reached.

The MacLeish family assembled in New Haven in late June to celebrate Archie's graduation — all except brother Norman, who had transferred from Williams to pursue studies in architecture at Penn and was busy with classes there. Leading the entourage was the patriarch, Andrew, still vigorous at seventy-six and firmly set in his ways. His wife, Patty, who sympathized with Archie's desire to be married, asked her son to arrange an interview with Yale president Hadley during the busy commencement period. Then she insisted that Andrew keep the appointment alone. Thus Archie's father heard from the president of the university, also a member of Skull and Bones, what he would not have credited from many another: that Archie had made a brilliant record at Yale, and that if Archie were his son, he would certainly stake him to the graduate study he ought to undertake and allow him to marry into the bargain. Patty MacLeish paced along the pavement, waiting for her husband to emerge from the president's office. When he did, it was with head high and the pleased observation, "Why, Patty, it seems our son is a lad of parts." Then they went over to Archie's room at Vanderbilt Hall to tell him what Andrew had decided. He would support him for three years of further education, as long as he did not marry until after the first year. With the end in sight, the delay no longer seemed insupportable. At the commencement ceremony the next day, Archie delivered his class poem with style and distinction.

At the time, Archie had not yet decided exactly what kind of further education he would devote himself to. At the midpoint of his senior year, he came close to committing himself to a future in the academic world. "MacLeish expects to take up the study of literature," the copy for the 1915 Yale *Class Book* read. Yet the more closely he observed his Yale professors, the less inclined he was to follow their example. In correspondence with Bangs, he discoursed on "professorial emulations and envies." Getting ahead was so much a matter of pecuniary necessity, so much a matter of life and death, that the men engaged in academic careers lacked the ability to "stand aside and smile. . . . It warps, feminizes and narrows them. They [Tinker, Berdan, and others] sneer at Mason behind his back and smile cat-like smiles before his naked brow. And Larry himself, please God, was not always so much a matter of irony and feline thrusts as now he is." The teaching of literature, he decided, was not for him. Yet he did not want to go west, and he disliked business.

"The alternative seem[ed] to be law," and that was the alternative he chose. MacLeish clearly regarded law school as a compromise. It was better than going into business, for the law might leave him some time — "summers, Sunday mornings, an evening now and then" — when he could write. What he most feared "was being caught in a regular day-in, day-out job." Besides, the redoubtable Aunt Mary urged him to take up the law. Her youngest brother, John Hillard, had been a promising law student at Harvard but had died of typhoid before graduating. Favorite nephew Archie, she felt, might well have the career her brother had been deprived of.

At the time of graduation, MacLeish's closest friend was Frank Bangs. His affection for Bangs and his feelings for Yale were intermingled in his mind, as Archie's sentimental letter of August 1915 shows.

> Never again shall I walk out into a soft June rain with its fragrances of hedge and flower and warm sweet earth but you shall walk with me and my heart shall smile for joy of our pilgrimages into immortality by way of a journey a'foot. Never shall wind

howl at eaves but a certain hearthstone in a room we both love
for all its affectations [Larry Mason's] shall beckon me in memory. Never shall stars shine shyly through elm leaves but I shall
lie on my back in a certain elm tree contemplating again the
comparative merits of ale and suicide. For you see, my dear
Frank, ours is such a friendship as hath little enow to do with
words and faces. . . . And I find that as New Haven drifts behind
me you stand out more and more vividly in my heart as that one
whom I will not willingly lose in this life nor in that eternal life
for which we so differently hope.

In future years Archie continued to look back on Yale with a sense
of nostalgia for the place itself, while becoming increasingly dissatisfied
with the education he received there. Similarly, his feelings for Bangs
diminished over time, as did those for others such as football star and
roommate Tommy Cornell. Archie forever recalled the night, junior year,
he'd taken Tommy to the infirmary with a charley horse that was driving
him crazy with pain, and another night, senior year, when the two of
them found out how to hit bats with tennis racquets. Eventually, though,
it seemed to him that Tommy "just stopped living after Yale — or
stopped growing older."

Ranald Macdonald, the short and energetic *News* chairman, did become a good friend in later life. And MacLeish kept in touch with the
likable Norman ("Nig") Donaldson, future editor of the Yale University
Press, and with Douglas Moore. Far and away his closest lifelong friend
in the class of 1915, however, was a man he hardly knew at Yale: Dean
Gooderham Acheson. Acheson had sailed through college with a degree
of conviviality Arch neither shared, since he was often in training for
one sport or another, nor entirely approved of. For his part, Dean
thought of Archie as overly tense and competitive, too concerned with
making a record for himself. At commencement, Dean's date was his
wife-to-be, Alice Stanley. Looking through the class book, Alice kept
coming across mentions of Archibald MacLeish as scholar, athlete, poet,
and so on. "Just who is this MacLeish fellow?" she asked. "Oh," Dean
replied, "you wouldn't like him." That feeling was to change at Harvard
Law School, where Acheson and MacLeish matriculated in the fall.

5

ADA AND THE MUSES

Law versus Poetry

Archibald MACLEISH entered upon his Harvard Law School studies with a confidence bordering on arrogance. He had been king of the hill at Yale, and went to his first classes proudly wearing his Phi Beta Kappa pin. Within the week, he attracted the attention of Professor Joseph H. Beale, "the most caustic of all the caustic users of the Socratic method." Joey Beale laid him out "naked on the floor," and left him wondering if he would ever attend another class. Instead of quitting, Archie put away his PBK pin and joined the fray. The law, he would demonstrate to Beale and everyone else, was just one more world fit to be conquered.

In the fall of 1915, Harvard Law was embarking on one of its greatest periods. The Socratic method, in universal use there, regularly generated classroom excitement. Among the interrogators at the rostrum, besides Beale, were Roscoe Pound, who was about to become dean, Austin W. Scott, an expert in constitutional law, Zechariah Chafee, Jr., the well-known champion of civil rights, and the brilliant young Felix Frankfurter, who made friends with the brightest of his students, MacLeish and Dean Acheson among them.

His real education started at Harvard Law, MacLeish remarked. Beginning with the notion that the law could provide him with a livelihood, he found himself caught up in its intellectual appeal. The law, he thought, provided "*the* great gateway to history." It gave him "a sense of the tradition of human conduct, action, knowledge, values, morality." For the first time, he realized what education was, and what the relation

between teachers and students ought to be. And as always he thrived
on the competition.

Stimulating as law school was, it occupied so much of his time and
energy that little was left over for poetry. This he bemoaned in letters
to his Boswell, Frank Bangs. Early in October, after only a week or two
at Harvard, he congratulated Bangs on leaving his publishing job with
Macmillan. Now Bangs was "saved out of the polluting mercilessness
of Things" and was free to dream. But Frank would have to dream for
Archie, too, since he was imprisoned in his studies. Two months later
he exemplified his plight in a parable:

> As to life: there was once a great number of fireflies who dwelt
> among certain rose-bushes in a certain arbor. And it happened
> that one among them was a philosopher. Now it is a character-
> istic of fireflies that when they are in a light mood they fairly
> irradiate; whereas when they are somber they are little better
> than emphasized shadows. Wherefore this philosopher among
> fireflies pondered in his heart upon the nature of his race, and
> he arrived at a tremendous discovery. For since momentary
> flashes of light were the great accomplishment of his race it must
> necessarily follow that Light itself was the great end and aim for
> which his race was created. And as he so ruminated in his secret
> soul, lo, the moon came climbing above the garden wall and
> seemed to hang in the branches of the rose trees — for you must
> know that this philosopher was accustomed to dream from under
> a toad stool. At once the philosopher became vastly excited &
> called to his race that he had found the great end and aim of
> life; and, so calling, he flew up and up above the rose bushes to
> the very verge of the garden wall, and all his folk with him, and
> on and on, and up and up till the garden was a mere shadow
> below — and still on and on till he and all his race were swal-
> lowed up in the white light of the moon & altogether destroyed.
> This is a fable.

Much as he might yearn to ascend to the heavens, that way lay devastation. Circumstances kept him earthbound, none of them more than
the need to pursue a vocation.

In a January letter to Bangs, Archie wrote that he was "completely
swallowed" not by the moon but by the law. "It is a perfect jungle,"
he insisted, articulating the thoughts of many a first-year law student.
"The farther in you go the deeper the tangle gets and the more lies out
behind you to keep in mind. I won't say that it has not its fascination
for it has. But it also fills me with a very real rebellion."

The rebellion derived from his conviction that he was born to write, not to make a success as a lawyer. For seven more years the competing claims of poetry and the law fought it out inside his mind. Occasionally the struggle led him to seek out alternate solutions. But always he was aware of the basic incompatibility of the two masters he was serving. They spoke different languages, for one thing: "Lawyers use words as signs standing for meanings whereas poets use them not only as signs but as sounds and as visible objects, as images, as metaphors."

In "A Library of Law," written before mid-1917, MacLeish expressed his disdain for the language of the law:

> Adjudicated quarrels of mankind,
> Brown row on row! — how well these lawyers bind
> Their records of dead sin, — as if they feared
> The hate might spill and their long shelves be smeared
> With slime of human souls, — brown row on row
> Span on Philistine span, a greasy show
> Of lust and lies and cruelty, dried grime
> Streaked from the finger of the beggar, Time.

In his fancy he wondered if even the "little letters there" in the lawbooks might not long for something finer than "the records of old sin," some trace of "that fair printed world of ancient song," some inkling of "the vanished magic of dead things."

Such was his drive for achievement, though, that Archie was able to report to his father that his "law school mark for the first year . . . was 76." That might not sound very high, but, he pointed out, the highest mark in a class was usually about 80 and any grade above 75 was an A. He expected to rank among the first ten in a class of two hundred, and hoped to be elected to "the much coveted Harvard Law Review." (He did and he was.) As usual he wanted to make certain his father properly valued what he had done. "Please ask some Harv. Law School man you know what an 'A' means," he wrote.

Marriage at Last

Once he had fulfilled his agreement with his father by finishing his first year of law school, Archie lost no time in marrying Ada. The wedding took place on June 21, 1916, in the old First Congregational Church of Farmington, Connecticut. The day dawned clear and bright, but as the ceremony was about to begin, a fierce summer squall struck. Latecomers staying at the village's Elm Tree Inn were soaked en route to the church, and caterers scrambled to move refreshments indoors from the lawn. Archie and Ada exchanged their vows amid thunder and lightning.

At last, five and a half years after they had met at Miss Hillard's table in the dining room at Westover, they were man and wife. Ada was pregnant, though she did not know for sure at the time.

Aunt Mary, having resigned herself to the marriage, characteristically took charge. As Archie put it, she "lifted the embargo, crossed the hills to Farmington, took over the wedding rehearsal in that most beautiful of all New England churches, instructed my about-to-be father-in-law in the art of stepping over a bridal train, loaned us Crossways [her home] for a stopover on our way to Bermuda, and generally conducted herself as though the whole thing had been her doing from the start — which, in a way, it was."

The society page of the local paper, wary of hyperbole, described the wedding as "one of the most important marriages of the season in the vicinity of Hartford." In attendance were Ada's parents, her friends and former schoolmates, Archie's entire family, and a contingent from Yale that included his brother Kenneth, who served as best man, Douglas Moore and Frank Bangs, and several members of his Skull and Bones club. Following the wedding, bride and groom withdrew for a private ceremony restricted to Bones members. Then they were off to Bermuda and a somewhat unsatisfactory honeymoon.

At sea, Archie wrote Bangs a curiously conflicted letter about his married status. "And so in all sweet things is sadness and in all happiness the bitter fragrance of burning leaves," he began. He felt joy, certainly, but also an "ache of memory" for dear days forever past. In Bermuda, Mrs. Edward Streeter lent the couple her cottage at Paget for the honeymoon. They soon discovered they were not alone. On the first night, Ada was sewing and listening to Archie read — a lifelong pattern — when she was startled by the sound of a book slamming against the wall. Archie had dispatched an enormous spider with the book, and dozens of gigantic black cockroaches were busy crawling up the same wall. Outnumbered, Archie and Ada hastily retreated behind the mosquito netting that surrounded their bed.

The next morning, when the housekeeper arrived to fix breakfast, Ada casually asked her if there were cockroaches in the kitchen. "Oh yes, Miss," she replied, "and they get into the icebox."

That was all the newlyweds needed to hear. Archie biked into Hamilton to find a hotel room, while Ada practiced a cough that would justify their moving from the cottage to a room nearer the doctor. While in town, Archie heard there were sharks off the point where Mrs. Streeter's cottage was located and raced back to rescue Ada before she dipped a toe in the water. They then packed up and left, Ada still coughing for the benefit of the housekeeper. No sooner were they safely ensconced in their hotel, however, than Ada let out a scream. There, in the bathtub, was a cockroach even larger than the ones they had escaped from.

As a married man, Archie was more conscious than ever of his financial responsibilities. His father's counsel, as always, aimed him in this direction. In April, while ordering his wedding suit, Archie tried to open a charge account at Brooks Brothers, and gave his father as a reference. Andrew MacLeish saw to it that his son was turned down. The whole reason he was furnishing Archie with quarterly funds, he explained, was to enable him to pay cash down and to impress on him "the supreme value of the maxim 'Pay as you go.' " He reminded Archie of the sage advice of Dickens's Mr. Micawber in *David Copperfield*: "Annual income £20, annual expenditure £19.19.6 — result happiness; per contra — annual income £20, annual expenditure £20.10 — result misery." It was a good time to make this point, Andrew believed, for as Archie set up housekeeping, he would inevitably be tempted to violate that excellent principle.

In order to earn some money on his own, Archie entered upon an intensive tour of duty as an instructor at the Roxbury Training School in Gales Ferry, Connecticut, "an institution of Yale men engaged in tutoring Yale men." He worked ten-hour days acquainting his pupils with the rudiments of *Macbeth* and Milton. He came out of the experience with "a verbatim knowledge" of Shakespeare's plays and "a pedagogic appreciation" of Milton's poetry. But it was exhausting work, and at summer's end he was glad to take the $400 he'd made and leave the "gaping countenances" of his students behind.

The money would come in handy "next March," he wrote his father on August 13 — a reference to Ada's pregnancy. Moreover, if brother Kenneth wanted to sell the Mercer car they'd been jointly given by Ben Billings, he was to "remember that the other half-owner is not only poor but a shyster lawyer to boot." No matter how pressing his financial needs, Archie was determined not to spend another summer as a tutor. His two remaining free summers he planned "to devote to the great mass of reading I have yet to do and for the doing of which my mind is so thirsty." Law and literature were incompatible, but he wanted to acquire sufficient background so that if he ever were able to turn to the creative work he most loved, he wouldn't have to stop for research and scholarship.

Law school did not entirely dam his poetic flow. He usually included a poem with his letters to Bangs, and authorized him to try to sell some of these to the magazines. Midway through Archie's first-year studies, Britain's poet laureate John Masefield came to read both at Yale and at Westover, where Aunt Mary was his particular admirer. She arranged

for Archie — and Bangs, whom he enlisted for the purpose — to drive
the great man from New Haven to Westover on January 14, 1916. At
Yale, Masefield was struck by the uncanny resemblance of Phelps Putnam
to the ill-fated English poet Rupert Brooke. He was still more impressed
with Archie, after reading his class poem. "That is fine," he exclaimed
to Bangs. "That is very fine!"

This was encouragement indeed, but increasingly Archie had a sense
that time, and other young poets, were passing him by. Soon he received
word of forthcoming books of poems from fellow Yale man Danford
Barney, from Charles Brackett, a Cambridge attorney MacLeish had met
and disliked, and from Edna St. Vincent Millay, not yet graduated from
Vassar. Naturally enough, he started to think of issuing a book of his
own. "I have reached two firm resolves," he wrote Bangs from Gales
Ferry: "(1) Never to *practice* law if I can escape it. (2) To publish a
volume if I can find a publisher . . . in two years." The second resolution,
at least, he was able to achieve.

Muses: Peabody and Sargent

Happily and newly married though he was, Archie was still susceptible
to the spell of female beauty. Bangs, who was inclined to think MacLeish
should not have married, introduced him to two such beauties in the
summer and fall of 1916. In each case Bangs himself was smitten. And
in the case of Grace Allen Peabody, Bangs was to become — for a time —
her husband. MacLeish met the beautiful and patrician Mrs. Peabody,
of York Harbor, Maine, and 830 Park Avenue, New York, on the beach
at Ogunquit late in July 1916. Bangs and MacLeish were out for a dawn
stroll on the beach when Mrs. Peabody and a companion, over from
York Harbor for an early morning swim, materialized out of the mist.
Grace wore a sea-green bathing suit and was beautifully bronzed by the
summer sun, with a reddish undertone to the bronze. She and Archie
tossed a tennis ball back and forth on the beach as the sun burnt away
the mist. The next day, Archie and Ada and Bangs lunched at her home
in York Harbor. Soon thereafter he wrote "Lilies," in which she is
depicted as

> Lily, Pan's red lily,
> Sunlight-drunken lily,
> Golden, golden lily tipped
> With dawn's drowned fire . . .

Nor was this the only poem she inspired. Four years later, Grace
accompanied Archie on a tour of New York's Cloisters in order to show

him the tomb of the abbess of Tours. Even in stone the abbess looked lovely, peaceful, happy, and young. In a sonnet, Archie speculated that she so appeared because she died confidently awaiting the arrival of the one perfect lover she was sure would come. Eight hundred years had passed, yet the illusion persisted:

> *And her two eyes that lift beneath the lash,*
> *Could he not kiss them even now awake?*

Early in October 1916, Bangs saw to it that the MacLeishes were invited to meet yet another flame of his, Margarett Sargent. Born to an old and distinguished Boston family, Margarett was an accomplished sculptor who worked with Gutzon Borglum. She was a talented amateur actress, a witty conversationalist, and a great beauty, with "unusually large light-blue eyes, a countenance pale as marble, and amazingly thick dark hair." MacLeish, like Bangs, was immediately attracted to her. "Many were," as her brother, the writer Daniel Sargent, laconically remarked. Archie wooed her with and through his poetry. She is depicted in "The 'Chantress" (originally called "Lo, the Lady Margarett"); "The Showman" is a portrait of her at a wedding; he took her as a model for Helen in "Our Lady of Troy."

Bangs, who continued to court Margarett during 1916 and 1917, was not entirely pleased with his friend's attentions to her. "I have seen M. S. quite a bit of late," Archie wrote Frank in February 1917. "She is all you claim for her — which is more than you say." He enclosed with the letter a "few lines which I dare not show her for fear of annihilation," the poem which begins:

> *Lo, the lady Margarett!*
> *Cunningly her fingers fret*
> *Witcheries in clay.*
> *She is Circe, sorceress.*

Bangs, sure that he was doing what Archie had expected, sent the poem to Margarett, along with a complaint: "Sargent, that Archibald should be casting such lines your way is beyond my comprehension." Weren't he and "Archibald" friends? Hadn't Archie just become father to a son?

Their first child, called Archibald, or little Archie for short, was born barely eight months after the MacLeishes were married. He almost arrived unattended. Awakened by labor pains shortly after midnight on February 25, Ada suggested that Archie fetch the doctor. "Nonsense, it takes nine months," he assured her. "Try to go back to sleep." But the pains intensified, and at Ada's insistence he ran off to summon help.

Shortly after the doctor arrived, she gave birth to a son. He was tiny and frail, but otherwise healthy. The event occasioned a poem in which Archie portrayed his son entirely as an extension of his wife:

> You are her laughter
>   Blown to a rose,
> Singing heard after
>   The song's at the close.
>
> You are the sorrow
>   Was dusk in her eyes,
> You are the morrow
>   Is night where she lies.

In some ways Archie regarded his firstborn as an intrusion on his marriage, for despite his admiration of other women, he was an uxorious man. Somewhat too short and too much given to putting on weight to meet the standards of classical beauty, Ada was a pretty and vivacious companion with a voice like an angel's, and she knew how to secure Archie. Adele Lovett, herself a stunningly attractive woman and for fifty years a close friend of both Archie and Ada, remarked that there was almost always some other woman Archie was interested in — and vice versa — but that these enthusiasms were never allowed to upset the basic soundness of the marriage. "Ada was too clever for that," she said. "She simply sat back and waited." And his romances undoubtedly stimulated his writing. "Ah, muses," his friend the poet May Sarton remarked. "Archie had to have his muses."

Whether they led to carnal knowledge is a question whose answer is not easily discovered. Late in life Archie confessed to his son Bill there had been one serious affair. He did not identify the woman. He was a reticent man, and gentlemen did not reveal such things. Only in his poetry, and most of all in poems he chose not to publish, does there appear what looks like concrete evidence.

On the basis of such poems, though, it seems likely that Archie did have an affair with Margarett Sargent. Margarett's granddaughter and biographer Honor Moore is inclined to think that both Frank Bangs and Archie MacLeish loved her platonically, after the ideal fashion advocated by Lawrence Mason at Yale. Yet the sheer number of MacLeish's published poems about her, and the internal evidence in these and in several unpublished poems, suggests otherwise. In May 1917 Archie saw Margarett for an hour at an outdoor wedding and was carried away by her wit. "Her words were swift as swallows in a gale," he wrote Bangs in a first draft of his poem "The Showman." "She was a blue brook broken to a thousand . . . bubbles by every conversational stone or water-soaked log of stupidity."

After World War I, Margarett continued to inspire him to verse, though — significantly — the postwar poems were never printed. What most attracted Archie physically was "the thunder of her hair" — her remarkably heavy, dark hair. He caught a glimpse of her on a Boston street in April 1919, "her eyes a jest, her hair a *dream unfurl'd.*" That very phrase crops up in a poem he set down on the back of his copy of James Barr Ames's *Cases in Equity Jurisdiction,* a textbook he was then studying at Harvard Law:

> *She is not beautiful as women are.*
> *Nor any living beauty, nor the sense*
> *Of perfectness in sorrow's immanence*
> *Nor any song, nor any wished-for star.*
>
> *But they who seek that face beyond the world*
> *Wherein earth's longing shall be blown at last,*
> *Whereof is Beauty but the shadow cast,*
> *Cry out, beholding now their* dream unfurled.

In the spring of 1920, Margarett married Quincy Adams Shaw McKean, and MacLeish's feelings for her went further underground. But her hair kept the memory alive in poetry he decided against publishing. Margarett appears vividly in the two poems that Archie recorded in his notebooks. In the spring of 1935, he wrote:

> *To have the hair of your nape in my*
> *Hand and the weight of your*
> *Dark hair in my hand!*
> *For the way I remember you —*
> *The way most I remember the*
> *Touch and the shape is the*
> *Coarse hair of the nape in my*
> *Hand and the warmth of it.*
> *The making of love I have lost.*
> *Who will remember*
> *The sun itself in the sky?*
> *It's the sun on the slight and*
> *Silver curve of a tree.*
> *It's the hair on the nape of your*
> *Comely neck I'm remembering.*

Sixteen years later, on August 10, 1951, she came back to him again in "Epitaph for a Young Man," another unpublished poem.

The thing I remembered most
Was the coarse dark hair
At the nape of her neck in love.
The dark feel of it filled my
Hand, waking and sleeping —

Even here.

A First Book

Beginning his second year in law school in September 1916, Archie and Ada moved into a rented house at 35 Bowdoin Street in Boston that Aunt Mary, naturally, had found for them. Early in the fall term Archie was elected to the *Harvard Law Review* together with eleven other second-year men, including Acheson and Day Kimball, another student who was to become his close friend. Kimball, he thought, was the real star of the class: "He had a marvelous mind, subtle, clear, and cool, a wonderful instrument to watch." MacLeish himself continued to rank among the academic leaders, though his mind was often concentrated on the book of poems he was trying to put together, and on the impending entry of the United States into World War I.

During the winter and spring of 1917, while Archie was working on new poems and shuffling old ones around, he broadened the circle of his literary acquaintances in Boston. There was a dinner, for example, with (American poet) "Josephine Preston Peabody Marks, Mr. Josephine P. P. Marks, and [English poet] W. W. Gibson," in which Josephine Preston Peabody held forth on the virtues of two poets Archie admired and she knew well: Edwin Arlington Robinson and William Vaughn Moody. In disagreements, Peabody was not to be bested. "She has a way of being very kind with one when one is in opposition," Archie wrote Bangs, "that makes one feel the Christian religion has its drawbacks." Soon thereafter he escorted the plainspoken, bucolic "Willy Wilf" Gibson to New Haven, where they had tea with Larry Mason at the Elizabethan Club. Gibson and Mason were immediately at odds. Mason was all brain and no flesh, Gibson quite the opposite. "I never think," Gibson said. "I don't like poetry I can't understand." Robinson, he said, was "too intellectual." "A pleasant vice," Mason drily observed, followed by silence and coolness. Archie also met the English poet Walter de la Mare, "a tremendous lover of Donne and a true metaphysician," and had a long and stimulating talk with him about life, death, art, and immortality.

In April 1917 Archie completed *Our Lady of Troy*, a one-act play in blank verse. Dealing with the last hours in the life of Faust, it was

MacLeish's most ambitious work to date and his first attempt at play-writing, a genre he was often to return to. Like most of his subsequent plays, *Our Lady of Troy* takes a plot from a well-known source and infuses it with a meaning peculiarly its own.

The scene opens at a tavern near Wittenberg as Faust awaits the midnight hour when the devil will appear to snatch him away. Three bibulous students recognize Faust and proceed to ask him questions. Was it true that he had the power to raise Alexander from the grave? Certainly not, Faust replies. The rational mind could

>   *analyze*
> *And test and know and fashion into word*
> *The thing that Is; but no thought ever shall*
>
> . . . .
>   *build new thing,*
> *Nor call up life or beauty from the void,*
> *Nor make the dead whose flesh is dead, alive.*

The students, paying no attention, urge Faust to raise up Helen of Troy. To demonstrate that his presumed magic is only trickery, he conjures up a hazy vision of her. The students are awestruck, but he rebukes them for their credulity. The vision is but an evanescent product of his craft, he declares,

> *And soul, and mystery, and stuff of dream*
> *Are rainbow-winking bubbles in the bowl*
> *That vanish and are nothing.*

Then the apparition moves, and it is Faust's turn to be awed as Helen speaks:

> *Lo! I am she ye seek in every maid*
> *Ye love and leave again. I am desire*
> *Of woman that no man may slake in woman.*
> *This thing am I, — a rose the world has dreamed.*

The dream, the power of the imagination, is ultimately more real than all his science, Faust admits in a final anguished speech:

> *"A rose the world has dreamed"; — and I, I stood*
> *Peak-high in those grey mountains of my mind*
> *And saw all truth, all science, all the laws*
> *Spread out beneath my feet. I sold all things*
> *To know that all I knew was all the world*
> *Of knowledge; and I bought — why, nothing then, —*

Or only this at last — a space to know
That out beyond my farthest range of thought
All knowledge shines — a radiance of stars.

Here art and beauty triumph over reason and science. There were more things in heaven and earth than "all the world of knowledge" could know.

With this twenty-page play as the leading item, Archie assembled a manuscript that included the sonnet sequence and class poem he had written at Yale, the poems inspired by Margarett Sargent and Grace Allen Peabody and the birth of his son, and a number of others — thirty-eight in all — and sent it off for consideration by Houghton Mifflin. He was eager to have publication arranged before he went off to war. When Houghton Mifflin turned it down, he decided to try the Yale University Press. On a spring weekend in New Haven, he went over his plans with Larry Mason and left the book, to be called *Tower of Ivory,* in his charge. It was issued by Yale on December 6, 1917, with a foreword by Mason. By that time Archie was serving in France.

6 ❖

THE GREAT WAR

Joining Up

By THE WINTER of 1917, it was clear that not even President Woodrow Wilson, who had run for re-election on that platform, could keep the United States out of the war. As the battles raged on in Europe, America's sympathies were increasingly drawn toward its old allies England and France, and against the hateful Hun. The war fever spread as German submarines, determined to cut off the flow of aid across the Atlantic, made repeated attacks on American shipping. On February 3 Wilson announced that the United States had broken off diplomatic relations with Germany. The next day, Archibald MacLeish wrote his father that he expected war within a fortnight, and that if the United States started building a great American army, he would "feel obligated to get officer's training in one way or another."

Both of his brothers made their commitments before Archie decided how best to serve his country. In the fall of 1916, Kenny took part in training exercises for potential naval officers. Then on March 26, 1917, he enlisted in the Naval Aviation Service with a number of his Yale friends and was sent to West Palm Beach, Florida, for flight training. Soon thereafter, older brother Norman joined the Pennsylvania Cavalry Corps. As a married man and a new father, Archie weighed his options with more caution.

The declaration of war came on April 6, two months — not two weeks — after the break in diplomatic relations. In his patriotic poem "The Easter of Swords (April 8, 1917)," Archie linked the event with the celebration of Easter Sunday.

Now out of this corruption has been born
This incorruption. Out of this decay,
This passionless, sick serving of the day,
This staleness — from this seed, this rotten corn

Of shame and doubt, has sprung this flowered thorn,
This burgeoned pain, this fire. We that were clay
Have lifted up our eyes — and lo! the spray
Of bright swords and the challenging high horn!

So Christ is risen, so the wakened soul
Has lifted back the heavy stone and stands
Aflame with morning; what then if it be
Death, not the lily, shining in his hands?
Already, ere the first reveilles roll,
Our death is swallowed up in victory.

On May 5, after "three or four weeks trying to decide where my duty lies," Archie wrote his father that his mind was made up. He had to reach a decision, he pointed out, since the new draft law did not exempt married men. Besides, something "stronger than draft laws" drove him to want to serve. "It means doing my part against a nation of madmen. It means giving my strength to tramp down an Idea of government and society as abhorrent to me as are crawling lice or dead things. It means, also, a blow for world peace in order that this small son of mine, this grandson who will bear your name and carry on your mortality, may live his life in freedom of wars and lust and lies."

Four days later he stated the case even more forcefully in another letter to his father. "I must serve," he asserted. "Else I were not your son." He backed up the point with a passage from Emerson that Andrew had once quoted to him: "What I *must* do is all that concerns me, not what the people think." He only worried that his wife and son might not prosper in his absence. "They would of course have to look to you in a measure," he observed.

The question was not whether to go to war but in what capacity. A stateside desk job was all wrong, Archie believed. The overage or physically infirm could do that work, whereas he was "athletic, intelligent and accustomed to handling men and absolutely fitted" for an officer's duty. He had thought of joining the spring Reserve Officer Training Corps camp at Plattsburgh, New York, but his mentors at the law school encouraged him to finish the year. He planned to wait until the next Plattsburgh camp in August. He would emerge as a lieutenant, and the resulting salary could help support Ada and little Archie. The only hitch was that he might be drafted in the meantime.

In reply, his father assured Archie that he would of course see to the welfare of Ada and the baby. In fact, he hoped they would move out to Craigie Lea if Archie was called. But Andrew MacLeish, now almost seventy-nine, did not think it right that he should be. "Our family, having given two out of its three sons, ought to be exempt from further demands." He even proposed finding a loophole to evade or delay the draft. "If you should come West," he wrote Archie, "the question might be raised, in case of conscription, whether you are not a legal resident of Massachusetts."

Archie could understand his father's feelings, but once he had decided to serve, he was eager to start doing so. August seemed unconscionably far away, and he began exploring alternatives to the ROTC camps. What he wanted was a military assignment in which he could do his duty without being killed — he owed it to his family to return from the war — and with, if possible, an officer's commission. The American Ambulance Field Service, already operating in France, provided one possibility. Late in May he asked several Yale professors and administrators, including President Hadley, to recommend him for the field service. They did so in glowing terms. "I always regarded him as one of the finest men we have ever had, a very strong man," read one letter of support. But the ambulance corps was already oversubscribed.

By mid-June Archie was considering two additional alternatives. One was a commission as a supply officer in the army aviation corps. Samuel B. Hemingway, an assistant professor of English and head of the Yale branch of the Intercollegiate Intelligence Bureau, supported him for this position, and for a time it looked as if MacLeish "might have an opportunity to buy copper wire after all." This plan fell through because of the War Department's directive that such posts should be reserved for men too old for more active service or for "younger men with slight physical defects."

So it was the other alternative, the Yale Mobile Hospital Unit, that Archie chose. Dr. Edward Streeter, whose wife had lent the MacLeishes her cockroach-inhabited cottage in Bermuda, encouraged him toward this decision. Under the leadership of Dr. Joseph Marshall Flint, head of surgery at Yale Medical School, the unit was training its personnel, mostly Yale graduates, at New Haven. Its mission was to set up a mobile field hospital that could function immediately behind the front lines, in order to provide the best and quickest care possible to the wounded. This sounded like useful work, certainly. The only trouble was that Archie, lacking any knowledge of medical procedures, had to enlist as a private. This did not appeal to him, but neither did being drafted into the infantry. Late in June he signed on with the Yale Mobile Hospital Unit.

Among others in this unit were three members of Arch's club in Skull and Bones: Lou Middlebrook, captain of the 1915 Yale baseball team; Lyon ("Nick") Carter, captain of the 1915 Yale track team; and MacLeish's former roommate Tommy Cornell. Three other classmates also enlisted, one of them Frank Bangs. Bangs was on his way to join the marines when he stopped at the Yale Club in New York City. There he met MacLeish. If he wanted action, if he "wanted to do the right thing and not be hurt," Archie argued, Bangs should join the Yale Mobile Hospital Unit. The marines might send him to Guatemala instead of Europe. The Yale unit was committed to operate just back of the trenches, and was leaving soon for France. Bangs, persuaded, came on board.

In August the unit's complement of a dozen medical officers, half a dozen nurses, and seventy enlisted men sailed for France aboard the SS *Baltic*. En route the difference between the commissioned and noncommissioned ranks was brought home in unmistakable terms. The officers and nurses were comfortable in their first-class accommodations. The enlisted men rode in steerage, and were served maggotty oatmeal for breakfast, horse meat for lunch, and hardtack and tea at every meal. Since most of the enlisted men were manifestly "officer material," they were particularly resentful of this double standard.

As the convoy drew closer to the U-boat–infested waters off the English coast, the ships ran without lights. One night Bangs and MacLeish were leaning over the deck rail of the *Baltic*, watching the white foam alongside the ship as it proceeded in total darkness. Archie went inside and emerged soon afterward with a sonnet, "Soul-Sight." It commingled memories of Margarett Sargent and his wife, Ada, he told Bangs.

> *Like moon-dark, like brown water you escape,*
> *O laughing mouth, O sweet uplifted lips.*
> *Within the peering brain old ghosts take shape;*
> *You flame and wither as the white foam slips*
> *Back from the broken waves: sometimes a start,*
> *A gesture of the hands, a way you own*
> *Of bending that smooth head above your heart, —*
> *Then these are vanished, then the dream is gone.*
>
> *Oh, you are too much mine and flesh of me*
> *To seal upon the brain, who in the blood*
> *Are so intense a pulse, so swift a flood*
> *Of beauty, such unceasing instancy.*
> *Dear unimagined brow, unvisioned face,*
> *All beauty has become your dwelling place.*

Two nights from landfall the troopships in the convoy separated, with a destroyer assigned to accompany each of them to port. The *Baltic* headed for the Irish Sea, where it was struck by a torpedo. The men in steerage felt a tremendous shock, then rushed to their lifeboat stations to see the destroyer laying down a pattern of depth charges. Fortunately, the ship was not seriously damaged, and it docked at Liverpool the following morning, on schedule.

Eventually the Yale unit made its way to Le Havre, where it boarded a slow freight. The officers occupied a passenger car, while the enlisted men were crowded into two boxcars bearing the legend "Huit chevaux ou quarante hommes" (eight horses or forty men). Their destination was Limoges, where they were to spend the next six months billeted in an empty Haviland porcelain factory. Not only was Limoges more than a hundred miles from the front, but the unit's equipment was commandeered to go to Italy. There was nothing much for the men to do. Occasionally they were invited to tea with members of the aristocratic Haviland family. At other times, Major Flint assigned them to digging drainage ditches and other make-work details. This was emphatically *not* the duty they had volunteered for. Like many of the enlistees, MacLeish wanted out. Unlike most, he was able to do something about it.

On a trip to Paris, Archie wangled an appointment at General Headquarters, American Expeditionary Forces, with Major Hugh A. Bayne, a member of General Pershing's staff. Bayne, Yale '92 and also Skull and Bones, lent a sympathetic ear to MacLeish's story. He and his fellow Bonesmen wanted to contribute to the winning of the war, Archie said, and they could certainly make a greater contribution as officers in some other branch than as timeservers in the moribund Yale Mobile Hospital Unit. In late November, working outside channels, Bayne arranged for his four fellow Bonesmen to be discharged from the Yale unit, enlisted in the field artillery as second lieutenants, and sent to Saumur for officers' training.

Major Flint, of course, was furious — he could see his command dwindling before his eyes — and took steps to make it extremely difficult for others to follow the example of the Bonesmen. Bangs had some reason to feel abandoned by his friend MacLeish. From Saumur, Archie assured him that he would not "give over the search till you are safely out of the Y.M.U." But the barriers had come down against further defections to the field artillery. As Bangs wryly put it in a 1928 account, "The mystic influences . . . which . . . rescued MacLeish, Carter, Middlebrook, and Cornell from fretful inactivity" provided "not even the comfort of bones" to their classmates left behind.

Intimations of Mortality

On December 6, 1917, MacLeish's *Tower of Ivory* was published
by the Yale University Press, in an edition of 757 copies priced at one
dollar. The curious title he chose deliberately, "as a sort of bold flouting of the philistines." According to Mason's foreword, the title "adequately represents [MacLeish's] predominating idealistic conception,
that against all the assaults of arid rationalism and crass materialism,
against all the riddles of endless speculation and brutal experience,
there is an impregnable tower of refuge into which man may enter, in the spirit, and find there the true values and eternal verities
which alone can make him victorious over the world." His only fear,
Mason wrote, was that readers might be so bewitched by the "lilt and
melodic charm" of the poems as to lose sight of their "vital underlying
idea."

Perhaps Mason overemphasized Archie's idealism. The book he described was one he might have wished to write himself. In *Our Lady
of Troy* and a number of other poems, MacLeish's verse did mirror
the program of the foreword. "Aweary of a world's reality," one
sonnet ends, "I dream above the imaged pool, Romance." But another
theme recurs at least as often: an overpowering sense of mutability
devouring time and leading on to death. MacLeish was young, only
twenty-five years old, but he distinctly heard the approach of time's
winged chariot.

The reviews of *Tower of Ivory* were mixed. A British notice, in an
omnibus review of five books by young poets, damned the collection as
much for its manner of presentation as for its contents. "Mr. MacLeish's
'The Tower of Ivory' is enthusiastically endorsed to the public by Professor Laurence [sic] Mason of Yale University, who probably finds more
to commend in the volume than any one less personally interested will
be able to do." The *New York Times* summed up its contents with a
faint measure of approbation. "When all is said this slim volume of
seventy pages has in it more poetry than the average run of minor verse
that falls into the reviewer's hands." Another American review, however,
praised MacLeish for his youthful accomplishment and predicted a bright
future. "Old truths come to him as new discoveries and old themes
arouse a fresh and blessed enthusiasm. He . . . is somewhere in France
as we write and if heaven is good to him he ought to count for a good
deal in American letters in days to come." John Masefield, visiting Aunt Mary Hillard at Westover School in January 1918, sent further words of encouragement about *Tower of Ivory*. "Let me wish
you a happy return from France at the end of this time, and many years

of happy quiet in which your mind will go on maturing and doing more and more of the beautiful work of which this book is so fine a promise."

"If heaven is good." "Let me wish you a happy return from France." The question of life or death weighed heavily on Archie's mind, especially after he transferred from the apparently safe Yale Mobile Hospital Unit to artillery, one of the combat arms. It was a subject he and his brother Kenny often touched on in correspondence, and during several meetings in France. Himself in great danger as a fighter pilot, Kenny did not at first approve of his older brother's shift to artillery. He was brought around by "a perfectly splendid letter" from Arch that arrived early in December 1917, the contents of which Kenny relayed to his fiancée, Priscilla Murdock: "Whatever happens to you, dear old boy, you can always know that I am back of you heart and soul. If you make your mark, I'll be the proudest man in the army. If you are unfortunate, I'll understand. If anything happens to you, I'll remember you as I have always thought of you, as one of the ——— etc. . . . and I won't grieve, because I'll know that you made a great sacrifice gladly for the sake of the things you stand for." "Isn't that *great?*" Kenny asked Priscilla, adding that Arch had just gone into the artillery. "He was right about going, too, for what we need more than a thousand men, is a *good* officer, and a *man!* He *is* the latter, and he *will* be the former." Arch's decision naturally worried Ada, but she wrote Kenny that "though her cowardly self cropped out now and then, and argued against added risk, she was just as happy most of the time, because she had the memories of a perfect year of happiness — and . . . very few have a whole year of perfect happiness in a lifetime."

Ada's welfare motivated Archie to write his father on January 30, raising "the question of the disposition to be made in your will in case of my predeceasing you." In the event of this "altogether improbable contingency," could he be sure that Ada would have "at least a life interest (& a full interest in case of little Archie's death) in that part of your estate which you have intended for me?" Such things were ordinarily not to be spoken of between father and son, he knew. But he was sure his father would forgive him under the circumstances, since he had nothing to leave to his wife and child should he fall in the war.

Archie need not have worried about Andrew's providing for Ada and — especially — for little Archie. They visited Craigie Lea in the fall of 1917, and grandfather was entirely captivated by grandson. "The baby and I got along famously," Andrew remarked. "He was very friendly with me, and he was the first person I tried to see each day upon my return home from business, when he would greet me with beaming smiles and stretch out his little hands to be taken by me." Upon their return to Craigie Lea the following summer, Andrew MacLeish reported to Archie that Ada was "well, brave, and cheerful, as a soldier's wife should be, and little Archie is the dearest little sunbeam that ever blessed a home. He is active and quick on his feet, bright and sunny in disposition, chatters away at a great rate, and is daily increasing his vocabulary. The maids and the women of the household adore him, and his aged grandfather doesn't know a sunnier, dearer burst of sunshine than wee Archie. He and I are good friends, and he ... likes to visit with me in my own room." Archie may have reflected that his father's room was off limits to him as a boy, and that Andrew had never doted on him as he did on his grandson. It would have been hard for him not to.

Archie's course in field artillery lasted three months, and then "the four rebellious hospital orderlies" were sent to French tractor school. It was April before he and Lou Middlebrook were assigned to the 146th Field Artillery, a well-equipped National Guard regiment from New Mexico awaiting action. By that time he had been rumored dead in the literary and artistic circles of New York and Boston.

The false report of MacLeish's demise stemmed equally from Frank Bangs's somewhat highfalutin epistolary style and from his uncertain penmanship. In a letter to Elizabeth Eyre, a talented visual artist and friend of Grace Allen Peabody, Bangs described a conversation between MacLeish and poetaster Danford Barney (who had also enlisted in the Yale Mobile Hospital Unit) shortly before Archie's departure. In arguing a point, Bangs wrote, MacLeish "winged into a finely adumbrated distinction." Eyre thought he had written that Archie "winged into a finely *ambuscaded destruction*." She took this to be Bangs's characteristically convoluted way of announcing MacLeish's death, and in a phone conversation passed on the news to William R. Jutte, a classmate of both Bangs and MacLeish. He in turn spread the report to Monty Woolley and Doug Moore, with whom he'd just been discussing the merits of *Tower of Ivory* at the Yale Club in New York. Within three days the rumor reached the Secret Service in Washington, which issued a formal denial. Jutte immediately wired Ada's mother to reassure her that her son-in-law had not been killed nor even hurt. Mrs. Hitchcock had heard nothing of the sort. Luckily, neither had Ada nor any member of the MacLeish family.

"The whole incident was not without its value," Archie wrote Bangs after an exchange of correspondence about the misunderstanding. "It induced a letter from [Ranald] Macdonald asking me for (1) a denial of the rumor or (2) if that were not possible, then a description of the details."

Before going to the front, Archie spent six weeks at Clermont-Ferrand, where he and Kenny had a memorable reunion on June 29. "It was perfectly wonderful being with him even for one short night," Kenny wrote Priscilla Murdock. The brothers talked of everything but what was most on their minds — Kenny's fiancée and Archie's wife. "I wonder if either of you got the messages we sent after we stopped talking and lay silent." At noon the next day Archie was ordered to the front as commanding officer of Battery B, 146th Field Artillery regiment. His troops were skilled in the use of the 155-millimeter rifles — known as *grands portes filous,* or GPFs — developed by the French and used with devastating effect by both the French and American armies. Though portable for short distances, the 155-millimeter GPFs were weighty weapons: hence the tractor school training in the operation and maintenance of the heavy trucks that took them into battle.

At tractor school, MacLeish had been briefly under aerial attack. "I have heard death overhead and have felt the swiftness of death and have seen the hand of death," he wrote Bangs at the time. But that was an isolated incident. At the front in July, where the Second Battle of the Marne was under way, death was everywhere around him.

During the Château-Thierry drive, Archie was sent forward to locate a site for his battery. The only place he could find that offered any cover at all was an apple orchard, so he moved his troops there and concealed them as best he could.

Two of his men came up to him, and one of them asked, "Lieutenant, why are we here?"

"You mean this apple orchard?" MacLeish said. "I've sited the battery here, and perhaps it's not the best possible choice, but we're stuck with it."

"No, no, not the goddam orchard," they said. "Why are we here in France?"

MacLeish puzzled over that for a minute, and then said the only thing he could think of. "We are here to make the world safe for democracy," he answered, parroting President Wilson's famous line. The men said thanks and walked away, seemingly satisfied. But Lieutenant MacLeish later regretted having produced so glib and "flagrantly improbable" an answer.

As he had feared, a German reconnaissance plane spotted their position. Thereafter he and his men, admirably located to launch their own fire, anticipated a counterattack from German artillery. Before it came, however, Archie and another officer were ordered back to the States to instruct units of the draft army forming at Camp Meade, Maryland, in the use of 155-millimeter GPFs. They did not want to go, he recalled. "The U.S. was full of officers fighting to get overseas. We were overseas and wanted to stay there." On his way back, MacLeish had just boarded a freight train in Paris when a German shell blew up the train station. The rest of the trip was uneventful, and MacLeish — promoted to first lieutenant — was working as operations officer of the Thirty-third Field Artillery regiment, Camp Meade, when he learned that nearly half of his men in France had been lost. It took a long time to shake the image out of his mind: his battery under the apple trees beside the Marne, with a German plane slowly circling above.

Archie was never quite sure why he was chosen to go home in the middle of one of the fiercest battles of World War I. He knew that Aunt Mary, a friend and advocate of Major Flint, had tried to reverse his decision to leave the Yale Mobile Hospital Unit. In a 1938 letter to Joseph Alsop, MacLeish mentioned the pressure that relatives — not his parents — brought upon him to stay in the Yale unit. "I shall never . . . forget the helpless feeling of rage which filled me when I thought that they were going to take, as indeed they did attempt to take, action in Washington." It may be that Aunt Mary made similar efforts to remove her fair-haired nephew from enemy fire when she heard he had been ordered to the front. But that was probably beyond her powers. As Archie said of her, "she had *folie de grandeur* and thought she could accomplish a lot of things that she couldn't." More likely he was selected as an instructor on the basis of his as usual excellent grades in field artillery school.

Ada and Ishbel were attending an outdoor concert at Ravinia Park on the August night when Archie wired that he had arrived in New York. Patty MacLeish pinned the telegram to Ada's pillow and was awakened later to see Ada dancing a sleepy baby down the hallway and shouting, "Daddy's coming home, Daddy's coming home!" Ada took the first train to New York, leaving little Archie at Craigie Lea. Father and the small son he had still to get to know were not reunited until Archie rented a duplex for his family in Jessups, Maryland, near Camp Meade. It was not, from Archie's standpoint, an entirely satisfactory meeting. Upon seeing the father he had no memory of, the child's first words were, "It is not a doggie."

Ada and little Archie did not stay in Maryland long. An influenza epidemic broke out at the camp, and as a precaution they went north to visit her family in Farmington. Once again a battery MacLeish had trained for combat was victimized. A third of his men died in the epidemic. Before the unit could again be readied for service, the armistice was signed on November 11.

Death of a Hero

According to his friend and fellow pilot Robert A. Lovett, Kenneth MacLeish was a very handsome, beautifully built man, and a fine athlete as swimmer, diver, and pole vaulter. He was also far more outgoing and cheery in disposition than his older brother. "There was much less of the dour Scot in him than in Archie," Lovett said. Lovett, MacLeish, Artemus Lamb ("Di") Gates, and F. Trubee Davison were among a contingent of fifteen members of the Yale class of 1918 who collectively joined the U.S. Naval Reserve Flying Corps midway through their junior year in college. The First Yale Unit, this group was called. They went into training a few weeks in advance of the United States' declaration of war. Kenneth MacLeish did so over the objections of his parents. Writing home, he explained his enlistment in the most idealistic and patriotic terms. He had thoroughly made up his mind to join the aviation corps, Kenny wrote. "That is the branch of service for which I am best fitted, and in which I could do most." He simply could not stay at home and let someone else do the fighting. "I could *never* be content at home if there was fighting of a real nature." War was a terrible thing, but the wanton brutality of the Germans was far worse. There were many things worth giving up his life for, and the greatest of these was "*humanity* and the assurance of Christianity."

Kenny's athletic skill and coordination made him a natural as a pilot. He first soloed at Hampton Roads, Virginia, in September 1917. "I was the first one of the new crowd to fly alone," he reported to his parents, and an exhilarating experience it was. He "rather quaked" in his boots when ordered to go up alone, but once he took off smoothly, the nervousness vanished. "The next thing I knew, I felt myself grinning from ear to ear and trying to whistle, though the wind blew my lips flat and the roar of the motor and the propeller entirely discouraged the attempt." He stayed up so long that it was almost dark when he made a perfect landing.

On October 13 Kenny was sent to France. In an exchange of correspondence, Patty MacLeish encouraged him to set down exactly how he felt about the possibility of losing his life in combat. "In the first place," he responded, "if I find it necessary to make the supreme sacrifice, always remember this: I am so firmly convinced that the ideals which I am going to fight for are right and splendid ideals that I am happy to be able to give so much for them. I could not have any self-respect, I could not consider myself a man, if I saw these ideals defeated when it lies in my power to help defend them." The statement, Patty MacLeish believed, showed "the rare beauty" of her youngest son's soul. As the daughter of Elias Brewster Hillard, she could hardly have felt otherwise.

Kenny's letter eloquently expressed that willingness to translate ideals into action that she inherited from her father and passed on to her children. The doctrine was to have a tremendous impact on Archie's life as well as on Kenny's.

According to Di Gates's account, during his year on active duty overseas, Kenneth MacLeish served as "an ordnance officer at a naval air station at Dunkirk, a fighting pilot over the lines, a bombing pilot against enemy bases, a Chief Tester at two of the Navy's largest airplane bases in Europe, and in numerous other capacities." Wherever assigned, he thirsted for action. He was happiest flying with Squadron 213, the Northern Bombing Group of the RAF, from March to June 1918, and was impatient when transferred away.

Early in September 1918 he was sent to Eastleigh, England, where as first flight officer he was to receive, examine, and in some cases repair the new DH.–4s sent from the United States and fly them across to Dunkirk. Bob Lovett, who was squadron commander of U.S. Naval Air Force no. 1 and acting wing commander of four embryo squadrons, secured approval to appoint Ken as squadron commander for USNAF no. 2, in charge of 386 men, 42 officers, and 10 airplanes designed for night bombing. Before cutting orders, Bob wrote Ken for his consent. To his surprise, MacLeish turned him down. He appreciated the honor, Ken replied, but squadron commanders were not allowed to fly, and he would curl up and blow away if he were kept from the fighting. "For the love of Pete, get me out of this hole and back to 213 [the RAF squadron]," he concluded.

Lovett, who was inclined to think his classmate was crazy from overwork or the English fog, tried once more. If Ken preferred, he could put him in charge of a day bombing squadron. This time the reply was even briefer: "Bob, there's no use trying to make a commanding officer out of me if I can't fight and fly." The message got through. A few days later Ken "flew a new bus over to one of the squadrons" at Dunkirk, and was about to fly back to England when the captain told him he was going out to Squadron 213 again. Kenny "nearly fell on his neck and kissed him" at the news.

On October 7 Kenny heard that Di Gates had been shot down. "I'm just crushed," he wrote Priscilla Murdock. "I've lost lots of friends, but Di was different. I've been brought up with him, and he's one of the two men that I actually *love* — Arch is the other." Gates survived, as it happened, but Kenny never knew that.

On Monday, October 14, Kenneth flew his single-seater Camel scout on an early morning patrol and brought down his first enemy plane. In the late afternoon he went up again, for the last time. Eight airplanes started out together, but the fliers became separated in the fog. Kenny stayed in formation with two English pilots. Somewhere over Belgium they spotted two German planes below them and shot them down. The low-flying Jerries may have been decoys, for immediately the three Allied planes were attacked from above by a swarm of eight German Fokkers. The fight was swift and savage. One of the English pilots escaped. MacLeish and the other were shot down.

No one actually saw his plane crash, and search expeditions turned up no sight of his Camel. For two and a half months thereafter Kenny was listed as missing in action, and his family and friends clung to the forlorn hope that he had been captured and was unable to report his whereabouts. His body was found on December 26 by Alfred Rouse, a Belgian solicitor and landowner who went that day to see what the Boche had left behind on his property at Schoore. As Archie recreated Rouse's journey in verse,

> The road was hard to find
> Even for me that sixty years or more
> Had trudged each market day from Bruges to Schoore
> And all the farm was ruin, and a pool
> Of horrid water, — not a cart nor tool
> Nor any wall upstanding, save the stack
> That shivered in the wind and warned us back.
> In all that place there was no living thing . . .

Kenneth's corpse was lying face upward on a pile of debris near a ruined outbuilding. He was wearing his flying helmet and gloves, and his coat was buttoned. His papers and valuables were intact, and Rouse found no trace of blood on his white shirt. The body had not been disturbed by humans. Rats had done their work on the unprotected head.

Some time later Kenneth's plane was discovered a few hundred meters away, apparently in good condition. Archie speculated that his brother had somehow brought the Camel down and died in an attack of poison gas. The British, he discovered, had in fact laid down such an attack approximately at that time, close by that place.

Archie was bereft. His beloved younger brother had made the supreme sacrifice he had pronounced himself willing to undergo. Over the course of the next half century, Archie wrote half a dozen poems that attempted to come to terms with Kenny's death. No other event in his life occasioned so much poetry, and — eventually — so much bitterness. In the first numbness, though, he regarded Kenny's passing without irony or rancor. His poem "Kenneth" celebrates the death of a hero.

He had no dream
Who was himself a music and a flame,
Who sought not glory, but himself became
The glory of his victories,
Who died
Clean washed in anger and the fighter's pride,
Unearthed of ease,
And down those burning skies
Fell like a shattered star.

Such were the delays in communication that the MacLeish family was not informed of Kenneth's death until the end of January. Archie meanwhile had risen to the rank of captain at Camp Meade. He so impressed his commanding officer, West Pointer Colonel Louis A. Beard, that Beard sent a memorandum to Washington stating that "there is not a flaw to find in any of his efforts" and encouraging his superiors to grant him a regular army captaincy, should he apply for one. Archie did not, of course. To accommodate returning veterans, Harvard announced a special law school session that would run nonstop from February to August. That meant that he could complete his third year in August 1919 instead of June 1920. Archie duly signed up.

While waiting for his discharge and for the start of the session, MacLeish returned to New Haven with Colonel Beard, who had been appointed commanding officer of the artillery ROTC program at Yale. On trips with Beard to New York and New England, he spoke about his experiences in the war. And he also served as graduate coach of the Yale swimming team, which had been inactive during the war. On Friday, January 31, he received a telegram from his half-brother Bruce that Kenneth's body had been found. Later that day he moved from New Haven to Cambridge, and missed Bruce's follow-up wire announcing a special memorial service for Sunday, February 2.

Archie was not on hand, therefore, for the memorial ceremonies at Glencoe Union Church. The day was bright and still, more like late March than early February. Young men who had trained with Kenneth acted as ushers. The Reverend Charles W. Gilkey, the MacLeish family pastor, read Archie's poem "Kenneth." Patty MacLeish was sustained in her grief by yet another letter Kenny had written home: "And the life that I lay down will be my preparation for the grander, finer life that I shall take up. *I shall live.* . . . You *must* not grieve! I shall be supremely happy — so must you — not that I have 'gone west,' but that I have bought such a wonderful life at such a small price and paid for it gladly."

Kenneth MacLeish's life was memorialized in a number of ways. Yale awarded him a B.A., *honoris causa*. His mother collected his letters and four poems Archie wrote about him into *Kenneth,* a privately printed pamphlet. The First Baptist Church of Evanston named an addition the Kenneth MacLeish Hall. He was posthumously awarded the Navy Cross "for distinguished service and extraordinary heroism." On December 18, 1919, his sister Ishbel christened the destroyer USS *MacLeish* at Philadelphia Navy Yard. And Ada and Archie changed their firstborn's name from Archibald, Jr., to Kenneth.

7 ❖

A. MACLEISH, ESQUIRE

Young Marrieds

ARCHIE MACLEISH performed brilliantly in Harvard Law School's special session of February–August 1919. Working "terribly hard because of the competition," he emerged as the leading scholar among fifty who completed their studies in that term. At commencement he was awarded the Fay Diploma for the member of the graduating class who "ranks highest in scholarship, conduct, and character, and gives evidence of the greatest promise." Despite his success, he felt no abiding commitment to the law, as occasional comments in his third-year textbooks suggest. "An important and rottenly worded rule," he noted in regard to one decision in his copy of *Cases on Corporations*. Later in the same book he observed of another ruling, "Most important Q, practically, tho' of no import intellectually."

Many of his happiest hours, in the spring and summer of 1919, were spent in Maurice Firuski's newly opened Dunster House Book Shop at the corner of Holyoke and Mount Auburn streets in Cambridge. The slender Firuski, Yale '16, offered a stock of six thousand old and rare editions and a congenial place for literary conversation. The bookshop became the center of Archie's "implausible hope to be a poet by night and a lawyer by day." At lunchtime he'd stand in the sun behind the store windows and read poetry until he "felt the cadences like pulses in his fingers." Then he'd buy a book or not, talk with Firuski, and walk back across the yard to where the law began.

It was in the spring of 1919 that Acheson and MacLeish solidified their friendship. During their first two years at Harvard Law, Archie tended to regard Dean as something of a playboy. Blessed with abundant charm and razor-sharp wit, the bachelor Acheson lived a far more convivial life in those years than did MacLeish. For a time he roomed in Cambridge with Cole Porter, who had transferred from law school to music school, and his evenings were occupied with other Yale companions from DKE, his fraternity, and Scroll and Key, his senior society. But law school worked its transformation on Acheson, and his marriage in May 1917 to Alice Stanley may also have played its part. An indifferent student at Groton and Yale, he became aware for the first time of the power of thought and "of this wonderful mechanism, the brain." Realizing that "excellence counted — a sloppy try wasn't enough," Dean graduated fifth in his class in the spring of 1918. After a brief stint in the navy, he returned to Harvard to write a short book on labor law under his mentors Roscoe Pound and Felix Frankfurter.

Although the Achesons and MacLeishes forgathered often in 1919, the friendship between Dean and Archie did not wholly communicate itself to their wives. Ada considered Dean somewhat overbearing and supercilious in manner, while Alice thought Archie overly ambitious and unduly given to enthusiasms. The two men were, in fact, very nearly opposites in temperament. Dean was, in Archie's words, "gay, graceful, gallant," but with an edge to his humor and a healthy skepticism about other people. This skepticism (some thought it cynicism) was confirmed by his two years' service as clerk to Supreme Court Justice Louis Brandeis, a post Frankfurter arranged for him late in 1919. Brandeis did not have "the slightest faith in mass salvation," Acheson observed in 1920. The business of the law as Brandeis saw it was not to create utopias, but to remove obstacles in the way of individual fulfillment. Archie, by contrast, was then and always idealistic about human potentialities, and often embraced particular causes and their spokesmen as pathfinders to some version of a secular holy grail. Whatever their dissimilarities, the two became fast friends. In his letters to Dean, Archie even proposed that they should set up practice together, or in three-way partnership with Day Kimball.

After the Achesons left for Washington, Archie and Ada began to see more of Bob Lovett, Kenny's friend and classmate, and of his beautiful wife, Adele. The Lovetts were very much to the manor born, Bob as son of the chairman of the Union Pacific Railroad, Adele as daughter of one of the brothers in Wall Street's Brown Brothers Harriman. When Lovett started Harvard Law in September 1919, the MacLeishes were the first to call on them. They lived only a few blocks from Archie and Ada's rented house at 9 Phillips Place, and in this case the wives became and remained close friends. This friendship survived despite Archie's oral and written tributes to Adele's beauty, and despite her considerable interest in literary matters and his career. In August 1920, for instance, he sent her a copy of Lytton Strachey's famous *Eminent Victorians* (1918), with an inscription that combined clever plot summary with flattery:

> Here's Cardinal Manning, a cunning divine,
> He'd a nose for the properest time to resign;
> Here's Matthias Arnold whose intricate soul
> Deprived him of wearing th'Episcopal stole;
> Here's Florence nee Nightingale mort Nightingale
> (She wouldn't have married Jove, Buddha or
>   Baal);
> Here's Gordon of China, courageous, erratic,
> Now shown up at last a religious fanatic;
> Behold them in gold and in white and in khaki
> All singing the glorious fame of L. Strachey
> (I think the refrain would have sounded more
>   catchy
> If Lytton pronounced himself soft as in
>   Strachey);
> As greatness of beauty since Adam first fell
> They all crave the curve of your lashes, Adele.

Undoubtedly the MacLeishes' closest friends during the four years (1919–1923) they spent in Cambridge and Boston were Kay and Harvey Bundy. Like Archie a middle westerner, Harvey had also attended Yale (Skull and Bones, class of 1909) and Harvard Law, and was practicing as a young attorney in Boston. His wife, Katharine Lawrence Putnam Bundy, was the daughter of William Lowell Putnam and Elizabeth Lowell, who were themselves distant cousins. As those names suggest, she was related to almost everybody at the center of Boston society. Her uncle, A. Lawrence Lowell, was president of Harvard; her aunt, Amy Lowell, was an eccentric and well-known poet. Harvey was gregarious and capable, Kay vigorous and intellectually active, and as a slightly older couple with a strong foothold in Boston society, they more or less adopted Archie and Ada. "Ada and Kay got along just like a pair of ducks," Archie recalled. Kay initiated her into the right sewing circles, and the Bundys introduced the MacLeishes into a community of talented young people that included Charles and Edith Curtis, Edward and Hester Pickman, and the artist Ives Gammell.

At dinner parties Ada was a great success for her cooking. All the women had grown up with servants, and only Ada had learned the mysteries of the kitchen. She could never eat her own desserts, though, since she was eternally trying to keep her weight down. Sometimes, after dinner, she would sing in her lovely, pure lyric soprano. Often the group would play word games, where Archie met his match in the brilliant Charlie Curtis, who was to become the youngest man elected to the Harvard Corporation and the assembler, with Houghton Mifflin editor Ferris Greenslet, of *The Practical Cogitator,* a best-selling philosophical anthology. Or they would write poems serially, each adding a line and all curious to hear the final result.

Soon Archie was admitted to the Tavern Club on Boylston Place, where leading Bostonian males assembled regularly for luncheon and on special occasions in the evening, as for the amateur plays written and performed by club members. He made his first visits to the club in a state of some trepidation, as a "young vulgarian from Illinois" in Boston and a Yale man in a Harvard setting. "I was persuaded that everyone in the Club was as voraciously well-read as Charlie Curtis," he wrote, "and that, if some of them were ostensibly doctors and lawyers, it was only because they preferred to do their writing or their painting on Sunday afternoons." His own uncertainty was met with the notorious Boston reserve that dictated, for example, that if one should see a friend coming down the street, the thing to do was to cross the street diagonally so as to avoid having to say hello. In Archie's case, he was confronted with the inescapable presence of President Lowell in a far corner of the Tavern Club's library. He had been told that members of the club addressed one another by their first names, but since he had never heard anyone refer to Mr. Lowell "by either the A or the L," he was absolutely at a loss for words.

The friendship with the Bundys was extended to include their children, and especially their sons McGeorge and William. McGeorge was born March 30, 1919, and four days later Archie composed a humorous "Ode in Reminder of Adversity" warning the proud father that he might yet "live to see (O fate too hard!) / Thy sons in sequence crossing Harvard yard." Eventually the prediction came true, as Mac Bundy — after graduating from Yale like his father before him — became dean of the faculty of arts and sciences at Harvard from 1953 to 1961. He went on from that post to serve as special assistant for national security under Presidents Kennedy and Johnson, as president of the Ford Foundation, and as an incisive commentator and writer on foreign affairs. Archie came to know Mac as he was growing up, and admired him for his accomplishments and for his aggressiveness. "He bites," he said approvingly of Bundy as a dean at Harvard. As Archie's own son Bill remarked,

"Mac Bundy was like a son to Dad," a surrogate son whose achievements it would have been almost impossible to equal.

What Next?

On May 1, 1919, his twenty-seventh birthday, Archie wrote his mother that he could not decide how to use his life. He would finish law school, but after that the future seemed uncertain: "My various plans circle around me like moons, now in eclipse and now in a full and alluring light." These plans included university teaching, journalism, teaching in law school, and, more or less as a last resort, practicing law. The appeal of each potential career he measured against two apparently competing standards: he wanted to do some good on earth, to be of service; and then again, he wanted time to write poetry.

His father agreed to support him during the 1919 special term at the law school, but he would be graduating at a time — the fall of the year — when few law firms were hiring. To make sure he had employment in the fall of 1919, Archie sent out overtures to Yale, Harvard, and Chicago for a teaching position. He proposed to teach not English but government, and Yale was probably his first choice. "I know I can teach government," he wrote Anson Phelps Stokes, the university secretary, on April 28, 1919. "I want to work at Yale." But the only opening there was in the department of history, and that department, perhaps influenced by MacLeish's declared desire to teach history only until he could be shifted to government, decided not to make him an offer. Both Chicago and Harvard came through, however. Chicago's offer was rather better, but Archie nonetheless opted for Harvard, a place for which he had come to feel "a very persuasive affection."

Almost immediately upon finishing law school, Archie undertook a two-part job in Harvard's department of government. First, he assisted Professor George Grafton Wilson in his course in international law: that was the basis on which he was hired. Second, he was given a course of his own in constitutional law, which he taught for the next two years. "I loved teaching that course," Archie recalled, and students enjoyed taking it as well. One of his best students was Samuel Eliot Morison, the eminent American historian-to-be, who sat in on the course as an auditor for the better part of a year, and after lectures would engage MacLeish in intense discussion.

In letters to Acheson, Archie expounded on his reaction to teaching. The contact of the classroom, he wrote, was "by way of being the greatest fun on earth. You are God in your own garden with all your omnisciences carefully brushed up." Yet how worthwhile was the profession itself?

"How many men do the really great teachers touch in such manner as to change their intimate prejudices?" Besides, while he was correcting "stupid papers on hackneyed themes," mighty things were being accomplished in the great world. "Doesn't it all come down to action in the end?"

He was nonetheless excited to be invited to lunch at the Harvard Club one October Saturday with Pound, Frankfurter, Chafee, and an English Labourite named Phelan. Afterwards Dean Pound discovered an example of metonymy in a Latin verse over the fireplace, quoted a sonnet of Santayana's, and casually asked MacLeish if he would be interested in teaching at the law school. "My knees clicked together," Archie wrote Dean, who was himself considering a career in law school teaching. Then he began to have reservations. He was flattered to be considered for a post at the nation's finest law school, but he would get only courses no one else wanted. Besides, teaching law would occupy all of his energy while he was still hoping for "something that will give me a little time for the writing of bad verses." In December, Pound made a concrete proposal, and after a week of agonized indecision MacLeish turned him down. "I can't see that there is anything in it except a sufficient salary and a tremendous prestige," he wrote Acheson. "God knows I don't want to train young men to make money practicing law." His interest in the law lay "in its analogical adaptations to new conditions, in its possibilities as an instrument of social service." And he would almost surely have to give up his ambitions as a writer. "You don't teach at the Harvard Law School and do anything else."

For a period of about two months at the turn of the decade, MacLeish seemed to have settled on a career in journalism. Through Frankfurter he had met Herbert Croly of the *New Republic,* the left-leaning New York journal of opinion, and he entertained some hopes of landing a job there. In any event, as he wrote Acheson in two December 1919 letters, journalism made more sense for him — and, he thought, for Dean — than the alternatives. His principal reason was that journalism offered a greater opportunity for making a difference in the world than either teaching or practicing law. "God save us, if a man is anything more than a potential prize vegetable it must be his purpose to act upon the world, not to wait to see what the world will do to him. It should be his ideal to free the world not to fatten himself." A career in practice promised both income and position, but was unlikely to change "the scope or direction of the growth of law" or to redeem "a class from bondage through the decisions of the courts." The trouble with teaching was that "you work at second hand. You are training *other men* who will work in *another generation* to effectuate the ideas you have developed or acquired." In editorial journalism, however, you could express these ideas to a broader audience and so exert your influence on the present and near future.

As a corollary to this argument, Archie urged Dean to join him in the new profession of journalism, which he characterized grandly as "a life of thought and study, and application of that thought and study to passing events." Dean was uniquely qualified for such work, he pointed out. "You write like an angel — or a devil — depending on your preferences and remembering Mr. Milton's delightful fiend. You do your own thinking. You have the best education these United States can offer. And you are tremendously interested in the goals of true journalism." Without much difficulty, Dean could land a place with the *New Republic*, or somewhere else. "Eventually we could hit it off together," Archie assured him. But if as he correctly feared Dean was "utterly cold" to this proposal, he should surely consider practicing law in Boston. That way at least they could renew their friendship.

Archie's tenuous resolve in favor of journalism melted away in mid-January after a fiery argument with Aunt Mary. First they argued "general industrial conditions and politics and Wilson: she thought I was a bolshevik and I thought she was a reactionary." Then they got down to Archie's career. Journalists, she told him, had no influence. Only men of affairs really exerted influence, and if Archie left the law for the Fourth Estate, he would be burning his bridges behind him. New York was dirty and expensive and absolutely the wrong place for Ada and Kenny. Archie was not persuaded at first, but after sleeping on her opinions, he had second thoughts. As he wrote his mother, it was certainly true that they "could live delightfully in Boston for an amount that wouldn't pay present rents in New York." And they liked Boston very much. "But it was hard," he concluded, coming to the bottom line, "to give up the idea of writing for which I have always lived."

Finally he decided "that perhaps by rigorously holding to my purpose of writing and rigorously sacrificing the ambition to be the greatest lawyer in Boston" he might be able to "write about as much after a year or two in practice here as in the mills of New York journalism." On that shaky basis, he accepted an offer from Choate, Hall and Stewart, one of Boston's most respected law firms, beginning September 7, 1920. Then, with the aid of a loan from Ada's father, the MacLeishes bought a small house at 44 Coolidge Hill Road in Cambridge and prepared to settle down. "It's an uninteresting outlook, isn't it?" Archie wrote his mother in April. "Most high hopes boil down to that at last."

From mid-June to mid-August 1920, Archie got his chance to try his hand at journalism. Croly hired him as a summer fill-in for associate editor Francis Hackett at the *New Republic*. With only a few days off to take (and of course pass) his bar exams, he worked out of the magazine's offices at 421 West Twenty-first Street in Manhattan. Among the staffers, Archie was most impressed with Walter Lippmann, who worked in the back room and turned out first-rate commentary with becoming modesty. Archie, meanwhile, produced two "skittish political verses" for the magazine, both focusing satirically on Warren Gamaliel Harding, the front-porch sage of Marion, Ohio, who was soon to be elected president. He also functioned as poetry editor. On a trip to Cambridge he persuaded Hervey Allen to submit some of his work and was able to write him on July 15 that the *New Republic* would accept two of his poems. The following day, he turned down some submissions from Stephen Vincent Benét, Yale '19.

While Ada and Kenny spent the summer months in Craigie Lea, Archie occupied Grace Allen Peabody's studio apartment in New York. The place was lovely, he wrote Acheson, "one large room opening into a bathtub, and garnished with wax fruit, velvet flowers, pictures by Italians . . . and a bed that makes up into a cross between a gondola and a rocking chair by day." The furniture was all wicker, and expensive. Archie found one chair he could safely sit in. Mrs. Peabody herself had decamped to York Harbor for the summer, but her lending the place to Archie may have increased the friction between himself and Frank Bangs, who continued to court her. The two Yale friends had not seen much of each other since the armistice.

> *Through half a circle of the careless sun*
> *The world has wavered and our love has run*
> *And only strangers tell me that you live . . .*

Archie had written Frank the previous year. Ensconced in New York, he made several further overtures, in vain. At the end of his stay, he wrote Acheson about his disillusionment with respect to Bangs. "I discovered what I should have known before, that the mere tie of a common experience in New Haven will not hold men together. When the man I knew best at Yale permitted six weeks to go by without an effort to see me and in spite of several efforts on my part to see him I was hurt — but wiser." In the process, he had learned what true friendships were made of, and he was determined that he and Dean should always remain friends.

Archie was not bereft in New York. There were other Yale friends to see, including Ranald Macdonald, whose wedding he had ushered for. Sister Blanche and brother-in-law Ben Billings invited him to a convivial weekend house party. There and among his more conservative classmates

MacLeish dodged questions about his place of employment. And he saw a good deal of Larry Mason, who was running the Brick Row Bookshop in New York. At Archie's summer apartment they concocted an elaborate hoax of an article, "The Next Philosophy," which produced considerable consternation when it was published, three years later, in the *North American Review.*

In the way of more strictly literary output, 1920 and 1921 were fallow years for MacLeish. His only serious poetry of that period appeared in the three-issue lifespan of *Parabalou,* a literary magazine issuing from "Will Warren's Den, Farmington, Connecticut," and devoted to printing the work of seven poets recently graduated from Yale, including, besides MacLeish, Phelps Putnam, Alfred Bellinger, Danford Barney, William Douglas, John Farrar, and Stephen Vincent Benét. The first issue, in June 1920, contained Archie's "Belgian Letter," about the discovery of Kenny's body; the third included his "Kenneth," with its salute to his brother's heroism. Of the sixteen additional poems, at least half concentrate on the inevitable effects of time on passion and love and beauty. Perhaps the most poignant and effective of these was titled simply "Sonnet":

> *It is not tragical that love should die*
> *Since youth grows fat and lovely women fade,*
> *And even old and bloody ghosts are laid,*
> *And young gods come where all immortals*
> *   lie,*
> *And wars cease: — under the forgetful sky*
> *The turf is sunken on the graves we made.*
> *All life's a tune that once is greatly played,*
> *Then whistled, then hummed for a lullaby.*
>
> *But oh it is past sorrow and past weeping*
> *That even now in this enchanted place,*
> *When moon is full and tides of wind are high,*
> *And beauty tossed along my pulses leaping,*
> *That even now, wondering at your face,*
> *I should be thinking love will surely die.*

Professional Duellist

MacLeish was sustained by two factors during his three-year tour of duty as a lawyer: his enjoyment of the competitive give-and-take of litigation and his admiration for Charles F. Choate, Jr., senior partner of Choate, Hall and Stewart. "Nothing I have ever done is more fun than the preparation of a brief or a good question," he wrote Acheson after six weeks on the job. Practicing law, he decided, "was simply the world's grandest covered-court game." You took them off the walls or on the bounce or on the fly, and took your shower afterward. Sometimes you won and sometimes the other fellow did. Yet either way "the effect on the human race or the welfare of society or the development of the individual [was] just exactly and precisely zero." Suppose your client kept the $900,000 he probably ought to pay. Nobody had gotten anywhere, no law had been made, no one cared except the families of the people involved. "It would be just about as useful to hire out as a professional duellist."

MacLeish was a very good duellist, however, and as time went on, the firm gave him more and more responsibility. In the summer of 1921 he wrote Acheson about a series of "great experiences . . . two arguments (tout seul) before the Supreme Judicial Court, a brace of demurrers and motions, a demurrer . . . in the United States Court, and an equity case and two jury cases in the offing." Yet he harbored a sense that he was meant for greater things than practicing law. "As a game there is nothing to match it," he wrote home. "But as a philosophy, as a training for such eternity as the next hour offers it is nowhere — a mockery of human ambition for reality."

Serving to stave off his incipient disillusionment was the impressive and magisterial figure of Mr. Choate. His mind was such an "intricate and bewildering mechanism," he wrote Choate's daughter Betty soon after joining the firm, that it seemed "an impertinence to dare to like him." He sought approbation from Choate as he had from his father, and with the same result. "I would do anything under heaven in the hope of that single syllable of commendation that never comes." Merely talking with "his chief" made Archie feel as he had under shell fire, with every nerve jumping. Yet working for such a man gave him real joy "even in this frivolous profession of ours," he commented in a letter to Betty ten months later. "It's not only that he has the most brilliant mind I have ever come in contact with either directly or in print. It is also that he has a personality to charm devils and Scotchmen."

Archie's relationship with the boss's daughter Betty Choate traced back to 1914, his junior year in college. Aunt Mary prevailed on him then to escort Betty, a Westover senior, to a school dance. (At the time, Ada was improving her musical education in Paris.) Undoubtedly Aunt Mary regarded Miss Choate as a better match for Archie than Miss Hitchcock. She came from a Boston family that had been prominent for generations. She was very attractive, with an aristocratic slenderness that contrasted with Ada's more rounded physique. And she was extremely interested in literature, as Ada was not. Archie was not to be swayed from his chosen girl, but he liked Betty enough to write a light-hearted poem to her in his 1915 "Songs for a Summer's Day." The subject is the new woman, and Archie turns the topic into the mock lament of a swain who has been rejected.

To B.C.

In the novels of Charlotte Bronte
There are maidens both stupid and gay,
There are maidens who blush
And maidens who flush
And maidens as merry as May.

There are ladies of volatile eye
And dames unbecomingly spry
There are spinsters aesthetic
And lasses pathetic
And all of them dreadfully shy.

But alack as the centuries pass
The Maid of Shalotte in her glass
Sees never a blush
Nor a ruffle-y flush
And never a shy little lass.

'Tis the era of women called "new"
And militants gentle as glue,
Of harsh suffragettes,
And powder and nets,
And neurotics with nothing to do.

And so when we're told of a girl
Whose ego is not in a whirl
Over Ibsen and votes
And eugenical notes
We yield her the palm and the pearl.

We yield her the palm and we pen
Soft sonnets and lyrics again,
'Till we find (Oh to die!)
That the reason she's shy
Is simply because she hates men.

Now the moral, if moral there be,
Is both moral and noble and free —
That the cause of all trouble,
The flaw in the bubble,
Is the presence of mankind — and me!

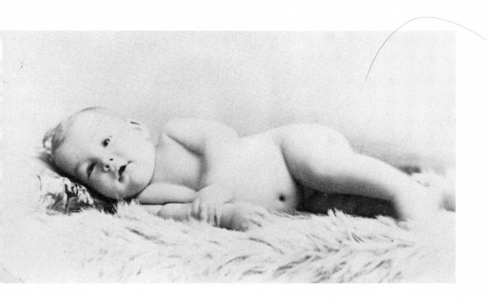

FIRST LIGHT

Archibald MacLeish, the second child of Andrew
MacLeish and his third wife, Martha Hillard
MacLeish, is shown above in the glory of
babyhood, a few months after his birth on May 7,
1892. At right the infant is cradled in the arms of
his mother, the former president of Rockford
Seminary. Below, the two-year-old Archie (at left)
appears with his older brother, Norman, and their
fierce-browed father. "God was father's father," he
later wrote.

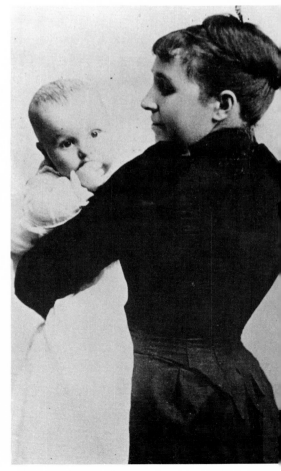

CRAIGIE LEA

Dressed up for childhood pictures against a sylvan studio backdrop are siblings Ishbel, Archie, and Norman, and Archie alone, about six, in full Scottish regalia. The kilt and the rest of the outfit reflected the country of his father's birth, as did the name, Craigie Lea, of their home in Glencoe, Illinois, on a bluff above Lake Michigan. Below, the adult Archie and his mother stand at the end of the landscaped pathway to the bluff.

BRIGHT COLLEGE YEARS

After prepping at Hotchkiss, MacLeish enjoyed a remarkably versatile career at Yale. A Phi Beta Kappa student and member of Skull and Bones, he excelled both in athletics and in literary circles. As a football player, he made a touchdown-saving tackle against Harvard in the fall of 1914, his senior year. He was also elected chairman of the *Yale Lit* that year (center, below). Arch's favorite instructor was Larry Mason, who served as mentor to MacLeish and his friend and classmate Frank Bangs.

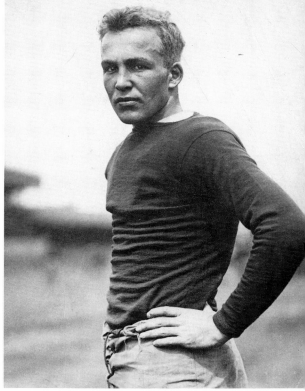

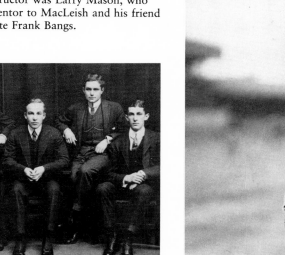

Lawrence Mason

Francis H. Bangs

MARRIAGE AT LAST

Archie decided early that he wanted to marry Ada Hitchcock, a girl he met while still in prep school. Their marriage was delayed until he finished Yale and his first year of law school. Ada, at the piano at left, was a talented musician who achieved considerable success as a concert singer during the 1920s, before devoting herself to her husband and their sixty-seven-year marriage. Below, Archie and Ada on their honeymoon to Bermuda, June 1916.

CASUALTY OF WAR

In France in 1918, a mustachioed Archie in field artillery uniform rendezvoused with his much-loved younger brother, Kenneth, a sunny and idealistic youth who enlisted as a pilot and was shot down over Belgium. It was a loss that MacLeish addressed in several poems, including the well-known "Memorial Rain." In addition, he and Ada changed the name of their first-born from Archibald to Kenneth. The lad is shown with his father, c. 1920.

HONOR MOORE

Margarett Sargent

MacLEISH AND MUSES

Physically attractive himself, MacLeish was susceptible to the beauty of women throughout his life. Two who inspired him to poetry during the years immediately before and after World War I were the artist Margarett Sargent, pictured at Gutzon Borglum's estate in 1918, and Grace Allen Peabody, in a portrait of 1917.

Grace Allen Peabody

Archie and Ada MacLeish

Stephen and Rosemary Benét, with dog

MERICANS ABROAD

hough Archie and Ada did not consider
emselves expatriates, they spent nearly five years
and around Paris, from 1923 to 1928. These
apshots were taken during an outing at Vernon,
the spring of 1924. Within a few months the
ishops returned to the United States, putting an
ean between them and what apparently was the
udding romance of Archie and Margaret Bishop.

John Peale Bishop and Alice-Lee Myers

Margaret Bishop

JOURNEYS EAST

From March to June 1926, MacLeish traveled to Persia as a member of the League of Nations committee looking into opium production in that country. He is at the extreme right in the group photograph, with commission chairman Frederic A. Delano at center. That same year Archie and Ada accompanied Sara and Gerald Murphy on a trip to Vienna. At home, he is pictured smiling at his daughter Mimi, c. 1927.

Apparently Archie did not see much of Betty again until after he began to work for her father in September 1920. Two months later he proposed that theirs might be one of the rare true friendships between man and woman. At least they could dream of such a great friendship, for "you know all there is to know and you are of those delicately-fingered women who can build as well upon quick-sand as upon stone." Thereafter he courted her by correspondence, addressing poems to her, comparing her to the fair shepherdess Marcella of legend, and serving as her instructor in a course of reading the masterworks. Kay Bundy, Adele Lovett, and Ives Gammell all assumed that Archie's and Betty's was a love affair, and the letters suggest as much, though it may well have remained platonic. "You I can never find, the pulse and stir / Of life that is essentially you," he wrote her in one sonnet. "You I can never touch, yet in your mind / If I might see how life's reflections fall," then might he know her at last. In another poem he stressed what had gone unspoken between them:

> Rumor and sigh of unimagined seas,
> Dim radiance of stars that never flamed,
> Fragrance of petals never strewn from trees, —
> Meaning of words unsaid and never named;
>
> So from a silence I have made you songs,
> So from a starless night a rose of stars,
> Can you not hear how all the stillness jars
> With music, and the darkness throngs?

As Archie characterized their liaison in literary terms, she was Marcella, "the most beautiful creature ever sent into the world," who in *Don Quixote* mercilessly spurns the bachelors who fall in love with her, while he played the imaginary part of Chrysostom, one of her lovers who dies of disappointed hope. So he wrote Betty after they met in a November 1921 snowscape: "How shall I recall seven black pines lifted high in a somber sky, weighted like kings with silver mail? How shall I find again hills ghostly in the slanting snow? Where shall I see Marcella, lithe and slender, blown to a flame of loveliness, swift-footed, laughing — impersonal as winter or the white north wind? And yet I am slave to those memories. They drift before me flickering with the changing light." A week later he sent her his version of the tale of Marcella and Chrysostom, with a closing imperative. "It is of the utmost importance to the kingdom and the empire that I see you forthwith. When?" And a week after that, he sent her yet another sonnet attesting to her elusiveness.

I never touch your thought but you are fled
Running the subtle deer of your delight
. . . .
And when you run to me, white feet, O white,
And sudden loveliness, it is not you.

In the March 1922 *Atlantic Monthly,* Betty published a travel piece about her trip to New Zealand, with stops at Panama, Samoa, and other intervening ports. In congratulating her, Archie insisted that it was time for her — she had not gone to college — to begin the readings he had set out for her. At least for a few months thereafter she followed this curriculum, sending him her comments on the reading and waiting for his counterreaction. Archie took his role as instructor seriously. On June 13–14, 1922, he produced a ten-page letter responding to her report on Plato and the Old Testament. In setting up the course, he placed particular stress on the Book of Job. Nearly forty years later, his adaptation of that story was to result in his greatest public triumph.

In 1923 Betty wrote two other articles for the *Atlantic,* and then her writing career subsided. That Archie was about to leave Boston may have had something to do with her silence. In one of the *Atlantic* pieces she tells the story of a Russian princess who yearns to express herself in writing. To purchase time for that purpose, she marries a man she does not care for. Then she meets another man, falls in love, and for a while is "content to talk, just endlessly talk, and feel a quiet sympathy" with him. "But talk won't do forever between lovers, and lips must meet if hearts and minds do." Hearing of the affair, her husband shuts her up in his home, and she withers away and dies. Betty Choate may have intended this story as a parable of her own experience.

Sometime in 1923 she and Archie had a final meeting in New York. Afterwards he sat in the Yale Club library, writing in a quiet penetrated only by the grind of cabs in the street and the click of an electric clock. It was ten o'clock at night, and she, the "slender girl in hazy blue" he had left only an hour before, would be playing bridge. If their relationship was over, Archie could not resist philosophizing about it. "Myself: Yourself: we have no reality but to others. I to you, perhaps; you certainly to me. And yet what marvels, what riddles we are — and to ourselves what unconquerable foes. I need you to laugh at me. I need you — to laugh at me." At a quarter to eleven he set down his last words: "Goodbyes are stupid. Particularly on the streets of cities. Particularly when one is struck dumb by the dumb fates. They can't be said on paper."

Oddly, the Yale Club in New York was the place Archie learned of another, even more painful ending. One of the reasons the MacLeishes had bought a house in Cambridge was that they expected their family to grow. On January 4, 1921, Ada gave birth to Brewster Hitchcock MacLeish, a son who bore family names from both parents' ancestry. Little Brudy, as they called him, lived but six months before succumbing to sudden infant death syndrome. On Saturday, June 18, Ada put Brudy down for a nap at noon, "as well and as lovely as he had been all his little life." At three the family nurse went to pick him up and he was dead. There had been no outcry. At that hour Archie was on his way to New York to attend a gathering of Kenny's former flying mates in the First Yale Unit. Ada had to face the horror "all alone — the doctor, the undertaker, the medical examiner." Then for a long time she sat with the poor discolored body. Bob Lovett met Archie at Grand Central Station, took him across the street to the Yale Club, and told him the news. Lovett stayed with him awhile. Then Archie boarded the midnight train back to Boston and was alone with his sorrow. He did not display his feelings to anyone. It was his duty, he felt, to be stoically strong in the face of tragedy.

Three days later Brewster was buried in the cemetery at Unionville, Connecticut, the town adjoining Farmington. "I am so sorry father never saw the little lad," Archie wrote his parents. "I don't think that a more beautiful baby ever lived." Everyone had been wonderfully kind, he assured them. "Ada and I have won to a very real peace and understanding." Where Ada was concerned, that assurance was premature. After a month or so she had a bad letdown. "I think she was trying to carry us both and it was too much for her," Archie reported. "She is such a wonderful, wonderful woman." Archie took her off for a holiday, and friends like Kay Bundy and Adele Lovett offered what comfort they could, but — in Adele's words — Ada was "like a dead person" for a long time. Late in the fall she became pregnant again, and on August 24, 1922, she brought another baby into the world, a daughter named Mary Hillard MacLeish after Aunt Mary, but soon called Mimi. "If her debut is an index of her career," Archie wrote later that day, "she will be inconsiderate and impulsive. And she *won't* be beautiful. But these things change." Best of all, Ada had come through the ordeal well and was quite happy.

During his early years in Boston, Archie was beginning to acquire his political convictions. Early in 1920 his young friend Christian Herter — later secretary of state under Eisenhower — persuaded him to run for president of the Hoover League of Harvard, and he was so elected. The club existed to encourage the (Republican) presidential candidacy of Herbert Hoover, who had made a national reputation as director of World War I relief work. He knew no better than to support Hoover at the time, MacLeish confessed late in his life. "I was a political ignoramus." His summer at the *New Republic* undoubtedly directed his political leanings leftward. In October 1920 he wrote Acheson that he could not support the Republicans because of Harding, the candidate the party had chosen in preference to Hoover.

A more significant episode occurred in May 1921. Some Harvard graduates had launched a campaign to censure or dismiss Zechariah Chafee at the law school. In *Freedom of Speech* (1920), Chafee argued that the Espionage Act of 1917 and the Sedition Act of 1918 violated the First Amendment by mandating fines or imprisonment for those found guilty of interfering with the draft or of encouraging disloyalty to the United States, a view that outraged certain right-wing alumni. MacLeish, however, had read his former professor's book and shared its conclusions. Moreover, he was using Chafee's arguments in his class on constitutional law.

When he heard of the attack on Chafee, he immediately sought to ally himself with his cause. In a letter to Arthur Holcombe, chairman of the department of government, he presented his views: "If it is improper to teach the theory of freedom of speech which Professor Chafee has adopted and to my mind established, and if it is improper to comment upon decisions and cases involving the application of the constitutional guaranty, and if it is improper to use a chair in Harvard University for the purpose of discussion of controversial questions, then it seems to me that I deserve censure from you and from your superiors in the University." If they were going to hang Chafee, he wanted to hang at his side. In reply Holcombe assured him that neither Chafee nor himself was in any danger of being censured by the university. Although the controversy soon faded away, Archie's reaction in this case served to predict his future passionate devotion to the cause of human freedom and his eagerness to enter into battle in its defense.

Conversations by Moonlight

MacLeish's contract with Harvard ran out in the spring of 1921, but by fall he was teaching again in addition to his workload at Choate, Hall and Stewart. This time he taught an evening course in civil procedure at Northeastern College of Law, and began to consider anew the possibility of a full-time career in the academic world, either in Harvard's department of government or in its law school. "My ancient and misplaced ambition to write lies dreadfully at the bottom" of the potential change, he admitted in a February 1922 letter to Bangs, with whom he had resumed genial acquaintance if not quite the friendship of old. Then, too, as he wrote Acheson, he continued to have "a profound suspicion of the practice of law" and of the materialistic considerations that kept him on the job.

"The Lord Chancellor Prepares His Opinion," Archie's only poem of 1922, vividly presented his case against the law. The magistrate of the title is writing his judgment in a lawsuit brought by a beautiful lady against a painter who made "a full heroic picture of herself," and displayed it publicly when she refused him payment. The lady sued because this "shameless painting," a wonderfully exact replica, was exhibited in a coffeehouse, where all who paid might stand and stare at her face. The Lord Chancellor decides that the courts are not equipped to deal with such questions, but only with rents and profits, estates and lands and livings.

> *Is beauty such a value as we know?*
> . . . .
> *Shall equity protect a woman's throat*
> *Against the painter's interest in his paint?*
> *The bill should be dismissed.*

So he argues, with convincing rationality. But in an interior monologue, the Lord Chancellor reveals that he has a still stronger motive to find for the defendant: he has seen the painting, and been swept away by it. But no one must know how moved he was:

> *How that still beauty on the canvas caught,*
> *Caught and held fast, as in the brain sometimes*
> *A gesture of the soul is caught and held, —*
> *How that still beauty stopped my mouth with awe*
> *And left my poor brain gaping.*

The world of law and the world of art, in MacLeish's poem, are mutually and irrevocably discrete.

The problem of vocation lay heavy on his mind throughout the fall and winter of 1922–23. In Washington, Dean Acheson was having his own doubts about whether to join the State Department or enter private practice. "Our real trouble," Archie wrote Dean in October 1922, "is that we don't want anything in particular: we just want the world." It was of no help "for moralists to remark that one can achieve anything he chooses to achieve. It's the labor of a lifetime to make a choice of an achievement." Yet once he shut off his reasoning powers, which could not be trusted "to decide anything of importance," the choice seemed clear enough.

The previous month in Maine, Archie had walked out alone onto the cliffs above the sea and watched the moon rise. "There was a land breeze blowing over moors covered with sweet fern and bayberry which had been cooking all day in the sun. The sea broke the rhythm of time. The moon devolved out of a rosy mist over the horizon." There he began to think of what he must do, and he knew at once. "I must go about looking at things, laboring to see them. If I could understand them too then so much the better. But first I must see what they were — not to a chemist, or a biologist, or a sociologist, but to so much conscious life as was in me to see them with. Then I must think about them and I must find words for them. Then I must write poetry of those words." But for the time being, common sense prevailed. Archie put aside this lifetime plan for poetry, went back to Choate, Hall and Stewart, and reason said, "Solid lad!"

Gradually MacLeish was building up to the most important decision he would ever make. In the months ahead he stole time for poetry and composed much of what was to become his second book of verse, *The Happy Marriage and Other Poems*. One day in February it occurred to him that he must either get out of the law then or not at all. It was quite clear that he was going to be "a good operating lawyer." If he stayed in the profession any longer, it would be impossible to break free. This realization came over him at the end of a long and tiring day at the office. Normally the way he got home was to walk several blocks from 30 State Street to Park Street Under, take the subway to Harvard Square, and walk to Coolidge Hill from there. As he approached the subway stop at Park Street, "there in icy, absolutely clear sky was the new moon with the old moon in its arms." He started down the subway steps, sniffed the fetid air, and changed his mind. He walked home instead, across the Common, all the way out Commonwealth Avenue, the whole length of Massachusetts Avenue to the Square, and the mile and a half beyond to his home. Along the way he debated his future. He was thirty, and he was beset with a nagging sense of a debt unpaid.

> Owe, I said. What do I owe? For what? To whom? No one can say I haven't worked, earning my keep in courtrooms before juries, teaching, tutoring . . . whatever — writing when I would take the time to write — first light — night late. . . .
>
> I understand, I said. It isn't work that matters. It's *the* work — the one work of art. I practice law and teach to make that other possible — to garner time. It isn't true I've wasted time. The war took two years out. There was law school. Teaching erases time by inches. Nevertheless, I have a book now. Not the book I meant to have — I know that. Nevertheless, the book I've written. . . .

I was opposite Eliot House when the moon went down. So that was what I'd done . . . had *not* done. I had prepared, provided, made arrangements for a time to come, for work to come, for art to come. There is no art to come: there's only art — the need, the now, the presence, the necessity . . . the sun.

It was the art I owed.

When he finally got home, Ada had put the children to bed and was impatiently waiting for him at her small piano, playing a phrase, listening for his footsteps, singing the phrase, listening again. In the long night ahead they talked it out, and the decision they reached was for both of them. They would go to Paris, where Archie would hire "the usual attic" and find out once and for all if he was a poet. He had tried all manner of combinations: teaching and writing, law practice and writing, journalism and writing. Now, at last, it was time to try writing alone. As for Ada, she could continue to develop her voice in the city where she had first learned to take music seriously. During the previous year in Cambridge, Ada had been coached by the Danish-born concert soprano Povla Frijsh, who encouraged her to pursue a career in singing. Her voice was "as newly wonderful, as clear, as excellently musical" as in the days immediately after the war, Archie wrote Dean. "In addition she has an increased power of expression which lifts you out of today into the time that never was." In Paris, she too would have her chance.

After only a few hours of sleep, Archie rose early and went to the office to tell Charles F. Choate, Jr., of their decision. To his surprise, he was told that the senior partner was waiting for him. Archie went into Choate's office, with its magnificent view of Boston Harbor beyond, and saw the whole firm standing around the room.

A tall, gray-haired man with a girl's skin, Choate was sitting there looking happy as a cat. "Archie," he said, "I think I'm going to tell you that we've decided to ask you to join the firm." Archie thought to himself, either now or never, took a deep breath, and said, "Mr. Choate, I came to tell you that I'm giving up the law." Angry and hurt, Choate turned absolutely scarlet at this news. Archie could see the color rising from his neck, and managed to get out before further words were spoken. Only later did he dare reveal the awful fact that he was leaving the law to write poetry.

Second Thoughts

Archie did not leave the firm at once, or without second thoughts. As it happened, he was already involved in the most interesting case of his legal career. He and Day Kimball, who had come to Choate, Hall and

Stewart along with Archie, were backing up James Loomer Hall, the firm's second in command, in a libel and slander suit involving some of Massachusetts's leading politicians. Their client was Joseph E. Warner, speaker of the state House of Representatives. In a 1920 campaign for the lieutenant governorship, Alvan T. Fuller, Warner's opponent in the Republican primary, had accused Warner of using his office for personal gain. At issue was whether Warner was in law partnership with Harold F. Hathaway, who had appeared before committees appointed by Warner on behalf of clients. If so, there would exist an obvious conflict of interest. Fuller so accused Warner in public meetings and in the press, and was unable to elicit either a confession or a denial from his opponent.

At one time Warner and Hathaway had been law partners, but it was not certain that this partnership had continued. Fuller's accusations apparently had their desired effect, however, since he was elected lieutenant governor. In due course Warner brought suit against him for libel and slander. The trial, according to Archie's letter to Dean in March 1923, "was tremendous." The courtroom was packed with petty politicians and newspapermen. Representing Fuller was John W. Cummings, "a grand old Victorian Irishman" who was president of the Massachusetts Bar Association, "a shrewd lawyer and an actor of parts." The examination throughout and the arguments on both sides were brilliant, Archie reported. When the jury remained deadlocked, he and Day Kimball persuaded Hall to let them try for a directed verdict. They went to the judge and made an impassioned appeal. It would be a shame to have all this time wasted without a decision. Why didn't he direct a verdict for their client of one dollar? The defense could appeal if they wished. "After a long fight [the judge] agreed. The poor old jury was called in and a verdict directed for Warner for $1 and the case reported. . . . And the newspapers have been trying ever since to find out who won. But it was a famous victory."

Three months later the verdict was overturned by the state Supreme Court, which found that the preponderance of evidence indicated that Warner and Hathaway were indeed partners and the jury should have been allowed to rule in favor of the defense, on the grounds that Fuller had only accused Warner of what was true. So Warner did not get his dollar after all. From Archie's point of view the reversal hardly mattered. "We knew damn well the appellate court would find against us. But we wanted that directed verdict and we got it."

At least temporarily the triumph was such as to make him reconsider leaving the law. Meanwhile, pressure was being brought to bear by the ubiquitous Aunt Mary, who had no doubts whatever that her nephew was about to make a mistake — again. Aunt Mary, who was a friend and admirer of Charles F. Choate, Jr., could barely fathom Archie's willingness to give up a promising legal career. She felt certain that, given seasoning, Archie — like Choate himself — could become a man of position, wealth, and influence. Writers simply didn't matter that much in her scheme of things. "The thought that Henry Thoreau might perhaps have been more influential than J. P. Morgan would never have crossed Aunt Mary's mind," Archie observed.

Besides, Aunt Mary was not at all sure — despite the encouraging words of Masefield — that her nephew had the makings of a poet in him. She made inquiries among members of the literary establishment in Boston and New York and from them elicited the opinion she was seeking — that Archie possessed little or no talent. This intelligence she passed on to him, along with a daunting question: "Why should a first-rate lawyer become a second-rate poet?"

The publication of "The Next Philosophy," Archie and Larry Mason's hoax in the May 1923 *North American Review,* only served to confirm her opinion. The essay employed hyperbole as a device of irony, and few proved capable of detecting it. The contemporary Czech Peter Sczornick, it claimed, was already "one with the immortals" and "beyond our pens to praise or injure." Sczornick's "great conception" was that the key to life lay in the Philosophy of Grammar. "Not only do words and sentences occur and recur in obedience to the rules of grammar, but man himself and the ideas and purposes of man fulfill the ambit of those laws, bear the relations of those principles, are understood only in the light of those commands." Sczornick's magnum opus, which MacLeish and Mason purported to have discovered in a French translation from the Czech, was thus divided into chapters that linked great abstract ideas with grammatical terms. "God: the Copula," for example, "Nature: the Predicate," "Love: the Genitive," and so on to "Death: the Period." When this nonsense appeared with all dignity in a well-known journal, Archie discovered some unintended consequences of a successful *jeu d'esprit.* He and Mason had demonstrated that the *North American Review* would publish hokum. But they risked being taken to task for *their* gullibility in regard to Sczornick, and for extravagantly overpraising the merits of his ridiculous philosophy.

Archie was not inclined to own up to the hoax (he did not do so for twenty years). When Aunt Mary objected that the article was damaging his reputation, he implored Frank Bangs by telegram to set her straight.

"FOR PLATOS SAKE TELL AUNT MARY YOUR OPINION NORTH AMER-ICAN ARTICLE. . . . STOP SHE IS VERY FEMININE STOP ALSO VERY STUPID STOP SHE IS ENGAGED CAMPAIGN TO SUPPRESS SCZORNICK AND ALL MY WORKS AND MAKE ME A LAWYER STOP STAND BY ME — ARCHIE."

According to Bangs, who dined with Aunt Mary in New Haven on May 23, he "was not successful" in explaining "The Next Philosophy" to Miss Hillard.

In raising the issue of reputation, Aunt Mary may also have been referring to the unhappy fate of Archie's co-author. Lawrence Mason had gone to Colorado in the fall of 1921 as a companion for a young man in poor health. The young man liked to drink, and so did Mason. In the spring of 1922, Mason exposed himself when drunk to a female librarian in Colorado Springs. He was forced to leave town, the rumor spread in the university world, and his academic career was ruined. So, as Bangs put it, "America lost one of its greatest teachers, all for a petty sexual aberration under liquor."

In an unpublished poem written in his eighties, MacLeish harked back to his arguments with Aunt Mary of half a century before. As he reconstructed the debate, he thought of poetry as a way of speaking not only for himself but for a generation of the young, some of whom had died before their time.

> *Who will speak for us now? I?*
> *Was it for this I felt the need to speak?*
> *to "write" as they say? Give up the law?*
> *deceive the expectations? By what*
> *right? says the Aunt.*
>   *I don't know.*
> *Who do you think you are? says the Aunt.*
> *That's just it, I said, I don't*
> *know.*
>   *And how will you learn?*
> *By writing when you don't know what to write?*
> *You have to have something to say before you can say it.*
>
> *I have something to say if I could learn to say it.*
> *Say about what?*
>   *Well . . . Kenny.*
>   *Your brother is*
> *dead. He was shot down. He died a*
> *hero's death.*
>   *He was shot down.*
> *He lay in the winter floods. They found his body*
> *After the Armistice. His face was gone.*
>
> *What has this to do with practicing law?*
>
> *Everything. He cannot speak.*
> *None of them can speak — a generation*

scattered across the Belgian Marches,
buried in the Netherlands, in France,
in Alsace, Germany. They have no voices.

There were thousands who came back —
survived it — marched in the streets

They too — they have no voices.

Aunt Mary fought the battle on other grounds as well. She wrote Ada, for example, that the climate and environment of Paris could be dangerous, even fatal, to young children. These tactics infuriated both Archie and Ada, but they probably helped his cause. When he went to Craigie Lea to secure his father's blessing — and his financial support — he feared that Andrew MacLeish, in his mid-eighties, would be unsympathetic to his admittedly risky plans. But as always Patty MacLeish was supportive. She let Andrew know about Aunt Mary's machinations, and he was damned if he would tolerate his sister-in-law's interfering in the life of his son. Besides, he had a Scotsman's respect for books and the makers of books. So he agreed to finance Archie on the same basis as he had in law school, at $3,000 for a year. "Maybe four can live as cheaply as one in Paris," Andrew said, and with the exchange rates as favorable as they were, so it turned out.

On May 2 Archie wrote his mother that the bridges were burned. They had sold their house for $1,000 profit and would vacate early in June. As Ada said, "We got no home." The night before, she had "made a tremendous hit" singing for a Boston society audience. The *New Republic* had bought two of Archie's poems and the *Yale Review* one. "Within 48 minutes" he would officially give notice to Mr. Choate that he planned to leave the office in the fall. For most of the summer he would live in Maurice Firuski's Cambridge apartment while Ada and the children stayed in Farmington. As best he could, he expressed his gratitude to his mother for helping to make their trip possible. "Your capacity for sympathizing with aspirations and plans and purposes which most people would think rash is one of the saving graces of life for me." He was driven to succeed, yet again, not merely for himself but to justify his parents' confidence in him.

Another who had confidence in Archie was the remarkable Amy Lowell, who was famous not merely for her imagist verse and her biography of Keats but for her substantial girth, her cigar smoking, and other eccentric habits. MacLeish first met Amy Lowell at a dinner party given by Kay Bundy, who was her niece. The poets, old and young, had a marvelous time talking. Afterwards, Archie sent Kay a poem in celebration.

Now, I shall put that evening by
For thinking on before I die —
How this she said, and thus she went,
That Lady of the long dissent,
How kings and centuries went down
Before the flicker of her frown,
And mighty poets, at her mirth,
Turned over in their English earth —

. . . .

Perhaps I've not seen Shelley plain, —
That gift was not in God's bestowal,
But I can overcome the pain, —
I dined at Kay's with Amy Lowell.

In their last months in Cambridge, Archie and Ada were invited to Lowell's house in Brookline on several occasions. She was living with Ada Russell, an accomplished actress who played much the same role for Lowell that Alice B. Toklas did for Gertrude Stein. Ada Russell took Ada MacLeish aside to chat while the two poets conversed, just as Toklas occupied Hadley Hemingway while her husband, Ernest, discussed prose with Stein. Often there would be other literary people at Miss Lowell's, including John Livingston Lowes, who was then teaching at Harvard. Her dinner parties started well into the evening, since she was a notoriously late riser. Once she invited the bohemian poet Maxwell Bodenheim to dinner at 9 o'clock in the evening. Thinking he must have misunderstood the invitation, Bodenheim arrived early, about 8:15 P.M. Lowell's sheepdogs came at him, and instead of trying to calm them down, he turned and ran. They tore the seat off his pants.

Archie, however, plainly profited from his acquaintance with Amy Lowell. Her work did not influence his own, but she encouraged his career, and the support of such an established poet was important to him. It was largely due to her backing, in fact, that Houghton Mifflin, her own publisher, agreed to publish his second book of poems. Over the summer he polished "The Happy Marriage," a sequence of thirty-three metrically varied lyrics that gave the book its title. To a large extent the title was intended ironically, for the sequence concentrates on the gap between ideal love and the actual experience of it in marriage. Some of the lyrics were autobiographical, MacLeish later observed, and others derived from his observations among the people he and Ada knew best in Boston, including Charles and Edith Curtis. Throughout, "The Happy Marriage" stresses the difference between the sexes. In MacLeish's view, man was given to dreaming of an impossible love, while woman waited for an actual love that would surely come. The distinction is developed by way of paradox in one of the sequence's sonnets:

> *Man is immortal, for his flesh is earth,*
> *And save he lives forever — why, he dies:*
> *Woman is mortal, for her flesh will rise*
> *In each new generation of her birth.*
> *She is the tree; we are the feverish*
> *Vain leaves that gild her summer with our own,*
> *And fall and rot when summer's overblown,*
> *And wish eternity and have — our wish.*
>
> *And man, immortal, marries his own dreams*
> *Of immortality in flesh and blood,*
> *And mortal woman, wiser than she seems,*
> *Marries her man for evil or for good, —*
> *Wherein perception sees what reason blurs:*
> *She was not his, but he was only hers.*

In marriage, husband and wife might say they were one flesh, but they remained "two nations" that could not "mix nor mesh." The wife was liable to feel betrayed by a husband who idealized another, whether in a platonic or a real sense.

> *Whom do you love, she said, when you look out*
> *So far beyond my eyes as our eyes meet?*

The issue of infidelity was one that Archie himself had raised some time before in an evening he spent in New York with Bangs, Mason, Frederic H. Cruger, and two extraordinarily lovely women, Grace Allen Peabody and Cruger's wife, Pinna, later a favorite of Edward, Prince of Wales. After dinner MacLeish posed a problem: were men and women inherently unable to find their quest for perfect love satisfied in the person they loved and married? The problem did not admit of solution, partly because none present were willing to speak frankly from their own experience. Pinna, for example, declined to make any comment in company, but promised she would discuss the matter privately with Archie. Perhaps she did so. In any case, his question was designed to stimulate such confidences and the degree of intimacy that would come with them.

Early in August, Archie went to Ogunquit, where he saw Grace again. In a letter to Bangs he rhapsodized on her charms. Somewhere in the sheltering dunes she "lies upon her back with her arms raised above her head so that if you lay beside her she would seem like some young Nike of the Greeks riding the prow of earth triumphant. . . . But if you lay beside her . . . you would not think this way at all. You would think with your fingers, with the flesh of your body, with the strong tug and compulsion of ignorant muscles that know only one use for loveliness." He could not express his feelings for Grace in words, Archie wrote, for that would be to invade a realm that was holy to Bangs. "I think of that lithe loveliness in the dunes — but I will not. Pity me."

Ada must have been aware of her husband's yearnings toward other women, but these did not forge a crucial division between them. Probably she would not have been surprised at the advice Archie gave to his friend Maurice Firuski, who was contemplating leaving one woman for another. If it was love, Archie wrote, necessity would tell Firuski what to do. Anything Maurice decided would be all right with him. But he cautioned him to remember that "you cannot build happiness on an injury to anyone else." And in any event, he should not act impulsively. "If Isabel still loves you you give her all the time you can. You will never regret it. Wait."

8

FEVER OF GREATNESS

Settling In

THE MACLEISHES SAILED for France on September 1, 1923. Aboard the SS *Lafayette,* as it went tooting across the Grand Banks in a raw fog, were Archie and Ada, six-year-old Kenny, and one-year-old Mimi, accompanied by Ada's mother and "a wonderful old Irish nurse" called Kathy. They were embarked on a great gamble, testing whether determination and talent might combine with the heady atmosphere of Paris to make an accomplished poet of Archie and a professional singer of his wife. Remarkably, the gamble paid off, and there was no minimizing the importance of Paris in the process, for they were going to the right place at the right time. At the beginning, the MacLeishes planned to stay a year in Paris. In the end, they stayed five.

But never, Archie always maintained, as expatriates, refugees from an unlivable country. It never occurred to them to settle overseas for good. They came to Paris not because they hated Boston — for they both liked it — but because they needed something that only Paris could give them. Nor were they members, charter or otherwise, of what has popularly been labeled the Lost Generation, after a remark Gertrude Stein appropriated from her garageman. It was the world they had come from that was lost, the old safe world of stability and order that was blown to bits in the war. The twenties in Paris were years of cultural rebuilding seemingly almost from scratch. The slate was wiped clean, and artists came to write upon it anew.

The devastating effects of the war struck MacLeish as he took his first walks along the wide avenues of Paris. He saw young women dressed in black who did not smile, old men, sour-looking middle-aged men, and boys — but, he realized, almost no young Frenchmen. Into that vacuum poured the youth of other nations more fortunate than France, and especially Americans. In 1921, six thousand of them inhabited Paris; in September 1924, thirty thousand. Some were indeed self-styled expatriates who lost no opportunity to attack their native land. Couldn't a law be passed, a 1924 letter to the editor of the *Paris Tribune* proposed, "requiring that muzzles be placed on all our young American intellectual aristocrats before they are turned loose in Montparnasse . . . soaking up various forms of alcoholic beverage and categorically condemning America and all things American?" Others were mere profiteers living well and cheaply on the exchange rates and philistines buying up only such art as they could easily fathom. These MacLeish devastated in a sonnet.

> Mr. and Mrs. *Longfellow Little who*
> *Disapproved of Picasso (having — the catalogue erred —*
> *Permitted themselves the emotions appropriate to*
> *The* Gouache of a Nude *while beholding the* Sketch of the Word
> Prone with Bananas) *who disapproved*
> *Of Picasso (and not that Picasso was Modern and not*
> *That Mr. and Mrs. Little were slow to be moved*
> *By Good Work — provided they recognized what*
>
> *It was they were moved by — but how could one tell if one ought*
> *To admire a thing unless one could say of it This is*
> *A glass, This is a girl? How could one love*
> *What might or might not be Important?) Mr. and Mrs.*
> *Little who disapproved of Picasso bought*
> *A Still Life. One knew what a Life was* of.

Or perhaps not.

But it was the others who mattered, those who had come to Paris because it was "the last of the great holy cities of the arts." A creative ferment was brewing there in the twenties. "It was Picasso and the changing forms" that confused the Longfellow Littles. "It was Stravinsky back to conduct the *Sacre* again": he conducted badly, as Ada knew, but nothing could spoil his *Rite of Spring.* "It was James Joyce, an Irishman from Trieste with the unpublishable manuscript of a novel which would set the world on fire." It was Alexis Léger (St.-John Perse) at the Quai d'Orsay and André Masson teasing the surrealists and Jules Romains. And it was the extraordinary American writers the MacLeishes soon came to know, Cummings, Hemingway, Dos Passos, and Fitzgerald among them. These artists were revolutionizing art, creating wonderful new music and paintings and books. It was inspiring.

"What lured us to Paris and held us there," Archie observed in the year he died, "was . . . the magnificent work being done by people from all over the world and in all the arts. . . . There were a lot of fakes, a lot of phonies, and there undoubtedly were people who had come as refugees, exiles. But what I remember are the individual human beings who I had the luck to know. The people who were good seemed to respond to that fever of greatness by becoming great themselves."

In Paris, Archie at last felt free to devote himself entirely to poetry. But first he and Ada had to get their bearings, find an apartment, establish a routine. They were met at the Gare de Lyons by Archie's cousin Frances and her husband, Billy Emerson, who took them to a *pension* in Neuilly. After two weeks of rancid cooking and brave attempts at mastering spoken French (Ada was a quicker linguist than Archie), they escaped from the *pension* and moved into the Left Bank flat that the Emersons left vacant on their return to the United States. The place wasn't big enough for them, and the *cabinet* gave off noisome fumes, but it served as a headquarters while they made arrangements for work and school. By the end of September, Ada had rented a studio in Passy for the morning hours, and Kenny was enrolled in kindergarten at the École Alsacienne, where one of his fellow students was the son of Richard and Alice-Lee Myers. The Myerses, both University of Chicago graduates, were old Paris hands. Dick worked for American Express, and composed on the side, while Alice-Lee seemed to know everybody and everything. She heard that a sizable cold-water flat on the fourth floor of an elevatorless building at 85, boulevard Saint-Michel might be available if the MacLeishes went quickly. They did, it was, and there they settled in for the balance of their first year.

The apartment was located directly opposite the Luxembourg Gardens, and the exchange rates were such that they were able to hire both a cook and a maid, in addition to Kathy. "I never have had such freedom before," Ada wrote Maurice Firuski in Cambridge. "The particular joy of mending Archie's socks is taken from me by Marie who doesn't fancy seeing Madame do anything useful." Mornings, Ada dropped Kenny off at school on her way to her studio, while Archie went upstairs to the *bonne*'s room and tried to write poems under a leaky skylight. At noon he picked Kenny up from school and brought him home. Archie tried (without much success) not to drink wine at lunch, in order to keep his mind clear for the afternoon's reading at the Bibliothèque Nationale, "where you can't possibly find the book you want and they have *no* artificial lighting." Twice a week he went to a gym to pull weights "and be sprayed by a fire hose afterwards." Once a week, he and Ada met for a long lunch at Aux Petits Riches, a bourgeois restaurant where the butter and the veal were excellent and they did not stint themselves on the wine. Occasionally there would be a dinner party, usually involving the Myerses, but most evenings they dined quietly at home. Weekends they took long walks along the Seine. "Think of us as most dreadfully happy," Ada wrote Firuski.

Not everything was perfect, of course. Archie, a lifelong worrier, worried about expenses, but concluded that as long as the franc stayed down, they would be all right. When the weather turned cold, he found out why so many artists worked in cafés: to keep warm. The gray Paris winter, relieved by "about two" sunsets a month, tended to depress him. Darkest of all were the days when he doubted himself. To avoid these, he compulsively stuck to his schedule. "He must learn to waste time, mustn't he?" Ada observed, but that was a lesson beyond Archie's capacity. The vagabonding Phelps Putnam turned up in Paris in the late fall and managed to tear him loose from his carefully planned routine now and then. It was not easy. Archie could not let time slip through his hands without discomfort.

For their first Christmas abroad, the weather was bright and sunny. Archie and Ada went to early mass at Notre-Dame, sitting high up in the gallery opposite the rose window and listening to the full choir of male voices ring through the gray stone arches. At home there was a Christmas tree, and Kenny sang French carols "with a perfect accent and not one idea what it was all about." They were touched when a cable arrived from Amy Lowell. "I should have sent her some cigars," Ada thought. After dinner, Archie and Ada walked for miles along the quays, marveling at their good fortune. But he could not help thinking of his sister Ishbel, who he knew was spending Christmas Day alone and far from home in a Colorado sanatorium. Earlier that fall she was found to have tuberculosis, and was sent to Colorado Springs to aid her recovery. (In the end, she spent nearly three years there.) You couldn't be cheerful on Christmas Day in a sanatorium, could you?

University of One

Ada was the first MacLeish to be recognized during the Paris years. In October, Povla Frijsh arrived for five weeks of intensive coaching, after which she pronounced her pupil ready for success as a singer of concert songs. "That is more than a compliment, it is a diploma," Archie wrote home to his parents. On the strength of such encouragement, Ada secured an audition with Nadia Boulanger on December 7. Boulanger was not herself a singing teacher but was the instructor of a number of composers then working in Paris, including the young American Aaron Copland, and a person of considerable influence in Parisian musical life.

Presumably Ada was seeking her advice as to a teacher, now that Frijsh was no longer available. "You are much too modest," Boulanger told Ada. "You shouldn't go around looking for teachers like a green girl. You should be doing concerts." Early in February, Boulanger arranged for Ada to sing a modern piece by Copland, with flute and clarinet accompaniment, in a program at the Salle Pleyel. The song itself was not wonderful, but Ada performed beautifully. With every prospect for further appearances of the kind, she worked hard to expand her repertoire in modern music.

Ada's voice, Archie wrote Amy Lowell, was ideally suited to "such songs as Stravinsky is now writing and Satie has been writing." These songs required extraordinary precision, perfect placement of the notes, and the capacity to produce those notes as if they had been made by a flute, yet with the quality of a human voice. Ada had what the French call *une voix blanche*, yet it was more silver than white. And to Archie, as to many of her listeners, it could be heartbreakingly beautiful. Ada was not lacking in ambition, and she was perfectly willing to seek out recognition by befriending critics and composers and impresarios. But Archie was still more ambitious for her and determined that she should have her chance. He believed in Ada's gift, passionately. And he wanted to disprove Aunt Mary's dire warnings that Ada's pursuit of a career would lead to the collapse of their marriage. About his own future he was considerably more doubtful. During the fall of 1923, he wrote half a dozen poems of varying length, and all of them were accepted by magazines such as the *Atlantic,* the *New Republic,* and the *North American Review.* He also completed a long verse play that was eventually, after revision, to become *Nobodaddy* (1926). But he was convinced that if he were really to succeed in poetry, he would have to educate himself. "Outside of the law I know nothing," he concluded. "I can't read Dante. I can't read the Greeks. I can't really read the Frenchmen and as for English poetry I have a college graduate's misinformation and nothing more." He was inclined to lay much of the blame on his undergraduate experience. "What a hell of a waste I made of four years at Yale!" he wrote Bangs in January. "PBK and a major in English taught me nothing of what I ought to know."

At the same time, he was discontented with the poetry he was then writing, even though it seemed to please Ellery Sedgwick at the *Atlantic.* "I don't like what I do," he wrote Amy Lowell on January 31. "In fact I dislike it very strongly." What he wanted was "a compact, precise edged poetry which could be terribly poignant, exquisitely moving." But in his own writing so far that was impossible. He needed to change, and to teach himself the way.

Midway through January 1924 he decided to stop writing, "except under pressure of compulsion," and to embark on a sound poetical education. "You *have* to read in order to write," he realized, and this was the time. He would learn Italian and read Dante in the original. He would read Laforgue and Rimbaud in French. He would go back to the beginnings of English poetry and read his way forward. And he would read the great moderns: Eliot and Pound and Yeats. The process, he estimated, would take two years to begin with, and a lifetime to keep up. This pragmatic approach to learning his craft was one he had to follow. "I am unfortunately so constructed that I need to know where I am going," he observed. "I am not sufficiently intuitive just simply to go."

Supplying the library for MacLeish's university of one was Sylvia Beach, a tiny, sharp-eyed woman from Princeton, New Jersey, who was owner and proprietor of Shakespeare and Company, a bookshop on the rue de l'Odéon. On her shelves she stacked the best of English literature, ancient and modern, and she had befriended most of the writers of Paris working in English. In Shakespeare and Company one might find James Joyce warming his hands over the log fire, or Hemingway shadowboxing as he talked in his flat midwestern accent. Sylvia lived with Adrienne Monnier, who ran a French-language bookshop across the street and occasionally invited writers and artists to her salon. Archie found these two havens within his first month in Paris: "Turning up from St. Germain to go home past the bottom of the gardens to the boulevard St. Michel one kept Shakespeare and Company to starboard and Adrienne Monnier's Amis des Livres to port, and felt . . . that one had passed the gates of dream." Gide was here on Thursday, he thought, looking at Adrienne's shop, and on Monday Joyce was there, at Sylvia's.

Archie became and remained one of the best customers of Shakespeare and Company's lending library. Four tightly written cards record the books he took out from his first visit, on October 11, 1923, through mid-April 1928. The borrowing was heaviest, and most obviously educational, during the first year and a half. MacLeish took extensive, closely scrawled notes on his reading. He started with the *Cambridge History of English Literature,* volumes one through three, and went on to Shakespeare and Chaucer and to Sir Philip Sidney, to Yeats's *Responsibilities* and Croce's *Aesthetics* and Lascelles Abercrombie's *Principles of English Prosody.* These books and dozens of others he mastered as if preparing for the toughest examination ever given, and administered by the toughest examiner: himself.

Certain of these books had a tremendous effect, among them T. S. Eliot's *Sacred Wood* and Ezra Pound's *Instigations.* Eliot's criticism led him toward a highly intellectualized poetry. "When we do not know enough, we tend always to substitute emotions for thoughts," Eliot wrote, and MacLeish agreed. Of course the impulse to create was itself emotional in origin, and of course it was emotion one wanted to convey. But the way to communicate such emotion, Eliot taught, was through expressing a pure perception of truth rather than a mere state of emotional arousal. "The difficulty," as MacLeish noted, was "to make the pure perception of truth live." Eliot also served as a guide to other works. In Dante, he believed, one found the key to this modern spirit in poetry, for *The Divine Comedy* was "compact with emotion and yet never once emotional." And *The Golden Bough*, Sir James Frazer's monumental study of archetypal themes in folklore and anthropology, provided an indispensable source for understanding what was basic and eternal in human history. By January 1924 Archie was deep in *The Golden Bough*, the abridged edition, and finding it "great stuff."

While Eliot was building a new philosophy, Pound was tearing down the old. As Archie later wrote of him, Pound was "the great dismantler, the great wrecker of brownstone fronts . . . imitation French chateaux and imitation Gothic railroad stations." He used his crowbar and sledge-hammer to demolish "the politely dead poetry" of the previous generation and of the whole world that accepted such poetry. This was a great service and needed doing. Yet Pound's most important contribution to MacLeish as a teacher was to reprint Ernest Fenellosa's essay on the Chinese written character in the back of *Instigations*. "This is one of the most important pieces of writing I have happened upon," MacLeish commented in his notebooks for February 1924. The business of poetry, Fenellosa argued from the Chinese example, was to express "concretely and vividly . . . the interactions of things." It followed that the verb, which made these connections, was by far the most crucial part of speech. In all cases the language of poems had to remain concrete. It was not enough for poetry "to furnish a meaning to philosophers. It must appeal to emotions with the charm of direct impression."

Out of these materials, Archie wove a theory that was to underlie much of what he wrote in Paris. His self-imposed course of reading did not, as he had feared, stem the flow of poems. Often his reading notes are interrupted by drafts of poems, suggested by an intersection between the ideas he was absorbing and his own experience. And the Paris years were to be unusually productive ones: five books in five years. Yet in June, Amy Lowell chided him that he was going at poetry the wrong way around. "The work must come first," she declared, "and the theory afterwards." One could learn by reading, certainly, but the primary thing was to feel deeply. "Give yourself a chance to feel as well as think," she advised him. "Do not simulate experience, plunge into it."

In fact MacLeish was at the time living a complicated emotional existence while holding himself strictly to his course of study. What puzzled him was how to convey the intricacies of such a life in poems. He did not himself inhabit the world of ideas very often, he knew. Most of the time his experience was made up of sense impressions, especially the senses of touch and hearing. "We go to our grave by way of door knobs and banisters and buttons and rough cloth and smooth cloth," he wrote in his notebooks. Often the journey was made painful by the women's high heels in the room above, or the yelping of a dog outside the window. Beyond the senses, he could detect no pattern to life. "Our thinking is all a sort of numb mumbling in which occasional words get themselves uttered. . . . Our relations with people — even the women we live with — are not continuous but momentary, fragmentary." How could such an inchoate and disorganized existence be put into words? "If you choose to reproduce the state of consciousness with its fog and the nameless objects looming out of the night, you run the risk of being foggy yourself. If you select instances and put them together you sacrifice to interest the thing you are trying to represent. You can only — in poetry at least — *describe*. Describe the inside of a consciousness as though it were a forest or a rock." That at least was the task he set himself as of spring 1924.

Through Sylvia Beach and Dick and Alice-Lee Myers, Archie and Ada soon became acquainted with a number of Americans living in Paris. Steve and Rosemary Benét were there, living on a shoestring while Steve prepared to write *John Brown's Body,* his long and eventually popular poem about the Civil War. The gadfly Lewis Galantière, who worked for the International Chamber of Commerce and spoke impeccable French, introduced them to his capacious circle of companions. The closest friends they made in 1924 were John Peale Bishop and his handsome wife, Margaret. Bishop, a classmate of Fitzgerald's at Princeton, was a poet and novelist who was very well read and interested in the aesthetic questions Archie was confronting. The two men bounced ideas back and forth, much as Archie and Frank Bangs had at Yale. Bishop insisted that a poet must use everything he knew, that there were possibilities even in the law. Taking his advice, MacLeish constructed a satiric poem on the legal conception of the corporation as a person. Here is "Corporate Entity," initially titled "The Sentimental Corporation" in notebok draft:

> The Oklahoma Ligno and Lithograph Co
> Of Maine doing business in Delaware Tennessee
> Missouri Montana Ohio and Idaho

With a corporate existence distinct from that of the
Secretary Treasurer President Directors or
Minority stockholder being empowered to acquire
As principal agent trustee licensee licensor
Any or all in part or in parts or entire

Etchings impressions engravings engravures prints
Paintings oil-paintings canvases portraits vignettes
Tableaux ceramics relievos insculptures tints
Art-treasures or masterpieces complete or in sets

The Oklahoma Ligno and Lithograph Co
Weeps at a nude by Michael Angelo.

In form this poem represented a departure for Archie. Obviously, it appropriates stilted legalese for the purposes of satire. It runs fourteen lines, but by its division into sections of eight, four, and two lines is differentiated from the two standard kinds of sonnet. All fourteen lines make up only one sentence, with no punctuation whatever until the final full stop.

These innovations may have been stimulated to some degree by the brilliant E. E. Cummings, another poet Archie got to know at this time. Cummings, a determined bohemian whose own eccentric punctuation functioned as a veiled attack on received conventions of all kinds, proved to be a nonstop monologist who loved to shock his listeners. He inveighed against the "disease" of poetry that consumed him, for example. As a consequence he sat in a shabby room, shivering in the cold and trying to keep warm by imagining the South Sea Islands. A plumber wouldn't do anything as foolish as that. He'd go out and get some coal to make a fire. Nor were poets superior to plumbers in any way. Poets and artists derived a shabby sort of satisfaction out of thinking themselves superior to better-adjusted people. Really, they were "unfortunate persons trying to capitalize their neuroses."

On and on Cummings would go, berating himself and his craft. At dinner with the MacLeishes one evening, he was holding forth, attacking himself, his laziness, his bad habits, his inability to work. Worst of all, he said, was "pissing his brains out in the belly of a whore." Ada dropped a spoon.

Cummings liked to poke fun at the literary discussions of Bishop and MacLeish. You can only write well, he maintained, if you know nothing. In debate Archie and John disposed of this "noble savage" argument. The ignorant were more likely to be infected by prejudice than the educated, they pointed out. Besides, literature was an art that demanded both expertness and knowledge. But Cummings only smiled his "glinting, solemn grin," and Bishop, realizing he'd been had, whinnied with laughter. "There was never a charm at once as taking and as withheld as Cummings' or a nature more generous and sensitive than John's," Archie observed in his notebooks. "Or a city that became them both better than Paris in that year."

Farewells

Busy as he was with his regimen of reading and composition, Archie was not yet fully committed to a life of poetry. On February 5, 1924, he wrote Charles F. Choate, Jr., about the possibility of returning to the law. At the moment, he told his former boss, he was in the middle of one of the hardest jobs he'd ever tackled (his self-imposed course of instruction). Yet he'd been a lawyer once, and might be one again. He couldn't expect to be "buoyed up" forever by an absurd rate of exchange. If he were to come back, he'd have to do it while he still knew some law. Archie continued until midsummer to pursue such options, including a post in Egypt. He rejected that alternative upon learning that the court he'd be working with was in Alexandria, where the cost of living was so high that he wouldn't make expenses. At that point he cut his ties with the legal profession once and for all.

The reception of *The Happy Marriage and Other Poems,* published March 1, may have contributed to this decision. The reviewers seemed to understand what he was doing, and when they found fault, it was with good reason. The *Independent* summed up the basic argument of the title poem admirably. According to convention, in a true marriage the lonely soul merges with another, and so ceases to be alone. But "The Happy Marriage" rejects this hypothesis entirely. For MacLeish, at this period, each soul was utterly and unavoidably alone. The brief review in the *Dial* praised the book for its "flashes of imagination," while criticizing its sometimes prosaic passages. MacLeish could not have agreed more: he had progressed to a much sparer style.

To his mind, the best work in the book consisted of a few poems he had written after coming overseas. Among these was "Chevaux de Bois," where life is compared to a merry-go-round:

> *Three hundred and sixty-five twirls*
> *To each of your annual whirls,*
>> *With a vorticle moon*
>> *For a sort of balloon*
> *And a meteorite in your curls,*
>> Ump! Ump!
> *And a meteorite in your curls.*

Here occurs the first instance of the most prevalent image in MacLeish's writing: insignificant man adrift in space on the spinning earth.

The MacLeishes naturally missed their Boston friends during the first months abroad. On January 1, 1924, Archie pleaded with the Bundys to make it a happy new year by coming to visit them in Paris. The Bundys did not make the crossing. Ada's parents did, staying at Foyot's, where Billy Hitchcock complained loudly when he was served coffee and rolls instead of a hearty New England breakfast. Trips around Europe helped to assuage lingering feelings of homesickness. With the Myerses, Archie and Ada traveled to the South of France and across to Italy in the spring of 1924. After staying up all night in their second-class railroad seats, they reached the Mediterranean ("O mare nostrum") in a misty dawn. The next day they motored to Ventimiglia in the rain, and then on to Genoa, Pisa, and Florence. There were many German tourists in Florence, and Archie found that hard to take. Otherwise, and despite the weather, it was a wonderful trip.

In May, Archie and Phelps Putnam journeyed to England for "a tour of poets and downs." In Oxford they visited Masefield, now a gruff old man who was guarded in his comments on the new verse. Masefield was grayer, and had acquired a limp and "a remarkable tendency to curse" since they had last seen him in New Haven, Archie wrote Frank Bangs. "He shoved Mrs. Masefield out of the room with one hand and closed the door back of her with the other." There was also a pleasant reunion with Walter de la Mare. But the two travelers did not see T. S. Eliot. As Archie wrote Amy Lowell, Eliot "gets ill when I am in the same country with him." He and Putnam had presented themselves at the bank where Eliot was working, and waited downstairs while an employee took their names up. In due course the employee returned with the news that Eliot was "not available." This disappointment aside, Putnam and MacLeish enjoyed their week in England. "Some vigorous bicycling in the country nearly finished off Phelpsie," Ada wrote Firuski. "It took a pint of port to renew his interest in life and letters."

At the end of May, MacLeish endured a week of drastic emotional suffering. Over the course of seven days, he lost a good friend and a lover, and bade a bitter farewell to the ghost of his brother Kenny. Archie's friendship with John Peale Bishop was compromised in much the same way that his earlier one with Frank Bangs had been. With Bangs, Archie undermined the friendship by courting the women — Margarett Sargent and Grace Allen Peabody — Frank was trying to marry. In Bishop's case, Archie went one step further by wooing his wife, Margaret. From letters, notebook entries, and poems, unpublished and published, it is possible to stitch together a plausible account of what happened between them. Looking back from his eighties, Archie could barely credit the "hysterical" nature of those documents, and did his best to rearrange the facts. He was never alone with Margaret Bishop in his life, he maintained. He thought her, in retrospect, nothing more than a "misplaced clubwoman" whose wealth had emasculated her husband. He did not feel that way in the spring of 1924.

Like Sargent before her, Margaret Bishop was tall with extravagant dark hair. MacLeish compared her beauty to that of the legendary Isolde, the goddess Astarte. As always basking in the admiration of beautiful women, he courted her — openly enough at first — with his near-hypnotic speaking voice. But the tie between them was not secured until she told him, with feeling, that the previous December, at Neuilly, she had been delivered of a first child, a son who arrived stillborn. Remembering the death of Brudie, Archie was moved by her sorrow and gave her what comfort he could. They began to meet privately, instead of at lunch or dinner with their spouses. Matters went far enough that they considered running away together, but that was not to be. It would be different, as she says in a 1926 poem of MacLeish's,

> *"If we had the choice*
> *To choose or not —"*

Then she went to her husband with a confession, or he discovered the affair in some other way. The Bishops decided it would be best to leave Paris and return to New York at the end of May. Otherwise they made no visible breach with the MacLeishes. If Ada knew of her husband's relationship with Margaret Bishop, she chose to ignore it. In a letter to the Lovetts, she mentioned "the event . . . or rather the tragedy" of the Bishops' departure, in her chatty manner of epistolary exaggeration. The farewell parties, she pointed out, "lasted about twelve hours each." But Archie *was* devastated by their leaving. Between May 26 and June 2, he repeatedly tried to work out his emotions on paper.

In an unpublished sonnet, for instance, he projected their shared grief for dead sons into the present anguish of separation from Margaret.

> *'Margaret,' I said, 'Margaret, what can I say,*
> *What can anyone say — my own dead son —'*
> *And I was weeping but not I thought for the one*
> *I left there on the hill that late June day,*
> *The last day I was young. And she turned away*
> *Her beautiful girl's head that none*
> *Was ever proud as hers and I saw run*
> *Her fingers over keys she did not play.*

And then she came into the room. I said
'They're dancing Noces tonight.' I said, 'This book —'
My heart hurt in my side; my hand shook.
For I had seen how on her young proud head
The sun fell sidewise and her eyes' look —
I could not think she ever must be dead.

On Monday evening, May 26, Archie mailed this poem to John Bishop with a brief note: "I send it to you as the inadequate record of one of the most heartbreaking experiences of my life. I send it to you and not to Margaret for you to decide whether she should see it. I am afraid my flowers were clumsy. I don't want to hurt her again."

The following day he wrote a long letter to both Bishops, in which he tried to explain if not to justify his conduct. He had lost all pride, he admitted. "Now when you think of her you think of him quickly so you won't think of her and when you think of her why there he is standing two yards above you." If he could undo what had passed between them, he would. "There are a great many things I would change if I could go back. I do not live skillfully," he admitted. Quoting Yeats's Aherne to the effect that "All dreams of the soul / End in a beautiful man's or woman's body," he insisted that what had happened was not a question of friendship. He knew they could "never meet again in the same way." That hardly seemed to matter in his present mood. "What matters is that I have in you two, words to clothe things which being wordless I never knew before." Two things, though, he could not leave unexpressed. "John Peale Bishop, novelist, poet, there is no man on earth I would rather have to friend. Margaret Bishop I love you. That is the end — of more than words." He posted the letter to the Bishops' steamer for them to read on the Atlantic.

On June 3 MacLeish once more wrote John Bishop, this time in the form of a free-verse dialogue on the inadequacy of memory. The speakers are MacIlliosa (MacLeish) and L'Eveque (Bishop). Toward the end comes this passage:

You, you within whose minds the moon
leaves incommun-
icable words
and the night birds
memories
briefer than they —

tell, tell me, O retell me these
and I
when I have heard you say,

when you are silent, will remember how
our mouths met
and will remember, will remember why —
what now
I have forgotten — why
she could so soon
forget.

Now that the Bishops were across the ocean, he added in a note, "the AX Bus no longer has significance nor the outline of the Trocadero from my window on the 6 E. Are there more poignant facts than these?"

In the years ahead Archie and John occasionally corresponded with each other, and there were several meetings, but Bishop could never feel the same way about him again. Margaret, apparently, did not write. It was over.

From the moment he arrived in Paris, Archie had been planning a pilgrimage to his brother Kenneth's grave. The opportunity came on Memorial Day weekend of 1924, so that he was in Belgium on Saturday, May 31, as the Bishops sailed across the Atlantic. As the brother of a hero of World War I, he was also an honored guest at the ceremonies commemorating the American dead. This put him in an awkward position, for Archie felt the war had been "an awful failure . . . a hideous mistake." It was, he concluded, "nothing but a commercial war." The rhetoric and propaganda that his brother passionately believed in was only "an enormous fraud." He was also outraged at the tactics of the United States Senate, and particularly those of Senator Henry Cabot Lodge of Massachusetts, in destroying Wilson's dream of a League of Nations strong enough to maintain peace. He went to Belgium for personal reasons only: for a moment of communion with his dead brother.

In Brussels he stayed overnight with Tom Daniels, second secretary in the American embassy and a Bonesman in the class of 1914. The next morning they started off with the largest wreath Archie had ever seen. At Ghent they lunched with Ambassador William Phillips and twenty others. At every stage of the journey, Archie felt his brother's bones in the earth, waiting, listening for him. At last they reached Waereghem, where Kenny was buried. In the cemetery the soil was sandy, the rhododendrons were dead, the grass would not grow. Kenny's name on the stone called out "like the cry of a hurt child." Archie removed a few withered flowers from his grave and replaced them with the magnificent wreath. Then he was overcome by "the most withering bitterness." It was "grotesque, absurd, silly that that beautiful boy should be lying under the sand in a field he never saw — for nothing — for nothing."

The sky was darkening as the Memorial Day observances began. The mayor made one graceful address in Flemish and another in French. The self-important American ambassador, reading French very badly, gravely uttered the sentiments that were expected of him. A priest led the crowd in prayer. The sky turned black. Archie felt nothing but the numbness of the earth, which seemed to be silently waiting. Lugubriously the band played "The Star-Spangled Banner," which the Belgian children sang in English, with incredible sweetness. Finally the heavens broke, and the torrent descended. Inside the shelter of the car Archie thought "about the flood of cool clean water beating onto the sand, sluicing onto the sand, clogging the sand with wet and slowly, slowly, seeping down into the dust, down past the roots of grass, past the roots of the dead rhododendrons, down between the cracked dry boards to the beautiful clean bones that lie there." With the purifying rain, the dead were no longer waiting. At last they could rest in the strange earth of a strange land.

So, Archie wrote his sister Ishbel about his journey to Waereghem, late on Memorial Day. Months later the experience worked itself out in one of his best-known and most powerful poems.

Memorial Rain
for Kenneth MacLeish

Ambassador Puser the ambassador
Reminds himself in French, felicitous tongue,
What these (young men no longer) lie here for
In rows that once, and somewhere else, were young . . .

All night in Brussels the wind had tugged at my door:
I had heard the wind at my door and the trees strung
Taut, and to me who had never been before
In that country it was a strange wind, blowing
Steadily, stiffening the walls, the floor,
The roof of my room. I had not slept for knowing
He too, dead, was a stranger in that land
And felt beneath the earth in the wind's flowing
A tightening of roots and would not understand,
Remembering lake winds in Illinois,
That strange wind. I had felt his bones in the sand
Listening.

. . . Reflects that these enjoy
Their country's gratitude, that deep repose,
That peace no pain can break, no hurt destroy,
That rest, that sleep . . .

At Ghent the wind rose.
There was a smell of rain and a heavy drag
Of wind in the hedges but not as the wind blows
Over fresh water when the waves lag
Foaming and the willows huddle and it will rain:
I felt him waiting.

. . . Indicates the flag
Which (may he say) enisles in Flanders plain
This little field these happy, happy dead
Have made America . . .

In the ripe grain
The wind coiled glistening, darted, fled,
Dragging its heavy body: at Waereghem
The wind coiled in the grass above his head:
Waiting — listening . . .

. . . Dedicates to them
This earth their bones have hallowed, this last gift
A grateful country . . .

Under the dry grass stem
The words are blurred, are thickened, the words sift
Confused by the rasp of the wind, by the thin grating
Of ants under the grass, the minute shift
And tumble of dusty sand separating
From dusty sand. The roots of the grass strain,
Tighten, the earth is rigid, waits — he is waiting —

And suddenly, and all at once, the rain!

A Second Year

For the summer, the MacLeishes rented a sturdily built villa perched one hundred and fifty feet above the Atlantic at Granville on the Normandy coast. On clear days they could see the Isle of Jersey to the northwest, and in any weather the sound of the sea ran through the halls. There Archie and Ada continued their artistic endeavors, undisturbed by social engagements. One morning as Ada was preparing some songs by Erik Satie on her rented piano, a nineteen-year-old boy showed up at the door. "Who's singing?" he wanted to know. "My wife," Archie answered. "But it is Satie. Nobody sings Satie," the lad said. "She does," Archie said. The boy was quite overcome by the miracle of hearing the contemporary music he loved in so unlikely a spot as Granville, a town with no reputation whatever as a center of culture. This was Christian Dior, who gave up his early passion for music to become a great fashion designer.

Granville proved an ideal vacation site for the children. They played on the beach and romped among the pines. And a French tutor came along to see to the development of their language skills. "Kenny is already fatter and eating like a horse and Mimi loves it," Archie wrote his parents on June 24. Physically, however, Kenny had to undergo treatment to straighten his legs. Kenny, it had been discovered, had suffered a bout of polio as an infant. Had he known of this affliction, Archie was to say, he would not have treated the lad so harshly.

The bond between father and son was as tenuous as the one between mother and son was strong. Kenny took after Ada in looks and in musical talent, while it seemed that everything he did annoyed Archie. "The truth is," he admitted, "that Kenny irritates me when we are together and I often bully him." He criticized his son for the way he talked and walked, and could not abide it when he cried. "What a miserable crybaby you are," he'd say, and send Kenny off to his room. Then Ada, to comfort her son, would sit on the stairs outside and sing until he fell asleep. When Archie was not critical, he tended to ignore the boy. In effect, he treated Kenny with the same sternness and lack of sympathy he had resented in his own father. And he felt justified in doing so on the grounds that such neglect was after all for the benefit of the child. "What I should like to give Kenny is himself," he wrote his parents. "Not being able to give him that what I should do is to prevent others from taking it away from him. And others will take it away not by opposition but by help. . . . It is those who go before and beat down the grass who lose you the way." Kenny would be better off, he believed, hacking his own trail through the wilderness.

It was different with Mimi, who at two was already displaying a streak of "Hillard-y" independence. She was "not exactly beautiful," Archie observed to his parents, for she looked exactly as he had in his baby pictures. "But she is as distinct a person as you could very well imagine with a delicious sense of humor [and] a way of her own." *She* decided when she would allow herself to be held in her father's lap. Archie declared her a "more than celestial child."

At Granville he adopted the writing routine he was to follow for most of his life. He wrote in the morning, exclusively. For the ear-sensitive MacLeish, the poems almost always started with a sound, "a rhythmic sound which clearly has a meaning but you don't know what . . . yet." When the sound became a phrase, a clause, a sentence, he knew he was at work. What he was after, in the end product, was "a believable speaking voice, a voice that will collect feelings the way lint collects on certain fabrics." Once begun, the drafts were set down in pencil, with an eraser kept handy. Often he tried two or three versions of the same incipient poem. Each day he stopped while he had momentum for the next: he did not know what he would do on the morrow, but he knew there was still "something moving inside." When a poem seemed complete, he put it away in a desk drawer, letting it ripen (or the opposite) like an apple. He did not want to publish green poems. After a few weeks or months, he pulled it out and looked at it again. What he did then was definitive. He would throw it away, or make revisions, or let it stand. Usually he sent the finished poem off to a magazine and waited for the verdict. Eventually most of the accepted poems were collected in books, and there — in galleys — came yet another temptation to revise.

In August the weather off the Atlantic turned foul. A tempest washed the beach away, and the winds, howling at night, spoke of menace. A small traveling circus came to town — "one tent, a very few animals, a few clowns, a few acrobats, and that was it." All the MacLeishes went one evening, watching the performers in the eerie light of torches: "One touch of the torch on the canvas roof and we were gone." The phrase that came to Archie a few days later, as he sat in his room high above the Atlantic trying to shut out the noise of the yelping dogs and of Ada singing Stravinsky, was "quite unexpectedly." Just that most unpoetic phrase, "quite unexpectedly," and then the repetition, "quite unexpectedly the top blew off." So commenced the composition of "The End of the World," another of his best and most widely anthologized poems.

> Quite unexpectedly as Vasserot
> The armless ambidextrian was lighting
> A match between his great and second toe
> And Ralph the lion was engaged in biting
> The neck of Madame Sossman while the drum
> Pointed, and Teeny was about to cough
> In waltz-time swinging Jocko by the thumb —
> Quite unexpectedly the top blew off:
>
> And there, there overhead, there, there, hung over
> Those thousands of white faces, those dazed eyes,
> There in the starless dark the poise, the hover,
> There with vast wings across the canceled skies,
> There in the sudden blackness the black pall
> Of nothing, nothing, nothing — nothing at all.

The jury is deadlocked on how to interpret this poem. To some, it reads like yet another statement of postwar disillusionment and emptiness: man confronted with a universe that has no connection with him and nothing to say. Yet others detect a kind of excitement at the very prospect of the tabula rasa out in space, awaiting those who will inscribe their message. Technically, most critics agree that the poem derives its power from the extraordinary contrast between the lively and busy octet — the hurly-burly of the circus underneath the tent — and the slow, measured pace of the sestet depicting the starless skies and ending in a memorable string of four negations. Because of this remarkable contrast, it is one of MacLeish's poems most often set to music.

At first, Archie and Ada had planned to stay overseas for only one year. Now, with both of them making progress but aware of how much they had still to learn, they determined to remain at least one more year. Aunt Mary, who had not given up on her determination that Archie should be a lawyer of importance, was tremendously disturbed by this news. She wrote Archie angrily that he was giving up a brilliant career and a chance to be a success. Knowing that she wished him only the best, Archie could not share her conclusions. Aunt Mary, he wrote Betty Choate, had an unfortunate way of confusing her will with the will of God. Besides, she "had about as much appreciation of art as of billiards." He could not forget her many past kindnesses, but he would not allow her future interference.

In early September, Archie and Ada went up to Paris and rented a veritable mansion with a lovely garden and rooms enough for everybody in suburban Saint-Cloud. They were now commuters, but the trains made the fifteen-minute run into Paris fifty-two times a day. Soon they met Gerald and Sara Murphy, who lived nearby, and began an intimate and lasting friendship. The Murphys were not rich by ordinary standards, but they believed in spending the money they had. As their story has become legend, the Murphys exist in the public consciousness primarily for their parties, and by all accounts these were wonderful. But Gerald, a Bonesman a few years before Archie, was also an accomplished artist, one whose work was celebrated by Fernand Léger as the only true American response to cubism. In his canvases, he strove to capture the thing itself in magnified detail. "He painted an Edwardian cigar box so totally representative of itself that it became its world," Archie wrote. "He painted a wasp so like a wasp that no one looking at it could take a wasp for granted ever again."

Both Gerald and Sara possessed charm. Something of a dandy in his dress, Gerald was a consummate host. Serene and beautiful, Sara managed to be gracious and at the same time to reserve a quiet corner of herself. In "Sketch for a Portrait of Mme. G—— M——," Archie portrayed Sara as he came to know her in the fall of 1924, when the Murphys were living in Gounod's old house in Saint-Cloud.

"Her room," you'd say — and wonder why you'd called it
Hers . . .

. . . .

Whether you came to dinner or to see
The last Picasso or because the sun
Blazed on her windows as you passed or just
Because you came, and whether she was there
Or down below in the garden or gone out
Or not come in yet, somehow when you came
you always crossed the hall and turned the doorknob
And went in; — "Her room" — as though the room
Itself were nearer her; as though the room
Were something she had left for you to see —

. . . .

. . . knowing it was not
A room to be possessed of, not a room
To give itself to people, not the kind
Of room you'd sit in and forget about,
Or sit in and look out from. It reserved
Something that in a woman you would call
Her reticence by which you'd mean her power
Of feeling what she had not put in words —

"There was a shine to life wherever they were," Archie said of the Murphys.

Through the Murphys, who were widely acquainted in the artistic community of Paris, the MacLeishes met Picasso and Stravinsky and Léger, and among their American friends John Dos Passos and his wife, Katy, who thereafter turned up like migratory birds every spring with flowers in their hands, arriving just in time for breakfast; F. Scott and Zelda Fitzgerald, whom they could never take seriously because of their reckless drinking; playwright Philip Barry and his wife, Ellen; humorist Donald Ogden Stewart and his first wife, Beatrice.

Ernest Hemingway, though, Archie found for himself. At Sylvia Beach's bookshop he picked up a copy of *in our time*, the pamphlet of brilliantly incisive vignettes Ernest published in the spring of 1924. Archie admired the writing, and wanted to meet the author. He could usually find Hemingway at the Closerie des Lilas late afternoons, Sylvia told him. There they met, and were immediately attracted to each other: two highly competitive middle-western middle-class young men, Ernest seven years the junior. At the time, Hemingway was a charming, sweet-natured person, MacLeish remembered. He was also blessed with a tremendous physical presence. As Archie later said of him, Ernest was the only person he'd ever known other than Franklin Delano Roosevelt who could exhaust the oxygen in a room just by walking into it. Although they had both grown up in the suburbs of Chicago, Ernest as a doctor's son in Oak Park, Hemingway at first pretended that he'd come from the wrong side of the tracks. Early in their friendship they boxed together, until Archie — thirty pounds lighter — got battered around too much. Later, on trips together, they compulsively raced each other on their bikes. Luckily there was no serious rivalry between them in literature, since Archie was destined for poetry, Ernest for prose.

After that first meeting, the MacLeishes invited the Hemingways to dinner. At the end of the evening, Ernest left with a corkscrew in his pocket. He returned it the next morning with a note. "If there is anything else missing in your home . . . ," he wrote, "send me a list." He also apologized for having arrived for dinner "in an advanced state of alcoholism" and for "having gone on and on all evening in doubtfully authentic reminiscences and dull obscenities." Actually, the dinner was a great success, and the supposed theft of the corkscrew remained a good-humored joke between them ever after.

"I am a poet"

At Granville, MacLeish began the long poem that was to become his third book, *The Pot of Earth*. In Saint-Cloud, working in a pink taffeta boudoir-studio, he finished the six-hundred-line poem and sent it off to Robert N. Linscott, his Houghton Mifflin editor, on October 31, 1924. In *The Pot of Earth,* as in much of his poetry, he hoped to articulate a universal truth. Therefore the poem is written for the most part in a kind of archetypal voice, and does not concern itself with the particulars of any individual's experience. "It happens that I cannot express myself in vignettes," he wrote Linscott unapologetically.

The epigraph, from Frazer's *Golden Bough,* tells the age-old story of vegetable life and death, as exemplified in the gardens of Adonis.

> These . . . were baskets or pots filled with earth in
>   which
> wheat, barley, lettuces, fennel, and various kinds of
> flowers were sown and tended for eight days, chiefly or
> exclusively by women. Fostered by the sun's heat, the
> plants shot up rapidly, but having no root they withered
> as rapidly away, and at the end of eight days were

> *carried out with the images of the dead Adonis and*
> *flung with them into the sea or into springs.*

The poem applies this symbolism to the biological pattern of its female protagonist. She, like the flowers and vegetables in the pot of earth, goes through the inevitable cycle of birth, growth, fertilization, giving birth, and death. At the end the woman has borne a child, which itself dies:

> *. . . I have borne the summer*
> *Dead, the corn dead, the living*
> *Dead. I am delivered.*

Then she too dies, to rot in the earth as the chestnut trees blossom.

The bitterness in this tale certainly owed a good deal to Brewster Hitchcock MacLeish's sudden death in the summer of 1921 and to Ada's devastated response. It may have owed something as well to the stillbirth of John and Margaret Bishop's first child, though there is nothing explicit in the poem that refers to any one person's loss. It was another kind of debt the poem owed — to the themes and the mood and even the rhythm of T. S. Eliot — that struck almost every intelligent reader. Like *The Waste Land* of 1922, MacLeish's *Pot of Earth* uses one of Frazer's vegetation myths as a parallel to modern life. And the influence of Eliot on MacLeish's verse is so strong to the ear that it occasionally resembles parody. This ominous, lugubrious passage from *The Pot of Earth* might almost have been drawn from *The Waste Land*'s "Burial of the Dead":

> *Silently on the sliding Nile*
> *The rudderless, the unoared barge*
> *Diminishing and for a while*
> *Followed, a fleck upon the large*
> *Silver, then faint, then vanished, passed*
> *Adonis who had once more died*
> *Down a slow water with the last*
> *Withdrawing of a fallen tide.*

Elsewhere the frantic colloquialisms and hint of madness in

> *Don't you want to dance?*
> *They're all dancing — that wonderful tune —*
> *Are you listening? Aren't you listening?*
> *The band*
> *start stuttered and*
> *Oh, won't you?*

are strongly reminiscent of Eliot's

"Speak to me. Why do you never speak. Speak.
"What are you thinking of? What thinking? What?
"I never know what you are thinking. Think."

The Waste Land cast "a net as difficult for a poet of today to escape as Joyce's *Ulysses* is for the writer of prose," Linscott wrote in response to *The Pot of Earth.* Houghton Mifflin would publish it in May, but he wished Archie had been able to wriggle free of Eliot. Yet once he'd read Eliot, MacLeish complained to Bishop, he could no more gaze at the world unaffected by the experience than he could go back to the innocence and ignorance of childhood. What was he supposed to do? "Recognize the great man's prior claims and shut up? And what if we can't shut up? Talk about the tragedy of the man who is ahead of his age: it is nothing to the tragedy of the man who comes after the man who is." Even Amy Lowell, writing to thank Archie for his article on her in the March 1925 *North American Review,* chided him for — so she had heard — falling under Eliot's influence. "I want to see you standing on your own feet and not diving head foremost after first one type of thing and then another," she lectured him in a sentence that exactly expressed what MacLeish's most severe critics were later to accuse him of. Having finished her monumental Keats biography, Lowell was not at all well. The following month, she was stricken with a fatal heart attack.

With his next book safely in press, Archie continued his process of education for poetry. In the winter of 1924–25, he concentrated on acquiring a reading knowledge of French poets such as Rimbaud, Laforgue, and Baudelaire. When Ada was busy and out of the house, he studied these poets with the assistance of Pierre Garanger, who taught philosophy in a Paris *lycée.* The private seminars did not last long. They disagreed about Rimbaud, for one thing. And at what was to be their last meeting, they were reading from the same book knee to knee when Archie felt Garanger's "blue eyes not looking at looking at me thinking his not my thoughts into me fucking me with his thoughts. I suffer like hell. I grin and say, well, well."

MacLeish was one of the few Americans in Paris who took the trouble to read French literature, Sylvia Beach pointed out. Through this common interest he met Marguerite Caetani, a Chapin from Boston who had married an Italian nobleman. She was founder and owner of the influential French literary journal *Commerce,* which was coedited by Paul Valéry, Valéry Larbaud, and Léon-Paul Fargue. In the spring of 1925, Archie was delighted when *Commerce* accepted a group of his poems for publication, undoubtedly with Caetani's endorsement. Prior to that time, his verse had appeared exclusively in American periodicals, albeit very good ones. But from 1925 to 1928 he began to publish in avant-garde little magazines that, whatever they paid, carried enormous prestige: *Commerce*, Eliot's *Criterion*, the *Dial*, *transition*.

While Archie's career as a poet was going forward, so was Ada's as a singer. She performed for Emma Eames, expanded her repertoire, and solidified her acquaintances "with as many critics and young composers as may be." When American writers and musicians came to Paris, they made it a point to look up the MacLeishes. During the visit of Sinclair Lewis and his wife, Grace, early in 1925, Archie and Ada were invited to their ground-floor flat on the rue de Rivoli. When they arrived, Lewis was lying in the bathtub fully dressed and drunk as a lord. Every now and then he would rise, pull down the shade, and get back in the bathtub — whereupon the shade sailed up again. Passersby collected to watch the show.

In the spring Gerald Murphy and Archie took a bicycle trip to Beaune. At a road mender's hut at Val de Mercée on Thursday the thirteenth of April, they read the following lines:

> *La vie est un desert, la femme un chameau.*
> *Pour voir le desert il faut monter sur le chameau.*

"Life is a desert, woman a camel. To see the desert one must mount the camel." As they left, they asked an old woman where the road led and got a sybilline answer. "Dans le pays," she said: into the lands. Then there was lunch by the rapid brook — "the vague sun, the vague green trees, the white lean bread, the cheese of St. Florentine, the Chablis (G.B. 1911) and the hunger to eat it with." Gerald was a fine traveling companion, Archie thought: knowledgeable about the wines, and curious and interested about whatever befell them.

During the early months of 1925, MacLeish was beginning to feel confident that the Parisian gamble was a good one, that he was on the right track. Increasingly he was certain of his vocation, he wrote Betty Choate in February. He was still obsessed with the shortness of time, but primarily because he wanted to get his next book finished — and the next after that. His work was far more important to him now than his romantic inclinations. "You for example," he told Betty, "could never again send me dazed and planet-struck up and down the drizzling sidewalks of the Charles River Basin." It was not that she had changed, but that he was moved by other things and saw the world differently. "I am stirred by poetry by music now as I wish I might still be by my less elaborate desires. That is to say — I never more see beautiful women. I see lonely and uncapturable gestures, swift nuances of an arm, curves of a breast, a throat — lines, forms, which as such crumple the words in my mind. But never a coordination of these things which becomes a person which becomes desirable. To write one must take the world apart and reconstruct it."

There in prose was the genesis of what was to become his most famous poem of all. In his notebooks for March 14, 1925, he set down "Ars poetica."

> A poem should be palpable and mute
> As a globed fruit.
>
> Dumb
> As old medallions to the thumb.
>
> Silent as the sleeve-worn stone
> Of casement ledges where the moss has grown —
>
> A poem should be wordless
> As the flight of birds.
>
> *
>
> A poem should be motionless in time
> As the moon climbs.
>
> Leaving, as the moon releases
> Twig by twig the night-entangled trees.
>
> Leaving, as the moon behind the winter leaves,
> Memory by memory the mind —
>
> A poem should be motionless in time
> As the moon climbs.
>
> *
>
> A poem should be equal to:
> Not true.
>
> For all the history of grief
> An empty doorway and a maple leaf.
>
> For love
> The leaning grasses and two lights above the sea —
>
> A poem should not mean
> But be.

The final much-quoted couplet embodies the central paradox of "Ars poetica," for the lines that tell us a poem should not mean but be carry a substantial burden of meaning. Yet even in this didactic poem, MacLeish works by metaphor for the most part: the globed fruit, the climbing moon, the empty doorway. In a gloss on the poem he sent to Norman Holmes Pearson in 1937, he went back to his notebooks for its sources. There he found Fenellosa's observation that metaphor was "the very essence of poetry," but not as exegesis or demonstration. Metaphor *itself* was experience. In his notebooks, too, was his reworking of Eliot's doctrine of the "objective correlative," a concrete representation that would convey emotion without involving the abstract slither of the merely personal. It would not do to gush on the page. The object of a poem was "not to recreate the poet's emotion in some one else. . . . The poem itself is finality, an end, a creation." In severely compressed form, "Ars poetica" conveyed most of the modernist aesthetic.

On May 1, *The Pot of Earth* came out to wider and more favorable attention than Archie's previous books. The influence of Eliot was noted everywhere, but not always in a fault-finding way. "If the young poet has taken a few hints from the elder one," Harriet Monroe wrote in *Poetry*, he has done so only so far as they suit his purposes. "*The Pot of Earth* is beautifully done," she declared. In *The Double Dealer*, John McClure agreed. MacLeish's poem was derived directly from *The Waste Land*, but MacLeish was good enough to be forgiven the echoes. The question should be "Is it good?" and not "Who did it first?"

Allen Tate in the *New Republic* cautiously concluded that MacLeish had "written an interesting poem; it is probable that he will write an important one." Others thought *The Pot of Earth* important in its own right. "Few poets of his generation have achieved more in their second volume," the *Dial* commented. MacLeish had marked out for himself "a definite and individual position in modern American poetry," according to Stephen Vincent Benét in the *Saturday Review of Literature*. "Is there any young American poet today better worth watching than Archibald MacLeish?" Katherine Lee Bates inquired in the *New York Evening Post*. Finally, the *New York Times* began its review with: "There can be no doubt that Mr. MacLeish is a poet." This was the judgment Archie had been waiting for and working toward. Happily he accepted it and made it his own. "I know I am a poet," the thirty-three-year-old wrote his parents on July 19, "and the rest can wait."

9

SHADOW OF THE NIGHT

Antibes and the States

GERALD AND SARA Murphy opened up Antibes in the summer of 1925, and the MacLeishes, with others, followed their lead. Prior to that time, the summer heat on the French Riviera was considered unhealthy, and everything closed down for the season. But the Murphys persuaded one hotel to stay open, bought a villa of their own, and took charge of daytime expeditions to the beach and occasional evening gatherings. Somehow the Murphys managed to conduct themselves with great style yet without extravagance. One of the best luncheons he ever ate, MacLeish recalled, was under the linden tree at the Murphys' Villa America. It consisted of perfectly boiled new potatoes and bread and butter, served on blue china and accompanied by an inexpensive white wine: nothing more. For the cocktail hour Gerald invented a Villa America special, which he presented in long-stemmed glasses with rims rubbed in lemon and dipped in coarse sugar. When asked about the contents of these drinks, Gerald was evasive. "Just the juices of a few flowers," he said. Philip Barry used the line in his play *Holiday*.

As it happened a tragic future lay in wait for the Murphy family. It was as if some cosmic enemy sought vengeance upon them. They had three beautiful children: "Honoria, an Alice-in-Wonderland little girl who melted with tenderness for animals . . . ; Baoth, a golden boy with a laughing delight in the world; Patrick, a child with the grave intelligence of a grown man — 'un monsieur,' as Picasso put it, 'que est par hasard un enfant.' " The children were cosseted and protected from all possible harm and, above all, from germs. Nonetheless, Patrick developed tuberculosis, and after a siege lasting several years and involving treatment in Switzerland and upstate New York, he died at sixteen. Midway through Patrick's long illness, his vigorously healthy older brother, Baoth, was suddenly stricken with spinal meningitis and carried off.

At Antibes in 1925, there was no inkling of these misfortunes. The MacLeishes were staying in the Villa Inshallah, a modest rented house that the Murphy children called the Chateau des Epinards because it somehow reminded them of spinach. For Honoria, Archie and Ada functioned as a second set of parents. Ada taught her how to make baking-powder biscuits on the miniature wood stove in her playhouse. Archie thrilled her with his high dives from the precipice of Eden Roc and with his beautiful speaking voice. She thought of him as a sort of Greek god, yet one who listened to her and called her by the pet name "Minoria."

In midsummer Gerald decided that he must have a boat. Accompanied by Vladimir Orloff, a Russian émigré who was a former naval cadet and a cousin of Diaghilev, he and Archie went to Marseille and returned with the *Picaflor,* an eight-meter Italian racing sloop that had been retired. Vladimir outfitted it with a new set of sails, and the three voyagers embarked for Antibes. It was a harrowing sail, for they ran into a fierce mistral they didn't know how to handle. Finally they put in at Saint-Tropez, short of their destination. Still, Archie was deeply impressed by Gerald's coolness and competence in the storm.

Picasso stayed with Gerald and Sara that summer at Antibes. Others also on the Riviera were the Barrys, John and Katy Dos Passos, and the Fitzgeralds. Scott "liked Archie MacLeish enormously," he wrote Bishop. Archie felt affection for Scott, too, though it was intermixed with caution. You never knew who was going to show up when you met Fitzgerald, he complained. In particular, he didn't cotton to Scott when his "eyes took on that Irish blur." Zelda joined her husband in reckless hedonism, and Archie was too much the puritan to feel comfortable around them.

By Labor Day the MacLeishes were back in the United States for the first time since leaving Boston two years before. They made it a long stay, with visits to New York, Boston, Farmington, and Craigie Lea. One reason for the return was an injury to his back Archie had suffered while diving at Eden Roc. His parents sent him to a specialist in Chicago, who recommended immediate and major surgery. Archie decided to wait, whereupon his condition steadily improved. Back in Europe, he consulted a Paris specialist who took X rays, diagnosed the problem as a congenital defect requiring no surgery, and strongly intimated that the Chicago surgeon must have been a quack. Archie wholeheartedly agreed, and suspected greed as his motive. "I think the sound of the name MacLeish was too much for him," he wrote his parents.

At Craigie Lea, Archie was saddened to witness the decline of his father, now fading at eighty-seven. In the spring, Andrew and Patty MacLeish had traveled to Colorado Springs to see Ishbel. During their absence, Bruce MacLeish's wife, Elizabeth, had tried her hand at some interior decorating of Craigie Lea, repainting the living room in grays and greens. On his return, Andrew did not recognize his beloved house. "Isn't this a fine hotel?" he remarked. Moreover, Andrew barely knew Archie when he arrived. It was "like watching the end of the procession," Archie confided to his notebooks: "Father, the old man, dead in life, living not in other places but away from all places — forgetting his own home, his own children." With artful persuasion, Patty MacLeish managed to keep her husband away from the office after that. Instead he roamed the halls of Craigie Lea, whistling "Merrily We Roll Along" over and over.

While in the States, MacLeish established contact with poets Wallace Stevens and Marianne Moore. From Farmington, Archie went up to spend an hour with Stevens in his Hartford insurance office. "You can write the waste of time off to charity," he wrote Stevens afterwards. "It meant a great deal to me." He also offered to ship Parisian goodies back to Hartford. "What kind of stuff exactly do you want — patisserie? — candy? — confections in gen'l?" Moore he met at a party the Bishops gave in New York, and she at once accepted Archie's poem "Nocturne" for the *Dial*, where she was poetry editor. Meanwhile, T. S. Eliot in London was considering other MacLeish poems for his *Criterion*. "Keep them as long as there remains the slightest chance that they will be of interest to you," Archie insisted. "Any plans I may have for them are secondary to, and conditional upon, your decision." After holding the batch of poems for months, Eliot decided to print two.

Back in Paris, the MacLeishes acquired at a very cheap rate a *pied-à-terre* at 44, rue du Bac. The place belonged to Count Étienne de Beaumont, an art connoisseur and patron they had met in Antibes. He had intended it as a studio for his friend Picasso, but the shape of the rooms and the light were not quite right, and so Beaumont made it available to Archie and Ada. Mornings they whisked Kenny off to school from their house in Saint-Cloud and took the train to Paris and the rue du Bac. Archie worked much better there, Ada wrote Firuski. At home "he smells foxes, or hears bells, or thinks the children may be falling downstairs." A Basque woman dressed in invariable black organized everything and fixed a marvelous lunch for the two of them. In midafternoon, Ada went back to Saint-Cloud to see to the children, and Archie worked on until dark. "Our studio," Ada wrote Firuski, "is . . . by far the most intelligent thing we ever did."

The day after Christmas, the MacLeishes went to Chartres for two days of rest and renewal. They spent hours in the cathedral letting time slip by, and took long walks in the Norman countryside, seeing no one but peasants and their beasts. They were wrenched from these rustic surroundings to the New Year's Eve costume ball at the Paris residence of the Pierpont Morgan Hamiltons. The champagne did not run out. Archie got mellow enough "to say the most atrocious things to the purest women he could find," while Ada was followed about by a wealthy Portuguese who insisted she would make a splendid mother for his children. The Fitzgeralds were in town, "almost always tight" but still attractive. So was Hemingway, "whose book [*In Our Time*] and whose person I admire tremendously," Ada wrote.

Persia

In January 1926 Archie decided to interrupt the productive Paris routine by signing on for a three-month trip to Persia (as it was then called). The League of Nations had appointed a three-man commission to go to Persia and look into that country's argument that because it had no effective transportation system, it could not survive financially without producing opium. The commission was composed of a Frenchman, an Italian, and as chairman an American, Colonel Frederic A. Delano, former chairman of the Wabash Railroad. Delano was looking for an aide to go along as his secretary and legal counsel. In Washington, Dean Acheson heard about this opportunity and wired MacLeish in Paris on January 15: "CAN YOU GO TO PERSIA AS COUNSEL-SECRETARY, FREDERIC DELANO, FORMERLY CHICAGO, PRESIDENT, LEAGUE COMMISSION OPIUM. YOU MEET DELANO HAVRE FEBRUARY 20TH, LEAVE GENEVA FOR PERSIA FEBRUARY 24TH, THREE MONTHS PERSIA INVESTIGATING, AFTERWARD HELP PREPARATION REPORT. COMMISSION FUNDS LIMITED. WOULD PAY EXPENSES AND ONE HUNDRED DOLLARS A MONTH. HOPE YOU GO. GREAT EXPERIENCE. DELANO DELIGHTFUL." Aside from Acheson's endorsement (and Archie was to end with a far different opinion of Delano), there was no sensible reason why MacLeish should have accepted this offer, but accept he did, for the lure of adventure called him. "You go into parts of Persia no European ever sees," he wrote Bishop. "It sounds exciting." Besides, Archie was rarely able to reject any proposal that involved traveling. "You must think of Archie's life," Ada said of him, "as that of someone who lives in a bustling port, all active and happy, and one day he looks up and sees a mountain, and thinks, 'well, I've simply got to go up there,' and he does and after a while he looks down at the bustling port and thinks, 'now I've got to get back down there.' "

Mountains, deserts, and exotic cities were all on the itinerary for the Persian trip. On January 23 Delano sent MacLeish a list of things to buy, including full equipment for extreme heat and extreme cold: Palm Beach suits and sweaters, sun helmet and heavy blankets, summer underwear and woolen underwear. Their route took them down to Egypt, where Archie was transfixed by the Sphinx, "an island in time." From in front he gazed up at the massive face that stared out beyond him "into the rising sun, its eyebrows lifted in an enormous wonder that is not wonder and upon its lips the broken, defaced, shadow of the smile with which man has so long faced the forces that destroy him." He was tempted to call the Sphinx a god, except that men had created its beauty. After traversing the desert, MacLeish was inspired to send Ezra Pound, a man he had never met, a one-sentence postcard from Iraq: "My dear Pound," he wrote. "Nothing here rhymes with Lepantos. MacLeish." Eventually the commission reached Persia, where it was confronted with a revolutionary change of scene. Archie described it as "an arid, impoverished, forbidding, and incredibly beautiful land, where men live in isolation behind their earthwalls with over-hanging peach boughs." That became his symbol for Persia: the peach bough over the mud wall. The commission traveled throughout the mountainous country, stopping at Persepolis, Ecbatan, Isfahan, Teheran, and elsewhere. Delano, MacLeish, and company saw more of Persia in two months than most of the Persians they met had seen in a lifetime.

Along the way, there were mishaps. At Fasā a fire destroyed part of the house they were occupying, and all the records and maps of the mission were destroyed. In the confusion, "some of the party, chiefly MacLeish," were robbed of articles of clothing. On the way to Kermanshah, Archie was ill with a high fever — probably, the doctor decided, owing to something he'd eaten. But what principally troubled Archie was his absence from Ada. As Delano wrote aboard the steamship taking them back to Marseille, "MacLeish has been very homesick. . . . He is a wonderful fellow and loveable, but very temperamental and at times difficile." Simultaneously Archie was recording in *his* journal withering comments about Delano, "a muddle-headed, goodhearted, meddlesome, belly-aching soft old man with disagreeable personal habits." Fussy, nervous, and constantly worrying, he served as "a terrible object lesson" to Archie, who recognized the same traits in himself. Worst of all, the old man could turn waspish at times. To Acheson, who had called Delano "delightful," MacLeish described him as "a cream puff stuffed with arsenic."

Delano was also lazy, and left the composition of the commission's report entirely to Archie. At the last minute he even asked MacLeish to write the report's preface for Delano's signature. "But that should be your own comment on the report — which you haven't yet read," MacLeish objected. "Never mind," the colonel proclaimed. "You draft something and I'll make whatever changes are necessary." So on June 30, his last day with the commission, Archie drafted Delano's preface. Therein he set down his own conclusions. Persia would continue to be heavily involved in producing and selling opium as long as there were no better roads in the country than those they had observed. He recommended, therefore, that a railroad be built to permit the transportation of other kinds of crops, and even spelled out one possible route the railroad should take. When the report finally came out, published by the League of Nations, MacLeish's draft was printed verbatim over Delano's signature. And the railroad that was built followed the route he had laid out for it.

The three-month separation caused by the trip to Persia hit both MacLeishes hard. After just three weeks apart, Ada wrote Firuski that she felt only half alive. She was working well, preparing for "a very important" concert on May 5, but otherwise was simply going through the motions. "I just have no real life apart from Archie," she wrote. In his journal, meanwhile, Archie intermingled testimony of his love for Ada with long descriptive passages about the landscape and the people they encountered en route. "Ten years of being married to you and I love you always more and more," he commented on March 9, at the very beginning. "And how I can lose a day of you I shall never understand. What a fool I am!" What they shared, he wrote the next day, was what other people gave their lives and dedicated their souls to attaining. Their love was such that "I shall never be able to say Was of it. It is like a kind of life going on underground in me."

As the weeks dragged on, Archie's journal entries began to sound almost desperate. "I am nothing — no one — away from you," he wrote in Teheran on March 23. "I relapse into a little boy trying to win a good word from the onlookers." Then on April 5, from Isfahan, he admitted that his coming was "an irremediable mistake." Apart from her, nothing could be beautiful to him. "O there are words to make Isfahan a thing of beauty. And there is a word to make it nothing, a mad dream which, horribly come true, confines and tortures me. And that word is your name." For the first time, he wrote, he feared death — her death, for against that he would have no defense, would only tear at the earth with cold fingers. "Forgive me. Forgive me if you can. You would not so hurt me as I have you." By the tenth of May, he would be back in Teheran to find her letters. He feared the moment as much as he longed for it, he wrote. "I am eaten by fears — as always — nameless and therefore more terrible." But what could he possibly have to fear from her letters?

He may have feared that Ada's professional career, the career he so passionately wanted for her, was drawing them apart. Certainly she was growing increasingly independent of him in her world of music. At times, too, she was the object of other men's admiration, including that of one particular impresario. Ada was eager to earn this man's good opinion, for he was a person of considerable influence. Madame Boulanger, Nadia's mother, warned Ada not to let him know she was married, for he would lose all interest in her if she did. So she withheld that information, and in due course the impresario invited her to accompany him to Salzburg, for what were manifestly less than honorable reasons. "Well, that's very flattering," Ada said. "I'll have to ask my husband, of course." She had temptations, in other words, and Archie's behavior gave her reason to consider giving in to them. One evening in Paris, Philip Hofer remembers, he went to a party with the MacLeishes. All evening Archie danced attendance on some great beauty from Boston. Ada would not dance with Philip at all, though he sat next to her all evening and was half in love with her.

On May 20 Ada moved from Paris to Antibes for the summer, bringing with her a Frenchwoman who was "one of the best accompanists in the world." The Murphys, and their animals, cheered her days in Archie's absence. She and Sara shared a cow, and the Murphy children were tending rabbits and guinea pigs. Finally, Archie arrived in Marseille on June 16. Ada, with Sara and Gerald, bribed their way onto the bridge of an ocean liner to watch his boat come in. Husband and wife had but one day together in Antibes before she accompanied him to Geneva, where he wrote the opium commission's report. They celebrated their tenth anniversary in Geneva "with so much champagne and so many roses," Ada wrote the Lovetts, "that the hotel management had its doubts about the sanctity of our marriage lines."

Archie's version of their reunion tells a different story. It appears in a poem called "Old Photograph," which he withheld from publication all his days. Richard McAdoo, his last editor at Houghton Mifflin, encouraged MacLeish to include it in *New and Collected Poems, 1917–1976,* but Archie, in his mid-eighties, said, "Not now." It appeared only after his death, in *Collected Poems, 1917–1982.*

> *Old Photograph*
> *There she is. At Antibes I'd guess*
> *by the pines, the garden, the sea shine.*
>
> *She's laughing. Oh, she always laughed*
> *at cameras. She'd laugh and run*
> *before that devil in the lens could catch her.*

He's caught her this time though: look at her
eyes — her eyes aren't laughing.

There's no such thing as fragrance in a photograph
but this one seems to hold a fragrance —
fresh-washed gingham in a summer wind.

Old? Oh, thirty maybe. Almost thirty.
This would have been the year I went to Persia —
they called it Persia then — Shiraz,
Bushire, the Caspian, Isfahan.
She sent me the news in envelopes lined in blue.
The children were well. The Murphys were angels:
they had given her new potatoes sweet as peas
on a white plate under the linden tree.
She was singing Melisande with Croiza —
"mes longues cheveux." She was quite, quite well.
I was almost out of my mind with longing for her . . .

There she is that summer in Antibes —
laughing
             with frightened eyes.

It is indeed Ada's eyes that dominate the snapshot — eyes that belie the laughing mouth, eyes that echo Archie's fear at what may have happened to their marriage during three months apart. In yet another poem written in 1926, this one never previously printed, Archie located a source for that fear in sexual betrayal, and combined that theme with his recent exposure to Near Eastern culture:

>   *The Treason*
>   *Saints and angels keep with me!*
> *My love lay by the apple-bloom tree.*
> *Her head was by my head, her knee*
> *In the bright brown sun of Araby.*
> *She heard the birds of that country*
> *And a man's face in a hood saw she.*
> *His knee lay on her loosened knee.*
> *This and all else told she me.*
> *Her mouth was by my mouth but she*
> *Naked lay in Araby.*

"Contemporary Portrait," a published poem of this period, repeats the motif of a woman's eyes revealing a silent, bitter truth her mouth denies:

The eyes are hers, the mouth is not her own.
The mouth smiles soft, remembers well, complies,
laughs, lifts a little, kisses — these are lies
when at the lid the tragic look is shown.

Ada may not have had an affair. The man beneath the hood remains unidentified, and may have been an invention. But in Archie's fevered imagination, he was real enough.

Season of Divorce

Antibes in the summer of 1926 was not what it had been the previous year. The word had got around, and the beach was overcrowded with — in Ada's phrase — "a group of New York people, movie producers, etc." Nor did the Murphys' friends seem as charming as in 1925. Fitzgerald, in particular, was behaving badly. His drinking kept him from writing, and in frustration he made life difficult for everyone around him. At a particularly elegant party the Murphys gave, he spied two homosexuals dancing together and began to dance beside them, glass in hand. Then he said to them, loudly, "Tell me — what do you *do?*" When the two men would not be provoked, Scott began tossing ripe figs into the glasses of the women present, so that champagne splashed on their gowns. At this point Gerald Murphy took Archie aside. "See what you can do to control Scott," he asked, for Gerald, like many another, thought of Archie as someone who could get difficult things done.

Archie managed to take Scott outside, and walked him down the road to the covered well at the *bastide*. There he sat Scott down and, standing over him, spoke with sweet reasonableness. "You know, Scott, the Murphys have gone to a great deal of trouble to make this party a success. And frankly, your behavior is ruining it." Fitzgerald rose up, furious. "You mean like this?" he asked, and belted MacLeish. The punch hurt, but Archie suffered no serious damage and did not retaliate. The next day the Murphys banned Scott and Zelda from the premises of the Villa America for three weeks.

Marriages were falling apart along the Riviera that summer. Noteworthy among these was that of Pierpont Morgan ("Peter") and Marie Louise ("Marise") Hamilton. Marise had fallen in love with a Canadian war ace. When Peter found out about it, he grabbed his wife by the backs of her arms and shook her, whereupon she "kicked him as high up as she could which was plenty." Peter came around to tell his side of the story to the MacLeishes at Antibes. The next day Marise did likewise. They decided to separate, and Peter asked Archie and Ada to move into their beautiful *rez-de-chaussée* flat at 41, avenue du Bois de

Boulogne in Paris. They could have the place rent free, and didn't even have to pay the butler. But Peter did ask them to pay the rest of the household staff, and to maintain the apartment until the dispute between himself and Marise blew over. It didn't blow over, and the MacLeishes nearly went broke paying the wages of a staff that included a maître d'hôtel, chef, five maids, and a governess. "You should see us!" Archie wrote his parents in October. "Three baths! And a mechanical piano. And me with a valet!!!" He and Ada were thus enabled to live at the very top level of American society in Paris without having much money themselves. The process may not have been good for them, Bob and Adele Lovett felt. "What this did for Archie in a vulgar sense," Lovett said, "was to give him a champagne taste on a beer budget."

The breakup of the Hamiltons, who were not really intimate friends of theirs, caused the MacLeishes little distress. It was different with Ernest Hemingway, whose marriage was also collapsing in the summer of 1926. Ernest spent much of the summer in Madrid, going to bullfights and writing stories. Archie wrote him there about his reaction to the typescript of *The Sun Also Rises*. "Jake stays with me," he commented. "So does Ashby [Lady Brett Ashley]. So do bulls. So do fish and fern leaves. . . . My one criticism is . . . that the novel is less of a block than your best stories are. But I don't see how it can help but be a success, both d'estime and d'argent. It has got the one rare thing — common life." While Ernest stayed in Madrid, his wife, Hadley, was almost literally confined in Antibes. Their son, Bumby, had come down with whooping cough, and the Murphys — ever wary of infectious disease — kept both mother and son under quarantine. Nor did Hadley feel she could leave Bumby, despite letters from Ernest asking her to join him in Spain. At long last he consented to come to the Riviera, but soon afterwards so did Pauline Pfeiffer, the other woman in the triangle. With Bumby better, the three adults set up a *ménage à trois* down the coast at Juan-les-Pins. At the end of the summer, Ernest and Hadley returned to Paris to set up separate residences.

These developments distressed Archie and Ada, for they genuinely liked Hadley, a woman of warmth and rare generosity. But their primary loyalty was to Ernest, and from the moment he arrived on the Riviera — bringing his just-completed story, "The Killers," for Archie to read — they knew that something was wrong. The four of them drove down the coast to have dinner at a hotel in Monte Carlo. Ernest asked Ada to dance; Archie asked Hadley, but she declined. A few minutes later Ernest stopped at the table and asked Archie angrily why he hadn't invited Hadley. Presumably, playing the gallant for the woman he was about to abandon may have salved Hemingway's conscience. At other times Hemingway was afflicted with "the horrors." These overcame him even in the bright noonday of the beach, but especially at night. He was torn between the two women he loved. He knew that he would have to choose, that people would be irreparably hurt, and that it was his fault. The least he could do was suffer, and suffer he did. "I've never seen a man go through the floor of despair as he did," MacLeish said.

Back in Paris, Ernest moved into Gerald Murphy's studio apartment at 69, rue Froidevaux. When they separated, Hadley stipulated that if Ernest and Pauline would stay apart for one hundred days and at the end of that time still wanted to marry each other, she would grant him a divorce. Rather surprisingly, the guilt-driven couple agreed. Pauline sailed across the Atlantic to present her parents in Arkansas, devout Catholics, with the unhappy news that she planned to marry a divorced man. Ernest remained in Paris, cut off from both his wife and his lover, and desperately lonely. Almost daily he came by the MacLeishes' posh flat on the avenue du Bois for companionship. In effect, Hemingway became part of the family during this period of trial, taking his meals with them, befriending the children, and keeping his bicycle in the front-hall parlor, much to the disgust of the Hamiltons' butler. Ernest and Archie took bicycle trips to Chartres and other points around Paris, both men pushing themselves to the limits of physical endurance as they raced forward in friendly but intense competition. Evenings, Ernest escorted Ada to the prize fights, where he truculently confronted anyone who so much as jostled her, and to the six-day bike races, where she pleased him by seeming to understand the tremendous effort of the racers.

In October, Ernest and Archie traveled to Zaragoza for the autumn bullfights. During this trip, MacLeish discovered two things about Hemingway. The first was that he could not bear to be left alone. Even at night, someone had to be within reach, or he'd be overcome by his "horrors." The second was that Ernest's rivalrous nature made it impossible for him to give full value to the accomplishment of other prose writers. For the most part, Ernest played the role of tutor in Zaragoza. At the museum, he knew exactly where to find the Goya etchings: in the basement, laid out on a large round table where anyone could have picked one up and carried it away. When it came to literary conversation, however, Archie felt himself at least the equal of the younger man. In particular, he praised the work of James Joyce and made the mistake of suggesting that Ernest might profit by reading more of Joyce's fiction. This drove Hemingway into the untenable position of attacking Joyce. "One thing led to another and we ended up not speaking to each other for about two days," Archie said. Since there were only the two of them, and they were sharing a room, this "got to be a little awkward." In "Cinema of a Man," Archie suggests how it must have been:

> *He walks with Ernest in the streets of Saragossa*
> *They are drunk their mouths are hard they say* qué cosa
> *They say the cruel words they hurt each other*
> *Their elbows touch their shoulders touch their feet go on and on*
> > *together*

If Ernest was temperamental in this period, so too was Archie, according to Alice-Lee Myers. "If he didn't like you," she said, "Archie was no pretender and it showed." In addition, he used to get crushes on people — both men and women — and these would lead to a tremendous emotional outpouring usually followed by disillusionment. Apparently Archie went through this process with Dick Myers, Alice-Lee's husband. First he admired Dick "because he was Irish and witty and full of enthusiasm." Then the infatuation subsided, and the two men quarreled. All in all, Alice-Lee recalled, MacLeish could be "very staccato," and it usually fell to Ada to smooth things over.

During the 1930s the friendship between MacLeish and Hemingway broke apart after a series of disputes still more unpleasant than the one at Zaragoza. In 1926–27, however, they were very close indeed. As Archie wrote Ernest in reminiscence on June 10, 1927:

> I could write a sweel history of my life out of the things pappy and me [MacLeish seems to have been the first to call Hemingway, then in his mid-twenties, by the name Pappy] have done together what with Bayonne and the smell of wet bark and the barges going by in the thin sunshine while we waited for it to be time to get into a garage and the flat light on the square at Tharagotha and the smell of melting snow on our pants at the station bar at Gstaad and all those swell talks we had with pappy up to his eyes in La Pedale and me trying to interest him in General Culture and that afternoon on the high land going out to Chartres with guys ploughing on the flat way off and the inside of my hip bones god only knows how sore and getting pleasantly stupified in front of the fire out on the Avenue du Bois in that blasted aptmt only pappy could take the curse off of.

And those feelings lasted, despite the troubles ahead. Ernest once said to Archie, "I don't love men." Neither did he, Archie said, yet he loved Ernest just the same.

On their return from Spain, Hemingway felt "about as happy as the average empty tomato can" in Pauline's absence. Often he was out of sorts. One evening at the MacLeishes, he read his scurrilous poem attacking Dorothy Parker, and so permanently alienated writer Donald Ogden Stewart. Archie took Ernest along to a French literary afternoon at Adrienne Monnier's, where "Gide and Jules Romains and others of that generation sat on stiff-backed chairs around a bookshop wall talking as though they had rehearsed all morning." Hemingway watched the floor and kept his silence. To get his attention, Gide drew him aside to explain how he punished his cat. He punished his cat, Gide said, by lifting him "by the scruff of the neck and saying PHT! in his face." It was not Ernest's kind of party.

At Christmastime, Hemingway accompanied the MacLeishes on a two-week visit to Gstaad, where Kenny was in boarding school at the Chalet Marie José. In later life Ken spoke with resentment about being shipped off to school at nine years of age. He was locked in a closet, he remembered, when he did not speak proper French. But he was sent there, according to Archie's letters, on the recommendation of doctors. The mountain air, it was believed, would help ensure his full recovery from infantile paralysis. The prescription seems to have worked. By Christmastime, Ada wrote the Lovetts, Ken was "a different child." He looked "like a rosy apple covered with freckles." Everyone went skiing, with Ernest taking over the job of coaching Ada. After a week she climbed a mountain — two hours' hard perspiring — and ran down. Then she and Ken won the mother-son skiing tournament.

Archie, also a beginner on the slopes, soon mastered the rudiments of the sport. After ten days he was even "jumping a little," Ada reported. The ambience of skiing interested him enough so that he attempted to write a short story on the subject, one of his rare ventures into fiction. "Don't you want to read it?" he asked Ernest. Hemingway didn't, especially, but took the story home and handed it back a few days later. "Never write about anything you don't know all about," he said. For a second opinion, Archie sent the story to Bob Linscott, who advised him against trying to publish it. The characters, Linscott said, lacked "the magic phrase or gesture that would make them three dimensional." Archie scrapped the story, and so ended his brief career as a writer of fiction.

Kenny and Mimi were both bewitched by Hemingway, who — so it seemed to Ken — paid more attention to them than their own father. He took Kenny fishing, for example. And one day he took him to see a slaughterhouse, an experience that fascinated and did not repel the boy. As for Mimi, she "was madly in love with Ernest." At four years old an elfin white-haired creature who "never smiled: she looked at you," Mimi wouldn't allow Ernest to address her in any language but French, which he "spoke like a butcher."

By late January 1927 the MacLeishes were back in Gstaad, this time to serve as chaperones to Ernest and Pauline, who were reunited at the end of the hundred-days agreement. Archie and Ada liked Pauline, who was younger, richer, and more stylish than Hadley, but they never felt close to her. "She always seemed like somebody you were about to meet," Archie said. Moreover, they were dismayed by the machinations Hemingway went through in order to be married in the Catholic faith. He claimed that he had been duly baptized as he lay wounded in Italy, when a priest came through the field station dispensing his blessings. Therefore he was a Catholic, and his previous marriage was null and void, Hadley had never been his wife, and Bumby was a bastard. "To see this farce being solemnized by the Catholic Church was more than we could take," Ada commented. When Ernest and Pauline were married in Paris on May 10, the MacLeishes did not attend.

While in Gstaad, Archie and Ernest met the eccentric and recklessly bohemian Harry Crosby, son of a Boston banking family. In 1922 Crosby persuaded Polly Peabody to leave her husband and fly with him to Paris. Polly changed her name to Caresse as a symbol of their new life together. For a time, Harry worked in the Morgan Harjes bank. They were then living in a balcony apartment above the Seine. Dressed in his banker's grays, Harry paddled to work each morning in a red canoe, with Caresse in her bathing suit in the bow. When he got out at the place de la Concorde, Caresse paddled home against the current to the whistles and applause of the onlookers on the bridges. The job did not last long, for Harry was committed to burning his candle at both ends and seriously courted his own death. Much of his energy went into philandering, some into writing poetry. Caresse, meanwhile, started the Black Sun Press to bring out limited editions of works they admired. MacLeish's poetry they admired a great deal. Early in 1927 Harry ranked him second among living poets, after Eliot and ahead of Cummings.

In his journal entry for December 28, 1926, Crosby recorded his encounter with MacLeish and Hemingway at a bar in Gstaad, where they drank the new wine. "H the realist and M the dreamer. . . . And M is quieter but they both have charm — rare in anyone, especially in men — nowadays. And M said he read very little. And H had been to the cock-fighting in Seville. And we drank. And H could drink us under the table. And everyone wanted to pay for the wine. And M won (that is he paid). And out into the cold and a hard walk uphill." Ernest and Archie both liked Crosby, who was himself blessed with charm. "You couldn't help being fond of him," Archie said. "He was frightening because it was perfectly apparent that he didn't exist — he didn't live in the real world at all. But if you could forget that, he was a charming person." Back in Paris, the Crosbys had the MacLeishes to lunch along with the painter Waldo Peirce, a friend of Hemingway's and a great bear of a man. On the letterhead of the Brasserie Lipp, MacLeish sent a note of thanks.

> Re Painters As Critics
> (for *private* consumption by HC and CC)
> *Poets should sing*
> *Hey ding-a-ling ling*
> *Says Peirce the brave painter*
> *(Good Egg too. No feinter)*
> *To which en pastiche*
> *Says the poet MacLeish*
> *(Good Egg too. No saint)*
> *Painters should paint!!!!*

Star Ascending

During and despite these many diversions, the MacLeishes' artistic careers continued to flourish. In October, Ada auditioned for Albert Carré, the honorary director of the Opéra-Comique, and as a consequence twice sang Mélisande with the whole cast. This was "the greatest event" in her life, she wrote the Lovetts in February, but hardly qualified her as an opera star. "Every American who can carry a tune says she is going to star in opera, and it makes me very weary." She *was* working with Carré, and he had told her she could sing *Faust* anywhere and *Romeo and Juliet* as well as Mélisande. "But it's another thing to do it," Ada pointed out. "Tenors are such a lousy lot and I don't like being mauled." She was having a grand winter, was going to do a concert March 2 and perhaps two more in the spring, but "kill that starring in opera stuff when you can."

Archie brought out two books of poetry in 1926. The first of these, issued by Maurice Firuski's Dunster House Press in May, was the verse play *Nobodaddy* he had substantially written during the fall of 1923. Two years later, after discussions with Conrad Aiken and Bob Linscott, he completely rewrote the second act and pronounced the play ready for publication. In *Nobodaddy,* which takes its title from William Blake's sardonic name for God, MacLeish once again — as with *Our Lady of Troy* and *The Pot of Earth* — appropriated a well-known story and altered it to conform to his purposes. This time he adapted the Adam-and-Eve, Cain-and-Abel story to dramatize "the condition of self-consciousness in an indifferent universe." In act 1, Adam and Eve eat of the forbidden fruit, and so become aware of themselves as isolated and lonely creatures, severed from their oneness with animal nature. In act 2, they flee from the Garden, and discover the pain of alienation in a universe that does not care about human beings or their values. Act 3 takes place thirty-five years later, in the desert east of Eden. Drought has destroyed Cain's crops and threatens Abel's flocks. Yet when Abel prays for permission to return to Eden and offers a sacrifice, Cain reacts with fury. "If we bow," he says, "we'll never stand upright on earth again." Abel may be willing to crawl before God, to sink back into the oneness with nature of the Garden before consciousness, but Cain is not. He stabs his brother with the sacrificial knife and runs into the dark.

MacLeish could hardly have diverged more radically from the biblical story. God is not an omnipotent deity but the life force in nature. Adam is humanity's first hero, not its first sinner. Eve is not the dupe of Satan but the instrument of man's rebelling against his animal origins. Abel symbolizes humanity's debilitating yearning to return to the womb of the natural world, and Cain becomes a heroic figure who dares to cut the cord. In effect, his tale reverses that of Genesis. In his own comment on the play, MacLeish celebrated the courage of Cain, condemned to be a fugitive and a wanderer all his days. "Cain, the son of those whose eyes were opened. The murderer of the brother whose offering was accepted. He who will not go back again to Eden. Who would not, even if he could. Who will go on. Who has the journey of mankind before him and the myth of man to bear." *Nobodaddy* was not widely reviewed on publication. Perhaps the best notice appeared in the *Independent,* edited by MacLeish's friend Christian Herter. Beginning with three reservations against the book — first, it consisted of a single poem seventy pages long; second, it was written in blank verse; and third, it was called *Nobodaddy* — the reviewer concluded that MacLeish had reworked the Bible story with originality into a powerful psychological drama of man's aloneness in the universe.

On his return from Persia, MacLeish began thinking about another long poem, one that was to achieve for him a measure of fame, or notoriety, when it emerged in 1928 as *The Hamlet of A. MacLeish.* The poem formed in his mind partly as a reaction to a letter of Bishop's wherein he remarked that modern terror had little to do with the demons of Elizabethan tragedy. Instead it was derived from "the horror of evil, of unexpected, sharply contrasted depravity, of helplessness before one's own nature — *not death, but life and its terrible possibilities.*" We are, MacLeish decided, afraid of our own lives. "Your modern is Hamlet —

but Hamlet without the ghost, without even the dead father, with nothing but the soliloquies — which are not overheard."

In the poem, then, he would confront himself directly, and especially his weaknesses: "my inability to have the appropriate emotions — my inadequacy — my ineffectiveness." In his preparatory notes, he elaborated on the worst of these weaknesses: his unhealthy reliance on the favorable opinion of others. "I profoundly lack grandeur-nobility (even the cheapest). I need justification and because I don't believe in myself I cannot have justification *chez moi.* Hence I seek it elsewhere. *I try to be a writer.* Which is why criticism so wounds me — I have no strength but the good opinion of others. Which is the real reason why my writing is what it is and why, at the same time, I dare not relinquish it. The true poet is a man who IS and incidentally writes." It seemed that his very existence required validation through the laudatory review, the letter of praise, the words of approbation from those in authority. "If a man writes to live in the sense that he risks his belief in his own validity on the reception of his writing by others he is already in hell." This brooding doubt about himself, not Prince Hamlet's awful uncertainty, was his torture on earth.

Originally he planned to call the poem "The Hamlet of L. T. Carnavel," a conjunction of *carnet* (notebook) and *navel.* Then he dropped the circumlocution and tried to describe honestly his own sometimes anguished life. For nearly a year after his Persian trip, he was at work on this "Hamlet."

Undoubtedly the most famous poem to come directly from that Near Eastern journey — the poem widely regarded as MacLeish's best — was "You, Andrew Marvell."

> *And here face down beneath the sun*
> *And here upon earth's noonward height*
> *To feel the always coming on*
> *The always rising of the night:*
>
> *To feel creep up the curving east*
> *The earthy chill of dusk and slow*
> *Upon those under lands the vast*
> *And ever climbing shadow grow*
>
> *And strange at Ecbatan the trees*
> *Take leaf by leaf the evening strange*
> *The flooding dark about their knees*
> *The mountains over Persia change*
>
> *And now at Kermanshah the gate*
> *Dark empty and the withered grass*

And through the twilight now the late
Few travelers in the westward pass

And Baghdad darken and the bridge
Across the silent river gone
And through Arabia the edge
Of evening widen and steal on

And deepen on Palmyra's street
The wheel rut in the ruined stone
And Lebanon fade out and Crete
High through the clouds and overblown

And over Sicily the air
Still flashing with the landward gulls
And loom and slowly disappear
The sails above the shadowy hulls

And Spain go under and the shore
Of Africa the gilded sand
And evening vanish and no more
The low pale light across that land

Nor now the long light on the sea:

And here face downward in the sun
To feel how swift how secretly
The shadow of the night comes on . . .

Unlike anything else he ever wrote, "You, Andrew Marvell" came with a rush. It "was there at the end of a morning and finished by night," Archie said. The physical images at the beginning were fresh in his mind, for he'd just come back from Persia across the Pitak Pass. That experience compounded by the emotional drain of his father's illness across the ocean work together in the emphasis on man's mortality versus nature's immutability. The title refers to Marvell's "To His Coy Mistress," which stresses the ephemerality of a human life measured against the eternal progress of "time's wingèd chariot hurrying near." But Marvell's argument is grounded in a lover's plea for consummation. Typically, MacLeish removes the theme from any single dramatic context and applies it to mankind generally. There is nothing in the poem to particularize whoever lies "face down beneath the sun" and feels "the shadow of the night" coming on. MacLeish writes of all of us on the spinning globe, feebly trying to keep pace with the passing of time, defeated even when we travel west to delay the setting of the sun. The form of the poem contributes to the sense of eternality. It is one long sentence, and it does not end. And the language is haunting in its musical power.

"You, Andrew Marvell" was written too late to be included in the collection of lyrics Houghton Mifflin had scheduled for November 1926 publication. It was also too late, Bob Linscott wrote Archie on August 20, to change the title from *Streets in the Moon* to *Under the Sun*. By any name the book was an extraordinary one, including among other poems "The End of the World," "Eleven," "Memorial Rain," and "Ars poetica." Not surprisingly, the passage of time constitutes an important theme in such lyrics as "Immortal Helix."

> *Hereunder Jacob Schmidt who, man and bones,*
> *Has been his hundred times around the sun.*
>
> *His Chronicle is endless — the great curve*
> *Inscribed in nothing by a point upon*
> *The spinning surface of a circling sphere.*
>
> *Dead bones roll on.*

A still more persistent motif in *Streets in the Moon* is that of man's difficulty in communicating with the cosmos. Out of Eden, certain descendants of Cain, including MacLeish, have lost the capacity to know nature.

> *In the doorway of the Bar*
> *Du Bon Port at Saint Tropez*
> *Sharp against the light*
> *The old sailor in the fez*
> *Stands face upward to the stars.*
>
> *Is it I then, only I,*
> *I who have such a need to know,*
> *I alone that cannot read?*

The most problematic poem in the book is "Einstein," presumably a portrait of modern intellectual man as scientist and rationalist, another descendant of Cain who, unlike the poet, has emerged triumphant. "Einstein" has occasioned a considerable amount of critical comment, much of it to the effect that the poem cannot be properly understood without a knowledge of the famous scientist's history and of his theory of relativity. But as David Barber has recently demonstrated, the poem was originally titled "Biography of Mr. Beck the Suicide" and submitted to the *North American Review* in 1923. The journal accepted the poem but never printed it, and at some time between 1923 and 1926 MacLeish changed the title and added a gloss of ten notes in the margin, as for example "Einstein hearing behind the wall of the Grand Hotel du Nord the stars discovers the Back Stair." None of these, however, seems to refer to actual moments in Albert Einstein's life.

It is no wonder, then, that Einstein was amused and puzzled when he read MacLeish's poem, probably in 1937. On his copy the great German physicist wrote this witty couplet.

> *Nützlich ist es dann und wann*
> *Wenn man nicht gut Englisch kann.*

In idiomatic translation: "Sometimes it's a good thing not to know much English."

Prior to publication of *Streets in the Moon,* MacLeish sent Linscott a list of poets and critics who should get advance copies. Included were Allen Tate, Louis Untermeyer, T. S. Eliot, Llewellyn Jones, Marianne Moore, Paul Rosenfeld, and Alexander Woollcott. Don't try Edmund ("Bunny") Wilson, he told Linscott. "He's agin' me for reasons more mysterious than I can fathom. For one thing he loves lady poets and for another he loves the oppressed. He can't forgive me the fact that I am male and used to play football at New Haven. I don't fit in anywhere. And what doesn't fit into his theories doesn't exist. Just the same, he's a damn fine critic and I wish I could please him." It may be that the trouble between Wilson and MacLeish was inspired in part by Archie's attentions to Margaret Bishop, the wife of Wilson's friend from Princeton days. For whatever reason, the two were always at odds, with the heaviest salvos yet to come.

The reviews of *Streets in the Moon* were still better than those of *The Pot of Earth.* Malcolm Cowley wrote a fine notice in the *Dial.* The strongest praise came from Yvor Winters in *Poetry,* who detected in MacLeish's poetry, "written . . . with a lunar clarity . . . the advent of one of the very few poets who . . . can rightly take a place beside the most distinguished poets of the preceding generation." *Streets in the Moon,* he observed, contained "a remarkably high percentage of completely and beautifully achieved poems." Tate was still more specific on this point. He asserted that fifteen of the book's fifty-two poems were "completely successful — an astonishing achievement." "Not for the beat of a line does MacLeish cease to be his own poet," Untermeyer concluded. No longer was he a poet of promise; he had emerged. If MacLeish was capable of "Einstein" and a dozen exquisite shorter poems, Conrad Aiken asked, "what mightn't he do next? One simply abdicates as critic, and flings one's hat in the air."

Archie's work also began appearing in anthologies. Untermeyer included six of his poems in *American Poetry, 1927: A Miscellany.* A section of his *Hamlet* ran in *The American Caravan: A Yearbook of*

American Literature (1927), edited by Van Wyck Brooks and others. Aiken printed four of his poems in *American Poetry: 1671–1928*. What's more, in the fall of 1926, Archie and Allen Tate explored the idea of preparing an anthology of their own. MacLeish consulted Linscott about the possibilities of publication, but the major work of the anthology was to reside with Tate. He was to make the selections and write the preface, leaving MacLeish in the role of an editor who could suggest but not demand a change of contents. Archie was prepared to pay the permissions costs for the right to reprint, he assured Tate on New Year's Day 1927. The job needed doing, and Tate should not have to make sacrifices in order to do it. Late in January, Archie assured him on another sticking point. "The work is yours, the responsibility is yours and the 'rewards' are yours," he pointed out. "Therefore the book bears your name alone." So encouraged, Tate began his chores as anthologizer, but — for whatever reason — the project was never completed.

Pleased though he must have been by reviews and recognition, Archie reached out for the endorsement of Ezra Pound and got his hand slapped. In November 1926 he sent Pound (then living in Rapallo) a batch of poems for possible publication in the *Exile,* the new review he was editing. He also promised Pound $100 of the $400 he needed to support the review for the first year. Included in the material was the third (or "Bleheris") section of *The Hamlet of A. MacLeish,* "You, Andrew Marvell," and this scurrilous piece of doggerel:

> As to Edmund Wilson the
> Apostle of Intensity
> Who prizes in poetic art
> The harder also softer part
> And makes his annual selection
> On the basis of erection —
> Also, hot as Charlie's auntie
> Plays the critical bacchante
> (But less naked than undressed) —
> He says He Likes The Ladies Best
>
> He used to like the gents but late
> Our Edmund's ceased to menstruate.

He liked the uncomplimentary lines on Wilson better than the "Bleheris," Pound replied. The latter, he thought, was too closely derived from his own *Cantos,* though also from Eliot, Gertrude Stein, and James Joyce. "Having a model in yr. ear you got the adhesiveness and agglutinativeness as well." He also thought "You, Andrew Marvell" derivative: "With the consciousness of having E.P. hovering over the work, it

Poem

And that was by the door (there)
                                    (and the new)
(Faint) leafy evening in the apple trees

And we would not forget this (anymore)

And even if we died there would be these
Remembered (touchings)
                              And we would return
From farther lands than any (that (were ever) named
To meet (within (the twilight of) that afternoon

Listen O my not now Ophelia (I)
(Think) there are not always (like a moon)
Rememberings afterward. [I think there are
Sometimes a few strange stars upon the sky.......]

Broken Promise

That was by the door.
Leafy evening in the apple trees.
And you would not forget this anymore
And even if you died there would be these

Touchings remembered.
                        And you would return
From any bourne from any shore
To find the evening in these leaves —
To find my arms beside this door . . .

I think, O, my not now Ophelia,
There are not always (like a moon)
Rememberings afterward:
                        (I think there are
Sometimes a few strange stars upon the sky.)

is perfectly easy to get out Herodotus and find some other city than Ecbatan." Pound knew he was swinging a heavy hammer, he wrote, but otherwise "the criticism is no use, and we get off into mere conversation and politesse."

This response left Archie seething, especially the remark about Ecbatan. He hadn't found Ecbatan in Pound *or* in Herodotus; he'd been there, twice, he wrote back. But otherwise Archie was all humility. It was true that Pound and later Eliot had liberated him from the past. Yet he still felt that much as he was indebted, and much as their cadences were ringing in his ear, his stuff was still his own. Pound turned the Ecbatan intelligence against MacLeish. "IF you have been there GOD-DAMN it you ought precisely to make that felt by putting in something that couldn't have been got from Herodotus." Then he added, "Come on down here and talk when you GIT ready." MacLeish did not go to Rapallo. Nearly three decades were to pass before he got to know Pound well, when he worked to release him from incarceration.

He thought Pound was crazy, he wrote Hemingway on February 14, 1927. And he was "getting fed up with the Ezraic assumption that he is a Great Man." Privately, though, he knew that Pound was a great line editor, for he had marked up and returned the draft of a poem (eventually called "Broken Promise") Archie had sent him. Here is the poem as Pound edited it, and the published "Broken Promise." Manifestly, MacLeish accepted nearly all of Pound's editing, especially the trimming away of excess verbiage and the occasional inversion, as in "Touchings remembered." Yet the most crucial revision of all — the change from "we" to "you" — was MacLeish's own. It is this alteration that justifies the title, and gives the now forgotten never-to-be-forgotten romance its poignancy.

An End to Paris

It was at Sylvia Beach's Shakespeare and Company that MacLeish met James Joyce, the myopic rail-thin Irish genius. Almost daily Joyce stopped by the bookshop, twirling his cane and eager for conversation. By 1926 the Joyces and MacLeishes had established a social pattern. They met for dinner once or twice a year; at Christmas, Archie and Ada sent him a case of the Alsatian white wine he fancied. Late in November 1926, Joyce came to dinner at the avenue du Bois apartment. It was the only "big, bang-up dinner" the MacLeishes gave while ensconced in the Hamiltons' grand flat. Sylvia Beach was invited, along with half a dozen others, including Bob Linscott, who was then visiting Paris for the first time. Linscott, a Lincolnesque figure who had educated himself in the stacks of the Boston Public Library while working as an office boy for Houghton Mifflin, was in awe at the prospect of meeting the author of *Ulysses*. Both he and MacLeish got out their copies of the book, published in France by Shakespeare and Company while banned in the United States, for Joyce to sign.

The evening began inauspiciously when "Joyce arrived with his bad eyes, and shook hands warmly with the butler." Embarrassed, he sat in a corner most of the evening, and in his befuddlement inscribed both copies of *Ulysses* to Archie. He warmed up after dinner, however, when Ada entertained the guests by singing. Joyce had a fine tenor voice himself. His wife, Nora, who never had a word of praise for her husband's fiction, used to regard him scornfully and say, "James Joyce the writer! And he could've sung with McCormack!" So Joyce joined the musical portion of the evening by teaching Ada "The Yellow Ale," an Irish ballad on the theme of the cuckold. She added it to her repertoire, and sang it in her March 1927 concert.

Prior to that time, Archie had had a chance to be of service to Joyce. In New York, an unscrupulous opportunist named Samuel Roth was printing bowdlerized sections of *Ulysses*, without permission, in his *Two Worlds Monthly* magazine. Roth was able to pirate the book because it could not be published in the United States and so was not under protection of copyright. This thievery outraged Joyce and Sylvia Beach, who immediately started a lawsuit and at the same time sought support from the leading literary and artistic figures of the age. A statement of protest was composed primarily by Ludwig Lewissohn, with MacLeish called in for revisions to ensure its legality. "The question at issue," the document concluded, "is whether the public (including the editors and publishers to whom his advertisements are offered) will encourage Mr. Samuel Roth to take advantage of the . . . legal difficulty of the author to deprive him of his property and to mutilate the creation of his art. The undersigned protest against Mr. Roth's conduct in republishing *Ulysses* and appeal to the American public in the name of that security of works of the intellect and the imagination without which art cannot live, to oppose to Mr. Roth's enterprise the full power of honorable and fair opinion." In effect, the protest asked the reading public to boycott Roth's magazine, though it did not explicitly say so. The statement also included a disclaimer artfully worded to stimulate even the hesitant to sign. "Some of us," it read, "may think it [*Ulysses*] might as well have never been published, but that opinion does not in any way mitigate the enormity of Roth's offense against the unwritten law and the decencies of his profession."

This document of protest, dated February 2, 1927, was eventually signed by 167 people, almost all of whom held some position of eminence in the international artistic community. Among them, to take a small sample, were H. G. Wells, Sherwood Anderson, Arnold Bennett, Benedetto Croce, Romain Rolland, Arthur Wing Pinero, Bertrand Russell, D. H. Lawrence, Luigi Pirandello, Miguel de Unamuno, Paul Valéry, W. B. Yeats, André Gide, Sean O'Casey, Maurice Maeterlinck, José Ortega y Gasset, Albert Einstein, T. S. Eliot, Somerset Maugham, Thornton Wilder, and Ernest Hemingway. Only two refused to sign: George Bernard Shaw and Ezra Pound. "That was just like Ezra," Beach remarked. The petition was then distributed to various newspapers and journals, which duly enlisted themselves on Joyce's side and against Roth's piracy. Roth was not deterred, and printed sections of *Ulysses* in three issues of *Two Worlds Monthly* before the courts intervened to stop him.

Pound, listening to a different drummer, did not think much of Joyce's writing at this period. He considered Joyce's long-term *Work in Progress* — eventually *Finnegans Wake* — "all a bad stunt." When Joyce showed him the manuscript of thirteen poems he had just completed, Pound handed them back without comment. "You don't think they're worth printing?" Joyce asked. "No, I don't," Pound answered. Next Joyce sent the manuscript in March 1927 to MacLeish, who was enthusiastic about it. His self-esteem restored, Joyce published it as *Pomes Penyeach,* and gave Archie one of the thirteen large paper copies that made up a limited edition of that title. On Halloween later that year, Archie was among the audience of two dozen who heard Joyce read the "Anna Livia Plurabelle" from *Finnegans Wake.* He could hardly summon up the words, he wrote Joyce afterwards, "to tell you how the pages you read us moved and excited me."

Though he never found Joyce warm, MacLeish liked him. He liked Joyce's "shyness and his stiffness and the sense of something vivid and maybe dangerous under it." Physically there was nothing at all prepossessing about him. With his little beard and thick lenses, he looked like "a very professional doctor — not a practicing one but a man about a hospital, rarely seen." Nonetheless, Archie wrote, "in Joyce you felt a hard, strong actuality that, if not greatness, was at least something you were always conscious of." And in his mind's eye, he forever saw the Irishman on the piano bench with Ada, lifting his tenor voice in the sad story of "The Yellow Ale."

Early in 1927 Archie took on the task of soliciting material for *Commerce,* the little magazine of Marguerite Caetani, the Princess Bassiano. Specifically he approached Elinor Wylie, E. E. Cummings, John Dos Passos, and Ernest Hemingway on her behalf. Hemingway sent along "Alpine Idyll" and "A Pursuit Race," but *Commerce* did not accept either one. MacLeish agreed with the decision, or at least half of it, for "A Pursuit Race" was the least successful story of Hemingway's he'd read. Caetani was also responsible for introducing MacLeish to St.-John Perse's *Anabase,* a poem he had read in French (before Eliot's translation) and found magnificent.

In February the MacLeishes and Murphys toured central Europe together, with stops at Berlin, Vienna, and Trieste, where Archie had agreed to look up Joyce's brother. They secured visas to enable them to go to Moscow as well, but gave up that idea when the rumor reached them that Russian beggars were confronting tourists, one hand extended for money and the other ready to throw lice at those who did not contribute.

Archie and Gerald may have had a falling-out during this trip. In June and again in August, MacLeish wrote Hemingway in some exasperation about the Murphys and about Gerald's "damn school girl quarrels" that made it hard to believe in his affection. "Relationships built on your personality and my personality just aren't relationships. I may be vulgar and prep school and all that but I still want friendships and no whipped up substitutes." Through the years, the MacLeish-Murphy friendship was to undergo several periods of strain. Usually, as in this case, they did not last long. Within the year, Gerald was to serve as godfather to another MacLeish child.

"It's time I had another baby," Ada wrote the Lovetts in January 1927, a "child of my old age." But with no such development in sight, she and Archie began to look around for a place of their own in France. In February they found a fifteenth-century farmhouse outside Versailles and very nearly bought it. The rent was only $200 a year, Ada wrote the Lovetts. "So we can afford to live in it whenever we want . . . and when we don't, just let it lie with a villager to look after it." Prices had gone up so steeply as the franc gained ground that they could no longer afford Paris. But thirty minutes away by automobile wasn't bad, and she could keep a studio in town. They were deep in negotiations to buy this place when they had a long talk and decided that they wanted to go back to America permanently, and if they were going to buy a house, it should be there. They resolved to spend the summer in the United States, and to look for a house in western Massachusetts near Aunt Mary's summer place in Ashfield.

Aunt Mary had decided that it was all right for her nephew to be a poet, especially since the Englishmen she relied on for her literary opinions "always mentioned" him as "one of the outstanding figures meriting the closest attention in his school of poetry," whatever that was. A partial reconciliation was effected, and Archie and Ada stayed in her Ashfield home while they conducted their search. Aunt Mary had lost little of her verve. Dean and Alice Acheson, on a visit, accompanied her to a country fair, where one of the booths offered for sale some glasses with pictures of naked women on them. Later she asked Alice, "Do you remember those filthy glasses we saw? What do you suppose I did with them?" "Oh, I don't know," Alice said. "Bought them and threw them out, I suppose." "Bought them?" Aunt Mary replied with indignation. "Certainly not. I took them!"

By summer's end, the MacLeishes had purchased a house and a sizable plot of farmland in Conway, Massachusetts, and arranged for the place to be remodeled. They then sailed back to Paris for their last months in that city, Archie minus the tonsils a Hartford doctor had removed. Harry and Caresse Crosby offered them the use of their apartment rent free, but Hugh Bayne, the same man who had wangled Archie's transfer to the artillery, made a still better offer, since his apartment at 8, rue Émile Augier was available for a longer period. The MacLeishes moved in there.

What Archie called "the world's worst winter" lay ahead. Kenny was back in school in Gstaad, and Archie interrupted his work to spend a month in Switzerland. Then he was called home to spend five weeks at Craigie Lea, where his father was suffering through his final days. Andrew MacLeish died on January 14, 1928. He was eighty-nine. With his passing, Archie was inclined to forgive his father the many inattentions that had so long plagued him. As he wrote Hemingway, whose own father committed suicide later that year, "I know how the death of your father changes him in your mind and he becomes what he was when you were very young and your heart is destroyed with tenderness for him."

The remaining days in Paris were uneventful except for Hemingway's freak accident and Archie's meeting with Kay Boyle. In March, Ernest and Pauline came to dinner with the MacLeishes, and after they went home, Hemingway pulled what he thought was the flushing chain for the toilet and managed to pull down a piece of the skylight, slicing open a gash on his forehead. It was Archie Ernest called for help at two in the morning, since he knew and respected MacLeish's talent for getting through emergencies. (Recently, in fact, the two of them had managed to extricate Hart Crane from a predicament with the French police.) Archie in turn called Alice-Lee Myers, who alerted the American hospital as they went to pick up Hemingway. Ernest was waiting for them on the sidewalk with a great towel around his head, still giddy with shock. A young intern stitched up the huge gash without anesthetic of any kind. "It was not the most beautiful job you ever saw," MacLeish observed. The stitches always showed.

The talented and beautiful writer Kay Boyle was an admirer of MacLeish's poetry before she came to Paris in 1928. The previous year she had spent at Stoke-on-Trent in England, where she used to sing the words to his "Signature Anonyme" as she pushed her daughter's pram among the hedgerows. Early in May 1928 she was invited to a party at the apartment of Eugene Jolas, co-founder of *transition*. As she was climbing the stairs, she was aware of a young man in a tweed jacket a flight below her, stopping to tie a shoelace so as not to overtake her. This was MacLeish. Inside the Jolases' party they talked, MacLeish in his tweed coat and gray trousers, Boyle in a brilliant orange velvet dress, and decided they liked each other. Archie was ever after one of her strongest supporters. "I think she is an even better writer than she lets herself be," he wrote her friend — and sometime lover — Harry Crosby. "She has the power and the glory."

A few days later the MacLeishes sailed westward across the Atlantic to settle into the house that would be their home for more than half a century. The customs people in Boston, remarkably, let them transport all their goods from France in a truck under seal. They broke the seal in Conway and passed customs on their front lawn. It was high time for them to return. Ada was six-months pregnant with the baby she wanted.

Reacclimation to their native land took some time. "For at least a year after we left Paris," Archie said, "we were still living in that city." In his poem "American Letter," dedicated to Gerald Murphy, he put his perplexity into words:

> *This land is my native land. And yet*
> *I am sick for home for the red roofs and the olives,*
> *And the foreign words and the smell of the sea fall.*
> *How can a wise man have two countries?*

And

> *Why should I think of the dolphins at Capo di Mele?*
> *Why should I see in my mind the taut sail*
> *And the hill over St.-Tropez and your hand on the tiller?*

Gerald was moved by the poem, naturally enough. And Scott Fitzgerald, homesick in Switzerland, where Zelda was institutionalized, committed whole sections of it to memory.

Looking backward two decades later in "Years of the Dog," MacLeish portrayed the Paris of the twenties as a breeding ground for fame.

> *Before, though, Paris was wonderful. Wanderers*
> *Talking in all tongues from every country.*

Fame was what they wanted in that town.
Fame could be found there too — flushed like quail in the
Cool dawn — struck among statues
Naked in hawthorn in the silver light.
James Joyce found it. Dublin bore him.
Could have sung with McCormack! Could he? He could.
Did he? He didn't. He walked by the winding Seine.

. . . .

Or the lad in the Rue de Notre Dame des Champs
At the carpenter's loft on the left-hand side going down —
The lad with the supple look like a sleepy panther —
And what became of him? Fame became of him.
Veteran out of the wars before he was twenty:
Famous at twenty-five: thirty a master —
Whittled a style for his time from a walnut stick
In a carpenter's loft in a street of that April city.

What Paris had done for Joyce and Hemingway, it did for MacLeish too. The young Boston lawyer of 1923 came back from Paris in 1928 one of the leading poets of his country and his time.

10

NEW FOUND LAND

Cricket Hill Farm

IT WASN'T FINANCIAL DISTRESS that brought the MacLeishes back to their native land. The boom continued into the late twenties, and with the death of Andrew MacLeish in January 1928, Archie inherited his share of Carson Pirie Scott stock. Feeling flush, he and Ada bought a flat in a modern Paris building near the Luxembourg where the Murphys also had an apartment. The plan was to live in Conway much of the year, then come to Paris for the fall and winter. No sooner had they returned to Massachusetts in May than they decided against this scheme. "We have given up our Paris apartment," Ada wrote Adele Lovett. "Beat that for fools." They were home now, and busy settling into their new house in Conway.

They'd found the place the previous fall after an extensive search. Initially they had purchased the old poor farm in Salisbury, in the northwestern corner of Connecticut, adjoining Lakeville and the Hotchkiss School. "We wanted two things," Archie recalled with laughter, "beautiful elm trees and a running brook. The poor farm in Salisbury had no elm trees and no brook, so we bought it." The price was $5,000, for a building that had begun as an inn in the eighteenth century and 230 acres of beautiful countryside. In correspondence Ada joked about the prospect of "wandering home to the poor farm to end our days." Actually, she was ready to wander away from it as soon as the papers were signed. Driving over to see their new property, she got more unhappy the closer they came. The place "smelled of the poor," she said. And she couldn't stand the cages they found in the attic for locking up the mentally troubled indigent.

So they continued to look around Ashfield, where they were staying in Aunt Mary's house, without much hope of success. Then Louise Bullitt — formerly Louise Bryant, once the wife of John Reed, the writer and communist, then married to William C. Bullitt and living in Ashfield — found what they were looking for on one of her horseback rides: the old Franklin Arms place in Conway. One Sunday the MacLeishes and the Bullitts and Adele Lovett, who was visiting from New York, came over and peeked through the windows. It was a big white house with pillars and a double-decker porch. Archie and Adele climbed up to the second story and peered in at the bedrooms with fireplaces, while Ada and the Bullitts were looking through the windows downstairs. They liked what they saw. "So, being very cautious people, we bought that house too," Archie said. They bid $5,000 for the house and more than three hundred surrounding acres, and were surprised when the owner, who ran a sporting goods store in Springfield, capitulated to that offer. For a short time the MacLeishes had "$10,000 worth of houses." Soon, though, they were able to sell the poor farm at a small profit to a Connecticut businessman who had been furious when the property was sold out from under him.

Ada's father contributed the money to buy the Conway house (Archie's inheritance had not yet come in), and posted a sign, "Do Not Trespass — Wm. H. Hitchcock," that did not fill Archie with joy. There was extensive remodeling to be done. The pillars and porch reminiscent of a southern plantation came down, and a brand-new brick wing was added, with a ground-floor music room for Ada's use and servants' quarters above it. "At that time," Archie pointed out, "you were expected to have servants." Kay Bundy lent them the funds for the addition, which was repaid with interest as soon as possible. A good Scotsman, Archie was ever uncomfortable about being in debt.

Almost immediately, Archie felt as if he belonged in Conway, where his maternal grandparents had spent their last happy years. Situated in the Connecticut Valley in western Massachusetts, Conway was a town of "old worn hills and rushing streams." Farming occupied most of the fewer than one thousand townspeople, who were friendly enough to help the neighbors but otherwise content to leave each other alone. The South River ran through the town, with the Bear River in the north end, and the Deerfield, which flowed into the Connecticut, to the east. Conway lay among the Hoosac Hills, with the Berkshires to the west. In good weather, there was a fine view of Mount Monadnock to the north. In every direction the scenery was human scale. The hills were not overpowering, and provided "the proper rhythm" for living.

Best of all, Archie found he could work there. With the help of a workman from Ashfield, he built a small stone house two football fields away from the main house. An oak, an apple tree, and a cedar stood guard over this rudely constructed edifice. In this work house he did most of his serious writing for most of the rest of his life. It was understood that he was not to be disturbed there during the morning hours. In the afternoons, there was plenty of outdoor physical work that needed doing.

The original saltbox house they bought had been constructed at the time of the Revolutionary War, and Franklin Arms and his descendants lived there up to the turn of the twentieth century, occasionally adding on as circumstances demanded. Then it had been taken over by an elderly couple from New York with southern roots, who affixed the exterior pillars and porches and also built a barn and a gazebo over the well. After they died, the Arms place remained largely unoccupied until the MacLeishes moved in.

Fresh off the boat from Paris, they drove by brooks and woodlands to the center of town, where a cluster of houses and the post office uneasily consorted with the grand Greek Revival library donated to the town by native son Marshall Field. Pine Hill Road carried uphill from the center, where it turned sharply west to run along the crest of the hill toward Bear River and Shelburne Falls one way and Ashfield the other. The Arms place, by now a substantial mansion, was situated on that crest. The MacLeishes decided to call it Cricket Hill Farm, as had the New York owners before them. (A decade later, upon discovering that there was another Cricket Hill in Conway, they changed the name to Uphill Farm.) Archie loved the house and the land, and owed it a debt that he could not adequately express in writing.

For a long time, he expected to write poetry about Uphill Farm. "There's a whole bird's nest of poems under the eaves if only I could reach them," he said. But the loved place warned him off. If he tried, he realized, "something would kick me downstairs." In his notebooks of the late 1970s, he conveyed something of his feeling for the place. "It was a New England house and therefore wooden and therefore built as you must build with wood in straight walls and square spaces — a kind of uprightness — simplicity — no decoration but the length and breadth, the fine proportions of the rooms themselves, each room alone and all together and the long-beamed attic over and the straight clean roof, but somehow no exclusion, no rigidity, but kindness. It was always kind, always welcoming to our return and generous and patient." The future often took the MacLeishes to other houses, other apartments, other towns. Ada once figured she'd set up thirty-two different households. But from 1928 on, Uphill Farm was always the place they came back to.

Immediately upon arriving from France, Archie and Ada plunged into the task of preparing their new home for occupancy. Workmen were still on the job, finishing the music-room wing, and a mighty clean-up job lay ahead. "I grunt around on weary feet I haven't been able to see" for weeks, the pregnant Ada wrote Adele, while Archie was cleaning coal bins and furniture "hip deep in dust." They took their meals with an old Yankee woman who lived nearby. "If we don't die of constipation we surely will from her tongue," Ada reported. On August 7, "the hottest day in the world," she gave birth to Peter MacLeish. The new heir lacked "the aristocracy of bone and modelling which has so far characterized our offspring," she wrote, but she liked the efficient look of his little square paws. By fall they were all settled at Cricket Hill Farm, except for Kenny, who was boarding at Avon Old Farms School in Hartford. His English teacher there, Alexander Campbell, recalled the eleven-year-old's first theme. In an attempt to emulate his father, Kenny produced a long poem in rhyme that began: "The night was dark as coal."

The Conway property had not only the brook the MacLeishes had been looking for but a pond as well. (Eventually Archie would create another pond, for protection against fire.) On Christmas Eve everyone but baby Peter went skating by moonlight on the pond's black ice. Soon thereafter they escaped for the winter. Pine Hill Road, it turned out, was often impassable during the months of snowfall. And they hadn't bothered to ask if the house was insulated, which it wasn't. The northwest wind came right through the wall of the baby's room and made his blond hair wave. So they moved to the sturdy comfort of Craigie Lea, where Mimi went to school and Ada continued to work at her music. The following year, and for a decade thereafter, the children spent the cool seasons with their Grandfather Hitchcock in Farmington, Connecticut. The house in Conway was not fully winterized until after World War II.

Hamlet to Díaz

MacLeish's critical reputation suffered a temporary setback with the publication of *The Hamlet of A. MacLeish* on October 16, 1928. This long poem is organized in fourteen blank-verse sections or scenes, accompanied by marginal comments or stage directions from Shakespeare's *Hamlet*. Whereas Shakespeare's Prince Hamlet is troubled by his doubts about what is true and what he should do — does the ghost of his father come from heaven or hell? is it right to take vengeance in his name? — MacLeish's modern Hamlet doubts both himself and the moral underpinnings of the universe. More than in anything else he had yet written,

Archie confronted himself in this poem. He excoriates himself for his yearnings after recognition, for example.

> Make verses! . . . ease myself at the soiled stool
> That's common to so swollen many! . . . shout
> For hearing in the world's thick dirty ear! . . .
> Expose my scabs! . . . crowd forward among those
> That beg for fame, that for so little praise
> As pays a dog off will go stiff and tell
> Their loss, lust, sorrow, anguish!

"Why must I speak of it?" he asked, yet speak he does of his most intimate sorrows in the exquisite self-disgust of the penultimate section.

> I'll tell the world.
> I'll make a book of it. I'll leave my rare
> Original, uncopied, dark heart pain
> To choke up volumes and among the rocks
> Cry I! I! I! forever. Look,
> My face here. I have suffered. I have lost
> A child, a brother, friends.
> . . . .
> Look, behold me
> Bearing my dead son's body to the grave.
> See how I weep. How many of them all
> Have lost a son as I have? Or see here:
> The Marne side. Raining. I am cold with fear.
> My bowels tremble. I go on. McHenry
> Hands me his overcoat and dies. We dig the
> Guns out sweating. I am very brave:
> Magnificent. I vomit in my mask.

No wonder then that the final section, with its refrain "It is time we should accept" is undermined by the closing quotation from Shakespeare's *Hamlet*:

> Thou wouldst not think
> How ill all's here about my heart!

The implication is strong that MacLeish must turn away from explorations of the self and toward wider concerns in the future.

It might be different if he could find something beyond himself to believe in. But when he hears the "voices calling the small new name of god,"

> It is always the same. It is always as though some
> Smell of leaves had made me not quite remember;

As though I had turned to look and there were no one.
It has always been secret like that with me.
Always something has not been said.

Nor could he discover solace in mythological quests for the sacred. In the "Bleheris" section, the Welsh storyteller takes on the lineaments of Gawain in his journey to the Chapel Perilous and the Grail Castle. Drawing on the story as it is recounted in Jessie L. Weston's *From Ritual to Romance* (a book Eliot made extensive use of in *The Waste Land*), MacLeish recreates the scene at the Chapel where a disembodied hand, black and hideous, snuffs out the one candle and Bleheris rides away choked by "the stench / Of death, of flesh rot." Death remains inscrutable, an evil that at least brings the petty ambitions of life to an end. The pessimism of the poem is cosmic, not merely personal.

By and large *The Hamlet of A. MacLeish* was received "with perfunctory reviews and tepid hostility," Archie commented. He was especially troubled by Conrad Aiken's comments in the *Bookman*. Acknowledging MacLeish's extraordinary technical skill — "he can say things with a brilliance, a suppleness, a power, which any living poet might covet" — Aiken nonetheless concluded that he remained "a slave of tradition," unable to throw off the influence "of T. S. Eliot, of Mr. Stevens, of various French poets of the last quarter century." The poem was therefore flawed by a falsity of tone. It was as if MacLeish were playing "a part which is not wholly natural to him." Here was the old charge of imitation, but expressed this time by a man and a poet whose opinion Archie respected. Certainly his book was influenced by Pound, by Perse, even by Aiken himself (though not by Eliot), he wrote in response. He had an ear "like a tweed suit in October" that picked up everything it heard. "But the experience l thought was mine, the emotion mine, the poetry mine."

In *Hound & Horn,* the journal Lincoln Kirstein was editing in Cambridge, R. P. Blackmur carried Aiken's charge of derivativeness several steps further. Not only had MacLeish appropriated the techniques of other poets, but he had attempted to adopt their feelings as well. As a consequence, the "great beauty of the verse has almost no reason for being: it holds nothing of the rare beauty of direct feeling." In conclusion, Blackmur pronounced the harshest of judgments: "As a poet Mr. MacLeish has no life of his own. He is compelled, in order to make poetry, to borrow the rhythms and materials as well as the modes of other poets. He does not add much and seldom transforms. The insight, the beauty, the wonder, of many of his lines cannot be taken at face value. . . . His poem is personal in the worst sense; it is essentially a ritual for himself alone."

Poleaxed by this review, Archie complained to Linscott that it seemed as if critics such as Blackmur were taking their opinions from Aiken. He wrote Kirstein, whose sister Mina was a neighbor in Ashfield, that he considered the review "an attack on my personal life, my literary honesty, and my integrity which has nothing of the usually expected critical detachment." And he sent the review to Hemingway, like himself a middle westerner brought up in an atmosphere of anti-Semitism, with an annotation characterizing *Hound & Horn* as "Kirstein's Jewish Harvard Monthly." Archie should ignore whatever "The Bitch and Bugle" had to say about him, Hemingway wrote back. The poem was "a damned wonderful poem — completely yours. It needs no Hamlet — no more than Ulysses needed that horse-shit Odyssey framework. But the framework doesn't hurt it and if it pleases you — fine — just as the Odyssey pleases Joyce." That letter meant a lot to Archie. "You must know how much I have always wanted to please you," he wrote Ernest. "But it was more than that here." He had hoped for everything from *Hamlet,* and Hemingway's assurance gave him "a rock to stand on in the seas of shit." Regarded from the distance of sixty years and more, Blackmur's diatribe seems almost purposefully wrongheaded. Dark as it is, Mac-Leish's *Hamlet* remains a powerful poem, and one in which the emotions are genuinely arrived at. "Hamlet is all right," Archie wrote Harry Crosby in March 1929, after most of the critics had had their say. "It will still be there when they get through."

The MacLeish-Hemingway friendship maintained its intensity despite the geographic distance between them. Ernest and Pauline had decided to move back to the United States and were spending part of the year in Key West. In November 1928 Hemingway came up to Massachusetts for a visit. He and Archie went to a Harvard football game, then drove over to Conway late in the evening. Daughter Mimi, upstairs, heard Ernest's voice and came dancing down from her room to see her old friend.

> *She ran to him,*
> *stopped, looked, screamed. It wasn't Ernest!*
> *wasn't Ernest! wasn't . . .*
> *She raced up the stair.*

Mimi was shocked by the scar Hemingway had suffered from the skylight accident in Paris. Ernest, however, was inclined to take her reaction as a judgment on himself, for destroying his marriage to Hadley. Archie and Ada reassured him, and after a while he went up to say good night to Mimi. As long as they were in the dark, everything was fine.

In December, after Ernest's father committed suicide, Archie warned him against becoming obsessed by "the way it happened. I know how your mind works round and round your pain like a dog in cover going over and over the same track." He must not let that happen now, Archie wrote his friend. "The consequences to you are too grave."

During this period Ernest repeatedly urged Archie to come down to Key West for the fishing on the Gulf Stream. At first MacLeish planned to make the trip the second week in January 1929, but those plans fell through. "I REGRET IT BEYOND TELEGRAPHABLE WORDS," Archie wired on January 5. "YOU HEREBY ACCEPT RENDEZVOUS WITH ME IN PARIS ZARAGOSSA MILANO AHWAZ OR THE SHETLAND ISLANDS FOR NEXT FALL LOVE ARCHIE." A month later he proposed a more immediate meeting. At Craigie Lea he had persuaded his mother that he ought to take a trip to Mexico to follow the path of the conquistadors, and she offered to lend him the money for the journey. At once he wired Hemingway asking him to join the trek, but Ernest could not get away. Still, "it was worth the remote chance and I knew you would want to if you could," Archie wrote.

The trip to Mexico was undertaken to provide background for the long poem on the Spanish conquest MacLeish had been contemplating since the summer of 1927. He was fascinated by "the obvious metaphor" of the dangerous journey into the unknown West and by the boldness Cortés displayed when he "burned his ships, cut himself off from Europe . . . made it impossible for anyone to go anywhere else but West with him." His poem, finally published in 1932 as *Conquistador,* covered the period from the beginning of Cortés's journey in the winter of 1519 to the *noche triste,* the destruction of Tenochtitlán in August 1521. Most strikingly, the speaker of the poem is Bernál Díaz del Castillo, himself an officer with Cortés, who was moved to write his history of the conquest in response to the official account prepared by Francisco López de Gómara. Gómara's version, as Díaz makes clear in his (and MacLeish's) introductory section, is flawed by its tendency to glorify the leading figures among the Spaniards, ignoring the contributions and the feelings of the ordinary soldier. In *Conquistador,* Díaz relates the story as from the viewpoint of such a man. Díaz obviously had little in common with Prince Hamlet. In choosing such a spokesman for his long poem, MacLeish was moving toward a more democratic poetry. After visiting Massachusetts in September 1928, Lewis Galantière observed that MacLeish seemed worried about being unable to find his public. "He feels himself to be writing in a vacuum." *Conquistador,* Archie hoped, would produce the wider audience he was seeking.

First, though, he felt it imperative to acquaint himself with the territory. In February 1929 he went down to Mexico to retrace the steps of the Spaniards. From Mexico City he took the train to Vera Cruz and hired a car to Jalapa, and after three days there found a young Mexican named Carlos Lascurain whom he hired as a guide and translator. Lascurain, who was engaged to an American girl, knew some English and represented himself as also knowing the Indian tongue. This he did not, so that as a guide he was not much help. But by following the maps in the back of Díaz's history, the two of them were able to follow the trail. Alternating travel by car, by mule, and by donkey, they crossed over the sierra to Tlaxcala and then back to Mexico City. It was fine country, MacLeish wrote Hemingway in Hemingway-style prose: "Around Jalapa it is like the Riviera only with rain and the air soft all the time and on the Mesa it is like New Mexico but absolutely clean and hard and in the mountains of Tlaxcala it is cedar forests and upland grazing, and between the volcanos it is all pine and you come out on the top and look a thousand miles." He stopped to see the American ambassador, Dwight Morrow, before leaving Mexico and discovered that a revolution had broken out in the *monte* between Vera Cruz and Mexico City. After chastising MacLeish for putting himself at risk during his journey, Morrow took him home to lunch. There he met Morrow's daughter Anne and her fiancé, Charles Lindbergh.

A more important encounter during MacLeish's stopover in Mexico City was with the frescoes of Diego Rivera. Rivera's depiction of the daily struggles of simple people, in the twentieth and not the sixteenth century, caught "a refracted glimpse" of a "new image of man," MacLeish wrote in his notebooks.

> It is true that Diego is a Communist. It is true also that no whole man can live on that dog biscuit. . . . But there is something else also. One says: What new dignity of man is this? Merely the noble savage repainted as the noble peasant or the noble pulque-drinker or the noble welder? Or something more? And one answers: Something more — and wonders how this guessed-at figure of mankind can move our generation of morbidly swollen egos with the reddened eyes and swollen faces. How can such men and women as we are find the image of our lives in the odor of labor and sun and a love simple and violent as the habit of the heart?

Despite their manifest propagandistic purpose, the frescoes moved him deeply. He began to think of what he could say, in his poetry, of the wonder and sorrow of his own time.

Parents and Children

Back in Conway by spring, the MacLeishes soon added to the animal population of Cricket Hill Farm. A huge white police dog called Finn McCool became almost a member of the household. Baby Peter took his first steps hanging on to the lips of Finn, who cried but allowed the indignity. And the poor dog suffered a worse fate when a neighboring housewife, unappreciative of Finn's amorous visits to her kennel, poured a kettle of boiling water over him. He survived the trauma but bore the scars the rest of his days. For livestock and poultry they acquired a Jersey cow, sheep and goats, chickens and turkeys. Their cow produced "a hundred dollar heifer calf" that, Archie reported in April 1929, "died on me this afternoon. *On* me. The poor wet thing limp in the bloody straw with the cunt ooze over it and the awful dignity of death lolling its foetal head into grotesque majesty." Everyone in the family had chores — Ken and Mimi were put in charge of cleaning the chicken house, for example — but Archie and helper Ray Bush did most of the work around the place. In June they spent two weeks laying a dam, with the aid of a pair of white horses. Using a great pile of rocks that a previous inhabitant had rolled downhill, they set these across the brook and then grouted in cement. At first it seemed "a magnificent engineering work," but before long the brook worked its way through the dam as though it weren't there.

In the process of building the dam, Archie dropped rocks on both his hands and could barely manage to push the pen as he wrote Hemingway on June 24 how much he admired the opening segments of *A Farewell to Arms,* then running as a serial in *Scribner's* magazine. "Your book starts slow and deep and real the way Tolstoy starts," he wrote him. "It is like the beginning of a year not the beginning of a book." By September he had still greater praise for Hemingway's novel. "You become in one book the great novelist of our time. . . . I think now you can forgive me my stupidity in Saragossa [when he had told Ernest he might profit by reading Joyce], for it was this achievement that I then wished for you."

With the economy going sour, Archie decided on raising turkeys as a source of income. He read up on the field, found there were no predatory foxes or turkey diseases thereabouts, and soon had dozens of big turkeys ready for sale. He and Ada sent postcards to their New York friends advertising "Cricket Hill turkeys, raised on crickets and milk," and transported them to the city in the back of an old Cadillac hearse. They made $300 or $400 out of these trips, but the business died out when "the foxes heard about the turkeys, and came back — they'd left for lack of game — and killed them." Later, disease took the cows and the dogs got the sheep: nature was not always the farmer's friend.

Despite such difficulties, the MacLeish family looks almost idyllically happy — almost — in the home movies that Alec Campbell, Ken's teacher and an admirer of Ishbel, took in 1929 and 1930. In October 1930 at Cricket Hill Farm, the film catches Archie and Ada working at opposite ends of a crosscut saw to bring down a tree. Then lusty work-man Archie takes a few vigorous swipes with an ax and down it comes. Finn McCool and curly-haired Peter, a beautiful child, oversee the lum-berjacks. In April 1929 at Craigie Lea, a blindfolded Ada reaches out to tag someone, while Archie dances around her just out of reach. Baby Peter appears again, along with a rather austere Ken, age twelve, holding a shotgun, and sad-eyed Mimi, six. Both Ken's shotgun and Mimi's expression had something to say about the inner workings of the family.

Ada's music room at Conway turned out to have wonderful acoustics, and for a time she continued to work there as diligently as she had in Paris. The American composers she had known in Paris — Aaron Cop-land, Virgil Thomson, Roger Sessions — all came back to the United States, and she presented their songs in concerts in Boston and New York. On November 3, 1930, for example, her concert was "brilliantly successful." Ada appeared also at the second Yaddo Music Festival in Saratoga Springs, and in the early-to-mid-1930s maintained an affiliation at Smith College in nearby Northampton. At Smith she taught students voice, and participated in concerts accompanied by composer-pianist John Duke. Ada's was not "a big voice," Duke found, but she was "a very finished artist and so musically intelligent that it was a pleasure to work with her."

Music provided her with a measure of independence that may have found expression in other ways as well. According to Kay Bundy, Ada "behaved outrageously" at the party Kay gave for the MacLeishes upon their return from France. Rumors circulated in Boston about her "run-ning around." Then the rumors stopped, and along with them Ada's musical career. "I couldn't leave the family, you know," she said years later. "That was all there was to that." Really it was her husband she bound herself to for the long decades ahead. With gaiety and charm she gladdened his sometimes dour days. With social deftness and competence she smoothed out all domestic arrangements. She took whatever burdens she could off his back, and protected him from troubles and invasions of privacy as best she could. Outside the house in Conway, she hewed a splendid flower garden out of the thin New England soil. Inside, her fingers flew as she knitted and chatted after dinner. If there was a hole in the conversation, she darned it with her wit. She shaped a life for herself and Archie that was very nearly perfect. It was a full-time job.

Since Ada's principal occupation was taking care of Archie, the children necessarily suffered. This was particularly true of Mimi, who was caught in the middle between two bright brothers. Even Peter began to feel that he was adopted, since he saw so little of his parents. For Mimi it was much worse. She was different from her brothers, a creature more of intuition than intelligence. And she was easily frightened, as when her older brother, Ken, persuaded her that the dust bunnies under her bed would bite her. The summers she remembers with fondness, particularly the afternoon outings when her father would play with her and young Peter. They went on exploratory walks, seeking the Pygmy Negritoes he had invented. He taught them to swim in the chilling waters of Upper Pond. In the evenings he read to them from the *Tales of the West Highlands,* which Mimi loved, and the Bible, which terrified her in its bloody passages.

During the long winter months Mimi was confronted with a very real creature who more than justified her fears. She and Peter lived in Farmington in her grandfather's house, under the supervision of a governess called Cie. "If you're not a good boy, your mother won't come to see you," Cie would tell Peter to gain obedience. But she and Peter got along well, for she liked little boys. Actually, he recalls, "she was a boy herself. She had an arm on her, and she could rifle a ball so it would go right through your hand." It was Mimi's misfortune that Cie detested little girls. In school, Mimi was the best player in dodgeball, so adept was she at dodging missiles thrown by Cie. Once this governess winged a set of shears at Mimi so viciously that they were embedded in the wall behind her. Often the two of them became locked in an unequal test of wills, as Mimi demonstrated her "black Hillard" streak of defiance. If Mimi slurped her soup, Cie pushed her face into it as a lesson. When she refused to finish her vegetables at lunch, Cie forced her to sit at table well into the afternoon. She did "terrible harm to Mimi," Ishbel observed.

Somehow neither Ada nor Archie realized what their daughter was going through under Cie's cruel regime. The girl blamed her mother for not seeing, and rebelled by refusing to do just those things Ada most wanted her to do: be ladylike and well-mannered, dress nicely and smile politely for company. Ken, meanwhile, responded to his father's lack of attention by taking risks and demonstrating his physical courage. Eventually he was to fly navy blimps in World War II and make some of the deepest underwater dives of his time, but in boyhood he hunted in and out of season with his shotgun — a practice he knew his father disapproved of. Peter, as the youngest child, managed to ingratiate himself with his parents. A sunny, attractive boy, he conformed to the very expectations his siblings had reacted against — and disliked himself for doing so.

Fortune Beckons

If Archie had been able to work at home and spend more time with his children, relations within the family might have turned out differently. But with the crash of October 1929, the dividends on the Carson Pirie Scott stock he had inherited started slowing down, and it became clear that he would have to find employment to support his family. He couldn't make any money farming. He didn't want to go back to the law. Luckily, opportunity arrived with a phone call from Henry Luce in New York. He was starting a business magazine called *Fortune* and was looking for writers. As a poet, MacLeish seemed an unlikely choice for such an assignment. According to Luce, however, the pool of possible staffers was composed of men who could write poetry and men who could read balance sheets. Those who could read balance sheets couldn't write. It was "easier to turn poets into business journalists than to turn bookkeepers into writers." Would Archie be interested in a job, Luce wanted to know. He would indeed, but he was also determined to finish *Conquistador,* the long poem that had been percolating in his mind. He told Luce about that, and the editor made him a proposition he couldn't refuse.

"All right," Luce said. "You can work for us as long as you need to pay your bills, and spend the rest of your time on poetry. How would that be?"

It was more than generous. In October 1929, the month of the crash, Archie went to work for a new magazine whose first issue had not yet appeared. He started on a half-time basis, at a salary of $5,000. Luce did not lose money on the arrangement. MacLeish proved to be the most productive writer on what may have been the best journalistic staff ever assembled. Sometimes half-time, sometimes full-time, during the next nine years he wrote more words for *Fortune* than anyone else.

Actually, this was not MacLeish's first job with Luce. When *Time* got under way in 1923, he had served briefly as education editor for the newsmagazine while continuing his law practice in Boston. But Archie was a stringer then, made few contributions, and was paid a paltry ten dollars a week. The *Time* connection figured not at all in his decision to leave for Paris, where, on their honeymoon, Harry and Lila Luce called on Archie and Ada. They had just returned from a trip into the *campagne* east of Paris, where, Luce said, in one hotel they could secure only an extremely small room with one narrow bed. "Lila had to sleep on the floor," Luce told the MacLeishes, apparently in earnest. It was Ada's favorite Harry Luce story.

Luce's original attitude toward MacLeish was something like awe. He was precisely four years behind Archie in school, first at Hotchkiss and then at Yale, where both climaxed their careers with election to Skull and Bones. Thus the two never met, and word of Archie's athletic and literary achievements came down to Harry unsullied by any personal contact. He was, for the younger man, "a god without clay feet." During the years at *Fortune,* and even thereafter, Archie was always something more to Luce than an unusually talented employee. For his part, MacLeish came to regard his boss as a genius of an editor-publisher, a judgment shared by many, and also as a subconscious democrat, a position shared by almost no one else at all. The hero worship Luce began with toward MacLeish somehow reversed itself over the years. It was important for Archie, nine years in Luce's employ, to feel that he had worked so long in the service of someone great.

The times could hardly have been less auspicious for the launching of a magazine designed to celebrate American business. That was what Luce had in mind, at least up to October 1929. A devout believer in the Protestant ethic, Harry Luce considered worldly success a sign of election and successful businessmen as the proper leaders of the country, in moral and intellectual as well as financial matters. At first the working title for his new magazine was *Power.* That was changed to *Fortune,* but the prospectus remained the same. "American business has importance — even majesty — so the magazine in which we are to interpret it will look and feel important — even majestic." Photographs would be used to complement text; the paper, the typography, everything about the magazine was to be first-class. *Fortune,* it was decided, would appear monthly, at the expensive price of one dollar a copy or ten dollars a year.

When the crash came resounding around everyone's ears, putting out a magazine conceived to glorify American business made very little sense. Yet the collapse and the extended depression that followed raised questions that people were intensely interested in. Instead of becoming an advocacy journal for American business, *Fortune* tried to figure out what had gone wrong and why. Intead of concerning itself with business for its own sake, *Fortune* in the depression became a general magazine devoted to the economic crisis in the country. Often it was not pro-business at all.

On *Fortune,* Archie was a star. An Alfred Eisenstaedt photo from those days shows him with his feet jauntily crossed atop his desk, wearing an unrumpled ice cream suit and gazing, slightly bemused, off to the right of the camera. The photograph depicts someone in command of his trade, as indeed MacLeish was. Let others sweat out their stories during all-nighters in the fifty-second floor offices in the Chrysler Building. His copy was produced in painstaking longhand, or two-fingered typing, accurately and on time. He kept no nighttime working hours. "Just throw the switch and let her run" is how he described his capacity to transform raw material into highly readable prose. He wrote nearly one hundred stories for *Fortune,* some of them as long as fifteen thousand words. At the same time, he was amazingly productive in his continuing career as a serious writer. During the 1929–1938 period of his employment, he published four volumes of poetry, three plays, a ballet scenario, a word-and-picture book on depression America, and more than thirty essays for other periodicals.

Nor were his stories for *Fortune* mere pedestrian prose. Archie demonstrated his flair for making hard facts memorable in his first piece for the magazine, in March 1930. The subject was apple pie. "Each weighs a rough three pounds. A knife will cut it. Three divisions will reduce it to six appropriate triangles. Each triangle will emit a faint warm smell of cinnamon and nutmeg. Subdivided with a four-pronged fork and tasted, the mouth remembers apples. Cheese consorts with it. Coffee leaves it sweet." Certain of his leads became legendary among Luce reporters. "History, stammering and automatic goddess, has a way of repeating herself like a worn phonograph record," he started a story on the farm strike in January 1934. And a December 1935 piece began: "There will be two candidates for the presidency in the fall of 1936 and both of them will be named Franklin Delano Roosevelt." (You were either for or against him, never mind his opponent). The combination of voluminous productivity and brilliant copy enabled MacLeish to command certain perquisites. For example, he was excused from "doing the corps," the stories on business corporations that Luce insisted upon and most of the *Fortune* staffers dreaded. Instead he was assigned to stories of national and international importance.

According to Eric Hodgins, who took over as editor of *Fortune* in 1935, he was directing an "insane, unreliable, alcoholic, and all in all, I think the most brilliant magazine staff ever to exist in America." MacLeish fit only the last of those adjectives, but a number of his colleagues qualified for all four. The other poet on board, for example, was the erratic and disheveled James Agee, whose first book of poems, the winner of the Yale Series of Younger Poets award, carried an introduction by Archie. For years Agee was given assignments that enabled him to

exercise his gift for "rich and beautiful prose." Then he was sent into
the poverty-stricken regions of the South, where, with the aid of the
photographer Walker Evans, he produced his masterly *Let Us Now
Praise Famous Men*.

Dwight Macdonald, who helped Agee land his job with *Fortune*,
started work on the magazine eight months before its first appearance
in February 1930 when Luce plucked him off the staff of *Time* to help
prepare the dummies. Along with MacLeish he was the most ardent
liberal among *Fortune* writers. Macdonald stayed with *Fortune* until
1936, when he was assigned to do a series of articles on the U.S. Steel
Corporation. During the fact-gathering and interview process, he fairly
terrified Big Steel's executives with his red beard and outspoken advocacy
of socialism. His articles distressed them still more, for he argued that
the biggest steel company in the world shortchanged its workers (whose
wages were kept low by shutting out the union), its customers (for
monopolistic practices kept prices artificially high), and its stockholders
(since management was so inefficient). Macdonald resigned in protest
when his last installment, headed with a quotation from Lenin, was
drastically altered by the magazine's editors.

Among those editors, the most significant figure was Ralph M.
("Mac") Ingersoll, who was later to found the short-lived liberal daily
PM, with financing from Marshall Field III, and to acquire a number of daily newspapers along the East Coast. The first *Fortune* editor,
Parker Lloyd-Smith, took his life in the summer of 1931 by jumping off
the roof of his apartment building. The last during MacLeish's tenure
was the eccentric Russell ("Mitch") Davenport, who took seriously the
counsel of astrologers and liked to fly his airplane to a certain altitude
where, he said, he could begin to hear a kind of symphony inside his
head. On the staff itself was the witty Wilder Hobson, Macdonald's
Yale roommate, a cousin of Thornton Wilder, and a devotee of Proust
and Dixieland jazz, along with Ed Kennedy, Charlie Wertenbaker, and
others who made up a "mixed bag of talents and oddballs, freaks and
geniuses." In those days of open inequality of opportunity according
to sex, Luce hired women to function as researchers, assembling and
gathering the information that the male writers and editors turned
into finished copy. Just as *Fortune*'s male staff came from Ivy League
institutions, and Yale in particular, almost all the female researchers
were graduates of the Seven Sisters, and especially Vassar. Over a period of time, an attempt was made to find a good working fit between
researcher and writer. MacLeish was fortunate in establishing such a
relationship with his primary researcher, Rhoda Booth, and later with
Eunice Clark, sister of the Pulitzer Prize–winning writer Eleanor Clark.

Women also staffed the proof room, where it was rarely necessary to change anything MacLeish submitted. On one occasion, however, the newly hired Mary Grace had to tell him, in some terror, that he could not use *protagonist* as the opposite of *antagonist*. Archie took the correction with only a hint of annoyance. He'd never use the word again, he said.

11

CITY OF GLASS

Cries upon the Air

FOR NICK CARRAWAY in *The Great Gatsby,* riding across the Queensboro Bridge in Jay Gatsby's circus wagon of a car, the view of New York City ahead offered a "promise of all the mystery and the beauty in the world." That was the summer of 1922, and seven years later, when MacLeish moved into the city, that sense of unspoken possibilities still clung to Manhattan. The crash seemed to breed a heightened recklessness. Stockbrokers defenestrated, and the death throes of the boom had begun. Yet people were drinking more than ever, in open defiance of Prohibition. And that brand-new institution the cocktail party invited irregular romantic attachments. New York remained a city of wondrous possibilities, a place where, as Nick puts it, "anything can happen . . . anything at all." On December 10, 1929, anything did.

From across the ocean Archie had kept in touch with Harry and Caresse Crosby. In March 1929 the Crosbys decided to print a special edition of MacLeish's *Einstein* for their Black Sun Press, and paid him the munificent sum of $200 for the privilege. The following month Archie sent Harry Crosby, whose *Transit of Venus* had just appeared, some encouraging words about his poems. "I think you have learned the smell of your own flesh. I think you should be well satisfied with where you are going." The devotedly reckless Crosby was headed straight for oblivion. He was determined to live his life on the edge. In his relentless pursuit of sexual love, he often spoke with bravado about ending his existence, and that of his lover, at the pinnacle of feeling. As early as 1921 he had written Caresse, then married to another man, that if she couldn't get a divorce, he would kill her and then himself so they could die in each other's arms. They averted that fate, but Harry held the thought. In his diary he repeatedly proposed possible methods of suicide, including leaping into Mount Vesuvius. This fixation became obsessive during the Crosbys' trip to the States in November and December 1929. "One is not in love unless one desires to die with one's beloved," his diary declared. The only happiness "is to love and be loved."

Crosby met Josephine Rotch Bigelow in Venice in the summer of 1928, when she was in Europe to buy her trousseau. They began a tempestuous love affair that continued after her marriage to an eminent Back Bay Bostonian, much like the one Caresse had left for Harry six years earlier. Harry called Josephine his "Fire Princess," and although he had other mistresses — often several at a time — she was the most serious and demanding of his lovers. And she was ready to do anything he proposed. On the 1929 trip to the States, he attended the Harvard-Yale game on November 23 (the ostensible reason for the journey), and then he and Josephine left for Detroit, together. They stayed at the Book-Cadillac Hotel, where they took opium pills "and all night we catapult through space J and I in each other's arms vision security happiness."

When he went back to New York to join his wife, his Fire Princess followed. On Sunday December 8, Harry asked Caresse to jump from the hotel window with him. She was not ready to do that. He seemed to think better of it too. The morning of Tuesday December 10, he bought steamship tickets for their return journey to France. Shortly after lunch, he and Josephine met at the studio of his artist friend Stanley Mortimer in the Hotel des Artistes. Mortimer let them in and discreetly left. At about 5 P.M., when he was due at tea with his uncle J. P. Morgan, Harry shot Josephine with a .25-caliber automatic. Perhaps two hours later, he shot and killed himself. It was nearly 10 P.M. when Mortimer found them, left hands clasped together and fully clothed save for bare feet. The soles of his feet were tattooed, a cross on the left and a sun symbol on the right. Harry's gold "sun-ring," which he had sworn to Caresse never to remove, was on the floor, stomped flat. In his pockets were the steamship tickets and a one-word telegram from another woman. "YES," it read. Harry died at thirty-one, Josephine twenty-two. The tabloids wrote about it for days.

Caresse could not bring herself to view the scene. She called Archie MacLeish instead and asked him to take charge. "That's quite a friend you've got there," the medical examiner told him. Archie accompanied the corpse to the morgue at Bellevue Hospital, again at the request of Caresse. She and Harry had promised to keep a vigil for each other, but she could not bring herself to do so. Archie assumed the task. "I sat for a long time in the vault with the body of poor Harry Crosby," he later wrote his mother. "He lay on a narrow couch under a dark red cloth. He had made a great noise with his death. But already I could hardly see his face." That troubled Archie, made him think of himself as insensitive, "an evil person."

To Caresse Crosby and to Harry's mother, however, he could hardly have been kinder. He dealt with the police and the doctor. He kept the vigil. He wrote Mrs. Crosby that her son "was always, however his desires may have realized themselves, on the side of the angels and against the authority and numbness and complacency of life." He had been reckless and free of soul, and these were dangerous qualities. "But without those fires lighted sometimes in the world it would be a dark and hopeless place. The pity is that you and Caresse must be so dreadfully, so deeply hurt." By cable he sent Caresse the most thoughtful of untruths: "ABSOLUTELY CERTAIN POLICE REMOVED RING BELIEVE ME ARCHIE."

One of MacLeish's first projects on *Fortune* was to enlist his literary friends — Hemingway, Dos Passos, Benét, Bishop — as contributors to the magazine. Generally these assignments did not work out well. The piece Hemingway mailed him on bullfighting on December 31, 1929, for instance, did not run until the summer of 1932, and in considerably altered form. Ernest and Pauline themselves appeared in New York toward the end of January 1930. "Please don't tell *anybody* that we're coming," Hemingway wrote Archie. "Want to see you and Ada and a couple of fights maybe and not be a writer in N.Y." When their boat arrived in New York, Ada was hospitalized after a hysterectomy that was "touch and go" for a while. Ernest came directly to the hospital, rushed over to her bed, and started to lift her up. "I thought I was breaking in two," she reported. Archie was not pleased about that, and declined to join Ernest in the condemnation of former friend Don Stewart. Nor did Hemingway escape the gossip of New York's literary circles. "Dotty [Dorothy Parker] says everything you heard in New York was shit and I guess I told you most of it," Archie wrote Ernest apologetically afterwards. For the second but not the last time, the friendship between the two writers suffered a strain when they actually spent time together.

In the spring of 1930, Archie finally traveled to Key West for the fishing expedition Hemingway had been urging on him, and this trip at least was a great success. Archie got along well with Ernest and with the two other companions he'd invited, artist Henry ("Mike") Strater and Key West sportsman Charles Thompson. Though he was no fisherman, Archie wrote, he couldn't "get that day on the Gulf Stream out of my eyes." In reply, Hemingway proposed a reunion of the four men the following year, this time for a three-month lion-hunting safari in

Africa, financed by Pauline's uncle Gus Pfeiffer. "You won't have to spend a sou after we leave N.Y.," he promised MacLeish. For the moment, Archie embraced this plan with enthusiasm.

On June 4, 1930, Houghton Mifflin published MacLeish's *New Found Land,* a slim collection of fourteen poems loosely organized around the theme of the contrast between the Old World and the New. The title was drawn from John Donne's line in an elegy to his mistress, "O my America, my new-found-land." The longest of the poems was "American Letter," which expressed MacLeish's conviction that his life must unfold in his native land.

> *This, this is our land, this is our people,*
> *This that is neither a land nor a race. We must reap*
> *The wind here, in the grass for our soul's harvest:*
> *Here we must eat our salt or our bones starve.*

With one notable exception, the reviews were excellent. Percy Hutchison in the *New York Times* blanched at the five-dollar price tag for the book (printed for Houghton Mifflin by Black Sun Press), but added that the contents were worth even that "immodest" sum. And if there were but fourteen poems, Eda Lou Walton observed in the *Nation,* every line in every one of them was "perfect." MacLeish had "passed through a period of fruitful experimentation into the full expression of his unusual talent," Horace Gregory commented in the *New York Evening Post.* Best of all was Babette Deutsch's opening paragraph in the *New York Herald Tribune:* "Here is a man who is moved by things which have moved poets and less articulate men for thousands of years: by the thought of the passing of empire and the swifter passing of a single life, by the changing seasons, more particularly the troubling betwixt-and-betweens, autumn and spring, by the problem of personal identity, by the sense of timelessness in a moment of love, by anonymous pains and passions still vibrant. Somehow he manages to stir our blood as his has been stirred. Somehow he communicates the tears in these things." Deutsch was referring to a few of the volume's better-known poems, among them "You, Andrew Marvell," "Immortal Autumn," and " 'Not Marble Nor the Gilded Monuments.' " In lyric poems such as these, Charles Norman declared, emotion and thought were beautifully joined.

"Immortal Autumn" itself was "the most beautiful single poem of [MacLeish's] generation," George Dangerfield asserted in the *Bookman,* and it has remained one of the dozen or so most often reprinted in anthologies. "I praise the fall: it is the human season," the poet announces, and he suggests why this is so — because in solitude we can communicate across the years.

But now in autumn with the black and outcast crows
Share we the spacious world: the whispering year is gone:
There is more room to live now: the once secret dawn
Comes late by daylight and the dark unguarded goes.

Between the mutinous brave burning of the leaves
And winter's covering of our hearts with his deep snow
We are alone: there are no evening birds: we know
The naked moon: the tame stars circle at our eaves.

It is the human season. On this sterile air
Do words outcry breath: the sound goes on and on.
I hear a dead man's cry from autumn long since gone.

I cry to you beyond upon this bitter air.

"Immortal Autumn," presented here in part, did not so appear in *New Found Land*. In that book MacLeish dispensed with punctuation almost entirely, a technique that challenged his readers' comprehension. The purpose, Morton Dauwen Zabel suggested in *Poetry*, was the same that Hemingway was aiming for in prose: to urge "the immediacy of his sensations by presenting them on a level of detached observation, connected by coordinating conjunctions and the simplest prepositions, but no longer by conventional periods and commas." The technique often fell flat, Zabel asserted, as in "the open banality" of "You, Andrew Marvell" "or the limp humility" of "American Letter." Zabel, with Edmund Wilson and a few others, never hesitated to denigrate Mac-Leish's poetry. (For whatever it's worth, these nay-sayers were all friends who shared similar political and literary convictions.) Yet about the lack of punctuation, if not about the poems themselves, Zabel was right. In revising for collected editions of his poems, MacLeish restored the commas and periods.

"Epistle to Be Left in the Earth," like "Immortal Autumn," ends with a cry across the generations. The epistle of this dark, prophetic, and powerful poem is a document written to convey to people of future generations what a man of this time has learned and what is still unknown. Like many MacLeish poems, it wonderfully repays reading aloud.

. . . It is colder now,
            there are many stars,
                        we are drifting
North by the Great Bear,
            the leaves are falling,

The water is stone in the scooped rocks,
*　　　　　　　　　　　　to southward*
Red sun grey air:
*　　　　the crows are*
Slow on their crooked wings,
*　　　　　　　　　　the jays have left us:*
Long since we passed the flares of Orion.
Each man believes in his heart he will die.
Many have written last thoughts and last letters.
None know if our deaths are now or forever:
None know if this wandering earth will be found.

We lie down and the snow covers our garments.
I pray you,
*　　　　　you (if any open this writing)*
Make in your mouths the words that were our names.
I will tell you all we have learned,
*　　　　　　　　　　　I will tell you everything:*
The earth is round,
*　　　　　　　there are springs under the orchards,*
The loam cuts with a blunt knife,
*　　　　　　　　　　beware of*
Elms in thunder,
*　　　　　　　the lights in the sky are stars —*
We think they do not see,
*　　　　　　　　　we think also*
The trees do not know nor the leaves of the grasses hear us:
The birds too are ignorant.
*　　　　　　　　Do not listen.*
Do not stand at dark in the open windows.
We before you have heard this:
*　　　　　　　　　they are voices:*
They are not words at all but the wind rising.
Also none among us has seen God.
(. . . We have thought often
The flaws of sun in the late and driving weather
Pointed to one tree but it was not so.)
As for the nights I warn you the nights are dangerous:
The wind changes at night and the dreams come.

It is very cold,
*　　　　　there are strange stars near Arcturus,*
Voices are crying an unknown name in the sky

A Leaf on Her Hair

In ". . . & Forty-Second Street," another poem in *New Found Land,* Archie sounded a far different note of celebration for Manhattan, an island that boldly declared itself by its skyscrapers.

> Be proud City of Glass of your
> Brass roofs & the bright peaks of your
> Houses!
>   Town that stood to your knees in the
> Sea water be proud, be proud,
> Of your high gleam on the sea!

The city had its excitement, but for family living it also had its drawbacks. Early in 1930 Archie and Ada and son Peter moved into a small rented house at 10 Henderson Place, off East Eighty-sixth Street. This arrangement did not last long before the dirt and the noise and the cost of living drove mother and child back to Farmington. Ada came to New York at times, and on occasion Archie traveled to Farmington for the weekend, but he was often away on trips for *Fortune.* "We both suffered from the separation," Archie recalled. In "Unfinished History," a poem published by the *New Yorker* on January 21, 1933, he envisioned the years ahead without assurance. "We have loved each other in this time twenty years," the poem begins, yet it ends with an unhappy thought:

> I wrote this poem that day when I thought
> Since we have loved we two so long together
> Shall we have done together — all love gone?
>
> Or how then will it change with us when the breath
> Is no more able for such joy and the blood is
> Thin in the throat and the time not come for death?

Later that same year, Archie had an opportunity to countermand this more or less public declaration of disaffinity. On September 20, 1933, the *New York Times* ran a story, datelined Vienna, announcing the marriage of Archibald MacLeish to Elizabeth Lofting, the only daughter of Hugh Lofting, who was the creator of Dr. Dolittle. The *Times* duly reported the accomplishments of the groom, and in its last paragraph noted that his first wife was "Ada Hitchcock, concert singer." MacLeish found out about the story when he stopped in to see Bill Bullitt in his New York office. "Anyone who would divorce Ada is a son-of-a-bitch," Bullitt roared. "Get the hell out of here." The *Times* was wrong, of course. The man who wed Miss Lofting was Archibald Fleming MacLiesh, as Archie informed the newspaper in a letter to the editor.

Regret to inform you I did not marry Miss Lofting in Vienna
yesterday, having passed the day quite comfortably in New York
and being, moreover, eminently satisfied with Miss Hitchcock,
who, I hope, reciprocates. Miss Lofting was presumably married
by a gifted young man who spells my name Archibald MacLiesh,
instead of MacLeish, and who had the misfortune to break his
or my back in Austria last Spring. Mr. MacLiesh also writes
verse which, fortunately for me, promises to be good. He has
also, fortunately for me, a middle name, which he will learn to
use. It would be a kindness if you would restore me to my wife,
who is an excellent soprano and mother.

The other MacLiesh, taking the point, published his subsequent work
under the name Archibald Fleming.

Even in Ada's absence, Archie did not lack for companionship in New
York. He did not socialize much with his colleagues on *Fortune,* but
soon established himself among writers, editors, and publishers in the
literary community. Malcolm Cowley recalled meeting Archie, for example, at a restaurant at Seventh Avenue and Twenty-third Street, where
New Republic staffers and others gathered on Wednesday evenings. He
looked youthful for his nearly forty years, Cowley thought, "tall and
slim, with a rawboned, handsome face as Scottish as his full name —
except for the forehead, which would have been high for any nation."
MacLeish also saw a good deal of Steve Benét, whose *John Brown's
Body* (1928) won the Pulitzer Prize in 1929 and sold many thousand
copies. He sought out friends from college days, including Ranald Macdonald and Doug Moore. The three of them, along with other classmates
such as Len Outhwaite, John Crosby Brown, Doc Merz, George Stewart,
Nig Donaldson, and, when he was in town from Washington, Dean
Acheson gathered several times a year for dinner meetings of what they
informally called the Chaos Club, the name drawn from the condition
of the nation's economy.

In 1931 Archie moved to less spacious quarters at 182 Sullivan Street
in Greenwich Village, where he functioned for the most part as a bachelor. In September, for instance, he asked Lincoln Kirstein, editor of
Hound & Horn, and his sister Mina Kirstein Curtiss to join him for
dinner at his digs. Mina and her husband, Harry Curtiss, had a home
in South Ashfield, adjoining Conway, and were among the first residents
the MacLeishes met after returning to Massachusetts. Harry Curtiss died
in 1928 after but one year of marriage, and though Mina kept the South
Ashfield home, she and her brother (later the nation's leading promoter
and producer of ballet) were often in residence at Sneden's Landing, on
the Hudson River. Mina was a free spirit who liked to tell tales. "You

know, I've had a rich sex life," she declared to new acquaintance Harry Levin. Then she proceeded to name numerous famous musicians and artists who had, she said, been her lovers.

The other woman he saw most often during the *Fortune* years was the amazingly beautiful Adele Lovett. Adele and Ada were as close as sisters. Adele came up to Conway for long summer visits alone, since her husband didn't much like visiting and was otherwise engaged in the affairs of international banking. She loved to take walks in the hills, and to be read to after dinner by Archie. The Lovetts lived in Locust Valley on Long Island, but kept an apartment in New York, where Adele liked to entertain writers and theater people. Archie was naturally included in those gatherings, and though they often argued about literature, he was not immune to her beauty.

In " 'Not Marble Nor the Gilded Monuments,' " his 1930 poem "for Adele," MacLeish reshaped Shakespeare's sonnet of extravagant tribute. "The praisers of women" who "Boasted those they loved should be forever remembered" were telling lies, he asserts in the opening stanza. He will make no such extravagant claim, the hardheaded poet says. Instead he will call up the picture in his mind that she is most remembered by. But this image confounds him by refusing to fade.

> *Therefore I will not speak of the undying glory of women.*
> *I will say you were young and straight and your skin fair*
> *And you stood in the door and the sun was a shadow of leaves on*
> *   your shoulders*
> *And a leaf in your hair —*
>
> *I will not speak of the famous beauty of dead women:*
> *I will say the shape of a leaf lay once on your hair.*
> *Till the world ends and the eyes are out and the mouths broken*
> *Look! It is there!*

Asked about Archie's intentions in this poem, which he did not reveal as dedicated to her until the *Collected Poems* of 1952, Adele said only, "That must be the way he felt at the time." In his notebooks there is a suggestion of what those feelings were. The note is about stories, and how they do not really reflect life. "Stories do not happen to people. One thing occurs Monday and another thing occurs Friday and the connection they have with each other" is made up to create the story. "Nothing is a story as it happens. Adele weeping, standing at the window in the night with the light behind her so that there is a flat glare on the window pane and only unreal flecks of lamps through it in the street below is not a story." It is, presumably, more real than any story.

During this period Archie also had a brief encounter with the young

British novelist Rosamond Lehmann during her trip to the United States. Tall, with almond-shaped eyes and an aura of vitality about her, Lehmann was "one of the most beautiful women of her generation," according to the English poet Stephen Spender. For a few intense days in New York, she and MacLeish spent a good deal of time together walking around the city. Then she was gone, but Archie was left with a dream that he could not get rid of, involving "jade lions and an intimation that the wind from the south was to be feared." These ingredients he folded into "The Night Dream," a poem that, whatever its provenance, resembles a love letter.

> . . . *Grace*
> *Folded my body with wings.*
> *I cannot love you she said.*
> *My head she laid on her breast.*
> *As stillness with ringing of bees*
> *I was filled with a singing of praise.*
> *Knowledge filled me and peace.*
> *We were silent and not ashamed.*
> *Ah we were glad that day.*

But after all, Archie pointed out, "This was a dream, Ah / This was a dream." The emotions in the poem came from that dream, and were not "felt for the body in question!"

However that may be, in his notebooks of the early 1930s he several times attempted to capture the poignancy of a woman's departure by ship and with it the end of an affair. Here is one of these in a barely legible draft:

> *She sailed at midnight on the* ——— *tide.*
> *The horn of the ship was a great sound in the city*
> *Descending street after street as the ship passed.*
> *Leaving at last in the alley a mute sound*
> *And the* ——— *bells and a dog & a dumb* ———.
> . . . .
> *And the door swung in the wind & my heart leapt!*
>
> *How shall we suffer endings while the hope*
> *Clicks at our anguish like an unlatched door*
> *That breaks the thought off and leaves nothing? Not the last,*
> *The long departing whistle after that*
> *Could change the dreadful trembling in my heart to*
> *Hopelessness and let me sleep of it.*

It was material for a novel, he proposed in his notes, or at least it would have been were not adultery so commonplace. In an unpublished May 1932 poem, he invokes from the *Inferno* a winter night. As the snowflakes are driven by the dark wind and the cranes go chanting their lamentations, Dante beholds the ghosts of guilty lovers in the eternal night of hell. All that had changed.

> Here in this country we have neither cranes
> Nor hell nor guilty lovers.
> The adulterous
> Pass to a novel on the evening train.

Not until "The Woman on the Stair" (1936) did he venture upon the concentrated "novel in verse" he had been contemplating. The subheadings mark off chapters in a love story that can have no happy ending: The White Poem, The Absence, The Treachery, The Quarrel, The Reconciliation, The Second Love, The Room by the River, The Remembrance, The Late Meeting, and The Release. Nobody in "The Woman on the Stair," MacLeish declared, was anybody he knew well.

Continuing Education

Hemingway he did know well, and he knew him still better after his automobile accident in November 1930. Out west in Montana with Dos Passos, Ernest drove off the road when blinded by headlights. The car turned over, and he broke his right arm. Pauline wrote Archie about the mishap. Since the break would take three to six months to heal, Ernest was afraid that the African safari planned for the spring might have to be postponed. For the time being, he was laid up in Saint Vincent's Hospital in Billings. "I wish you'd write to Ernest and cheer him up," Pauline wrote. Archie did better than that. He flew out to Montana, a dangerous trip that took two days, and presented himself at Hemingway's bedside. Ernest was "surrounded by nurses and looking rosy and fine with a magnificent, glossy, black beard." He gave MacLeish a savage look and said, "So! You've come to see me die, have you?" That brutal remark, Archie eventually felt, derived from a cross-grain streak in his friend that had little or nothing to do with the man who wrote with wonderful "innocence of eye." He was beginning to learn that Hemingway was at once an irreplaceable and an impossible friend.

Archie's visit had at least one constructive result. Once he calmed down, Ernest urged MacLeish to join him in publishing his books with Scribners. All publishing was an unfortunate business, he thought, but Scribners was much the best house. So he wrote Max Perkins to get in

touch with Archie at *Fortune.* MacLeish was receptive to Perkins's overtures. He was finishing *Conquistador,* and had hopes that it would turn
into a big book. Besides, he was upset with Houghton Mifflin for publishing *New Found Land* in an expensive format and failing to advertise
it sufficiently.

When he completed *Conquistador* in November 1931, a decision had
to be made. At Houghton Mifflin, Bob Linscott was fully aware that
Archie was shopping the poem around, but he probably did not know
that Perkins at Scribners was the rival. In a glowing reader's report to
his boss Ferris Greenslet, Linscott commented that *Conquistador*
"smelled more strongly of longevity than any manuscript" he'd ever
read. He expected it to win a Pulitzer Prize. Greenslet immediately wrote
MacLeish with congratulations, offering him the same sliding scale of
royalties and advertising support normally invested in novels. Feeling
very much wanted, Archie accepted. The outcome was what Perkins had
anticipated. He knew Houghton Mifflin would "make a fight" for *Conquistador,* and though he very much wanted to publish it at Scribners,
he was probably relieved that it worked out that way. A gentleman
publisher, Perkins did not fancy himself as raiding another company's
authors. "I do feel troubled about the Linscott end of the matter," he
wrote Archie. From his bargaining position, Archie sought and obtained
yet another concession from Houghton Mifflin — a promise to bring
out a collected edition of his poems if *Conquistador* proved a success.

Archie's friendship with Gerald Murphy, like that with Hemingway,
had been going through a time of trial. The Murphys had moved to
Montana-Vermala in the Swiss Alps, in hopes of curing their son Patrick's
tuberculosis. In September 1930, Gerald came back to the United States
alone to visit his parents. Although he was in New York the entire time,
he did not get in touch with Archie and Ada. This was no ordinary
oversight, for the two couples had become extremely close during the
last years in Paris. Gerald had decided in advance not to see Archie
because he felt unworthy of his friendship, and Sara was unable to change
his mind. In an abject letter of apology written January 11, 1931, Gerald
tried to explain himself. Since the age of fifteen, he confessed, he had
been painfully unsure of himself. Because of these feelings of inferiority,
he had "never been able to feel *sure* that *anyone* was fond" of him. On
the surface he had presented a confident facade, but it was only a shell.
When he came to the United States, he was deeply unhappy and unwilling
to "risk disfiguring" his friendship with the MacLeishes. Gerald added
in closing that he hoped his letter would not offend Archie. "I *know* I
could have *told* you this without offending you," he added.

Moved by his letter, the MacLeishes decided to accept the Murphys'

invitation to join them in Switzerland for a holiday. Sinclair Lewis, on
the same boat during the return voyage, remarked of Hemingway, "I'm
afraid he's a great man." Archie was inclined to agree, despite the un-
pleasantness in Billings. He was also beginning to feel the same way
about Harry Luce. With *Conquistador* finished, and feeling the pinch
of finances, he went to work for *Fortune* full-time in the fall of 1931.
"This writing in the recesses of hack work is Hell," he wrote Linscott
about October 30. "But we are as poor as the rest of the world this
year." The following spring the MacLeishes were even poorer when
Carson Pirie Scott stopped paying dividends entirely. With hard times
getting harder, Time Inc.'s executives took a voluntary 10 percent cut,
and at the same time asked the staff to work harder. "At present two
full time writers are turning out the whole of this bleeding book
monthly," Archie complained to Hemingway in June 1932.

Increasingly during the months ahead, MacLeish felt overburdened
at *Fortune*. "If you were here," he warned the re-expatriated John Peale
Bishop in April 1933, he would have taken a journalistic job of some
kind and lost his freedom of mind as Archie had. "We have absolutely
nothing now but what I earn here and . . . it has meant that I have written
nothing [except for *Fortune*] for a year. Which I cannot endure." The
following month he wrote in the same vein to Hemingway. "As for
me — well its the same old hellofit. I am now doing a story on Morgan,
a story on the Port of New York Authority and a story on Marshall
Fields all for the August issue. And I can't even get to Conway for every
weekend." It helped to some degree that Time Inc. gave him a $500
bonus in July 1933 for "the swell job" he'd been doing, but what he
really wanted was time. Finally, in November 1933 he and Harry Luce
reached an agreement to that end. "Let us assume that $12,000 a year
is for you a satisfactory 'earned income,' " Luce proposed. "Then I would
say that you can earn $24,000 in 18 months at *Fortune*. That gives you
six months off in a two year period," in addition to briefer holidays,
some of them in conjunction with stories for the magazine. That remarkable offer was not made casually, nor to anyone else on the payroll.
But, Luce concluded, he hoped Archie would not begin his six months
off in the near future. For the next few months, in particular, they needed
him on the job. It was the spring of 1934 before MacLeish managed to
get away from the office and back to Conway. Soon thereafter Robert
Frost came by to suggest that he screw his standard of living down to
nothing and escape *Fortune* altogether. But Archie felt trapped by family
expenses, and he knew they would be getting larger all the time; in the
fall, for example, son Kenny would be going to college.

Besides, he realized that *Fortune* was providing him with the education of his lifetime. "Not only did I see the United States at Mr. Luce's expense," he later acknowledged, "but I got to know . . . a lot about its goings-on." One of the harshest lessons was that romantic individualism had died. On April 20, 1931, he elaborated on the point in his notebook. "The necessary effect of Industrial Civilization has been to make every member of the community dependent in one way or another upon every other. . . . And it is a matter of history that a surplus of the metal silver in India may so depress the currency of South American countries that men in Collinsville Connecticut won't eat." The second lesson was that those in charge of American industry were ill equipped to fight off the depression: "A sadder, stubborner, more timorous, whistle-in-the-grave-yard lot never before lived on earth." Walking from the Chrysler Building to Grand Central Station to take the train to Farmington, he passed people he had known in school trying to sell him apples or pencils. This hurt, and it spurred him like many others to envision a better way. In an essay of the 1950s, MacLeish characterized the spirit of the times in one long, powerful sentence.

> That was the Thirties when nobody was young any longer and next to nobody was rich and a great many people had nothing at all to do and almost as many had less than they should have had to eat and there was room to spare in the subways and scarcely a seat in the parks and the heart smoldered with indignation like a peat fire under-ground in the wet moss and the dead leaves but smoldered too with a kind of fiery hope so that men and women walked the streets together or sat around tables together and talked of a new world, a new and better beginning, and tried to make it happen in a theater somewhere, or in a fresco on a post-office wall, or a government plan to refinance farmers or to get the textile industry off its back.

Terrible as they were, those depression years were a time of hope, and even in the darkest of the writings Archie invariably suggested that if men would only work together, they could make things improve. Nor did he hesitate to assign blame. The worst of the depression, he believed, resulted from a failure of intelligence. In a *Saturday Review of Literature* essay of January 16, 1932, he directly addressed the "Young Men of Wall Street," such friends as Ranald Macdonald and Bob Lovett among them. The generation presently in control was going to leave "capitalism where it found it, intellectually defenceless and unarmed," he declared. It was up to the younger generation to give the nation something to believe in. The communists were already making their bid, and it was hard to resist. "Look at the Rivera frescoes in Chapingo and see what force moves through them. Read the manifestoes of the Soviets and see to what emotions they appeal. And ask yourselves what reason there is in heaven or earth or out of it why a man earning five dollars a day should believe in capitalism in any of its forms." Capitalism needed spokesmen to counteract that siren song of communism, and the job was too important to trust to the mawkish, nauseating, and false copy of publicity writers and advertising men. "If you can create an idea of capitalism which men will support with their hope rather than their despair, you will inherit the world," he stated in conclusion. "If you cannot, you and your children and ourselves with you will vanish from the West."

From February through July 1932, MacLeish's six-part series on housing ran in *Fortune*. (Harcourt, Brace and Company brought it out as a book by "The Editors of 'Fortune'" in October 1932, but it was all Archie's.) He began by depicting the morning ritual of Sinclair Lewis's fictional George Follansbee Babbitt. Babbitt awoke on the sleeping porch of his home in Floral Heights, turned off his "nationally advertised alarm clock with the cathedral chimes, and stumped down the hallway to the white tile bath. There, surrounded by the glass towel rack and the glittering medicine cabinet and the flush plumbing of his American citizenship, he shaved." *Babbitt* was satire, certainly, but it also failed to reflect the way most people lived. For the great mass of Americans, "whose incomes, even in times of prosperity, lie downward of $2,000 a year," did "not inhabit Mr. Babbitt's world. They don't wash in Mr. Babbitt's bathroom. An incredible percentage of them don't wash in any bathroom at all." The truth was that "less than half the homes in America measure up to minimum standards of health and decency." The cause, MacLeish asserted, was not so much poverty as the greed of union leaders and contractors who cooperated in defrauding the public. He came down hardest on union bosses like "Umbrella Mike" Boyle of Chicago, who saved $350,000 ("It was with great thrift") from a salary of $35 a week, and Con Shea, whose motto was "Every man must belong to the union or go to the hospital." But such racketeers could not thrive without the support of the building trades, he pointed out. "Behind every crooked business agent there was a crooked contractor." Between them they pocketed enormous sums, and saw to it that only shoddy buildings were erected.

The zeal of the reformer drove MacLeish's pen, and it was natural for him to support the presidential candidate in 1932 who promised a New Deal for the American people. In his travels for the housing series, Archie had seen at firsthand the ramshackle Hoovervilles thrown up by the unemployed in a futile attempt to make a livable environment out of nothing. President Herbert Hoover, he thought, was criminally remiss in not ameliorating conditions. All his sympathies went out to the Democrat, Franklin Delano Roosevelt, as two *Fortune* articles during the campaign showed. In August 1932 Archie wrote a piece on Hoover's private fortune. The subject was far from sensational, but MacLeish was so angered by the lies the president had told him about his early career that his article read like an exposé. Still more partisan was an essay titled " 'No One Has Starved,' " an insensitive remark of Hoover's that was demonstrably untrue. Written but not signed by MacLeish, the article was illustrated by Reginald Marsh paintings graphically depicting the filthy Hooverville shacks on the outskirts of the nation's cities.

In December 1933 MacLeish was assigned to write a piece about where President Roosevelt's New Deal was taking the country. With many American businessmen alarmed about the administration's apparent drift toward socialism, MacLeish's "What's to Become of Us?" struck a reassuring note. Roosevelt was "a product of the American tradition," he declared. Therefore he could be expected "to hold to individualism and the profit system but to insist that no man should be able to exploit the profit system to the injury of others." Only those who sanctioned "industrial banditry" could object to the government regulations he was initiating. Luce and MacLeish had an off-the-record meeting with Roosevelt before the article went to press. Afterwards, Archie recalled, "Harry grabbed me by the arm . . . and said, his face young and open as a boy's, 'What a man! What a *man!* ' " Luce's enthusiasm did not last. MacLeish's did. Tactfully, Roosevelt did not thank Archie for his favorable comments on the future of the New Deal. Instead he complimented MacLeish for another article of his in the same December 1933 issue, on inflation.

In 1933 also Archie produced a much-praised three-part series on the manipulation and the decline and eventual suicide of the Swede Ivar Kreuger, the most notorious international stock swindler of his day. The research for the series was done in Europe by Allen Grover. Grover's Wall Street background enabled him to make sense of Kreuger's complicated swindles, and he understood the importance of noting even the smallest details. MacLeish turned this material into a kind of prose poetry. The story ended in Paris, where Kreuger took his life. At the beginning, MacLeish's account went inside the Swede's mind, or rather his senses, as he left his Paris apartment. "The stair smelled as it had always smelled of hemp and people and politeness — of the decent bourgeois dust. . . . Mr. Kreuger breathed it softly as he went down around the caged-in column of the ascenseur. He had a delicate sense of smell for flowers and cities and fabrics and wines and foods." Later that day he stopped at a gun shop, an encounter MacLeish turned into a brilliant scene.

> A clerk received him in the lighted shop. 'Monsieur desires . . . ?'
> 'An automatic — a revolver — it makes no difference which.'
> Monsieur was very calm, in no way excited, nothing to make a
> man suppose. . . . 'Perhaps the 6.35 mm. Browning?' The 6.35
> mm. Browning was too small. 'The 7.65 then?' *'Non, plus gros!*
> *Plus gros!'* 'The army type? The 9 mm.?' Yes, the army type.
> Monsieur was familiar with the action of these arms. He was
> aware of the law which requires the sale of cartridges by the
> box. He bought four boxes. He gave his name and address: M.
> Ivar Kreuger, Numéro Cinq, Avenue Victor-Emmanuel III, au
> troisième.

The next morning — March 12, 1933 — he awoke with a cold. On his desk lay a telegram commanding him to meet with representatives from the Bank of Sweden. Shortly after 11 A.M., while his housekeeper was off to do the marketing,

> Mr. Kreuger drew the bedroom blinds evenly and neatly to the
> sill. He smoothed the unmade bedclothes and lay down. The
> street sounds had grown fainter through the darkened blinds.
> Looking up he saw the fat, gold stucco cherubs in the ceiling
> corners of the room. Odd witnesses! He turned his black coat
> back and laid aside the leather-covered large gold coin above his
> heart. For a long time he had worn it there as fetish or as guard
> against some shot, some madman. . . . Mr. Kreuger snapped a
> cartridge in the army type, the 9 mm. He placed his feet together
> neatly side by side. He shot himself an inch below the heart.

This was vivid reportage by any standard, but Luce was not entirely satisfied. "Arch was not edited into enough plain explicitness," he thought.

Journeys Westward

It was characteristic of the ever contrary Ernest Hemingway to castigate Archie for "selling out" to *Fortune,* never mind his need to support himself and his family. After hearing Ernest go on in this vein, Ada did not particularly care if she ever saw her old admirer again. Although Ernest continued his gestures of antagonism, Archie was more forgiving. Somehow he seemed to understand that Hemingway was driven by a dark inner vulnerability to break off friendships just as he broke off marriages.

In December 1931 Ernest reacted with ill humor to Linscott's request for a blurb to be used in advertising *Conquistador*. He believed in MacLeish and in his poem completely, Hemingway wrote Archie, but he had no facility for blurbs and was aware that there might be objections, "ethically and tactically," for him to be promoting his friend's book. Only grudgingly did he supply two lukewarm comments. Yet two months later he was urging MacLeish to come to Key West and offering him a loan to pay for the trip. Archie did not take him up on the loan, but in March he did make a return visit to Key West. That trip ended disastrously, though from correspondence and interviews it is difficult to ascertain exactly what went wrong.

It is clear that four men — Ernest, Archie, Mike Strater, and Gus Pfeiffer — set out for Dry Tortugas and were marooned for days by a norther. "As a result we saw a little too much of each other," MacLeish recalled, and tempers grew short. When they got back to Key West, Archie told Ernest that someone ought to prick his balloon, and Ernest told Archie his prick wasn't big enough. This childish exchange turned serious when neither man would back down. Archie moved out of the Hemingways' house into a hotel, and the next day he flew back to New York. His follow-up letter to Ernest, dated April 7, 1932, commences with the bad news that Carson Pirie Scott dividends had stopped entirely and the trip to Africa, now scheduled for the fall and winter ahead, was definitely off. "I suppose I have always known that I couldn't really go," he confessed. That letter also contained a curious passage about a fire at Dry Tortugas and a suggestion that Archie had panicked. He was in fact always frightened by fire, especially after a bad grass fire at Conway very nearly swept the house away with it. But what bothered Archie, he wrote, was that Ernest seemed not to trust him. "I know that you do not believe in trusting people but I thought I had given you about every proof a man could of the fact of my very deep and now long lasting affection and admiration for you and it puzzled me that you should be so ready to take offense at what I did."

By return mail Hemingway replied that he trusted Archie "more than completely as a friend." He admitted that he was bossy and irritating and quick to take offense. "But to hell with that," he added, and with talking about it. As to Africa, they wouldn't take anyone in Archie's place, so if he could get free at the last minute, he could just get on the boat and come along. Maybe they could go somewhere else together, later. It was too bad about the "uneasiness" between them, he concluded, but when people really cared for each other, there was bound to be uneasiness.

Another person Archie had strong feelings about, his Aunt Mary

Hillard, died in 1932. Overtly, the feud between them had ceased after the MacLeishes came back from Paris, but Archie's resentment of her meddlesome ways still smoldered. The year before she died, Aunt Mary visited Conway and asked Archie to come down to Westover in the fall to read to her students. He said nothing at all, simply looked at her, and shook his head slowly from side to side. He did attend the funeral in Waterbury. "Just the standard Episcopal obsequies" it was, and she would have been disappointed, he felt sure. "At last I've made my peace with Aunt Mary," he said to Ishbel as the coffin was lowered into the ground.

On March 30, 1932, *Conquistador* was published. In the prologue to this long poem, the voice of the modern poet — a latter-day Odysseus — calls up the ghost of Bernál Díaz to tell the story of the Spanish conquest of Mexico. Díaz presumably speaks as would a common soldier, albeit one with a remarkable sensory apparatus. The dominant pronoun of his account is "we," not "I." He is one man speaking for all. "Unless poetry can not only perceive, but also *feel,* the race of men to be more important than any one man, we are merely fighting back against the water," MacLeish observed. It is a vicious tale of conquest he relates, as the Spaniards under Cortés murder, betray, and rape the Mexicans who stand between them and their plunder. *Conquistador* vividly illustrates the abuses of colonialism and the horrors of war. Yet there is something other than greed driving Díaz and the others onward. They are possessed by a *Drang nach Westen,* the hypnotic pull of the journey westward that history demanded.

> The west is dangerous for thoughtful men:
> Eastward is all sure: all as it ought to be: . . .

Díaz comments, but it is the heart and not the head that mysteriously calls him onward:

> But as for us that returned from that westward country —
> We could not lie in our towns for the sound of the sea:
> We could not rest at all in our thoughts: we were young then:
> We looked to the west.

That journey, in short, took on universal overtones even beyond the prototype of America as quintessential western land.

MacLeish's first note for the poem he began writing in 1929 was this: "The Conquest of the New World which is the metaphor not only of our continent but of our time — as 'America' is the metaphor of all human hope — as 'west' is the metaphor of the dreamed-of future. . . . The heroism and the nobility and the pathos of an indestructible belief in that kingdom in the west, our search for it, our discovery of it, our conquest and its forever loss." More than by any other single image, he could not shake from his mind the image of the burning ships Cortés set afire at Vera Cruz so that his men would have no alternative but to follow him. In subsequent notes MacLeish further worked out the significance of this sixteenth-century saga for his own time.

> The poem is in the mouth of Bernal Díaz. He is against the heroes. . . . He knows. He is trying to give the lowdown. "Here's Gomora's [official, subsidized] story — the story you all read with the big names and the imperial decorations and all that shit. And here's what happened and here's the men who did it and where are they now? In the bellies of the tigers and the serpents and their women forgotten or down here in Guatemala with a mud hut and a street full of children. . . .
>
> But that is only a tone, a manner. The material of the poem has a great power of its own. . . . As well as I can understand my own mind, it compels me because it is a symbol . . . of the life of our race on this earth. That sailing westward into the unknown bay, those reports of richness and wonders . . . to the west, the will to seize them, the long marches, the endless battles, the finding of its beautiful city (and then its capture and destruction) . . . it is like the life of a man with its first enchantment — the universal dream of happiness and glory beyond — the laborious and dangerous attempt to seize it — the success which destroys the dream itself. . . .
>
> That or the adventure of those of our time into the unknown world beyond the . . . islands and the cities and the cultivated lands. "West" into the new land.

And what was this new land? The Spanish conquest of Mexico, he believed, marked the end of the movement westward. "The margin of unknown earth" disappeared, and with it the faith in a terrestrial paradise. "There was no longer an earthly habitation for our dreams. And we turned inward, to the unknown within us, to science which is the translation into symbols of the physical world." It remained for the twentieth century to penetrate that unknown continent. In that sense, MacLeish wrote, "the conquistadors *are* my generation."

Very little of MacLeish's program for *Conquistador* communicated itself to those who reviewed it. Llewellyn Jones of the *Chicago Evening Post* rightly called attention to the westering theme implicit in Díaz's disgust at the aftercomers who made their habitations in the promised land and so robbed it of its fascination. The settlers brought carts with beds and boards and pots and kettles and stale clothes.

And the west is gone now: the west is the ocean sky . . .

And Harriet Monroe in *Poetry* astutely observed that MacLeish's work was "an epic of races rather than heroes."

For the most part, however, those who most admired the poem did so for the wrong reasons. Along comes "Mr. Archibald MacLeish's muse encased in stout Spanish armor, and bearing a sword dripping with the blood of the Tlaxacans and the Aztecs," wrote Herbert Gorman in the *New York Evening Post*. The result was "an impressive and moving performance . . . , a poem vibrating with masculine emotion and stained with barbarous colors and compact with terror and beauty." *Conquistador,* Gorman concluded, was "quite the best" of MacLeish, "a tremendous advance" over *The Hamlet of A. MacLeish.* The loudest huzzah of all came from Archie's friend Lincoln Kirstein in *Hound & Horn.* In *Conquistador,* Kirstein asserted, MacLeish had written "the finest consecutive narrative since [Browning's] *The Ring and the Book,* the single narrative worthy of the inheritance by an American, and what is far more important, a poem which is a rehabilitation of a language, raising new standards in symbols and reasserting the idea of heroism."

Technically, Kirstein and others applauded the poem's form — a deft terza rima dependent on assonance rather than end rhyme for its coherence. Another unifying factor, Allen Tate pointed out in the *New Republic,* was "the clarity of sensuous reminiscence" pervasive throughout. "There is not one moment of action objectively rendered in the whole poem," he commented. "There is constantly and solely the pattern of sensation that surrounds the moment of action." Throughout Díaz is concerned less with telling what happened than with how it felt. The technique was rather like that Hemingway was using in prose, Tate observed.

As for the poem's applicability to the contemporary world, only Horace Gregory detected such a link, and it was not one MacLeish had overtly in mind. Acknowledging the poet's mastery of "a loosely woven music that once heard can never be forgotten," Gregory drew an analogy between *Conquistador* and the open letter Archie had written to the "Young Men of Wall Street." The poem was thus a jeremiad, warning today's "sons of Caesar" that the conquistadors of an earlier time, once thought of as the heroes of the age, were now dead and gone. Most commentary from the left, however, criticized the poem for its lack of relevance to present conditions. For MacLeish, according to the *New Masses* review by V. J. Jerome, history was but "the flat wash for his watercolor verbiage, his landscapes, seascapes, nightscapes, and self-escapes from reality." As an artist, he was representative "of the class views of the bourgeois intelligentsia" and of "the failure of the middle class in a period of dying capitalism." The very subject matter troubled Isidor Schneider in the *New York Herald Tribune.* Despite "its superb poetry," *Conquistador* had nothing to say to the modern reader. "Mr. MacLeish must make a bolder and more direct settlement with his world." To this conclusion, Laurence Stallings in the *New York Sun* responded with a one-word rebuttal: "Tomatoes!" Archie himself did not so lightly dismiss such criticism. In the poems and plays of the next half dozen years, he vigorously and repeatedly confronted the issues and the problems of his own time.

What most bothered MacLeish was yet another attack on his work in the form of a letter from the cranky and idiosyncratic Ezra Pound. Again, as during the Paris years, Pound detected in Archie's poetry a pale imitation of his own. "Naturally I don't see the surface traces of the Cantos on Conquistador as you see them," MacLeish pointed out in response. "It would be odd if the author of the Cantos didn't see them, however." He had begun his work on *Conquistador* with four guiding ideas, with Pound's among them.

> *Angle*
> 1) Use the material a la Perse — universalized — i.e. no proper names of any kind — the human race of mankind for actors. . . .
> 2) Use the material in the manner of Pound: assume the wars of the conquest and follow them at a distance . . . "the presentness of the past" — "make the thing live"
> 3) Use the material from the angle from which Bernal saw it, but exaggerate that obliquity — the old man veteran of wars and hardship ignored by fame, writing of his deeds . . .
> 4) Use the material in straight objective narration.

So much he was happy to acknowledge, but he was unwilling to regard his poem as merely derivative of Pound. Farrar and Rinehart had just asked him for a favorable comment on the *Cantos,* and he had complied, MacLeish wrote Pound with some pique. "You would probably prefer the praise of someone whose work you respected. If so just instruct them. I shall thoroughly understand." Pound sent no such instruction to the publishers.

If Pound's reaction annoyed Archie, he was merely amused by the review in the British publication *New Verse,* which averred that *Conquistador* could not be a good poem because the conquest of Mexico was not a proper subject for poetry. That assertion inspired him to send an epistle in doggerel to Stephen Spender, an English poet who had dared to like his poem.

My dear Sir: did YOU *know*
The Conquest of Mexico
Was totally inappropriate for poetic presentation?

But never mind WHAT *you knew:*
It's quite so: it's so true!
The proprietor of a magazine has informed the British nation.
. . . .
Alas the poor provincial poet!
Let him learn while truth will show it
That history's what happens to an Englishman at Eton.

Whatever the critical carping, *Conquistador* earned its justification in May 1933, when it was awarded the Pulitzer Prize for poetry. Archie and Ada were in Paris at the time, on assignment for *Fortune.* One morning he opened the hotel room door for his copy of the Paris edition of the *Herald Tribune,* and there on the front page he was with his Pulitzer. He never forgot the ecstasy of that moment. Back in New York, the $1,000 awards were distributed at the first ceremony ever held for the Pulitzers. The other winners were T. S. Stribling for his novel *The Store,* Frederick Jackson Turner for history, Allan Nevins for his biography of Grover Cleveland, and Maxwell Anderson for his play *Both Your Houses.*

Robert Frost, writing Ferris Greenslet of Houghton Mifflin his congratulations, allowed that MacLeish's poem was "right for the year" and would have been a good choice for any year. Four hundred years earlier, old Díaz had said that his story ought to be told "otherwise than in the dry manner" of his own voice. That was "as good as asking MacLeish to do what he has done." Hemingway mailed Archie a jocular letter edged in sarcasm. Now that he had the Pulitzer, Ernest wrote, Archie had nothing left to work for "except the Nobel prize, the French academy and Westminster abbey — MacLeish a success at last — From the training table to a seat with the immortals." Archie at forty-one knew better than to think that any award guaranteed him a place among the elect. But the Pulitzer functioned as a sign of recognition — not of his ultimate worth as a poet, but recognition that he was a poet, and that he existed.

12

PUBLIC POET I

Not Man but Mankind

DURING THE DECADE of the 1930s, Archibald MacLeish dramatically changed the direction of his poetry and his life. Like every sensate American, he felt the effects of the depression. For the first time, he was forced to support himself and his family without benefit of stock dividends or subventions from his parents. As a working man, he developed a sense of solidarity with other workers. The Rivera frescoes of simple laborers he had seen in Mexico in 1929 took on an added poignancy and power. For *Fortune* he went out into the country and saw the urban unemployed huddling in the squalor of the Hoovervilles, middle-western farmers spilling on the highways milk they could not sell, hungry coal miners striking for a living wage in Pennsylvania. Something had gone desperately wrong at the heart of capitalism, and in talking with the leading industrialists and financiers of the day, also for *Fortune,* MacLeish could discover no light of intelligence strong enough to ward off the dark. In such times, he came to believe, a poet could not stand aloof. As he wrote Carl Sandburg in July 1936: "You and I have a considerable responsibility. We are poets but we are also men able to live in the world. We cannot escape our duty as political animals."

It was not a popular position to take, then or later. At the time, MacLeish was attacked from both the left and the right. And his reputation has certainly suffered from his willingness to besmirch his art with the grit and grime of social issues. Yet, given his heritage and his upbringing, he could hardly have done otherwise. The pragmatic idealism bequeathed to him by his mother and his maternal grandfather ran strong in his veins. Like them, he felt obligated to teach and minister in the public interest as best he could. As early as 1916, fresh out of Yale, he had envisioned the prospect of performing that service through his writing. "I shall never attempt poetry," he wrote in that year, "till there is in me a great truth crying to be *preached*."

He did not pursue that ministerial goal for fifteen years. The delay was occasioned by a number of circumstances, among them his involvement in and disillusionment with World War I, his studies at Harvard Law School and brief career as a lawyer and part-time college instructor in Boston, his escape to Paris in the mid-1920s and immersion there in the study of poetry and particularly of the high modernists. But with the return to the United States and the onset of the depression, MacLeish finally embarked on the course he had set himself at the beginning. Even before the country's economic foundations started crumbling, he repeatedly excoriated himself for undue selfishness and introspection. In *The Hamlet of A. MacLeish* (1928), for example, he berated himself for shamelessly catering to the approval of his audience. To his mind, merely to take pleasure in writing poetry was not only not enough; it was wrong. "I am an evil person," he wrote his mother on February 12, 1930. "I take no happiness but in the sonorousness of certain words. It is a very wrong thing. Poetry is not always in me & sometimes coming out. I go to it as a man goes to what he loves & is ashamed of. I go to it out of my life. I come back ashamed." He would not feel right about himself until his poetry and his life were of actual use to others.

In two articles of the early 1930s, MacLeish attempted to work out the proper role of such a poet. "Nevertheless One Debt" (July 1931) argued that the days of bourgeois individualism were over. "It is no longer A MAN against the stars. It is Mankind." The one debt of poetry was to provide this collectivity with "an image of mankind in which men can again believe." Narrowing down in his open letter "To the Young Men of Wall Street" (January 1932), he suggested that the economic system would go under unless the new generation of bankers and executives presented the people with "a conception of Capitalism in which a man [a *generic* man] can believe." But the phony constructs of the publicity and advertising flacks could not do the job. According to "American Mythos," an unpublished satirical poem of September 1932,

> *What this country needs is its own mythology:*
> *Ask the professors of poetry: ask anyone:*
> *What this country needs is its own mythology.*
> . . . .
> *What this country needs is a bigger better*

> *Brighter mythology made to remake the Americans:*
> *Something in tweeds with a hat and expensive manners:*
> *As the world's leading industrial metal-bearing*
>
> *Publicly prosperous people our god man*
> *Should imitate popular practice: he should be rich:*
> *His face should absorb a suitable sun-tan handsomely.*

And so on.

The following month MacLeish published in the *New Republic* his "Invocation to the Social Muse," a widely misunderstood poem that aroused a good deal of controversy. It is a long poem, but the first few stanzas catch the tone.

> *Señora, it is true the Greeks are dead.*
>
> *It is true also that we here are Americans:*
> *That we use the machines; that the sight of the god is unusual:*
> *That more people have more thoughts: that there are*
>
> *Progress and science and tractors and revolutions and*
> *Marx and the wars more antiseptic and murderous*
> *And music in every home: there is also Hoover.*
>
> *Does the lady suggest we should write it out in The Word?*
> *Does Madame recall our responsibilities? We are*
> *Whores, Fräulein: poets, Fräulein, are persons of*
>
> *Known vocation following troops: they must sleep with*
> *Stragglers from either prince and of both views.*
> *The rules permit them to further the business of neither.*

And the poem ends with

> *I remind you, Barinya, the life of the poet is hard —*
> *A hardy life with a boot as quick as a fiver:*
>
> *Is it just to demand of us also to bear arms?*

A lively exchange of correspondence followed, debating whether poets should enlist in the cause of revolution and whether it was fair to characterize them as whores. The level of the debate (despite the fact that it was joined by such luminaries as Allen Tate, John Peale Bishop, and Yvor Winters) bore testimony to the risk of trusting too much to irony, even where the clues to the ironical intention lie thick. Many readers who are keenly sensitive to unreliable narrators in prose continue to think that the persona speaking in a poem does so with the voice of the poet. But the speaker of "Invocation to the Social Muse" is not Archibald MacLeish.

To begin with, the "social muse" invoked is a curious mixture of European nationalities — Spanish, French, German, Russian. The poem thus repudiates the call to action of a foreign muse, specifically the muse of communism. And MacLeish is no more ready to propagandize on behalf of such a cause than for Hoover or "Mister Morgan," who appears in the poem as not among the "handful of things a man likes." In addition, the demeaning portrait of poets as whores willing to sleep with "stragglers" of either camp for "a fiver" is the kind of deliberate vulgarity that calls out for contrary interpretation. The trouble is that elsewhere in the poem MacLeish does seem to speak straightforwardly and without irony, as for instance:

> The things of the poet are done to a man alone
> As the things of love are done — or of death when he hears the
> Step withdraw on the stair and the clock tick only.
>
> Neither his class nor his kind nor his trade may come near him
> There where he lies on his left arm and will die,
> Nor his class nor his kind nor his trade when the blood is jeering
>
> And his knee's in the soft of his bed where his love lies.

Yet even in those lines the metaphor of whoring continues, and that is not to be taken literally.

What "Invocation to the Social Muse" asserts is that poets should stay independent of doctrinaire thought of whatever origin, and that they should maintain this independence despite the lure of easy acceptance by the armies of dogma. At the same time, they must not fear to take a position once they have arrived at it for themselves and not out of expediency. Almost no one seems to have gotten the point, however. Advocates of proletarian literature were offended. So were defenders of poesie pure. "Following its publication," MacLeish wrote Bishop, "I was summoned to a full editorial dinner of the New Republic plus [Edmund] Wilson where I was required to defend my self for two hours."

If neither a barking dog of capitalism nor a tail wagger for communism, what was the poet to throw his energy behind? What image of mankind should he present? Perhaps it was unrealistic to expect the twentieth-century poet to function as an unacknowledged legislator, but MacLeish, like Shelley, believed that what he wrote could and should make a difference. Through the education he was receiving at *Fortune,* which took him to the center of power in Washington, MacLeish began to associate his cause with that of the new president. It was not mere happenstance that "Invocation to the Social Muse" was published ten days before Franklin Delano Roosevelt's election. In his interviews with

Roosevelt and his cadre of insiders, Archie was particularly impressed by the New Deal's willingness to take action, to try to change the future rather than waiting for the past to reformulate itself. Always avid for competition, MacLeish liked nothing better than to enter into the fray, and felt he recognized a kindred spirit in Roosevelt. They were both shaped, to a degree, by the concepts propagated at their prep schools of noblesse oblige and life as a struggle. Future battles might not be won on the playing fields of Groton and Hotchkiss, but schoolboy combat was certainly mandated there. Everyone, for example, was expected to play football. Both by schooling and by inheritance, MacLeish was drawn toward participation on wider playing fields. As he later put the point in conversation with Mark Van Doren, "If you have a man of a rather active nature and a rather competitive nature, he is bound to want to get involved in his time just to see what things taste like. He may not learn anything by it, but he's bound to want to do it."

In "1933," his Phi Beta Kappa poem delivered at Harvard in June of that year, MacLeish declared his confidence in the new president and the New Deal. The mythological framework for his argument came from the eleventh book of the *Odyssey,* where Odysseus in Hades meets Elpenor, the youngest of his men, who had been consigned to hell after dying in a drunken fall from Circe's roof. Elpenor, now chastened, tells him what hell is like. It is like the United States of 1933.

> *Millions starving for corn with*
> *Mountains of waste corn and*
>
> *Millions cold for a house with*
> *Cities of empty houses and*
>
> *Millions naked for cloth and the*
> *Looms choked with the cloth-*
> *weave . . .*

Odysseus himself observes the denizens of this infernal region,

> *Great captains, emperors,*
> *Princes, leaders-of-men*
>
> *Their rumps turned round to the wind*

and

> *Fools booming like oracles*

and young men

> *Watching for shifts in the breeze.*

Odysseus asks for advice as to the best route home to Ithaca, but Elpenor counsels him to press on instead. There can be no return to the quiet days before the war, he says.

> For myself — if you ask me —
> There's no way back over sea water,
>
> Nor by earth's oaks, nor beyond them:
> There is only the way on.
>
> You had best, trusting neither to
> Charts nor to prophets but seamanship,
> Take to the open sea . . .

And Elpenor tells him how to proceed:

> You have only to cross this place
> And launch ship and get way on her
>
> Working her out with the oars to the
> Full wind and go forward and
>
> Bring yourselves to a home:
> To a new land: to an ocean
>
> Never sailed.

In propounding this advice, "1933" closely resembled the Pulitzer Prize–winning *Conquistador* of the previous year, in which the continuing journey westward is apotheosized. The thing to do was to go forward, trusting to no dogma but "working it out" pragmatically: precisely the method of the New Deal. Roosevelt's "great perception," Archie commented in a discussion of this poem, was that the American inclination to look backward to a supposedly golden past was not the way to turn, that "we had to move ahead into a wholly new conception of the operation between government and people. But nobody wanted to look ahead; that way lay disaster. Each day was worse than the last. . . . And people went out windows because they couldn't face the thought of what the next morning was going to be like." But "1933" announced the necessity of accepting the disaster and then going forward from there.

In putting his poetry at the service of a political agenda, MacLeish defied the prevailing canons of literary criticism. In the 1930s there were two competing schools of thought as to the ideal relationship between poetry and society. The still surviving supporters of genteel romanticism elevated poetry into an art that was so pure and so private it could not survive contamination with public issues. Then the high modernists, whose doctrines were rapidly gaining ascendancy, declared their alienation from "the tragic shoddiness" of their own time, and tended, like Eliot, to seek direction from the traditional past. Both camps believed that fine craftsmanship and communication to a wide audience were necessarily at odds. As Malcolm Cowley asserted, "A conflict truly exists between the private world of poets . . . and the world of public issues. . . . The poet thinks in terms of individual persons and objects; the public man deals with movements that affect the masses. The poet tries to invent his own language . . . while the public man has to find words that will be universally understood."

MacLeish chose not to accept this as an unbreachable division, and he has suffered for it. Critics brought up in the orthodoxy of high modernist poetics condemned his writing of the 1930s as mere "rhetoric" — that is, "work intended for an audience with designs on that audience." What resulted, most agreed, were "neither good poems nor good speeches." MacLeish had "certainly abandoned poetry for social protest," the leading New Critic John Crowe Ransom declared in 1938. MacLeish had too often been lured from his calling as a lyric poet to the public arena, Frederick Morgan commented in 1953. "Some nervous compulsion" caused him "to retreat from the hard task of making verse, and to seek refuge in a more reassuring external reality." But why must it be true that excellent poetry may not have a worthy moral or social or political purpose? "In practice," as Stanley Fish sums up Ransom's views on the subject, "this means an exclusive focus on technique as it exists apart from any social or moral end, a focus that promotes rapt contemplation as the only attitude that can properly belong to an activity defined in opposition to the business of everyday life, or to the everyday life of business." And there were plenty of examples of great public poets in English and other literatures, as MacLeish was to point out. Watching his much-loved native land in what appeared to be its last transport, MacLeish was temperamentally unable to resist the attempt to communicate both his outrage and his hope to as many as possible. He took it as his mission "to integrate the role of the poet and the public man."

Frescoes and "Fascism"

In the early 1930s, when the New Critics had not yet taken up their positions, those who most objected to MacLeish's poetry were the Marxist faithful. He presented a confusing target, to be sure, for even as he denounced the tycoons as insensitive money grubbers, he belittled the comrades for their lack of understanding about American history and culture. This was the method, in particular, of *Frescoes for Mr. Rockefeller's City*, published June 22, 1933, in pamphlet form for the bargain price of twenty-five cents. The price and the format were at the opposite pole from his elegantly printed *New Found Land* (1930), a boxed volume brought out to sell for the princely sum of five dollars. Patently, MacLeish was reaching out for the widest possible audience. As he observed in a 1935 essay, "An art which lives by the production of little books to lie on little tables . . . is not an art in flower."

Frescoes is primarily concerned with the relation of Americans to their native land. MacLeish's notebook entries reveal his preliminary thinking on this theme.

> The material here is America, the continent. Coasts, seas, lakes, corn, the always west wind, the never northward rivers.
>
> But it is this continent translated into men. . . . (This because I so feel it.)

He did not want to be misconstrued as advocating a return to nature, for in an industrial age that was impossible. But he did want to portray "man-on-the-earth instead of man in the abstract." The organization had to be dramatic, "existing in time as well as in design. And — for me at least and from henceforth — it must be capable of human action."

With this background in mind, he sketched out the argument of his poem.

> Here in America, to me an American now living here, there is this fact: a great continent, a great section of the earth until a dozen generations ago unknown has been discovered, changed, overrun, and at last completely subjugated. The railroads have been built and the farms fenced and the banks have strung their spider webs over the whole face of the land. . . .
>
> But this is the wrong relation of man and earth — exploitation — promotion — Mr. Hoover . . .
>
> This poem then is the poem of the relation between man and the earth worked out by satire and by praise and it celebrates always the true: it satirizes the false: it uses the actual names of actual men and the actual events of actual history: it imagines a true and actual civilization instead of the false and sour communism . . . or the hoggish capitalism.

Finally, his book would take its inspiration from the Diego Rivera frescoes he had seen in the Mexican Ministry of Education, murals that conveyed "a sense of the beauty of man on this earth in his labors . . . and the ugliness of man false to the earth — exploiting her."

Rivera's Mexican murals were very much on MacLeish's mind as he wrote his poem early in 1933. At the last minute before publication, Rivera's difficulties with the Rockefellers in New York provided him with a title for what he had already written. The artist had been commissioned to paint a number of panels in the Great Hall of the RCA Building going up in New York's Rockefeller Center. The basic motif agreed upon was "Man at the Crossroads Looking with Uncertainty but with Hope and High Vision to the Choosing of a Course Leading to a New and Better Future." As a communist, Rivera knew exactly where the hope and high vision would come from. In one of his panels he depicted Lenin in heroic form, "guiding the exploited masses toward a new social order." This was not to the taste of the Rockefeller interests. In May 1933, amid considerable public controversy, they saw to it that Lenin was deleted and Rivera paid off and dismissed. Archie had some inside knowledge of the issue, for he had written an article on Rockefeller Center for *Fortune*'s January 1933 issue. It must have seemed that the title came to him unbidden, as from some magical agency.

Frescoes for Mr. Rockefeller's City is divided into six sections, or panels. The first, "Landscape as a Nude," presents the American earth as a naked, beautifully fecund, ruggedly unique motherland.

> *She lies on her left side her flank golden:*
> *Her hair is burned black with the strong sun:*
> *The scent of her hair is of rain in the dust on her shoulders:*
> *She has brown breasts and the mouth of no other country: . . .*

Dominating the second panel, "Wildwest," is the intrepid Crazy Horse, who died rather than abandon the land he loved. He is killed to make way for the railroad, whose various minions — Perham, Cooke, Morgan — had no feeling whatever for the country they were wresting from the Indians.

> *It was all prices to them: they never looked at it:*
> *why should they look at the land? they were Empire Builders:*
> *it was all in the bid and the asked and the ink on their books . . .*

Crazy Horse, by contrast, had achieved a right relation to the land, a giving of the self in response to its generosity.

> *When Crazy Horse was there by the Black Hills*
> *His heart would be big with the love he had for that country*
> *And all the game he had seen and the mares he had ridden*
>
> *And how it went out from you wide and clean in the sunlight . . .*

The foreigners who built the railroad across the West — the Irish and the Chinese and the others — speak from their graves in the third panel, "Burying Ground by the Ties." Although they did not come to America in order to "lie in the bottoms" with the trains going over them, they take a measure of pride, tinged with irony, in their accomplishment.

> *Do not pity us much for the strange grass over us:*
> *We laid the steel to the stone stock of these mountains:*
> *The place of our graves is marked by the telegraph poles!*

These honest workingmen are contrasted with the plump Mr. Pl'f in "Oil Painting of the Artist as the Artist," the fourth panel. An expatriated aesthete who clips his coupons in Europe, Mr. Pl'f is distressed by the "vulgarity" and oversized mountains and rivers of his native land.

> *There is much too much of your flowing, Mississippi:*
> *He prefers a tidier stream with a terrace for trippers and*
>
> *Cypresses mentioned in Horace or Henry James:*
> *He prefers a country where everything carries the name of a*
>
> *Countess or real king or an actual palace or*
> *Something in Prose and the stock prices all in Italian.*

MacLeish confronted the "Empire Builders" again in his fifth section. The speaker is the museum attendant, presenting "The Making of America" in five panels by the robber barons: Harriman, Vanderbilt, J. P. Morgan, Mellon, and advertising man Bruce Barton. Beneath the paint on these panels is discovered a letter from Meriwether Lewis to his uncle, Thomas Jefferson, telling of the plenitude of the western lands he is exploring on the Lewis and Clark expedition. "Many men will have living on these lands," he writes. "There is wealth in the earth for them all and the wood standing." Lewis did not anticipate the rapacity of the bankers and tycoons, the "Makers Making America."

> *They screwed her scrawny and gaunt with their seven-year panics*
> *They bought her back on their mortgages old-whore cheap:*
> *They fattened their bonds at her breasts till the thin blood ran from*
> *   them.*
> *Men have forgotten how full clear and deep*
> *The Yellowstone moved on the gravel and the grass grew*
> *When the land lay waiting for her westward people!*

Up to this point, *Frescoes* reads very much like a revolutionary document. But in the sixth and final panel, "Background with Revolutionaries," MacLeish openly satirizes those who have enlisted in the communist cause. The section is headed by a mocking epigraph:

> *And the corn singing Millennium!*
> *Lenin! Millennium! Lennium!*

Then it proceeds to scornful vignettes. There is the provincial New York Jew, for example,

> *Also Comrade Levine who writes of America*
> *Most instructively having in 'Seventy-four*
> *Crossed to the Hoboken side on the Barclay Street Ferry.*

Joining him is the fallen-away Episcopalian in search of a new faith:

> *Also Comrade Edward Remington Ridge*
> *Who has prayed God since the April of 'Seventeen*
> *To replace in his life his lost (M.E.) religion.*

Then there is the would-be artist who hopes that communism will compensate for his fading virility:

> *Even Comrade Grenadine Grilt who has tried since*
> *August tenth for something to feel about strongly in*
> *Verses — his personal passions having tired.*

Presumably these comrades are bound together by doctrines such as the one presented in ignorant broken English:

> *Aindt you read in d' books you are all brudders?*
> *D' glassic historic objective broves you are brudders!*
> *You and d' Wops and d' Chinks you are all brudders!*
> *Havend't you got it d' same ideoloogy? Havend't you?*

The slogans of communism have nothing of substance to offer in the present crisis:

> *For Marx has said to us, Workers what do you need?*
> *And Stalin has said to us, Starvers what do you need?*
> *You need the Dialectical Materialism!*

In a coda at the end of the poem, MacLeish speaks in his own, italicized voice. *"She's a tough land under the corn, mister,"* he announces. Though "screwed scrawny," the earth remains and with it the possibility of a future. In any event, he concludes, *"There is too much sun on the lids of my eyes to be listening"* to the illiterate ranting of the revolutionaries. That sunlight on the eyes, MacLeish later said, was "continental light, continental sunlight." Lenin's "ideology" was as irrelevant to the spirit of the nation, which is bound up in the communion of people with the land, as that of J. P. Morgan.

In the *Yale Review*, Eugene Davidson welcomed *Frescoes* as the work of "a satirical controversialist. . . . Mr. MacLeish is writing of a contradictory, sometimes blatant civilization, and he is one of the few who can make poetry of it." Cleanth Brooks, in his 1939 *Modern Poetry and the Tradition,* felt that the poem was greater than the sum of its parts. The satirical sections that might otherwise be regarded as "cheap jesting" took on "the effect of bitter taunting" in the full context of the theme. *Frescoes* might not be remarkable for fine passages, Brooks concluded, but it ranked as MacLeish's "most ambitious successful poem." Considered from a distance of half a century and more, his six panels present a powerful mural of what had gone wrong in the United States at the bottom of the depression. Some latter-day critics complain that MacLeish offered no solution to the crisis — that it was not enough to display unbridled capitalists raping the land and unenlightened communists pretending to care about it. But that is to confuse poetry with prophecy. *Frescoes* showed how it was, to one keen observer's eyes, and delivered a vague hint at the end of how it might be. More than that was beyond the poet's reach.

The severest criticism came from the left, from the avowed communists Mike Gold and John Strachey. In the pages of the *New Republic,* one month after *Frescoes* was published, Gold argued that MacLeish was "an unconscious fascist." *Frescoes* preached a "mystic nationalism" characteristic of fascist rhetoric, he asserted. "The Rocky Mountains should be left to their snow and eternal stars. They are no answer to make to the demands of six million unemployed men and women Americans." A second sign of fascism lay in MacLeish's contempt for Marxists, and especially for Jewish ones. In a burst of rhetoric closing his review, Gold insisted that the comrades would go on "repeating in our vulgar dialect, despite Hitler and MacLeish, 'Aindt you read in d' books you are all brudders?' " Even the poet's attack on the robber barons reflected the origins of fascism in "the revolt of the lower middle class, a cruel and futile rage of little traders who have been wiped out by chain stores, bankers and big business."

Strachey made the same point against *Frescoes* in his 1934 *Literature and Dialectical Materialism.* "On the one hand," he pointed out, "there is this perfectly genuine emotion of revolt against the great bankers, and on the other hand, in the last section of the poem, there is the equally strong revulsion against the actual masses — against the urban masses in particular. For these masses are largely either Jewish, or ill-educated, or foreign born." These same two emotions of revolt and revulsion, according to Strachey, "appeared in the rank and file of every fascist movement in the world."

MacLeish responded to this criticism by changing one letter of *Frescoes.* Sensitive to the charge of anti-Semitism, as well he should have been, given his mother's passionate involvement in the National Conference of Christians and Jews, he converted Comrade Levine of the once-and-ancient trip to Hoboken into Comrade Devine. The alteration was made immediately, in time for the reprinting of *Frescoes* in *Poems, 1924–1933,* published in December 1933. Otherwise he made no response to the criticism from the left. William Rose Benét, the brother of his friend Stephen Vincent Benét, spoke for him instead from his "Phoenix Nest" column in the *Saturday Review of Literature.*

Far from displaying the first stages of the fascist mind, it seemed to Benét, MacLeish was "merely trying to understand his own country and his own time." The trouble with Gold was that "he would have the poets turn propagandists for a particular political and economic thesis. If they refuse to do this, they are simply speaking out of turn and wasting his time." That way lay the death of art: "If you reduce poets to propagandists you kill poetry deader than a door-nail." Political poetry was or could be a good thing. MacLeish was to be admired as one of the very few American poets who were trying to get a perspective on their own country. More poets should be so engaged, Benét believed. At the same time, each must work "in his own way, preserving the most strict individual honesty."

American Manifesto

Late in the summer of 1933, Archie attended a reunion of the World War I naval aviation unit with which his brother Kenneth had flown. On hand were his friend Bob Lovett, who had been commander of the organization, Di Gates, Trubee Davison, Dave Ingalls, and the other Yale men who had served with his younger brother. Despite or because of the good companionship of the evening, Archie came away from it incensed. Not only had his brother's gallant sacrifice been in vain, but now it seemed quite forgotten. In the heat of the moment he wrote "Lines for an Interment," a poem whose bitterness is directed "at the nature of memory and what happens to . . . great hopes and great tragedies."

> Now it is fifteen years you have lain in the meadow:
> The boards at your face have gone through: the earth is
> Packed down and the sound of the rain is fainter:
> The roots of the first grass are dead.

So he began, and moved on to castigate the then fashionable deterministic attitude toward the Great War. Now that the Germans with cropped hair were back in the Midi and the English were "drinking the better beer in Bavaria,"

We are all acting again like civilized beings:
People mention it at tea . . .

The Facts of Life we have learned are Economic:
You were deceived by the detonation of bombs:

You thought of courage and death when you thought of warfare.
Hadn't they taught you the fine words were unfortunate?

In the same September 20 issue of the *New Republic* where this poem
appeared, MacLeish contributed a review of Laurence Stallings's book
The First World War. According to his review, Stallings failed to differentiate between two views of that war. The participants in the war,
including himself and his fallen brother, thought they were involved in
"a war of parades, speeches, brass bands, *bistros,* boredom, terror, anguish, heroism, endurance, humor, death" — in short, a human war.
But as it was now reconstructed by communist doctrine, the war's actors
were not humans at all but impersonal and terrifying forces. Moreover,
those who adopted this revisionist view of the war were as fanatical and
intolerant about it as the idealistic phrase makers of 1918. "American
intellectual Marxism is as like the Liberty Loan fanaticism of the war
years as one opposite can be like another." To prove the point, MacLeish
added, one had only to note the hysteria with which the literary Marxist
lashed out at those who did not conform to the official dogmas. He was
thinking of Mike Gold's accusations, almost surely. Within the year he
had still other antagonists on the left to deal with.

On December 7, Houghton Mifflin published MacLeish's *Poems,*
1924–1933, a selection they had agreed to bring out when contracting
for *Conquistador.* By no means a collected edition — it omitted the first
two books of poems entirely — *Poems* presented, in the author's words,
"those pieces I can now reread without embarrassment." Included were
the whole of three long poems: *The Hamlet of A. MacLeish* (leading off
the book), *The Pot of Earth* (in the middle), and *Conquistador* (at the
end). Interspersed between were most of the lyric poems MacLeish has
come to be best known by in various anthologies: "You, Andrew Marvell," "The End of the World," "Ars poetica," "Memorial Rain," and
" 'Not Marble Nor the Gilded Monuments.' " Also reprinted were the
politically oriented *Frescoes* and the Harvard Phi Beta Kappa poem,
"1933."

Most of the reviews took up the issue of the presumed impasse between politics and art, and chided MacLeish for either neglecting his
aesthetic duty in the cause of propaganda or quite the opposite. Speaking
for the aesthetic wing, Eda Lou Walton saluted MacLeish as "one of
the fine lyric poets of our time" but deplored his recent involvement in

political squabbling. "His art has been injured by his compulsion to fight — in poetry — when, obviously, his is not the mind or the technique of the controversialist." *Poems, 1924–1933* and the best poems in it would outlive contemporary arguments, the middle-of-the-roading Alfred Kreymborg asserted in the *Saturday Review of Literature.* Yet MacLeish could be even greater if he immersed himself in the cause of humanity. "Will the self lose distinction by trying to embrace the universal self? Is not a racial theme greater than a personal?" In the *American Mercury,* R. P. Blackmur traveled farther left along this line. The trouble with MacLeish was that he took himself too seriously, and his themes not seriously enough. "Dante was serious about his poem, but was serious about himself only incidentally. For Mr. MacLeish the accent is the other way round." Conrad Aiken in the *New Republic* argued that to achieve his full potential, MacLeish must move either one way or the other: "walk either inward on himself, or outward to the world."

It was the unpleasant duty of Bob Linscott at Houghton Mifflin to keep Archie informed of such responses. By way of reassuring himself, MacLeish wrote his editor early in 1934 that after all his work was "just as good or just as bad after an attack [even from Aiken] as it was before." Yet he could not shake off his eagerness for approval from "the termite army of critics." "I have a passion for fame," he acknowledged. "And I am very doubtful as to the extent to which my work really deserves to enjoy it." Therefore, he marched directly into the line of fire.

The poet-critic Rolfe Humphries zeroed in on MacLeish and let loose a burst of invective in the June 1934 *Modern Monthly,* a Trotskyist periodical edited by V. F. Calverton. Humphries began his diatribe with the Gold-Strachey charge of unconscious fascism. Although he denigrated MacLeish for his "political foolishness," Humphries dismissed the issue as basically unimportant, since "the poetic man may be sound and healthy while the political man . . . is hopelessly degenerate and corrupt." Besides, he had a more damning bill of particulars to press.

Basically, Humphries resurrected the often advanced complaint that MacLeish's poetry was derivative of Eliot, or Pound, or Perse, or whoever — resurrected it and added his own dose of vitriol. "I do not mean that Mr. MacLeish is influenced by this contemporary, or borrows to advantage from that one; I mean much more; I mean that he depends on this one or that one for his very existence." Then he provided chapter and verse, working primarily with the patent similarity between *The Pot of Earth* (1925) and Eliot's *Waste Land* (1922). As for *Conquistador,* that long narrative poem "synthesized the manner of Ezra Pound and the matter of Bernal Díaz" and certainly did not deserve the Pulitzer Prize. MacLeish, as a poet, was but a hollow man. "It is my own conviction that if you are looking for a poet you will find nobody home in the earthly tenement known as Archibald MacLeish; but you will find a fellow who would like to be considered a poet, who knows various arts of the necessary disguise, who is a talented, industrious and successful mimic of poetic activity." At the end Humphries summed up his case with the critic's old device of pretending to be charitable. "Let us not be unkind; let us co-operate; let us meet Mr. MacLeish half-way; let us try to find one poem that is memorable."

This review, condemning all of MacLeish's mature work, was so mean-spirited as to suggest a concealed animus against the poet. In fact the attacks had not begun, Archie wrote Linscott, "until after the Pulitzer Prize & the publication of *Invocation To The Social Muse.*" Relatively unrecognized poet-critics like Humphries had every reason to be jealous of MacLeish's success, particularly when it was packaged in a man whose patrician appearance reflected his overprivileged social background and his upper-class educational training. Although he was by no means well off in 1934, MacLeish recognized that in the prevailing climate even relative "affluence [was] a social sin." And despite his apparent sloughing off of the political issue, Humphries had still more reason than earlier communist critics to savage MacLeish. For in two separate articles, early in 1934, MacLeish had not only dissociated himself from communism; he had also had the effrontery to advocate a home-grown American democratic revolution.

At the beginning of the year, in an article titled "The Poetry of Karl Marx," Archie attempted to silence the debate about the proper subject matter for poetry. "It is just as silly to say that a poem can't be a poem *if* its subject is the Young Communists as it is to say that a poem can't be a poem *unless* its subject is the Young Communists," he pointed out. Then in the April 1934 "Preface to an American Manifesto," whose very title promised a quarrel with orthodox Marxism, he outlined his own deepening political convictions. The current American revolutionary movement had stalled, he wrote, because it was "conceived, delivered, and nurtured in negatives." Since its one wish was to destroy the existing order, it was willing and even eager to establish a repressive regime for that purpose. Never mind that it was "a pleasure — almost a duty" to hate greedy and arrogant capitalists; people still needed to believe *in* something, for "from hatred there springs no life." Only democracy offered hope instead of hatred, freedom instead of repression. The minds of the nation's citizens were fired by Roosevelt "because they are sick to nausea of the rich bankers and their economists upon the one side and the wise revolutionaries and their economists upon the other, repeating over and over that the world is ruled by incontrovertible economic laws which it is not only blasphemy but idiocy to oppose, and which lead inevitably to certain fixed and inescapable conclusions." That kind of inert determinism he was not willing to accept, and neither in his view were the American people. "They may, for a time, fight from hatred. But only to hope will they give themselves entirely. And only writers writing out of hope can lead them to anything more permanent than the barricades."

Although the critical reception of *Poems, 1924–1933* was less than enthusiastic, MacLeish achieved a resounding artistic success in another medium during the spring of 1934. This was the ballet *Union Pacific,* for which he wrote the libretto. The idea of undertaking such a project came from Nicholas Nabokov, a composer and first cousin of Vladimir Nabokov, who turned up in New York in the early thirties. Nick was "an irresistible man," and when he proposed that they should do a ballet together, Archie went along with him despite knowing next to nothing about the form. "Just write down what you want to have happen on stage and I'll set it to music," Nabokov told him. So MacLeish raided the reading he'd done for *Frescoes,* and came up with the notion of depicting onstage the climactic moment in the opening of the West: the meeting at Promontory Point, Utah, where the Chinese railroad builders coming east from San Francisco met the Irish workmen toiling west from Omaha, and a golden spike was driven to signify their union. The point of the ballet, as he sketched it out, was that the railroads were made by the men who built them, not by the men who paid for them.

MacLeish's plot outline included singing, drinking, and whoring as well as driving the golden spike. To accompany this action musically, he suggested to Nabokov that he draw on Gerald Murphy's extensive collection of American folk and barroom music from the 1880s. Nabokov wove fragments of this material, ranging from Negro spirituals to Creole banjo music and "Yankee Doodle," into his modernistic score. It was this native American music, MacLeish felt, that carried the ballet. Nabokov next arranged for the Ballet Russe de Monte Carlo to add *Union Pacific* to its repertoire. The producer of the ballet company was Colonel W. de Basil, who turned out, in MacLeish's words, to be "a white Russian crook." The lead dancer and choreographer was the brilliant Léonide Massine, who took the words and music supplied him and added movement. To finance the production, Archie solicited $1,000 advances from Sara Murphy, Lila Luce, and others, with an assurance that they would be repaid out of proceeds from the first performances.

Early in April 1934, Nick and Archie took the train to Philadelphia to witness the premiere of *Union Pacific,* arming themselves for the evening in the club car. Opening night was a wild success. According to the reviewer Siegfried Wagener, first-nighters stood on their chairs to applaud as the spike was driven. It was "as refreshing as a glacial wind on a midsummer day to find somewhere in the world a public that is not completely obsessed with economic worries" showing its enthusiasm in this way, he commented. The ballet itself he found noteworthy because for the first time "a purely American theme has been thought out and presented in choreographic form and set to music." Soon after *Union Pacific* was performed to popular acclaim in New York, in Chicago, and in Europe. On June 5 Eugene and Marie Jolas, Sylvia Beach, and James and Nora Joyce wired MacLeish congratulations on its triumphant premiere in Paris. At Covent Garden two weeks later, the London audience demanded eight curtain calls. *Union Pacific* was the hit of the season for the Ballet Russe de Monte Carlo, and it was performed for several years, amid a flurry of futile legal attempts to secure payment for its originators. Neither Nabokov nor MacLeish nor the investors ever got a penny from Colonel de Basil.

In conversations with others and dialogues with himself, Archie gradually solidified his thinking about how the artist might best address the national crisis. "Talk about really doing something about what we believe in, both as regards literature and democracy," Steve Benét noted in his diary after a long evening's discussion late in 1933 with MacLeish, publisher John Farrar, and writer Hervey Allen. By this time MacLeish was adamant in his conviction that communism was not the answer. Earlier in the decade, infuriated by the collapse of the economy and Hoover's inaction, he had come very close to announcing to his wife that he was going to join the Communist party. But he looked at Ada, said nothing, and never joined. "I may have been fruit ripe for the picking," he explained, "but deep down I hated the Communist conception of the relation of the state to the people it governed." Besides, he believed that the poet must saturate himself in his own time and not in theories about that time set down a century earlier in another land. Most communists, he discovered, knew almost nothing about the United States. One evening he and Carl Sandburg attended a party convention, where they heard incredibly ignorant statements from "grade-school intellectual types about the American situation, the American economy, American history." Archie and Carl started laughing, and "were literally, physically, thrown out!" They ended up on the sidewalk, still laughing.

Sure that a writer had to do more than merely mouth the slogans of the party, MacLeish in his notebooks considered the most effective artistic response. Since the social problem was essentially dramatic, he felt, it could best be handled dramatically. The commercial theater with all its artifice was dying, but the new workers' theater offered a hearing for the best and most honest work he could do. On such a stage he might be able to affect the life of the time. But what should he convey there?

In a 1932 note he sketched out the plot of a three-act play in which the villagers of a remote rural community imprison and finally kill the king, the queen, and the princess of the ruling family they still revere, despite the revolution that has overtaken them. A cold revolutionist named Bill tells the people what must be done. They have been exploited and abused, and must now exact revenge. In the end, Bill himself is forced to kill the princess, out of the logical necessity of his convictions, though he has fallen half in love with her. The play ends as Bill returns shaken from his brutal deed. Dead white in pallor and barely able to stand, he reads to the populace from a bulletin ordering the planting of winter wheat.

That putative plot did not reach the boards, nor did another based on the notion that modern man was split in two: in a world where economic individualism was impossible, he had to struggle to preserve the individualism of his own soul. In his notes MacLeish outlined a verse play on this theme in the form of a musical revue called *Gallagher the Great*. The drama was to end when even Gallagher proved insufficiently great to maintain his individuality. This idea, conjoined with the bank panic of 1933, led to MacLeish's play *Panic*. The play ran for only three nights in March 1935, yet generated controversy out of all proportion to the brevity of that run.

Panic, Prejudice, *Public Speech*

MacLeish undertook the writing of *Panic* almost as a duty. The playwrights of the day were not presenting the industrial scene, he thought, because they did not know enough about it. He had gained that knowledge. His work at *Fortune* and his contacts with the left had educated him in a way available to few other writers. He intended *Panic*, like *Frescoes*, as a criticism of both capitalism and communism. In a long memo to Henry Luce written shortly before his play opened, he devastated the big businessmen of the day, both individually and as a group.

> Mr. Lambert struck me as a very vain man with a good bit of sexual reason for being so — the kind of bird you run into around the theatre. Mr. Young struck me as a combination of lawyer and pedagog with no particular capacity for original thought. . . . Mr. Morgan struck me as a healthy and childish Britisher probably inhabiting the early Nineteenth Century. Mr. Avery struck me as a garrulous and boring case of premature senility entirely

preserved in ginger. Mr. Dulles struck me as a sound, methodical, unimaginative and laborious man in whose hands anything would be safe unless the unexpected happened too quickly for him to get around to expecting it. Anything I said about Mr. Morgan's Mr. Whitney would be libellous. Tommy Lamont is a nice boy with a good C plus mind. Parker Gilbert is a bloodless intelligence saved from decay by continuous refrigeration. John W. Davis is a curious example of weight without force, honor without luster and mind without perception.

They were all honest men, Archie acknowledged, but as the rulers of industries and money pools they ought to have power of mind and vigor of personality, and that they didn't. "For five years," he continued, making his complaint more general, "they have been fearful, vacillating, bewildered and void. Their one hope has been to hang on. Their greatest fear has been the fear of falling off. . . . They are incapable of leadership. They are sterile. They sound empty when they are struck." And they would probably want to lynch him when they saw *Panic*.

As this diatribe suggests, MacLeish laid much of the blame for the collapse of the nation's economy at the door of capitalists for their weakness and poverty of imagination. John D. Rockefeller, Sr., he had heard, ordered all the houses within sight of his estate painted green so that he might not be exposed to the slightest shock to his sensibilities in his declining years. But trying to cling to the past and painting over the present would do no one any good. Also at fault in the crisis, Archie thought, was the debilitating Marxist doctrine that the future was determined by unalterable economic forces. In *Panic*, therefore, he invented a protagonist, the powerful J. P. McGafferty, who seems to have the capacity for leadership that Morgan and Lamont and the others lacked. McGafferty takes a stand against the panic, and for a time reassures those who have been making a run on the banks. "He is a man," as MacLeish noted, "who believes he is free to act and who has acted and who finds himself, at the top of his fortunes, face to face . . . with a religion of human destiny which leaves him no room for action." So as conditions worsen and his closest colleagues succumb to fear, even McGafferty loses confidence in himself, comes to believe that he is but a pawn in the hands of all-powerful forces, and commits suicide. He falls not because capitalism is dying, but because he accepts the prophecy that it must die. At least that was what MacLeish meant to convey, though the message was not apparent to most who saw the play.

During the summer of 1934, on a six-month leave from *Fortune*, he fashioned a verse drama on this theme, using the framework of the Oedipus legend and retaining in the actual production the device of the

Greek chorus. *Swellfoot McGafferty* he was going to call it, or *J. P. McGafferty*. Then the title was altered to *Panic,* and arrangements made for both publication in book form and a stage production in March 1935.

The play was the first production of the new Phoenix Theater, co-founded by John Houseman and Nathan Zatkin. Bob Lovett agreed to underwrite the costs, which were held to a minimum. The budget was too small to attract an established actor such as Edward G. Robinson or Paul Muni for the lead. Instead, Houseman located a nineteen-year-old named Orson Welles. As the audition began, Archie's eyes narrowed "in exasperation." How was this mere boy supposed to play one of the most powerful men in the world, a tycoon in his late fifties? When Welles opened his mouth, Archie found out how: with a miraculous voice that combined "infinite delicacy and brutally devastating power." Involved in the production besides Houseman and Welles were director Jimmy Light of the Provincetown Theater, Jo Mielziner for lighting and sets, and in charge of movement, the great Martha Graham.

All that talent was put in the service of a play scheduled for a two-night run at the Imperial Theater on Thursday and Friday, March 14–15. The house was scaled from $5.50 for down-front orchestra seats to a mere fifty cents in the balcony. Zatkin said he expected boos from both areas, since MacLeish was "anathema to both left-wingers and fascists." The opening night audience was made up mostly of the $5.50 seat holders, who hissed distinctly at the playwright's unfavorable de-piction of bankers and businessmen. Should he take a curtain call? Archie asked director Jimmy Light. "Don't you dare go out there," Light told him. The Friday audience was no better, but the play was nonetheless extended to an extra Saturday-night performance sold out at fifty cents a seat through the Communist party journals *New Theatre* and the *New Masses*. After the production, it was understood, MacLeish was to ap-pear onstage for a "critical symposium." The Saturday-night audience made up for the previous ones, Archie felt. "They did not come to like that play," he wrote Houseman. "They went away liking it — more than liking it." But it was a classic case of what the psychologists call selective perception. The proletarian theatergoers saw precisely what they wanted to see, a play about the downfall of capitalism. They did not choose to hear the principal point he was trying to make: that the country and its economic system were not *fated* to fail at all, and that one man strong enough to believe in himself more than historical determinism could turn the tide.

After the curtain, the house lights went up for the promised discussion. Sweating from a 103-degree fever, MacLeish was confronted by three party intellectuals, V. J. Jerome, John Howard Lawson, and Stanley Burnshaw. He was expecting an all-out attack, but the criticism was muted. Why had Archie made the play's principal espouser of the communist line a blind man? Why had he let his bankers speak in five-beat lines and his proletarians in lines of but three beats? Why had he not dramatized the uprising, or at least the potential uprising, of the working class? Archie did his best to prevent his inquisitors from rewriting his play for him and went home to sleep off his fever, feeling he had more than held his own.

The party line on MacLeish had softened considerably since the "unconscious fascist" charges of the previous two years. Increasingly he was perceived as a possibly valuable ally. To some extent Archie himself was responsible for this altered view. Although he never joined the movement, he had several friends who did, John Dos Passos (*Panic* was dedicated to him and his wife, Katy) and Malcolm Cowley among them. And though ideologically he hated the Marxist conception of a predetermined destiny, he also detested the tangible abuses of the capitalist system constantly on view around him. So he was persuaded by the party to join a committee of inquiry dispatched to Philadelphia to investigate the Ohrbach department store strike that started in December 1934 and was settled on March 9, 1935, the week before Archie's play opened. Unsurprisingly, MacLeish found himself on the workers' side in this dispute, especially after the police made wholesale arrests of those who tried to picket the store. When he went to testify on the pickets' behalf in Essex Market Court, he was practically shoved into a seat by a bailiff. Later, after the attorney for the pickets mentioned the Pulitzer Prize and a few other things about him, the same bailiff tried to help him on with his coat as he left. "I don't think anything that happened to me in ten years has made me so mad," Archie told an interviewer from the *Daily Worker*.

The *Daily Worker* piece, on Friday March 15, was divided between a laudatory view of MacLeish's part in the Ohrbach strike and a straight Marxist interpretation of his play. At the end, the article announced the final performance of *Panic* scheduled for the following night, and the symposium to follow. It seems fair to assume that most of those in the audience were faithful readers of the *Worker* and knew in advance what attitude to take toward MacLeish and his play. In the event that they had missed their cue, party agitprop expert V. J. Jerome spelled it out for them during the postperformance discussion. *Panic* had as its theme "the doom of capitalism," he declared, "a doom that proceeds out of the very being of capitalism, organically, by an inexorable dictate," in that statement effectively dismissing the basic argument of the play.

MacLeish had not yet "advanced" quite enough in his thinking, Jerome acknowledged. He did not yet proclaim the necessity of a revolution to overthrow the ruling class. But he had made progress, and the auspices were good. Based on the author's "present point of transition," Jerome anticipated a time not far hence when MacLeish, "America's most splendid singer," would sing the epic of the proletariat.

Although it was given a London production a year later, *Panic* was not a wonderful play. It read rather better than it played, probably, though in both forms it elicited widely varying critical reactions. "As lean as a Greek drama," John Chamberlain commented in the *New York Times;* "a pale pretentious drama," Lewis Gannett countered in the *New York Herald Tribune*. Perhaps most enthusiastic was Ben Ray Redman in the *Saturday Review of Literature*. In the poetry of the play, he asserted, MacLeish reduced the complexity of real life to symbols that were "at once a simplification and an artistic intensification of reality." His verse drama provided an effective answer to the nonsensical position that poetry was "not a fit medium for the expression of our days." Cowley not only read the play; he also saw the Saturday-night performance, and for the most part his impressions were favorable. But he did criticize MacLeish for failing to individualize his characters, with the exception of McGafferty. His bankers, dressed in short London jackets, were all peas in a pod, whereas the author might have brought them to life by letting one emerge as a Falstaff type, another as a Uriah Heep. Similarly, the people in the street all spoke in one voice, without individuality. What was missing, therefore, was human conflict. "Even a poetic drama," Cowley concluded, "has to be drama first of all."

Late in 1935 *Fortune* assigned MacLeish to produce a long essay on Jews in America. Growing up as a well-to-do white Anglo-Saxon Protestant in the Midwest, he tended to stereotype and denigrate Jews like many others in his situation, notably including such writers as Pound, Eliot, Hemingway, and Fitzgerald. Thus he could refer in a June 1932 letter to Hemingway to a $100,000 plant in Lowell, Massachusetts, "knocked down . . . to a kike for dollars six thousand" and later in the same letter to "the sour academic kikes and their bogus communism." Thus in January and February 1934, he and grain executive F. Peavey Heffelfinger of Minneapolis could agree no longer to disagree about an inaccuracy in MacLeish's story because its source was a not-to-be-trusted "Chicago Jew."

Individually, Archie was a particular friend (as well as former student) of Felix Frankfurter, of Lincoln and Mina Kirstein, and, then and later, of many other Jews. But generically he tended to apply the traditional slurs, remarks that had she heard them would have set his mother's teeth on edge. Martha MacLeish, who was to her son and to many who knew her no less than "one of the forces of nature," devoted the last decades of her life to preventing and destroying prejudice as an officer of the National Conference of Christians and Jews. In Glencoe, for example, the village council set aside an exceedingly narrow strip of the public beach for use by blacks. As soon as she heard about this, Martha MacLeish announced publicly that her lakefront property — rather larger than the one provided by the village — would be open to the black community. That act of courage and independent spirit was more than equaled in 1941, after bigots painted a swastika on the Glencoe synagogue. Archie's mother, then in her mid-eighties, summoned the community officers to her home. Marshaling the considerable moral authority at her command, she drew herself up to her full five feet and addressed councilman Ben Parks. "Ben, I've known you since you were a boy. I know that this is not the kind of thing you will be able to live with unless you take prompt and vigorous action against the desecrators." Driven by the sheer force of the tiny woman before them, the Glencoe village council moved at once to condemn the bigotry and punish its perpetrators. As Archie said of his mother in admiration, "She had that whole town turned upside down by five o'clock in the afternoon."

It was the Nazi barbarities in the mid-1930s that occasioned *Fortune*'s story on American Jews. MacLeish's article, written expressly to head off fascist-fomented prejudice in this country, began with an epigraph from Professor L. B. Namier of Manchester University that pointed to the issue as a worldwide concern. "When the head of Louis XVI fell, all the monarchs of Europe felt their necks; when the blow fell on the head of German Jewry, many of us other Jews began to wonder what the future had in store for various branches of our people." Most of the animus against Jews, MacLeish suggested in a preliminary memorandum, derived from the belief that they were "becoming too powerful in politics, in finance, in business, in the professions." His article, therefore, took care to dismiss that preconception. "There is no basis whatever for the suggestion that Jews monopolize U.S. business and industry," he wrote. Nor was anti-Semitism rife in the country, if the term was taken to mean the deliberately incited racial phobia that led to the pogroms of contemporary Germany. He estimated that there were "no more than 15,000 loyal Jew-hating group members" in the country, cited the finding of the National Conference of Christians and Jews that there was less prejudice against Jews in 1935 than at the beginning of the depression, and concluded that anti-Semitism in America was "a very sick donkey."

Archie sent his article in advance of publication to a number of distinguished Jewish figures, including Frankfurter, Felix Warburg, Louis Kirstein (Lincoln and Mina's father), Judge Julian Mack, and Professor Morris Cohen. All of them, he reported to Luce, felt "the piece was valuable and should give offense to no one." It appeared in the February 1936 *Fortune,* together with a list of anti-Semitic organizations and data on the concentration of Jews in fields such as motion pictures. On April 13 Random House brought out *Jews in America* as a book. According to the practice of Time Inc., the credit for authorship went to "The Editors of *Fortune.*" But it was MacLeish's work all right, as was the dedication to Carl Sandburg. In the process of writing it and thinking it through, he arrived at an understanding of the question that effectively prevented him, ever again, from making offhand denigrations of an entire people.

The title of *Public Speech,* a slim volume of eleven poems by Archibald MacLeish published March 16, 1936, declared the poet's underlying purpose. In these poems he meant to communicate to as wide an audience as possible, and about matters of importance to everyone. Not all of the poems were political in orientation. "The Woman on the Stair," for example, presents the course of a love affair in psychologically sensitive fashion. But in all of them the poet was seeking to replace the traditionally subjective themes of the past with those of near-universal application. Three of them are even called "speeches," in which MacLeish speaks as from the rhetorician's platform. In "Speech to Those Who Say Comrade," he presents his version of brotherhood. Men become brothers not by sharing ideology but by sharing fear or harm or hurt or indignity.

> *The brotherhood is not by the blood certainly,*
> *But neither are men brothers by speech — by saying so:*
> *Men are brothers by life lived and are hurt for it.*

"Speech to a Crowd" advances the point by its exhortation to action. His listeners should no longer wait for others to tell them what to do.

> *There is only you. There is no one else on the telephone:*
> . . . .
> *Waiting for messages out of the dark you were poor.*
> *The world was always yours: you would not take it.*

The last of these hortatory speeches, "Speech to the Detractors," deplores the access of envy that makes contemporary people unable to admire the great. "Why then must this time of ours be envious?" he asks.

> *We cheat ourselves in cheating worth of wonder.*
> *Not the unwitting dead*
> *But we who leave the praise unsaid are plundered.*

If this was instructive, it was also poetry, and poetry of a plainspoken power heretofore unknown in MacLeish's work. Even the irony of "The German Girls! The German Girls!" became a savagely patent pillorying of the brutal and lovelessly carnal "mounted men," or Nazis:

> *Smellers of horse-sweat, swingers of polished boots,*
> *Leather crotch to the britches, brave looters,*
> *Lope over flowerbeds, wheel on the well-kept lawn,*
> *Force your knees in the negligée under the awning,*
> *Bold boys with a blouse, insolent handlers,*
> *Bring you the feel again, bring you the German man: . . .*

The reviewers of *Public Speech* were lavish with praise. MacLeish was hailed for his mastery of technique, and particularly — in Cowley's formulation — for his invention "of a new verse form, easy and flexible enough to contain all sorts of material from daily life, yet never so loose . . . that it gives an effect of slovenliness." At the same time he was acclaimed, as William Rose Benét put it, for combining this technical skill with "a vital interest in what is actually going on." Unquestionably, Ruth Lechlitner declared in the *New York Herald Tribune*, MacLeish was "the most *important* poet writing in America today." With the alteration of but one adjective, C. G. Poore in the *New York Times* concurred: he was "the most *influential* poet writing in America today." Whether you knew of MacLeish or not, Poore added, any reader would recognize in *Public Speech* "the sweep and confidence and precision of mature work." Even the communist press was now admiring. Isidor Schneider in the *New Masses* detected a "strengthening of ideas . . . sharpening of comprehension" in these new poems, and in a kind of backhanded apology for previous attacks took this improvement as "evidence that for all its excesses proletarian criticism has been helpful."

With both the establishment and the left in his corner, MacLeish had virtually achieved the status of a cultural icon. Instead of tussling with him as they used to, Linscott pointed out, the critics "sort of walk around your base with their hats in their hands admiring with awe." That was pleasant enough, and MacLeish himself "was happier about *Public Speech*" than about any of his earlier work. There was only one problem: the book did not sell. Even by his previous standards, and he had never been a best-seller, *Public Speech* sold poorly, despite being priced at only a dollar in an attractive format by Farrar and Rinehart. "What disturbs me," MacLeish wrote John Farrar, "is the apparent falling off in sales when the book has been well received critically, and when the price has been intentionally lowered in order to extend the reading of

the book among those whom I particularly want to reach." Linscott
somewhat uncharitably suggested that the problem was due to insufficient advertising, but then again Linscott was upset that MacLeish had
deserted Houghton Mifflin for Farrar and Rinehart. What was certain
was that although the reviews might elevate MacLeish to the skies, here
on earth he was still not attracting the public he hoped for.

13

MIDDLE OF
THE JOURNEY

On Trial with Ernest

THROUGHOUT THE MID-1930s, Archibald MacLeish contin-
ued to produce quantities of copy for the columns of *Fortune*. As a result
of his eminence and his sympathy with the New Deal, he covered the
government beat in Washington, turning out stories on inflation, taxa-
tion, the NRA (National Recovery Act), and social security. But he was
also dispatched on special assignment to destinations far more distant
than Washington, D.C. He did farming stories in Iowa and Montana,
and he journeyed to three different continents — Europe, Asia, and
South America — for Luce's magazine. Despite these frequent trips, during this period MacLeish solidified his family relationships and reached
new, and sometimes bitter, levels of understanding about his friendships.

On a trip to England and France in the spring of 1933, he combined
his journalistic duties for *Fortune* with a voyage around the Mediterranean on the Murphys' new hundred-foot schooner, *Weatherbird*. In
England he was doing research for a story on Harry Selfridge, the Amer-
ican-born "merchant prince of Oxford Street." One Sunday he saw much
of the English isle when "young bucko Selfridge" hoisted him into the
sky in the rumble seat of his Puss Moth for a morning trip to Cambridge,
a teatime visit in the west counties, and back to London for the evening.
"Imagine any other country calling a [flying] machine a Puss Moth," he
wrote Hemingway. He escaped to Paris on the day before Good Friday,
accompanied by a mob of English tourists munching on buns "so as not
to have to eat that horrible French food." Aboard the *Weatherbird* there
wasn't much to do, but the company and the food were fine, and he
and Ada came back rested.

No sooner had they returned to the States than a wire arrived from Hemingway, who was outraged by Max Eastman's *New Republic* review of his book on bullfighting, *Death in the Afternoon*. "Bull in the Afternoon," the review was called, and that was bad enough. What most troubled Hemingway, though, were Eastman's slurs against his manhood. Hemingway wore "false hair" on his literary chest, Eastman wrote. "It is of course a commonplace that Hemingway lacks the serene confidence that he *is* a full-sized man," he added. Delighted to serve as his friend's paladin, Archie immediately wrote Bruce Bliven, editor of the *New Republic*, objecting to the scurrilous remarks. In fact it *was* "a commonplace" among "the young sensitives" who envied Hemingway his accomplishment to impugn his masculinity, MacLeish pointed out. His letter set out to correct this slander. He had thrice seen Hemingway in danger, Archie wrote, "once at sea, once in the mountains and once on a Spanish street." He had also seen others in similar positions during the war. But no one had ever impressed him "as strongly as has Mr. Hemingway with his complete confidence in his own courage, nor has any other man more completely justified that confidence in the event." As for the issue of virility, he could only refer Mr. Eastman to the birth records of Paris and Kansas City.

Bliven declined to print the letter. Instead he showed it to Eastman, who wrote Archie in return that he had intended nothing of the sort, please believe him. Nor would Bliven publish a three-sentence counterattack from Hemingway himself. He was "through with politeness in letters," a frustrated Archie wrote John Bishop. "Hereafter I am going to hit where and when I can and take whatever they have to send back." At the same time, he assured Hemingway that no one but Ada knew of Ernest's cable and no one ever would as far as he was concerned. Besides, he would have written to object to Eastman's foul, filthy article without Hemingway's wire. There the matter rested until, four years later, Hemingway and Eastman met unexpectedly in Max Perkins's office at Scribners and engaged in a brief, inconsequential wrestling match.

Although his attempt at championing Ernest's cause hadn't worked out, Hemingway was moved to remember Archie's kindnesses to him over the years: coming out to Billings to visit him after he'd broken his arm, for example, and keeping his "god damned head working" during the Paris winter of 1926–27, when he was leaving Hadley for Pauline. *Winner Take Nothing*, his next book of stories, published in October, was dedicated to "A. MacLeish." The ambiguity was deliberate. When Archie thanked him for the dedication, Ernest said, "What makes you think you're A. MacLeish?" By not spelling it out, Hemingway managed to acknowledge a debt to Ada as well as to Archie.

Besides inviting a response to the Eastman "false hair" review, Ernest asked another favor of Archie in the summer of 1933. Jane Mason, the beautiful and sexually adventurous young wife of Grant Mason, Pan Am's man in Havana, landed in Doctors Hospital, New York, and Ernest — who was almost certainly her lover — asked MacLeish to visit her there. Jane's hospitalization was a consequence of not one but two accidents. In the first of these, she drove her Packard down a forty-foot embankment to avoid an oncoming bus. A few days later, she jumped off the second-story balcony of her home in Cuba and broke her back. Her husband chose to regard this as a grandstand play for sympathy, and shipped her off alone for recuperation and psychiatric treatment in New York. Hemingway, who regarded Grant Mason as "Husbandus Americanus Yalemaniensus Twirpi Ciego," was more sympathetic to Jane's plight. She had had the bad luck to marry the wrong husband, he wrote Archie, and it was "no fun to break your bloody back at 25." At the same time, characteristically, Ernest could be cruel about her situation. He'd tried to write a story, he said, that began, "Every spring Mrs. M. wanted to marry someone else but in the spring of 1933 she broke her back." She had done herself this injury, it was widely thought in Havana, out of her despairing love for Ernest. How much of this Archie knew is unclear, but he had already visited Jane in the hospital at Ernest's request once before, when she came to New York for a minor operation in May 1932. So he of course went to see her again in 1933, and this time stayed long enough to become friends. Or at least they were on good enough terms so that when they met in London two years later, she tried to arrange a private interview for Archie, who was writing a *Fortune* article on King George V, with the Prince of Wales. She was by this time something of a celebrated international beauty, one who had just been on safari in Africa "with 14 men" and in England was bidden to dine with the prince (who would before long give up his claim to the throne by marrying another previously wed American woman).

Apparently, when she got back to Cuba from these adventures, Jane told Hemingway that his friend MacLeish had made a pass at her, though she had only "sisterly feelings" toward him. Those were the only kind of feelings she was invited to have, Archie wrote Ernest early in 1936. Her remark had "a damned unpleasant connotation," and Archie "resented the hell out of it." Jane Mason, he said by way of summing up, "was the only person that I can think of offhand who does what she does, and the only one who has done what is to date the most considerable injury anyone has done me: the effective destruction of one of the few human relationships I ever gave a deep damn about." Hemingway was now disillusioned about Jane also. "As for your sisterhood pal she is a bitch say i and am documented," he replied. It seems clear that Jane Mason's physical attractions and fickle ways helped to break down the Hemingway-MacLeish friendship.

This relationship followed a pattern in the 1930s. Ernest would eagerly encourage Archie to join him at Key West. Usually Archie could not take the time, and when he did, he wished he hadn't. This was the case during their Dry Tortugas journey in 1932, and again in May 1934. On the latter occasion they were fishing on the Gulf Stream, and MacLeish hooked a sailfish. Hemingway had warned him in advance to give the sailfish plenty of slack, since striking too soon might jerk the bait out of his jaws. But Archie, seasick in the rough weather and excited at the sight of the sailfish leaping, could not resist the temptation to strike. According to Arnold Samuelson, a young would-be writer who went along on that trip, Ernest shouted a series of commands to accompany this episode. "Don't strike until I tell you. There! He hit it! Slack to him! *Slack to him!!!* Shit! Why the hell didn't you slack to him?" Once again, as during the episode of the fire in 1932, Archie had not lived up to Ernest's expectations under the pressure of action. In the aftermath of this visit, Hemingway wrote Waldo Peirce that from this point on he was only going to like the people he liked, not the bastards who liked him.

Archie went away stung by Ernest's criticism, yet soon was prepared, "sullen resentful Scot" though he was, to forget the insult and resume the friendship. In July 1934 he wrote Ernest that he'd been asked to do an article on him by Henry Seidel Canby at the *Saturday Review*. Go ahead, Ernest wrote back. "If you don't he will get somebody that no likum dog." But stick to the work and lay off his person, Hemingway advised. He wasn't interested in reading about his family or his religion, his war experiences or his high school sports career. In the end MacLeish decided not to do the article. "I knew Ernest well enough to know that anything I wrote about him would be wrong." The aborted connection with the *Saturday Review* proved to be fortunate, however. In June 1935 the magazine was considering an article on Hemingway by the psychiatrist who had treated Jane Mason. MacLeish heard about this, got hold of a copy, found it to be "just shit," and persuaded the editors not to run it. Alerting Hemingway to these events, Archie added that he hoped Ernest wouldn't think he'd been "interfering again," as in the *New Republic* fiasco. By now Hemingway was again urging MacLeish to join him on the Gulf Stream, this time at Bimini, where beautiful women, exotic food and drink, and gigantic fish awaited him. Then he inserted a jocular dig at Archie's recent contacts with the left. "Shit Mac you must come down and get to know the individual as well as the Masses and the Classes."

In the course of their friendship, Hemingway repeatedly found MacLeish unworthy in one way or another, and lashed out at him as a consequence. Wounded by these outbursts, Archie was still inclined to forgive them, especially since Ernest himself usually felt contrite before long. But it was an uncomfortable role Archie was asked to play — that of a man seven years Hemingway's senior constantly in the dock as the younger man passed judgment — and eventually he declined the part. Another complication was that the two were forever engaged in a competitive contest of one sort or another, physical or mental or artistic. On one of Ernest's visits to New York, Bob and Adele Lovett took him and Archie to the recently opened Radio City Music Hall. Before the show, Ernest pulled up his shirt, displayed his stomach muscles, and dared Archie to punch him in the stomach. Archie did so, not terribly hard. Then MacLeish said, "Well, that's not so good. Look at my stomach," which was always very flat and hard. There they were, two of the prominent American writers of the century, competitively displaying their abdominal musculature in the lobby of Radio City Music Hall.

Adele Lovett's interest in literature led her to a close friendship with yet another American writer. Early in 1934 she was staying with Philip and Ellen Barry in Southampton, and Phil asked her to look at the typescript of John O'Hara's first novel, *Appointment in Samarra*. Phil had been asked to comment on it, but was shocked by the book and didn't know what to say. Adele sat up one night and read it straight through. It was, she thought, a masterpiece. Except for Faulkner's *Sanctuary*, she had never read a more brutally unpleasant novel, but she had a sense that every word of it was absolutely true to experience. She told O'Hara how she felt about his novel. In gratitude he gave her the typescript, and came to rely on her as a guide to the imposing social world he was eager to belong to. O'Hara was added to the roster of luminaries who showed up at the Lovetts' for parties after Broadway first nights. Among others on hand at such gatherings, typically, were Robert Benchley (also an intimate friend of Adele's), Dorothy Parker, Hoagy Carmichael, Robert Sherwood, Franklin P. Adams, Frank Sullivan, the Barrys, Averell Harriman (Lovett's business partner), and of course MacLeish. For a time, Archie also used the butler's room at the Lovetts' house on Eighty-third Street at the East River for a place to write in peace, away from the bustle of the *Fortune* offices.

MacLeish's own boyhood feelings of social inferiority came flooding back in June 1934 as he prepared to deliver the commencement address at Hotchkiss, where he had first confronted the snobbery of old-money eastern families. "It was a memorable occasion," he wrote Bernard De Voto afterwards. "I got up and told them why I felt as bitterly as I did about the place and what they could still do to take the curse off." Oswald Garrison Villard, in the audience to see a son graduate, told Archie it was a brave speech. Villard didn't know the half of it, MacLeish observed. It took all the courage he had "and a hell of a lot more" to dress down the prep school of his youth.

Wounded Friends

Back on the job in New York, Archie enjoyed from his boss and fellow former Hotchkiss boy Harry Luce the kind of respect and trust that Hemingway was loath to bestow. Luce sought out Archie's opinions about the magazine, which was rare among mere *Fortune* staffers. In addition the two men felt affectionate toward each other in their mutually reticent way. When Luce was considering a divorce, the first person he confided in was Archie MacLeish. Luce met Clare Brokaw midway through 1934 at a dinner party, and saw her again a few other times later in the year. Pretty, blond, and extremely bright, Clare was a divorcée who knew how to attract men. According to a *New Yorker* profile of her, at parties she would assess the crowd, decide which male was worth talking to, and then zero in by asking him "endless questions about whatever subject temporarily interested her and which he is informed about." At the time Clare was an editor at *Vanity Fair,* where she had been unable to persuade her employers to start a new picture magazine. Harry Luce showed more interest, though she thought him rude at first. He had an annoying habit of suddenly looking at his watch and breaking off conversation with her. But one night early in December, at a party given by Elsa Maxwell, they had a long talk over champagne, and he told her the startling news that she was "the one woman" in his life and he intended to marry her.

The situation was complicated by the fact that he was very much married, and it was this dilemma he presented to Archie MacLeish. Archie was at work in his office when Luce called on the morning of December 7, 1934. They arranged to meet in the ballroom of the Commodore Hotel, a block away. When Archie arrived, Harry was sitting in a corner, smoking nervously. Luce "was shaken, overwhelmed, infatuated," MacLeish remembered. He told Archie the whole story and got the answer he wanted. Love was "all there was," MacLeish told him. If that was so, Harry reasoned, he had to leave Lila because of his love for Clare.

In 1935 MacLeish turned down two separate job offers to stay in

Luce's employ. The first of these, doing public relations for the NRA in Washington, he probably did not consider seriously. The proposal came from Averell Harriman, and in turning it down on February 11, Archie pointed out that he had only recently returned to *Fortune* after a six-month leave and so would not feel right about jumping ship. Luce himself objected on similar grounds, despite Harriman's plea that he should release Arch (as both men called him, out of homage to the nickname of Yale days) as a matter of public service. Luce also disliked the "special pleading" that would apparently be involved in the public relations work. He couldn't "see Arch doing that with any gusto."

The other, more attractive offer — director of the Harvard University Press — came from Harvard president James Bryant Conant in the spring. On May 14 MacLeish wrote Conant that he could not take the post for two reasons. For one thing, he had been appointed to the editorial committee of *Fortune,* an elevation in status and responsibility. For another, he wasn't at all sure that running the press, even with three months off annually, would fit his purposes as a writer any better than his work in journalism. Conant did not let the matter rest at that, and four weeks later Archie wrote him again with a still more definite refusal. He shouldn't take the job, he explained, unless he was "willing to give up all thought of writing for some years to come." And since he worked in order to have time to write, that simply didn't make sense. Conant accepted the decision with reluctance, for in the process of talking the matter over, he had conceived an admiration for MacLeish.

So it was, a few months later, that MacLeish and Ralph Ingersoll had breakfast with President Conant to float a new idea: a monthly *Fortune* survey using the polling techniques developed in market research to assess public opinion on issues of the day. Conant was immediately excited by the implications. The survey, he exclaimed, could "revolutionize the functioning of democracy." And with its brain power in statistics and the social sciences, Harvard could make the concept go. Then Conant bethought himself and backed down as to the university's involvement. "We can't do it," he said. "We couldn't even begin before we'd be involved in politics." Encouraged by Conant's enthusiasm nonetheless, *Fortune* plunged ahead with its survey, which provided remarkably accurate measurements of public opinion. It predicted within 1.2 percentage points, for example, the margin of Roosevelt's landslide victory over Alf Landon in 1936. Taking note, Roosevelt himself began to consider the survey's results, notably on questions leading up to World War II, before taking action.

In the fall of 1935, Archie spent the entire wheat season with farmer Tom Campbell in Montana. The experience taught him even "more about the disadvantages of raising winter wheat in a dry climate" than he'd expected to learn. But there came out of it one of his finest articles for *Fortune,* "The Grasslands" of November 1935. Luce congratulated him on the piece, though he, like practically everyone else in the organization, was distracted by the effort to produce the picture magazine Clare Brokaw had proposed. It emerged, eventually, as *Life,* and for some years was tremendously successful. But in its formative stages in 1936, the staff put out an unnamed dummy, containing pictures too obviously designed to shock rather than enlighten. There was a lynching, for instance, and a murderer in the death chair, and a nudist colony. "One nude is a nude," MacLeish commented on seeing the photos. "Twenty nudes are just bare."

Fortune paid the bills for MacLeish from 1929 to 1938. But it did more than that for him, and undoubtedly he was right to believe that journalism linked better with poetry than, say, flacking for a government agency or directing a university press. Writers weren't "mechanical spiders," he observed in a 1960 interview: "We're spiders that have to produce our own fluff *from* somewhere." *Fortune* assignments taught him things he needed to know and helped him build up that supply of fluff, and so he did not — in retrospect, anyway — regret the time he spent in journalism instead of poetry. What was hard was switching back and forth. "It takes me a couple of months after I stop journalizing to dissolve the tension in sunlight and get the weight off the gravel so the water can come up through again." And the satisfactions were very different, too. "I can work my hair out twelve hours a day at *Fortune* and have no happiness — only the kind of jag which comes from using up time in a necessary duty." With poetry, it was precisely the opposite. "There's no fun in doing it as there is fun in doing a piece of journalism but there does come briefly at the end and soon lost something that the greatest piece of journalism ever attempted is incapable of giving."

Trying as were his relations with Ernest Hemingway, Archie's friendship with Gerald and Sara Murphy intensified as they went though their time of trials. The Murphys returned to the United States in order to obtain treatment for younger son Patrick's tuberculosis in a sanatorium at Saranac Lake, New York. In October 1934 Archie wrote the boy about a wounded animal he'd discovered at Conway the night before.

> Last night it was dark coming up from the pond. . . . There had been hunters in the woods beyond and the chipmunks driving the dogs crazy and the sun coming in sideways under the leaves the way it does only in autumn. . . . I was tired coming up and not paying attention and when there was a little rustling in the

leaves in the woods I hardly looked. Something like a toad was moving through them — something almost the same color as the elm leaves. But I thought it was too late for a toad and I followed it. It barely ran. When I caught up with it I thought at first it was a field mouse but too big — a head the size of a rat. Then I saw its tail, broad and flat and gray with a fine gray fur — like no tail I had ever seen in my life. I picked it up by the tail's end and it ran a little with its feet, its fore feet wide apart, its hind feet smaller and close together. I thought as I carried it that it was very hot in my hand. . . . When I came to the kitchen under the bright light over the sink I saw what it was. I saw the web of delicate skin running back from the front legs to the hips, white underneath and gray on top. It was a young flying squirrel, sick or hurt or for some reason unable to move. I sent the dogs in and went back into the woods and put it in the bole of a great maple covered with leaves. It lay still there. All night in the brilliant moon I thought of it there and wondered about it. Somehow it had fallen and been hurt or perhaps some partridge hunter had hit it. Its fur was softer than any squirrel.

Patrick was delighted with his letter from the poet, especially since he was rarely well enough to venture forth on outdoor sojourns. Over the years his condition gradually worsened, with each spell of improvement followed by a deeper relapse. Gerald and Sara suffered through these agonies with him, and then in March 1935 their vigorously healthy son Baoth was stricken with spinal meningitis. He died, with Hibernian irony, on March 17, after his mother sat beside him for four hours willing him to breathe. At the funeral service in New York, the devastated Sara rushed outside onto Park Avenue as Archie followed. Suddenly she stopped, raised her clenched fists to the sky, and cursed God. Two months later an apple tree was planted in Baoth's memory, and Archie read his poem, "Words to be Spoken," during a memorial service at Baoth's school. Patrick lingered until January 1937, when Archie and Ada once again tried to comfort parents who were beyond comforting. Never again did Sara Murphy believe this world a fit place to live in. Never again did Gerald take up his artistic career: as if in atonement for some unspoken sin, he devoted himself entirely to running Mark Cross, the family specialty shop in New York. He threw everything out of his room in their New York apartment save a bed and a chair — white plaster walls, a white bed and chair. "Did his friends try to dissuade him?" Archie was asked. "How could they?"

Gardens East and West

In March 1936 Archie sailed to the Orient, where he and fellow *Fortune* staffer Wilder Hobson did the spade work for the magazine's single-subject issue on Japan. Initially Archie was booked to fly across the Pacific on the maiden trip of the *Hawaiian Clipper*. When the flight was scrubbed, he crossed on board the SS *Majestic* with Ada and Adele Lovett as companions. Archie and Adele fought like hawks en route. They fought so much, in fact, that Ada began to wonder if her husband was not in love with her friend. It was not that way at all, Adele reassured her. "Archie doesn't like anybody to know anything he doesn't know," she explained, and since she had read a great deal, had a good memory, and was used to saying exactly what she thought, she did not hesitate to enlighten or correct him. They traveled third class, "below the water line," Ada wrote the Benéts. Even in those infernal regions, messages reached Mrs. Lovett that certain gentlemen in second cabin were willing to make her acquaintance.

The Japan issue was the brainchild of Harry Luce, who correctly anticipated the emerging threat of that island nation. In collecting information, MacLeish and Hobson kept one basic question in mind: "How long can Japan continue her phenomenal commercial, industrial, and military expansion?" Among Archie's letters of introduction was one from Harry Crosby's mother to her cousin, American ambassador Joseph Grew. Such bona fides were of little use in dealing with the Japanese police and customs officials. They confiscated two of Archie's books, and actually called Adele Lovett back to Yokohama from Tokyo for an interrogation when they found a book on the Chinese soviet (not hers) lying atop her steamer trunk. Speaking in English to harbor police who seemed to understand nothing of what she was saying, and to a chief inquisitor who rudely continued to shave himself, she angrily told them that she had come to Japan because she wanted to see their beautiful country and particularly its gardens. Now, however, she had to conclude that they were not nice people. The book they had found was not hers, she insisted. What interest could she possibly have in the Chinese soviet? Her husband was a banker. Her father and grandfather and great-grandfather had all been bankers. Her great-grandfather had founded Brown Brothers bank. Finally she produced a letter of credit for $3,000, an enormous sum at the time. This went around the room, and where nothing else had worked, this document convinced the Japanese that they were not in the presence of an extraordinarily attractive western spy. They bowed and smiled and apologized. The chief inquisitor stopped shaving long enough to say, in perfect English, "There's been a mistake. You can go."

The Japanese had reason enough to be suspicious in the spring of 1936. The nation had been shaken by a military coup of young right-wing officers on February 26. The plotters succeeded in killing Finance Minister Takahashi, General Watanabe, and Colonel Matsuo (who died while standing in for his brother-in-law, Premier Okada). The belligerent rebels wanted stronger garrisons, larger stockpiles of armaments, and consolidation of the country's gains against China. Presumably they singled out Takahashi as a target because he had advised against issue of red-ink bonds to finance further military adventures. On the surface the coup failed, for Emperor Hirohito appointed the relatively liberal Admiral Osumi to form a new cabinet. Behind the scenes, however, the hawkish young fascists were taking the reins, as MacLeish soon discovered in his travels around Japan. "Knowing what Wilder and I found out in Japan," he wrote in retrospect, "it was perfectly obvious that something like Pearl Harbor had to be in the future. These people had nowhere to go except to war."

The *Fortune* issue on Japan did not quite say that. In part it dwelled on the marked differences between customs of the East and West. For example, wherever Ada and Adele went, with their western clothes and confident attitudes, they were objects of curiosity. Japanese pointed at them, laughed at them, even touched their skin. And the custom of using night soil for fertilizer had its effect on the olfactory system. In "your country," Archie wrote Hemingway, the countryside in spring smells of earth and rain. Here "it smells of crap." Yet in his account of the life of farmers on the southern island of Kyushu, MacLeish isolated two traits that made the Japanese liable to wage wars of expansion. The first was their extraordinary solidarity. A Japanese villager, he wrote, "has resources which the Westerner does not have. He has the association of his fellows. If he wishes to build a house, his neighbors help him build it. If he wishes a loan of money, he forms a society of his friends to provide the fund." So the poor man in Japan "is part of the life of many men and his destiny is theirs. The whole village is together." The second characteristic was population density. "Nowhere else in the world is there such a concentration of humanity upon arable land." In Japan, the fields "are too narrow for the men who feed upon them." Either the inhabitants would have to continue their practice of infanticide or they would have to stretch their tentacles to appropriate more space, more land.

So much at least was implicit in the special issue in September. It was very nearly banned in Japan because the cover reproduced the chrysanthemum, the sacred symbol of the imperial household, in its official sixteen-petal design. Only Hirohito could use the sixteen-petal symbol, it was discovered at the last minute, and *Fortune*'s artists airbrushed out one petal on the cover chrysanthemum. "For a 16-petal offence," the magazine commented, "*Fortune* would have been banned in Japan for 30 years." As it was, the Japan issue could hardly have been more timely, and it enjoyed a lasting success. When John Kenneth Galbraith arrived in Japan on General Douglas MacArthur's staff in 1945, the American peacemakers frequently consulted the *Fortune* issue for insights and information; the Japanese Galbraith met still spoke with admiration of "Archibod MacReish and Wider Hobson."

Archie turned out many thousands of words for the Japan issue, and did so in record time. Fellow staffer Perrin Stryker recalls seeing him at *Fortune*'s offices, a bandanna round his brow, singing an aria as he clutched his finished copy. The accomplishment warranted a long holiday with the family in Conway. Marriage was in the air that summer of 1936. Ishbel married Alexander Campbell, who had been Kenneth's English teacher both at Avon Old Farms in Hartford and Fountain Valley School in Colorado. According to family lore, Andrew MacLeish had given his daughter Ishbel only one piece of advice on the question of matrimony. "Whatever ye do," he is supposed to have warned her in his Scottish brogue, "dinna marry a Campbell," for the Campbell clan had perpetrated the 1692 massacre of the Macdonald clan, in which the first to fall was a female MacLeish. Despite the admonition, Ishbel and Alec's marriage was an exceedingly happy one. Archie gave the newlyweds a piece of land, with an old schoolhouse still standing on it, at the bottom of his property. They remodeled the schoolhouse and spent most of their summers there. Uphill Farm, Archie and Ada's house was now called. The Campbells named their place Downdale.

June 1936 marked the twentieth anniversary of Archie and Ada's wedding, and they celebrated the occasion with a barn dance in Conway attended by friends from Boston, New York, and Washington. Ken, studying at Harvard, invited his Radcliffe girlfriend, Carolyn de Chadenèdes, for a visit, and the eighteen-year-old girl was enchanted by his parents. They seemed almost perfect, she thought. It was only years later, after she and Ken were married, that Carolyn began to think otherwise. She came to the conclusion — and it was one shared by all three MacLeish children — that Archie and Ada were so tightly bonded together as husband and wife that they had little time or energy or love left over for their offspring.

In Mimi's case it was her mother who got the blame. Mimi believed that only a mother who chose to remain blind to reality could have permitted the persistent abuses she suffered at the hands of Cie, her governess. Yet when she had the opportunity to make such an accusation herself, she did not dare to do so. Once Mimi was away at summer camp, she talked freely about Cie, and the camp director wrote Ada that if she cared about Mimi she ought to get rid of her governess. When Ada asked Mimi about this letter, however, the girl simply remained silent. Mimi was deathly afraid of what Cie might do to her if she found out that she had complained. Mimi was finally liberated from Cie's dominion when she was sent off to Westover, but by her lights the school was not much of an improvement. She thought it was full of snobs with highfalutin manners, and said as much. Whatever else she might be, Mimi was determined not to be like her mother. Whereas Ada was always neat and feminine, beautifully dressed and groomed, Mimi wore old clothes and no makeup in rebellion. She simply made up her mind, as Archie said, that she wasn't interested in being pretty.

Although bitter about her mother, Mimi felt genuine affection for her father. But these emotions were called into question when, very probably in the summer of 1936, Mina Kirstein told Mimi that she and Archie had been lovers. Perhaps seeking a surrogate mother, Mimi had become devoted to Mina, who lived a few miles away from Uphill Farm. She would go over to visit, and to have long talks with Mina. On the day Mina "confessed" the affair, Archie found Mimi crying in the apple orchard and discovered what she had been told. It was "an outrageous lie," he later insisted, part and parcel of Mina's habit of claiming intimacy with various leading artists in the world of music. Besides, he pointed out, Mina was greatly overweight, and he would never have been attracted to such a woman. Yet according to Mimi, when she asked him directly about the supposed affair, her father would not reply. "My father was not a liar," as she put it, "and he did not answer."

It was also in the late 1930s that Mimi's younger brother, Peter, was renamed William Hitchcock MacLeish. Ada was the only child of Billy Hitchcock, and when her father began to moan that he had no one in the line named after him, Peter became Bill, except that for many years thereafter both names were used more or less interchangeably. Naturally this led to some confusion. For some time the boy thought that Bill was a nickname for Peter. By whatever name, he was a likable, agreeable child, and — to the eyes of most outsiders — very much his father's favorite. Archie used to take him for long walks together, during which he would call him Mr. Stanley after the explorer. The purpose was to expose the boy to the wonders of the natural world, so occasionally Archie would say, "Mr. Stanley, do you see that?" and point out a fish jumping in the pond or a bluebird in the bush. On one day that Bill has not forgotten, his father gestured at a pile of dog shit in the path and said, "Mr. Stanley, look at that!" Father and son dissolved in laughter.

There were other good times around the house, now and then. Ken and Bill were musically inclined, like their mother, and after-dinner impromptu concerts featured the boys on bagpipes or guitars and Ada on piano, with all of them singing. Archie, despite his fine speaking voice, and Mimi, with her unmistakable monotone, were not encouraged to participate. Normally Archie and Ada dressed for dinner, and the children were admitted to the dining room only after they had reached a certain age. But the formalities could break down, as one evening when Archie was eating watermelon and Ada cantaloupe for dessert. As much by accident as purposely, Archie spit out a seed. "Now, really, Archie," Ada remonstrated, which led him to project one seed after another in her direction. "You'll regret this, Archie," she told him, and pursued him from the dining room to the bedroom, where he dived under the bed and she smushed him in the face with her cantaloupe.

It was Ada's job to provoke gaiety and to make guests feel comfortable, both of which she did with notable skill. In conversation she could rattle on with pleasure and a certain wit. For their twentieth anniversary party, Bob and Adele Lovett drove up from New York in a brand-new Chrysler with such amazing features as a record player and air-conditioning. Lovett proudly showed off his automotive chariot to the company, but Ada had the last word. "It's absolutely wonderful, Bob," she said, "but I don't see where the septic pool is." The following year, on December 29, 1937, she sent Adele an age-old sentiment for the new year in the form of a limerick.

> In the Garden of Eden sat Adam
> Contentedly stroking his Madame
>   He chuckled with mirth
>   As he thought, on this earth
> There were only two balls, and he had 'em.

The Achesons were frequent summer visitors to Conway, often accompanied by their three children, who were roughly of an age with the MacLeishes. The two families invented an outdoor game played in the pine woods adjoining the pond. The Achesons — Dean and Alice, David and Mary and Jane — would go to the far end of the woods, and the MacLeishes would start out at the near end. The object of the game was to get one member of your family through the woods and underbrush to the other end without being discovered. If you were spied by the opposition, you were out of the game. The children were the best players, for they were harder to spot crawling on their bellies. Both Archie and Dean took the game very seriously, and felt a thrill of triumph at getting one person through the enemy lines.

With his plaid trousers, neatly trimmed moustache, and pan-Atlantic accent, Dean seemed totally out of place on the farm. But he was allowed to direct the bulldozer that fashioned the narrow road between Uphill and Downdale, and it was known as the Acheson Memorial Highway. For daughter Mary, and only for her, Acheson let down his veneer of dignity entirely by performing his crocus dance. First, he put some heavily dramatic Russian music on the record player and began to dance. Then he fetched out his handkerchief and behind it acted out the plight of a poor little crocus shivering through the cold and wind and finally blossoming with the spring. It made quite a sight, Bill recalled: "One of the most powerful men in America dancing a delicate dance of the unfolding crocus to the music of Stravinsky."

Times like these were the more memorable because they occurred so infrequently. Often the children felt excluded from their parents' lives. In Bill's metaphorical view, Archie and Ada occupied a garden, and the children looked in at them from behind a wall. They saw two beautiful people inside, dressed in shimmering garments and having a wonderful time. Once in a while, when they were allowed to come in, life seemed almost magical, but soon they were returned to their observation posts outside. They were admitted only by invitation from their mother, whose role was to act as gatekeeper and protector for her husband. But for Ada Taylor Hitchcock, Bill believes, Archibald MacLeish might have begun and ended as a highly successful lawyer only. She kept the world away so that he could get his work done. He knew it, and adored her for it.

14

PUBLIC POET II

The Antifascist Cause

ARCHIBALD MACLEISH CALLED HIMSELF, with some pride, a "writer who keeps up a running quarrel with his time." In the late 1930s that quarrel was with the fascism that was systematically doing away with individual freedoms in Hitler's Germany, Mussolini's Italy, and war-torn Spain. The Spanish civil war was merely a warm-up for a far-ranging conflict, MacLeish felt sure; in much of his writing from 1936 to 1939, he strongly advocated United States support of the Loyalist cause before it was too late. To spread the message as widely as possible, he learned to use whatever means were available, including the new medium of radio. And to gain as much support as possible in the fight, he was willing to associate himself, though always at arm's length, with the communists.

Two pieces MacLeish contributed to the *New Masses* in August and September 1936 illustrate the tenuousness of this association. He would not have written for that party publication at all unless he shared some of the goals of American communism. Yet in each of his articles — on Maxim Gorky and Carl Sandburg — he used his space to differentiate himself from the party line. Gorky was virtually apotheosized by the communists because he had fought for the revolution and created a proletarian literature. But his doctrinaire biographers, MacLeish pointed out, were at a loss to account for Gorky's occasional differences with Lenin and his continuing concern with the Old Russia. Gorky did not fit the standard formula. He thought with "the direct sensuous mind of the artist: the stupid, blunt, shrewd, delicately-fingering artisan mind of the artist," and not with the lockstep logic of the committed intellectual. As an artist, he had to dig out of the earth "the tangible materials, the wind-proof stone, the time-withstanding brick with which these men of concepts can deal." For MacLeish, this was the greatest tribute Gorky could be paid and the greatest lesson his life could teach. In America there was no shortage of intellectuals — that is, party agitprop specialists — to place the bricks according to a preordained blueprint. What was needed were more artists who could make the bricks in the first place.

The communists could also learn a great deal, MacLeish asserted in his rave review of *The People, Yes,* from an artist such as Sandburg. His book of poetry "ought to be required reading for every man in every American metropolis who calls himself a revolutionary," for these urban revolutionists rarely knew anything about the American people or the country they inhabited. "I remember being told recently by a group of young men at City College that love of the land was a childish emotion to be put aside with childhood," MacLeish wrote. These young men did not understand what Sandburg showed: that "people belong to their countrysides." Out of *The People, Yes,* according to MacLeish, came "the smell and the sound and the movement of all men everywhere," but also and in particular of the people on this continent. The one great American tradition Sandburg emphasized was belief in these people and their right to govern themselves. Only a revolutionary party that restored government to the populace, not one that merely mouthed these sentiments, could succeed in the United States.

Both of these articles followed the pattern MacLeish employed in most of his political prose. As John Timberman Newcomb points out, these essays normally took the form of "a dialectic consisting of a *critique* of injustice, misrepresentation, and oppression, and an *affirmation* of alternate values and methods for social transformation." In these cases the misrepresentation came from doctrinaire party intellectuals unable to fathom Gorky's independence and ignorant of the very country they meant to transform. In affirmation, by contrast, MacLeish celebrated the virtues of the artist and of the native democratic tradition. The *New Masses* editors understood well enough that they were being criticized in these contributions. But they printed the pieces anyway, and for good reasons. That such an eminent poet should choose to speak from the pages of the party magazine conferred on the *New Masses* the sort of authority — if not respectability exactly, then a wider credibility — they very much wanted to achieve. Besides, MacLeish was clearly on their side in regard to the Spanish war, and the word had come down from Moscow to make common cause on this basis, to construct a popular front involving an entire spectrum of varying political beliefs, united in joint opposition to the spread of fascism.

MacLeish demonstrated his dedicated antifascism in two important ways following the outbreak of the Spanish war in July 1936. First, he was instrumental in organizing the group that made *The Spanish Earth*, a documentary film about the war. Second, he joined the communist-originated League of American Writers and played a highly visible role at its second congress in New York.

The Spanish Earth began with a conversation between MacLeish and John Dos Passos. Disturbed by the coverage of the war in the press, they decided that a motion picture presenting a "clear, objective statement of the facts" about the background, origins, and development of the conflict would represent "the most effective anti-fascist document which could possibly be presented to the American people." As director the two writers secured the services of Joris Ivens, a prizewinning Dutch filmmaker and, in MacLeish's words, "a communist who never let communism get in the way of his work." Ivens, he believed, would not, like many radical novelists, merely "set out . . . to discover his preconceptions." Dos Passos and MacLeish next formed a corporation called Contemporary Historians, and in collaboration with the playwright Lillian Hellman wrote a scenario for the film. Ivens sailed for Spain on December 26 to begin work, while Dos and Archie did their best to raise funds for the project.

In February 1937 Hemingway joined the corporation. Soon he was traveling around Spain with Ivens shooting film for the motion picture and quarreling with Dos Passos about its contents. Dos wanted to show the impact of the war on the common people, focusing on one particular village. Ernest was more interested in demonstrating the military side of the conflict, in various locations. Hemingway gave himself to the project in several ways, not least by contributing at least $2,000 toward production costs, and in the end his views prevailed. He not only wrote the narration to accompany *The Spanish Earth;* he also spoke it on the sound track.

The film was ready for showing — all but the sound track — at the second congress of the League of American Writers in New York, June 4–6, 1937. MacLeish was among twenty-two prominent writers who issued the call to the congress. The list included critics Van Wyck Brooks and Carl Van Doren, novelists Erskine Caldwell and Upton Sinclair, playwrights Marc Connelly and Clifford Odets, poet Langston Hughes, and humorist and Hollywood screenwriter Donald Ogden Stewart. MacLeish was tapped to serve as chairman of the opening session of the congress, at Carnegie Hall. "Why they chose me I don't know," he reflected later, "except that at the time I was an editor of *Fortune,* so I was the other side. Also, I could produce Hemingway, who they particularly wanted, and nobody else could."

A few hours before the opening session began, MacLeish was summoned to a meeting of a group of communist leaders. Some of those present tried to tell him what he should say as chairman, but Archie was having none of that. They would find out what he was going to say when everyone else did, at the congress. When he got to Carnegie Hall, it was jammed with 358 writer-delegates and 3,500 spectators, with another thousand turned away outside. Archie was exeedingly nervous as he looked at the crowd and his fellow speakers on the platform. Stewart and journalist Walter Duranty were on hand, as planned. But Hemingway had not yet turned up. This was to be Ernest's first public speech, and he was in a bar summoning up his courage with the help of alcohol and his companion Martha Gellhorn. Just as disturbing to MacLeish as the absence of Ernest was the presence of Earl Browder, secretary of the Communist party. Archie had *not* expected to occupy the same platform with Browder, who was after all not a writer.

As chairman, MacLeish had the privilege of making the first speech. After reading messages of support from Albert Einstein, C. Day Lewis, and others, he forcefully made his points. To those who contended that fighting fascism might foment war, he responded that the war had already begun. What was happening in Spain was no political allegory. The actors were not actors: they truly died. The cities were not stage sets: they burned with fire. "And in that war, that Spanish war on Spanish earth, we, writers who contend for freedom, are ourselves, and whether we so wish or not, engaged." Since that was the case, it would be pusillanimous to stay silent. He knew that many people would attack the intelligence and even the integrity of those who stood with the communists in opposition to the menace of fascism, that they would be regarded as dupes who were being "used" by the communists. To this charge he answered "that the man who refuses to defend his convictions for fear that he may defend them in the wrong company, has no convictions" and that "no writer worthy the name ever refused to make his position clear for fear that position might advantage others than himself — even others whom he had no wish to help." The assembled communist faithful received this message without enthusiasm, in anticipation of more stirring and less backhanded speeches of support to come.

Hemingway arrived well "inbibulated" about 10 P.M., just as Duranty was finishing his talk. "Why the hell am I making a speech?" he muttered in the wings before going onstage. Once there, he was the hit of the meeting. As a writer-observer in Spain, he said, he had grown accustomed to war, but he could not grow accustomed to murder, and the fascists fighting in Spain with the aid of German and Italian planes and tanks were nothing less than murderers. "Every time they are beaten in the field they salvage that strange thing they call their honor by murdering civilians," he declared, to tumultuous applause. The meeting concluded with a showing of selections from *The Spanish Earth,* with Ivens supplying occasional remarks — "at this point you would hear machine guns" — to make up for the lack of sound.

The following week MacLeish called on scholars to join writers in the fight against fascism. In his poem "Speech to the Scholars," read at Columbia University's Phi Beta Kappa ceremonies, MacLeish argued that this war was different from others in history, since the agencies of propaganda were now being used in sophisticated and cunning ways to seduce people into believing the lies of totalitarian states. Under such circumstances, his poem concludes, scholars had no choice but to defend the truth with every weapon at their disposal.

> *I say the guns are in your house:*
> *I say there is no room for flight:*
> *Arise O scholars from your peace!*
> *Arise! Enlist! Take arms and fight!*

These sentiments, as printed in the *Saturday Review of Literature,* so troubled President Conant that he undertook to refute them in his baccalaureate sermon at Harvard. Letters debating the issue went back and forth between Conant and MacLeish. "I believe it is easy to lose the very things one wishes to preserve by declaring war in favor of them," Conant asserted. For MacLeish, not to fight was simply to bow the knee and accept tyranny. But this correspondence, despite its source in disagreement, was conducted in a spirit of mutual admiration, and Walter Lippmann, then serving on the Harvard board of overseers, intervened with MacLeish to suggest that the quarrel was really a matter of misunderstanding.

Later in 1937 MacLeish took his campaign against the fascist forces in Spain to the highest reaches of the United States government. Acting on behalf of an informal group outraged by the U.S. policy of nonintervention, he and playwright Robert Sherwood called on President Roosevelt. Why, they asked FDR, didn't the United States aid the duly elected and democratic government of Spain in its war against Franco's rebels and the German and Italian fascists who manipulated them? Didn't he realize that not to act was to invite the spread of fascist dictatorships? The president calmed their passion as best he could, but would make no promises. They emerged with the sense that Roosevelt favored the right side, and the beginnings of an awareness that he was powerless to act on his convictions, since his hands were tied by the Neutrality Act.

Neither Conant nor Roosevelt lost any respect for MacLeish as a consequence of his early and vehement conviction that the United States must go to war. His stance did alienate a great many people, however, including literary artists determined to steer clear of political issues, and right-wingers and fallen-away communists suspicious of his apparent adherence to the party line emanating from Soviet Russia. In his April 1937 article "The Struggle in Spain," the second in the *Fortune* series *Background of War,* MacLeish sought to differentiate his position from that of the party regulars. "The real struggle of our time," he declared, was not between communism and fascism "but the much more fundamental struggle between democratic institutions on the one side and all forms of dictatorship, whatever the dictator's label, on the other." The lesson of Spain was that the dictatorships most to be feared were those of Nazi Germany and fascist Italy.

Radio and Photograph

At seven o'clock on the evening of April 11, 1937, Orson Welles's orotund voice delivered the first lines of MacLeish's verse play *The Fall of the City* to a nationwide CBS radio audience. The setting was the city of Tenochtitlán, where, legend had it, a woman had risen from the grave to warn of the coming of a conquering army. On the radio, however, neither the place nor the time was specified. What MacLeish had in mind was a play-as-parable, conveying how easily people anywhere could be persuaded to accept what they construed to be their fate.

Welles, in the role of the announcer, provides an eyewitness view of events in the great square where the citizens assemble. He sees the woman rise from the tomb and utter her dire prophecy:

> *The city of masterless men*
> *Will take a master.*
> *There will be shouting then:*
> *Blood after!*

Next a messenger arrives with the news that a conqueror has landed. The assembled crowd grows panicky, but a pacifist assures them that reason and truth will win out and there is no need to resist. Amid further reports of the conqueror's progress, a group of priests counsels the fearful people to renounce the things of this world.

> *In the day of despair when the heart's bare:*
> *Turn to your gods!*

Only a veteran soldier speaks out in opposition to the pacifist and the priests. There is nothing worse than doing the strong man's will, he tells the people. "The free will fight for their freedom." But the citizens are not persuaded to fight, for they believe the enemy to be invincible. "The city is doomed!" they conclude, and bow down before the conqueror as he walks into the square, his armor clanking. There they remain prostrate so that only the announcer can see that the armor houses no one.

> The helmet is hollow.
> The metal is empty.
> The armor is empty.
> I tell you there is no
> One at all there.

The Fall of the City was the first verse play written for radio, a medium that came into its own in the thirties. During the first six months of 1937, for instance, international audiences heard King Edward VIII renounce the throne of England for the sake of the woman he loved, Franklin Delano Roosevelt insist that we had nothing to fear but fear itself, and a horrified announcer describe the burning of the dirigible *Hindenburg* as it prepared to land. Radios were selling at a rate of 10 million annually. Whole families gathered around their sets to listen to Edgar Bergen and Charlie McCarthy, Major Bowes and the "Amateur Hour," Amos and Andy, Jack Benny and Mary Livingston. MacLeish's play ran opposite the "Jack Benny Show" on Saturday night, yet it commanded an audience of tremendous size. According to Frank Brady, "More people heard the message of a single poet and a single poem that night than at any other time in history." Most of them were hardly aware that it was poetry they were listening to. The imagination took over and transported them to the square, where the announcer and the pacifist and the priests and the others painted a picture for their ears.

MacLeish's half-hour play was one of the first broadcasts of the Columbia Workshop, CBS's experimental division under the leadership of Irving Reis and Norman Corwin. The show was produced cheaply, with Welles and Burgess Meredith working for low wages and a small army of New Jersey women and schoolchildren persuaded to occupy the Seventh Regiment Armory and produce the required crowd noises at their own expense. Yet it is still regarded by some historians of the medium as "the best thing ever to originate in the workshop — or in radio theater as a whole." The network proudly put out a leaflet of laudatory comments from the audience. "After a few moments," one listener wrote, "I closed my eyes and was actually in the Square. There was no microphone; gone was my receiving set — both obliterated." Another commented that never before had she been so stirred "by a little black box which stands on my bookshelves and habitually pours forth a stream of advertising, swing, and Negro comics." Also in the audience was an aspiring dramatist named Arthur Miller, who concluded that "radio . . . was made for poetry and MacLeish lifted it to a gorgeous level." A few months later CBS rebroadcast the play, this time from the Hollywood Bowl.

The new medium of radio served MacLeish's purposes well. In no other way could he have delivered his warning against the fascist oppressors to so many people in so many corners of the country. And his warning, like that of the woman risen from the tomb, proved prophetic when the Nazi tanks clanked into Austria in March 1938, meeting scarcely any opposition. By that time MacLeish was at work on another half-hour radio play on a similar theme. *Air Raid*, broadcast October 27, 1938, by the CBS Columbia Workshop, once again depicted the advent of a conqueror, except that this one hurls destruction from the skies on innocent women and children. The inspiration for the play was Picasso's famous painting *Guernica*, with its vivid rendering of the German bombing of that undefended Spanish city in April 1937. When he first saw Picasso's images — "the dead child and the shrieking woman, the kneeling woman, the running woman, the stabbed horse, the shattered soldier, the arrogant triumphant bull" — MacLeish immediately began to hear the carnage in his mind's ear. *Air Raid* was a product of his outrage.

As with *The Fall of the City*, the play uses the device of an on-the-spot announcer (Ray Collins, from Welles's Mercury Theater), reporting on the anticipated slaughter in some contemporary but undesignated country. Dawn has come, the announcer says, and the town goes about its ordinary business:

> *They are flushing the cobblestones with water*
> *The sidewalks are slippery with sun.*
> *It smells of a summer morning anywhere:*
> *It smells of seven o'clock in the morning in*
> *Any town they water dust in.*

Broadcast four days before the famous *War of the Worlds* used the same technique of apparently reliable reportage by an announcer to frighten thousands into believing that an invasion of Martians was under way, MacLeish's *Air Raid* lacked the specificity of Orson Welles's adaptation of H. G. Wells's story. Welles's Martians land in New Jersey and proceed toward New York, with bulletins relating their progress. MacLeish's planes come from no particular enemy and bomb no particular place: what he wanted to convey was the generic horror of modern warfare, where women and children become the innocent victims of technological monsters.

In his play's town the women gossip about their farms and their men and their clothes as they go about their work. When the siren sounds, a police sergeant tries to herd them into cellars. But, they ask, who will look after the cleaning and the cooking and the childbearing? War was men's occupation, the women insist; let them look to it. Even when the planes arrive in formation, they will not scare. They go into the marketplace to show their skirts and shawls — "It's us, do you see!" — as death rains from the air. The sergeant had been right. "It may have been thought: this enemy kills women / Meaning to kill them!" But until it happens, no one will listen to him. Like *The Fall of the City, Air Raid* achieved an "intolerable timeliness." The October broadcast, according to *Time,* provided a "straight projection" of the Nazi *Anschluss* against Czechoslovakia the month before.

Both radio plays appeared in inexpensive printed editions as well, and so attracted critical attention. Generally, the reviews praised the capacity of the plainspoken verse to recreate the experience of war. "This is not *an* air raid but all air raids," the *Christian Century* declared, "the announcement, the incredulity, the expectation, the suspense, the diminishing margin of minutes — ten, six, three — the crescendo of sound, the piercing shriek, the single questing voice — silence." To some tastes, though, *Air Raid* read and sounded like "fear-mongering." That was the phrase Louise Bogan used in writing to Rolfe Humphries, both of them charter members of the Anti-MacLeish Club. "Working it all out psychologically," she commented, "I *should say* that he is now ready to murder some women, subconsciously."

With *Air Raid,* MacLeish abandoned his career as a radio dramatist. It was stimulating to reach an audience in the hundreds of thousands. "But just think," he said. "It takes half a year of work to write such a performance and radio saps its value in thirty minutes. On the stage it might run for months." Besides, he was stimulated by the work then being performed on the stage, in particular the gritty realism of such playwrights as Clifford Odets. Archie kept in touch with the dramatic world through his friendship with Houseman and Welles, both of whom were involved in putting on Marc Blitzstein's operetta *The Cradle Will Rock*. Blitzstein's plot line drew an analogy between a down-and-out prostitute selling her body and American working men required to sell themselves to big business in order to survive.

The Cradle Will Rock was financed by the WPA Federal Arts Project,

SETTLING IN CONWAY

The MacLeishes returned to the United States in 1928 and moved into the house in Conway, Massachusetts — Uphill Farm — that was to be their home for more than half a century. At left, Ada and Archie fell a tree with a crosscut saw, and Archie prepares to toss a stick for the family dog, Finn McCool, to fetch. Below, MacLeish is shown with a basket of peaches grown on the property.

AT SEA WITH ERNEST

Hemingway, MacLeish said, was an "impossible friend," yet the two men were close companions in Paris, and Ernest repeatedly invited Archie to join him in Key West for fishing expeditions on the Gulf Stream. Above, fishing on Hemingway's boat with Captain Bra Saunders, c. 1930, MacLeish appears to have made a strike. Twenty years later, the serious deep-sea fisherman Hemingway sent Archie and Ada a picture of "one of the big ones" he brought in.

ON ASSIGNMENT

MacLeish saw a great deal of the United States and traveled to Europe, Asia, and South America during his nine years with Henry Luce's *Fortune*. In 1935 (right) he spent the winter wheat season in Montana with farmer Tom Campbell. The following year (below) Adele Lovett accompanied Ada and Archie on a journey to Japan. MacLeish and fellow *Fortune* staffer Wilder Hobson wrote the entire special issue of September 1936 devoted to that country.

THE OUTDOOR LIFE

During summer vacations, the MacLeishes forgathered in Conway to work the farm and explore the territory. At left, Archie in his work gloves strides along with son Bill; below, sons Kenneth and Bill bend their bows, c. 1938 and 1940. According to neighbor Warren Harris, the lads were regular hellions in their youth.

CALL OF DUTY

During 1938 and 1939 MacLeish directed
the beginning Nieman program, which
brought practicing journalists to study at
Harvard. He is shown above with the first
Nieman fellows, among them the irreverent
and hatless Edwin A. Lahey. Felix
Frankfurter, at left below, was instrumental
in President Roosevelt's decision to call
MacLeish to Washington as librarian of
Congress, while Dean Acheson, beside him,
used his connections in Congress to help
insure confirmation. At right, Robert Frost
links arms with Archie at the 1940 Bread
Loaf conference. Two years earlier, Frost
started a small fire to disrupt MacLeish's
reading there.

ON THE JOB, 1942

In three photos from that year, Librarian of Congress MacLeish supervises the morning staff meeting in his office, chats with dancer Martha Graham and LC benefactor Gertrude Clarke Whittall (his black eye came from a run-in with a crowbar at his home in Alexandria), and lunches with President Roosevelt and Mrs. Samuel Rosenman at the presidential retreat, Shangri-La (later called Camp David).

THURSA BAKEY SANDERS

MARGARET SUCKLEY COLLECTION, FDR LIBRARY

WAGING PEACE

In December 1944, MacLeish was sworn in as assistant secretary of state as part of a reorganization fashioned by President Roosevelt. The new team, above, included Will L. Clayton, Dean Acheson, Joseph C. Grew, Secretary of State Edward R. Stettinius, MacLeish, Nelson Rockefeller, and James C. Dunn. MacLeish's job was to persuade the American people of the need for worldwide cooperation toward peace. At the conclusion of the United Nations conference in San Francisco in 1945, Archie and his right-hand man, Adlai Stevenson, took a one-day trip to Yosemite Park. They are shown, dwarfed by the falls, with MacLeish's valued secretary, Thursa Bakey, between them, and an unidentified man at left. Later that year, MacLeish and Ellen Wilkinson, representing Great Britain, signed the constitution of UNESCO in London.

NINETIETH BIRTHDAY

On August 17, 1946, the children and grandchildren of Martha Hillard MacLeish assembled at Craigie Lea to honor her ninetieth birthday. Archie thought of his mother as one of the great North American women, "no doubt about that," and from her he inherited boundless energy and an obligation to serve the republic. The two of them are shown at right, while in the photo above are Mrs. MacLeish, her stepson, Bruce — like his father, president of Carson Pirie Scott in Chicago — Ishbel, Norman, and Archie.

which withdrew its support prior to the sold-out performance in June 1937. The doors of the Maxine Elliott Theater were padlocked and guarded by federal authorities when the irate first nighters arrived. But at the last minute Welles and Houseman located an empty theater twenty blocks away, loaded an old piano into a truck, and marched the audience to what Archie thought "the most exciting evening of theater this New York generation has seen." Blitzstein himself sat down at the piano under a dusty spotlight and began to introduce his play. He thought he was going to have to act out all the parts himself, since Actors Equity would not permit the performers to take the stage. "A street corner — Steeltown, U.S.A.," Blitzstein began, but when he launched into the prostitute's song in his raspy voice, actress Olive Stanton stood up in one of the boxes and took the words from his mouth. For the rest of the evening, the actors picked up cues and played their roles from their seats. The audience was enthralled, perhaps because — as MacLeish speculated — the Brechtian device by which the actors admitted they were actors actually added to the "honest realism" of the production.

In April 1938 MacLeish published *Land of the Free*, which used yet another popular medium — a "book of photographs illustrated by a poem" — to communicate his ideas to a far-ranging sweep of the American people. The book consisted of 88 photographs and 338 lines of free verse called the "sound track." Most of the photos were drawn from the collection of the Farm Security Administration, which had hired some of the nation's most talented artists to record the devastating effects of the depression. Dorothea Lange took 31 of the 88 photos used; others came from Walker Evans, Arthur Rothstein, and Ben Shahn. The title carried a burden of irony, for what did picture after picture of sharecroppers and homesteaders on relief and migrant fruit pickers and child laborers, shown in an environment of ramshackle dwellings and eroding grain fields, have to do with the Land of the Free?

MacLeish's spare, colloquial verse ran alongside this documentation of human misery. The poor and downtrodden speak with a collective voice in the first-person plural; their refrain is, "We don't know, we're wondering." Would the dream of freedom die with the dust storms and the vanished jobs? In proletarian fashion, MacLeish suggests that freedom may have disappeared along with prosperity. Even the right to assemble and to petition seems to have withered away, at least for working people on the picket lines:

> *. . . try it in South Chicago Memorial Day*
> *With the mick police on the prairie in front of the factory*

> *Gunning you down from behind and for what?*
> *For liberty?*
> . . . .
> *. . . try it at River Rouge with the Ford militia.*
> *Try it if Mister Ford's opinions are otherwise,*
> *Try it and see where you land with your back broken . . .*

In *Land of the Free*, MacLeish attempted to find words for the purgatory of the depression, for what had happened to American hopes and expectations. The voice that utters his words is all but defeated. "It was pretty hard to feel any hope about those people," he said. "They felt very little about themselves." Nonetheless, there is a hint that the skies may clear at the end. The last four pictures show a May Day procession, a union meeting, the celebration of the end of a strike, and a Dust Bowl farmer.

> *We wonder if the liberty is done: . . .*

they ask. Then, they speculate, perhaps "there's liberty a man can mean that's / Men, not land." And finally they end in doubt:

> *We wonder*
> *We don't know*
> *We're asking.*

Reviews of the book all remarked on the power of the photographs. As Archie later said, the "cameras caught something more than just eroded land. They caught eroded human beings." As for MacLeish's "sound track," one critic thought it somewhat contrived, yet another so admired its fusion with the photographs that he thought the book "ought to be got into the hands of every man, woman, and child in the United States."

Yeats, Frost, and "Public Speech"

In the spring of 1937, Archie spent six weeks at Princeton as "a visiting member of the faculty." His duties, as envisioned by Dean Christian Gauss, involved giving a series of lectures on contemporary literature, meeting informally with students in groups to discuss aesthetic and political controversies, and seeing them individually to critique their writing. This "poet-in-residence" experiment, financed by the Carnegie Corporation, proved less than satisfactory. One problem was that MacLeish was on campus for only six weeks, and only in the evenings, since he continued his *Fortune* duties during the day in New York.

Another was that the students who turned out for the evening lectures and open houses and consultations received no academic credit for their time and effort. Nonetheless, the university and the poet parted friends. MacLeish gave Princeton the manuscript of his play *Panic* as a farewell gesture.

To his alma mater, Yale, in December 1937, he made the more substantial gift of the manuscript of *Conquistador*. The next month, on January 7, 1938, he presented the Francis Bergen lecture, "Public Speech and Private Speech in Poetry," to a packed audience at Sprague Hall. The same day, an exhibition of his works opened at the Yale University Library, with a catalogue prepared by Arthur Mizener. With wry modesty, Archie downplayed the exhibition. "There is a point beyond which mediocrity cannot be inflated to look like the real thing," he wrote, "and I think that point has been well reached at Yale in the Rare Book Room." What he had to say in his Bergen lecture, however, was dead serious and from the heart.

"Public Speech and Private Speech in Poetry" represented MacLeish's most extended endorsement of the need for artists to speak with a public voice. To support that contention, MacLeish declared that the greatest ages of poetic creation had always been characterized by public speech. Milton and Dante had always written of the great world and its trials and opportunities. In contrast, he viewed with scorn the British poets of the nineteenth century, both the Victorian "teacup" poet and that ridiculous figure "the private speaker, the whisperer to the heart, the unworldly romantic, the quaint bohemian, the young man with the girl's eyes."

Modern poetry was in the process of re-establishing its connection with the actual world, engaged in "a struggle to regain that conception of poetry in which a poem, like a war or an edict, is an action on this earth." The way had been prepared by Eliot and Pound, who had begun to move in the right direction, and especially by Yeats, the "best of modern poets," who knew better than to claim his difference from other men. "He is quite simply a man who is a poet," MacLeish stated. Yet even Yeats balked at moving into the area "where the poetic revolution crosses the revolution in the social and political and economic structure of the post-war world." To underscore the point, MacLeish invoked Thomas Mann's comment that for our time "the destiny of man presents its meaning in political terms."

The following year, in his essay "Poetry and the Public World," Archie went on to contend that in our time there was no true separation between the private and public realms. "Indeed the public world with us has *become* the private world, and the private world has become the public. . . . The single individual, whether he so wishes or not, has become a part of a world which contains also Austria and Czechoslovakia and China and Spain. The victories of tyrants and the resistance of peoples halfway round the world are as near to him as the ticking of the clock on the mantel. What happens in his morning paper happens in his blood all day." It remained for poetry to communicate that sense of involvement. Despite the warnings of the literary dilettantes to avoid such matters, "the real wonder [was] that poetry should deal so little with a public world which concerns it so much."

The Yale students who heard his Bergen lecture rose to give MacLeish a standing ovation. Here, they must have thought, was a poet who *mattered*. His message was not universally applauded, however. Walter Prichard Eaton, also in the audience, drew from his talk the annoying implication "that the individual doesn't count, the mass is all, and that art which doesn't concern itself with the economic and social regeneration of mankind simply isn't art — it's teacups." And William Butler Yeats himself took exception in the form of his poem "Politics," published in January 1939, the last year of his life. "Politics" was a direct response to MacLeish's observation that Yeats was too depoliticized to write the kind of poetry — public speech — the times demanded. Yeats even used the Thomas Mann quote about the destiny of modern man presenting itself in political terms as an epigraph to his poem.

> How can I, that girl standing there,
> My attention fix
> On Roman or on Russian
> Or on Spanish politics,
> Yet here's a travelled man that knows
> What he talks about,
> And there's a politician
> That has both read and thought,
> And maybe what they say is true
> Of war and war's alarms,
> But O that I were young again
> And held her in my arms.

It is hard to conceive of a more eloquent rebuttal to the argument for public speech than Yeats's moving poem of private feeling. But by no means did he speak for all, or even most, writers of the time. Many of them found MacLeish's political conviction and manifest humanitarianism exceedingly attractive. When he came to read at the Bread Loaf Writers' Conference on August 27, 1938, he was greeted by an enthusiastic and receptive group of listeners. Under the leadership of Theodore Morrison and Bernard DeVoto, Bread Loaf was the nation's leading summer conference for aspiring writers. The uncrowned but universally recognized King of Bread Loaf was Robert Frost. Frost, who had opened the 1938 session with a reading of his own the week before, was not happy about the climate of adulation surrounding MacLeish's evening. He did not welcome apparent pretenders to his throne (not that anyone in attendance would have disputed his title). And in his conviction that "griefs, not grievances" were the stuff of poetry, he could hardly have disagreed more completely with Archie's literary-political stance. Moreover, Frost was at the time suffering through the sorrow of his wife's recent death. But for whatever reasons, he behaved very badly on the night of August 27.

At MacLeish's reading Frost sat near the back, twisting a pile of mimeographed notices and occasionally gesturing with them to indicate his reaction to a particular line or phrase. Midway through the reading, he said, in a stage whisper, "Archie's poems all have the same *tune*." Then he began to rustle the papers in his hand loudly enough to cause some disturbance. Nonetheless, the reading went on successfully. When MacLeish announced his much-admired "You, Andrew Marvell," murmurs of approval emanated from the assemblage. At this stage, Frost had had enough; he somehow managed to set fire to his batch of papers, and commanded everyone's attention as he beat out the fire and waved away the smoke.

Nor was the King of Bread Loaf through for the evening. After the reading, a number of conferees adjourned to a cottage where drinks were served, and MacLeish was persuaded to read his radio play *Air Raid*. Once again, Frost's back went up. He rattled his ice cubes and intruded with comments that began as friendly joking and went on to barbed attacks. Finally DeVoto said something like, "For God's sake, Robert, let him read!" Archie, who must have understood Frost's feelings, chose not to take offense. At the end of the evening, he came over to talk with Frost. "Jesus H. Christ, Robert," he told him. "You're the foundation and we all know it." That was what he needed to hear, Frost replied. He was an old man, he said, and he wanted to be flattered. Then they chatted about less personal matters amicably enough. "God-damn everything to hell so long as we're friends, Archie," Frost remarked in parting. Years later MacLeish summed up his feelings about the great poet. Frost, he said, was "like a horse you could get along with if you came up beside him from the okay side."

An End of *Fortune*

MacLeish's passionate commitment to the Loyalist cause in the Spanish civil war played a part in another falling-out in the long quarrel that was his friendship with Hemingway, and in his resignation from *Fortune*. The Hemingway dispute involved money. Ernest had contributed generously to underwrite the costs of making *The Spanish Earth*. For his investment in the film he was issued unsecured "pro-rata notes paid if as and when" any profits were available. Then, in the summer of 1938, Ernest met Ralph ("Mac") Ingersoll, who was vacationing in Key West, and discovered that Ingersoll, Luce's right-hand editorial man at Time Inc., and Luce himself had been given preferred notes for *their* cash, so that they would be repaid ahead of other investors. At this point Hemingway decided that MacLeish had cheated him, and recollected that someone — perhaps Joris Ivens — had promised him that for his last $1,000 of support, he would be paid back "out of the first money the film brought in." MacLeish knew that he had made no such guarantee to Hemingway, and had done so in the case of Ingersoll and Luce only because of a last-minute financial emergency: creditors were pressing, and it seemed possible that the film might have to be scrapped entirely unless funds were raised in a hurry. It was difficult to understand Ernest's apparent rancor, Archie wrote to Ingersoll, for initially he'd had to persuade Hemingway to take a note at all.

On July 28, 1938, Ernest wrote Archie a particularly snide letter. MacLeish's contribution to the film (aside from time and energy) had been a paltry one hundred dollars, Hemingway pointed out, and he enclosed a check for twenty dollars to defray even that cost. Feelings between MacLeish and Hemingway were further strained at this time by Archie and Ada's disapproval of his impending divorce from Pauline and his ongoing affair with Martha Gellhorn. In addition, Hemingway was going through an exceedingly cranky period, even for him, that saw his friendship with Dos Passos end in bitter recriminations. For Ada, at least, his behavior in connection with *The Spanish Earth* was the last straw. "I wish to state in writing," she announced, "that the MacLeish family . . . will find it entirely convenient to stay out of Pappy's way for all time."

Archie, however, was inclined to forgive and try to forget yet again. "I knew you did not think very well of me — or as well as you had," he wrote Hemingway early in August 1938, in response to the hundred-dollars letter. "But it seemed to me absolutely incredible that you should think me dishonest." Archie assured Ernest that his support of *The Spanish Earth* had been crucial. "You put much more money into it than any other individual and you did much more about it than any one except Joris himself," he wrote by way of appreciation and calming the waters.

Archie might also have pointed out, but did not, that in the two previous months he had waged a small campaign against the suppression of Hemingway's novel *To Have and Have Not* in Detroit. The book was banned from the bookstores and libraries of that city because of complaints from the Catholic church. The real reason for the suppression, according to MacLeish, was Hemingway's "known sympathy for the Spanish Government in the civil war in Spain," where the Catholic church had aligned itself with Franco's forces. So he argued in an open letter sent first to the *New York Times,* which refused to print it on the grounds that the suppression was under court consideration, and then to the *Nation,* where Max Lerner was delighted to run it. Behind the scenes, MacLeish wrestled with the League of American Writers about the proper form of his letter. The league wanted it to come as from their organization, MacLeish as from individual writers. In the end, the letter of protest was co-signed by Van Wyck Brooks and Thornton Wilder and concluded its argument with language Archie insisted upon: "We put this with cogent emphasis not only as members of the League of American Writers but as individuals; not only as writers but as American citizens."

As early as February 1936, Walter Winchell had alerted readers of his nationally syndicated column to the stirrings of trouble in the Luce publishing empire. "Some *Fortune* eds are liberals," Winchell reported. "They are said to be alarmed over *Time*'s 'Fascist attitude.' " From inside the Chrysler Building, MacLeish spoke as one of the liberals — the others included Eric Hodgins, Wilder Hobson, Dwight Macdonald, Charles Wertenbaker, and Allen Grover — who thought *Time* was losing the impartiality a newsmagazine ought to maintain. "We think *Time* is an indispensable adjunct to American living," MacLeish wrote Luce after the Winchell column appeared. "We think it is beautifully edited. We know damn well we couldn't do the job as well. But there is enough truth in the Winchell dope — however he came by it — to call for names and numbers." Along with his memo, Archie included Macdonald's documentation of "the names and numbers": examples of *Time*'s bias.

This bias became flagrantly obvious following the outbreak of war between President Manuel Azaña's leftist government and Francisco Franco's right-wing challengers in Spain. Laird ("Goldie") Goldsborough, foreign news editor of *Time,* was manifestly pro-Franco — and so, if he could help it, would be the readers of *Time.* Azaña was described by *Time* as "frog-faced" and "obese and blotchy." He was quoted as having said of himself, "The only person whose views are always correct is Azaña!" He was characterized as a coward who stole out of Madrid as soon as the bombs started to fall. Franco, by contrast, was a soft-spoken, serious man of "soldierly simplicity," yet blessed with humor.

Instead of calling the government forces Republicans or Loyalists, *Time* referred to them as "Reds." Similarly, those who fought for Franco were not rebels but "Whites." Nor did *Time* alter its tune when the Germans and the Italians sent their troops and their planes to aid the "smiling Generalissimo Franco." Goldsborough had established the pro-Mussolini line at the time of his attack on Ethiopia. Haile Selassie was "squealing for protection" in this "dreary little war," *Time* informed its readers. Besides, weren't "Socialists, Communists and rattle-brained Liberals" from around the world enlisting in the International Brigades to fight for the "Reds"?

It did not take a genius at propaganda analysis to decide which way the magazine was tilting. By heritage Luce was inclined to favor Goldie and the fascists. They had both the rich and the religious on their side, and as the child of a missionary he had grown up with a devout respect for both groups. Nonetheless, MacLeish eagerly set about trying to convert Luce to his views. In a series of memos, he and Goldie contended for the heart and mind of Harry Luce. MacLeish objected to *Time*'s "presentation of the Spanish civil war as though it were some sort of spontaneous cockfight between Whites and Reds." Objective journalism, he insisted, would have made it clear that Franco's fascists, backed by landowners and by the church, were the unjustified aggressors against a lawfully elected government. For Goldsborough, however, the government's partisans were simply "Communists" and Franco's supporters "men of property, men of God and men of the sword."

Basically the dispute boiled down to whether the contending camps were properly understood as the communists versus the fascists, as Goldsborough believed, or the "Fascist International" versus the democracies, as in MacLeish's formulation. Archie's views on this issue, Goldsborough pointed out to Luce, precisely matched those of the Soviet ambassador in Washington. He always enjoyed "the suave writings" of MacLeish, once he got around to reading them, but thought that his articles, like most in *Fortune,* went on far too long. MacLeish was not easily daunted, however. Admiring Luce as he did, Archie chose to consider him an unconscious liberal, "a progressive . . . meant to make common cause with the people." Therefore Archie organized a dinner for Luce at the Century Club in December 1937, where other guests such as Felix Frankfurter and President William Allan Neilson of Smith College were to awaken his presumably dormant liberalism. But this dinner, like others Archie would arrange in the future, was unable to make a small-*d* democrat out of Henry Luce. He never openly declared himself on the issue of the Spanish civil war. But neither did he take any steps to stop Goldie's slanting of foreign news in *Time* magazine.

Outraged by *Time*'s continuing profascist bias, Dwight Macdonald quit at *Fortune*. MacLeish stayed on, adopting the position shared by Allen Grover that "wicked and irresponsible" as Goldie was, Luce was not entirely to blame since he was "rather naive about politics." Throughout 1937 Archie angled for a raise and/or a promotion in the ranks of *Fortune*. In the late 1930s he had arrived at a work schedule that kept him on the job for nine months a year, with a three-month summer in Conway for his poetry. His salary was about $15,000 a year, which made him one of the highest-paid journalists in the country. He was also given some stock in Time Inc. as a reward for his efforts.

Still, Archie could not help feeling envious of other, younger men who were earning larger salaries in editorial and administrative positions. Time Inc., he observed in retrospect, was a highly competitive institution, "a real rat race" where people "would cut your throat as soon as look at you." Unattractive as this atmosphere was, Archie could not resist entering the competition, and so he regularly badgered Luce about higher pay. In a May 1937 letter he summed up for his boss what was troubling him. Was *Fortune* "going to be able to make provision for a writer who, for whatever reason, wished to remain a writer but who, malgré tout, was getting older & facing heavier expenses & who, malgré tout, had a certain personal competitive sense?" It was hard to believe that the company should reward a man doing the actual productive work of writing the magazine less than "the same man doing something *about* the production of the magazine." But that, he supposed, was the way business hierarchies structured themselves, and he was stuck on the pyramid like everyone else. Either he had to climb the pyramid or get off. Since he couldn't do the climbing and continue to write his poetry on extended leaves, he proposed getting off, or at least changing his status from an editor of *Fortune* to an outside contributor.

Luce talked Archie out of that halfhearted attempt at resignation, and may have encouraged him to play a larger role in editorial policy. In October 1937, at any rate, Archie presented Luce (along with Mitch Davenport and Eric Hodgins) with a proposal to brighten *Fortune* by using shorter, livelier articles in the front of the book and moving supporting data to appendixes in the back. Specifically, he recommended that for each article writer-researcher teams should produce about 10,000 words, and then the writer should boil that copy down to 2,500 words by concentrating on the "interesting and exciting and intriguing aspects of the material." Whatever hard data were cut in the rewrite could then be packaged as reference material, along with an acknowledgment of sources consulted. In everything except practicality it was an excellent proposal. Almost everyone agreed that *Fortune* articles were far too bulky, at times even soporific. But few *Fortune* staffers were as prolific as MacLeish, and practically none of them would have been willing to write 10,000 words per article in order to delete three-fourths of them.

If he did not, like Mac Ingersoll, reach the top of the Time Inc. pyramid, MacLeish was at least allowed to cover what stories he chose. In the winter of 1938, he chose to "take over" the last two parts of a four-part series on South America. By way of preparation, he spent nearly three months in Chile and Argentina, from mid-January to April 1938. Accompanying him as researcher was the beautiful young Catherine Carr, who was selected for the assignment for two reasons. She had a good command of Spanish, and she and Archie were lovers. According to her friend Lael Wertenbaker, Catherine was a warm, vivacious, and very bright young woman who "went through *Fortune* like a whirl-wind." After Archie she had an affair with Mitch Davenport, and eventually she married another *Fortune* hand, Fred Rodell. The liaison with MacLeish broke up at least in part, Catherine told Lael, because Archie took himself — and, probably, their relationship — too seriously.

Whether or not this in-house romance influenced his decision, soon after his return to New York, MacLeish resigned from *Fortune*, effective June 30. He left in order to accept the post James Bryant Conant offered him as curator (director) of the new Nieman journalism program at Harvard. The job paid substantially less than he was making at *Fortune*, but it was to be half-time, leaving MacLeish free to write more of his poetry and plays. His departure occasioned an exchange of letters with Harry Luce. He was sorry they hadn't seen more of each other in the past few years, Luce wrote Archie on July 18, 1938. Then he rhetorically inquired, "Do I need to say how much I appreciate your splendid work on FORTUNE during all this time?" In reply, Archie told his former boss that the answer was yes, Luce did need to say as much, and oftener. The last piece of his Harry had praised was "The Grasslands," and that had run nearly three years earlier, in November 1935. Once there had been a real camaraderie at *Fortune*, but the company had grown enormously and become more impersonal, so that now "not more than a dozen or so people know each other's names." More than ever before, then, Luce *did* need to tell his associates when their work was good. This vehement response may have surprised Luce. Certainly it surprised Mac Ingersoll, who had been Archie's managing editor at one time. "It would never have occurred to me to tell Archie that I admired his work," Ingersoll said. "Everyone at *Fortune* took his superiority for granted, including Luce and myself and his fellow writers." Neither Luce nor Ingersoll understood how eagerly Archie had sought to be rewarded for his accomplishments since the childhood days when his father ignored them. Six years MacLeish's junior, Luce was hardly a father figure, but he was a figure of authority whose articulated approval meant a great deal to Archie.

MacLeish must have been pleased, therefore, when Luce's letter of September 1 reached him in Conway. The previous fall, Harry said, he had come up with the idea of an editorial page for *Fortune*, "and another of my ideas was that you might be persuaded to be The Editor of FORTUNE, specifically responsible for the contents of that page." That had not happened yet, but it might someday, and he wanted Archie to know about the possibility. Obviously Luce was holding the door open a crack for MacLeish's possible return. Just as clearly, Archie did not slam it shut. It was "heart-warming" to hear of Luce's plans for him, he replied, and good to know that something might develop in the future. But most of Archie's letter had to do with the wedding of his son Kenneth to Carolyn de Chadenèdes, which had taken place in Conway on Wednesday, September 7. The weather had not cooperated.

> Tuesday was a beautiful day
> Thursday was also brilliant
> The wedding was Wednesday

Still, it was a tremendous thing to see the marriage of "a pair of incredibly beautiful children of twenty one and twenty with not a cent between them." Archie cried "like a — well what DOES cry that way?"

The Nieman Year

When the $1.35 million bequest landed on his desk in 1937, Harvard's President Conant was naturally pleased. But the gift came with strings. Agnes W. Nieman, the donor, specified that the money was to be used in honor of her late husband, Lucius, the founder of the *Milwaukee Journal,* "to promote and elevate standards of journalism in the United States and educate people deemed especially qualified for journalism." How should these ends be realized? The last thing Conant wanted to do was to start another journalism school, so he cast around for alternative ideas. The library sensibly proposed building a collection of journalistic texts and extending its newspaper and magazine holdings by way of microfilm. But that took only a small portion of the funds. The rest, Conant decided, might best be spent along the model established by the Littauer program. With a gift from Lucius Littauer, Harvard had set up a graduate center in public administration where selected government representatives came to study. The same thing, Conant reasoned, could be done for working journalists as for working government employees, with one important difference. The Littauer fellows were working toward graduate degrees. The Nieman fellows, as Conant envisioned them, would receive no academic credit for their studies, but neither would they be restricted by any special degree requirements. When he proposed this plan to his board and then to a group of newspaper executives, it met with a lukewarm reception. But Conant found in MacLeish an eager supporter of his idea, and went ahead anyway.

The Nieman program, as Archie understood it, said to the nation's leading journalists: "Here is Harvard University, it is yours, you can use it in any way you want to and nothing will be required of you. . . . You will get no degree, what you have is the use of the university." That, he thought, was tremendously innovative and imaginative, and he was easily persuaded, since his career at *Fortune* seemed to have run its course, to take over as director. Conant's plan still needed fine-tuning. Anyone chosen for a Nieman fellowship, it was determined, should have at least three years' experience as a working journalist, by which — at least initially — was meant newspaperman. Each would be paid the same amount at Harvard as if on the job. Fellowships would last for only one year, after which the recipient must agree to return to his previous post. And the person in charge, bearing the burdensome title of "Curator of the Nieman Collection of Contemporary Journalism," was to function as "a guide, counselor, and friend" to the visiting journalists and as an intermediary between them and the university.

This was the job MacLeish began in September 1938, at a salary of $5,000, one-third of what he had been earning at *Fortune*. To save money, he moved in with newly married son Kenneth (who was studying for a master's degree in anthropology) and his bride in Cambridge, while Ada and the younger children lived in Farmington with her father. Archie's most immediate task, he found, was to persuade Harvard's eminent professors to accept the Nieman fellows as auditors in their classes. Some were suspicious of the motive or the sincerity of these newspaper people, who might disrupt class meetings, write scathing exposés, or otherwise make themselves nuisances. But Archie was persuasive, and located valuable allies for the cause in Felix Frankfurter of the law school and historian Arthur Schlesinger, Sr. The Nieman fellows themselves constituted their own best argument, however. From the very inception of the program these journalists made a significant contribution to the university with their curiosity, enthusiasm, and talent for expressing themselves. Archie explained their effect on Harvard by way of metaphor. "You know in the spring of the year when the lawn won't come up, the best thing to do is to go get a plank, drive ten penny nails through it, go around the lawn and pound the lawn and let air in it. I think the Nieman experiment . . . let more air into Harvard than anything that has happened in this century."

MacLeish also served as host and organizer of weekly dinners for the fellows. At each of these, a distinguished journalist talked briefly, followed by general off-the-record discussion. Occasionally faculty members with a special interest in the topic under discussion came along for these convivial gatherings. Frankfurter and Schlesinger were regulars. The group met at a restaurant in downtown Boston where the space was cramped but the food excellent. Mac Ingersoll, as the first outside speaker, outlined some of his ideas for the new daily newspaper that eventually became *PM*. John Gunther, who was second, spoke about foreign correspondence. Others included Walter Lippmann, Heywood Broun, Henry Luce, Alexander Woollcott, William Allen White, Harold Laski, and Raymond Gram Swing.

The initial Nieman group of nine newspapermen — five reporters and four editorial writers — was selected from a field of 309 applicants. Six were college graduates, three Phi Beta Kappas. Two had not finished college, and one had not gone beyond high school. The average age was thirty-one, and all had been in newspaper work for at least five years. Geographically they came from New England, the Middle Atlantic, the Middle West, and the South. Most had been employed by major newspapers such as the *Boston Globe, Chicago Daily News, St. Louis Post-Dispatch,* and *Baltimore Sun*. One was with the *Paducah* (Kentucky) *Sun-Democrat*. Whatever their origin, the Nieman fellows were drawn to Harvard's academic offerings like ants to sugar. Almost all of them attended courses in the social sciences, and everyone took at least five courses. The scholarly Frank Snowden Hopkins, a *Baltimore Sun* reporter, took ten, on subjects ranging from American constitutional government to Byzantine history. Archie went to see Conant about the Byzantine course. The entire year's work, he reasoned, would do no more than prepare Hopkins to write one general article on Constantinople in the eighth century. Should he discourage him? Certainly not, Conant replied. "We have offered him the university, and *that* is in the university." In fact, Hopkins found the course at least as valuable as the others he took. Byzantine history was particularly "suggestive for our times," he observed, because it presented "the record of a society which survived repeated crises through its ability to put through internal reforms at crucial periods in its eleven centuries of existence."

Louis Lyons of the *Boston Globe* had a similar experience studying medieval history under Gaetano Salvemini, the distinguished historian exiled from fascist Italy. Salvemini's lectures on the Italian city-state, he discovered, had relevance to "city machines anytime anywhere." Although he received no grades, Lyons wrote final exams in several courses, and elicited from the historian Samuel Eliot Morison a comment that "you newspapermen certainly know how to take examinations." Like about half of the Nieman fellows, Lyons participated in Felix Frankfurter's seminar in administrative law. The star of that seminar, and of the first batch of Nieman fellows, was thirty-six-year-old Edwin A. Lahey of the *Chicago Daily News,* a brilliant, tough-talking labor and crime reporter who had never previously spent a day on a college campus.

According to MacLeish, "Lahey was fresh as paint, and Irish enough to get away with it, but just barely." Within a few weeks, he knew most of the Cambridge cops by name and had relieved the other fellows of their excess funds in poker games. But he did not idle away his time at Harvard. In addition to courses with Frankfurter and Salvemini, Lahey took one in accounting and statistics. What was the point of that? Lyons asked him. "I'm going to know how to squeeze the water out of a municipal budget," Lahey replied. Interviewed by the *Harvard Crimson* after two weeks on campus, Lahey allowed that he was "daffy" about the place. "The Ivy has got me. There's something of the illusion of antiquity at Harvard that I've never had. . . . Do they allow you to bring whiskey into the dormitories?" Irreverence was his watchword, and he did not hesitate to do his own share of educating. In a talk at the Harvard Union, for instance, he advised the sons of rich families present to forget about making money and consider a career on behalf of labor instead. "In this stage of labor relations," he declared, "violence and the sitdown strike are the only weapons against repression."

When Lahey discovered a course he liked, his enthusiasm drew some of the other fellows along. Such was the case with Granville Hicks's tutorial in American history. Social critic and historian of American literature, Hicks was one of the "counsellors in American history" Conant appointed as an experiment for 1938–39. He was also an avowed communist, and before long his presence at Harvard created a furor. Alumni were outraged, and spoke in disgust of the "Kremlin on the Charles." The trouble began with a rally to raise funds for the *New Masses* on the evening of October 12, 1938. Before a crowd of four hundred, Hicks provided a short history of the magazine and passed the hat for contributions ranging from five-dollar bills to small change. Joseph North, a *New Masses* editor recently returned from Spain, spoke of seeing Harvard men there, fighting valiantly for the Loyalist cause. And MacLeish argued vigorously for a left-wing press in the United States, if only because it advanced views contrary to those of the majority. "Freedom of the press is only truly freedom of the press," he said, "when it protects those who would destroy freedom of the press."

The *New Masses* rally was widely reported in the Boston newspapers. Soon thereafter Hicks came under attack, and the feisty Lahey defended him in a letter to the metropolitan journals. The Boston press was guilty of wasting white space on an innocuous meeting in Cambridge, Lahey wrote. The reports of "public demands" for Hicks's resignation were especially suspect, because they were issued by those windbags who, every newspaper office knew, would express an opinion on anything for the sake of publicity. If the red-scare stories about Hicks had circulation appeal, he concluded, "Lord have mercy on Boston." Hicks stayed on the job, and left the Communist party the following year when the Soviet Union invaded Finland.

Two weeks after the *New Masses* meeting, MacLeish read from his poems as the first of three 1938–39 Morris Gray lecturers on modern poetry, with Frost and Mark Van Doren to succeed him. A few days later he traveled to the Midwest to talk at the University of Chicago, Rockford College, and the University of Iowa. His mother had a dinner for Archie at Craigie Lea, where one of the guests was Hadley Hemingway Mowrer, now the wife of Paul Mowrer, a colleague of Lahey's at the *Chicago Daily News*. In December, Archie was appointed, along with Morison and Frankfurter, to a fifteen-member national commission to plan for the conversion of FDR's Hyde Park, New York, estate to a presidential library. As Morison pointed out, "It will be the first complete and intact collection of records ever available to historians as it has been the custom of Presidents to take their papers with them." Early in January, Roosevelt chose Frankfurter to succeed the late Justice Benjamin Cardozo on the Supreme Court, a development that gave MacLeish a friend and mentor in the highest reaches of the government.

Considering the critical bombardment he was under at the time, Archie needed all the friends he could get. His persistent enemy Louise Bogan tore off a poem one night in the fall of 1938 in which she scathingly criticized the contemporary culture for failing to recognize true artists.

Come, drunks and drug-takers; come, perverts unnerved!
Receive the laurel, given, though late, on merit; to whom and wherever deserved.
Parochial punks, trimmers, nice people, joiners true-blue,
Get the hell out of the way of the laurel. It is deathless. And it isn't for you.

Although she had more than one road-blocking laurel-seeking time server in mind, MacLeish was high on her list. She sent the poem first to *her* mentor and friend, Edmund ("Bunny") Wilson, who liked it, and then to the *Partisan Review,* which printed it. Perhaps inspired by Bogan's effort, Wilson outdid her in a direct diatribe against MacLeish, a poet he and Bogan and Morton Dauwen Zabel had taken to referring to as "MacSlush."

On January 13, 1939, the *New Yorker* printed Wilson's brutal "The Omelet of A. MacLeish." In the time-honored tradition of parodies, Wilson's echoed the idiosyncracies of MacLeish's verse. "The Omelet" — the title an obvious pun on *The Hamlet of A. MacLeish* — is written in the terza rima without rhyme Archie used in *Conquistador;* his trademark all-purpose colons appear everywhere; his persistent self-questioning is made fun of, and catchphrases are repeated from well-known poems "(Señora, I could go on like this forever: / It is a strange thing to be an American)." All of this is done with the considerable skill one would expect of Wilson. But he went much further than the usual parodist to a direct assault on the talent and the character of "A. MacLeish." In Wilson's sixty-line diatribe, MacLeish is presumably preparing the omelet that constitutes his written corpus. He stuffs into it whatever he can of the work of others — the old charge of undue appropriation revisited, with malice.

> *Eliot alarmed me at first: but my later abasement:*
> *And the clean sun of France: and the freakish but beautiful fashion:*
> *Striped bathhouses bright on the sand: Anabase and The Waste*
> *   Land:*
>
> *These and the Cantos of Pound: O how they came pat!*
> *Nimble at other men's arts how I picked up the trick of it:*
> *Rode it reposed on it drifted away on it: . . .*

The other, and more damning charge was that MacLeish had trimmed his sails and refashioned his convictions to win the favor of others, particularly on the left. Thus, Wilson writes, though MacLeish's omelet has become "a national institution and gets into Fanny Farmer," he is still obliged to reopen it "and put a little garlic in" in order to "placate" the "shrieking outlandish reproaches" of the communists. Like them, he repeats the "fierce cries of 'Aesthete!' and 'Fascist!' " Like them, he rails at the "Bankers and builders of railroads." But MacLeish is not done shifting with the wind, Wilson declares. "Wired for sound," he "is doomed to go on doctoring his omelet." Perhaps the true poet "need not be a madman or even a bounder" (a veiled reference, very likely, to Archie's courting of his friend John Peale Bishop's wife). But surely he must be more than A. MacLeish himself, who is merely, in Wilson's closing lines,

A clean and clever lad
                    who is doing
                            his best
                                    to get on . . .

Wilson's attack was the most vicious and the most widely circulated
MacLeish had been subjected to. His immediate reaction was to fight
back. For a time he considered a lawsuit. Instead he launched some
private fire of his own in the form of letters to Bishop and Hemingway.
"When did Bunny Wilson's bile bladder burst, do you know?" he inquired of Bishop. "Seems to have gotten into his brain as well as all
over his hands." In writing Hemingway, who had also suffered from
Wilson's venomous criticism, he extended the burst-bladder metaphor.

A LETTER TO MR. HEMINGWAY
on the subject of Mr. Edmund (Bunny to his Princeton Club-
mates) Wilson, author of *The Triple Thinkers, I Thought of
Daisy* and various other works who, having declined to take part
in the wars has set himself up as a character-assassin behind the
lines.

> *As one on whom*
> *The Triple Stinker publicly hath stunk . . .*
> . . . .
> *Move over Hemingway. Your Spanish pants*
> *Are stained but there's no Wilson on your coat . . .*
> . . . .
> *The load you got was envy. Bad enough!*
> *The wounded ego of a man gone rotten*
> *Sticks to the pant-leg and will stain the stuff.*
> *But what you got was nothing to the blast I've gotten.*
>
> *I took the whole frustration on the nose —*
> *The wish to be a poet: the ambition*
> *To Think of Daisy in immortal prose*
> *The hope to publish in a limited edition*
> . . . .
> *Move over Ernest till I rinse my shirt*
> *And see for what they spend* New Yorker *money:*
> *The blast was like a mule's that feels the quirt.*
> *The nuisance . . .*
>   *Look!*
>   *It isn't even goat.*
>   *It's bunny.*

Undoubtedly envy did play some role in Wilson's visceral abhorrence
for MacLeish. Archie was entirely too successful for his own good at

almost everything he attempted, and it was easy for his enemies to suppose that he must have gained recognition by calculation and expediency rather than merit. Quite possibly, too, Wilson resented the connections Archie had acquired through his background and education ("The Omelet" evokes with mock solemnity "the shudder of Tap Day" at Yale). Then again, Wilson and MacLeish were very nearly temperamental opposites. Archie was publicly hearty and optimistic, Wilson shy of meeting others and extremely crusty in manner. In addition, Wilson may have felt it his duty as John Bishop's friend not to forgive MacLeish for his attentions to Margaret Bishop in Paris. Add to this their ideological differences — as a disillusioned former communist sympathizer, Wilson distrusted the advocates of an antifascist war — and there were reasons enough why Bunny should have vented his wrath on Archie. "Mention MacLeish," Donald Hall recalls, "and Wilson would draw his guns."

From the perspective of half a century and more, what is most striking about MacLeish's political stance in the 1930s is that he was right. When the democracies failed to intervene in Spain, they established a precedent that led to further piecemeal grabs by the fascist powers and eventually to war. What also seems clear is that Wilson was wrong about MacLeish: his views evolved more out of principled idealism than personal opportunism. It was true that in the early 1930s he advocated a nearly complete separation of art and politics, and that in the late 1930s he declared that poetry must be public rather than private speech. But the latter position grew logically out of the conviction, ingrained in him by heritage and reinforced by schooling, that the only life worth living was one of actual service.

MacLeish made common cause with the communists in the fight against international fascism, but he did not go out of his way to ingratiate himself with the comrades. On the contrary, he seized every opportunity to distance himself from the party, even when he was speaking or writing from a platform — Carnegie Hall, the New Masses — provided by that party. In particular, two Marxist-derived positions were anathema to him. The first was economic determinism, an arid philosophy that in his view threatened to rob human existence of all meaning. The second was the elevation of propaganda over art, for — though MacLeish came to advocate public speech for the creative writer — he never believed that one should be willing to compromise artistic values in the service of articulating political slogans. In short, he remained his own man, always on the side of democracy and of individual freedom even when these were unpopular positions. In the thirties as in later decades, MacLeish's politics often bucked against the tide of the prevailing orthodoxies. As he was to prove time and again, most notably during the heyday of Senator Joseph McCarthy, he was not a man to back down from verbal combat with powerful foes.

As the year shepherding the Nieman fellows drew to a close, Ezra Pound came to speak at Harvard, and for the first time Archie met the poet he had been corresponding with, off and on, for more than a decade. Pound spent his time at Harvard letting everyone know what an awful place it was. The students were being cheated of their $400 tuition fee, he told them. They were not getting "the straight tip on Economics and American History." The straight tip, as Pound saw it, was that fascism posed no danger. "It is as idiotic to be anti-Fascist in America as it would be to start a movement to prevent Javanese temple dancing in Massachusetts." At a party later at Theodore Spencer's house, Pound continued in the same vein. MacLeish thought he was not only in error but boringly so, and left as soon as he could.

By early May he had informed President Conant that he would not be back in the fall, for he needed a year off to "dig into a long poem." The Nieman program was off to a good start, both men agreed, and it continued to prosper in succeeding years under the leadership of Louis Lyons, who took over the position of director. The Nieman experience had given Archie far more of an admiration for Harvard, for the brilliance of its scholar-teachers and the variety of its offerings, than he had felt as a law student and part-time instructor in the late 1910s and early 1920s. Harvard struck him, alas, as substantially superior to the Yale he had attended as an undergraduate. But there was nothing for him there at the moment, and in the spring of 1939 he was looking forward to an extended period of writing poetry that would matter in the world. Then the phone call came from Washington.

15

MR. M. GOES TO WASHINGTON

A Call from On High

BRIEF AS MACLEISH'S LEADERSHIP of the Nieman program was, it was crucial in shaping much of the rest of his life. In the long run, the warmth of the associations he established during 1938–39 worked to incline him toward the academic life. More immediately, his deepening friendship with Felix Frankfurter led to six years of service in Washington under President Franklin Delano Roosevelt. Frankfurter not only gave the Nieman project his unqualified support in the fall of 1938; he also enlisted Archie as co-editor of a volume of his collected papers. In the foreword to this 1939 book, MacLeish stressed the judge's brilliance and his famous classroom intolerance for pretentiousness and pose. Former students would "remember very well a blue ironic eye behind a brightly polished eye-glass," he wrote. "We remember also a voice which can crackle under a fool's complacence like dry wood under an empty kettle." Yet the most remarkable thing about Frankfurter was not his mental acuity but his appetite for life. As Archie depicted him, Frankfurter was "that rarest of God's creatures, a simon-pure, unmitigated intellectual with a limitless relish for living," for food and drink and good talk, for the touch of people and the sound of laughter. He was a man who shared his ideas and revelations in innumerable phone calls and letters: "Have you read this?" he would ask. "Did you see that?" "Yesterday I was thinking . . ." In short, MacLeish's Frankfurter was blessed with a natural warmth and a genius for friendship. He was also eager to advance the careers of his friends and protégés whenever the opportunity presented itself.

That opportunity arose in the spring of 1939, when Frankfurter, a newly appointed associate justice of the Supreme Court, received a memorandum from President Roosevelt. For months FDR had been stewing over the problem of finding a replacement for seventy-eight-year-old Herbert Putnam as librarian of Congress. What did Felix think of Archie MacLeish for the post? "He is not a professional Librarian nor is he a special student of incunabula or ancient manuscripts," the president acknowledged. "Nevertheless, he has lots of qualifications that said specialists have not."

Frankfurter heartily endorsed the idea, and in a long reply made a series of points in support of his former student. The most eminent librarians of the past fifty years, he pointed out, had not been technically trained for the work. Subordinates could keep the day-to-day operations going easily enough. But the director of a great library should have imaginative energy and vision. "He should be a man who knows books, loves books and makes books." MacLeish was manifestly such a person; but more than that, he was also acquainted through his work with the developing media of radio and motion pictures. Then in an irresistible brief, Frankfurter summarized MacLeish's wide range of accomplishments and capabilities:

> It must be remembered that Archie was one of the leaders of his class at the Law School, proved his metal as a very able lawyer, was invited to join the Harvard Law School Faculty, then pursued his poetic career, was the most effective editor of *Fortune,* and this year showed astonishing personal and organizing faculties in connection with the Nieman Fellowships at Harvard. He unites in himself qualities seldom found in combination — those of the hardheaded lawyer with the sympathetic imagination of the poet, the independent thinker and the charming "mixer." He would bring to the Librarianship intellectual distinction, cultural recognition the world over, a persuasive personality and a delicacy of touch in dealing with others, and creative energy in making the Library of Congress the great center of the cultural resources of the Nation in the technological setting of our time.

Frankfurter sent a copy of his May 11 recommendation to Archie, and the following day MacLeish was called to New York for a talk with Congressman Kent Keller, chairman of the House of Representatives Committee on the Library of Congress. By Monday May 15, Archie had made up his mind — or thought he had — to turn down the position if it was offered. In a letter to Felix, he admitted that he was capable of doing well a number of things that didn't usually go together. In his versatility, he knew, he was not at all "the kind of person with whom the word artist is commonly associated." Yet an artist he was determined to be, and so could not sensibly accept even the place of great honor and distinction for which Frankfurter was advancing him. In the course of saying no, Archie's letter sounded more like maybe. It was possible, he wrote, that he had reached the place in his life where he must turn from poetry to public service, but if so, he probably wouldn't be "of much use . . . because the one thing I have ever wanted to do with all my heart was to write poetry." Then he added a postscript. He'd just had a phone call from the White House inviting him to lunch with the president on Tuesday May 23. He was loath to waste FDR's valuable time, but had already wired the White House that he would come. What did Felix think he should do?

Frankfurter urged him to come to Washington, and arranged a breakfast for MacLeish with himself and Roosevelt brain truster Tommy Corcoran. What they talked about, in Felix's house overlooking the Potomac, "was the Republic and the obligation to serve it," a message that appealed powerfully to the canons of service Archie had inherited from his mother and maternal grandfather. "You and you alone," he wrote Frankfurter when leaving Washington, "have dared to believe that men do enter Government . . . because they believe in the Republic and wish to serve it." Fresh from that meeting, he went on to the White House to confront Roosevelt's charismatic blend of personal charm and public authority. Afterwards he took the train back to Farmington tortured by doubts.

Almost all the indicators pointed toward a negative decision. He knew he was being asked to make a long-term commitment — Putnam had been librarian of Congress for forty years! — and that the work would require so much of his energy as to make the writing of poetry virtually impossible. "It's a job from which no traveller returns," as Gerald Murphy put it. Seeking advice, he consulted Harvard librarian Keyes Metcalf. Metcalf told him that being librarian of Congress was primarily an administrative position, that a good deal of reorganization would probably be necessary, and that an important part of the job would involve seeking funds from congressional committees. "That's not what I want to do with my life," MacLeish responded, and that, Metcalf thought, was the end of the matter. Archie's friend Kenneth Murdock, of the Harvard English department, exhorted him to decline. Nothing could be worse for him as a poet than to become librarian of Congress, Murdock told him. He needed the time to write. As for Ada, she understood that sooner or later Archie would have to earn some money, since poetry paid no bills, and their dividends were not sufficient to see the children through college. Still, she could not be enthusiastic about the move to Washington.

On Sunday May 28, Archie wrote the president that he must reject his offer. The difficulty was one of time, he explained. He could not believe that the job of librarian of Congress would leave him time to practice his art. "Either the art or the library would suffer, and either result would be disastrous to the man." He hated to say no: he had been "going round and round the apple tree for four days but I end up every day at the same place." Then he added in conclusion: "I should be proud indeed to be useful to you in any capacity which did not deprive me of the trade I follow." Roosevelt was not accustomed to being turned down, and so Tommy Corcoran called and informed Archie that he was lunching with the president yet again, and this time Archie capitulated. FDR made him feel that librarian of Congress was the most important job in the world. He painted visions of the library as a great educational institution for the country at large, with fleets of bookmobiles roaming the illiterate South. He praised the essential democracy of the national library, a place where any citizen — old or young, rich or poor, black or white, scholar or schoolboy, executive or laborer — could go to read a book without so much as asking leave. Archie left fired with enthusiasm, the captive of the president forever.

"Mr. Roosevelt," MacLeish was wont to say in later years, "decided that I wanted to be librarian of Congress." But there was more to it than the persuasive powers of the president. Archie did after all need a salary, and he was reluctant to go back to Harry Luce, hat in hand. Besides, it was his pattern when presented with a difficult challenge to face it down. In this case he said: "I just stopped thinking about it. I decided to take it on and do what I could do as well as I could do it." There were those on the sidelines who deplored MacLeish's choice, who saw it as the act of an overambitious and overbearing man. So Dwight Macdonald, his former *Fortune* colleague, characterized Archie as, basically, "a power guy." It was true that his six years in Washington would draw him close to the very center of power — closer than any other American man of letters. Yet perhaps the strongest factor in changing Archie's mind was his lifelong determination to be of use. If there was one thing he had learned from his mother, it was that his life should make a difference. He had tried through poetry and drama to make good things happen; now he would try through the more conventional channel of public service. In retrospect, he looked back on his "improbable and impossible" tour of duty as librarian of Congress as "about the best thing that ever happened" to him, for it gave him a chance to experience the life of public responsibility, at least for a while. Archie took the job President Roosevelt offered him, then, because he could not do otherwise. He was, in the words of his fellow poet Richard Wilbur, "a naturally high-minded man," one of the "passionate serving kind."

Roosevelt made MacLeish's decision easier by assuring him that he would be able to find time for his writing. According to legend, FDR told him that he could polish off his duties as librarian of Congress before breakfast. In his June 1 letter of acceptance, Archie specifically mentioned this assurance as his final precondition. To underline the point, he asked for the summer off before assuming his post. He was hard at work on a long poem — *America Was Promises* — and could not take up his duties until October 1. In a wonderful reply, President Roosevelt granted the three-month leave and made gentle fun of his appointee's devotion to his art.

> Dear Archie MacLeish: —
>
> It is one of those curious facts that when I got your first letter I took to my bed with a severe attack of indigestion — and that when your second letter came I found myself able to rise and resume my normal life.
>
> You make me very happy and the nomination will go to the Senate in a few days. I will take care of the matter of approval by the Senators from your State.
>
> It is perfectly all right about your taking office after the Summer is over — say the end of September or the first of October. And I am also very clear that you will be able to take "time off" for writing, especially if you like travel to distant parts where you could also improve your knowledge of ancient literature. For example, as Librarian of Congress, you should become thoroughly familiar with the inscriptions on the stone monuments of Easter Island — especially in their relationship to similar sign writing alleged to exist on ancient sheepskins in some of the remoter lamaseries of Tibet. If you go on such a trip I would like to go along as cabin boy and will guarantee that I will not interrupt the Muse when she is flirting with you!
>
> As ever yours,
> Franklin D. Roosevelt

The Opposition

Given his political sensitivity, President Roosevelt may have anticipated the storm of protest his nomination of Archibald MacLeish would generate. MacLeish, however, certainly did not. The president made his announcement on June 6, and within minutes a staffer on the *Washington Evening Star* relayed the word to David C. Mearns at the Library of Congress. Pausing only to check the name in *Who's Who*, Mearns rushed to the office of Martin Roberts, who was acting librarian in the summer-long absence of Herbert Putnam in Maine. Roberts at once called Putnam with the unlikely news about MacLeish. "Mr. Mearns said he's a P-P-POET!" Roberts stammered into the phone.

The reaction of Roberts and, one assumes, of Putnam was as nothing compared to the consternation among the officers of the American Library Association, who had for months unsuccessfully sought an appointment with Roosevelt to advance the candidacy of one of their own, ALA executive secretary Carl H. Milam. As the librarians began to muster their forces for an onslaught against the nomination on professional grounds, the first volley of political opposition came from J. Parnell Thomas, Republican congressman from New Jersey and a member of the House's Special Committee to Investigate Un-American Activities, also known as the Dies Committee. On June 7, from the floor of the House of Representatives, Thomas coined a new phrase to condemn by association those who, like MacLeish, had once shared some of the views of the Communist party. This nomination and others, Thomas insisted, indicated that Communist influences were at work in the White House. He did not accuse MacLeish of actually belonging to the party. He was instead, according to Thomas, one of its leading "fellow travelers."

Pressed by administration supporter Sam Rayburn, Democrat from Texas, to define his term, Congressman Thomas said a fellow traveler was one "who is absolutely sympathetic with the Communist cause, but for various reasons does not care to be a party member." Was he calling MacLeish a communist? Rayburn demanded. Thomas dodged the question by widening his accusation. Rayburn could hardly deny, could he, that the administration had been appointing either communists or fellow travelers to key positions in the government. "I do deny it!" Rayburn roared. "And I think the gentleman's statement is little short of slander." Having apparently drawn blood, Thomas returned to the attack a week later with more particulars. Specifically he focused on the 1937 League of American Writers meeting in which Archie, as chairman, had introduced Earl Browder, adding the erroneous information that MacLeish had been elected vice president of the league. Thomas was clearly relying on the dubious principle of guilt by association. "To a large extent," he intoned, "we may know a man by the company he keeps."

A fellow New Jerseyite, Dean Christian Gauss at Princeton, wrote Archie his congratulations: "The inevitable has happened. You have already been honored by having been officially called a communist. . . . I have heard FDR called so many times. I'd like to be called one too, so can't you get me in on it?" But MacLeish could not take the matter so lightly. Recalling his differences with the party faithful over the years, he declared that "no one would be more shocked to learn I am a Communist than the Communists themselves." Nor did he particularly welcome the support of the League of American Writers, which pointed out in rebuttal to Thomas, first, that it was not a Communist-front organization (a point on which reasonable men might well disagree), and second, MacLeish had never been an officer (the truth, pure and simple).

The second serious challenge to Archie's appointment came from the embattled American Library Association. Milton James Ferguson of the Brooklyn Public Library, the ALA president, expressed his outrage in a flurry of similes. Giving this post to a nonprofessional librarian, he said, was like "making the skipper of a racing yacht the Chief of Naval Operations." He had the highest respect for MacLeish as a poet, but could "no more think of him as Librarian of Congress than as chief engineer of a new Brooklyn Bridge." It was about the same, he said, "as appointing a man Secretary of Agriculture because he likes cut flowers on his dinner table." The *New York Herald Tribune*, in an editorial written by Geoffrey Parsons and headlined "A Shocking Nomination," agreed without resorting to spurious metaphors that the man in charge of the world's greatest library should be well acquainted with running libraries. As it happened, the ALA was holding its national meeting in San Francisco in mid-June, and there Ferguson and Milam marshaled their forces. They wrote and circulated a petition, signed by 1,400 librarians present. Appointing MacLeish, it maintained, would be a calamity. Librarianship was "not a literary pursuit" and writing was "not of itself a suitable preparation for it." The Library of Congress would almost certainly deteriorate under amateur leadership. The appointment of a nonlibrarian would be a slap in the face of the nation's thirty thousand librarians, and would deter talented young people from entering the profession. In addition to launching this petition, the ALA executive council urged its members to bombard the Senate with letters and telegrams expressing their objections, and to contact local newspapers seeking editorial support of their views.

Before beginning this full-scale campaign, the ALA decided to give MacLeish a chance to withdraw from consideration. Keyes Metcalf was chosen to call Archie from San Francisco with this proposal, and did so, though not without some discomfort. MacLeish responded no, vigorously and without hesitation. In the first place, he told Metcalf, he was not going to withdraw under fire, for that would be cowardly. As ever, he would not shrink from the battle. Second, he was not going to renege on his word to President Roosevelt. "Keyes," he said, "have you really thought about what you're asking me to do? The president has . . . sent my name up to the Senate and you're suggesting that I should now undercut his nomination and go back on my commitment." "Well," Metcalf said, "I see your point."

So the issue was joined, and Archie soon found that he had plenty of allies. Several newspapers, including the *New York Times, Hartford Courant,* and *Boston Herald,* heartily endorsed his nomination. And from the first, there were defections within the ALA. Milton C. Lord of the Boston Public Library wrote MacLeish from San Francisco that what "the library crowd" was saying at that moment was "not to be taken in any sense personally." They had no alternative but to howl, but when the howling was over, Lord and many others would be ready to aid MacLeish in any way they could. More openly, M. Llewellyn Raney of the University of Chicago libraries denounced the ALA campaign as "badly overplayed" and "marked with such persistence and intolerance as to awaken resentment in Washington and revulsion among the soberer, scholarly element at San Francisco." Chicago's Raney enthusiastically backed MacLeish, partly out of admiration for his parents. MacLeish, like Putnam, was a lawyer, he pointed out, and that was entirely appropriate for the director of the library of the nation's lawmakers. He was also equally at home in the arts "as one of the four leading American poets now alive." It was true that he had not attended a professional school of library science, but neither had thirty-four of the thirty-seven persons presently occupying executive positions at the Library of Congress. As a Scotsman he could be relied on to manage the library's finances with frugality. Finally, Raney struck a counterblow against Ferguson and Milam. "MacLeish did not seek the place," he concluded. "He was besought. Can his two critics say as much?"

Such support was heartening, but MacLeish and his friends looked for still other champions. Charles Curtis approached Harvard president Conant, who decided to remain neutral in the controversy. In a letter to MacLeish, Conant explained his reasons: "I am so regretful at your leaving Harvard and what I assume is a farewell to your career as a poet that the less I say on the subject the better." Metcalf wrote Frankfurter that for his part he could not endorse the nomination, since he could not believe that Archie would "be happy in the work, or willing to stay in it for any length of time" and he feared that the appointment would handicap the movement for professional training of librarians. "I cannot congratulate you," he wrote MacLeish directly, "but I can assure you that if the appointment is confirmed I shall help you in any way that is within my power."

In Washington, Dean Acheson used his wide contacts within the Congress to ensure his friend's confirmation. In a letter to Senator George L. Radcliffe of Maryland, a member of the Senate committee on the library, Acheson emphasized his long and intimate acquaintance with MacLeish, and in particular praised his capacity for leadership. "At the Law School," Acheson's letter read:

> he was a leader both scholastically and in the intellectual life of the School. He had in those days, as he has now, the gift of friendship, and there are few who can spend a half hour with him without catching the fire of his enthusiasm and wanting to go with him on whatever task he has in hand. His courage has been shown on the football field, as an officer in the Field Artillery during the World War, and by his willingness to stand for the right as he has seen it against any opposition.

Senator Radcliffe was persuaded, but not everyone Acheson contacted could be brought to vote for MacLeish. In particular, he could not sway Senators Warren Barbour of New Jersey and Warren Austin of Vermont from opposition. The problem was the charge of fellow traveling. As Barbour put it in a letter to Acheson, "If the information I have received about MacLeish and Earl Browder and all the rest of it is really based on fact, I wanted to tell you, old man, that I am afraid it may be impossible, after all, for me to vote for his confirmation." At this stage, Acheson brought the weight of his alma mater to bear. On June 21 Yale University awarded MacLeish an honorary Doctor of Letters degree, the fourth among dozens of such degrees he was eventually to accumulate. The same day, Reeve Schley, a member of the Yale Corporation, wrote J. Parnell Thomas that he could assure him of one thing: that MacLeish was "not only far from being a communist but, on the other hand, [was] thoroughly detested by the communistic party." Acheson sent a copy of Schley's letter to Senator Barbour, who could not be budged because he was under "tremendous" pressure from fellow New Jersey congressman Thomas to do a good deal more than vote against the nomination. Nonetheless, Barbour said he would leave the task of making the case against MacLeish to Senator Austin. Austin himself promised Acheson only that "I shall not make the claim that Mr. MacLeish is a Communist."

Indeed he did not, though he managed to raise the issue. "My contention will not be that this man is a Communist," Austin stated in the course of his opening speech at the confirmation hearing of June 29. (Nor did he contend that MacLeish was a criminal or a wife-beater.) But he did quote from articles and reviews that he felt illustrated the nominee's radicalism and excessive idealism — qualities to be expected from a fuzzy-minded poet, perhaps, but not to be countenanced in a position of responsibility. In his long statement Senator Austin read into the record the Ferguson-ALA petition against MacLeish, and an autobiographical sketch Archie had written for the 1931 edition of *Living Authors*. The manner of the sketch was ironic and self-deprecatory, but Austin was disposed to take literally such statements as "War: went abroad in a hospital unit so as to do the right thing but not be hurt. In France got shifted to the field artillery out of shame," and "Went to Harvard Law School to avoid going to work. Led my class in last year." It was necessary for Senate Majority Leader Alben Barkley, Democrat of Kentucky, to interrupt with the intelligence that MacLeish was using "a Pickwickian, facetious way of referring to himself, because nobody could lead his class at Harvard without doing a considerable amount of work." Undeterred, Austin went on to cite objections to the appointment from the *New York Sun,* the *Baltimore Sun,* and the *New York Herald Tribune.* In conclusion, he asserted that "in this particular case there is no evidence whatever which tends to show that this brilliant littérateur and poet has any qualifications at all for an executive, for an administrator, or for a librarian."

Senator Barkley himself led the defense. He cited encomiums for MacLeish and his appointment from various newspapers. "So warm and generous a spirit, keenly sensitive to the finest cultural traditions, aflame with love of liberty, can hardly be a danger to the Library of Congress," the *New York Times* opined. His appointment, said the *Boston Herald,* was "not only good but brilliant." Barkley produced letters of enthusiastic support from librarians Raney and Alexander Laing of Dartmouth, and from businessman and philanthropist Louis Kirstein. In dealing with what he called "the effort to make light of Mr. MacLeish because he is a poet," Barkley discovered a precedent in the case of James Russell Lowell, both poet and ambassador to the Court of St. James's. Moreover, he insisted, MacLeish was "much more than a poet," no mere moongazer but lawyer, editor, educator. During the committee hearing, he added, the nominee had been so impressive that members unanimously approved sending his name to the Senate floor. As for the outpouring of opposition from the ALA, it was entirely possible he would have received a thousand letters and telegrams against the appointment from librarians without prodding, Barkley admitted, but the fact was that "the secretary of the organization did ask them to write." It was worth noting, too, that not one of those communications attacked "the character, or even the views of Mr. MacLeish on political, social, or economic problems."

When it was time to call the question, Barkley played his last card, in effect reminding those on the fence that any defections from the president's choice would be duly recorded. He asked for a roll-call vote, and added that he was confident there would be, "if any, not more than a few votes against the confirmation of the nomination." With the full strength of the Democratic party and FDR behind him, Barkley proved to be absolutely right. The final tally was sixty-three in favor, eight opposed, and twenty-five not voting. "Your majority," Corcoran wrote MacLeish, "was disgraceful!"

Now the fence-mending process commenced. Ralph Munn of Pittsburgh's Carnegie Library, the newly elected president of the American Library Association, wrote MacLeish on July 1 conveying the ALA's "sincere good wishes for your complete success." He regretted that the organization's "attempt to secure a professionally trained librarian had to take the form of a protest against your confirmation," but assured him that these were the only grounds for opposition. "We all recognize and admire your personal qualities and talents." MacLeish responded that he regarded the protest as "quite natural" and that he bore no lingering resentment, though he did regret "the tactics adopted by certain representatives of the ALA." It was important that they all work together in the future. There the issue rested, for the moment. It remained for Archie to prove to his detractors what an amateur librarian could accomplish.

First, however, he had *America Was Promises* to finish. He spent most of the summer in Conway working on that long poem and trying to put thoughts of what awaited him in Washington out of his mind. On July 10 he stopped by the local post office and got postmaster Charles Dacey to give him the oath of office. "We did it through the wicket," MacLeish said. By that time he had already learned from Tommy Corcoran that he would have opportunities to serve the president in ways that had nothing to do with the Library of Congress. "Don't you think you'd better begin to think about a Rhodes Scholarship scheme for South American students?" Corcoran asked. There was one other thing he wanted, too. Couldn't Archie use his connections to persuade some eminent historian — Sam Morison, perhaps, or Charles Beard — to publish an article "debunking the Third Term myth": the notion that American presidents were somehow prevented by something more than 150 years of custom from serving beyond eight years. The purpose of such a piece was obvious. Roosevelt would be coming up for a third term in the fall of 1940.

To solidify relations with his appointee, FDR invited Archie and Ada to spend the July 21–23 weekend at Hyde Park. The festivities included a clambake at the nearby estate of Secretary of the Treasury Henry

Morgenthau, Jr., and possibly — so Ada anticipated — one of the Roosevelt's famous hot dog picnics. "I hope it won't count against me that I hate hot dogs," she wrote Sara Murphy. Aside from that, her feelings about Archie's post were mixed. She was afraid he wouldn't have any time for his own writing, yet she was glad of anything that would give the family "a home all together."

The highlight of the weekend was provided Sunday morning by fellow house guest Alexander Woollcott, the well-known writer and columnist. Archie and Ada went off for a brisk walk while Eleanor Roosevelt was at church, and returned to spy Woollcott sitting on the porch in a pair of shorts. As they got closer, they could see clearly that one of Alec's testicles was on display, hanging out of his shorts. They were about to say something to him when Mrs. Roosevelt's car drove up and she alighted. She must have seen what they did, the MacLeishes thought, but she said only, "Well, Mr. Woollcott, how lovely to see you on my porch."

In private conference with the president, MacLeish discovered something of his views about the Library of Congress. The pay levels were "too low all along the line," Roosevelt told him. At the same time, he said, "a lot of thoroughly nice people there . . . would simply have to be removed." The library had grown moribund over the last decades of Putnam's tenure, and badly needed modernizing. Archie began to envision his role as that of an unpopular newcomer, disturbing the status quo. A luncheon meeting with Putnam at the Century Club in New York did nothing to alter this view. Putnam fully intended to come into the library regularly as librarian emeritus, he announced. Later, in a conference with Luther Evans, who was then directing the Works Progress Administration (WPA) Historical Records Survey at the library, Archie said he supposed the staff must be quaking in their boots anticipating his arrival and the changes he would bring. It wasn't that way at all, Evans insisted. He knew nearly every division chief at the library, and almost all of them were thirsting for real leadership. "Putnam's been in his dotage for several years," Evans said. "You're going to have a warm welcome at the Library of Congress."

The Librarian Profiled

The man Franklin Delano Roosevelt chose for librarian of Congress was forty-seven years old in the autumn of 1939, though his leanness made him look younger. The same impression was conveyed by his characteristic vigor of movement; aides had to scurry to keep up with him as he walked the halls. His hairline was receding, but that only served to emphasize the nobleness of his Palladian brow. He was thought by most to be an unusually handsome man, and he took care to keep himself in fit condition. He knew the forks, and practiced the prevailing canons of deference to women and the elderly. By far his most appealing attribute was his voice, which could be almost hypnotic in its effect. Although he did everything else at full throttle, in public appearances he spoke slowly, even haltingly, as if each word were a pearl to be strung on the course of his utterance. Even the pauses were musical. He had "the most beautiful voice, man's or woman's, I have ever heard," Jill Ker Conway said of him. "If he read you the small type on the back of an insurance policy, you'd buy it," another friend remarked. Much of his considerable power of persuasion came from that voice. "Isn't it lucky Archie's on the right side?" E. E. Cummings once said. "He'd be a dangerous man on the wrong side."

Being in the right — being *passionately* in the right — mattered a great deal to MacLeish, who was ever ready to struggle against injustice. There was nothing self-serving about this combativeness. He was just as outraged at infringements on the personal liberties of others as of his own. Archie was a "cause seeker," with a crusader's instinct, Bob Lovett said. At the same time, he was not given to empty gestures. As an old-fashioned liberal, he wanted not only to do and say the right thing, but to achieve his ends against whatever opposition presented itself.

"My God," he blurted out in the course of an interview, "life is a fight, and if you pretend you are not in a fight you aren't talking about life." But he also said that "life was like panning for gold — all of the bad things go through the screen and only the nuggets stay on top." He was equipped for the struggle, in other words, with a strong personal sense of optimism, a natural ebullience reinforced by the progressive outlook of his middle-western upbringing and the forward-going affirmation and ambitiousness inculcated at Yale, particularly in Skull and Bones. There were good reasons for him to be optimistic. He was, for instance, fortunate in his ancestry and in his financial situation. As librarian of Congress, he earned a salary of $10,000, the same as that of Cabinet officials. Quarterly dividends from Carson Pirie Scott ran to about $1,600 during this period, and he fleshed out that income with honoraria for speeches, payment for articles, and royalties from books. He and Ada spent almost all of their money. They sent their children to expensive boarding schools and colleges. They took pleasure in living well. Archie dressed in the tweeds and Brooks Brothers suits of the Ivy League gentleman, and Ada in dresses made to her order. They bought wine by the case from importer Frank Schoonmaker in New York.

Yet work always came ahead of play for MacLeish. He worked as he moved, very fast and with great concentration. He constructed his days in a precise routine to eliminate waste of time. His desk was well organized. He was invariably on time, sometimes ahead of time. From childhood on he was obsessed by the feeling that there was too much to do and not enough time to get it done. "And why, then, must I hurry?" he had asked in his 1925 poem *The Pot of Earth*.

> *There are things I have to do*
> *More than just to live and die*
> *More than just to die of living.*

He worked hard at everything he undertook, and would not let exhaustion prevent him from finishing the job. When he took a break from mental labor, he used the spare moments for manual tasks: moving the strawberry bed, erecting fence posts, cutting saplings. And he took pride in doing everything right. Duty with a capital *D* was ingrained in him. In a 1968 conversation, Mark Van Doren remarked that occasionally he found it very pleasant to do nothing at all. "It's beyond my powers," Archie responded. "How have you learned how to do that?"

It followed that he was often impatient with others who did not work as hard as he did or with as much dedication. He disdained mediocre performance, and was openly intolerant of the shoddy. This forthright scorn made him a difficult and demanding boss, and in private life cost him a number of friends. He was nearly always at odds with one friend or another, Bob and Adele Lovett thought, and largely because of this judgmental strain in his nature. A 1935 letter of Ada's to Adele tells one such story between the lines. Archie had seen Philip and Ellen Barry and thought them quite unfriendly. "Poor dear," Ada sympathized in her letter, "he . . . can't seem to realize that what Ellen forced from him about Phil has forever closed that chapter. I hate losing old friends, but human nature being what it is, I can't blame them." Whatever Archie said about his friend, it led to a break that even Ada, with her masterly social skills, could not repair.

Candid about others, Archie withheld something of himself in relationships with them. As the poet Donald Hall, one of his students, said, he "was a good man, a kind man, a generous man, but there was something timid even in that generosity." He seemed to thrive on a sort of easy geniality, a gemütlichkeit that warded off intimacy. Others characterized him as "friendly but aloof," or "always affable but almost never cordial." Manifestly he did not want to reveal his inner self. "I was very close to Archie," John Conway remarked, "but never felt I really knew him." Whenever the talk veered toward the personal, Archie gently and firmly moved it in another direction. He "was a secret man," his son Bill wrote, "as tightly chambered as a nautilus." What MacLeish said of Picasso was true of himself as well. "Everybody knew" Picasso but "nobody knew" him, Archie said. "He was a very agreeable man but you got no part of him."

To some extent this concealment derived from his heritage. Scots and Yankees alike are notorious for their reticence and respect for privacy. But also, the carapace around his inmost self was constructed to protect the public man from intruders. As he wrote Edward Hoagland, another of his brilliant student-writers, "when you are young it is possible to hide. When you get older and are caught up in life — particularly if you love life and want to live it — you have to be out on the street and your only safeguard there is the persona." For MacLeish, the persona was one of consummate agreeability, mingled with self-deprecation. He was very good at telling anecdotes that made fun of himself, but did not especially welcome others' doing so. And from behind that genial facade he was given to delivering profound statements, often peppered with stories about his contacts with the great men of his time.

To most this persona was charming; to others it could be insufferable. Such detractors thought him autocratic and arrogant, entirely too full of himself. He was "not one to hide his light under a bushel," as Alice Acheson observed. It was not surprising that he should have hurt himself diving off Eden Roc; he dove beautifully, and was not reluctant to demonstrate his form in company. He liked dressing up, too, whether in the dinner jacket of Washington's formal gatherings or in full Scottish regalia. For dressy occasions he wore a pair of black patent leather shoes adorned with black carnations. And in later years he acquired a number of hats for daily use: a Scottish bonnet with ribbons in back, a beret, a Greek fisherman's cap.

At the same time, his vanity did not preclude a genuine interest in the welfare of those who attracted him by way of their own ability, whether realized or potential. He reveled in his association with people of accomplishment, and desperately craved their good opinion. He also went out of his way to befriend and advance the careers of young writers of talent, as many have testified. At bottom, the plumage he donned may have concealed a lack of self-consciousness rather than the opposite. "You know," he once said to his son Bill, "I never think about myself." Certainly he did not know himself very well. There were moments, recorded in his notebooks, when he would wake in the morning and be unable to recognize himself: "There is a bathroom still in a house on Bowdoin Street in Cambridge where the grey light of a winter morning is reflected in a mirror that should have held my face but held instead a face I'd never seen — a face I *did not remember* ever having seen."

That sense of otherness, perhaps, is one reason why so much of his poetry deals in universals rather than particulars — in Adam and Eve, the generic conquistador, the latter-day Hamlet.

The face he presented to the world was one of easy self-assurance, interpreted by some as smugness. Privately, he was far less sure of himself than he seemed. He was terrified of fire. He did not want Ada to drive for fear of a possible automobile accident. Late in life he was beset by such worries. He worried about the weather, and the next day's tasks. If there was nothing to worry about, he would invent something. Eventually he suffered from ulcers, an affliction brought on or at least exacerbated by worry. He was also hypersensitive to noise; at one point during his years in Washington he had to be restrained from assaulting a workman operating an air hammer outside his office. He sometimes had trouble sleeping, as yet another notebook entry reveals: "August-September. The year stands at dead center. And I with it. . . . A hot sun but meaningless in its heat except to kill — grass, leaves, earth even. One does not sleep from one day's end to the beginning of the next. . . . Life is dead to me as is the year."

These symptoms belied his surface equanimity. Taken in combination, they sound like signs of depression. But Archie did not let himself touch bottom. He was once asked what might have caused Hart Crane to step off the stern of a ship into oblivion at the age of thirty-three. The difference "between those who ended their lives at the very moment they shouldn't and those who stumbled on," he said, was not simply that the stumblers had clay feet or lacked the sensitivity that led to despair, but that they felt life as both tragic and in the true sense comic: "the laughing face of the dead girl." All of us despair, he added, but some survive, whether because of good parents, good health, good digestion, a good wife, or finally an unwillingness to give up contemplating "the shine of the world." Archie never lost his boyhood sense of wonder. The glory of the natural world — excepting the drear days of August-September — gave him reason to rise again all his mornings, whoever might face him from the mirror.

These were some of the characteristics of the ambitious and complicated man who drove up to the monumental Library of Congress building across from the Capitol on the morning of Monday, October 2, parked his car in the garage space reserved for him, and strode upstairs to get to work.

16 ❖

BRUSH OF THE COMET

The Best Job in Town

PRESIDENT ROOSEVELT WAS WRONG, of course. Archibald MacLeish, the ninth librarian of Congress, could not finish his work before breakfast — nor before dinner, often. He worked long and hard in an effort to propel the institution he had taken charge of into the twentieth century.

The Library of Congress began modestly enough, with an appropriation of $5,000 in 1800. Thomas Jefferson was the leading advocate of the project, and when the British burned the books along with the Capitol in 1814, he sold his personal library to the country as the foundation for a new national library: 6,487 books for $23,950. The holdings had grown to 55,000 volumes by 1851, when another fire destroyed three-fifths of them. Rising yet again from the ashes, the library moved into its massive pillared main building in 1897, amid assurances that the structure would serve all conceivable needs "for a century and a half to come." Within a generation the collection had outgrown its repository, and Congress authorized the erection of a second building. On April 5, 1939, the fortieth anniversary of Herbert Putnam's accession to the post of librarian of Congress, the annex was dedicated. Designed as a "giant bookstack," the five-story annex contained space for 10 million books. Its dedication represented a fitting capstone to the long leadership of Putnam, who in his forty years had built the collection from 1 million to nearly 6 million volumes, with a staff of 1,100 and an annual budget of approximately $3 million.

Externally, MacLeish found the Library of Congress in good shape.

On the inside, the place was in a state of disorganization. The trouble began with Putnam, a classic example of an executive who stayed too long on the job. Putnam ran the Library of Congress like a feudal fiefdom. Even at the age of seventy-eight, he had to be maneuvered into retirement.

A small, mustachioed, red-haired man, the patrician Putnam was the son of the founder of the publishing house that carried the family name. A Phi Beta Kappa graduate of Harvard, with a law degree from Columbia, he was appointed librarian of Congress in 1899 following fifteen years in library and legal work. During his tenure, he ruled the LC absolutely, by force of personality. Putnam did not approve of wasted motion. His own speech was meticulous and precise, his letters rarely more than two or three sentences long. Subordinates were not allowed to take notes in his presence: they were to memorize their orders and execute them. His employees described him as remote, aloof, a man of "impenetrable dignity." In an article, one of his staff members referred to him as "the Tallest Little Man in the World." Over the years, David Mearns wrote, his relationship to his staff came to resemble that of the Great White Father to an aboriginal tribe. "He was venerated. He was endowed with extraordinary gifts. He was changeless and timeless. He was a spirit cast in the image of other men but too carefully socked and booted ever to suggest affliction with ceramic feet." He also had the capacity, despite his iron reserve, of inspiring employees with a sense of mission and of commanding their loyalty.

In several ways, Putnam is regarded by historians as a great figure in the development of the Library of Congress. His principal accomplishment was developing the LC's holdings, so that it assumed rank as one of the world's finest repositories of learning. In addition, Putnam envisioned the library as a national resource, working in concert with other libraries throughout the United States. Under his leadership, the LC devised its classification scheme, standardized cataloguing processes, and inaugurated a system of uniform printed cards. By law, American books came to the LC for copyright and possible addition to the collection. The chosen volumes were duly classified, and the information about them was recorded on cards. These cards were then sold to other libraries, so that readers looking for a book according to author, title, or subject could locate it by the same process whether in Minneapolis or Atlanta or Steamboat Springs.

While Putnam had overseen the LC during its period of most remarkable growth, he had neglected many of the problems that growth entailed. The rapid acquisition of books, for example, led to an appalling backlog in processing them. Personnel were paid notoriously low salaries, even by government standards, and for years Putnam resisted all attempts to improve levels of pay. Worst of all was the administrative structure — or lack of it — by which he attempted to govern the LC. He was forever creating new divisions and departments, with all lines on the table of organization tracing back to himself. He inherited nine such administrative units in 1899 and within a year expanded the number to eighteen. By the time he retired, the number had risen to thirty-five, and each department chief reported directly to Putnam alone. In the early years he had been able through his formidable intelligence to operate in this way. But over a period of time, the system proved beyond the capacities of any mere human, even one who betrayed no hint of clay feet. This organizational pattern produced considerable duplication of effort, kept staffers from working together to solve problems, and led to neglect of certain crucial library functions.

The situation was worsened by Putnam's working schedule. During his valedictory years as librarian, he used to arrive at 7:00 A.M. and call it a day after his 12:30 lunch. He also decamped to Maine for a full three months each summer. During these absences Martin Roberts, his chief assistant librarian, was nominally in charge, but Roberts could do nothing without consulting Putnam. As MacLeish was to characterize the situation, the Library of Congress in 1939 "was not so much an organization in its own right as the lengthened shadow of a man — a man of great force, extraordinary abilities, and a personality which left its fortunate impress upon everything he touched." It was folly to speak of succeeding such an eminence, he added. "To succeed Mr. Putnam was a good deal like inheriting an enormous house at Stockbridge or Bar Harbor from a wise, well-loved, strong-minded, charming and particular uncle who knew where everything was and how everything worked and what everyone could do but had left no indications in his will."

It did not particularly gladden MacLeish to know that Putnam, though in retirement, had been designated librarian emeritus and given an office down the hall from his own. (The LC was bachelor Putnam's life, and he still came into that office well into his nineties, often disagreeing with and disapproving of his successors' actions.) Those who had worked for Putnam in the past naturally tended to look to him for guidance. And every change MacLeish made could be construed as an implicit criticism of the previous regime. So MacLeish did not include Putnam among the small group of officers he met with each morning. The librarian emeritus's feelings "were mortally hurt" by this decision, Archie recalled, but there was no other way. If Putnam had attended, "he would have been sitting there listening to talk about himself which he would take personally."

Under the circumstances, it was something of a triumph that Putnam declared himself MacLeish's enthusiastic supporter in the fall of 1939. Accepting the J. W. Lippincott Award for library service in a ceremony in New York, Putnam tried to put to rest the American Library Association's objections to MacLeish. These protests, he told an audience that included principal protester Milton J. Ferguson of the Brooklyn Library, were directed against "the theory" of MacLeish. The "facts of him" were quite otherwise.

> There is first the Scot in him — shrewd, austere, exacting, but humorous. There is the poet in him — whose stuff is not made of mere dreams but of realities — the contrasts of beauty and ugliness, joy and despair, success and failure.
>
> Then the humanist, keenly sympathetic to all that calls for social sympathy. The lawyer — trained to analysis through determination of exact issues. The soldier, pledged to duty under discipline. And finally there's the orator, capable of vivid and forceful speech.

As for his own contribution as librarian emeritus, Putnam said, he was supposed to "perform such offices as the President may prescribe." So far, the president hadn't prescribed any.

Nor, it turned out, did FDR offer much by way of instructions to his appointee as librarian of Congress. For a time, Archie was in the dark about what was expected of him. According to a family joke, his daughter, Mimi, wanted to know what her father would be doing. "Are you going to hand out the books?" she asked. Archie laughed, and then began to wonder why he was laughing, for he knew little more than she what his duties were, and wasn't it the business of all libraries to make books available to the public? In one of his early speeches after assuming the LC post, MacLeish expounded on his puzzlement. "Nothing is more difficult for the beginning librarian," he remarked, "than to discover in what profession he is engaged." Most professions defined themselves, but a librarian was "so called not for what he does, as the farmer who farms or the lawyer who laws, but from the place in which he does it. And the words which earlier librarians have written of their calling tell, if anything, less than the name itself."

It soon became clear that it was up to him to create his own job description. Characteristically, he assigned himself to a task of extraordinarily wide compass. As administrative chief, he instituted a series of shifts and innovations that amounted to a total reorganization. As an eloquent advocate for the profession, he brought wider recognition to the LC and elevated the status of the nation's librarians. Through his connections he vastly broadened the cultural and intellectual activities of the library and its associations with artists and scholars. Finally, he used the office of librarian of Congress as a platform from which to speak out on behalf of democracy and its preservation in a time of crisis. No librarian of Congress, before or since, has been so visible to the American public.

In undertaking these tasks, MacLeish moved with a speed that was astounding in bureaucratic Washington. It was, a colleague wrote, as if a "brush of the comet" had swept down upon an institution that had lain moribund for decades. Archie could do so much so fast because, in a very real sense, he had no superior to restrain him. He had contacts with both the executive and legislative branches, but took orders from neither. He was appointed by the president, and a telephone with a direct line from the White House sat on his desk, but FDR rarely consulted him about the operations of the library. Yet he reported not to the president but to the Congress. It was after all the Library of *Congress* he was running; the Senate had confirmed his nomination, and a congressional committee passed the budget. At least in the beginning phases of his tenure, MacLeish was careful to cultivate congressmen who showed a special interest in the library. In effect, though, as long as he maintained cordial relations (something that became more difficult as FDR assigned him to chores of partisan coloration), he could count on little or no interference from the Capitol. Having five hundred bosses was very much like having none at all. Librarian of Congress, he discovered, was "really the best job in Washington," for it offered the maximum of freedom to act.

Opening Windows

From the Putnam administration MacLeish inherited two valuable lieutenants. Martin Roberts, who understood the labyrinthine ways of the LC as well as anyone, stayed on the job as chief assistant librarian. And the able and competent Henry Boudinot, who had been secretary to Putnam, assumed the same position with MacLeish. Within a week or so, however, Archie called down to personnel for a second secretary to handle the vast amount of correspondence. He wanted someone with a college education, who was also expert at typing and shorthand. Thursa Bakey, a 1938 graduate of American University assigned to the Copyright Office, met the specifications, and soon she started reducing the stack of mail from friends and job seekers, congressmen and librarians, people who wanted MacLeish to speak and people who wanted special attention from the LC. Thursa expected to stay only a few weeks. Instead she became MacLeish's trusted assistant for the next half-dozen years.

No other person worked with him so long or so closely during his career in government.

At the beginning, Thursa was of two minds about being secretary to Archibald MacLeish. She certainly admired her boss, as did co-secretary Boudinot. "I would say we were in awe of him," she recalled. He was brilliant, with an unusual range of knowledge. He spoke eloquently, with an amazing command of the language. He was, they knew, a writer of renown. As a supervisor he was generous and understanding when they made mistakes. He showed an admirable sense of humor in response to Bakey's first goof, for example. She booked him into the Palmer House in Chicago, but the reservation was for the wrong night, and when he arrived the hotel was full. When he got back from his trip, MacLeish offered to enlighten his secretary about the latest fashions in ladies' hats. The hotel had put him up for the night in a millinery shop off the lobby.

Yet during the early days she often thought of resigning, for the workload was so heavy and incessant. MacLeish, she realized, "could do twice as much work as anyone else in half the time." Just when one pile of letters was cleared away, he would sail off on new projects. When he called her into the office, it was nearly always with five things to do rather than one. They scarcely had time for lunch; MacLeish often ordered in and continued working through the noon hour without interruption. When he had a speech or long report pending, he escaped to a study room on the top floor of the annex. When the White House called, he dropped everything and left. Invariably he would return to his desk from such absences with additional tasks that needed doing as soon as possible. MacLeish was, in short, "a glutton for work," and expected his associates to share his compulsion. In the end, it was only her conviction that she was "working for a very special person" that kept Thursa on the job.

Soon it was decided that Henry Boudinot would act as the librarian's official secretary and Thursa Bakey as his personal secretary. MacLeish called Thursa into his office to explain that he expected absolute discretion in handling such personal matters as social engagements and financial affairs. He was, as she put it, "a very private man." In her capacity as personal secretary, Thursa kept her boss's checkbook, arranged his travel and hotel accommodations, replied to invitations, organized official cocktail parties, reminded him of appointments with the dentist, passed on messages from Ada, and even saw to it that the laundry and dry cleaning were picked up — these in addition to the usual typing and filing and calendar keeping. "T Pls call the Star & ask how we can get a paper delivered" he asked her in one note. "We pay by the week. Little girls with apple cores in their chubby fists. Sometimes the paper comes. Most often it doesn't. I consider myself robbed!!!" Or "T: Will you figger this out & let me know what to do AMacL," to which Thursa replied, "Mr. M. The weight of your car is 3670 pounds. At .40 per hundred, the cost of the license is $14.68. This is what you paid last year. tmb" "Will you be working on your Annual Report while on vacation?" she queried. "Not if I can help it," he answered. "I'm going to lie in the dry grass on the highest hill & watch the hawks." A likely story, that!

Such were the standards of formality that secretary and boss remained "Miss Bakey" and "Mr. MacLeish" for two full years before she was persuaded to call him "Archie," and even then only outside the office. Nonetheless, she came to understand him well. "I knew what was going on; I knew how he worked; I knew when not to bother him; I knew his moods; I knew who his friends were; I knew what he liked to eat; I knew when to make appointments for him and when to direct visitors elsewhere." No wonder that Archie eventually wrote of her, in an all-purpose letter of recommendation, that she "exhibited qualities of intelligence, personality, tact, imagination, loyalty, skill and plain hard work, rare either in government or out of it."

One of MacLeish's idiosyncrasies, Thursa discovered, was that he insisted on absolute quiet. The librarian's office was large, bright, and decorated in the same Italianate style as the main halls: "a painted vault," Archie called it, with pillars supporting nothing and a domed ceiling where "nymphs, largely nude, [were] floating around." When visitors dropped by to see him, they were intercepted in the area outside by his secretaries. If excessive conversation then ensued, MacLeish would use the intercom to sing out, "Tell whoever is out there talking to go do it elsewhere." Eventually visitors were shunted across the hall to await appointments, and a heavy velvet curtain was installed within Mac-Leish's office to baffle the noise. So sensitive was Archie to harsh sounds that he and Ada moved from one side of Thirty-third Street in Georgetown to the other to avoid the cacophony made by the radios of police cars from the station around the corner.

Certain visitors, among them Carl Sandburg, were exempt from his insistence on noiseless surroundings. Sandburg burst in unannounced early in MacLeish's tenure, waving a burning cigar. He didn't say a word to Archie, didn't even look at him. Instead he walked slowly around the room, surveying the ornate surroundings. He went to the door, cleared his throat, and said, "Over the poet's cocoa was rococo," and walked out. The two poets were jointly involved in a mixup on November 30, 1939, when MacLeish drove Sandburg to the wrong building for his evening lecture appearance. They stepped outside the car to reconnoiter, and both men locked their doors behind them, leaving the car keys, Sandburg's guitar, and the copy of *The People, Yes* he planned to read from imprisoned inside. Then they sped their separate ways, Sandburg to the site of his appearance, MacLeish to get a duplicate set of keys in Georgetown. Archie liberated the car and delivered the guitar in time for Sandburg to finish his performance with "Frankie and Johnny" and an old slave song he'd learned from an ancient woman in South Carolina "with a face like a relief map of Asia." Sandburg like no one else managed to make MacLeish relax. "He was," Archie said, "a darling man."

Many well-known people paid calls on MacLeish as librarian of Congress, Thursa Bakey recalled. Among them were journalists Walter Lippmann and Raymond Gram Swing; radio commentator Edward R. Murrow; writers Lillian Hellman, Ernest Hemingway, Thornton Wilder, John Dos Passos, John Gunther, and Alexander Woollcott; magazine editors Freda Kirchwey, Edward Weeks, and Henry Seidel Canby; ballet impresario Lincoln Kirstein; sculptor Jo Davidson; philanthropist Lessing Rosenwald; Henry and Clare Boothe Luce of Time Inc.; Charles Poore of the *New York Times* and Mrs. Ogden Reid of the *New York Herald Tribune;* Supreme Court Justice Felix Frankfurter, a frequent caller; and Gerald and Sara Murphy.

Other memorable visitors included Archie's mother and half-brother Bruce. They posed no threat to Archie's sensitive ears, sitting in total silence until he was free to see them. Seeking a degree of sociability, Thursa looked up and smiled at Martha Hillard MacLeish, who in response "dipped her head a quarter of an inch" but did not change expression. Very nearly her opposite was Archie's father-in-law, William Hitchcock, "a little dumpling of a man who strutted when he walked and led with his stomach." MacLeish and his father-in-law did not get on well. After one of his visits Archie told Thursa, "You know, it would never occur to that man that anyone else might go through a door first." The bouncy Billy Hitchcock fell fatally ill during the summer of 1940, leaving only child Ada with a substantial inheritance. In addition, by provisions of his will each of the three grandchildren received a bequest of $10,000, and Archie one of $1,000. MacLeish took that as a direct affront. As for his own finances, Archie was losing confidence in the leadership of Carson Pirie Scott, now that Bruce MacLeish was about to retire as president. In March 1940 he proposed to Lincoln and Mina Kirstein's father, Louis, the head of Filene's department store in Boston, that he investigate the possibility of buying out Carson Pirie Scott.

As librarian of Congress, MacLeish immediately differentiated himself from his venerated but haughty predecessor. On the afternoon of his first day on the job, he held an informal reception for his department heads. Shortly thereafter, he invited administrators to a cocktail party at his home in Georgetown. These gestures did not go unappreciated. Most of the staff knew the LC had become a stodgy institution, run much as it had been at the turn of the century. They were ready for a breath of fresh air, and MacLeish promised to open the windows. His lieutenants at once sensed his tremendous drive and his unusual personal qualities: "a first-rate mind, which absorbed and penetrated and understood; energies that could be at once exhausting, graceful and yet dynamic; marked powers of concentration and concern for rationalization; an insistence on definition; and a gift of expression beyond any similar gift they had ever known." Many were eager to serve at his side. "If Archie asked you to do a job," David Mearns said, "you'd do it happily if you had to work around the clock."

Within a week of assuming office, MacLeish looked in on every one of the library's divisions and departments, introducing himself and asking for cooperation. His very appearance proclaimed a new day dawning at the Library of Congress. "Goodness," Thursa Bakey thought when he came by the Copyright Office, "I never knew librarians were so handsome or dressed so well." Putnam came to work in a wing collar and a swallowtail coat. MacLeish wore tweeds, soft collars, and bright ties. Whereas Putnam's office had been out of bounds to almost everyone, MacLeish announced that he would take time to talk to any employee who wished to see him. This was a mistake, for his days were soon occupied in listening to petty grievances. Boudinot and Bakey were forced to intervene, making appointments only for those few who had ideas about improving the library's services and referring the majority with personal complaints to their immediate supervisors. One such petitioner was the wife of a security guard who said her husband was meeting his girlfriend while on duty and wanted MacLeish to put a stop to it. Thursa suggested that she try to straighten the matter out with her husband, for approaching the librarian or even the captain of the security guards might well lead to her husband's dismissal. She did not pursue her complaint further. MacLeish's open-door policy did not please all of his officers, either. Luther Evans, who was eventually to succeed him as librarian of Congress, felt that Archie gave too much attention to malcontents, listening to rumors and criticism instead of giving his full support to responsible, highly placed administrators. If so, it may have been because of the personnel problems that confronted him during his first weeks at the LC. Some of those in high places, he discovered, were considerably less than responsible.

Putting Out Fires

Putnam's management style, at least in the latter years of his long service as librarian of Congress, was to concentrate on those areas of most interest to him — acquisitions, for example, and interlibrary co-operation — and to assume other operations would take care of themselves. Often they did not. MacLeish got a whiff of one such neglected field on a tour of the LC's subterranean regions. Somewhat reluctantly, the building superintendent guided him three stories below ground level, where they came upon a terrible stench. "It's those god-damned motion picture films," the superintendent explained. With American films, as with books, two copies were submitted to the LC to secure copyright. Putnam had taken little interest in these and consigned them to a cellar closet. When the superintendent opened the door, the odor was over-powering. On the floor lay something that looked like a mass of black jelly. Much of the film was ruined, but MacLeish sent everything that hadn't turned into crust to the Museum of Modern Art, which salvaged some priceless historical footage, including film of McKinley speaking from a rear railroad platform during the presidential campaign of 1900.

Then there was the problem of disposing of squatters — veteran LC users who had taken possession of study rooms (supposedly reservable only for one week) and were "doing everything in them but light house-keeping." Champion among the squatters was an elderly fellow who called himself a research statistician. For ten years he had occupied a spacious area equipped with two desks and a collection of over five hundred books from the library stacks. Despite orders to the contrary, he flatly refused to leave his bailiwick or to return the books. He even advertised for a secretary to assist him, directing candidates to "apply Library of Congress." Competing with him for the chutzpah award was a retired schoolteacher who had occupied a study room for nine years. She was a writer, she said, but no one had been able to find anything she had ever published. When the annex opened, she applied for a brand-new study room, inking out the one-week condition and substituting "For Life" instead. Shortly before MacLeish arrived, her application was approved with this revision.

Rather more serious troubles awaited MacLeish in the Legislative Reference Service (LRS) and the Rare Book Room. The LRS was estab-lished in 1915 as a service to the Congress, a place where representatives could call on competent reference librarians "to prepare such indexes, digests, and compilations of law as may be required." Obviously it was especially important that this service operate efficiently and well, since the LC's budget depended on congressional appropriations. Yet in advance of assuming his duties, the new librarian received several communications from disgruntled congressmen complaining that their requests had been ignored or poorly handled. The situation was complicated by the fact that Wilfred C. Gilbert, the director of the LRS, had been a classmate of Archie's at Harvard Law School. Gilbert wrote MacLeish his congratulations on the same day that President Roosevelt made his choice known. As an "admiring member" of the law school class of 1919, he reminded Archie, "I watched and listened with delight as you . . . 'talked back' to the professors." And of course, Gilbert added, he stood ready to contribute to the success of MacLeish's administration in any way he could. Yet as the complaints began to pour in, it became apparent that the LRS needed fresh leadership.

On arrival, MacLeish made it clear that queries from the Congress were to take precedence over other functions. In November he brought Luther Evans on board to steer the LRS, demoting classmate Gilbert to deputy director. He also conducted a survey of LRS operations, inviting senators and representatives to comment on improvements they desired. The survey disclosed, first, that there were not enough researchers to respond adequately to the increasing volume of congressional requests, and second, that those researchers now on the job were badly undercompensated. In addition to calling for more staff, MacLeish attempted to make the LC more accessible by establishing a Browsing Room stocked with the latest books for the use of members of Congress and their families.

Unlike Gilbert, the flamboyant V. Valta Parma, curator of the Rare Book Collection, would neither accept demotion gracefully nor go quietly, though *go* is precisely what both Putnam and MacLeish wanted him to do. To his credit, Parma had been instrumental in building the LC's rare book division over a period of twelve years, personally retrieving from the library's nooks and crannies nearly 90 percent of the one hundred thousand volumes shelved and catalogued in the Rare Book Room, and adding to that number by purchasing many others. But Parma also managed to alienate nearly everyone who worked with him, including Alice Lerch, the woman he hired as his chief assistant. Moreover, he followed unethical practices in buying books, and may have been guilty of accepting kickbacks from dealers. On July 1, 1939, Putnam began the process of easing Parma out. Henceforth, Putnam decreed, Parma would spend one-half of his time preparing a bibliography of the LC's juvenile holdings — under a grant from J. K. Lilly, Inc., that Parma himself had negotiated — and the other half on the Rare Book Collection, with his $4,600 salary split down the middle. While he worked on the bibliography, chief assistant Lerch was to take charge of "routine administrative duties." In mid-September, Parma asked to resume his former status, since he had employed an assistant for the bibliographic project. At first inclined to agree, Putnam then changed his mind. Effective September 25, less than a week before the new librarian was to take office, he directed Parma to detach himself completely from the Rare Book Room, thereafter devoting himself to the juvenile bibliography until the Lilly grant ran out. His salary from the LC was to continue only through the period of any annual leave he had accumulated.

A letter from Parma was on MacLeish's desk on October 2, 1939. Putnam had given no reason for removing him from the rare book division, he claimed. He was eager to discuss the matter with MacLeish. The following day, the new librarian received an FBI report, ordered by Putnam, that spelled out Parma's irregular dealings. Among other things, the investigators found that Parma had on a number of occasions purchased rare books for the LC from Mrs. W. M. Walbridge, who it turned out was in fact Mrs. Parma. By way of explanation, Parma later wrote MacLeish that Walbridge was his wife's professional name, which she invariably used in buying and selling books, that under the name of Walbridge she had once *given* the LC "a book of such rarity [unnamed] that its value exceeded the total amount she received for [selling the Rare Book Room] the collection of Children's Books," and that it did not occur to him that there could be "anything compromising" in such transactions. The confusion about names extended to Parma as well as to his wife. Born Albert C. Pratt, he was so known until he married Madama Pallas Parma (a.k.a. Mrs. W. M. Walbridge) and adopted her name as his own.

Although the FBI investigation failed "to disclose any violation of a Federal Criminal Statute," the report was nonetheless forwarded to MacLeish for such action as he deemed appropriate. Armed with this information, he wrote Parma on October 4 that of course he would be glad to meet and talk the matter over. At the same time, he expressed his "strongly held opinion that a new administrator should in general accept the acts of his predecessors as binding upon himself." More than a month elapsed before the two men met, with MacLeish repudiating a suggestion that they meet outside the library, in a social setting. When Parma finally presented himself, resplendent in elevator shoes, flowing tie, and a wide-brimmed hat crushed flat on one side, it was with threats of possible consequences if he were not restored to his former position. Rumors were being spread by Alice Lerch and Martin Roberts that he had stolen books from the Rare Book Collection, he maintained. These were damaging to his reputation, and his friends at the Associated Press were eager to tell his side of the story. In addition, the LC might well lose the $30,000 Lilly grant in his absence.

When these warnings did not avail, Parma widened the scope of his campaign. He contacted Colonel Frederic Delano, who had been Archie's employer on the 1926 League of Nations mission to Persia, and Delano in turn carried the protest to his relatives, the president and Mrs. Roosevelt. Either President Roosevelt must grant him a hearing, Parma told Delano, or a congressional investigation of the library "will surely result." Both Delano and Eleanor Roosevelt wrote MacLeish about the Parma question, and FDR asked him about it at the end of a luncheon meeting. Archie assured them all that Parma knew exactly why he was being let go, whatever he might say to the contrary, and that he had been given every opportunity to present his case. He also offered Parma a lesser position, unaffiliated with rare books, at least for the duration of the Lilly grant. Finally, on December 27, 1939, the still indignant Parma resigned.

As a last gasp, he managed to carry out one of his threats. He persuaded the *Washington Star* to present his case against Putnam and MacLeish. "Little birds on Capitol Hill twitter that while the voice at the Library is the voice of Jacob MacLeish," Frederick William Wile wrote in a January 29, 1940, article, "the hands still running the establishment are the hands of Esau Putnam." Wile characterized Parma as "by common consent America's first rare bookman" and quoted North Dakota Representative Usher L. Burdick as deploring "the treatment meted out to this scholarly, patriotic" public servant. Parma did not seek reinstatement, Wile pointed out, but "his friends in and out of Congress" were considering a congressional investigation. None came to pass.

Reorganization and Outreach

He did not set out to reorganize the Library of Congress, MacLeish commented in an October 1944 article. What happened was that one problem or another demanded action, and each problem solved led on to another that needed attention. Most of these difficulties were traceable to the archaic table of organization he inherited. During the summer of 1939, two former LC employees traveled to Conway to enlighten him about the unworkability of this structure and to offer their services in effecting the necessary reforms. MacLeish put them off, observing that he was sure he would find competent staff when he got to Washington. One of his first acts as librarian was designed to involve such staff members more actively in the library's operation. He called a daily conference, made up of division chiefs, the chief assistant librarian, and other administrators. These meetings functioned as a forum for hammering out decisions on important questions of the day. MacLeish for the most part kept his silence, except to calm tempers when the debate grew rancorous. The important thing for the division chiefs, who had stood silent before Putnam through the years, was that the new man expected them to contribute their opinions, and that he seemed to value them. The conferences also helped him determine who among the staff were best qualified to take on additional responsibility.

Besides consulting the staff regularly, MacLeish sought advice from outside experts before making changes. The LC's fiscal operations, for example, were at best "complicated, diverse, and difficult to control." Primary funding came from congressional appropriations, but income was also received from private grants, from two branches which each grossed more than $300,000 per year for issuing copyrights and selling catalog cards, and from services such as photoduplicating and recording. Yet no uniform plan for handling funds was in place, so that each area followed its own procedures. In the fall of 1939, MacLeish brought in five investigators from the General Accounting Office to unravel the fiscal threads. They were unable to report back until April 1942.

Fortunately, most of the committees MacLeish appointed moved much faster than that. Before he came to Washington, he was approached by a number of librarians who urged him to "do something" about the delay in the LC's cataloguing. Soon after taking office, he appointed a committee to look into the backlog in processing. It was composed of internal officers, who consulted leading librarians from around the country for their ideas. On December 9, 1939, the report was ready, revealing that 1,670,161 volumes — one-fourth of the LC's entire holdings! — had not been catalogued, with arrearage piling up at the rate of thirty thousand books a year. Another 373,721 volumes languished in the binding department. Putnam clearly had been far more interested in accumulating books than in making sure they were catalogued and put into use.

To guide the library's further growth, MacLeish also appointed a "committee on acquisitions policy," again with instructions to consult eminent specialists outside the LC. Of the forty subject areas they examined, the committee reported that twelve areas received "relatively adequate attention" from division heads and consultants, that thirteen subjects were "partially and inadequately provided for," and that in fifteen areas no one was responsible for initiating orders. In practice, to take a few examples, this meant that the LC was acquiring most of the books it needed in United States history and in music and the fine arts;

that it was doing a fair job in religion and geology; and that it was falling behind in education and the biological sciences. As one consequence of these findings, MacLeish in 1940 formulated three "Canons of Selection." Although it was impossible to collect everything, new and used, from all countries, the canons held that the LC should possess, first, "all bibliothecal materials necessary to the Congress and to the officers of government of the United States," second, "all books and other materials . . . which express and record the life and achievements of the people of the United States," and third, "the material parts of the records of other societies, past and present, and . . . full and representative collections of the written records of those societies and peoples whose experience is of most immediate concern to the people of the United States." These general principles were then applied to the hundreds of specific subjects covered by the LC classification scheme, with the result that some topics were collected far more intensively than before while at least two, medicine and agriculture, were assigned to other, more specialized national libraries.

A grant from the Carnegie Corporation, whose head, Frank Keppel, had been bitterly opposed to MacLeish's selection as librarian, facilitated this work. In September 1940 the LC established a program of fellowships for young scholars to examine holdings in their fields of expertise and recommend purchases to fill in the gaps. The first five fellows surveyed the collections in modern European history, population, Romance languages, geology, and library science. A major side benefit of this program, which lasted until 1944, was to provide — in MacLeish's words — "the increasing liaison between the Library of Congress and American scholarship that the Library so pointedly needs."

Leading scholar-practitioners in library science served on the single most important committee MacLeish appointed, the special Librarians' Committee to analyze the LC's operations. On April 10 MacLeish announced the formation of this committee, made up of Carleton B. Joeckel of the University of Chicago as chairman, Paul North Rice of the New York Public Library, and Andrew D. Osborn of Harvard. These three were soon joined by three others, Keyes Metcalf of Harvard, Quincy Mumford of the New York Public Library, and Francis R. St. John of Baltimore's Enoch Pratt Free Library. In two months' time these leading librarians produced a three-hundred-page report. Its findings did not surprise MacLeish, who had been on the job only briefly before he knew that a drastic shakeup was mandatory. As new librarian, for instance, he was constantly in the position of being asked to approve papers emanating from one or another of the LC's thirty-five divisions. Often he did not know whether what was in front of him was a good or a harebrained proposal. "Since I have a constitutional disinclination to signing documents I do not know to be right," he pointed out, "the situation was difficult, not to say downright impossible." What he needed was a small number of intermediate-level officers to report directly to him and to field most of this paperwork. Yet he was reluctant to decree such a transformation on its own, for it would be interpreted as a slap against Putnam. So he waited for the authority of his Librarians' Committee before swinging into action. He was confident that they would tell him to do what he planned to do.

The major conclusion of the June 15 report, sure enough, was that "the Library cannot be an efficient operating agency until its organic structure has been thoroughly overhauled." On June 28, less than a fortnight later, MacLeish divided the library's functions into the three major departments of administration, processing, and reference, with all existing divisions assigned to these departments as appropriate. He appointed Verner W. Clapp head of the Administrative Department, Luther Evans chief of the Reference Department, and Quincy Mumford (on loan from the New York Public Library) in charge of the Processing Department. Soon thereafter, Evans was assigned to do double duty as chief assistant librarian, following the death of Martin Roberts. As of July 1 MacLeish had streamlined the cumbersome and unwieldy system bequeathed to him by Putnam. Instead of thirty-five, only five reported directly to him: Clapp, Evans, Mumford, the director of the Law Library, and the head of the Copyright Office. In less than a year, MacLeish had carried out an administrative reorganization that affected nearly every staff member and division. The LC's hardened arteries were functioning healthily again. The blood began to flow.

MacLeish's practice of bringing in advisers from major city and university libraries assuaged the lingering bad feelings aroused by his appointment. He also won over detractors with his public advocacy of the librarian's calling and its undervalued status. In his March 1940 budget message to Congress, he asked for a whopping increase of more than a million dollars, from $3,107,707 to $4,189,228. Most of the increase was in three areas: acquisition of books in underrepresented subjects, new positions to reduce the backlog in processing and to bolster the research staff in the Legislative Reference Service, and improved pay levels for nearly all LC employees. MacLeish's case for higher compensation was picked up and circulated in a *New York Times* editorial of April 21, 1940. The average salary for a full-time employee in the Library of Congress, other than maintenance workers, was a mere $1,948 per year, the *Times* pointed out. Fifty-six staff members holding graduate degrees made less than that. Salaries were so uncompetitive that the library was constantly losing employees to business or other government agencies; often it could not fill positions that called for high qualifications and offered low rewards. Moreover, the paltry compensation at the national library reflected the general salary level in libraries throughout the country. Library workers were paid much less than comparably trained professionals in other fields. If federal and civic budgets could stand any increase at all, the *Times* concluded, they could stand it in this category "where the service is so unselfish and the rewards at best never large."

MacLeish did not get his million-dollar budget increase. The Congress did, however, authorize a boost of $367,591, the largest granted the LC in a single year up to that time. The $270,000 in additional funds MacLeish asked for in acquisitions was disallowed on the grounds that the LC should first attack its "accumulated arrearage." One hundred and thirty of the 287 new positions MacLeish requested were authorized, including 56 in processing. As for salaries, the Congress provided no immediate relief, instead directing the Civil Service Commission to reclassify the entire library staff. This process took time: it was not until 1944 that the Civil Service finished its reclassification survey. As a consequence, 600 — or almost exactly half of the LC's positions — were upgraded on the pay scale, while 616 positions, most of them custodial, remained unchanged and a mere 8 were downgraded. Although the process was laborious, MacLeish had at least called the Congress's and the nation's attention to the sorry state of library salaries and put machinery in motion for some amelioration of that condition.

In articles and speeches the new librarian proclaimed the importance of the profession. Books were "not dead things," he emphasized, nor were librarians merely deliverers of books to readers. They were also "keepers of the records of the human spirit," he asserted in the June 1940 *Atlantic Monthly*. "In such a time as ours, when wars are made against the spirit and its works, the keeping of these records is itself a kind of warfare. The keepers, whether they so wish or not, cannot be neutral." The proper role for librarians, he believed, was as champions of the cause of liberty, as it found expression in free speech and free thought. Addressing the annual meeting of the American Library Association in Cincinnati on May 31, 1940, less than a year after the group had denounced his selection by FDR, he told his hearers that they must "become active and not passive agents of the democratic process." "We have never had such leadership in things of the spirit from LC," Evelyn Steel Little, Mills College librarian, wrote Archie in response. "It has merely been the sacred mountain from which rules and cards, equally sacred in form, descended." MacLeish had given the profession a proper sense of its mission. "Your calling librarians to Washington to sit in council has destroyed the bogies held up to us a year ago," Little pointed out. And his stirring public statements had "replaced all fear with respect and enthusiastic loyalty. . . . We're with you and more power to you!"

The Congress was similarly impressed. Normally, Joseph Alsop and Robert Kintner observed in their *Washington Star* "Capital Parade" column, "one would suppose that poets and Congressmen would mix as well as oil and water." Instead, MacLeish's performance during the two-day hearing on the LC budget converted the relationship into a love feast. Congressmen discovered that MacLeish "was one of the most likable men in Washington, and knew his job down to the ground." The outcome — an increase of more than $350,000 in an economizing year — was a triumph for the new librarian. Before the House of Representatives voted on the appropriation, members of the committee on the library praised "the industrious and intelligent manner in which Mr. MacLeish has entered upon his duties." He has worked prodigiously, they asserted, and deserved the House's support. Charles A. Plummer, a no-nonsense Vermont Republican, drew applause when he rose to "make public acknowledgment of an error of judgment" in opposing MacLeish's confirmation.

At the same time he was operating officer of the LC, MacLeish served as a kind of national caretaker of culture. "Roosevelt's minister of culture," David Mearns called him, as in that role he inaugurated new programs and revitalized existing ones at the library, primarily but not exclusively in music and literature. Early in November 1939, for instance, the LC took over editorial direction of two WPA programs — the Federal Writers Project that was preparing state guidebooks, and the Historical Records Survey. It was only appropriate that the LC should do these jobs, MacLeish observed. As "the place where the American tradition was deposited," its function was "to educate the people to the value of their own culture." To preserve an important part of that culture MacLeish secured a $41,250 Carnegie Corporation grant in April 1940 for construction of a sound laboratory and purchase of portable recording equipment. Intended primarily to make the LC the center for American folk music, the laboratory eventually proved useful in transcribing radio broadcasts and building an archive of readings by major American poets. MacLeish "struggled and screamed and groaned" to secure this grant, according to music division chief Harold Spivacke. In succeeding, he managed to overcome the bias of those on the Carnegie board who regarded him as an untrustworthy left-winger. And indeed, there was more than a trace of radicalism in the songs of Leadbelly (Huddie Ledbetter), Woody Guthrie, and the other folk musicians in the LC recorded for posterity.

Classical music also played a part in the library's cultural offerings. Exiled by the war in Europe, during 1940 and 1941 the Budapest String Quartet spent half the year in Washington as the LC's "resident" chamber ensemble. The quartet presented a series of concerts in the Coolidge Auditorium, using the Stradivarius instruments presented by benefactor Gertrude Clarke Whittall. Tickets to these performances were free to the general public. Encouraged by FDR to realize the institution's potential as a museum, MacLeish established an Office of Exhibits for the first time in the library's history. Visitors were attracted to the halls and galleries to view displays of photographs, maps, handbills, pamphlets, and letters, in addition to books and manuscripts.

MacLeish took special interest in broadening the LC's role in international cultural affairs. He brought a number of important overseas artists to the LC as consultants, with an implicit understanding that they might spend much of their time cultivating their art. A Brazilian painter and a Chilean poet were secured through the auspices of the Hispanic Foundation. Harry Luce of *Time* financed a scheme to lure Chinese writer and ambassador Hu Shih. Other private gifts enabled the library to employ two of the greatest writers of the twentieth century, French poet St.-John Perse and German novelist Thomas Mann.

MacLeish had admired Perse's work since he read *Anabase* during his Paris days. Perse, he learned, was the pen name for Alexis St.-Léger, a Frenchman born in Martinique who worked as a civil servant on the quai d'Orsay. Léger took no part in the literary life of Paris, though, and MacLeish did not actually meet him until the fall of 1940. Through the years Léger had risen to become secretary general of the French Ministry of Foreign Affairs. As a leader of the fallen regime, he was exiled from his country following the German occupation of France. At this stage a benefactor — the poet Katherine Garrison Chapin, wife of U.S. Attorney General Francis Biddle — approached MacLeish with the suggestion that Léger be employed to survey the library's holdings in French literature. "I can assure you that the work itself interests me greatly," Léger wrote MacLeish in accepting on December 4, 1940. He planned to devote himself to it fully, preserving "the greatest possible measure of solitude, silence, and withdrawal in my retreat."

After his arrival at the LC, Léger and MacLeish became fast friends. For a time, Léger's mail was delivered to the librarian's office, and he would stop by at the noon hour to pick it up and chat for a few minutes. On two successive occasions when he came by, Thursa Bakey was eating an orange for lunch. Both times, M. Léger with Gallic gallantry bowed, picked up her right hand, and put it to his lips. Thereafter she gave up oranges for lunch.

"Now that you have come to us and have a room here," MacLeish told Léger in one of their first conversations, "perhaps you will be able to return to your real work as a poet." The Frenchman clicked his heels like a dragoon and said, "Jamais la vie!" Never! But less than a year later, Léger sent Archie an invitation to lunch at the U.S. Senate restaurant. On the walk back, he handed MacLeish an envelope. "Please take this, dear friend," he said, "and please do not open it until you have gone into that office of yours and locked the door." Inside was the manuscript of his long poem, *Exil,* along with a note. "Here's my poem on exile," it read. "It is yours. Do whatever you want with it. It has at least afforded me the opportunity of making this gesture of confidence towards a poet I admire and a man I love."

What MacLeish did was to send *Exil* to *Poetry,* where it was published in French in the March 1942 issue, along with an article by Archie on Perse/Léger. In the article, Archie quoted from a letter of Léger's about his travels in Central Asia. He might say with profundity that the Asia experience had given him "a broadened gauge of space and time," Léger admitted. Instead, he offered a story. In the middle of the Gobi Desert, someone translated for him the beautiful guttural pronouncement of a migrant lama: "Man is born in the house, but he dies in the desert." For days he puzzled over the deeper romantic meanings of the phrase, until in a lamasery on the border of the desert he had it explained to him in brutally mundane terms. "A dying man must be exposed outside the tent so as not to infect the dwelling-place of the living." So much, Léger added, "for the incurable associations of ideas of literary culture!"

Thomas Mann's service to the Library of Congress, underwritten by Eugene and Agnes Meyer of the *Washington Post,* was briefer and less demanding than Perse's. Under conditions of the arrangement arrived at on December 8, 1941, the day after Pearl Harbor, Mann agreed to be in Washington two weeks during the year, to give one lecture during that period, and to provide advice and information as requested about the collections of Germanic literature. This appointment came under some critical scrutiny because of the war. Announcing the appointment on January 16, 1942, MacLeish was careful to point out that Mann's "devotion to the cause of democracy led him to self-imposed exile from Nazi Germany." And in introducing Mann for his November 17 speech at the LC, MacLeish referred with pride to the novelist's service as consultant "in Germanic literature — a great literature which no evil, no obfuscation, no hatred, no venom can ever destroy." Nonetheless, anti-German feeling ran high. The following year, an indignant letter to the *New York Herald Tribune* accused MacLeish of endowing the German writer with a $9,000 annual stipend, though he continued to live in California. The amount was much less, Archie responded, and the position was endowed not by him but by friends of the LC.

However it may have been with Thomas Mann, MacLeish himself interceded on behalf of British poet W. H. Auden. In mid-October 1939, Auden asked Archie to support his application to be included in the immigration quota for Great Britain, with the goal of eventually becoming a United States citizen. MacLeish was happy to comply. "I can think of no other man of letters I should rather see received in this democracy," he wrote Auden, who was duly admitted under the quota on November 24.

Closer to home, MacLeish was interested in advancing the cause of American poetry in any way he could. Soon after taking office at the Library of Congress, he was invited to give a poetry reading at a Washington meeting of the American Association of University Women. At first he accepted, then canceled the date upon discovering that the group offered no honorarium. It was not so much that he needed the money. During his tenure at the library, he normally returned fees issued him for readings. But he felt he owed it to his fellow poets who earned their living by their craft not to read without a stipend. A quick inspection of the LC card catalog underlined the sorry status of contemporary American poetry. The library, he found, had very few books by the leading poets of the time, and almost none of his own.

It was curious, then, that the LC should already have had a poetry consultant in residence when MacLeish arrived. The poet was Joseph Auslander, the personal choice of shipbuilding magnate Archer M. Huntington, who donated the money to set up the consultancy in 1937. Auslander was not a particular favorite of MacLeish. In a 1926 letter to Pound, MacLeish described him as "a word fellow" with "the labial not to say digital dexterity of a masturbating monkey and as little fecundity." In his influential anthology of *Modern American Poetry*, Louis Untermeyer characterized Auslander as "inclined to overdecorate" and "to rely on the frayed trappings of the poetic stock-room." Shortly before he was called to the LC, Auslander's wife died, leaving him with an infant daughter. He then married twenty-two-year-old Audrey Wurdemann, who in 1935 won the Pulitzer Prize for poetry. Besides appointing Auslander to be poetry consultant in 1937, Putnam approved a post for Wurdemann as her husband's secretary and for Kenton Kilmer, the son of Joyce Kilmer (of "Trees" fame), as his assistant.

Immediately after Archie took over, he encountered two examples of how widely his tastes diverged from those of Auslander. The first concerned the interior decoration of the Poetry Room, an addition to the library Auslander had persuaded Huntington to underwrite. The room should be "warm and rich and inviting," Auslander felt. On these grounds Archie did not object, but he did oppose making the room into a kind of religious sanctuary. "In principle," he wrote Auslander in October 1939, "I am against the idea of putting stained glass windows in the Poetry Room." The second case involved NBC radio personality Ted Malone, whose broadcasts tended to reduce poetry to pretty sentiments in rhyme. Malone was about to begin a series called "Pilgrimages in Poetry" — broadcasts from poetically appropriate sites like the Poe cottage in New York and Emerson's Concord home. Malone planned to open the series with a broadcast from the LC's new Poetry Room. Auslander — and, presumably, Putnam — approved of the idea. Malone asked MacLeish to speak "to the masses of America in the cause of poetry" during this program, but Archie refused, not wanting to give the impression that the LC was in any way sponsoring the show. Thus he was outraged when the broadcast claimed that the library was its "honorary sponsor" and implied that the poet-librarian himself had planned it.

Exasperated by Auslander, MacLeish put into effect a scheme to ease him out of his position. Instead of one more or less permanent consultant in poetry, he proposed that the job be rotated annually among the best American poets. In clearing this plan with benefactor Huntington, Archie pointed out that both the library and the poets chosen would benefit from the arrangement. It would be "a grand thing for American poetry," he felt sure. In time "the award would become . . . one of the greatest distinctions in American letters." Huntington was persuaded, and Auslander could not reasonably oppose the idea, especially since it was understood that he would stay on the LC payroll as gift officer, with a higher salary, when the poetry consultantship was rotated. "Go ahead, and more power to your elbow," he wrote MacLeish in late August 1940. But that he very much wanted to keep his post was evident in the flurry of poetic activity he engendered during the fall of 1940. The most notable and worthwhile of Auslander's projects was a series of poetry readings in the Coolidge Auditorium, the first such performances ever sponsored by the library. Robinson Jeffers inaugurated the program, which was underwritten by Eugene and Agnes Meyer, in February 1941. In introducing Jeffers, MacLeish observed that too often American libraries and universities had taken the position that "the only good poet is a dead poet, and sometimes that the only good poetry is dead poetry." It was not altogether desirable, he added, "that the government of a democracy should ignore its poets as this government has done in the past."

Following Jeffers in the 1941 schedule were Robert Frost, Carl Sand-

burg (with guitar), and Stephen Vincent Benét, all of whom drew enthusiastic and sizable crowds. Auslander twice asked MacLeish to be
one of the readers. Archie, sensitive to the obvious conflict of interest,
twice declined. "It's just too goddam bad that a poet with so much fire
and truth in his belly and so much music in his mouth should be shut
off from the people whose hearts would be lifted by his voice and his
words," Auslander wrote in regret at his boss's refusal. Neither Auslander's burst of activity nor his fulsome flattery deterred MacLeish from
his determination to replace the consultant in poetry. It did not prove
easy to find a replacement, however. Even before he came to Washington,
MacLeish was shopping the job around. By the summer of 1940, he had
unsuccessfully offered the position to at least four of his friends and
acquaintances.

The first man he approached was John Peale Bishop in the summer
of 1939. Bishop, comfortably settled in South Chatham, Massachusetts,
said he would think it over. While he was cogitating, MacLeish tried
Stephen Vincent Benét on October 31, 1939. Steve could take the consultantship the following summer, he suggested, and use his time in
Washington to assemble material for *Western Star,* the long poem he
was working on as a follow-up to *John Brown's Body.* Benét turned the
proposal down. Next, in February 1940, MacLeish proposed that Allen
Tate take the post. Tate was interested, but delayed acceptance because
of illness and, probably, because of political differences. Rather embarrassingly, Bishop visited the Tates in Princeton shortly after Archie's
letter of invitation arrived. "Tate told me that you had just offered him
the job you offered me . . . and which, as I recall, I did not refuse,"
Bishop wrote MacLeish. "Now it's all right with me if you've changed
your mind. But I would like to know where the hell we stand." After
smoothing Bishop's feathers, Archie made yet another offer, this time
to Carl Sandburg in June 1940, but Sandburg, like Benét, declined.
Although no successor had been found by the following year, MacLeish
officially transferred Auslander from consultant in poetry to gift officer
on December 8, 1941. Another eighteen months elapsed before Allen
Tate assumed the vacant position.

17 ❖

THE DRUMS OF WAR

Promises

ARCHIBALD MACLEISH did his inside job as librarian of Congress expeditiously and well. Within two years he transformed the LC into an efficiently operating twentieth-century institution, with an expanded program of cultural outreach. But he was determined to do far more. His function as he saw it was that of the nation's librarians magnified: not the "neutral, passive, negative profession of the guardian and fiduciary" but the "affirmative and advocative profession of the attorney for a cause." The cause was that of democracy embroiled in a struggle to the death with international fascism. With the zeal one might expect of the son of a reforming college president and the grandson of a crusading minister, he set out to educate and persuade, cajole and sermonize. During the 1939–1945 period, he produced dozens of political essays and public addresses. In June 1941 he delivered four separate commencement speeches in less than two weeks — at Union College, the University of Pennsylvania, Wellesley College, and Stanford University. Like no predecessor before him, MacLeish used the platform of librarian of Congress to emerge as a national spokesman.

On November 28, 1939, the British ambassador presented MacLeish with one of four known copies of the Magna Carta for safekeeping at the Library of Congress until the end of the war in Europe. The great English charter was displayed in the same gallery as the Declaration of Independence. "To Thomas Jefferson," MacLeish observed, "the deposit, beside the Declaration of Independence, of this Charter of the liberties of those from whom we won our independence, would not have seemed

incongruous but just and fitting — an affirmation of the faith in which
this nation was conceived." But such faith could not be maintained by
sitting back and letting events take their course, as Great Britain had
learned through its policy of appeasement. A few days later, *America
Was Promises,* the poem MacLeish completed during the summer of
1939, was published. It was, in effect, a call to action.

At the last minute, MacLeish tried to change the title of his twenty-
page poem to "America *Is* Promises." His friends in Washington were
"very much concerned as to the effect of the poem on the witch-hunters,"
he explained to Bruce Bliven at the *New Republic,* where the poem
appeared in advance of book publication. But the magazine had already
gone to press, and *America Was Promises* had to do without the inspirational effect of the present tense. However it was called, MacLeish's
poem seemed affirmative enough to most readers.

From the discovery of Columbus — "from the first voyage and the
first ship there were promises" — MacLeish declares. These promises
had been variously interpreted. To Jefferson, a child of the Enlightenment,

> *The promises were Man's: the land was his —*
> *Man endowed by his Creator:*
> *Earnest in love: perfectible by reason:*
> *Just and perceiving justice: his natural nature*
> *Clear and sweet at the source as springs in trees are.*

Jeffersonian Man was to ride west, carrying his books and his seeds with
him, "Building liberty a farmyard wide."

Jefferson's agrarian dream was undone by profit seekers "Practicing
prudence on a long-term lease," "Just and perceiving justice by the
dollar." To "Old Man Adams," the promises were made to the best of
these, an aristocracy not of nature but of wealth and talents. History
proved Adams wrong just as it had Jefferson.

> *The Aristocracy of Wealth and Talents*
> *Moved out: settled on the Continent:*
> *Sat beside the water at Rapallo:*
> *Died in a rented house: unwept: unhonored.*

Unlike his contemporaries,

> *Tom Paine knew.*
> *Tom Paine knew the People.*
> *The promises were spoken to the People.*
> *History was voyages toward the People.*

Whatever was truly built the People had built it.
Whatever was taken down they had taken
    down.

For the People to fulfill these promises, they needed only to express themselves and assert their rights. But the People remained mute, while their enemies did not.

The time came: the time comes: the speakers
Come and these who speak are not the People.

Oddly, it is the dead in the worldwide battle against fascism who utter the poem's oracular message, the dead of "Spain Austria Poland China Bohemia" who say:

"The promises are theirs who take them."

If the People do not take them, others will. In a peroration, MacLeish exhorts his Brothers, his Generation, to action.

America is promises to
Take!
America is promises to
Us
To take them
Brutally
With love but
Take them.

Oh believe this!

MacLeish explained what *America Was Promises* was about in Whit Burnett's 1942 *This Is My Best*. From the beginning, America promised wealth, well-being, escape, and freedom. But these promises would not come true by themselves, like the ones in fairy tales: "They must be made to come true." The final "Oh believe this!" he intended as a hopeful exhortation, for, he thought, he could sense the country surging forward under the leadership of Roosevelt. Those who felt as he did were moved by the poem. Walter Lippmann wrote Archie that he thought it was "one of the half dozen greatest poems ever written in this country, and the greatest written *about* this country since the most inspired things of Walt Whitman." Archie's friend Nicholas Nabokov, who also detected a resemblance to Whitman, composed a cantata as a setting for the poem; it was broadcast in April 1940 by the CBS Radio Workshop.

Critical reviewers generally took an opposite view. As Louise Bogan expressed it, *America Was Promises* represented "MacLeish's saddest and most conglomerate attempt at 'public speech' to date. . . . The difficulty is that he is writing political poetry, even a kind of official poetry, and therefore the strict checks and discipline of poetry written for itself . . . do not hold." In her view he was "a private, a lyric, poet through and through," and should have allowed himself to remain one. Morton Zabel went still further in condemnation: "*America Was Promises* is a text-book in error and tastelessness." In his usual acerbic style, Randall Jarrell later disposed of the poem as a "malicious parody of MacLeish's public-speaking period." It is hard to dispute the essential point behind such objections: that in his pursuit of public poetry, Archie had sacrificed the power of deeply felt private emotions. In selecting *America Was Promises* for reprinting in a volume of the "best" work of several authors, he clearly committed an error of judgment. By no valid critical standard could this didactic, hortatory poem be ranked at the top of his body of poetry, or anywhere near it.

Yet 1939 also marked the publication of Cleanth Brooks's influential *Modern Poetry and the Tradition,* a book in which MacLeish's literary reputation may have reached its zenith. Brooks included MacLeish with Frost and Auden as practicing poets who could be regarded as logical successors to the great modernists Yeats and Eliot. The tribute carried more weight because of those Brooks left out, Stevens, Williams, and Cummings among them. *Conquistador,* he declared, "surely must be judged one of the finer accomplishments of modern American poetry." And MacLeish's other poems were "remarkably sound," though often lacking in dramatic tension and more concerned with humankind in general than any particular person. Notably, though, Brooks largely ignored the public poetry of the later 1930s. It was the work of this period and of the early 1940s that made MacLeish, as Karl Shapiro wrote, into both

> A poet of bitter enemies and a
>   man
> Of vast influence in our literature.

Once in Washington working for the Roosevelt administration, Archie had little time or inclination to write poetry. After *America Was Promises,* it would be nearly a decade before he published a book of poems. During this period his reputation as a poet declined precipitously. And when he raised his voice on other issues, as he often did, it earned him still more and bitterer enemies.

Responsibilities

MacLeish was not easily converted to the cause of militarism. "No man who saw anything of the last war," he wrote in 1933, "can help but hate and fear the possibility of a repetition." In June 1935, replying to a questionnaire in the *Modern Monthly,* he adopted an uncompromisingly pacifist stance: "I should do everything in my power to prevent the United States going to war under *any* circumstances." By 1939, however, he had become one of the nation's strongest advocates of support for Britain and France and full-scale preparation for war. He was chided for the inconsistency by Zabel, who attributed MacLeish's change of mind to the worst possible motives. "There isn't anybody smarter than Archie MacLeish when it comes to knowing how . . . to jump onto band wagons." That kind of vituperative accusation left out of account the course of history between 1935 and 1939. Manifestly, Archie's uncompromising 1935 statement had been wrong. Circumstances *did* make a difference, and he became progressively more hawkish after he traveled to Japan, and Franco's forces overran Spain, and Austria and Czechoslovakia fell before Hitler's *Blitzkrieg,* and the Battle of Britain commenced. By the time he came to Washington, MacLeish was prepared to speak out militantly against the threat of fascism. In his 1940 poem

> OPEN LETTER TO THE POET ARCHIBALD MACLEISH WHO
> HAS FORSAKEN HIS MASSACHUSETTS FARM TO
> MAKE PROPAGANDA FOR FREEDOM

Sandburg suggested two distinguished precedents for his actions:

> *Thomas Jefferson had red hair and a violin*
> *and he loved life and people and music*
> *and books and writing and quiet thoughts —*
> . . . .
> *And yet — for eight years he fought in a war —*
> . . . .
> *And there was his friend and comrade*
> *Ben Franklin, the printer, bookman, diplomat:*
> *all Franklin asked was they let him alone*
> *so he could do his work as lover of peace and work —*
> *Franklin too made war for eight years — . . .*

Implicit in Sandburg's poem was the conviction that some wars simply had to be fought. Any doubts Archie may have had about World War II vanished with the fall of France on June 14, 1940. When the news came of the Germans marching into Paris, Mearns discovered MacLeish at his desk, in tears. It was as Yeats had predicted in "The Second Coming," he said. The rough beasts were slouching toward Bethlehem. The center could not hold. The world had cracked open like an egg, revealing a vacancy at the heart of western civilization. The next day, in a luncheon conversation with Harold Ickes, Archie advocated the declaration of war that would not come for another eighteen months.

Actually, the fall of France only confirmed the message he had been expounding throughout the spring of 1940. In two separate speech-articles, he excoriated his fellow artists for failing to prepare the nation for war. One could not expect much of Hollywood, MacLeish felt, though he was offended by the movie capital's policy of offering only "escape . . . from any reality in any language." But with scholars and writers it was different. Neither group, he declared in the highly controversial "The Irresponsibles" (presented to the American Philosophical Society as an address on April 19, 1940, printed in the *Nation* on May 18, and in pamphlet form shortly thereafter), would accept its due responsibility "for the common culture or for its defense."

At one time, he maintained, men of letters like Milton, Voltaire, and Bartolomé de Las Casas felt obliged "to defend the disciplines of thought not in their own but in the general interest." Such men were not alive now, or if they were, they were keeping their silence. The modern scholar, according to MacLeish, retreated behind the facade of the disinterested scientist. "He knows because he cannot help but know, reading his papers . . . he knows this fire has consumed the books, the spirit, everything he lives by, flesh itself — in other countries. He knows this but he will not know. It's not his business." Writers were also irresponsible, MacLeish argued. They escaped by seeing the world as gods "see it — without morality, without care, without judgment. People look like this. People act like that." It was enough to show them looking thus and acting so, never mind why. Any suggestion that they owed a debt to defend the culture they had inherited would strike them as ridiculous. Modern artists "do not save the world. They practice art."

Archie's second speech, "Post-War Writers and Pre-War Readers," delivered May 23 and published in the *New Republic* for June 10, particularized his charge. Here he named names of writers who, he believed, had made young American readers so "distrustful of all words, distrustful of all moral judgments of better and worse," that they were incapable "of using the only weapon with which fascism can be fought — the moral conviction that fascism is evil and that a free society of free men is worth fighting for." Novels like Dos Passos's *Three Soldiers* and Hemingway's *A Farewell to Arms* did not merely attack "the hatefulness and cruelty and filthiness of war." They were also "filled with passionate contempt for the statements of conviction" used to justify the war of 1914–1918. Readers were led to the conclusion that not only "the war issues but *all* issues, all moral issues, were false — were fraudulent — were intended to deceive." He himself had no right to judge these writers, Archie acknowledged. In his own virulent reaction against the waste and carnage of the First World War, he had tried to say the same things himself. But he was now convinced that unless the "pre-war readers" of the present day could see that there were and must be "final things for which democracy will fight," the country could leave its planes and battleships unbuilt, for they would not be needed. Literature had virtually unmanned the nation.

"The Irresponsibles" and "Post-War Writers and Pre-War Readers," taken together, generated a substantial amount of controversy in the months leading up to Pearl Harbor. Among scholar-intellectuals, Merle Curti of Columbia wrote MacLeish to object that he had unfairly tarred the entire tribe of historians with his brush. In reply, MacLeish turned the argument back upon Curti. Which historians could he name, Archie asked, who truly faced the danger of fascism with "all the strength, all the imagination, all the resources of courage and inventiveness, all the watchfulness by day and night, all the last reserves of hope and skill and pain which men must use whose lives and more than lives are put in danger?" Willard Thorp at Princeton, by contrast, agreed with MacLeish and carried his point one step further. Passionate social commitment played no part in the academic game, Thorp stated. Scholars in search of "ultimate truth" were supposed to avoid unseemly displays of advocacy.

MacLeish's most influential ally, however, proved to be Van Wyck Brooks. In a series of public writings and statements, Brooks applauded and expanded on "The Irresponsibles." MacLeish's pamphlet might "turn the tide in American literature," which had for too long been "drugged by fatalism," he observed. The canon of literary modernism was overcrowded by such life-despairing authors as Eliot, Pound, Joyce, Mencken, Hemingway, O'Neill, and Dreiser, Brooks believed, excepting only Frost, Sandburg, and his friend Lewis Mumford from his blanket condemnation.

Hemingway did not accept such criticism quietly. In an ad hominem response in *Time* (June 24, 1940), he suggested that MacLeish must "have a very bad conscience. Having fought fascism in every way that I know how in the places where you could really fight it, I have no remorse — neither literary nor political. . . . If MacLeish had been at Guadalajara, Jarama, Madrid, Teruel, first and second battles of the

Ebro, he might feel better." In addition, Ernest located a logical inconsistency in Archie's thesis. "Young men wrote of the first war to show
truly the idiocies and murderous stupidity of the way it was conducted
by the Allies and Italy. Other young men wrote books that showed the
same thing about the German conduct of the war." So if Germans learned
how to fight the next war and Americans did not, MacLeish could hardly
blame the books. "Or," Hemingway added in a vicious final sentence,
"do his high-sounding words blame us because we never advocated a
fascism to end fascism."

Six months later, following his characteristic pattern, Hemingway
wrote MacLeish a friendly letter in which he jocularly inquired, "Can
it be I am becoming an Irresponsible?" The two had not met since the
Spanish civil war, at which time, Ernest confessed, he "was so self righ-
teous and chickenshit to coin a phrase . . . that often look back on that
so un-belle epoque with vivid horrorous." In any case, he was coming
to Washington and proposed to see MacLeish. The two met briefly early
in 1941. "Archie was fine," Hemingway wrote Sara Murphy. "I made
it all up with him because what are people doing nursing old rows at
our age?"

Most of the attacks on MacLeish's two articles came from the old
left. First to enter the lists was Edmund Wilson, who, like Hemingway,
focused on Archie's deficient logic. The books of Dos Passos, Hemingway, and Company had *not* "done more to disarm democracy in the
face of fascism than any other single influence," Wilson held. Books
were not that important: if the German Erich Maria Remarque's *All
Quiet on the Western Front* had really been influential, "the Nazis would
not now be in France." The real "literary irresponsible" was MacLeish
himself, who in his jingoistic advocacy of international conflict acted as
if "he had never heard of the class war . . . the fundamental conflict of
the contemporary world."

On that last point, Wilson was echoing the doctrines of the League
for Cultural Freedom and Socialism, an organization largely made up
of former communists who as of the summer of 1939 conceived the
enemy to be not Nazi Germany but repressive government at home.
"We demand COMPLETE FREEDOM FOR ART AND SCIENCE. NO DICTATION
BY PARTY OR GOVERNMENT," the League declared in a statement signed
by thirty-four writers and intellectuals "concerned about the present
drift of the United States to war reaction and war." They repudiated
the policies of the Kremlin, but they were unwilling to "abandon the
ideals of revolutionary socialism."

In "The Irresponsibles," however, MacLeish clearly had. His speeches
were "representative of this new gleam-in-the-eye, tough-muscle sort of

haranguing," Burton Rascoe thought. In his November 1940 diatribe against MacLeish, Rascoe portrayed him as a would-be führer, laying down the law about what writers should write. The opportunistic MacLeish was forever changing his spots, Rascoe observed. "What sort of mind is it that can yell for this Stalin in Carnegie Hall, work on *Fortune*, get its owner's picture and a two-page-spread signed advertisement in *Life* endorsing a paste-up movie ["The March of Time's" militant *The Ramparts We Watch*, summer 1940], and all in the name of idealism?" In his "newly fashionable incarnation," MacLeish was dispensing "totalitarian he-man hooey." He had "the same idea as Hitler" but didn't know how to express it.

To many observers it seemed that MacLeish was wrapping himself in the flag. Dwight Macdonald accused him of "patrioteering." Bernard DeVoto spoke of him as a "crisis patriot." In the fall of 1941, the *Partisan Review* solicited reaction to "the Brooks-MacLeish thesis." Brooks, MacLeish, and Mumford were nothing more than "ideological policemen" and "frightened philistines," James T. Farrell asserted. MacLeish had dwindled into an apologist for official policy, others commented. In developing this line of thought, Zabel invoked Montaigne: "Meanwhile let us follow that great teacher Epaminondas, and boldly declare that there are some things not allowed, even in fighting an enemy; that the public interest does not require all things of all men; that all things are not permissible to a man of honor because he happens to be in the service of his king, his country, and the laws."

As ever, Archie felt himself embattled and did not hesitate to excoriate his adversaries. In two letters to Phelps Putnam early in 1941, he remonstrated with his old friend for accepting the representations of his opponents. After supplying a point-by-point refutation, Archie went on to characterize the slanders as coming from "isolationists, pro-fascists, communist-fascists, and the whole literary gang who always run with the cur dogs." Furthermore, Putnam seemed unaware that "a desperate world situation" lay festering beneath the whole nasty name-calling business.

The dispute had barely quieted down by April 1942, when Stephen Vincent Benét wrote Farrell what may have been the most evenhanded assessment of the literary-political quarrel. On the one hand, Benét wrote, he did "not believe in throwing overboard a lot of the best writing of the past thirty years because it was 'gloomy' or 'depressing' in tendency." On the other hand, he could not agree with Farrell that Brooks and MacLeish "wish to 'politicize' writing, set up a certain kind of State writing, put artists in uniform or do the various things of which they have been accused." Farrell had also objected that lyric poetry was hardly an appropriate form "in which to predict historic events," probably a snide reference to *America Was Promises*. Why not? Benét wondered. "I don't think poetry should put its head in a bag — I don't think it should be the exclusive possession of an intellectual few." Of course, he would burn no books and suppress no writers — and neither would MacLeish.

In his repeated calls for United States involvement in the war, Archie managed to offend others than writers and left-wingers. Notable among these were members of the America First movement, isolationists determined not to be "sold" again as they had been by the propaganda leading up to World War I. Prior to the fall of France, a substantial majority of Americans was opposed to entering the war in Europe. When MacLeish told the American Library Association late in May 1940 that the war was really being waged "against us as Americans" and that at least some of those who disagreed with this viewpoint were "dishonest and treasonable," delegates from four CIO unions in Cincinnati (a city with a sizable German-American population) took vigorous exception. "We agree with 93 per cent of the American people who, irrespective of their sympathies with the combatants, are determined to stay out of war," they announced by way of rebuttal.

The national mood underwent a transformation in succeeding months, owing in part to increasing sympathy with England during the Luftwaffe's incessant pounding. Undoubtedly the on-the-spot broadcasts of Edward R. Murrow from London contributed to this change. His tense, measured voice brought the reality of the war into American living rooms, as he spoke against a background accompaniment of air-raid sirens, exploding bombs, and antiaircraft fire. "You burnt the city of London in our homes, and we felt the flames," MacLeish said of Murrow. "Without rhetoric, without dramatics, without more emotion than needed be, you destroyed the superstition of distance and of time." For his own part, Archie uttered the cry for liberty whenever the opportunity presented itself. "Democracy in action is a cause for which the stones themselves will fight," he declared from the steps of Boston's Faneuil Hall on November 20, 1940.

Repeatedly he attempted to bestir his fellow Americans to action by way of patriotic messages. In July 1940, for example, he prepared a draft for an "American Declaration of Faith, 1940" on behalf of the coordinating Council for Democracy. This draft was sent to seven others for alterations — Hamilton Fish Armstrong, Felix Frankfurter, John Gunther, Freda Kirchwey, Henry R. Luce, Robert E. Sherwood, and John Steinbeck — and presumably in the course of rewriting did not develop into "the spiritual rallying point" the council had hoped for.

The following year, Archie composed lyrics for two different songs hymning the wonders of freedom. The opening chorus of the second, written in August 1941, ran:

> We were born free men.
> We'll be free until we die.
> There'll be some to tell us when.
> There'll be some to tell us why.
> We'll live the way we choose.
> And we'll talk the way we please.
> The earth will take our shoes
> But God alone will have our knees.

For CBS's "Free Company," he wrote a radio play called *The States Talking* that was broadcast in the spring of 1941. The colloquy of voices from different regions of the country was intended to disprove the Nazi claim that "the States would never amount to anything because of their mixed blood," that "the pure-bred nations of the old world . . . would run the world and the rest of it." MacLeish let the States speak for themselves in refutation.

> Have they seen our kids says York State: the tall girls
> the small elegant breasts they have like Egyptians
> the long legs with the delicate slender bones
> . . . .
> Have they raced our boys says Michigan — fast as black snakes:
> Quick on the gun as quail: the sweet striders:
> . . . .
> Have they seen our farms says Texas?
>   and who ploughed them.

Often MacLeish was called on to speak on occasions of national celebration. Wintering in Scottsdale, Arizona, his mother heard Archie's talk over the radio on Washington's Birthday 1941. "You certainly are giving great service," she proudly wrote her son the next day. Herself a dedicated adherent of intervention on the British side, she reported her impression that American sentiment was rapidly changing in that direction, despite the howls of isolationists. Then in her motherly way she cautioned Archie not to exhaust himself by overworking, for his service would be needed for a long time to come. "If necessary," she added, "tell the President I say so."

The rising tide of feeling against Nazi Germany that Martha MacLeish detected reached new heights after several incidents of submarines' torpedoing U.S. merchant ships. On the night of October 16, 1941, for example, Nazi U-boats sank thirteen vessels in a convoy of fifty-three ships in the North Atlantic. Among these was the *Bold Venture,* an American-owned freighter sailing under the Panamanian flag. President Roosevelt reacted angrily, but the debate in the Senate was so blandly isolationist that Archie was moved to a sarcastic protest in verse:

> *They sank the* Bold Venture *and Senators said:*
> *"She should have been riding at anchor instead.*
> *If only she'd stayed in a port of her own*
> *The Nazi Command would have left her alone."*
> . . . .
> *They sank the* Bold Venture *and Senators said:*
> *"If sailors would only lie quiet in bed*
> *And shipping could only be tied to a rope*
> *The Nazi Command wouldn't hurt us — we hope."*

Senator Claude Pepper of Florida read the poem on the Senate floor on October 28. "I wish you could have seen the Senate," he wrote Archie. "You could have heard a pin drop . . . the attention was so rapt."

Two weeks after the sinking of the *Bold Venture,* Eleanor Roosevelt assigned MacLeish to a patriotic task. She wanted him to devise a pledge of faith in democracy for millions of Americans to sign. The pledge was to be brief enough to print on a card and ringing enough to proclaim itself on posters. Archie took a crack at the job, and on November 8 invited Carl Sandburg to do the same, but neither of them could find words to fit so restrictive a formula. In all his endeavors — speeches, articles, radio plays, poems, songs, and pledges — MacLeish sought to enlist his fellow citizens in what he called *The American Cause,* the title of his forty-three-page book published in November 1941. The cause was democracy — the eighteenth-century democracy of our revolutionary ancestors who believed in the liberty of the individual, and not the nineteenth-century democracy of the status quo. The only way to restore this democracy, MacLeish believed, was through action, and if need be through warfare. "Democracy is always something that a nation must be doing," he declared.

The President's Man

MacLeish's militant views on the war in Europe closely paralleled those of President Roosevelt, and Archie was in a position before Pearl Harbor — on the periphery of the administration — to express them more forcefully. Throughout his years in Washington, Archie regarded himself very much as FDR's man. The president had, after all, declared his confidence in him by appointing him librarian of Congress. Then in succeeding years, FDR assigned him a series of important jobs. Flattered by these indications of Roosevelt's faith in him, Archie was altogether captivated by the president's famous charm: "He was just the most attractive human being who ever lived." In addition, FDR somehow made Archie, and his other loyal lieutenants, feel that they were working together, not only for the public weal but as an act of friendship. If the president asked him to do anything, he jumped.

From the start, Roosevelt patently felt that MacLeish's contacts in the world of journalism might be used to generate favorable publicity for his policies. Thus Archie gave a dinner party for Mac Ingersoll on June 1, 1940 — seventeen days before the first issue of Ingersoll's liberal New York daily newspaper, *PM* — with administration insiders Dean Acheson, Felix Frankfurter, Robert H. Jackson, Francis Biddle, Harold Ickes, Tom Corcoran, and Benjamin Cohen. Ingersoll, Archie thought, had been the "best *combination* of editor, writer, idea man, administrative and business executive in Time, Inc." (Luce, when he'd worked at the trade, had been a better manuscript editor.) Therefore MacLeish had high hopes for the success of the short-lived *PM,* a paper that promised to follow the New Deal line. Ingersoll admired MacLeish as well, and adopted his definition of objectivity as a guide to the new paper. "It is current-day fancy," Archie observed, "to consider a journalist objective if he hands out slaps and compliments with evenhanded impartiality on both sides of the question. Such an idea is, of course, infantile. Objectivity consists in keeping your eye on the object [and] describing the object as it is — without regard to the feelings of anyone." The following year, on March 9, 1941, Luce himself was the honored guest at another Washington dinner of Archie's, this one atttended by Acheson, Biddle, Frankfurter, Bob Lovett, William O. Douglas, Robert Patterson, and James Forrestal. The dinner's purpose, Alice Acheson recalls, was to persuade Luce to take a more liberal, pro-Roosevelt view in his publications. It did not succeed.

One interesting if insignificant assignment MacLeish undertook for FDR involved selecting the best in current mystery and detective fiction for the president's reading pleasure. In June 1940 Archie called on Alec Woollcott to nominate books for this special bookshelf in the White House. Woollcott himself was in Washington in February 1941, playing the lead role in *The Man Who Came to Dinner.* The MacLeishes threw a supper party for him opening night, and the Roosevelts gave another later in the run of the show.

Far more important was MacLeish's role as a speechwriter for Roosevelt. During the campaign of 1940, he was frequently called on to work with Harry Hopkins, Sam Rosenman, and Bob Sherwood in drafting speeches. Archie's first assignment, a solo job, involved producing language for the laying of the cornerstone of the Jefferson Memorial. "I worked like hell for three days," he wrote Rosenman later, "and . . . although he never said a word to me, the President apparently liked the result." Usually Roosevelt's speeches were the result of collaborative efforts. His cadre of speechwriters assembled around five P.M. in the room above the Oval Office. FDR passed around the Old Fashioneds and a discussion ensued, with the president asking questions rather than giving orders. "What do you think about this approach?" he would say. Sometimes these sessions went on past midnight. MacLeish was "an effective collaborator," according to Rosenman. He "never quarreled over language. And he had a grand sense of humor — a real asset at three in the morning when ideas didn't seem to come or when the President was getting . . . a little ruthless with bright ideas."

About eleven o'clock one evening, while MacLeish, Sherwood, and Rosenman were struggling over a speech, Roosevelt and Hopkins came in tired and hungry. As it happened, Archie and Ada had expected guests for dinner who couldn't come, and a whole platter of fried chicken was sent back to the kitchen untouched. So a White House car was dispatched to Georgetown to pick up a bushel of chicken. When Ada opened the icebox door, however, only two drumsticks remained. "Knowing the toting habits of the ladies of Washington's kitchens," Archie later wrote Mearns, he could guess what had happened. The two drumsticks didn't go very far toward assuaging the pangs of hunger. The next day an advertisement with a photo of a plateful of succulent Birds Eye Country Fryers arrived at the MacLeish house, initialed by the president and signed by Hopkins, Sherwood, Rosenman, and Roosevelt's secretary, Grace Tully. "Dear Ada," the covering copy ran. "This is called to your attention as a suggestion for solving your housekeeping problems of which we understand you have plenty."

In stitching a speech together, FDR sometimes combined passages from all of his speechwriters. Mearns was sitting at newspaper publisher Jonathan Daniels's house one night listening to one of FDR's fireside chats over the radio. Sherwood, Rosenman, and MacLeish were also in attendance; each raised his hand when the president uttered a passage he had written. Malcolm Cowley also began to pick up echoes of Archie's prose in these radio broadcasts. They were easy to detect, he thought, because Roosevelt's style was so much more down-to-earth than MacLeish's. In fact, high-sounding rhetoric was exactly what the president wanted from MacLeish. In his 1941 inaugural address he delivered a ringing if somewhat abstract affirmation of faith in democracy, most of it contributed by Archie. "It is not enough to clothe and feed the body of this Nation," the speech proclaimed. "For there is also the spirit." To preserve our democratic way of life, we must "muster the spirit of America, and the faith of America."

MacLeish served FDR well as a supplier of inspirational rhetoric. He was less successful when he attempted to take foreign policy into his own hands. In the summer of 1940, MacLeish strongly supported Roosevelt's position that the United States should give fifty overaged destroyers to Britain to bolster their navy. This step could be taken far more effectively, he reasoned, if it had the support not only of President Roosevelt but also of Wendell Willkie, his Republican opponent in the upcoming election. So he telephoned Mitch Davenport, his old friend from *Fortune* and now one of Willkie's leading advisers, to sound him out as to the Republican challenger's views. Impulsively and rather naively, Archie apparently assumed that he could do away with partisan differences on this issue by means of a phone call. Somehow Arthur Krock of the *New York Times* got wind of this, and chastised MacLeish and FDR in print for using underhanded techniques to discover what the opposition was up to. That was not Archie's intention; he simply wanted Britain to win the war. After reading Krock's article on the front page of the *Times*, he called Ada and told her to get ready to pack. Then he sat in his office waiting for the phone to ring. At eleven A.M. it did. Missy Lehand at the White House was on the line. "Well, you did put your foot into it, didn't you?" she said. "The boss says to tell you, 'That's the boy'!"

Archie, who knew he had pulled a boner, was grateful for the president's tolerance. A friendship grew up between the two and their families, although Archie was never, except as a speech drafter, really a member of Roosevelt's innermost circle of advisers. In January 1941, for instance, Archie and Ada accompanied Eleanor Roosevelt to a National Symphony Orchestra performance with Igor Stravinsky as guest conductor. A year later, when Mrs. Roosevelt had to be out of town, she asked Ada to serve as her hostess at an after-theater party in the White House. The MacLeishes also accompanied the president on retreats to his cottage in the mountains and on cruises aboard his Coast Guard cutter. Archie understood that he was a resource for Eleanor Roosevelt as well as for her husband. In the summer of 1941, she commandeered his services for the Summer Student Leadership Institute she established at Campobello Island, discussing the "principles of progressive democracy" with a group of thirty college students (other "faculty" members were Frankfurter, William Allan Neilson, who was president emeritus of Smith College, and Mrs. Roosevelt herself). MacLeish admired Eleanor Roosevelt tremendously. She was, he thought, as truly selfless a person as he had ever known. She saw problems in human terms. "Things got simpler where she was," he wrote of her. "Good became good again, and nonsense nonsense, and evil evil." Yet he never felt easy with her in the same way that he did with the president.

The day MacLeish remembered best, a Saturday outing on the Chesapeake Bay aboard the Coast Guard cutter, Mrs. Roosevelt did not come along. For much of the morning, FDR sat way aft, working on his stamp collection and laughing with Ada. Then in the distance Archie spied the MacLeish family boat, a lumbering vessel called the *C.J.* for *Creeping Jesus*. Aboard, he knew, were son Ken, then working in Washington as a cultural anthropologist for the Department of Agriculture, and his wife, Carolyn. Also on board, Archie knew, were two revolvers that Ken was not supposed to have. Seeing the Coast Guard cutter, Ken made for shallow water. FDR, when Archie told him what was going on, decided to have some fun with young MacLeish. He ordered the captain to overtake the *Creeping Jesus,* which didn't take long. Not until the two ships were alongside did the president and Archie and Ada show themselves and wave at the young couple. In relief, Ken and Carolyn danced a jig on deck.

Summer of '41

Bill MacLeish has never forgotten the expression on his mother's face one day in Washington when he was about twelve years old and the two of them were taking a walk along the Potomac. They stopped for a moment while Ada stared out over the river, a look of absolute devastation on her face. Bill did not ask her what was wrong; he knew that she would not have told him. But he is inclined to connect his mother's distress, that day in 1940 or 1941, with a conversation he had with his father thirty years later. Had he ever had a serious affair? Bill asked Archie. "Yes," Archie answered, "and it damned near killed me."

The woman may have been Catherine Carr, who accompanied him to South America in 1938. So much is suggested by MacLeish's poem "Voyage West," published in the February 1941 *Yale Review*. It is one of a handful of poems Archie wrote during his six-year tenure in Washington, and the only one that is personal rather than political in nature. Here is "Voyage West," as it appears in MacLeish's *Collected Poems*:

> *There was a time for discoveries —*
> *For the headlands looming above in the*
> *First light and the surf and the*
> *Crying of gulls: for the curve of the*
> *Coast north into secrecy.*

That time is past.
The last lands have been peopled.
The oceans are known now.

Señora: once the maps have all been made
A man were better dead than find new continents.

A man would better never have been born
Than find upon the open ocean flowers
Drifted from islands where there are no islands.

Or midnight, out of sight of any land,
Smell on the altering air the odor of rosemary.

No fortune passes that misfortune —
To lift along the evening of the sky,
Certain as sun and sea, a new-found land
Steep from an ocean where no landfall can be.

Even at first blush, this poem carries metaphorical connotations beyond its ostensible subject matter: the terrible "misfortune" of discovering a newfound land when the time for discovery is past. The title and the references to "Señora" and "new continents" seem to link this implicit meaning to the voyage he and Catherine Carr made to South America. That might be only guesswork, save for the headnote to the poem Archie supplied for its original appearance in the *Yale Review* (this was omitted for later reprintings). "It is perhaps a disastrous thing to confuse a continent with a woman," he wrote, "but when it is done it has happened. Also there were the parakeets in the trees and the column of gnats imperceptibly contriving the evening." He was, one surmises, bidding unhappy farewell to an affair that had run its course "north into secrecy" yet could not last, since the map of his life was not subject to alteration. The explicit gloss on the poem he provided — continent = woman — may have been intended as a gift to Catherine, since the parting was painful enough to "damned near kill him," or as a gesture of confession to Ada.

Bitter as this affair may have been to both MacLeishes, they emerged from it bound to each other. Ada became increasingly for Archie the embodiment of the good wife, organizing their days smoothly and practicing the womanly graces with great skill. She was somewhat more oriented toward high society than her husband, and her speaking voice showed the influence. On one occasion, Thursa Bakey recalls, Ada apologized for getting wax on the telephone receiver. She'd been waxing "flaws," she explained. Assuming she meant "floors," Thursa asked why she didn't let her houseman do that work. "Oh, he wouldn't know how," Ada replied. Then it dawned on Thursa that Ada had been waxing *flowers*, not *floors*. Archie himself enjoyed the company of the elite, especially those who combined their advantageous inheritance with careers of accomplishment. Only once did he and Ada clash on an issue of social propriety. Ada badly wanted daughter Mimi to have a coming-out party. Mimi said she'd run away from home rather than go through such an event. Archie intervened on his daughter's side. "What are you thinking of?" he said to Ada. "In the middle of a war?" Mimi skipped away, victorious.

The entire family assembled at Conway for three weeks in the summer of 1941, the last time they would all be together before the United States entered the war. Archie and Ada celebrated their silver wedding anniversary in June with a party for their closest friends, including the Achesons and Lovetts and Murphys. Alexander Woollcott had specifically not been invited, since Dean Acheson could not abide him. Nonetheless, Alec drove down from his place in Vermont, arriving as the anniversary feast was about to commence. Ada greeted the man who came to dinner unasked as graciously as she could. "You know and I know that you shouldn't be here, Alec," she said, "but since you are, we're delighted to have you."

Archie's mother also came for the occasion, as did sister Ishbel and Alec Campbell. On a picnic outing during her visit, Martha MacLeish was walking along the banks of the Deerfield River and lost her footing. Alec Campbell, a few steps behind her, saw her turn turtle and start sliding toward the water. When he rescued her, Mrs. MacLeish was roaring with laughter. Most eighty-five-year-old women would have called for an ambulance, Campbell thought, but Martha MacLeish, like her son Archie, was endowed with tremendous physical vigor. Mother and son also looked amazingly alike.

As the MacLeish family dynamics worked out, Mimi rebelled against her mother and Ken against his father, while Bill did more or less what his parents expected of him. Bill performed creditably at the prep schools he was sent to, first at Fountain Valley School in Colorado, where his uncle Alec Campbell was teaching English, and then at Deerfield Academy. He dutifully attended the debutante dances Mimi had shunned, standing miserably among the stags while the strikingly pretty Jacqueline Bouvier danced by in the arms of more socially prominent boys. In due course he went to Yale, Archie's alma mater, and made Skull and Bones there; older brother Ken had declared his independence by attending Harvard. Despite his seemingly tractable nature, Bill admired the defiant spirit of Ken, his senior by more than a decade. Ken was avid for danger:

he flew "lighter-than-air" ships on submarine watch during World War II, and later became a record holder for the depth of his underwater dives. Ken also liked weapons, possibly because his father did not, and introduced his younger brother into whatever mischief the Conway countryside afforded.

According to the Warren Harrises, who bought a portion of the land at Uphill Farm in the thirties and so became the MacLeishes' nearest neighbors, "Billy and Kenny were devils." As soon as Bill was old enough to carry a gun, the two of them went hunting. They shot a beautiful wood duck, which so disgusted Archie that he hung it up where the boys would see it every day. They shot a deer out of season, and concealed its carcass under the garden shed. When there was no game in sight, they shot at trees and chimneys, littering the fields with 30-0-6 cartridges. The game warden from Shelburne Falls thought it was Warren Harris doing all the shooting. "I watched with binoculars and I could never get you," he told Harris. "Well," Warren said, "I don't think you'll find that it was me that was doing it."

In his 1984 story "Stalking," Bill describes a perilous game that he played with his brother. Ken (called Shep, in fictional disguise) teaches his worshipful younger brother (Paul, in the story) about the use of various deadly weapons: rifle, knife, revolver, bow and arrow. Shep is on leave from training as a fighter pilot, and thinks his younger brother needs to be educated about killing. One day he fires an arrow straight up into the sun, and Paul follows its flight until he loses sight of it, then in terror stands as close to Shep as he can. To tease Paul, Shep moves one step this way and two that, never taking his eyes from the arrow until it slams into the ground six feet behind them.

The game itself involves stalking each other with bow and arrow. In preparation, they drink a quantity of champagne, stolen from the cellar, and use the corks as padding for the arrows. The padded arrows, they find, hurt terribly but do not break the skin. Shep sets down the rules. They will stalk each other, and attempt to get in the first shot. No aiming at the head, for that might cause brain damage. No charging at the opponent, and no shots from closer than twenty yards. When they play the game, though, something terrible happens. Paul shoots his brother from a considerable distance. Shep comes staggering out of the woods, an arrow stuck in his belly and his khaki shirt stained red. Paul starts running for help, when Shep calls him back. He has not really been hurt. Paul's arrow had missed him. He'd simply broken it off to make it look as if it were embedded in his body, and used some berries for the stain. The game is over, and Paul has learned a lesson. "Now you know what it feels like to kill a man," Shep tells him. Now he was ready for war.

PROPAGANDIST
FOR DEMOCRACY

War of Words

ON SUNDAY, December 7, 1941, Archie and Ada MacLeish drove out to Harewood, the Achesons' place in Sandy Spring, Maryland. The two couples took a walk, cleared some brush for a bonfire, and enjoyed a picnic lunch in the woods. Early in the afternoon, the MacLeishes left so that Archie could keep an appointment in Washington. Fifteen minutes later he hurried back with the news he had heard on the car radio. The Japanese had attacked Pearl Harbor. Dean put away his tools, and both men sped back to their jobs in the capital. The weekend — the long weekend between wars — was over.

Within two weeks the Library of Congress completed a calculated removal of its most valuable books and manuscripts to fireproof buildings. The project moved quickly because MacLeish had instituted contingency plans nine months before. The Declaration of Independence, the Constitution, the Bill of Rights, the Gutenberg Bible, the Stradivarius instruments, and the Magna Carta traveled in hermetically sealed containers to the vaults at Fort Knox, Kentucky. About seventy thousand volumes were carried in twenty-nine truckloads to three different sites — the University of Virginia in Charlottesville, Washington and Lee University and Virginia Military Institute in Lexington, Virginia, and Denison University in Granville, Ohio. The Union catalog was moved to Charlottesville, and the main catalog was microfilmed and stored safely outside Washington.

In other ways the LC made itself useful in the prosecution of the war. It held by far the nation's largest repository of books from and about

Japan, and security was stepped up to make sure that none of these disappeared. Volumes that had been gathering dust for decades suddenly became valuable sources of military intelligence. One such was an imposing tome called *Rainfall in Burma,* with an account of meteorological conditions that the air force would consult when they began to fly the hump in the China-Burma-India theater. A Division of Special Information was immediately established to ferret out such resources; later it became the Research and Analysis Branch of the Office of Strategic Services (OSS). The bibliographic staff devoted itself to making summaries, preparing lists, and otherwise conducting research for those in command.

The LC was not uppermost in MacLeish's thoughts during the early days after Pearl Harbor, however. He was primarily concerned with the reaction of the American people, the logical preoccupation of the post President Roosevelt appointed him to on October 24, 1941. As the impending war drew nearer, FDR had established the Office of Facts and Figures (OFF) in the Office of Emergency Management (OEM), and he named Archie director. He was not relieved of his duties as librarian of Congress, simply given this additional task to perform. The executive order outlined the purpose of OFF in this way:

> Subject to such policies and directions as the President may from time to time prescribe, the Office of Facts and Figures shall formulate programs designed to facilitate a widespread and accurate understanding of the status and progress of the national defense policies and activities of the Government; and advise with the several departments and agencies of the Government concerning the dissemination of such defense information. The Office of Facts and Figures shall rely upon the services and facilities of existing agencies of the Government for the dissemination of information.

Such was the organization's charge, except that after December 7 the word *war* — war information, war policies — supplanted *defense.*

Several things are notable about the language of this executive order. The first is its vagueness. Fiorello H. La Guardia, a strong early proponent of OFF in the White House, envisioned it primarily as a morale-boosting organization. In preliminary drafts he advocated such specific steps as establishing a speakers bureau, persuading radio commentators to broadcast the government's views, supplying canned editorials and articles to small-town newspapers, and using outstanding personalities from abroad to bombard their native countries via shortwave. "All this could be put into sonorous and lengthy language," La Guardia observed in a memo to the president, "but it all boils down to getting across actual and accurate information, as well as sugar-coated, colored, ornamented matter, otherwise known as 'bunk,' but very useful." As OFF director, MacLeish was sensitive to the need for carrying the government's message to the people, but he would certainly have quarreled with La Guardia as to the usefulness of bunk. OFF, he insisted, would neither pervert nor color the facts and figures and would "not use bally-hoo methods." If the American people were provided with a "widespread and accurate understanding" of the nation's policies, he had no doubt that they would support its cause to the death. OFF, then, would pursue a "strategy of truth," give the people the information they required.

This proved easier said than done, because the president — or Samuel Rosenman, who drafted the executive order — did not endow OFF with sufficient authority. It was empowered only to "advise with the several departments and agencies of the Government concerning the dissemination of [war] information," and advisory powers were insufficient to get the job done. In addition, OFF was only one of several government information agencies FDR set up. Already conducting a day-by-day news operation within OEM was a Division of Information run by Robert Horton. In charge of the Office of Government Reports (OGR) was Lowell Mallett, who was coordinating the government's motion picture program. Colonel William J. ("Wild Bill") Donovan, soon to head the Office of Strategic Services (OSS), was disseminating news overseas out of the Office of Coordinator of Information (OCI). This sort of alphabet soupiness attracted a scornful response from the press. Under a "Here's Where We Get OFF" headline, a *New York Herald Tribune* editorial sarcastically welcomed the new agency as "the answer to the prayers of a bewildered people. The Office of Facts and Figures, or OFF, will coordinate the Office of Co-ordinator of Information (or OCI), report on the Office of Government Reports (the frequent reference to this as OGRE is just a typographical error), press-agent the Innumerable Press Agents of the Individual Departments (often called the PAIDS) and will under no circumstances do anything whatever that anybody else is doing already." Reading this, President Roosevelt may have smiled, for he knew exactly what he was doing. He did not want to set up a powerful centralized information service like the Committee on Public Information President Wilson had been criticized for establishing in 1917. Creating multiple agencies with limited powers kept control of wartime news and information where he wanted it: in his hands and those of his press secretary, Stephen Early.

This policy was immediately demonstrated in the aftermath of the bombing of Pearl Harbor. Journalists came clamoring to OFF for full information about the attack, but MacLeish and his aides knew only what they heard on the radio. The president and the war and navy departments maintained a controlled silence, a pattern that was followed throughout the war. MacLeish was made uneasily complicit in this way of managing the news when, on December 16, FDR appointed him to an eight-member committee of the Office of Censorship. Whatever hat he was wearing, however, Archie held steadfastly to the view that the people of the United States were fighting the war and deserved to know as much about it as possible, except for military information that would aid the enemy.

Those in the literary establishment who were critical of MacLeish for his hawkish sentiments in advance of the war now regarded him with scorn for selling out to the lure of power. In the opinion of Louise Bogan and writer Caroline Gordon, to take two examples, he had dwindled into a mere propagandist for the administration. In the root sense of the word — *propagare* in Latin means "to put forth" — he was indeed expressing in OFF the democratic convictions he shared with the president. But to him there was no necessary distinction between the truth and what his detractors labeled American propaganda. Nazi Germany, he thought, was attempting to divide Americans along ethnic or racial or religious lines. They were sometimes assisted in this campaign of divide and conquer by America Firsters and right-wing newspapers that depicted Roosevelt as a warmonger in thrall to Jewish money interests. The Nazis and misguided American "divisionists" were lying. He and OFF would tell the truth instead, for the truth was the most effective weapon in psychological warfare. OFF proposed to put "all the facts, meaning the profound facts of belief, as well as the superficial facts of statistics," before the people. "The crucial battleground of this war," he declared, "is American opinion."

MacLeish directed OFF for less than eight months before the agency was dissolved. They were months of living hell. Not only was he drastically overworked, but he had almost no cooperation from the president. FDR had set up OFF only because of the insistence of La Guardia and Mrs. Roosevelt, Archie soon discovered. With little backing from the top and a weak executive order, Archie had to struggle to establish even the beginnings of a budget. He ran afoul of J. Edgar Hoover and his Federal Bureau of Investigation (FBI) in recruiting a staff. He was subjected to verbal abuse by segments of the press. Worst of all, he failed in his basic mission of delivering the facts to the nation. For a man as driven to succeed as Archie MacLeish, that rankled.

The only saving grace was the loyal and talented staff that worked for OFF. On November 4, 1941, MacLeish requested a budget of

$100,000. At the time, he contemplated hiring only a small staff. With the outbreak of the war, the dimensions of the task widened drastically, and the need for personnel along with them. Seven months later, OFF employed 350 people, many of them professional writers. Allen Grover was borrowed from Time Inc. to help organize and staff the agency. Henry Pringle, the distinguished biographer from Columbia University, served as informal dean of a group that included Charles Poore from the *New York Times,* Marty Sommers from the *Saturday Evening Post,* poet and editor Malcolm Cowley, McGeorge Bundy, son of Archie's Boston friends Kay and Harvey Bundy, and Arthur Schlesinger, Jr., son of the Harvard professor of history.

After Pearl Harbor, MacLeish — and Grover — had the pick of a glut of applicants for writing posts in Washington. The wonder was that Archie managed to surround himself with the most amiable and effective members of a notoriously temperamental group. In part, the staff's unity derived from the shared conviction that they were engaged in work of crucial importance to the nation. MacLeish at once set up a publications division, later followed by a radio division and a poster division, by which to communicate "the facts of belief." "We had to state the American cause," as he later put it. "The American cause was our cause, and by God we weren't ashamed of it." OFF put out pamphlets about the war production drive and the techniques of German propaganda. It issued a *Report to the Nation* on the progress of the war early in 1942, and put together a radio program called "This Is War" that in its militancy alienated both intellectuals and still-doubting isolationists.

Occasionally outside personnel were called in to undertake specific duties. After Roosevelt enunciated the "Four Freedoms" in his 1942 State of the Union address, he directed OFF to prepare a pamphlet on the subject "for the widest possible distribution." Given that mandate, MacLeish assembled four of America's leading writer-scholars in Washington to discuss the contents of the pamphlet. Theologian Reinhold Niebuhr was brought in to write on freedom of religion, Max Lerner of the *Nation* on freedom from fear, Cowley on freedom from want, and E. B. ("Andy") White of the *New Yorker* on freedom of speech. White was also assigned to take everyone else's drafts and stitch them together into a coherent piece of work. The procedure was not one White approved of. There had been entirely too much talk at the session in Washington, he thought, and the drafts submitted seemed "forbidding and dreary." Nonetheless, he completed *The Four Freedoms* in slightly over three weeks, culling from it all "pretty writing" and including "an absolute minimum of statements" he did not himself understand. Even though cleansed of excessive rhetoric, the pamphlet still read like the collection of abstractions it was. The experience left him without enthusiasm for further writing assignments from the government. Martha Gellhorn, Hemingway's wife, repeated one soldier's comment after hearing a Four Freedoms broadcast. "Just freedom would be all right with us," he said. People were getting sick of words, Ernest wrote Archie. Perhaps. But supplying the words was MacLeish's business.

Home Front Enemies

Malcolm Cowley, one of Archie's first recruits, brought OFF under the scrutiny of the FBI. As soon as he could find office space, Archie summoned Malcolm from the *New Republic*. In a letter of January 11, 1942, Cowley reported on his reactions to bureaucratic Washington. "You can get a vague picture of a government agency," he wrote his lifelong friend Kenneth Burke, "by imagining the business of General Motors being run by the faculty of . . . Columbia." The difference was that, unlike in the commercial world, people were struggling for power and not money. His own salary was $8,000, which he thought rather lordly. On the negative side, the FBI was trying to get him fired. "Every second writer in the country" wanted a job exactly like his, and he had to depend on MacLeish to save it for him.

Five days after Cowley's letter to Burke, Representative Martin Dies, chairman of the House committee investigating un-American activities (HUAC), singled out Cowley as "one of the chief communist intellectuals in the country." He traced seventy-two separate connections of this "high-salaried government employee" with "the Communist party and its front organizations." MacLeish, who knew of Cowley's disaffection with communist policies and harbored no doubts about his loyalty, dismissed the charge as the predictable behavior of red-baiting Congressman Dies and journalist Westbrook Pegler. The following month, when *Time* magazine joined the attack on Cowley in its February 16 issue, he indignantly wrote Harry Luce specifying the misrepresentations in the article. An injury had been done to Cowley, to *Time,* and to OFF, which was "already working under pretty heavy handicaps of manufactured prejudice," Archie pointed out. He advised Luce to look for serpents at the bottom of the Time Inc. cesspool.

In the end, though, MacLeish was unable to keep Cowley on the OFF payroll, because of his extensive connections with the Communist party during the 1930s. During late February and early March, Cowley sought in vain to counteract the inaccurate picture of his activities supplied the FBI by, he thought, former communist sympathizers who in renouncing their faith were moved to find traitors everywhere. Cowley was so busy trying to clear himself that there was no time for the work he had been hired to perform. Finally he decided to resign, effective March 31, and went back to Sherman, Connecticut, to hoe his garden and write for the *New Republic* for the duration of the war. MacLeish gave him a testimonial luncheon as a farewell. "I was not born to be a martyr," Malcolm told his co-workers.

Cowley's unhappy experience led MacLeish to an exchange of correspondence with FBI chief Hoover. The bureau's investigative reports on his staff routinely came to MacLeish, as director of OFF. Time and again he came across such phrases as "——— was said to be associated with various Liberal and Communistic groups" during the Spanish civil war. Archie wrote to Hoover in January 1942 objecting to this kind of thinking and proposing that FBI agents should be subjected to a course of instruction in history. "Don't you think it would be a good thing if all investigators could be made to understand that Liberalism is not only not a crime but actually the attitude of the President of the United States and the greater part of his Administration?" Shouldn't the agents be told that "the people we are at war with now are the same people who supported Franco in the Spanish civil war?" In the beginning, though, MacLeish's attitude was not antagonistic. Perhaps in wartime a certain amount of witch-hunting was inevitable, he wrote Hoover amelioratively on February 3. Meanwhile, he thanked God that people like J. Edgar were running the law enforcement agencies. For his part, Hoover replied that he was doing his best. He — or his minions — also placed MacLeish's name on a list of faculty for the FBI's Training Division, but he was not actually called upon to enlighten FBI agents.

In the light of Cowley's impending resignation and FBI investigations of two other candidates (names censored) for OFF, MacLeish could no longer contain his indignation. He jumped channels and wrote directly to his friend, and Hoover's superior, Attorney General Francis Biddle complaining that FBI agents "seem not only to be out of touch with intellectual currents, they seem to be in other currents of a most suspicious nature." He had already written Hoover about this, he told Biddle, and received from him "a very pleasant but not precisely responsive answer." Busy as he was, couldn't Biddle do something about it? What Biddle did was to send a copy of Archie's letter to Hoover. In replying to Biddle, the FBI chief appropriated the high ground. Naturally he welcomed suggestions about improving the bureau's ability to conduct thorough and impartial investigations, Hoover wrote. But presenting the facts fairly and completely while satisfying "extremists" like Dies on the one hand and MacLeish on the other was "as difficult as steering a course between Scylla and Charybdis."

MacLeish did not know, and would probably have been astounded to discover, that Biddle had forwarded his complaint to Hoover, and thereby made him a dangerous enemy for the rest of his life. Nor did Archie know that the FBI was already in the process of compiling an extensive dossier on himself, in the wake of a "personal and confidential" proposal from Hoover to Biddle of December 5, 1941. Eventually the FBI file on MacLeish ran to six hundred pages, longer than that on any other American writer. In part this was due to his involvement in government service, and in part to his eagerness to express himself on controversial issues, but the sheer volume of the file probably also owed something to Hoover's animus against him. J. Edgar Hoover did not take criticism lightly, and he was known to bear grudges.

Besides rehearsing MacLeish's connections with the League of American Writers and various other antifascist and procommunist groups of the late 1930s, the FBI report noted Archie's aggressive pro-Russian stance after Pearl Harbor. In an April 15, 1942, speech for Russian war relief, for example, he lamented that there were people even in the United States "who would rather see this country lose this War alone than win it with the aid of other countries they do not care for." The right-wing American press, which sometimes did seem to fear ally Soviet Russia more than the fascist powers the United States was fighting against, understood MacLeish's accusation clearly enough, and gave as good as they got. During MacLeish's brief period at OFF, he was persistently embroiled in disputes with these publications, particularly the *Chicago Tribune* group and the Hearst papers.

From its inception, OFF was subject to jibes and jabs from journalists. They called it the Office of Fuss and Feathers, the Office of Fun and Frolic. They poked fun at the idea of putting a poet in charge. One cartoon depicted a dreamy MacLeish with a book under his arm titled "Sonnets." His staff was belittled as "a weird assortment" of long-haired intellectuals and unreliable creative writers, most of them paid much more than they deserved. And the newspapers complained, with some justification, that OFF was not in fact disseminating the information it was supposed to deliver.

Most of the attacks, however, concentrated on MacLeish personally. In effect, he invited the combat. Zealous to ensure American victory, he carried on what he called "my one-man battle against the America First influence." In a series of speeches in the spring of 1942, he lashed out against three newspapers in the *Tribune* group: the *Chicago Tribune,* published by Colonel Robert ("Bertie") McCormick, and the *New York News* and *Washington Times-Herald,* published, respectively, by McCormick's relatives Captain Joseph Patterson and Eleanor ("Cissy")

Patterson. By and large, these papers favored a "noninterventionist" posture that would require the United States to fight only when war threatened its borders. They were strongly opposed to bailing out Great Britain, and accused Roosevelt of having tricked the nation into war by virtue of his unfortunate anglophilia. They stubbornly resisted any alliance with the Soviet Union. To circulate such ideas in peacetime might rightly be construed as a proper exercise of freedom of the press, since the First Amendment was designed to encourage circulation of differing opinions. But in time of war, MacLeish believed, these papers were doing more than expressing partisan political views. They were in fact — he did not say "traitors" — nothing less than enemies of the people. In the words of his March 19, 1942, speech at the Freedom House dinner: "The man who attempts, through his ownership of a powerful newspaper, to dictate the opinions of millions of Americans — the man who employs all the tricks and dodges of a paid propagandist to undermine the people's confidence in their leaders in a war, to infect their minds with suspicion of their desperately needed allies, to break their will to fight, is the enemy, not of the government of this country, but of its people."

In his April 17 address to the American Society of Newspaper Editors, Archie went further in his diatribe against elements of the American press "actively engaged in influencing American opinion in directions which lead not to victory but to defeat." The press needed to police its own members, he maintained, and cited a specific case to prove the point. "When a powerful newspaper-owner can publish without criticism from his colleagues a secret document of vital importance to the security of his country — a document which could not have issued from its place of safe-keeping by any but dishonorable means — people of ordinary common sense and common observation are inclined to wonder why." The well-informed among the editors in attendance knew what he was talking about.

On December 4, 1941, the *Chicago Tribune* and its sister papers had printed the news that United States intelligence had broken the Japanese code. Obviously this was secret information, and undoubtedly its publication assisted the enemy-to-be. Along with Secretary of the Navy Frank Knox, President Roosevelt was convinced that the *Tribune* had been guilty of sedition. Early in 1942, a grand jury was empaneled to look into the case, but was unable to assemble enough evidence to warrant an indictment. The navy itself declined to cooperate, on the grounds that any further disclosures could also aid the enemy. On his own, Roosevelt later directed the Justice Department to conduct a content analysis of editorials and news articles of the *Tribune* group and

Hearst newspapers from December 7, 1941, to May 1942, looking for profascist and pro-German propaganda. Although the study found no consistent pattern along these lines, FDR remained dubious about the loyalty of Bertie McCormick and the Pattersons. He went so far as to order surveillance of Joe and Cissy Patterson.

In yet another talk, this one to the Associated Press on April 20, MacLeish appropriated a line from Gilbert and Sullivan to identify the newspaper owners he was objecting to: "a publisher from Chicago . . . and another from New York (to say nothing of their sisters and their cousins and their aunts in other cities)." It was not long before the sisters and cousins returned his fire. In the June 4 *Washington Times-Herald*, MacLeish was labeled a "fellow traveler" who was campaigning with "Communists and other proletarians" to "intimidate newspapers that are fighting to preserve the American way of life." A month later, Cissy Patterson herself had her innings. As reported by the *Chicago Tribune* press service, her Sunday July 5 article under the fictitious byline of Georgiana X. Preston took "another devastating verbal poke at a political pink who had the temerity to question her patriotism. . . . The Bald Bard of Balderdash, Archibald MacLeish." Cissy's article on MacLeish was the third in a series directed against those "who are attacking noninterventionist papers," the first two subjects having been Harry Luce and Marshall Field III, founder of *P.M.* Among other things, Patterson accused Archie of presiding over an "array of literary floosies engaged in turning out its hate at salaries equivalent to those of major generals."

When he got wind of this effusion, FDR sent Archie a letter:

> July 13, 1942.
>
> Dear Archie:
>   I welcome you to the "Society of the Immortals." Bertie McCormick started it many years ago, even before we entered the first World War; and he incorporated it in 1919 when he broke Woodrow Wilson's heart and made him the first of the Immortals. The trouble is that Bertie, Joe Patterson and Cissie deserve neither hate nor praise — only pity for their unbalanced mentalities.
>
> As ever yours,
> FDR

At this time, MacLeish was also subject to some of the abuse Ezra Pound was broadcasting from Mussolini's Italy. Commuting between Rapallo and Rome, Pound began making these broadcasts (eventually 125 of them) following America's entry into World War II. He was not always coherent on the radio — "I lose my thread at times," he confessed on March 8, 1942 — but he hammered away at his vitriolic themes. The root of evil lay in usury, and the Jews were history's worst usurers. The war was being fought to protect and advance Jewish interests, and Roosevelt himself was part of the conspiracy. Speaking "from Europe for the American heritage" via shortwave, Ezra lamented "that any Jew in the White House should send American kids to die for the private interests of the scum of the English earth . . . and the still lower dregs of the Levantine." The United States would not be at war now, he told his listeners, if they had "had the sense to eliminate Roosevelt and his Jews or the Jews and their Roosevelt at the last election." As it was, "you are not going to win this war," Pound insisted. "You have never had a chance in this war."

As for MacLeish, according to Pound's April 23, 1942, broadcast, "He has been given a gangster's brief and he has been entrusted with the defense of a gang of criminals and he is a-doing his damnedest." Then in an astounding and baseless accusation, Pound demanded that Archie "say openly why he handed out four billion dollars in excess profits on the gold [market?] between 1932 and 1940, handing it to a dirty gang of kikes and hyper-kikes on the London gold exchange firms."

Clearly, much of what Pound said smacked of treason, since he remained an American citizen. Just as clearly he was, in his obsessive hatred of Jews, at least slightly mad. In the April 1942 issue of *Poetry,* Eunice Tietjens declared that the time had come "to put a formal end to the countenancing of Ezra Pound," now that he was deliberately attempting "to undermine the country of his birth through enemy propaganda." MacLeish himself took little notice of Pound's rantings. He had other things on his mind.

Getting OFF

Looking back on the Office of Facts and Figures, Archie was inclined to blame its demise on his journalistic enemies. "The American press won its fight against OFF," he wrote, "which was a good deal like a railroad train winning its fight with a snail on the right of way." The real trouble with the agency, however, lay in its lack of authority: its pitiful status as snail set up for the crushing.

That the auspices were ill emerged immediately after Pearl Harbor, during President Roosevelt's press conference on December 9, 1941. The subject was future government policy in issuing war news. Two standards would be applied, the president said. First, the news must be true, and second, it must not give aid and comfort to the enemy. Decisions on applying these standards, he added, would be left to the heads of the War and Navy departments. Roosevelt did not mention, much less stress the importance of, the Office of Facts and Figures, which he had established six weeks earlier to coordinate the flow of information from government departments. The press got the message, and did not rely on OFF as a channel for dissemination of news. In its brief existence, the agency issued fewer than ninety news stories, most of them in response to enemy propaganda. Meanwhile the army and navy, each with its own information office, produced hard data about the war through official communiqués, or more often observed journalistic silence on the basis of the "aid and comfort" clause. Even good news was withheld, regardless of the opportunity this gave the Japanese to score propaganda victories. Frustrated by the unwillingness of the Navy Department to publicize the American breakthrough at the Battle of the Coral Sea, Robert Sherwood wrote Archie that "sometimes there is nothing which can give so much aid and comfort to the enemy as silence on our part."

MacLeish did his best to appropriate authority for OFF through yet another position, his chairmanship of the Committee on War Information. This committee was composed of policy-making representatives from the State, Treasury, War, Navy, and Justice departments, OGR, OCI, OEM, the Lend-Lease Administration, and later the Office of Civilian Defense (OCD) and the Coordinator of Inter-American Affairs. Included in its distinguished membership were Attorney General Biddle himself from Justice, John J. ("Jack") McCloy from War, and Adlai Stevenson from Navy. To solidify relationships, MacLeish also appointed OFF deputies to various departments, among them Robert Kintner, Christian Herter, and Barry Bingham.

The Committee on War Information (CWI) took on a broad spectrum of problems. Not only did it advise on information matters and lay down principles regarding security, but CWI also outlined general propaganda objectives and recommended subjects for publications and radio programs.

One of the CWI's goals was to minimize differences of opinion between departments before they got into print. Public confidence in the government was naturally eroded when the War Department and the Office of Production Management (OPM) issued conflicting figures on the amount of aluminum and steel needed for successful prosecution of the war, or when the secretary of the navy made pronouncements on foreign policy that were at odds with State Department positions. For such reasons, cabinet members and bureau chiefs were directed, as of January 29, to clear any public addresses they planned to make with MacLeish at OFF. (In the light of this directive, a *New Yorker* cartoon depicted a secretary telling her boss, "Mr. MacLeish O.K.'s your speech for clearance, sir, but he wants to point out a dangling participle.") The agency was also empowered to serve as a clearing-house for government radio messages. Through close liaison with the networks, OFF coordinated arrangements for coverage of important events, commandeered radio time for major addresses, and developed special programs such as "This Is War." The agency also took over the job of issuing posters, allocating space as available among competing departments. Perhaps most important, OFF issued two pamphlets and completed work on half a dozen more that reached circulation in the tens of millions.

Insofar as was possible, all of these materials — speeches, broadcasts, posters, pamphlets — were coordinated to meet the objectives of various war information campaigns such as those concerning the production drive, sacrifice and the enemy, and the United Nations. In order to know what message to send, MacLeish set up a public opinion research organization. Through sophisticated polling techniques, this organization reported on what government information was getting across to the citizens and what additional information was required. This public opinion research operation, like much of what OFF did, was not contemplated in the agency's original executive order. Manifestly MacLeish was endeavoring to broaden the function of the agency, so that it would serve both to coordinate information and to bolster public morale. Despite his dedication to the task, and that of his extremely capable staff, these objectives were beyond the reach of OFF. It simply lacked the authority to get the job done.

MacLeish's communications with the White House in the winter and spring of 1942 reveal his increasing frustration. As early as January 16, he wrote Grace Tully asking that the president change the name of his organization. His colleagues "would much rather work in the Office of War Information than the Office of Facts and Figures," he pointed out. And since the interdepartmental advisory committee was called the Committee on War Information, the new name made sense. The request was turned down by the Bureau of the Budget on the grounds that the whole information field needed to be reorganized.

This was hardly news to MacLeish. On February 20 he submitted his plan for reorganization. A policy-making committee like the CWI should be established, but this time given "adequate authority to enforce its decisions." Otherwise, several of the alphabet agencies, including OFF, should be liquidated or folded into a surviving central office empowered to direct both foreign and domestic operations. "A tremendous amount of confusion and duplication would eventually be avoided" in this way, he wrote, but "the real gain . . . would be in rationalization of an anarchic situation." He was ready himself to step down, he added.

On March 24, however, he retreated from this position somewhat in a letter to Sam Rosenman. If a new Office of War Information such as he proposed — a similar recommendation had come from Milton S. Eisenhower, who had been appointed by the Bureau of the Budget to look into the tangled information field — were to be authorized, he was available to head it, if only because he'd become "intensely interested in the broad information job" over the course of his six months at OFF. He was well equipped to handle the policy-making end of the work, he thought, but "an experienced, hard-boiled, totally extrovert, highly energetic operator" should run the production end, and he was "certainly not that man." His personal ambitions hardly mattered, though. If leaving him out achieved the desired goal, so be it. "The centralized organization of the government's information service is so vitally important that nothing, and least of all any question of personalities, ought to stand in its way."

At this time MacLeish was fully aware that his dual role as librarian of Congress and head of the Office of Facts and Figures threatened to be costly to the LC. Luther Evans was effectively overseeing the LC reorganization in his post as acting librarian. But the Congress, and especially Republican congressmen, took exception to Archie's doubling up. MacLeish was supposed to be running the Library of Congress — *their* library. Instead he was engaged in information and propaganda efforts for the administration, and in writing speeches for President Roosevelt. Representatives were not inclined to be sympathetic when MacLeish observed, at the House Appropriations Subcommittee meeting of February 19, that "like a lot of other people in town I have stopped sleeping and given up Sundays." When the appropriations bill came to the floor on March 18, Everett Dirksen of Illinois proposed an amendment to slash the book budget from $173,000 to $55,000, which would in effect have prevented the library from purchasing any books except for continuations. Although the money was later restored by a House-Senate conference committee, Dirksen's amendment actually passed the House on a 62–42 vote. An indignant MacLeish characterized the proposed cut as "an attack . . . upon an institution of learning." At least in part it was also an attack upon himself.

These troubles were as nothing compared to his ongoing battle to tell the American people the truth about the war. His principal adversaries in this contest were the War and Navy departments. In an April 9 letter to Frankfurter, MacLeish set forth his complaint. After months of debate, the CWI had adopted a statement of information policy, according to which there were to be three regularly issued communiqués. One was to report on war production, another on casualties, and the third — from the Joint Chiefs of Staff — on overall progress of the war. This policy, which was duly announced to the press, was not being followed. Casualty lists were not appearing, nor were reports of ship sinkings, information that the Navy Department had promised to supply. The deadline for the Joint Chiefs' communiqué had passed, because army and navy representatives could not agree on what to say or how to say it. And the production communiqué, which the War Department had agreed to, was being blocked by the department's own intelligence branch.

MacLeish and OFF were already under considerable fire from the press. Now, though, the agency stood to lose all of its surviving credibility in the journalistic world, if the War and Navy departments failed to make good on the commitments their representatives within the CWI had agreed to. Archie was not going to lash out publicly against the armed services, he wrote Frankfurter, but he did threaten to resign in protest. What was involved was a breach of faith, and the breach was not of his making. As he angrily put it, "I am willing to give everything I possess to this cause except my reputation for basic honesty."

MacLeish did not resign his position. He remained director of OFF until — on June 13, 1942 — President Roosevelt established the Office of War Information that Archie had proposed five months before. The man chosen to lead this centralized organization was highly respected CBS newscaster Elmer Davis, an Indianan, a Rhodes Scholar, and a liberal whose distinctive nasal twang was familiar to millions of radio listeners. In choosing Davis, FDR followed a recommendation that E. B. White had advanced in the *New Yorker*. The first step he'd like to see the government take in the war, White wrote (anonymously) in the March 14 "Talk of the Town," was "the unification of the information bureaus and the appointment of Elmer Davis to head them up." Privately Archie may have coveted this position himself. "In government," as he commented thirty years later, "you're always a little sore when you're pushed out, even if you've asked to be pushed out." But he hailed Davis as "a grand choice," and agreed at FDR's insistence to serve as assistant director of OWI for policy development. Writing McGeorge Bundy, he looked back at the whole sorry business of OFF as "one of the deepest satisfactions of my life ... instead of one of the bitterest disappointments." The reason was the human warmth of the staff that worked together there against all odds. "Whatever else OFF was," Archie concluded, "it was a group of devoted people who felt about each other as members of an organization rarely feel."

Matters of Opinion

OWI profited from a number of mistakes that OFF had suffered through. It was in fact as well as theory the coordinating agency for information, combining within itself such previously competing organizations as OFF, the Foreign Information Service, OGR, and the division of information of OEM. Milton Eisenhower was recruited as deputy director for administration, leaving the director free to concern himself with wider issues. Best of all, OWI was inaugurated with an executive order that had teeth: "The director of the new Office of War Information will have authority, subject to powers held directly by the President, to issue directions to all departments and agencies of the government with respect to their information services. He will have full authority to eliminate all overlapping and duplication and to discontinue in any department any information activity which is not necessary or useful to the war effort." These words gave Davis the kind of clout at OWI that MacLeish had yearned for at OFF.

One of Archie's first tasks for OWI was to organize the agency's main overseas base in London. Working with James Warburg, MacLeish concentrated on setting up an information program that included broadcasts to American troops stationed in Britain. He also established liaison with British propaganda and information leaders, with an eye to ensuring that the same story was told on both sides of the Atlantic. During this trip, Archie went down to West Ham east of London, a town that had been bombed mercilessly during the Battle of Britain. "They got bombed," he discovered, "because the curve of the river made a mark that the bombers could see on a moonlit night. . . . That was their sin; they lived in a place where the moon shone on the river." He could not get the sight of that devastated place and of its bewildered inhabitants out of his head.

People like these needed to know what they were fighting for, he declared in his July 30, 1942, Rede lecture at Cambridge University. Placing particular emphasis on American opinion, MacLeish said he sensed in the nation "a forward thrusting and overflowing of human hope and human will which must be given channel or it will dig a channel for itself." In his view it was the proper and necessary function of OWI to provide this channel by helping the American people to decide what they were fighting for, what kind of world they wanted to live in after the war was over. A fervent internationalist, MacLeish strongly advocated One Worldism, and a United Nations organization that would keep the peace and advance the mutual interests of its members.

Once again, as with OFF, Archie was attempting to widen the scope of his assignment. This time Milton Eisenhower opposed him from within OWI. The agency should encourage discussion of the forthcoming peace, but only in a climate of objectivity, Eisenhower held. Above all the OWI "should continue to be thought of primarily as an *information* agency." So the lines formed: MacLeish and Robert Sherwood on one

side, Eisenhower and Gardner ("Mike") Cowles on the other, and Elmer
Davis in the middle. In memoranda MacLeish argued that for OWI to
follow Eisenhower's guidelines was to dwindle into "a mere issuing
mechanism [of information] for the government departments." In the
end Eisenhower's views prevailed.

As early as August 12, two months after the inception of OWI,
MacLeish wrote Davis that he wanted to resign. He gave three reasons.
First, he occupied an untenable position as assistant director for policy,
since "operational policy" was made by the planning boards working
under Sherwood (for overseas information) and Cowles (for domestic
information), and "high policy" was shaped in the morning meetings
Davis himself held — meetings in which MacLeish did not participate.
Second, he was conscious of the mounting responsibilities he had left
behind at the Library of Congress. Third, he thought he could be of
"more use to our common cause" outside of the agency than inside it.
In that way, Archie wrote, "I shall be able to speak in public on issues
on which I feel I must speak, without involving you or OWI."

In closing, MacLeish assured Davis that he was "filled with admiration" for the work he had done in so short a time at OWI. Still,
MacLeish was constitutionally unsuited to play a secondary role in any
institution, or to conceive of himself as in the wrong. In his retrospective
account of OWI, Davis lamented "one personnel problem which came
up again and again . . . the problem of the brilliant and zealous individual who cannot work as part of a team." Among others, Davis probably
had in mind Sherwood, whom he tried, unsuccessfully, to persuade FDR
to dismiss as head of overseas operations. Or he may have been thinking
of the cantankerous group of writers, Henry Pringle among them, who
resigned from OWI en masse when required to disseminate views of the
government they did not share. On departure these writers chucked their
personal files out the window to colleagues waiting below. But Davis
may have meant MacLeish specifically when he observed that "in any
organization that is going to get any work done you cannot do much
with people who are convinced that they are the sole authorized cus-
todians of Truth, and that whoever differs from them is ipso facto
wrong." Like the legendary judge, Archie was sometimes wrong but
never in doubt.

It was this habit of mind that especially infuriated the *Tribune* group
and the America Firsters, particularly since they were certain that their
precisely opposite views were incontestably correct. When Davis declined
to accept MacLeish's resignation, he remained with OWI through the
fall of 1942, while the McCormick-Patterson axis continued its assault
upon him. In his "Capitol Stuff" column of September 28, John F.

O'Donnell of the *Washington Times-Herald* accused MacLeish of throwing a lavish dinner for OWI regional directors at taxpayer expense. What was worse, *Time* magazine picked up the item and ran it the next week, thereby giving it circulation in the millions. "My grief and anguish are in part personal and in part professional," Archie wrote Harry Luce in exasperation. As a friend, surely Harry owed him the courtesy of checking with him before going to press. And on professional grounds, Archie wrote, "I never expected to see you . . . act as a typhoid Mary for Cissy Patterson's particular brand of filth."

According to MacLeish, O'Donnell's attack "was a carefully contrived piece of vilification" intended to embarrass OWI at the appropriation hearing scheduled the same day his column appeared. And O'Donnell had his facts all wrong. MacLeish, who had been asked to speak at the dinner, was not the host, nor was it paid for out of the public coffers. Paul C. Smith, assistant director of domestic operations, hosted the dinner and paid the bill himself. *Time* printed a retraction, but the *Times-Herald* did not.

Bothersome as such sniping may have been, it was the wartime personnel shortage at the LC that eventually moved MacLeish, on January 26, 1943, to insist on resigning from OWI. "The only solution," he wrote Davis, was to return to his duties as librarian of Congress fulltime. In a private letter of appreciation, Elmer Davis thanked Archie for helping him get acclimated "in relations with Congress, in information as to backgrounds around town, and not least in representing OWI in relations social and diplomatic with our foreign brethren and with other agencies of the government." At OFF, Davis added, MacLeish had done much of the spadework on which OWI was trying to build. "I would not say that we have yet got a completely satisfactory structure, but you interposed yourself as target for many bricks that, once thrown, are not likely to be thrown again." True to form, the *Times-Herald* saluted MacLeish's resignation from OWI with a sneering couplet:

> *Oh, West is West and East is Eash*
> *And so is Archibald MacLeish.*

With Archie gone, Davis observed, the *Tribune* papers would have to find a new target "among the prose writers."

19 ❖

MAKING THE PEACE

Poets at the Library

By THE TIME MacLeish returned to the LC from OWI, he and Ada were settling into a house outside Washington, the Robert E. Lee boyhood home at 607 Oronoco Street in Alexandria, Virginia. The buyer of record in the October 27, 1942, transaction was Ada Hitchcock MacLeish, with the purchase made possible through her inheritance from her father. Ada herself was not idle during the war years. Along with friends such as Annie Burr (Mrs. Wilmarth) Lewis, Jane (Mrs. Cass) Canfield, and Helen (Mrs. Walter) Lippmann, Ada worked for the Red Cross. Eventually she rose to become director of camp and hospital services, a job that occasionally took her away from home on tours of inspection. Appalled at the primitive conditions of a desert training base near Indio, California, she hitched a jeep ride to General George S. Patton's headquarters and told him to make his troops more comfortable. Patton, who was preparing his soldiers for combat in North Africa, knew better than to argue with her or to change their regimen.

A major project awaiting Archie in the spring of 1943 was the Jefferson bicentennial. MacLeish, who admired Jefferson above all other Americans, was intimately involved in the April 13, 1943, observances. The principal public event was the dedication of the Jefferson Memorial. Archie wrote FDR's speech for this occasion, and the president delivered it verbatim, the only time that ever happened. Within the library, a special exhibit was mounted showing the drafts of the Declaration of Independence, and the LC published Julian Boyd's definitive *Declaration of Independence: The Evolution of the Text*. Boyd, librarian of Princeton

University, was among fifteen writers and scholars MacLeish assembled for a seminar on the morning of April 13. His idea was to bring together a number of leading American thinkers "to discuss, with no audience but a good stenographer, their notions as to the relation of Mr. Jefferson's general position to the problems of this present racked and riven world." Or, if Jefferson "could see and feel and know what we do, what would he say to us?"

Two of those invited to that seminar produced a measure of consternation. One was Malcolm Cowley, whom Archie had lured to the session partly to make up for his unhappy experience at OFF. The FBI did not let Cowley's appearance go unchallenged. Midway through the morning seminar, a man in a three-piece suit materialized in front of Thursa Bakey's desk, identified himself as an FBI agent, and produced a long white envelope sealed with wax. He was to deliver this document to Mr. MacLeish personally, the FBI man said. When Thursa tried to stall him until the noon break, she was presented with the letter to open and read. Signed by J. Edgar Hoover, it stated that, according to the bureau's informants, Cowley was a communist and hence should not be included in the ceremonies honoring Thomas Jefferson. Called out of the seminar, MacLeish read this letter, had a short discussion with the agent, and went back inside. Cowley left soon thereafter, before the afternoon and evening observances.

The other controversial seminarian was Wendell Willkie, FDR's opponent in the 1940 election. Members of the seminar were honored guests for the dedication ceremony, so when President Roosevelt arrived at the Jefferson Memorial to deliver his speech, there was Willkie in the front row before him. Not until Grace Tully called him from the White House later that day did MacLeish realize what he'd done. Willkie was "a devoted Jefferson man," Archie knew, and had been invited on that basis. The partisan issue never crossed his mind. The bad news, Tully said, was that the president didn't like seeing his opponent at the Jefferson dedication. The good news was that he liked the speech Archie had written for him well enough to forgive him.

Though writing speeches instead of poems, MacLeish kept in touch with the profession in other ways. In 1943 and for two years thereafter, he served as editor of the Yale Series of Younger Poets, inheriting the position on the death of Stephen Vincent Benét in March. In a memorial tribute to his fellow Yale poet, MacLeish observed that Benét's life "was a model. . . . He was altogether without envy or vanity. He never considered appearance, or tried to present himself as anything but what he was, or paid the least attention to the prevalent notions, the fashionable preconceptions, of what a poet ought to be." MacLeish's first choice as editor and judge of the Yale Series was *Love Letter from an Impossible Land,* a manuscript by a young naval aviator, William Meredith.

In July 1943 MacLeish at long last was able to appoint a replacement for Joseph Auslander as consultant in poetry. Auslander, who had been relegated to gift officer in December 1941, was ineffective in that role. Although he and his wife had succeeded in attracting a number of donors to the LC, Auslander lacked the orderly mind and the bibliographic knowledge such a position required. In one case he persuaded a donor to contribute $500 for a copy of Oliver Wendell Holmes's poem "The Chambered Nautilus," though such copies normally commanded no more than $75. Transactions like that, as Mearns put it in a report on Auslander's activities, "alienated the respect for the Library of Congress" among leaders in the book trade. Nonetheless, both Auslanders stayed on the LC payroll until March 1944, when they resigned to "return to literary work." In the chaotic quarters they left behind, Verner Clapp discovered among the several thousand books some that belonged to the Auslanders personally, some to the LC, some whose ownership could not be determined, and at least one book belonging to Harvard. "The place," Clapp wrote, "is a jumble of personal and official property — unopened express packages, lemonade sets, loose papers, and accumulated files of all sorts."

Allen Tate officially took over as consultant in poetry on July 1, 1943, for a one-year term. Within the month, a significant event in the history of American poetry occurred: on July 26 Ezra Pound was indicted for treason by a federal grand jury in the District of Columbia. Several months earlier Hemingway had written MacLeish asking for the hours of Pound's broadcasts from Italy. "Sooner or later he will have to be tried, of course," Ernest remarked, and he wanted to hear his "old pal Ezra" in case he was eventually called on to testify. The day after the indictment for treason, Archie sent Ernest photostatic transcripts of Pound's radio rantings, along with his assessment that "poor old Ezra is quite, quite balmy." Ezra was "obviously crazy," Hemingway agreed, and though he deserved punishment, he should not be hanged or martyred. He stood ready to do "anything an honest man should do" for Pound, Hemingway concluded, showing more charity and compassion for his old mentor and boxing companion from Paris days than for virtually any other literary friend of his life.

MacLeish, characteristically, did something about it. First he sent Hemingway's letter to Tate and asked for his advice. "I have never had anything from Pound but vituperation and obscenity," Archie wrote. Nevertheless, he emphatically shared Ernest's conviction that Ezra "should be dealt with in some other way than by martyrdom." The danger was that an American army, occupying Italy, might summarily try him and hang him. Next he wrote his old friend Harvey Bundy, who was serving as assistant secretary of war under Henry L. Stimson. Could Bundy see to it that orders were given to prevent "summary disposition of the case by the military authorities in Italy" so that Pound might later be tried in a civil court, where the judgment on this "half-cracked and extremely foolish individual" might more precisely fit his crime? Eventually, that is what happened. Pound was not interned by army authorities until May 1945, and was brought to Washington, D.C., for civil trial late that year.

Working out of a main-floor office in the LC with a pair of crossed Confederate flags on the wall, Tate set a high standard for his successors as consultants in poetry to follow. As his duties were spelled out in a memorandum from Mearns, the consultant was to survey the existing collections in English and American literature, initiate recommendations for purchase, seek gifts of books and manuscripts, confer with visiting writers and scholars, prepare bibliographic materials, and answer questions about poetry "from poetry groups, and women's clubs, and program makers, and catch-penny anthologists, and talent testers, and moon-struck (perhaps moon-stricken) novices too ponderous to be raised by Pegasus." Tate did all these things, and more. He got under way, for example, MacLeish's plan to develop a collection of poetry recordings. In time, many American poets came to Washington to make these recordings, and to establish a connection with the LC. Tate was also instrumental in bringing three of his closest literary friends to work at the LC: John Peale Bishop as resident fellow in comparative literature, Katherine Anne Porter as resident fellow in regional American literature, and Robert Penn Warren to succeed him as consultant in poetry.

Archie also urged Bishop to come, pointing out that both he and Tate "would be heartbroken" if he couldn't. Through the years, and despite the compromising circumstances of their parting in Paris during the 1920s, Bishop and MacLeish corresponded regularly and warmly. Bishop was an acute if generally favorable judge of Archie's poetry, and MacLeish invariably respected John's literary views. Perhaps he considered Bishop's stay in Washington a chance to bind the ties of friendship closer. This was not to be. Bishop arrived in Washington in November 1943, and two weeks later suffered an incapacitating heart attack that sent him home to South Chatham, Massachusetts. He died in April 1944. "John loved [Archie] I think more deeply and sensitively than any other of his many fine and wonderful friends," Margaret Bishop wrote Ada in response to a letter of condolence.

Katherine Anne Porter's experience was a happier one. She was fas-

cinated by the pamphlets, journals, and diaries she found in the recesses
of the LC. Two of these documents she brought to the attention of
Robert Penn Warren, who followed Tate as consultant in poetry for
1944–45. One provided the germ of Warren's novel *World Enough and
Time*, the other led to his poem and play *Brother to Dragons*.

Perhaps Tate's most important contribution as consultant in poetry
was the establishment of the Fellows of the Library of Congress in
American Letters, a group that met for the first time in May 1944. The
inaugural members were Tate himself, Porter, Katherine Garrison
Chapin, Willard Thorp, Mark Van Doren, Van Wyck Brooks, Paul
Green, and Carl Sandburg. At their initial meeting the fellows encouraged the LC to pursue its acquisition of books and other literary materials
and manuscripts, and to make these available to visiting writers and
scholars with as few restrictions as possible. This step, along with the
poetry readings at the Coolidge Auditorium and the poetry recordings
made by the music division, brought the LC into a literary relationship
with the nation's writers for the first time. Prior to that time, Red Warren
commented, a writer "wouldn't have come in out of the rain" to use
the LC.

Warren recalled his tour of duty at the LC with high good humor. "I
helped to win the war there," he said. One morning an army captain
telephoned with an urgent request. General So-and-So had written a
poem, and wanted the consultant to straighten out the meter. Warren
remembered only the first two lines,

> We are the boys who don't like to
>   brag,
> But we certainly love our dear old flag.

Warren did what he could for the general. "That," he pointed out, "was
my contribution to the war effort." More seriously, he profited from
the lively exchange of ideas among the Fellows in American Literature
and found time for his own writing, just as MacLeish had thought
consultants in poetry should. Retrospectively, MacLeish regarded the
rotating consultantship as the major accomplishment of his years as
librarian of Congress. There was "more of the purpose of the LC in a
glimpse of Red going up the steps than in any canon [of selection or
service] I ever set off," he said.

At the same time, however, he was disappointed in two attempts to
arrange a post for T. S. Eliot. In April 1943 MacLeish proposed to
Thomas W. Lamont of Wall Street that Eliot be brought across the
Atlantic as consultant in Anglo-American literature, along the lines of
the arrangements made with Perse and Mann. Though active in Anglo-

American affairs, Lamont was not sufficiently attracted by this idea to finance it. In March 1944, on a trip to England, MacLeish approached Eliot directly with the offer of the consultantship in poetry. After mulling the matter over, Eliot turned him down. He was loath to sacrifice his current salary at Faber and Faber, publishers, and to lose time from the writing he had planned to do, he explained. But Eliot, who had taken British citizenship, was also sensitive to the way his appointment might be regarded by the American press and public. "It would be natural for many people to presume that I had come primarily in the British interest, or even for some clandestine purpose." Then the fact that he was on the payroll of the United States government "might inflame the suspicion into a grievance."

Late in 1944 MacLeish confounded longtime antagonist Louise Bogan by appointing her a fellow in American letters. Bogan, who was pleased to join such illustrious company, accepted without delay. Then at a cocktail party for the fellows in Washington, she confronted her bene-factor — a man whose poetry she had excoriated in the most damning terms for the past decade. After circling to avoid him and taking a few drinks, she finally came up to Archie and said, "I can't stand this any more. Why did you do it?" He said, "Why did I do what? Throw this cocktail party?" "No, no," she said. "Why did you appoint me?" Only, he said, because she seemed the best qualified person available. "But don't you know?" she asked. "Yes, I know," Archie said. "I read, and I don't think it makes the slightest difference." It was rare, Bogan decided, "to find a person being magnanimous, after receiving what no doubt seemed to him a series of 'slights.' " No doubt it was.

Fighting for Freedom

Although MacLeish remained librarian of Congress until December 1944, he began plotting his escape from that position eighteen months earlier. The job, he knew, was an important one, but he was eager to play a more active role in the prosecution of the war. President Roosevelt, responding to such an appeal on June 9, 1943, said he could well understand Archie's feelings and promised "to keep a weather eye open" for such a slot, though it was going to be "difficult and I honestly believe impossible" to find anybody to replace him at the LC. Then FDR went on to propose that MacLeish oversee the preparation of a history of the war. "Possibly, you could head up a small committee of not more than half a dozen people, who would sift the current material, put it in monograph form and trust to God that some Sam Morison would come along after the war and put it together." That would be "war work of most decided value," Roosevelt pointed out. "It is not dry history or the cataloging of books and papers and reports. It is trying to capture a great dream before it dies."

Archie was immediately interested, and in a long memorandum of July 3 spelled out an alternative proposal. The navy, he had found, was already using Harvard's Morison as a historian, but the army lagged behind. "Why not," he proposed, "let me give myself leave-of-absence for six months, or nine months, to go out and do one of the campaign histories" the army was now planning? That way he "could really do something about a part, at least, of this war." In August, Hemingway wrote MacLeish with a similar suggestion. Was there any chance, Ernest asked, that "we might send guys to the war" not to write propaganda but "something good"? Could he get an assignment like that? MacLeish promised to look into Hemingway's proposal in discussions with Jack McCloy of the War Department. As it worked out, neither Archie nor Ernest became a battlefield historian, though the army did establish a branch using professional historians to chronicle the years of combat.

While Archie was lobbying for a more active wartime job in the government, he was also in touch with Time Inc. about a possible assignment in England. He and Harry Luce explored this option during a luncheon on August 28, 1943, but upon due consideration MacLeish decided against Luce's "very flattering invitation." If he could shake free of his administrative responsibilities, he wanted to get back to his own writing, he explained. Five years had elapsed since he left *Fortune* for Harvard. "During that period I have written one poem, and a couple of books of speeches, but the real work I want to do has been backing up behind the dam." At least he hoped it had been. Nonetheless, he did not want to rule out a future return to Time Inc. under a part-time arrangement like the one he and Luce had arrived at in connection with *Fortune*. Luce, however, apparently took MacLeish's refusal as a final, if genial, severing of the ties with his magazines. The two of them had struggled through "one hell of a 'crisis'" together, though often on opposite sides, he wrote Archie. "Will we ever be able to sit peacefully like the old men at the gates of Troy and gossip about it all, making sounds like so many cicadi? And would a Helen passing by distract our attention from so many remembered tumults?" Not, Harry thought, "before another decade or two of rough-and-tumble." Meanwhile, he did persuade Archie to serve as a charter member on a pet project of his, the Commission on the Freedom of the Press established under the sponsorship of Time Inc. and the Encyclopaedia Britannica in the fall of 1943.

MacLeish underestimated the number of poems he produced during the years in Washington. He actually wrote five poems in this period, most of them in reaction to events of the day. Nazi U-boat activity, for example, inspired "Bold Venture" in October 1941. And on September 11, 1943, two days after Harry Luce mailed his Helen of Troy letter, MacLeish published "A Poet Speaks from the Visitors' Gallery" in the *New Yorker*. The visitors' gallery is that of Congress, the poet who speaks is manifestly Archie himself, and his subject is the continuing abuse spewed forth by the Roosevelt-hating right-wing press. Specifically, the speaker warns members of Congress not to rely on the paid minions of these irresponsible newspapers to memorialize them. They may be inclined to snigger at poets, but would do well to remember that

> We write the histories.
> . . . .
> History's not written in the kind of ink
> The richest man of most ambitious mind
> Who hates a president enough to print
> A daily paper can afford or find.
>
> Gentlemen have power now and know it,
> But even the greatest and most famous kings
> Feared and with reason to offend the poets
> Whose songs are marble
> and whose marble
> sings.

A month later, Republican Hugh Scott of Pennsylvania read a rebuttal in rhyme into the *Congressional Record*. In her "Sycophantic Archibald," Charlotte C. Starr asserted:

> The poets who can take a name
> And make it great, for future's fame,
> Are not the poets Archie knows,
> For men who write great poems, or prose,
> Are not concerned with politics — . . .

MacLeish, however, certainly was, and he chafed at the boundaries imposed on his political activities, to take that adjective in its broadest sense, by the requirements of his office as librarian of Congress. On November 12, 1943, he wrote President Roosevelt again, asking that his resignation take effect as soon after January 1 as possible. "I can be considerably more useful in back of my own typewriter than back of a Library desk, and I want to get into the fight again as soon as I possibly can." He also had a successor in mind: Julian Boyd of Princeton. Boyd's reputation as a scholar and librarian was excellent. He believed in the same principles MacLeish did. He "would not only take over the wheel easily and smoothly: he would also drive the car."

The "fight" MacLeish had in mind emerged in "The Young Dead Soldiers," written during one of the darkest hours of World War II. "Everything was going wrong," Archie recalled. "The Russians were biting back, we'd lost the Philippines," he'd heard of the terrible death of young Richard Myers, son of his friends from Paris days, Richard and Alice-Lee Myers — the lad burned in the cockpit of his plane — and then a note crossed his desk asking for something to spur the sale of Victory Bonds. With this tangle of ideas running through his head, he wrote "The Young Dead Soldiers" in about seven minutes one morning. Not until he'd finished did he realize that he had created a poem, not a prose piece.

> *The young dead soldiers do not speak.*
> *Nevertheless, they are heard in the still houses: who has not heard them?*
> *They have a silence that speaks for them at night and when the clock counts.*
> *They say: We were young. We have died. Remember us.*
> *They say: We have done what we could but until it is finished it is not done.*
> *They say: We have given our lives but until it is finished no one can know what our lives gave.*
> *They say: Whether our lives and our deaths were for peace and a new hope or for nothing we cannot say; it is you who must say this.*
> *They say: We leave you our deaths. Give them their meaning.*
> *We were young, they say. We have died. Remember us.*

Without question, Archie's sentiments in this poem were the same as those aroused by the death of another young pilot of World War I, his brother Kenneth. Such deaths could be given due remembrance only through "peace and a new hope." In that sense Kenny's death had never been justified. After World War II, however, Archie was determined to do whatever he could toward making the kind of peace the young soldiers were dying for. This was the fight he saw ahead, the cause he meant to devote himself to. Yet again, poetry would have to wait.

In 1943 and 1944 MacLeish attended meetings of a secret committee on the peace, set up by President Roosevelt and supervised by Sumner Welles. These sessions were held in Welles's private office, so that Archie wondered if Cordell Hull, the secretary of state, even knew of the existence of the committee. At any event, he became convinced in these meetings that it would be folly not to decide what kind of world the American people wanted to evolve out of the war, well in advance of final victory. To let things drift would allow the proponents of reaction to re-establish the status quo, just as they had after World War I.

In his remarks during the Metropolitan Opera radio program on Christmas Day 1943, MacLeish spoke of several dangerous options for the future. What do we mean when we speak of peace? he asked. "Is it the old lethargic peace we mean . . . the peace that lasts from one war till the next?" "Is the peace we mean the peace of those who used to tell us, If we leave them alone they'll leave us alone. . . . It takes two to make a war. . . . The Atlantic is three thousand miles across and the Pacific is broader?" "Is it the peace of those who tell us the best treaty of peace is the biggest Navy; of those who say, Grab for the bases, Hang onto the islands, Buy up the airways. . . . Kick the foreigners out and lock the gate after them?" "Is the peace we mean the armed peace, the war without warfare, the peace that devours the peace-makers, bleeding them white?" His generation, Archie said, had been guilty of two wars within twenty years, and had learned through bitter experience that peace could only be "*made* by continuing labor, increasing labor, labor that does not end with a meeting or a conference." Unless we are willing to do that hard work, he told his audience, "then let us in common decency be quiet and not talk of peace."

In his Blashfield address to the American Academy and Institute of Arts and Letters in May 1944, he advanced the positive side of the argument. With peace must come freedom for all. "The war must be a war truly and visibly for the freedom of mankind, and the peace must be a peace for liberty in fact, not liberty in speeches. . . . If the peace that ends this war of freedom against fascism is a peace of arrangements, a peace of adjustments, a peace of facts, of grades, of balances, more will be gone than the chance to make a peace. If even now, even at this late last moment, the great abstractions of democracy can take their honest meanings, and have their truthful way, more than a war will have been fought and won." In talks like these, Archie spoke as from a secular pulpit. He recognized the ministerial tone himself. "Many of my recent speeches, if you come to think of it, are more like sermons than anything else," he wrote his mother in February 1944. The things he had to say were more effectively said outside the church than inside it, yet he could not help being reminded of the Hillard blood coursing through his veins.

During his government service, MacLeish became increasingly aware of the similarities between his experience and that of other people from around the world. His thinking became steadily more internationalist.

Thus he was receptive when Muna Lee, a Mississippi-born poet married to Luis Muñoz Marin, the governor of Puerto Rico, came to him with the idea for *The American Story,* a series of ten scripts broadcast on NBC radio in February, March, and April 1944 and published as a book in December of that year. The underlying theme was that of the early discoveries along "all the American coasts." Whether the discoveries were made by the Spanish and Portuguese or by the English and Dutch and Scandinavians, the pattern was similar, and the struggles with the tribes in the interior came about in much the same way, Muna maintained. She did the research for the broadcasts, and Archie stitched the material together, rising at five A.M. to write the scripts before his regular working day.

According to MacLeish, the purpose of *The American Story* broadcasts was "to bring together from the ancient chronicles, the narratives, the letters, from the pages written by those who saw with their own eyes and were part of it, the American record — the record common to all of us who are American, of whatever American country and whatever tongue." What bound men together, even more than common blood or common speech, he believed, was their "common experience of the earth." The first show, "The Admiral," dealt with Columbus, and was included in *The Best One-Act Plays of 1944.* The show MacLeish himself liked best dealt with the Inca civilization and was called "The Discovered." Therein the narrator traces a parallel between ancient settlements on all the continents.

> We speak of the discovery of America, thinking of Columbus sailing westward through the promises and portents, or thinking of Frobisher and Magellan at the two ends of the endless line of surf, trying the bays and inlets for the passage to Cathay, or of Cabot or Cartier or Thorfinn on the northeast coast. But in one sense America was no more discovered by these men than China was discovered by Marco Polo or Europe by the first Mongolian horseman to cross the Carpathians. There were men before the discoverers in those countries, and in America also there were men, and festivals and palaces and cities made of stone and gold.

In March 1944, during the run of *The American Story* on NBC radio, MacLeish was called to England to represent the United States at the Conference of Allied Ministers of Education. At this meeting plans were laid for rebuilding education in Europe after the war, and MacLeish made a number of connections that later led to his service on UNESCO. He also buried the hatchet with Geoffrey Parsons of the *New York Herald Tribune,* who had consistently deprecated him in editorials since his appointment as librarian of Congress. When the conference was over, MacLeish and Parsons found themselves riding together on a train trip to Shannon Airport in Ireland. They had lunch, and a drink or two. As the train passed through Foynes, Geoffrey challenged Archie to compose a limerick on the spot. He did so, Geoffrey put it on the wire, and it went around the world within a few days.

> A certain young lady from Foynes
> Collected His Majesty's coins:
> The threepenny bits
> By the quick of her wits,
> And the crowns by the quick of her loins.

In September 1944, with an eventual Allied victory seemingly assured, the LC recalled its most precious documents from Fort Knox and once again placed the Declaration of Independence and the Constitution on public display. Robert Penn Warren, asked to write an article about the event, noted that the deteriorated parchment of the Declaration had been repaired with "Japanese tissue." MacLeish was on the phone as soon as he read that phrase, which Warren changed to "paper fibres moistened with rice paste." With the war winding down, MacLeish submitted his resignation as librarian of Congress on November 8. The reorganization of the LC was now complete, he wrote the president, and the wartime measures for the security of the collections had been successfully carried out. Roosevelt accepted Archie's resignation, though he did not have a replacement in the wings. Julian Boyd declined the post, in order to continue his editing of the Jefferson papers at Princeton. As alternatives MacLeish proposed Vannevar Bush of the Carnegie Institute, Dean Theodore Blegen of the University of Minnesota, John Gauss of Wisconsin, Kenneth Murdock of Harvard, Wilmarth Lewis, and, with some reluctance, Luther Evans, who had functioned as acting librarian during MacLeish's enforced absences at OFF and OWI and was now chief assistant librarian.

As MacLeish described him to Roosevelt, Evans was "a good all-around executive" whose years of loyal service entitled him to consideration. Archie did not, however, regard him as "a man of intellectual distinction." In fact, he recommended Evans for librarian of Congress only "as a last resort." As that wording suggests, relations between MacLeish and Evans had cooled since Archie's return to the LC on a full-time basis. Evans had twice presented his resignation in protest, once when Archie overturned an efficiency report to give one of Evans's subordinates a higher rating on ability to get along with his staff than he had given Evans himself. According to David Mearns, Evans was very unlike MacLeish in personality — a somewhat loud Texan with a wonderful laugh, a table pounder. "I can't defend Luther against the charge of bad manners," Archie wrote Allen Tate. "His manners are just normally bad. And they are made worse by the fact that . . . it takes him days to do what most people do in an hour." On his side, Evans felt that MacLeish consistently undercut him by crediting complaints against him from chronic troublemakers. And he thought also that Archie "exercised himself a good deal to try to keep me from being appointed his successor." Nonetheless, it was Evans that President Harry Truman chose to succeed MacLeish. He took office on June 30, 1945.

In evaluating MacLeish's performance as librarian of Congress, his loyal lieutenant David Mearns wrote that "his drive was tremendous, and the fresh air that he brought with him was invigorating. Working with Archibald MacLeish was almost never easy, but it was almost always fun. His spirit of mission was contagious; he gave libraries (and particularly his own Library) a consciousness of new duties and new responsibilities." Herman Henkle, director of processing under Mac-Leish, thought him the best administrator he had ever worked for. To begin with, Henkle pointed out, MacLeish stressed the importance of planning and setting objectives, as in the canons of selection and of service. Then he reorganized the LC in order to carry out those objectives. And throughout he recognized that the staff made the institution run, and gave his lieutenants the backing and the opportunity for advancement they deserved. MacLeish was "the most articulate librarian we've ever had," and whatever he had to say was listened to, according to Frederick Goff, head of the rare books division after Parma. Nor did it hurt that he had, literally, a private line to the White House on his desk.

If there was one quality about MacLeish that everyone who worked for him was struck by, it was his extraordinary speed — in movement, in thought, in expression. He got a great deal done in very little time, and was impatient with others, like Evans, who could not go as fast. Quincy Mumford, another future librarian of Congress, was amazed at Archie's versatility, his capacity to switch without pause from one task to another. As a boss, Mumford recalled, MacLeish "wanted it done *now*." No wonder then, as Keyes Metcalf wrote, that in reorganizing the LC and widening its services, MacLeish "plunged boldly ahead at a pace that few if any trained librarians would have attempted." Among other ways in which he brought the library into the middle of the twentieth century, MacLeish appointed its first woman director of a department and the first black director. In the space of five years, the institution underwent a nearly incredible metamorphosis. Yet the outstanding characteristic of the MacLeish regime, Evans noted in the LC's 1945 annual report, was not "that so much was consummated in so short a time, but rather that there is now so little to repent." Experts rank MacLeish one of the three great figures in the institution's history.

Mausoleum No. 2

When Archie wrote President Roosevelt his letter of resignation on November 8, 1944, he assumed that his days in Washington were over. FDR decided otherwise. No sooner did he relieve MacLeish as librarian than he appointed him assistant secretary of state for cultural and public affairs. Archie's name was sent up to the Senate for confirmation along with six others tapped to serve under the new secretary of state, Edward R. Stettinius, who had succeeded Cordell Hull. Joseph C. Grew was nominated as undersecretary, and Dean Acheson, Will L. Clayton, James C. Dunn, Julius Holmes, and Nelson Rockefeller as assistant secretaries along with MacLeish. "I think it is thrilling that you are not leaving us," FDR wrote Archie on December 1. "The only trouble is that you jump from one mausoleum to another." In reply, MacLeish could not resist a punning reminder that "a rolling stone gathers no Mausoleum."

Archie was powerless, as always, to resist the president's wishes. Nor did he want to, in this case. His immediate task as assistant secretary of state was to sell the concept of the United Nations to the American people. It was a cause he deeply believed in. Only through the United Nations, he thought, could a workable and lasting peace be forged. First, though, he had to be confirmed. He very nearly wasn't.

Among the six nominees to the State Department, MacLeish was the lone liberal, and the one most closely identified with the president. This made him vulnerable to the conservative anti–New Deal wing of the Senate Foreign Relations Committee. Asked for his views on MacLeish, Republican Senator Henrik Shipstead of Minnesota said only, "I understand he is a good ghost writer." Senator Bennett Champ Clark, Democrat of Missouri, declared himself more forcefully against the appointment. MacLeish lacked the qualifications to be assistant secretary of state, he told the press. "He has never performed his duties as Librarian — he has merely been a propagandist."

In his opening statement to the Senate Foreign Relations Committee hearing, MacLeish outlined what he understood to be his responsibilities in the new position of assistant secretary for public and cultural affairs. First, he was to direct "the information policies and activities of the department at home and abroad," and second, he was to direct the department's activities in the area of "cultural cooperation," including "the exchange with other countries of scientific, technical, artistic, lit-

erary and professional knowledge." The principles that would guide
him, he told the senators, were those of freedom of the press and free
exchange of information. In his view, the more the countries of the
world knew about and shared with one another, the better.

With the formality of the opening statement out of the way, Senator
Clark moved to the attack. Did MacLeish consider it part of his duties
as librarian of Congress to be an active propagandist? No, Archie replied,
but it seemed to him that as a citizen he had the right to express his
views, and besides, he had been asked by the president to perform that
role in OFF and OWI. Next, Clark raised the issue of Archie's suspect
political past, citing particularly his introduction of Earl Browder at the
League of American Writers meeting in 1937. Asked pointblank if he
were in favor of communism, Archie said that he had fought it for fifteen
years and "would always fight it in any society" in which he lived. At
the same time, he said, "as regards getting along in the world with a
great power which has adopted for itself communism, I believe we must
get along with it."

After a day's delay, Senator Clark continued his interrogation. During
the interim he had done some digging into MacLeish's writings — ironically, with the aid of the LC's legislative research branch — and was
now prepared to use his words against him. In the process he casually
took what Archie had written out of context. This was especially true
of one passage that outraged Clark in MacLeish's 1934 "Preface to an
American Manifesto": "The great American capitalist and his son and
his daughter-in-law and his banking system might well have been be-
gotten explicitly for hatefulness. They are greedy, they are arrogant, they
are gross, they lack honor, their existence insults the intelligence. It is a
pleasure — almost a duty — to hate them." Did MacLeish really mean
that it was "a pleasure — almost a duty" to hate capitalists? Not at all,
Archie replied, for what he was describing in the quoted passage was
the stock figure of the capitalist that the communist writers of the thirties
set up to attack. Moreover, he had explicitly argued in his essay that it
was this attitude of hatred that doomed the American communist movement to fail, because "from hatred there springs no life."

Undaunted, Clark redirected his fire to MacLeish's poetry. He read
aloud a somewhat baffling passage from "The Lost Speakers" (1936)
and the sonnet "Immortality" from Archie's undergraduate book of
verse, *Tower of Ivory* (1917). "Since the new Assistant Secretary is
supposed to impose culture on the whole world," Senator Clark said,
perhaps he will "tell us what [these poems] mean." MacLeish was not
about to explicate his verse in a congressional hearing. Instead he repeated a famous anecdote about Robert Browning. Asked to explain

the meaning of a passage, Browning replied, "When I wrote that, God and I knew what it meant; but now God alone knows." To take the curse off the implication that MacLeish was a fuzzy-minded aesthete, Roosevelt supporter Claude Pepper of Florida asked Archie to confirm that he had played quarterback at Yale and had fought at the Battle of the Marne. "Yes, sir," Archie answered. "I was on the front in the second Battle of the Marne; and in addition to writing poems at Yale, I did play on the football team."

So the hearing ended, and with it, one would have thought, all serious opposition to MacLeish's appointment. In fact, though, the committee was evenly divided. In his "In the Nation" column for the Friday December 15 *New York Times,* Arthur Krock commented that MacLeish was "unpopular with most of the conservative Democrats and almost all Republicans as well as with some New Dealers." According to Krock, Archie was afflicted with "the divine afflatus," which imbued him with strong opinions strongly expressed and an impatient and intolerant attitude toward anyone who disagreed with them. In addition, Krock went on, "the undercurrent of the attack on him from one quarter is that in previous administrative jobs he has not done very well or kept to the lines of his commission, and that he is too hot a partisan of his patrons in the White House to turn out State Department material in which information instead of administration propaganda will be the end-product."

"If you see Arthur Krock," Archie wrote Secretary of State Stettinius immediately after reading the *Times,* "I hope you will congratulate him for me on his attempt at assassination this morning." In the event he was not confirmed, Archie told Stettinius, he thought it would be "a great mistake" to send his name up again, even though the president had proposed that course of action. The Senate Foreign Relations Committee, meeting in secret session later that day, initially did turn down MacLeish's nomination by a vote of twelve to eight. Then Senators Pepper of Florida and James E. Murray of Montana, who had voted against all the nominees because they did not like the choice of former cotton broker Will Clayton, switched their votes, creating a ten-ten tie. Committee chairman Tom Connally of Texas, trying to produce a favorable vote for all the administration's nominees, ruled he would hold the balloting open until midnight, so that two absent members — Robert F. Wagner of New York and Gerald P. Nye of North Dakota — might record their votes. Wagner telephoned in his vote in favor of MacLeish. Nye telegraphed his vote against MacLeish, but the wire arrived after midnight and so was not counted. The committee forwarded MacLeish's name to the Senate, eleven to ten. A few days later, all six of Roosevelt's nominees were confirmed by the full Senate. The vote on MacLeish was the closest: forty-three in favor, twenty-five against, and twenty-eight abstaining.

After bidding farewell to his companions at the LC, MacLeish moved to the State Department December 19 and immediately set about acquiring a staff and translating his job description into action. A complement of three was assigned to his immediate office, including Haldore Hanson as an administrative assistant. But his right-hand man was State Department veteran John Sloan Dickey, who as director of the Office of Public Affairs oversaw half a dozen divisions and several hundred employees. Within forty-eight hours after the announcement of the Stettinius team, Dickey had a telephone call from Acheson, inviting him to lunch at the Metropolitan Club. At the lunch it took Dean some time to come to the point, which was Archie's appointment. "Archie's probably my closest friend," Acheson said, "but I'm afraid he may be a disaster as assistant secretary. If ever there was a man temperamentally unsuited for administrative work, and particularly the administrative jungle of the State department, that man is Archie MacLeish."

What Dean wanted John Dickey to do was first, to keep Archie from plunging ahead with idealism and impulsiveness, not to say naiveté, into areas where he would be ridiculed by others, and second, to protect him from the more vicious and smooth-talking animals of Foggy Bottom. As a consequence, Dickey often did counsel MacLeish to slow down in the months ahead. "You'd be wise not to rush into this," he'd say, while an annoyed MacLeish accused him of always anticipating trouble. Yet Dickey came to admire MacLeish tremendously, largely because of his drive to get things done. "He wanted results," Dickey said. "He wanted to work for the things he believed in." In the Department of State, those qualities were rare.

Dickey was troubled by the low opinion Acheson and MacLeish had of Stettinius. They regarded the secretary of state — a handsome man with prematurely white hair who had come to the government by way of General Motors and United States Steel — as an intellectual lightweight, "a very well-intentioned boy scout." According to Acheson, it was not true that President Roosevelt was "his own secretary of state," as the rumor had it. The nature of the two positions made that impossible. But Roosevelt could prevent anyone else from being secretary of state, and appointing Stettinius had that effect. Archie flatly refused to write speeches for Stettinius. He would do that for FDR, but for no one else. In fact, it was in part to compose speeches for the secretary of state that MacLeish recruited a special assistant. This was Adlai Stevenson, the young lawyer from Illinois who had impressed him as "one of the most valuable men" in Washington during the days of the Committee on War Information.

Stevenson came to work late in February 1945. Early in March, MacLeish wrote Thursa Bakey from Hot Springs, Virginia, where he was taking a short holiday, to "please tell A.S. that I thank God for him every night and every morning." His week's vacation with Ada and the Murphys hurt Archie's conscience "like a stone bruise on the heel," he wrote his mother. "What a thing is a Scotch forebear! To say nothing of having Elder Brewster looking over your biological shoulder twenty-four hours a day every day of the year." Yet there was no reason for guilt, for he desperately needed the rest. The Senate hearings had taken more out of him than he realized. And at the State Department, he'd found, "there is always more to do than can be done & it is always urgent."

His job shook down into domestic and overseas components. At home he served as a kind of "ambassador to the American people," and the very vagueness of this role attracted all sorts of requests. Serge Koussevitzky of the Boston Symphony Orchestra called for an appointment, which was of course granted. What Koussevitzky had in mind, it developed, was a position for his niece in the State Department. On another occasion a delegation of blacks, headed by Mary McLeod Bethune, confronted MacLeish with their complaints about unequal treatment of black soldiers in army camps. Bethune, a woman of sixty "articulate as an angel," brilliantly and very forcefully laid out her case. "Black men are dying in this war," she said. "We want some responsible consideration." As the group was leaving, she stole back into Archie's office alone. "Your mother opened the door for me," she said. "I am Mary McLeod Bethune, and your mother opened the door for me at Hull House in Chicago many years ago. I owe her everything I am." Moved, Archie not long after made a speech on the subject of discrimination against blacks in the military that did not — as he knew it would not — endear him to President Roosevelt.

His primary stateside function was to communicate with the American people about what the State Department was doing, and especially about its plans for a lasting peace through the United Nations. The basic framework for the UN was hammered out in two meetings at Dumbarton Oaks in Washington, the first between the United States, Great Britain, and the Soviet Union in August–September 1944 and the second between the United States, Britain, and China the following month. The resulting proposals were presented in a series of seven half-hour "Building the Peace" NBC radio broadcasts on Saturday nights, beginning in February 1945. Archie wrote and participated in all of these broadcasts, where questions and responses from the public were aired. As Dickey recalled, it was "terribly important" to both of them that communication with the American people be a two-way street, and the radio series, which reached an audience of 6 to 8 million people weekly, produced an unprecedented volume of comment in the mails and the media. "No foreign policy in a democracy is any better than the public support it has," MacLeish maintained. "And you can't have public support without public knowledge."

Not all of the radio shows went smoothly. One Saturday night NBC tried a hookup between MacLeish, Dickey, Acheson, and others in Washington and Secretary of State Stettinius in Mexico City. Supposedly the watches were synchronized, but when the director in Washington finished his countdown and Archie launched into his introductory remarks, the voice of Stettinius came across the airwaves loud and clear. "Shut up, you fellows," he said. "We'll be on the air in thirty seconds." For some reason, Mexico stayed thirty seconds behind Washington throughout the half-hour show. As Acheson recalled, some "stations cut out Washington; others cut out Mexico City; some left them both on; some cut them both off." After the chaos was ended, Dickey succumbed to a fit of hysterical laughter. Yet the mixup may have had the unintended effect of humanizing the nation's leading diplomats. To a considerable degree, Edwin Lahey observed at the end of the broadcasts, "Archie MacLeish has convinced a lot of Americans that this really is their State Department, and not the private preserve of the lads in the striped pants and the homburg hats."

Overseas, MacLeish faced the challenge of trying to achieve cross-cultural understanding. Modern electronic communications, he wrote, were "as capable of altering the social structure of the world" (once the clocks were coordinated) "as modern air transport is capable of altering the geography of the world." The Parliament of Man that Tennyson dreamed of was at hand, now that it was possible for the peoples of the world to leap the boundaries of time and address one another directly. As for the message the United States should convey, "We want men and women in other continents to know what our life as a people is like, what we value as a people, in what we are skilled and in what not skilled — our character, our qualities, our beliefs. . . . We want them to know our habits of laughing and of not laughing so that they will hear not only the words but the tone too and understand it. We want them to have the sense of us as men and women as we wish too to have the sense of them."

This kind of shared understanding, Archie believed, could only be achieved through open channels, through the freedom of exchange of ideas that was "basic to our whole political doctrine." Within the State Department, however, many officers emphatically opposed the policy of "open covenants openly arrived at." "Less information is put out than the country has a right to expect, and far less than the press desires," MacLeish wrote Undersecretary Grew on February 19. "An affirmative and conscious desire to tell as much as possible must take the place of the present inclination in many quarters to tell as little as possible and only to tell that when it is no longer possible to be silent." Grew may have blinked at Archie's imperative tone. He did nothing else. Secrets were the very stuff of international negotiations.

Neither of them, for instance, knew what President Roosevelt chose to keep to himself about the United Nations agreements that he, Churchill, and Stalin worked out at the Yalta Conference of February 4–11, 1945. The Security Council, it was understood, was to be made up of five nations: the United States, the United Kingdom, the Soviet Union, France, and China. What was not revealed for nearly a month after the end of the conference was that Russia had insisted on a veto provision within the Security Council. The veto rather undermined the emphasis on the solidarity of the Big Three that MacLeish and Stevenson had been emphasizing over the radio. But at least absolute equality would prevail in the UN General Assembly, they pointed out; all nations, whether large or small, would have one vote. Thus it was with considerable dismay that Archie and Adlai found out, through a leak to the *New York Herald Tribune* early in April, that at Yalta, Britain and the United States had agreed to support the Soviet Union's request for *three* votes in the General Assembly in return for its promise to support a request from the United States for three votes, if such a request were ever made. (It was not.) This revelation made it clear to the press and the public that those charged with providing them information had not themselves been fully informed. MacLeish's credibility in particular was damaged. A cartoon on the front page of the April 5 *Washington Evening Star* showed a dapper Stettinius in swallowtail coat with a sweating MacLeish in shirtsleeves with a pencil behind his ear. "Why don't you tell the people the facts?" Stettinius asks. "Why doesn't somebody tell *me* the facts?" MacLeish responds.

A week later, on April 12, 1945, Franklin Delano Roosevelt died at his winter retreat in Warm Springs, Georgia. FDR, whose health had been deteriorating for some time, had come back from Yalta exhausted and ill. MacLeish and press secretary Jonathan Daniels were the last to see him on official business before he left Washington for Georgia. At 11:45 A.M. March 29, they met with Roosevelt in his upstairs study. It was a beautiful day, but the light from the window revealed a haggard man before them. "I saw that light on his face, and knew he was dying," MacLeish recalled. By midafternoon the president was scheduled to leave for a period of recuperation in Warm Springs. In the meantime, MacLeish prepared a press release for his signature. Roosevelt changed a phrase in the first paragraph and wearily pushed the paper back to MacLeish and Daniels. Looking it over in the hall, they realized that FDR's alteration made nonsense of what followed. "We had to go back into the room of that gaunt man," Daniels remembered, "and ask him to reconsider."

MacLeish called Stevenson into his office at the old State, War, and Navy building on Seventeenth Street when word came of the massive cerebral hemorrhage that killed Roosevelt. "The president is dead," Archie said quietly. He was to write the proclamation of death. In order to help, Stevenson looked up the precedents, the statements issued when earlier presidents had died in office. Characteristically, what MacLeish wrote — in language reminiscent of the King James Bible — looked forward rather than backward.

> It has pleased God in His infinite wisdom to take from us the immortal spirit of Franklin Delano Roosevelt, the 32nd president of the United States.
>
> The leader of his people in a great war, he lived to see the assurance of the victory but not to share it. He lived to see the first foundations of the free and peaceful world to which his life was dedicated, but not to enter on that world himself.
>
> His fellow countrymen will sorely miss his fortitude and faith and courage in the time to come. The peoples of the earth who love the ways of freedom and of hope will mourn for him.
>
> But though his voice is silent, his courage is not spent, his faith is not extinguished. The courage of great men outlives them to become the courage of their people and the peoples of the world. It lives beyond them and upholds their purposes and brings their hopes to pass.

The next day, MacLeish and Robert Sherwood paid tribute to their chief in nationwide radio broadcasts. Archie, after speaking briefly in a program for American schoolchildren, broke down under the emotional strain and was unable to continue. Only when Roosevelt was gone did he realize the depth of his feeling for the president. "We did not know we would weep so for him," MacLeish wrote in his "April Elegy," which compared FDR's death with that of Abraham Lincoln eighty Aprils before. "We did not know we would sit in our chairs, at our desks, our hands still. There were many who loved him, but even those who loved him did not know."

One World

For MacLeish, Roosevelt's passing invested the United Nations Conference on International Organization with the aura of a holy mission. The task that confronted the delegates from fifty nations in San Francisco was to establish a charter that would bind them together in a spirit of peaceful cooperation. Though not one of the eight official U.S. delegates, Archie traveled to San Francisco with them in advance of the April 25 starting date. For the next two months he campaigned for the United Nations. In a signed article for the *San Francisco Chronicle* on April 26, he declared his conviction that the conference was "*not* an effort to create a new world — a new and indivisible world," because that world already existed. "We've been pretending that we didn't know it's just one world," he wrote, while everywhere people were discovering their interdependence. "If there are world ills, there should be world resistance to such ills. If there are hopes common to mankind, there should be methods as extensive as mankind to bring the hopes to pass." The importance of the conference to establish the United Nations could not be overemphasized, and the endeavor was far from utopian. "No more realistic or sensible or necessary labor was ever undertaken by any meeting in the history of mankind," MacLeish concluded.

Archie had three separate jobs to perform at the San Francisco conference. First, with Stevenson, who soon joined him in a suite on the fourteenth floor of the Mark Hopkins Hotel, he participated in what was humorously known as Operation Titanic, which was set up to issue briefings to the press — as a supplement to the regular news releases — about what was going on in negotiations between the United States and other nations over the specifications of the charter. Stevenson, in particular, proved skillful in providing background information, and occasional leaks, to the press. He also learned to say "yo" in response to questions as an ambiguous blend of "yes" and "no."

Second, MacLeish conducted another national series of eight weekly Saturday-night broadcasts from San Francisco, reporting to the radio audience about the progress of the conference. In these broadcasts he did his best to allay fears among conservative groups about the ill effects of concessions to the Soviet Union. The two nations had worked together during the war under the "most difficult geographic, economic, and psychological circumstances," he commented on May 26. At Dumbarton Oaks, at Yalta, and in San Francisco they had reconciled their differences and arrived at common understandings. "The vital interests of the United States and the Soviet Union conflict at no point on the earth's surface," he declared. There was "no necessary reason" to suppose that "the United States and the Soviet Union should ever find themselves in conflict with each other, let alone in the kind of conflict reckless and irresponsible men have begun now to suggest." As the cold war was to prove, he was overoptimistic about the course of U.S.-Soviet relations, and his words would come back to haunt him.

Third, he became involved in writing and editing portions of the United Nations charter, and particularly its preamble. On June 8, as approval on the charter neared, Archie wrote Ed Stettinius that "he had never seen a more complete literary and intellectual abortion" than the preamble as then constituted. The preamble "should be *written* — not constructed like a cross word puzzle out of political and academic odds and ends." It should have the power to "move men's minds." He enclosed a draft of the way he would go about composing the preamble. "It has all the raisins which are in the original, but an attempt has been made to combine them into some kind of pudding." Several drafts later, the preamble to the United Nations charter emerged from his kitchen in one long ringing sentence.

> *We the peoples of the United*
> *Nations determined*
>
> to save succeeding generations from the scourge of war which twice in our lifetime has brought untold sorrow to mankind, and
>
> to reaffirm faith in fundamental human rights, in the dignity and worth of the human person, in the equal rights of men and women and of nations large and small, and
>
> to establish conditions under which justice and respect for the obligations arising from treaties and other sources of international law can be maintained, and
>
> to promote social progress and better standards of life in larger freedom,
>
> *and for these ends*
>
> to practice tolerance and live together in peace with one another as good neighbors, and
>
> to unite our strength to maintain international peace and security, and
>
> to ensure, by the acceptance of principles and the institution of methods, that armed force shall not be used, save in the common interest, and

to employ international machinery for the promotion of the economic and social advancement of all peoples,

have resolved to combine our efforts to accomplish these aims.

"Tuesday, June 26, 1945, was a great day," MacLeish said over the armed forces radio network. United States superfortresses flattened ten Japanese war factories, while "across the Pacific in San Francisco, the delegates of fifty allies in this war against the Axis sat down, one by one, at a huge round table and put their names to the Charter of the United Nations.

"Two big strides: one toward the end of this war, the other — one hopes — toward the end of all war."

A month later the United States Senate approved the charter by the impressive margin of eighty-nine for, two against.

Soon after Archie's return from the San Francisco conference, his daughter, Mimi, was married to Ensign Karl Grimm at the MacLeish house in Alexandria. Mimi met her husband in Chicago, while she was studying at the National College of Education in Evanston and he was taking naval officer's training nearby. Archie and Ada tried to prevent the marriage, Archie going so far as to inquire of the dean and president of Olivet College, Michigan, about his putative son-in-law's record there. The basic grounds of the objection were social: young Grimm was the son of working-class parents, his father having risen from factory worker to time-and-motion man. This mattered not at all to Mimi, though it mattered a great deal to her mother. Mimi and Karl were married on July 12.

With the war against Japan still continuing, few of the couple's friends from Chicago could arrange to attend the wedding. Most of the guests were friends of Archie and Ada's. Felix Frankfurter was on hand, though he could not, as Mimi had hoped, officiate at her wedding. Supreme Court justices were not licensed to perform such ceremonies in the state of Virginia. Lord Halifax, the British ambassador, attended, as did Harold Ickes, Adlai Stevenson, and Ed Stettinius. Dean Acheson brought a Revolutionary War sword to cut the cake with. Sara Murphy lent Mimi her own very elaborate wedding dress, encrusted with pearls. Standing in this gown at the bottom of the staircase in her family's eighteenth-century house, her aunt Ishbel recalled, "for once in her life Mimi looked like a picture out of *Vogue*." Ada had seen to that. Characteristically, what Mimi remembers best about the day is wanting to get out of Sara Murphy's beautiful but cumbersome wedding dress.

On the day after FDR's death, MacLeish formally submitted his resignation as assistant secretary of state. This was routine procedure throughout the government, to enable President Truman to make his own appointments. On July 3 Truman replaced Stettinius with James F. Byrnes, and the assistant secretaries began to anticipate a similar fate. With the UN conference over, MacLeish proposed Stevenson as his successor. Adlai was not interested. "I don't think I 'rate' your job should the Secretary accept your resignation — that is, I have no distinction and little experience in the field of information, cultural relations, etc.," he wrote Archie on July 26. "I'm just a low order of country lawyer with a congenital taste for public service, politics, politicians and the public trough where my family have been nibbling, frugally, albeit, for several generations." Stevenson went back to Illinois, declaring that he was "prouder of having had a part in the information job on Dumbarton Oaks than anything in these four eventful years." He asked Thursa Bakey to send him a signed photograph of MacLeish, his boss on "the best detail" he'd yet had.

In mid-August, Joseph C. Grew resigned as undersecretary of state, and President Truman named Dean Acheson to succeed him. This surprised some Washington insiders, for the plain-speaking president and the elegantly turned out easterner made an odd couple. Yet there was a bond between Truman and Acheson: they were both realists who understood the ways of politics. MacLeish's resignation was accepted on August 17. "All of us realize the wonderful work you did to bring about the adoption of the [United Nations] charter," President Truman congratulated him. "I know that you wanted to be released from the government service more than a year ago," he added. "It was good of you to remain and I do not feel that I should now ask you to make a greater sacrifice."

At the time, MacLeish was still smoldering about his experience in the State Department. The rigid policy of secrecy chafed him, and he was often impatient, Dickey recalled, in dealing with people who were not as quick or imaginative as he was. "Archie was not a management person," Dickey said, at least not in the area of personnel management. At the same time, he was operating in a jungle where few of the animals were to be trusted. Archie's resentment was evident in his letter of congratulations and condolences to Acheson upon his assuming the post of undersecretary. "I hope to God," he wrote Dean, "you won't have to eat too many pecks of dirt over the next twelve months and that the serried legions of the apple polishers won't too completely and too profoundly disgust you." He was beginning to realize what "that caustic and cryptic philosopher, John S. Dickey," who had left to become president of Dartmouth College, meant when he told him, "You don't owe any of these birds anything."

In retrospect, MacLeish looked back on his six years in Washington as time well spent. "What I know about the Republic and what I know about the innards of American history, I owe to those years in Washington," he said. Although he had been silenced as a poet for the duration, it was "a proper loss" if it was a loss at all. "If the art of poetry is, as I deeply believe it to be, the art of making sense of the chaos of human experience, it's not a bad thing to see a lot of chaos." And he left his mark behind him. The bare record of his years in Washington might "look like a design for frustration," Jonathan Daniels said of MacLeish. But "few minds touched so many other important minds. . . . His was a spirit that could not be locked in a vault, painted or not. America will scarcely ever know how much he contributed . . . beyond his tasks as librarian, propagandist, briefly as diplomat." Be that as it may, Archie gladly left Washington in the fall of 1945 "to work again as a free man, a poet laboring in his own time with the instruments of his own talent, not to work for other masters." Or so he thought.

On November 18 another poet who was not a free man arrived handcuffed at Bolling Field in Washington to be tried for treason. Ezra Pound had been held at the U.S. Army Disciplinary Training Center in Pisa, Italy, since May 24. T. S. Eliot, learning of his arrest, wrote and cabled MacLeish to ask what could be done for Pound, particularly "in the way of enlisting the support of poets and men of letters." The whole affair, in Eliot's opinion, should be quickly disposed of and forgotten. But that was not possible, given the state of public opinion. The best hope for Pound, MacLeish intimated, lay in the area of such "mitigating circumstance(s)" as might be established by psychiatric examination. Oddly, Pound twice asked that MacLeish be approached about the possibility of serving as his lawyer. Apparently Archie never heard of his proposal, and probably he would have been surprised, considering Ezra's repeated attacks upon him as a person and a poet. Julien Cornell, a young lawyer with strong civil rights convictions, was instead enlisted to defend Pound. "I find myself pulled in opposite directions by the whole Pound business," MacLeish wrote Cornell on December 6. He admired Ezra deeply as a poet, yet felt "only the most complete contempt" for his wartime broadcasts. Archie did not exert himself to see Ezra before his trial, which ended with no verdict and his confinement in Saint Elizabeths Hospital in Washington.

MacLeish underwent a process of decompression following his resignation from the State Department. For half a decade and more he had worked at a frenetic pace on issues of national and sometimes international importance. Often he could hardly wait to get to his desk in the morning to discover what new crisis awaited him. "I'd enjoyed power for the first time in my life, had quite a taste of it," he explained to his son Bill, "and it was hard to make the bridge and go back to being myself." To keep himself too tired to think, back in Conway where the phone hardly rang at all, he spent long hours chopping down saplings and sawing wood.

The pangs of withdrawal from power were considerably eased when Secretary of State Byrnes named him to head the United States delegation to the organizational conference of the United Nations Educational, Scientific, and Cultural Organization (UNESCO) in London, beginning November 1. Dean Acheson sounded Archie out about the assignment in advance, and MacLeish agreed to go, as long as he could be chairman and wouldn't have to waste his time sitting around waiting for others to make up their minds. MacLeish was a logical choice for the position, both as a previous participant in the March 1944 meeting of the Allied ministers of education and as an eloquent spokesman for the cause of international cooperation and understanding. At the London UNESCO meeting of November 1–16, 1945, Archie headed a delegation of fifteen, most of them educators. The distinguished astronomer Harlow Shapley, director of the Harvard College Observatory, was included — as MacLeish said — "to put the S in UNESCO."

British Prime Minister Clement Attlee made the keynote address at the conference. "Do not wars, after all, begin in the minds of men?" he asked. Weren't the peoples of the world "islands shouting at each other over seas of misunderstandings?" Attlee's words gave MacLeish the inspiration for the first sentence of the constitution that UNESCO adopted two weeks later. "Since wars begin in the minds of men," he wrote, "it is in the minds of men that the defenses of peace must be constructed." Ideally, he envisioned UNESCO as helping the peoples of the world to "root out the prejudice and ignorance which have separated them in the past." This prospect was within reach, he believed, through improved means of communication that made it possible for people to address one another directly across national boundaries. The UNESCO conference marked a second step (after the drafting of the UN charter) toward realizing "the great dream of human peace through understanding." Nor was he the only one to have such high hopes. The delegates came away from their damp and dreary London meetings with a constitution in place and a sense that they had participated in a historic enterprise. It was, the English author J. B. Priestley said, "the most underrated conference in all history."

For a number of reasons, UNESCO did not fulfill the heady expectations of its founders. From the beginning there were financial disputes, with nations whose educational establishments had been damaged or wiped out by the war seeking funds for reconstruction programs from countries reluctant to make such commitments. Given only advisory powers, UNESCO could rarely make anything happen that was opposed by any of its members. The Soviet Union kept its distance, not even sending representatives to the originating conference. The United States itself gave the organization considerably less than its full support. In a December 30, 1945, letter to Acheson, MacLeish complained that the organization was already being stripped of two of its most important functions: overseeing both the exchange of scientific information and the international activities of the mass media. To his way of thinking, the second function was the more important one. Even the League of Nations had advocated cooperative exchanges between scholars and scientists. But UNESCO proposed to increase understanding not only through associations of learned societies but among ordinary people as well through "popular education and the modern instruments of mass communication — newspaper, radio, motion picture."

The principal reason for the failure of UNESCO to shape "the minds of men" toward peace was the persistence of nationalism. Theoretically, the organization was to be staffed by civil servants free from the taint of national self-interest. Actually, they could not be found. Soon UNESCO was drawn into ideological disputes between East and West. Within the United States, anticommunist elements regarded UNESCO as an undeclared enemy. The organization, a retired U.S. Army major general testified to the Congress, was "designed to break down Americans' faith in American government and dilute American loyalty to American institutions." As the cold war intensified, the U.S. commitment to UNESCO progressively withered away. In 1984 the United States withdrew from the organization entirely.

Most of those troubles lay beyond the horizon in 1946, when MacLeish was lobbying hard for UNESCO. For the winter he and Ada rented James Warburg's New York apartment on Seventieth Street east of Madison. In March the MacLeishes and Warburgs drove to Florida together on vacation. During an outing on Biscayne Bay, they discovered a fifteen-foot motorboat that had turned over in high winds. The owner of the motorboat, a New Jersey businessman, drowned in the mishap, but Archie plunged into the water and rescued two of his floundering passengers.

In November 1946, a year after the founding conference in London, UNESCO met in Paris to get its operations under way. William Benton, who had succeeded MacLeish as assistant secretary of state, was chairman of the U.S. delegation, and MacLeish deputy secretary. Britisher John Maud (later Lord Redcliffe-Maud) vigorously supported MacLeish for first director of UNESCO, as did Léon Blum of the French delegation. Archie's connections with France, both in World War I and during the 1920s, made him a logical choice, Blum thought. Only two months before, MacLeish had been made a "Commandeur de la Lègion d'Honneur" in a Washington, D.C., ceremony presided over by Ambassador Henri Bonnet.

Enthusiastic as he was about the potential of the organization, Archie backed away from taking its reins. He "had run out of oxygen," he said. He needed to go back to being himself. So English scientist Julian Huxley was elected director, and Archie settled for a position as the lone American on the five-member executive council. Four months later he resigned, after chiding his fellow council members for substituting "broad generalizations for specific action." Idealist though he may have been, Archie could measure success only by way of action. It seemed to him that UNESCO was liable to degenerate into "a bureaucratic educational operation" instead of the last best hope for peace and understanding among the peoples of the world.

On November 19, 1946, the opening day of the UNESCO meeting in Paris, MacLeish was elevated in absentia from the National Institute to the more exclusive American Academy of Arts and Letters. His principal sponsor was Robinson Jeffers, joined by Van Wyck Brooks, Thornton Wilder, Wilbur L. Cross, Edna St. Vincent Millay, Walter Lippmann, Carl Sandburg, and Robert Frost. (Sinclair Lewis declined to second him.) In advancing Archie's candidacy, Jeffers described him as "a poet of originality and power, a writer of distinguished prose, and a persuasive speaker" who was "also notable for public service of various kinds." Once before, in July 1940, MacLeish had been nominated to the American Academy, but had not been elected, probably because of the furor over "The Irresponsibles." This time he was duly elected to occupy chair 38 in the academy, succeeding Ellen Glasgow. He proved an unusually active member, although the academy — like the State Department and UNESCO — disappointed him with its inertia.

In addition to his involvement with UNESCO, MacLeish spent much of his time in 1945 and 1946 in New York, working on the report of the Commission on the Freedom of the Press that Harry Luce had chosen him for. In February 1946 he sent his "second draft of the General Report" on the commission's deliberations to fellow member Beardsley Ruml. The report was still in preliminary form, however. More than a year elapsed before the commission published its *Freedom of the Press: A Framework of Principle,* under the authorship of Harvard philosophy professor William Ernest Hocking. Notably, Archie took exception to some of the report's conclusions by way of footnotes. To the assertion that "as addressed to society, *there are no unconditional rights,*" he objected that the rights specified in the Declaration of Independence — to life, liberty, and the pursuit of happiness — were *not* conditional.

Where ownership of the mass media was concerned, however, MacLeish emphasized not rights but duties. Freedom of the press was a right belonging to all the people, but as a practical matter that freedom could be exercised only by the small minority who had access to the press. That minority therefore had an obligation to circulate the widest possible range of ideas in its publications, he maintained. It was crucial in a democracy to recognize the opinions of those who had something to say but no press to say it with. Otherwise, MacLeish shared the report's conclusions that three dangers loomed for the future of a free press: its drift toward monopoly, its failure to meet the needs of society through overemphasis on the trivial and sensational, and its morally questionable practices such as "distortion, bias, outright lying, and suppression." The press had better begin to police itself, the commission concluded, for freedom of the press was an "accountable freedom."

20 ❖

A NEW LIFE

Freedom Fenced In

THE YEARS AFTER World War II were dark ones for MacLeish. He thought of himself as having deserted his art to serve his country, and for a time it seemed as if his art would not readmit him. "When I left Washington," he later told his student, the poet Stephen Sandy, "I went to my farm, out in Conway. The weather was cold and wet and it sank into you, a damp wind streaming down from the golden Berkshires, and I tried to light a fire outside, but the wood was wet, the wood was green and would only smoke and sputter." He sat there on the ground and thought, "It's just like me, I'm that way inside, I just won't burn inside."

To such doubts about his capacity to write poetry was added an overwhelming sense of malaise, both personal and political. Death came calling horribly when Katy Dos Passos was decapitated in a September 1947 automobile accident. Archie and Ada gave what comfort they could to Dos, who had been driving, but the errand of mercy turned bitter when Edmund Wilson appeared in the hospital room and declined to shake Archie's hand. Three months later, on December 19, 1947, Martha Hillard MacLeish died at ninety-one. The mother who always believed in Archie, who gave him an ideal to live by, was gone.

Vigorous to the end, Martha MacLeish fought on the side of the angels into her tenth decade. She expressed her liberal views, both locally in Glencoe civic affairs and nationally, as in a March 1946 letter to President Truman imploring him to grant a loan to Great Britain. To her, as to her son, this issue, like all issues, could be reduced to moral terms. England had protected us in the war while we prepared to fight, she pointed out. "If we have any gratitude and honor, we should now seize our opportunity to repay her." She shared Archie's journalistic biases, too. Mrs. MacLeish reminded the president that she was part of "a large and growing liberal element" that was thriving in and around Chicago "in spite of the Chicago Tribune."

In August 1946 the family assembled at Craigie Lea to observe her ninetieth birthday. After the toasts in her honor were over, Martha MacLeish rose to praise her late husband. "Now I think we have had enough about me," she said. "While we are all together I want to tell the grandchildren and great grandchildren of Andrew MacLeish . . . why they should be proud to bear his name." At Rockford College, in November 1946, Archie gave the principal address honoring "Martha MacLeish, Citizen." She possessed a fundamental quality of the American character, he said: "confidence not only in ourselves but in life, belief in the goodness of life and in the goodness of humankind." In short, she believed in the American dream, and in her long service to education and racial and religious tolerance had done her best to make it come true. "I am proud to be her son," Archie concluded. "I am even more proud to be her countryman."

Midway through 1947, Martha MacLeish broke a rib in a fall. Characteristically, she made light of her mishap, but while hospitalized she contracted pneumonia, suffered an incapacitating stroke, and faded off into an extended period of semiconsciousness. In a last lucid moment she told her assembled children — Norman, Archie, and Ishbel — that it was all right, she was ready to go. "It has been worth while," she said. "It has been very worth while." Her mother was remarkable, Ishbel observed, for her fine balance of mind and heart. "She never had the hardness of a cold, impersonal mind, nor the softness of an undisciplined heart. It was this . . . that made her so greatly respected and so deeply loved." In two separate poems, Archie refused to accept the idea that his mother was, in any final sense, dead. She was with him as eternally as the waves.

> You think a life can end?
> Mind knows, nor soul believes
> How far, how far beyond
> The shattering of the waves,
> How deep within the land,
> The surge of sea survives.

Among other ways, his mother's example inspired MacLeish in his postwar battle on behalf of civil liberties. The war had been fought, he believed, for freedom. But in the red scare that followed World War II, as it had World War I, that goal was sacrificed to the presumably more pressing need for national security. The United States and the Soviet Union embarked on an extended but undeclared war that dictated the policies of both nations. Against the specter of worldwide Soviet domination, any hint of prior sympathy or association with communism became cause for suspicion. The House Committee on Un-American Activities (HUAC) casually ruined the reputations and careers of those it decided to investigate. Motivated by fear, informers saw their chance and took it. Motivated by fear, employers shied away from those who were called to testify but would not inform. Silently, blacklists began to circulate. Noisily, loyalty oaths were demanded.

Against such enemies to freedom, MacLeish was avid for combat. As he argued the issue abstractly with Harry Luce, freedom was not something to be "defended . . . like man's other possessions." Freedom, he insisted, "is not something you *have:* it is something you *do.* The only way you can defend it is to exercise it." Especially it could not be defended by "extra-legal police and extra-judicial committees . . . if instead of trying to build a wall around our freedom to keep others out we would increase our freedom until it overflowed the world, we would have less to fear." Now Americans were in a moral slough, "our minds and our newspapers full of panic fears and Maginot lines and the hypocritical protestations of men who have proved their devotion to the cause of freedom by doing everything they could to destroy it." Then he quoted Erich Fromm's *Escape to Freedom* to Luce, to the effect that "positive freedom consists in the spontaneous *activity* of the total, integrated personality." It was action that counted, and act MacLeish did, in public and with considerable courage.

He first spoke out against HUAC at a March 1948 gathering of scientists assembled in New York to protest the loyalty investigation of Dr. Edward U. Condon, director of the United States Bureau of Standards. Without charging Condon with any specific wrongdoing, HUAC chairman J. Parnell Thomas described him as "one of the weakest links" in the security screen protecting the nation's atomic bomb secrets. In outrage, MacLeish objected that the committee was acting as prosecutor and judge, announcing judgments in advance of prosecution, and doing so under cover of congressional immunity to libel suits. Defamation of character was just as effective in silencing free speech as rubber hoses or automatic rifles, he said. In his view the Thomas committee had "done more in a year and a half to breach the defenses of freedom and to introduce the wooden horse of terror into the United States than all the Communists on earth."

In July 1948 Archie took the lead in a freedom-of-expression case involving the liberal magazine the *Nation*. The board of superintendents of the New York City schools had canceled the schools' subscription to this eighty-year-old publication after it ran two articles critical of practices in the Catholic church. Working with editor Freda Kirchwey, MacLeish drafted "An Appeal to Reason and Conscience," arguing that the board's actions violated constitutional guarantees of freedom of inquiry and of separation of church and state. One hundred and seven distinguished citizens signed this appeal, among them Eleanor Roosevelt, former New York governor Herbert H. Lehman, Charles Seymour, president of Yale, and Robert M. Hutchens, chancellor of the University of Chicago. This firepower did not persuade the superintendent of schools, William Jansen, to restore the *Nation* to the list of approved magazines, however. Angry and disturbed, MacLeish declared that the highhanded way the *Nation* had been barred from school libraries heralded an era of "the exclusive list and the forbidden title." The *Daily Worker* — not precisely the journal Archie was aiming to reach — praised him for that ominous prediction in its May 31, 1949, issue.

The FBI duly took note of MacLeish's activities in both the Condon and the *Nation* controversies and yet again when he lashed out against the vicious treatment of Laurence Duggan. Duggan, forty-two, a fourteen-year State Department veteran, was president of the Institute of International Education when, at 7 P.M. on December 20, 1948, he fell to his death from the window of his sixteenth-floor office on West Forty-fifth Street in New York. Before midnight, Representatives Karl Mundt, acting chairman of HUAC while Thomas was under indictment for fraud, and Richard M. Nixon informed reporters of testimony about Duggan before their committee. The files revealed that Isaac Don Levine had testified on December 8 that nine years previously the ex-communist Whittaker Chambers had stated to Assistant Secretary of State Adolf Berle that Duggan was one of six State Department officials who had given Chambers confidential information. When this hearsay evidence, twice removed, appeared in the morning papers, the inference was clear that Duggan's death had resulted directly from HUAC's investigation of communist infiltration of the State Department. "Fall Kills Duggan," the *New York Times* headline read. "Named with Hiss in Spy Ring Inquiry." The next day, however, Chambers disavowed Levine's testimony. He hadn't received any documents from Duggan, Chambers said. He hadn't even known Duggan at the time, though he did regard him as procommunist. No corroboration of Levine's testimony was sought. Duggan was never informed of these charges against him, nor was he invited to appear before HUAC. Nonetheless, five hours after he died, Mundt and Nixon chose to besmirch his name.

Who was Laurence Duggan? He was, according to former undersecretary of state Sumner Welles, "one of the most brilliant, most devoted and most patriotic public servants I have ever known." As the *Times* pointed out in an apologetic editorial, he was head of an organization that arranged for exchange of students among countries in the hope of achieving better understanding among peoples. On December 24 the *New York Herald Tribune* printed MacLeish's poem "The Black Day," written in a blaze of indignation and dedicated to Duggan's memory.

> God help that country where informers thrive!
> Where slander flourishes and lies contrive
> To kill by whispers! Where men lie to live!

> God help that country by informers fed
> Where fear corrupts and where suspicion's spread
> By look and gesture, even to the dead.

> God help that country where the liar's shame
> Outshouts the decent silence to defame
> The dead man's honor and defile his name.

> God help that country, cankered deep by doubt,
> Where honest men, by scandals turned about,
> See honor murdered and will not speak out.

The following month, Archie became chairman of the Laurence Duggan Fund, established to advance "the work of international education and understanding to which he had devoted his life."

In "The Conquest of America," published in the August 1949 *Atlantic Monthly,* MacLeish summed up his convictions about the nation's postwar descent. In military and economic terms the strongest country in the world, he wrote, the United States had nonetheless been conquered by Russia. All its actions were dictated by the USSR. In foreign policy, "whatever the Russians did, we did in reverse." In domestic politics, no one could be elected to office without demonstrating his hatred of Russia, and no law could be enacted "unless it could be demonstrated that the Russians wouldn't like it." Archie no longer maintained, as he had in February 1946, that America's interests and those of Russia were in conflict no place on the globe. In fact, he denounced the Soviet government for continuing its brutal crackdown on individual liberties. But that was no reason for the United States to give up its independence, and to compromise the freedom of its citizens, in the name of opposing the Russians. MacLeish's article elicited damning responses both from the *New Leader,* which the FBI recorded for its files, and from *Pravda,* which the FBI either ignored or was not monitoring.

It was in a mood of disgust over promises unfulfilled that Archie wrote *Actfive,* the long title poem of his 1948 *Actfive and Other Poems.* This was public poetry yet again, but the patriotic optimism and exhortation that characterized his work of the thirties was gone, replaced by a bitter irony. What he hoped to do in *Actfive,* MacLeish said, was to address the problem of where man stood at the end of World War II. "He had defeated an enormous danger, but was he alive? Was he getting anywhere?" The answer, unhappily, was no.

Actfive is divided into three scenes. The first opens with a stage direction reminiscent of *Hamlet:* "THE STAGE ALL BLOOD." God is departed, and so are the King and the King's son. The only figure in sight is the lifeless form of Man.

> *Now man is murdered and, where once he stood,*
> *Armed and in terror, ignorant, rank with blood,*
> *Cruel and desperate, stained with such a stain*
> *As earth nor fire, sea nor the dear rain*
> *Shall wash from heart or hand, his murderers remain.*

Yet "Every age must have its hero — / Even the faint age of fear": so MacLeish calls for one who will give meaning to

> *. . . these broken stones these*
> *Broken bodies violated brains*
> *Corrupted spirits shriveled hearts.*

The second scene, a masque or dumb show, introduces and dismisses various candidates for hero of the age: the scientist, the tycoon, the revolutionary, the dictator, the pacifist, the religionist, the Ego, and the crowd. Where Archie had earlier reposed his faith in the resilience and good sense of the American people, he now depicted them as cowed and weakened.

> *The many added together are not more but*
> *Less than each since each one fears*
> *And all are only each divided*
> *By the fears of all the others —*
> *By the trembling at your side:*
> *By the breathing at your ear.*

The climate of fear is chilling: no one dares to speak, to lead.

Yet in scene 3 the hero appears in the shape of mere flesh and bone, animated by the heart: man stripped of his hopes and dreams yet undefeated. It is a hard-won affirmation.

> *Abandoned by the guardians and gods,*
> *The great companion of the metaphor*

> Dead of the wars and wounds (O murdered dream!)
> The city of man consumed to ashes, ashes,
> The republic a marble rubble on its hill,
> The laws rules rites prayers philters all exhausted,
> Elders and the spiritual aids withdrawn —
> Abandoned by them all, by all forsaken,
> The naked human perishable heart —
> . . . .
> Stands guard: bears truth: knows fear and will outface,
> Unarmed at last before the vast ordeal,
> The death behind us and the death before.

Such a creature,

> Minute upon an immense plain
> Where vultures huddle and the soft
> And torpid rats recoil and crawl,

knowing only the void in the night above, knowing no surcease from despair, must somehow dare to "Endure and love." Such a one was FDR, though MacLeish invokes his example not by name but by description: "the responsible man" who

> . . . dies in his chair
> Fagged out, worn down, sick
> With the weight of his own bones, the task finished,
> The war won, the victory assured,
> The glory left behind him for the others.

But where shall such another be found?

The source of MacLeish's pervasive malaise is spelled out in the ironically titled "Brave New World," the concluding poem of *Actfive and Other Poems*. Here he addresses Thomas Jefferson directly to explain what has been lost since the Declaration of Independence. Once "freedom made free men." That was no longer true.

> What's changed is freedom in this age.
> What great men dared to choose
> Small men dare now neither win
> Nor lose.
> . . . .
> Freedom that was a thing to use
> They've made a thing to save
> And staked it in and fenced it round
> Like a dead man's grave.

In addition to these poems of political statement, several lyrics that presaged MacLeish's return to a more private verse appear in *Actfive and Other Poems*. Among the best are half a dozen love poems, including "The Linden Trees," "Excavation of Troy," and the expressive "What Must," which begins:

> *We lay beneath the alder tree*
> *Her breast she leaned upon my hand*
> *The alder leaf moved over me*
> *The sun moved over on the land*
> *Her mouth she pressed upon my mouth*
> *I felt the leaf beat in her breast*
> *I felt the sun move in her hair*
> *But nearer than the leaf the sun*
> *I felt the love go deep in me*
> *That had no season in the earth*
> *That has no time of spring or birth*
> *That cannot flower like a tree*
> *Or like one die*
>   *but only be.*

As against these evocations of carnal love, Archie set down his "Poem in Prose" for Ada, though

> *She has no more need for praise*
> *Than summer has*
> *Or the bright days.*
> . . . .
> *Wherever she is there is sun*
> *And time and a sweet air:*
> *Peace is there,*
> *Work done.*

What little critical attention this book of poems generated tended to compliment these short lyrics at the expense of the longer public poems. Selden Rodman in the *Saturday Review of Literature* chastised MacLeish for recklessly disregarding "the artistic consequences of imposing a blunt political content on one of the most subjective and volatile of styles." Yet in a dozen personal lyrics, Rodman added, one heard what Archie once said he listened for in poetry — "the sound of the axe as it enters the living wood." *Time*'s more negative review described the results of *Actfive and Other Poems* as "certainly minor, still echoing the big, pretentiously philosophical tones for which his poetic equipment is essentially unsuited, but here & there MacLeish is at home again with the private emotions that he can make ring true." The title poem was a failure, Hayden Carruth noted in *Poetry,* because MacLeish was more concerned with his message than his craft. *Actfive* was not a good poem, Robert Fitzgerald commented in the *New Republic,* but at least it was better than the "infantile" *America Was Promises.*

Such brutal notices were distressing enough, but Archie was still more disturbed by the silence of most reviewers, particularly those on the New York newspapers. MacLeish published his book with Random House in New York, moving down the coast from Boston's Houghton Mifflin in the wake of his editor Bob Linscott. In March 1948 Linscott warned him over lunch at the Century Club that he must expect to be massacred by the critics and offered him the option of withdrawing his manuscript. According to Linscott, the principal reviewers and editors in New York had agreed either to ignore *Actfive and Other Poems* or to savage it in print. Archie decided to go ahead with publication, only to find that Linscott was right. He was being punished, MacLeish felt, for abandoning poetry to serve the government, and for his own attacks on the literary establishment in "The Irresponsibles" and elsewhere. In his last years he maintained that even the *New York Times* had not reviewed the book, but there his memory played him false. The *Times* did print a brief, so-so notice by Peter Viereck on November 21, 1948, more than three months after publication. It was titled "Indignant Sing-Song."

Archie bitterly resented the reception of *Actfive and Other Poems,* his first book of poetry in nine years. In a letter to the editor of the *New York Times* in February 1949, Helen Wolfert pleaded his complaint for him. His publishers had brought the book out in August with very little fanfare, she pointed out. Then from the book sections "came the long yawn of silence." As the months passed, a few reviews emerged, but almost none of them bothered to tell the public what the title poem was about. Instead they "told other poets which cliques MacLeish did not fit into. For there are not only poetry cliques but poetry clique reviewers as well."

English S

Archie's disappointment over *Actfive and Other Poems* was soon assuaged by an invitation from Harvard. In March 1949 the distinguished comparatist Harry Levin of Harvard's English department sounded MacLeish out over a lunch at Joseph's in Boston. Was he interested in becoming the Boylston professor of rhetoric and oratory? The chair, which honored literary talent, had most recently been held by Robert Hillyer and Theodore Spencer, but it was an ancient professorship — the university's first — and the initial incumbent was John

Quincy Adams. The pay was $10,000 a year and the right to tether a cow in the college yard. Archie immediately consulted Felix Frankfurter, who counseled him to accept. "It seems to me the Boylston Professorship is made to order for you," Frankfurter wrote. "You don't have to stay there for life, any more than you did at the Library of Congress." (President Conant, on the Boylston search committee, had raised this point from the other way around: would Archie be willing to accept a long-term commitment, especially after his contact with the great world of national and international affairs?) Frankfurter also observed that although no one could be free on every front, at Harvard Archie would be free on a sufficient number of fronts to have "the ultimate freedom" he wanted. He could, in other words, write as well as teach. Reassured and eager as always for a new challenge, Archie telegraphed his acceptance to Levin. So commenced what he called the happiest period of his life, the thirteen years at Harvard that ended in 1962 when, at seventy years of age, he was forced to retire.

Archie had taught before, on a part-time basis, in the years after law school, as a once-a-week writing consultant at Princeton in 1937 and, at John Dickey's invitation, as a visiting lecturer at Dartmouth during 1948–49. But he had never before entered upon the profession — notably, his mother's profession — on a regular full-time basis, planning a curriculum, setting exams, and interacting with students. So in the summer before he took up his duties, he sought advice from a number of sources both about what to teach and about how to teach it. Very little direction was forthcoming from Harvard. Levin would say only that Archie would see his boss every morning when he looked in the mirror to shave. Beyond that, he was on his own. The charismatic F. O. Matthiessen, who had not supported MacLeish's appointment, wryly suggested that he might like to take over his Shakespeare course. Friends Kenneth Murdock and Perry Miller, who *had* supported his choice, advised Archie to take it easy and stop worrying, but that was not his nature.

Mark Van Doren, whose courses at Columbia were legendary, was more helpful. Archie drove down to Cornwall, Connecticut, to seek Van Doren's advice about how to teach. "You already know how," Mark insisted. "You only talk about the things you're interested in, and you already do that very well." Then he added: "You have to like your students. You have to be patient with them, listen to them, and care about them." Mark and Archie had known each other since the 1930s, but this meeting solidified their friendship. There was a real warmth between them, though as Dorothy Van Doren pointed out they were very different in personality — Archie intense, Mark seemingly calm.

But they liked to be together, they admired each other's work, and they wrote poems for each other.

As to the subject matter of his courses, it was assumed that MacLeish would teach some version of the advanced writing seminar that had been offered by previous Boylston professors. MacLeish called this course English S, and made it into one of the best writing classes ever offered.

The very idea of teaching "creative writing," a phrase MacLeish cordially detested for its implication that other kinds were not creative, involved a paradox: "You have to have a writer who can write before you can teach him how." At Harvard, he had a remarkable number, including Donald Hall, Robert Bly, George Plimpton, George Starbuck, Ilona Karmel, George J. W. Goodman ("Adam Smith"), William Alfred, Charles Bracelen Flood, John Simon, Harold Brodkey, Edward Hoagland, Elizabeth Marshall Thomas, James Chace, Benjamin DeMott, Jonathan Kozol, and Stephen Sandy. Competition for the twelve spots in his English S class was intense at the start, and became even fiercer after students like Karmel and Hoagland began publishing novels straight out of the course. He took a dozen students a year for thirteen years. "It would have been unusual luck to get one real writer out of the whole group," he said, "but I think there may have been ten or twelve."

MacLeish's first English S class, in 1949–50, was very nearly his last. The chosen dozen included two future prizewinning poets, Hall and Bly, and several World War II veterans disinclined to accept any pearls of received wisdom. In such company even MacLeish's appearance weighed against him. He "had the long bony face of an aristocrat, the good looks of a rich man, and the smile of an administrator," Hall recalled. "So of course we distrusted him immediately." Hall, Bly, and company "waited for him, that first day, like lions for a Christian." Whatever he said, they took exception to. At the second meeting Archie was speaking about "Hemingway's world" when Hall broke in to leap for the throat. All that talk about writers' "worlds" was nonsense, he said. There was only one world, and good writers wrote about it. Flustered, Archie beat a retreat, and when he brought in his response the following week, buttressed by arguments from Plato, Aristotle, and Hegel, Hall didn't even show up for class.

The quarrelsome Bly proved a still more obstreperous antagonist. It was wonderful that MacLeish could recite Pound's "Slow Return" beautifully, and talk familiarly of Ezra into the bargain, Bly thought, but that didn't mean that he was going to tolerate "any authoritarian bullshit" from him. He considered MacLeish lacking in intellectual integrity, and contradicted him at every turn. After three or four such episodes, Archie called Bly into his office for a private discussion. Sitting against the western window of Widener W, with the glow of the sunset behind him, Archie looked for all the world like one of the handsome Crusaders on the south porch of Chartres. Bly, however, would not be cowed.

"Robert," he began. "I don't know what to do. Most of the things I say you reject loudly and eloquently. What can we do to change things?"

"What do you think, Mr. MacLeish?" the young writer responded.

"Well, either we all agree to be gentlemen in class, or I jump out the window," indicating the one behind him.

"All right, then," Bly said. "Go ahead and jump."

Archie, who had no previous experience with the uncompromising arrogance of youth, decided not to fight. For the rest of the year, he canceled seminar meetings entirely, instead conferring with each of his students individually. He also learned from the experience, so that in future versions of English S he rarely spoke at all in the classroom. Students ordinarily read from a story or poem or play, and then their work was dissected by others in the seminar, with Archie holding his fire for a final comment or two, and for private conferences.

Forty years down the road, both Bly and Hall acknowledged their debt to MacLeish. Bly particularly valued his teacher's restraint. "Archie could have exacted revenge," he observed. "He could have dressed me down or turned me in to the dean for insubordination or embarrassed me in front of others, but he did none of those things." As a result, Bly feels, his healthy impulse toward rebellion was not muted, and he was able to found and run *The 50s,* a journal opposed to old-fashioned poetry and on the lookout for revolutionary writing around the globe. Recognizing talent when he saw it, MacLeish swallowed his resentment and nominated Bly's long poem on an Indian woman who killed her white husband in the Dakota uprising for the Garrison Prize at Harvard. His Indian protagonist spoke in Shakespearean blank verse, Bly recalls, yet his poem addressed an important and controversial topic, and it won the prize. A few years later MacLeish tried unsuccessfully to secure a fellowship for Bly at Iowa. After that, Bly sent him all his books as they came out. "I like your book and I'm glad you did it," Archie wrote about one of them, "but I didn't teach you anything." That was not quite true. MacLeish "taught us to stop sitting on English poetry, like a hen on eggs," Bly said, and in a more personal way, "He taught me something about nobility."

Don Hall was a junior doing very well at Harvard and on the *Advocate,* the literary magazine, when he entered English S. MacLeish thought he was not stretching himself enough, and put him on a regular writing schedule, two hours a day. Then he absolutely dumbfounded Hall by accusing him of *laziness,* a fighting word to a Connecticut Yankee like Hall. He objected that it was not true, that he was working every day. Only in retrospect did he realize that MacLeish was correct. Each student in English S was required to complete one major project, which could be a poem, a play, a novel, or a work of nonfiction. The entire course grade depended on that project. Hall wrote a verse play, called *The Minstrel's Progress,* mostly in tetrameter couplets. It was easy for him to do; there was nothing intellectually or spiritually challenging about it, and MacLeish graded it B+. When Hall, who was not used to getting Bs in English classes, wrote to complain, Archie reminded him that the grade was based on the long project alone, and that Hall's play was not ambitious enough. It was in that sense that he was lazy. Years later Hall heard Henry Moore say that a sculptor could tap tap tap eighteen hours a day and still be lazy. By then he knew what Moore was talking about.

George Plimpton, another English S student in MacLeish's first year, initially planned to write a novel about patricide for his major undertaking, but the book fizzled out and he switched to an exposé on the hush-hush topic of the senior societies at Yale, and particularly Skull and Bones. Since MacLeish was a Bonesman sworn to secrecy, this put Plimpton in the unusual position of attending tutorials with a teacher who was honor bound not to discuss the subject of the student's work. In the end, Archie awarded him an A. It wasn't a novel, he commented, but there were a lot of anecdotes in it that could be used in a novel. Also he was impressed by how much Plimpton had found out.

In the spring of 1950, MacLeish went to bat for yet another of his English S students. This lad, not so much criminal as Nietzschean in his belief that supermen need not be restricted by convention, had taken a hundred or so books from Widener Library without bothering to check them out. A college official happened to spy this cache of books in his room, and the next day the student stuffed the books in pillowcases and dumped them in the hallway of a dorm, along with one or two he'd made the mistake of actually signing out of the library. Confronted by the dean, Archie's student stonewalled. Then he went to MacLeish, looked him square in the eye, and said, "I did not take those books." That was good enough for Archie, who spoke to the dean on his behalf. At this stage the dean called the student in and told him that Harvard would take no further action, but that since they couldn't clear up the matter on campus, he was going to have to call in the police. "In that case," the student said immediately, "I took them."

In a way this story was symptomatic of MacLeish's good nature and the way his students reacted to it. Some found his equability irritating. He wanted too much to be liked, Donald Hall remarked, and his students were suspicious of this quality. At Christmas Archie invited his English S students to a party at his house in Louisburg Square. Each was to read something he'd written, and Bly persuaded Hall to read a satirical poem called "The Poet as Social Worker." It was not written as an attack on MacLeish, but could easily be interpreted that way, and Don was unprepared for the distress it caused his teacher. Nonetheless, Archie subsequently advanced Hall's career in several ways, sending his first book of poems around to publishers, for example, and recommending him to Harvard's Society of Fellows. For generosity of spirit, MacLeish could hardly have done more. He had clearly taken Van Doren's advice to heart: he cared about his students.

To none of his young writers did he give more of himself than to William Alfred and Ilona Karmel. A charming leprechaun of a man whose brilliance as a playwright culminated in the Broadway success *Hogan's Goat,* Bill Alfred came to English S in the fall of 1950 as "that most dangerous of time-bombs for a teacher of writing: a Graduate-Student with extravagant aspirations." Within months Archie converted him into "a writer, a person who thinks less of the effect he is making than of how much truth he has managed to get down on a page." In Alfred's mature estimation — and he was in a position to know, having taken English S two years running — MacLeish was "the best teacher of writing" he ever encountered. Part of the effectiveness derived from his storied past as librarian of Congress and assistant secretary of state, as friend of the great writers and statesmen of his time. "He brought the outside world into the college," Alfred said. "There was a kind of generous worldliness about him — a sort of glamour." Yet mingled with this glamour was a willingness to give young talent the benefit of every doubt. Early in the 1950–51 academic year, one of his students — like Alfred a graduate student — submitted a short story about a poet and a novelist. The poet in the story, a second-rater, was modeled on Archie, while the novelist was by contrast a great writer. The student read this story out in class, but MacLeish refused to be upset. Only much later in the term did he take a measure of revenge, when this same pretentious young man of twenty-four or twenty-five remarked that "the older I get the less music I can listen to with pleasure, the fewer people I enjoy. It's as if I'm walking on a jetty to the sea, with people dropping off behind me." That particular balloon Archie could not resist puncturing. "Look around you," he advised. "That may be a burlesque runway you're on, not a jetty."

MacLeish's greatest gift to Alfred, as to other expectant writers, was to make him feel he could accomplish something really important. For Archie, "every goose was a swan." In the spring of 1952, he invited the most comely of his English S swans to lunch at Conway, where he served them martinis à la MacLeish: shaken violently and placed in the freezer to render them "cold as the devil's heart." They toasted their future that day — Charlie Flood, John Simon, Ilona Karmel, Bill Alfred. "We pledged our hoping," Bill recalls, with the glittering gin in the icy glasses. And Archie made the pledge something to live by with the look he gave them. "Part assessing stare, part angry blessing," he dared them to believe in themselves, their work, their country.

Nor did Archie's encouragement stop at the end of the course. MacLeish did what he could to advance Bill Alfred's career, just as he had for Don Hall and Bob Bly. Specifically, he encouraged Alfred to send his blank-verse play *Agamemnon* to *Botteghe Oscure,* where his friend Marguerite Caetani was prepared to accept it. When Bill completed his doctorate, he helped him wangle a year off in London with an Amy Lowell Traveling Fellowship. And when Alfred returned, Archie argued forcefully and with success that Harvard's English department should hire him to teach. In their shared commitment to literature there sprang up a friendship between these two — Alfred the Roman Catholic son of a Brooklyn bricklayer, and MacLeish the Scottish-Puritan child of middle-western fortune — which transcended boundaries of age and class and religion.

As much, or more, was true of Archie's relationship with Ilona Karmel. She was born a Polish Jew in Cracow, where her family was unable to escape the Nazis during World War II. Her father was arrested in 1942 and never heard from again. Shortly thereafter Ilona was caught and sent to work, at fourteen, as a scrubwoman in a German barracks. Toward the end of the war, she was confined to the Buchenwald concentration camp, making antiaircraft shells in a munitions factory by day and writing poetry on the back of worksheets at night. Shortly before liberation the women of the camp were being herded along a road when a group of drunken German soldiers in a tank tore into them. Four of them, including Ilona, were run over. It was thought that she would not walk again.

After the war, however, American relief agencies sent her to a hospital in Stockholm, where she made a remarkable recovery. She taught herself English in the hospital, to go with her native Polish, the Hebrew she had learned in school, and the German she had absorbed during her confinement. On the strength of these language skills, she was admitted to Hunter College in New York City, where a story of hers won the *Mademoiselle* Prize. In 1950 she transferred to Radcliffe, and with the encouragement of Elena Levin, the wife of Harry Levin, presented herself to MacLeish as a potential student in English S. There she was, Karmel recalled, four feet eleven with a cane, "in nearly impenetrable English declaring her desire to be a writer." Archie decided to admit her if only because he had never before known anyone remotely like her. It was a happy decision.

They confronted each other with a deep reserve, hers based on formal European manners and respect for elders, his on native reticence. He was a gentleman of the old school, she thought, not someone you could know very well. Thus he was always "Mr. MacLeish" to her, though as time wore on she looked to him as a sort of idealized father figure, while he became protective of her and referred to her, in public, as "my Ilona." Despite the reserve, she said, "there was a love between us. I always had the feeling I could completely rely on him."

MacLeish was not much impressed with her prizewinning story. "Too easy and sentimental," he declared. At one of their first conferences, though, she outlined another story that was running through her head, about three women in a Swedish hospital. In her machine-gun English, she talked for an hour and a half while Archie listened and listened. Finally he interrupted her. "My dear," he said, "this is not a story, this is a novel." And so it was, though it took her more than two years to complete it. The novel was *Stephania,* which was sold, through Archie's auspices, to Houghton Mifflin and published as a Literary Guild selection in 1953. The novel was dedicated to MacLeish.

If it had not been for Archie, Karmel said in 1988, she could not have made a career as a writer and — at MIT — as a teacher of writing. "He created an atmosphere in which we all wanted to work." From seminar, the students would adjourn to Jim Cronin's in Harvard Square for fifty-cent stew and quarter beer, and talk about their craft long into the evening. Once in a while Archie contributed a shrewd insight in conference. Bothered by a shifting point of view in one of Ilona's stories, he sent her to Tolstoy for a model, and she fixed the problem accordingly. But his greatest contribution for Karmel, as for Alfred, was in making her believe in herself, and that was not easy. "I was not Miss Self-Confidence, believe me." She was especially troubled by how slowly the novel was going, but he assured her it did not matter how long it took. The book was something that had to be done and would be done, no matter what. Nor would he allow her to speak ill of herself. "You are not to use the word 'fail' of this labor even if you have not succeeded," he wrote Karmel, on the Browningesque principle that reach should exceed grasp. "One does not say of a rocket that it failed to reach the moon — only that it went very high."

After graduating Phi Beta Kappa from Radcliffe, Ilona took a number of jobs to help support herself. She was packing candy at the New England Candy Company (NECCO) when word arrived of the Literary Guild selection. One of the book club's readers had become ill, read *Stephania* in the hospital, and fallen in love with it. With the $15,000 bonus, Karmel quit her job, which had taught her only that there was nothing to be learned on the assembly line. Overjoyed at her success, MacLeish went on to try to make a "beautiful" woman out of her, as Ilona put it. Her leg needed occasional "refurbishing," she understood, but Archie sent her to the best orthopedic surgeon in Boston, in hopes that she could with treatment be able to walk without a cane. Unfortunately, the tests disclosed that her condition was worsening, and she had to go to the hospital for another operation. The medical bills were paid behind the scenes, by Archie or by contributors he enlisted. The question was never discussed between them.

To George ("Jerry") Goodman, as to Karmel and Alfred, MacLeish's English S opened up a new world. MacLeish seemed to know everybody in the establishment, and to move comfortably in that company. When he invited his students to Louisburg Square, or introduced them to editors and publishers, it almost seemed as if they belonged. For English S, Goodman wrote a comic novel about a bumpkin newspaperman covering a youth rally in Berlin, fashioned along the lines of Evelyn Waugh's *Scoop*. MacLeish liked it, and Goodman went on to write four other novels before settling into his identity as "Adam Smith." What he dreamed of in those days, though, was not becoming the nation's best-known commentator on financial issues and institutions. What he dreamed of was becoming the next Irwin Shaw, skiing in Europe and making love to beautiful actresses. Such were the hopes and expectations of English S.

The star of the course from 1952 to 1954 — like Alfred and James Chace, he took it twice — was Ted Hoagland, one of America's finest prose stylists. Hoagland actually had two mentors at Harvard, and they could hardly have been more different. From MacLeish he discovered the benefits of professionalism, of sticking to a schedule and getting one's work done. Looking at MacLeish, Ted learned that you did not have to be out of control or malicious or self-destructive to be an artist. It was not that MacLeish was without appetites. They were taking a walk one day when Archie, at sixty, spied a good-looking high school girl in bobby sox. "If I ever get 'sent up,' " he said, "it will be because of something like that." Hoagland's second mentor was the poet John Berryman. A thin, nervous embodiment of the writer as Wild Man, Berryman in his summer-school class taught that craziness could be healthy and useful too. Totally opposite figures, the two naturally employed conflicting teaching styles. Reading a student's story in class, Berryman would be shaking so hard from hangover that the pages rattled in his hand. And he was cruel to the untalented or misguided, whereas MacLeish gentled them along. Hoagland adopted MacLeish's techniques as his own, teaching by way of dialogue, praise, and inspiration, not by rearranging nuts and bolts. In his view the primary task of the teacher of writing was to provide an example of productivity and integrity and dedication to the craft, and then to get out of the way.

Over the course of time, MacLeish became a father figure to Ted, his own father having abdicated the role. Hoagland's novel of circus life, *Cat Man,* came out of English S, and MacLeish took it around to Houghton Mifflin, which accepted it with alacrity. Ted proudly showed the manuscript to his father, who read it, decided it was obscene, and incredibly, without telling his son, wrote the publishers attempting to stop publication on those grounds. (Houghton Mifflin's lawyer, Archie's friend Charlie Curtis, could find nothing obscene about the novel, though he did detect a strain of sadism.) At commencement in June 1954, both Hoagland parents earnestly pleaded with MacLeish. Their son, they said, had this ridiculous idea in his head that he was going to be a writer. Couldn't Archie do something to dissuade him?

On the contrary, Archie encouraged young Hoagland, first by comparing him to Hemingway, later by suggesting his likeness to Thoreau. Hemingway was great, he reminded Ted, not because he left the adjectives out but because when he used them, they blazed. It took Hoagland some time to find his voice as a nature essayist rather than a novelist, but even during his lean periods Archie urged him to go on with his writing. At one stage Ted was subsisting in a five-dollar-a-week Pinckney Street boarding house in Boston. When a letter from MacLeish arrived, he left it on the hall table to impress the other roomers. The two men corresponded often during the decades ahead. Archie commiserated with Hoagland about his divorce, which he thought was a bad idea. "Why did you have to do that?" he wanted to know. Usually, though, he wrote to applaud Ted's books, and it gave him real pleasure when one of them, *Red Wolves and Black Bears* (1976), was dedicated to him.

At the beginning of each academic year, Ada MacLeish wrote Gerald and Sara Murphy on October 1, 1953, she lived with a man in anguish. Archie was snowed under with manuscripts from prospective writing students and felt terrible about the ones he had to turn down. Sometimes he made mistakes, and the fall of 1953 was one of those times, and the mistake was John Updike. As Updike recalls, he applied for English S not once but twice, and was turned down both times, though one of his roommates, Charlie Neushauser, was "repeatedly" admitted to "MacLeish," as they called English S.

One instance Updike vividly remembers. His submission was "a play in verse about a Shakespearian fool in love with a princess, and outside of MacLeish's office in the upper reaches of Widener Library, when I went to see if I had been admitted, my poor play was lying in a scattered heap of other manuscripts, all of which except mine had a few comments scratched on them. On my play, not a word. *Pas un mot,* as the French say." Updike was disappointed but not crushed. He took other writing classes at Harvard with Theodore Morrison and Kenneth Kempton and Albert Guérard, and wrote and drew for the *Lampoon* besides. As for MacLeish, over time he was able to persuade himself that Updike had never applied. "If only I could have had him in English S," he remarked in 1980.

Mistakes aside, MacLeish's English S may have been the most successful writing course ever offered, as measured by the success of its enrollees. The requirement of completing a long project provided his students with the salutary knowledge that they were perfectly capable of getting a book-length manuscript down on paper. The form of the manuscript hardly mattered. Often, as with Ted Hoagland and Jerry Goodman, undergraduate novels segued into nonfiction. The same was true of James Chace, who made his mark as an analyst and commentator on foreign affairs, and of Jonathan Kozol, whose *Death at an Early Age* — an exposé on the dreadful teaching of America's disadvantaged children — won the National Book Award for 1967. Kozol, who graduated from Harvard as a Rhodes scholar, took English S in both his junior and senior years. At the time he was on track to become a doctor, but MacLeish's course derailed him. Kozol tried poetry for a time, producing, as he put it, "an endless number of impassioned and atrocious poems." Stick to prose, MacLeish advised him. In the fall of senior year, Archie told him he'd have to do some serious work over Christmas to earn an A. For Kozol, a junior Phi Beta Kappa, any other grade was unthinkable. So during the Christmas holiday he wrote a short romantic novel, turned it in, and got his A. That, he thought, was the end of that. But classmate George Starbuck, stringing for Houghton Mifflin, shopped the manuscript to the publisher, and they brought it out as *The Fume of Poppies.*

At commencement MacLeish took young Kozol aside for a talk. He should put his novel behind him and go on to better things, Archie told him. The title was terrible, nearly as bad as *Tower of Ivory,* his own undergraduate book of verse. Before long, he predicted, Jonathan would be as eager to have *The Fume of Poppies* go out of print as he had been to see *Tower of Ivory* disappear from circulation. He was right about that. Although *The Fume of Poppies* enjoyed unusual success for a first novel and was even sold to the movies, Kozol soon came to despise it.

As with many other veterans of English S, Kozol kept in close touch with MacLeish after graduation. When Jonathan decided to throw over his Rhodes Scholarship in order to live and write in Paris, Archie, perhaps thinking back on his own early escape from the law, wrote him a wonderfully generous letter saying that he was undoubtedly right to leave Oxford, since otherwise he might be trapped in a life that was wrong for him. When he came back from Europe, still without bearings, Kozol went to see MacLeish at Conway and asked him about the possibility of returning to Harvard for graduate work. Kozol could certainly do that, Archie responded, but he hoped he wouldn't. He had the feeling that something more important was waiting for him. A week later Jonathan saw a notice on a bulletin board in Harvard Square asking for volunteer teachers at the Freedom School in Roxbury. He volunteered, was appalled at what he found, and wrote *Death at an Early Age* to tell the rest of the country about it. Consciously or not, he had been infected by Archie's conviction that good honest writing, from the mind and heart, could make things happen.

La Désirade

Notable as English S was, MacLeish was far better known among Harvard students for his lecture-discussion course on poetry. He first offered "An Approach to Poetry," advertised as "intensive study of a limited number of texts considered not in their historical perspective but as illustrative of the age and experience of poetry," in the fall of 1950, as a replacement for a similar course given by F. O. Matthiessen. (Depressed by the course of events in his private life and on the national scene, Matthiessen had jumped to his death on April 1, 1950.) "Professor MacLeish was far and away the most logical choice for the job of continuing to teach" Matty's course, Harry Levin commented in the registration issue of the *Harvard Crimson*. The *Crimson*'s readers obviously agreed. "An Approach to Poetry" was assigned to a room in Sever Hall that could accommodate 275 students. Many more showed up for MacLeish's first class on September 28, 1950, and he moved the group outside into the sunshine to address them on the steps of Memorial Hall. The *Crimson* ran a picture of his alfresco lecture. Some of his colleagues, who felt rather put in the shade, were tempted to warn Archie about the cult of personality.

From the start, MacLeish knew the basic point he wanted to make in this course: "that art exists in the context of life; that art is an action on the scene of life; that art is a means of perceiving life; of ordering life; of making life intelligible; and thus also of changing it." Poetry as he conceived of it was inseparable from experience. "Only in poetry," he argued, "does *man* appear, man as he really is in his sordidness and his nobility. Elsewhere in the University man is a clinical specimen, or an intellectual abstraction, or a member of a mathematical equation, or a fixed point in a final dogma. Only with us is he himself . . . himself in all his unimaginable — unimaginable if literature had not perceived them — possibilities."

How best to get this message across posed a pedagogical problem. Archie was soon frustrated by an apparent lack of response to his lectures. "What SHOULD I do with this poetry course of mine?" he wrote Levin. "Should I go on wrestling with the angel twice a week for a class in which only a few — if I can judge — see the angel there?" To remedy matters, he turned the course into one-third lecture and two-thirds discussion. Borrowing a technique from his brilliant British colleague I. A. Richards (who used it himself in seminars, not in large classes), he assigned his students to read one poem at a time and to record their reaction to that poem on a single six-by-eight-inch card the day before the class was to meet. On occasion they were responding to a long poem, like *The Rime of the Ancient Mariner*. More often, the assigned poem was quite short. Whatever the length, this method forced his students to think about what they had read, and to record what they thought. That way they came to class committed.

What MacLeish did next was to use the students' cards to teach the course. This required a laborious process of reading and sorting through the cards. Invariably, he discarded a certain number from students who were feeling dull that day or who weren't much good, ever. On those remaining he would underline points that seemed particularly interesting, and from these underlinings shuffle his cards to work out an order that moved from one topic to another more or less smoothly. This technique was much harder than lecturing, Archie came to realize, for every class meeting demanded substantial preparation. "I don't suppose anyone ever spent so much time over lectures," he wrote to Walter Kaiser, who was one of his graduate assistants in that class, "but then no one ever went about it in so idiotic a way." Yet the reward was worth it, for now the students were eager to wrestle with the angel. Moreover, this method enabled him to learn from his students in a very real sense. What star students such as George Steiner and Radcliffe Squires had to say on their cards often uncovered fresh insights. "I *see* the poem again through their eyes, with all its light and odor and darkness about it," he said. From Anne Lindbergh, the daughter of Charles and Anne Morrow Lindbergh, he learned more about Emily Dickinson than from any professor or critic he ever read.

Dickinson's poetry became a mainstay of that course, along with that of a few other poets. "He was superb on Chinese poetry, Rilke, and Rimbaud," Squires recalled. Harvard was not then "a teaching college," as Squires put it, yet MacLeish taught with brilliance and charm — and with obvious enthusiasm for the subject. It was important to find a viable pedagogical approach, but the real secret of Archie's success in the classroom, according to his colleague W. Jackson Bate, lay in that enthusiasm. "Students will forgive almost anything if you really like what you're teaching," Bate said. "Archie did, and communicated it."

Since MacLeish was his own boss as Boylston professor, he was able to arrange his teaching schedule accordingly. A few years after assuming the post, he established a pattern of teaching during the fall term and spending much of the winter in Antigua in the Caribbean. Archie and Ada discovered the island during the Christmas holidays of 1950 on a visit with Mortimer and Frida Seabury of Boston, who were charter members of the new Mill Reef Club. The club was founded by Robertson ("Happy") Ward, who was also the architect of many of its first houses. Ward bought up three hundred acres on the windward end of the island in 1946, and began searching for prospective members. A New Yorker, Ward sought out candidates throughout the East Coast and Midwest. He did not want Mill Reef to become the winter enclave, say, of Philadelphians alone. Nor did he want the club to become solely a playground for the rich. Charter members were expected to build homes on parcels of land along the water, but initially, at least, it was stipulated that no house should be constructed that cost more than $20,000 to build.

"Well, we have found it," Ada wrote the Murphys on January 11, 1951, "the island we always imagined might exist." Located in the Lesser Antilles, some fifty miles from Nevis and Guadeloupe, Antigua had been a British possession since the time Horatio Nelson sailed into its beautifully protected English Harbour. A small island of about 108 square miles in area, Antigua survived largely on the basis of producing sugar, but by the late 1940s that business was dying out. "You can live well with two servants and a car for $400 a month, and when we all have to retire what could be handier?" Ada commented.

Oddly, it was the 1940 sale of fifty overaged destroyers to Britain — which MacLeish had supported — that expedited the postwar tourist development of Antigua. In return for the destroyers, the British allowed the United States to install ten airstrips on British possessions for reconnaissance purposes. One of the airstrips was on Antigua, which made the island accessible by air, if only just. In the early 1950s the Mill Reef special flew from New York on Friday night, stopping at Puerto Rico about 10:30 P.M., and after refueling landing at Antigua by midmorning Saturday. Philip and Mabel Reed, who were to become close friends of the MacLeishes, remembered coming down for the first time on that long flight. As the plane landed, a fire engine raced alongside. This gave the passengers a moment of uneasiness, but the plane slowed safely to a halt, and when the cabin door opened, there was a steel band to greet them.

The island's greatest asset was of course its wonderful climate: warm days and cool nights, with the trade winds blowing. It was "the best climate in the world," Archie thought. He and Ada bought a two-and-a-half-acre strip of land along the water for $7,500 and authorized Happy Ward to design and build a $17,500 house by the next winter. La Désirade, they decided to call it, after the name Columbus gave to his landfall on the second voyage, at a little island off Guadeloupe. Theirs was a "cinder block house with a living room and two bedrooms [later, the MacLeishes added on to the house] on top of lime rock fifteen feet above and fifteen feet back from the clearest water a man could hope to find." It was hot in the midday sun, but MacLeish worked well in the mornings in a small green studio thirty yards away from the house. With the shutters open, the sound of the surf dominated the braying of the donkeys.

For the MacLeishes, who came to Antigua every winter from 1950–51 to 1976–77, Antigua represented more than a retreat from the harsh New England winter. The island offered an entirely different way of life. At Harvard, most of their social life revolved around the literary and political and intellectual communities. Mill Reef, by contrast, and despite founder Happy Ward's intentions, was inhabited almost entirely by wealthy and successful businessmen. Dean and Alice Acheson came down regularly for nearly two decades, beginning in 1953, but no one else remotely like Dean or Archie wintered there. To redress the lack, the MacLeishes often invited house guests. Bob and Adele Lovett came only once. Mark and Dorothy Van Doren visited twice, but that was enough. Everyone was perfectly sociable, but as Mark observed after the second stay, "God damn the rich; I can't stand them."

Archie and Ada, however, discriminatingly made friends among the rich — those who were intelligent as well as shrewd, engaging as well as forceful. As his Harvard colleague John Bullitt commented, Archie "enjoyed the company of the literate and the powerful, and why not?"

Their closest friends during the early years in Antigua were John and Betty Cowles and Phil and Mabel Reed. Cowles, who was president of the *Minneapolis Star and Tribune* and at one time served as head of the Harvard Alumni Association, was a brash, inquisitive man with a healthy capacity for the enjoyment of life, Betty a clever and strong-minded companion. Phil Reed, chairman of the board of General Electric, played marvelous four-hand piano with Ada, and Mabel was charming and sunny. With John H. P. ("Jay") Gould, the men developed an afternoon habit of playing Crokie, a partnership version of croquet. This was a traveling contest, for the Reeds, Goulds, and MacLeishes all installed Crokie lawns and used precious water from their catchments to keep them green. Whatever the partnerships, all the men played the game with enthusiasm, and took the result seriously.

Although the MacLeishes rarely attended large parties in Antigua, they did considerable drinking with their friends. Lacking private telephones, Archie announced the advent of the cocktail hour by blowing on a conch shell. Then he mixed one of the meanest rum punches in creation: one part sweet (simple syrup), two parts sour (lime juice), and nine parts rum, with freshly grated nutmeg on top. Several of these could do substantial damage, and in Antigua almost everyone drank more than on the mainland. "That was a heavy, heavy drinking crowd," his son Bill said. Archie partook, though he kept his drinking, like everything else, under a measure of control. His consumption of liquor during the island winters probably contributed to his recurring bouts with ulcers, Bill believes.

Every day the natural life of Antigua stimulated the senses. Small yellow land birds — banana twerps, Archie and Dean called them — skittered about in the jungly foliage. Ada grew orchids in the garden out front. Strangest of all was the way time slipped by. "There isn't any time down here," Archie reported to the Levins. "It neither flows nor freezes. It just isn't."

Archie did not adjust easily to casual island attitudes. He established his own routine, exercising on the beach each morning, working till noon, and taking a long swim in the "liquid velvet" water before lunch. When they lunched at the Mill Reef Club, Ada would be driven across, while Archie swam the three-quarters of a mile across the bay, wearing a rubber cap to protect what hair he still had from the sea water. He was a strong swimmer well into his sixties. His son Ken loved to visit Antigua, where the two men would go snorkeling or spearfishing amid the reefs.

Following Crokie and the cocktail hour came an early dinner and bedtime. Even at Mill Reef, Archie expected punctuality of himself and others. On one occasion when Ken and Carolyn were staying with them, the four MacLeishes were invited to dinner at the house of the bluestocking Boston hostess Hester Pickman. They arrived on time, or rather, in Carolyn's recollection, "one minute early." Dusk had fallen, the full moon was rising, and their hostess was nowhere to be found.

"Well, where is she?" Archie demanded of the servants.

"She's gone tropping," they said, meaning that she'd gone for a walk to look at the moon.

They waited a few minutes, then Archie got up and announced, furiously, "Well, we're leaving." Shortly thereafter, as they were sitting around La Désirade with a drink in hand but no dinner in prospect, Hester arrived full of apologies, bearing a tray of hors d'oeuvres and a bottle of rum. "Won't you come back and have dinner after all?" she asked, but Archie could not be mollified. "You have a watch, don't you?" he demanded.

Curiously, Archie's intractability on this occasion and Hester's moon-gazing are both reflected in his one-act verse play about Antigua. *This Music Crept by Me upon the Waters,* its title drawn from *The Tempest,* was written in 1952, published in *Botteghe Oscure* in April 1953, broadcast by the BBC in June 1953, and performed by the Poets' Theatre in Cambridge that fall. Set in the Antilles among the well-to-do, a dinner party assembles as the play begins. While they wait for one tardy couple, the hostess, Elizabeth Stone, is bewitched by the rising of the moon. This is paradise, she thinks, and happiness is there for the taking, could she only give herself to the moment. The natives knew how:

> *They have no time to lose. They live*
> *Now. Not late, not soon, but now.*

The last to arrive are Peter and Ann Bolt, and the suggestion of a previous bond between Peter and Elizabeth is underlined when it is revealed that he too has been moonstruck. They talk together, as the feeling between them intensifies. Heretofore Peter has been driven by what remains to be done. As he tells her:

> *All my life I've lived tomorrow*
> *Waiting for my life to come:*
> *Promises to come true tomorrow,*
> *Journeys to begin tomorrow.*
> *Mornings in the sun tomorrow,*
> *Books read, words written.*
> *All tomorrow.*

The expectation grows that he and Elizabeth will seize the night and run off together. But a mock crisis intervenes. His wife, Ann, has been lost sight of. It is thought she may have plunged from the rocks into the sea, and Peter dashes off to see what has happened. Ann is not in danger; she is in the kitchen fixing potatoes. But the moment of illumination has gone, and will not come again. Peter and Elizabeth had been confronted by an overwhelming sense of happiness "*now,* now and forever." She was ready to take it, and he was not.

"Happiness is difficult," another character observes, speaking for MacLeish. "It takes a kind of courage most men / Are never masters of." In an interview Archie elaborated on the point. Women could live in the present, and so could a Provençal peasant, but the modern American male — and particularly the American businessman — could not. He necessarily faced the future, like Peter Bolt. "The defeated hero of that little play has lived his entire life looking forward toward self-aggrandizement." Distance it from himself though he may, *This Music*'s "defeated hero" bore an unmistakable resemblance to Archibald MacLeish himself. Antigua was paradise, but paradise palled when you had things to do. Antigua was perfection, but two or three months of perfection was all he could stand. Then he needed the sustenance of the actual world.

THE VIEW FROM SIXTY

Harvard's Wonders

IN A SHORT POEM called "With Age Wisdom," Archibald Mac-
Leish summed up his sense of well-being as of May 1952.

> At twenty, stooping round about,
> I thought the world a miserable place,
> Truth a trick, faith in doubt,
> Little beauty, less grace.
>
> Now at sixty what I see,
> Although the world is worse by far,
> Stops my heart in ecstasy.
> God, the wonders that there are!

MacLeish had not become suddenly Panglossian. In many ways, and
particularly on the political front, the world was "worse by far" than
the one he had known forty years earlier. Nonetheless, his life shaped
itself into a happy and productive pattern: spring and summer in Cambridge and Conway, autumn teaching at Harvard, winter in Antigua.
Of these settings, Uphill Farm at Conway remained his treasured home.
In a letter to his brother-in-law Alexander Campbell, he sang the joys
of an October weekend visit, when he "walked down past the pool to
the pond and back along the wood road to Mr. [Warren] Harris' meadow
blue green under yellow maple leaves and through your birch bars and
up across your down dale meadow to the gate again. What a miracle it
is to live (when one can) in the one place in which it is a miracle to
live!"

Glorious as Conway could be, Harvard contributed still more to his euphoric mood. His four months of academic duties were not so time-consuming as to prevent the writing of poems, essays, and verse plays. The contact with brilliant (if sometimes intractable) students helped keep him young. He enjoyed the fellowship of amiable and distinguished colleagues. Many of his fellow professors were, like himself, intimately involved in national and international affairs. And though he and Ada never really settled in Cambridge-Boston, instead occupying a succession of homes, they delighted in the social ambience of that community.

Archie's closest friend in the English department was probably Kenneth Murdock, an expert on colonial American literature who had served a five-year term as dean of the faculty of arts and sciences. The two men, who got to know each other during Archie's 1938–39 Nieman year, were fellow Scotsmen, both belonging to the clan MacPherson. Kenneth's wife, Eleanor, shared with Archie a passionate interest in the poetry of John Keats. MacLeish himself contributed a poem — "The Little Boy in the Locked House" — to the *Coolidge Hill Gazette,* an occasional newspaper that the Murdocks' son Charlie put out with the other neighborhood children. Perry Miller, the other colonialist in the English department, also became a good friend of MacLeish's, as did Harry Levin. Through his affiliation with Eliot House, Archie soon formed lasting connections with younger scholars such as Canadian historian John Conway and W. Jackson Bate, the prizewinning biographer of Keats, Coleridge, and Samuel Johnson. In addition, he went out of his way to become acquainted with the young writers who were brought to the campus under the auspices of the Society of Fellows or as Briggs-Copeland lecturers, programs that enabled them to teach part-time while they continued their writing careers.

The poet Richard Wilbur and his wife, Charlee, were early beneficiaries of the MacLeishes' companionship. Archie and Ada entertained often and with style. "Things were planned" at their dinner parties, Wilbur recalled. Archie might appear in kilts. Ada would sing "Loch Lomond" or "Down by the Salley Gardens" in her marvelous voice. A special wine might be served. Yet guests were invariably made to feel important by Archie's manifest interest in their lives and careers. His interest in Wilbur eventually became almost paternal, as it expressed itself not only in acts of kindness but in acts of counsel. Archie, Wilbur sometimes felt, "bestowed more of his feeling on me than on his own children."

It meant a great deal to poet May Sarton, a Briggs-Copeland fellow, to be included in Archie and Ada's "dazzling dinner parties." MacLeish "had a genius for drawing people out, for making everybody feel they were brilliant," she said. Most of all, she was struck by his generosity, which was exceedingly rare in the "very tight envious mean world" of literary politics, where people were constantly pushing others off the heights in order to make way for themselves.

This generosity was demonstrated in the case of yet another young poet I'll call Philip Williams. Williams, who was not teaching at Harvard but was associated with a group of poets including Edwin Honig, Richard Ellmann, and Richard Eberhart, was arrested for the unlawful act of watching a homosexual ejaculate. Word of his arrest reached MacLeish, who appealed to his friend and Harvard overseer Judge Charles Wyzanski for leniency. The erring Williams was let off with a year's probation, and ordered to see a psychiatrist. As Honig said, Archie "did what mattered" for Williams, who was trying to live the life of a poet with almost no means of support whatever.

Within the Harvard community, Archie and Ada were called on to entertain almost every person of importance, artistic or political, who came through campus. In the fall of 1950, these dignitaries included both Carl Sandburg ("Let me know whom you would like to see at dinner," Archie wired him) and T. S. Eliot. Eliot enjoyed his dinner party very much, he wrote afterwards. This came as a surprise to Archie, for Eliot had spent most of the evening, whether out of shyness or hauteur, looking at his navel.

As Boylston professor, Archie was more or less insulated from the mundane concerns of the English department. He was not expected to serve on departmental committees, for example. At one meeting, Harry Levin said, there was a dispute on the department's library committee, and someone remarked, "Well, for heaven's sake, this is a library committee and we've got the former Librarian of Congress in the department. Why don't we consult him?" Wisely, Archie stood up and said, no, he wouldn't presume to interfere in this matter. By keeping his distance from departmental politics, he made himself more valuable on issues that did concern him.

He was, for example, extremely influential in attracting the best and brightest to Harvard. Appointments to the Harvard faculty are made differently than at other American universities. When there is a vacancy, an ad hoc committee is established to consider applicants — or, more usually, nominees — and make a recommendation. What is unusual is that this committee is made up of professors from *outside* the department with the vacancy. The charge of such committees, according to Henry Rosovsky's book on the way Harvard is governed, is no less than to find the best-qualified candidate in the world. Given such elevated expectations, the tendency of such committees was to opt for reputation over potential. The result, according to Jack Bate (who chaired the English department during much of MacLeish's tenure), was the frequent selection of "extinct volcanoes," as philosopher Alfred North Whitehead called them, or "extinct molehills," in Bate's phrase.

Fortunately, though, the ad hoc committee's nominees had to pass muster with the dean of the faculty of arts and sciences and with the president of Harvard. After September 1953, when Nathan Pusey took over as president and McGeorge Bundy as dean, Archie's voice carried considerable weight in their decisions. His long friendship with Mac Bundy's parents — and with Mac himself, in one of those unusual bonds that stretch across generations — made it certain that his opinion would be taken into consideration. According to Jack Bate, MacLeish's advice was invaluable, for he was quick to spot talent, good at evaluating it, and eager to appoint gifted young teacher-scholars. He was instrumental in the appointment of Bill Alfred, in Bate's estimation "a superb teacher," and offered to fly up from Antigua to speak to an ad hoc committee on behalf of David Perkins.

One task that fell to MacLeish as Boylston professor was to chair the committee that selected the Charles Eliot Norton professors. Originally designated as a chair of poetry, the Norton professorship had long since been broadened to include artists of all kinds: Robert Frost, Igor Stravinsky, Thornton Wilder, and so on. This one-year post, which paid a salary equivalent to that of the highest-paid professor on the faculty, required only six lectures a year, but holders of the chair were expected to live and work at Harvard during the academic year. Among those MacLeish helped bring to Harvard on these attractive terms were E. E. Cummings, Aaron Copland, Paul Hindemith, Ben Shahn, and Edwin Muir, the Orkney poet and Kafka translator he considered one of the foremost living poets in English. The benefit to the institution derived as much from the presence on campus of these distinguished artists as from their lectures. Shahn, for example, took over a studio, nailed the door open, and started to work. Undergraduates crowded around to watch and to talk with the great man.

Archie also took an active role in the off-campus Poets' Theatre, founded in 1950 to provide playwrights, and particularly playwrights working in verse, with a stage for their work. And he was among the most vigorous supporters of the long campaign for construction of an adequate theater on campus. As early as 1951 he spoke out on the question, pointing out how important it was to encourage student participation not only in conventional dramatic and musical performances but in radio and television as well. In 1954, with the aid of Bundy, Harry Levin, and John Mason Brown, he participated in inaugurating a national fund-raising effort for such a theater. It was not until the fall of 1960, however, that the $2 million Loeb Drama Center, financed by New York banker John L. Loeb, opened with a performance of Shakespeare's *Troilus and Cressida*.

Taking on McCarthy

MacLeish was one of the first to fight back as the tentacles of McCarthyism clutched and tightened around the heart of the nation. In February 1950 the junior senator from Wisconsin made his famous speech in Wheeling, West Virginia, claiming that a certain number of State Department employees — the number changed from one press conference to the next — were in fact communists. The timing could hardly have been better for capitalizing on fear of the Soviets. In Canada, a code clerk in the Russian embassy had defected with lurid tales of Soviet espionage in the United States. One veteran of the State Department, Whittaker Chambers, accused another, Alger Hiss, of belonging to and spying for the Communist party. China came under the domination of Mao in October 1949, and it looked as if Korea might be next.

Archie at once recognized Joe McCarthy as an even greater threat to the republic than the enemies he warned against. On May 27, 1950, he wrote Dean Acheson, who had become secretary of state in the second Truman administration, imploring him to take a stand against McCarthy and in favor of a real peace with the Russians. Perhaps he was naive to think that the cold war could be halted through diplomatic action. Undoubtedly Acheson thought so. Yet for Archie the issue was clearcut: all that was required was leadership. "You can't compete with Joe in scaring people about Russia," he wrote Acheson. "As long as you do that you are the kite-tail to his Holy War. The way to handle Joe is to take the play away from him. And the way to take the play away from him is to clear the atmosphere of frustration and fatality which makes it possible for McFharthies to breed. And the way to do that is to act — to move — to lead."

At Harvard, Archie found considerable support for his position. The economist John Kenneth Galbraith, whom he had first met during Galbraith's World War II service in the Office of Price Administration, felt even more strongly than he that the United States was forcing the Soviets into a posture of opposition by its own truculence, less because of any real threat to national security than out of distaste for communism as an economic system. Galbraith argued this case forcefully against Acheson one evening at the MacLeishes. At that time Archie aligned himself alongside his old friend Dean — more out of friendship than conviction, Galbraith felt.

MacLeish was not disposed to stay silent as McCarthyism began to make inroads into the academic community, however. In September 1950 he joined several Harvard colleagues in protesting the dismissal of twenty University of California professors for refusing to sign the loyalty oath recently enacted by the state legislature. And in the following month, MacLeish, his former law professor Zechariah Chafee, Jr., and historian Arthur Schlesinger, Sr., publicly urged repeal of the McCarran Act because it sacrificed "the American tradition of individual liberty" to the cause of national security.

MacLeish held no brief for communism or for the Soviets. The grab for power in Eastern Europe and elsewhere made it clear that they were not to be trusted. Fundamentally, he believed, communism amounted to "an attempt to impose upon human society a kind of police control which is going to determine what men do, how they think, what they believe." The irony was that in its eagerness to fight communism, America was adopting the same kind of oppression. He hammered away at this point in speeches of May and June 1951 at the University of Virginia and Wellesley College. "When the members of a Congressional committee [HUAC] destroy the life of a man or a woman without a trial or hearing, even though they do it in the name of the protection of this republic against Communism, they are not protecting this republic against Communism," he declared at Virginia. Similarly, "when a misguided and thoroughly stupid board of education in Jersey City withdraws from the schools, with much public notice, four books about poetry by that saint on earth Mark Van Doren because Mark Van Doren is alleged to be associated with a certain number of associations which are alleged to be on the list of the Attorney General, that board of education is not defending individual liberty against the police state. It is actually engaging itself in the operation of the police state." Nor were the 130 (out of 131) Texas legislators who voted for the expulsion of a professor of economics at the University of Texas — because he said in a lecture that capitalism was decadent — protecting free enterprise thereby. The professor may have been both wrong and foolish, but that did not matter. What the legislators were doing was imposing official conformist views on individual citizens. In this country, Archie insisted, "we do not believe in official truth" — or at least we did not before the rise of McCarthyism and the epidemic of laws restricting free speech and free thought which it spawned. And for MacLeish it seemed clear that hemming freedom about in this way would only do away with it. "The defense of freedom under attack," he wrote, "is more freedom."

MacLeish collected a series of essays on this theme in *Freedom Is the Right to Choose,* published late in 1951. The reviewers were generally admiring. "These essays are more than beautifully written," one commented; "they are filled with the ardor of a firm conviction, supporting a high ideal." The United States needed such a spokesman now, another observed, as it had once needed Tom Paine. MacLeish, like Paine, wrote his essays out of total conviction, but he confined his deepest and bitterest feelings to his notebooks, as in the unpublished poem "The Blow Flies."

> *This nation, more powerful than any —*
> *Alexander's or Caesar's or T'ai Tang's —*
> *Is in danger of death: not from weapons or armies*
> *Or enemies over the two salt seas*
> *Or hidden enemies within, but friends*
> *Those pretending to be friends,*
> *Pretending to pray for us, preaching in freedom's name,*
> *Who deposit instead in the sweet flesh of the people*
> *The blow-fly eggs of hatred and terror and ignorance.*
> *The fat grubs have hatched & the festering sores*
> *Of treason and infamy know their loathsome fathers.*
> *A people divided: suspicion fostered and fed:*
> *Government itself debased by slanders:*
> *Citizens hounded & hunted with obscene lies:*
> *Liberty raped on the public floor of liberty!*
> *Hypocrite priests of hate! Hypocrite listeners!*

Such a diatribe may have been more explicit or simply uglier than Archie thought appropriate for print. The jeremiad he produced for public consumption in the latter half of 1951 took the form of a verse play, *The Trojan Horse.* Verse drama was the form he was working in during those years, and the one he was urging on such students as Hall, Bly, and Alfred. At a Harvard summer-school symposium, he even ventured the suggestion that all the participants might write their next plays in verse. "Well, I damn well won't," Lillian Hellman responded. A one-act play, *The Trojan Horse* was broadcast by the BBC in January 1952. The play is allegorical, directed at the enemies within. Specifically, MacLeish had Senator McCarthy "and his foul ways" in mind. "Well, they talk about people wrapping themselves in the flag! He wrapped himself in the wooden horse of patriotism." To underline the message, publisher Paul Brooks included a note with Houghton Mifflin's limited edition later in 1952: "If this play helps us to recognize a wooden horse when we see one it will have served an important purpose."

In a preface written twenty-five years later, Archie elaborated on his intentions. He wanted to explore how it could have come to pass that when "an insignificant and unrespected member of the United States Senate launched an attack on the integrity of the American government he was supported by so large a body of American opinion that even his bravest and most admired opponents in the Senate were silenced for a time." There were card-carrying communists in the State Department, McCarthy said, and though there was no proof, people believed him. There were traitors in the Defense Department, he said without evidence, and was believed. "Even the people themselves, he said, were guilty of treason: teachers, students, librarians, intellectuals, scientists, actors and actresses, artists, writers. . . . The country was rotten with Communism. There were spies and conspirators under every bed."

The whole thing was a fraud, of course, as obvious a fraud as the Trojan Horse itself with the armed Greeks hidden in its belly. The mystery was why such frauds should have succeeded. "Why had the Trojans taken the huge horse in, breaching their own walls to let it pass? Why had our deluded generation of Americans accepted McCarthy's enormous fabrication made, not of wood but lies?" Such was the pervasiveness of McCarthyism that though there was no mention of his name in the text, even the Groton schoolboys to whom Archie read his play knew at once who and what it was about. In *The Trojan Horse,* a wise blind man sees the danger ahead:

> *Bring that enormous image in*
> *To make official patriots of us,*
> *Sweating our public love by law,*
> *And all of us will fear each other.*

As they roll the horse inside the gate, he detects the unmistakable sound of humans shifting position within and tries to warn his fellow Trojans. But he is not listened to, except by a young girl trying to understand the peculiar behavior of the adults around her.

Mary Manning Howe, an Abbey Theatre actress married to law profesor Mark DeWolfe Howe, directed *The Trojan Horse* for the Poets' Theatre, in a double bill with *This Music*. The Howes' daughter Susan played the part of the young girl, very effectively, and won Archie's enduring affection. A few years later, at her request, he gave the commencement address at Beaver Country Day School, "because someone had asked him to whom nothing could be denied." And after she went to New York to seek her fortune on the stage, failed, and developed anorexia, he wrote her a wonderful letter. Both Felix Frankfurter and Bill Alfred had told him of her illness, he began. "Light as a feather they say you are, both of them, but then you always were. I can see you now drifting with that blind man across the meadows in front of Troy. . . . If you are lighter than that you will lift away with the winds which you mustn't for they have no claim to you at all and we have — all of us who have been waiting for you." In time, Susan Howe became a poet herself.

While he was in Antigua for the winter of 1952, Archie had a letter from Adlai Stevenson, now governor of Illinois. He was considering a run for the presidency, Adlai said, though he was not at all sure of his qualifications. Nonsense, Archie assured him. The very fact that he raised the question made him an attractive candidate to MacLeish. At midsummer Stevenson was nominated for the presidency, and in his acceptance speech said much of what he had written Archie six months earlier. He wondered if he was fully qualified for the job and had not pursued the nomination, but he was proud to accept it and would campaign as hard as he could. To men such as Acheson and Frankfurter, that speech was indicative of Stevenson's indecisiveness. He was really too nice a man to lead the country, they felt, but Archie disagreed. He'd seen Adlai under pressure in San Francisco and Washington, he told them, and there was never any question where he stood on any issue that mattered. Dean and Felix were unconvinced, and so, it turned out, were the voters, though it may well have been true that no one could have defeated war hero Eisenhower in 1952.

In May and June, Archie underwent the first and most severe of at least four separate attacks of stomach ulcers. The doctors confined him to bed for four weeks, and instructed him to cut down on his consumption of bourbon. Archie was inclined to blame a different source for his ulcer. "I call it McCarthy after its father," he wrote Van Doren.

Once recovered from his ulcers, he began drafting speeches for Stevenson. In this endeavor he was united with former FDR speechwriters Sam Rosenman and Robert Sherwood, along with Bernard DeVoto, Arthur Schlesinger, Jr., and John Kenneth Galbraith. Specifically, Adlai wrote Archie asking for remarks to deliver to the American Legion convention on August 27. He hoped he could keep the debate "on a level of honor, dignity and public enlightenment," Stevenson wrote, "and for that purpose there is only one MacLeish." Most speeches, Adlai felt, were full of "the everlasting appeals to the cupidity and prejudice of every group which characterizes our political campaigns. There is something finer in people; they know that they *owe* something too." Taking his direction from these comments, MacLeish produced a talk on the proper meaning of patriotism. He tried it out at a Cambridge dinner party first, where Mark Howe objected that it was "all phrasemaking, all rhetoric." Yes, but rhetoric of a high order.

AT LEISURE

After six years in government service, MacLeish returned home to Conway, in 1946. At first he missed the heady atmosphere of serving the nation on the front lines and found it difficult to resume his life as a poet. But he worked regularly each morning in his stone house (below), and in due course, when his hand was in luck, the poems started coming.

BENEVOLENT DUTIES

In these two photographs, Archie plays the role of family patriarch to three of his grandchildren. Above, he reads aloud from Walter de la Mare to Kenneth's children, Kim and Ellen Ishbel, for a national library program in 1960. At left, he and Bill's daughter Meg prepare to launch a duck in the fountain at Uphill Farm, c. 1956. Ada saw to it that the grandchildren did not disturb him at work.

DECADE OF SUCCESS

Called to Harvard as Boylston Professor in 1949,
MacLeish entered a period of remarkable productivity.
His *Collected Poems, 1917–1952* won both the Pulitzer
Prize and the National Book Award for 1952; he is
pictured above with the other NBA winners of that year,
Bernard De Voto for nonfiction and Ralph Ellison for
fiction. At the end of the fifties, he achieved his widest
popular recognition with *J.B.*, a play that won both the
Tony Award and the Pulitzer. In the rehearsal photo
below, Archie is shown, head in hands, with the question
that tormented his hero. Others involved in the
production, including director Elia Kazan, "who shares
all your guilt," signed their names in the margins.

Show me my guilt, O God!

FREEDOM FIGHTING

Ever combative in the cause of
individual liberties, MacLeish spoke
out early and publicly against the
smear campaigns of Senator Joseph
McCarthy, above right, who attacked
Harvard professors in general and
MacLeish in particular in 1952. Later
in the decade, MacLeish orchestrated
the campaign that led to the release of
poet Ezra Pound from St. Elizabeths
Hospital in 1958.

WINTER RETREAT

For twenty-five years beginning in 1950, Archie and Ada spent most of their winters in Antigua. At right are the regular foursome for afternoon Crokie contests: John H. P. ("Jay") Gould, John Cowles, MacLeish, and Philip Reed. Below, Archie and his son Kenneth, strong swimmers, go snorkeling at Green Island in 1960, and Ada and Archie sit on a wall above the sea, c. 1968.

FRIEND, LEADER

Perhaps Archie's dearest friend was the poet, critic, and charismatic teacher Mark Van Doren, shown above at an alfresco breakfast during the filming of their CBS television program in the summer of 1962. On October 26, 1963, MacLeish shared the platform with President John F. Kennedy at the dedication of the Robert Frost Library at Amherst College. Four weeks later, Kennedy was shot and killed.

BACK TO THE ROOTS

In the spring of 1970, Archie accompanied his son Kenneth, a *National Geographic* editor, on a trip to the windswept island of Barra, in Scotland's Outer Hebrides. At right, Archie wears his Scottish costume with Ada, c. 1975. Ken's death from cancer in 1977 was a devastating blow to his parents.

A LIFE MARKED

Like his parents before him, Archibald
MacLeish lived into his ninetieth year.
Toward the end, he abandoned the stone
house to work inside, in Ada's music room,
as in the picture above. Archie died on April
20, 1982, and was buried in Pine Grove
cemetery, where a boulder from Uphill Farm
marks the family plot.

"When an American says he loves his country," the MacLeish-Stevenson speech declared,

> he means not only that he loves the New England hills, the prairies glistening in the sun, the wide and rising plains, the great mountains, and the sea. He means that he loves an inner air, an inner light in which freedom lives and in which a man can draw the breath of self-respect. . . . Men who have offered their lives for their country know that patriotism is not the fear of something; it is the love of something. Patriotism with us is not the hatred of Russia; it is the love of this republic and the real liberty of men and mind in which it was born and to which this republic is dedicated.

There, for the wider circulation that a presidential candidate could give it, lay the gist of MacLeish's complaint against McCarthyism.

His efforts to stop McCarthy and his cohort became more pointed and overt as the campaign of 1952 approached its climax. Early in July, MacLeish lashed out at the enemy twice in the New York newspapers. "The Wisconsin-Nevada Axis," his satirical poem in the July 2 *New York Herald Tribune,* directed bipartisan scorn against Senator Patrick A. McCarran, Democrat of Nevada, as well as Senator Joseph McCarthy, Republican of Wisconsin.

> *Says McCarran to McCarthy,*
> *What's platform or party!*
> *We sport the same feather:*
> *Let's fight this together.*
> *I'll tear them in two*
> *If they criticize you.*
> *Says McCarthy to McCarran,*
> *Sweet Rosie of Sharon,*
> *My truth and my honor*
> *Shall fly to your banner.*
> *If they light into you*
> *They're Commies, that's who.*

And so on for six doggerel verses. In tribute, Charlie Wyzanski wrote Archie he was all for ridicule as a way of dealing with the ridiculous. MacLeish's poem, Wyzanski said, outweighed "a ton of pamphlets from the American Civil Liberties Union and all the commencement speeches delivered on the topic of civil liberties."

A few days later in a letter to the *New York Times,* MacLeish defended Zechariah Chafee from McCarthy's charge that he was "dangerous to America." As "the foremost living authority on, and defender of, the fundamental American freedoms of speech and press," Chafee might well be dangerous to McCarthy but hardly to Americans who believed in individual freedom, he wrote.

These public forays against a powerful and reckless demagogue required some courage. A month before the election, they drew blood. On October 9 MacLeish, Arthur M. Schlesinger, Sr., and Mark DeWolfe Howe announced a nationwide fund-raising effort aimed at unseating McCarthy and Senator William E. Jenner, Republican of Indiana, in the upcoming balloting. The two senators, they asserted in a letter of appeal, represented "the greatest menace the American liberal tradition has faced in our lifetime." In announcing the drive, the *New York Times* noted that "none of the three Harvard professors ha[d] been a target for Senators McCarthy and Jenner." That soon changed.

On October 10 Jenner characterized his Harvard antagonists as "pink boys" who "hate America." And the following day, Senator Karl Mundt, the South Dakota Republican, chimed in. McCarthy bided his time, waiting until his nationally televised speech of October 27 — subject: Stevenson's record of being "weak on communism" — to retaliate. McCarthy accused Stevenson of harboring advisers whose loyalty was in question. According to McCarthy, these included Arthur Schlesinger, Jr., Bernard DeVoto, and, most notably, Archibald MacLeish. In his speech McCarthy accused MacLeish of having "been affiliated with as vast a number of communist fronts, according to the Un-American Activities Committee, as any other individual whom I have ever named." When the *Harvard Crimson* called Archie for a response, he pointed out that the senator from Wisconsin had never previously mentioned his name, nor to his knowledge had the committee on un-American activities. Only now, after MacLeish's appeal for funds to fight McCarthyism, did the senator attack. "The pattern is clear," MacLeish pointed out, "and so is the implied threat to all others who criticize the Wisconsin senator."

Archie humorously remarked later that Ken Galbraith was rather put out at being omitted from McCarthy's list. No, Galbraith said, it was a distinction he was glad to do without. But Archie could confidently write Harry Levin on July 4, 1953, about the dubious report that McCarthy "has discovered a Communist plot to murder him. . . . One might as probably discover a plot by the children to murder Santa Claus."

The Harvard administration under Nathan M. Pusey, who assumed the presidency in September 1953, was soon forced to take a position for academic freedom and against McCarthy's demands that certain faculty members (MacLeish not among them) be dismissed. The local chapter of the American Association of University Professors, under the leadership of young law professor Kingman Brewster, organized a meeting to honor Pusey and other administrators and members of the board for their courage. In a joint statement, MacLeish and Samuel Eliot Morison denounced Senator McCarthy and his Senate internal security subcommittee for attempting to "place thought in prison and universities in chains." The issue, Archie told the audience, was not whether communists should teach, for no one "should teach who is not free to find the truth for himself." The issue was whether such decisions should be made by free institutions of learning or by the agencies of government. On this question, Pusey — and Harvard — declared their independence at a meeting at Sanders Theater on a rainy, dismal afternoon in the fall of 1953, with the president and the fellows of the university onstage and the AAUP members down front. There was a sense in that room, MacLeish remembered, of Harvard standing for all the things a great university should stand for. Moreover, he felt that Harvard's courage in repudiating McCarthy at a time when almost no one else dared to do so marked the beginning of the end for the politician from Wisconsin.

Mastery

At the end of November 1952, MacLeish brought out his *Collected Poems, 1917–1952*. The dust-jacket copy hailed him as "a poet who has survived" to emerge as "the most significant poet now writing in America." Even allowing for publisher's puffery, many reviewers were inclined to agree. For one thing, the sheer weight of MacLeish's accomplishment over thirty-five years commanded respect. Yet Archie by no means included everything he had written. He excised almost all of his first two books of poetry, cut discriminatingly from later volumes, and left out most of his work in verse drama, including *Nobodaddy, Panic, The Fall of the City,* and *Air Raid.* Then he added forty-one new poems to the mix, resulting in a book that, in Hayden Carruth's estimation, contained "407 pages of poetry and not a verse that shouldn't be there." Reading through the *Collected Poems* was a humbling experience for a previously critical reviewer, Carruth acknowledged. "For all these amputations, for all our rusty scalpels and contrary diagnoses, the patient lives. We are left with little to say. Perhaps there wasn't anything wrong with him in the first place."

As if to make up for its shoddy reception of *Actfive* four years earlier, the *New York Times* reviewed MacLeish's 1952 collection prominently in both its daily and Sunday editions. Richard Eberhart praised MacLeish, in the Sunday book review, for taking poetry out of the library and offering it in "a highly intelligible style to the many rather than the few." The book was a major achievement, and the whole bulked larger than the sum of its parts. "There is something basically lithe, wiry, direct and clear-seeing" about MacLeish, Eberhart concluded. "We feel him as distinctly American." Charles Poore in the daily *Times* described MacLeish as "the Renaissance man of the Lost Generation. He has had more careers than you can shake a Who's Who at," yet in the Renaissance tradition remained "a man who writes memorable verse while old worlds are dying and new worlds are being born." His range, his grasp of technique, and his ideas all stamped him as "the most significant American poet."

As against such raves, the reaction of the critics in the quarterlies was lukewarm at best. Frederick Morgan in the *Hudson Review* detected "little sense of growth" over the decades. MacLeish's talent was basically a thin one that had "managed to crystallize itself, accidentally as it were, in a handful of fine poems." Essentially Morgan rehearsed the usual complaints against MacLeish: he was too imitative at the beginning and too political later on. In his comments for the *Yale Review,* David Daiches singled out yet another failing. To his mind, MacLeish was too aggressive in presenting himself to his audience. When he began his early poem "Immortal Autumn" with "I speak this poem now with grave and level voice," and addressed the reader directly in many other poems, MacLeish was openly violating the doctrine of impersonality preached in high modernist poetics and the New Criticism. "We should never be allowed to see the poet arranging his gestures as we read the poetry," Daiches ordained. "The poet should be lost in the poem." Reed Whittemore in the *Sewanee Review* tried without much success to fit MacLeish's body of work into a convenient critical category. Some of the verse might be called Democratic Pastoral, he decided, but no label really fit. He was left to develop a list of the best poems, and it turned out to be a longer list than he would have arrived at for most modern poets.

Perhaps the most heartening observation in any review was Richard Wilbur's that "among MacLeish's lyrics of the last two years are things (*Calypso's Island,* for instance) as good as he has ever done." In a letter of congratulations, Allen Tate also expressed admiration for "many of the new things," citing particularly "The Sheep in the Ruins" and "Hypocrite Auteur." Such poems conveyed a sense "of great power held in reserve," Tate commented. As for the collection as a whole, Tate generously added that he had written at least as much verse as Archie, "but not nearly as much as would stand the light of day."

Collected Poems ranked as a strong contender for the major poetry awards, I. L. Salomon wrote in the December 27, 1952, *Saturday Review.*

In fact, Archie's volume swept the field, winning the Bollingen (shared with William Carlos Williams), the National Book Award, the Shelley Memorial Award, and his second Pulitzer Prize.

For his next book of verse, MacLeish returned to the Garden of Eden story he had explored thirty years before in *Nobodaddy*. As in the earlier volume, *Songs for Eve*, published in September 1954, reinterprets the biblical story to the poet's purposes. Not all of the twenty-eight short "songs" making up the sequence are addressed to or spoken by Eve, but there is no question she is the central figure of the piece. Only through her agency was Adam, "that browsing animal," enabled to fall upward from earth to consciousness, and so to God. Only the carnal and vicariously creative Eve made this fortunate fall possible. In *Songs for Eve*, as in *The Happy Marriage*, the sexes are radically differentiated, but here the differences work for the best, as in "Adam in the Evening":

> *Beauty cannot be shown*
> *But only at remove:*
> *What is beautiful is known*
> *By opposites, as love.*

> *Counter, the mind can see.*
> *When first Eve disobeyed*
> *And turned and looked at me,*
> *Beauty was made.*

> *That distance in the blood*
> *Whereby the eyes have sight*
> *Is love — not understood*
> *But infinite.*

Songs for Eve declares its author's optimism throughout.

It was always difficult to assess any new book, Archie wrote Ferris Greenslet at Houghton Mifflin (his publishers again, from *Collected Poems, 1917–1952* on), but if he knew anything about the art of poetry, *Songs for Eve* was "the farthest" he had gone so far. Almost all the reviews were positive, if not as positive as that. Eberhart in the Sunday *Times* hailed MacLeish's mature reimmersion in the pure waters of the lyric. Sara Henderson Hay thought the volume "a joy to read, and think about." John Ciardi called it "one of the books that must not be missed." The acerbic Randall Jarrell took exception in the *Yale Review*. "The sharp, bright, sometimes quite interesting, sometimes quite mannered series of poems about the Garden of Eden is pleasant to read, and would be even pleasanter to believe," he observed. Manifestly, he could not credit MacLeish's attempt at turning the Fall on its head. And in an opening sentence clearly intended to devastate, Jarrell echoed Frederick Morgan's judgment on the *Collected Poems.* "It seems to me," he began, "that Archibald MacLeish has made overpowering demands upon his own delicate lyric talent."

The jaundiced views of such rival poets as Jarrell and Morgan may have been influenced by a perception that whatever his merits, MacLeish had already enjoyed far more success than comes to most artists. Besides, they may have felt, Archie was too genially acquainted in those circles where decisions were made on the award of prizes, Pulitzer and otherwise. In December 1953, in fact, he rose to the very pinnacle of the nation's cultural establishment when he was elected president of the American Academy of Arts and Letters.

Since his elevation from the National Institute to the American Academy in 1946, MacLeish had been an unusually vigorous member. As he moved through the chain of office from secretary to chancellor ro president, he actively sought to bring other distinguished writers into the organization. Between 1948 and 1951, for example, he nominated William Faulkner, Robert Sherwood, W. H. Auden, E. E. Cummings, and Wallace Stevens for membership in the academy. Archie was also influential in seeing that writers he admired received whatever honors the academy could bestow. Presenting the Award of Merit medal to Thomas Mann in 1949 (who was in Sweden at the time), he quoted the German writer's letter of acceptance. He was honored by the award, Mann wrote, but not persuaded that his work deserved it. Goethe had said it beautifully: "Rarely do we satisfy ourselves; all the more comforting it is to have satisfied others." The following spring MacLeish presented the Howells medal to Faulkner (who was in Mississippi at the time), again drawing from the absent novelist's letter of response. He could not be there to accept in person, Faulkner explained, for "up until he sells crops, no Mississippi farmer has the time, or money either, to travel anywhere on." But he was certainly grateful, for "nothing makes a man feel better than for his fellow craftsmen publicly and concretely to depose that his work is all right." Another nonattendee was Ernest Hemingway, who was awarded the academy's gold medal in May 1954, four months after he was critically injured in not one but two airplane crashes in Africa. Reports of Hemingway's death circulated widely at the time, but — so Archie wrote his old friend — even when a reporter called to ask him for a memorial comment, he never for a moment believed that Ernest could be dead.

Throughout the period of his most active involvement in the academy, from 1947 to 1956, MacLeish persistently tried to make the body more politically sensitive, on two fronts. Initially he was interested in expanding the academy's contacts with foreign artists and with similar organizations in other countries. He hoped that such connections might lead to an international "Republic of Letters." Then, after 1950, he thought the academy should adopt public positions vigorously supporting freedom of expression and opposing government attempts to stifle the exchange of ideas through red tape and classification of documents, loyalty oaths, and outright censorship.

When McCarthy, for instance, sent his young lieutenants Roy Cohn and G. David Schine to Europe in order to cull books written by those of politically incorrect orientation from United States Information Service libraries, Archie urged the academy to express its outrage publicly. If the present climate of virulent anticommunism were to continue, he pointed out, "Picasso's paintings would be removed from American museums as a matter of course." If an anti-Catholic movement should take hold in the future, "Dante would be expunged from all library shelves." In the face of so vicious an attack on the freedom of the arts, he could not conceive "of an institution calling itself an American Academy of Arts and Letters" keeping quiet.

MacLeish's views, however, did not prevail. A number of academy members were adamantly apolitical, and others were determined to maintain the organization as no more than an extremely exclusive private club. Even during his three-year term as president, Archie was unable to persuade his fellow academicians to take stands on issues affecting the arts, and twenty years later, when there was a movement to combine the institute and the academy, he was inclined instead to question whether *either* society justified its existence. At the end of his three-year term as president, he was ready to conclude that individual members of the academy "were more effective in the defense of the arts, and the humanization of life, in our single and separate capacities than in our capacity as members of an organization."

Despite his frustration at the academy's inertia, MacLeish was a remarkably effective leader in other ways. Felicia Geffen was executive secretary from 1941 to 1973, serving such presidents as Paul Manship, George F. Kennan, Malcolm Cowley, Mark Van Doren (who succeeded Archie), Douglas Moore, Allan Nevins, Aaron Copland, Glenway Wescott, and Richard Wilbur. None of these worked with Archie's intensity or command of detail, she recalled. He would meet her for a half hour between trains at the Century Club and race through an agenda of half a dozen items, ranging from the seating chart at the May ceremonial to the award of a small sum of money to an indigent poet. Always, he wanted more funds spent on helping the arts and less on mere maintenance. In addition, Geffen recalled, Archie "was a superb presiding officer" who pulled such occasions together with his charm and humor.

Some of those same attributes proved useful during the 1954–55 academic year, when Archie served as interim master of Harvard's Eliot House. The largest and one of the oldest of the Harvard houses, Eliot was widely regarded as a haven for eastern prep school students, not to say snobs. Preppies or not, Eliot residents were expected to excel in scholarship, athletics, or some other field. In 1950–51, for example, both of Harvard's Rhodes scholars came from Eliot, as well as seven of its twenty-four first-elected Phi Beta Kappas. In the words of John H. Finley, the house master MacLeish replaced during his visiting appointment at Oxford, "a man has to be somebody to get along at Eliot house."

During his term in residence at Eliot, Archie performed the conventional duties of the master. To fulfill the social engagements expected of them, he and Ada moved into the master's lodgings for the year, and regularly entertained students at tea. In December he was dragooned into acting in the house's traditional Christmas farce, a "social travesty" called *The What D'ye Call It*. Archie also was available to listen to undergraduates' complaints, and to guide them with advice. In the spring of 1955 Rob Cowley, the son of his friend Malcolm Cowley, decided to fall in love, develop writer's block, and let his studies go to hell. Rob was about to be "rusticated," as his father expressed it, when Archie stepped in to reduce the penalty to probation and enable the lad to recover his bearings.

Archie's senior tutor at Eliot House was John Conway, a Canadian who had lost an arm in World War II. The two immediately hit it off. In time Conway was to become one of the closest of the several younger men Archie accepted as surrogate sons. A bachelor, Conway was a regular at the MacLeish Thanksgiving dinners, and some years later, when he married fellow historian Jill Ker, she too formed an extremely close friendship with both Archie and Ada. As senior tutor of Eliot House, Conway took care of the administrative duties, while Archie carried off the social side of the job with gusto. His particular innovation was to arrange for notable people to come to dinner and to talk with selected students. Among the guests were Dean Acheson, J. Robert Oppenheimer, Judge Learned Hand, Robert Frost, John Crowe Ransom, and Felix Frankfurter. These visits ran to a pattern. First there would be a dinner for the guest and perhaps eight to ten Harvard faculty professors in his field of interest. Drinks would be served: Archie wanted the conversation to flow as freely as possible. Meanwhile, a score or so of Eliot students would assemble in the master's study for a glass of beer. After dinner the distinguished visitor and the faculty members, brandy snifters in hand, would join the students for a discussion session "as easy and civilized . . . and as pleasant for all concerned" as possible.

These evenings were either enormously successful, as John Conway adjudged them, or quite the opposite, in the opinion of Jack Bate. For Conway 1954–55 was an *annus mirabilis* in the history of Eliot House because of the dignitaries Archie lured to campus. Their very presence had a way of stimulating the imagination of the undergraduates, of giving them a vision of what they might become.

For Bate, however, those Eliot House evenings verged on the ridiculous. Only eminent faculty — and no students — were invited to the dinner preceding the discussion. Archie himself usually wore a dinner jacket and his tasseled pumps. When the two groups assembled afterwards, Archie first asked the faculty members to pose questions, and only then threw the floor open to the students. This process rather overwhelmed the students, who tended to remain silent. After a few such evenings, Ada called in Bate and Conway and asked them what could be done to stimulate student participation. "Stop asking the faculty," Bate advised.

The most successful visitor was Frost, partly because the awkwardness about questions and answers was effectively averted by his deafness. Since he could not hear what others were saying, the poet simply held forth, at length. "Everything he remembered, he called up," Archie said. The hour grew late as he continued his monologue before an enraptured group of students. About half past ten, a rather tired MacLeish said: "Gentlemen, Mr. Frost has been extraordinarily generous and kind to us. I think we should thank him and give him an opportunity to go to bed." But as the students began to clap, Frost broke in. "Archie," he said, "if you are tired, why don't you go to bed?" That brought down the house, and Frost talked on for another hour and a half.

Earlier in 1954 MacLeish had attended an eightieth birthday dinner for Frost at Amherst. The older poet had just come back from New York, where he had been paid every possible honor at a banquet, and Frost began to reflect on the issue of his future reputation. What he really hoped to do, he said, was to leave behind him "a few poems that will be hard to get rid of." That was exactly right, Archie thought. It sounded modest enough, but of course it wasn't, for a poem that was hard to get rid of was a voice that was hard to get rid of, and the voice was the poet himself. It was not praise that mattered, but to be in the company of those a few of whose poems would last.

22 ❖

MEANS OF ESCAPE

Liberating Pound

As A HAPPY side-effect of the winters in Antigua, the MacLeishes were transported round the world on air and sea ships belonging to their friends. They regularly flew to and from the island with John and Betty Cowles on the *Minneapolis Star and Tribune* plane. There were more leisurely trips on yachts owned or rented by the Cowleses, Phil and Mabel Reed, J. Noel (owner of the Westchester county newspapers) and Elena Macy, and Laurens (inventor of the Hammond organ) and Roxanne Hammond. In April 1956 the Cowleses and MacLeishes stopped in Cuba to see Ernest Hemingway. It was the last meeting of Archie and Ernest, one they had been building up to for a long time.

As early as August 1948, after Archie sent him "Years of the Dog," his reminiscent poem about the 1920s in Paris, Hemingway was campaigning for a reunion. Married to his fourth wife, Mary Welsh, and settled at the Finca Vigia outside Havana, he suggested that Archie and Ada come to stay with them. He was not difficult anymore, Ernest wrote, and was old enough to know that he loved them both. Ada, especially: he would rather have made love to Ada than to any woman he ever met. In fact, he added, she was the only woman he ever wanted to sleep with that he hadn't slept with. That piece of braggadocio was very much in the spirit of this particular letter from Hemingway. Elsewhere he claimed to have killed "26 krauts (armed) sures" during his eight months as a war correspondent with the Twenty-second Infantry Regiment. Archie restricted the letter for years, to protect Ernest's reputation.

Both MacLeishes were pleased by the success of *The Old Man and the Sea* in 1952. Everyone kept asking him about the symbolism, Ernest wrote Archie, but actually the old man was an old man and the boy a boy and so on. Having Archie praise the book reminded him of writing "The Killers" in Madrid and bringing it to Juan-les-Pins in the summer of 1926 for MacLeish to pronounce judgment on. "Oh pappy," Ada wrote in response to *The Old Man and the Sea,* "no one sees as you do and writes as you can." Reading the book left her feeling that "when we see each other again, we can take up a little bit before where we left off." Ernest thought so, too. What had loused up their friendship was the strain of the war and his bad marriage to Martha Gellhorn, he thought.

The anticipated 1954 get-together in New York, when Ernest was to receive the gold medal of the American Academy, was prevented by Hemingway's plane crashes in Africa. In the moment of what seemed to be his death, Ernest wrote Archie on March 2, he learned two things: that he loved "Miss Ada" very much and that he loved Archie like a brother. Physically, he could not attend the ceremony. Otherwise, he wrote, "I'll be there only won't be visible." Winning the gold medal put him in mind of the Nobel Prize. That he could never win, Ernest predicted, because he was the only author who knew how to make dynamite out of TNT and sand. Yet win the Nobel he did, before the month was out. MacLeish celebrated his friend's accomplishment in a poem.

> *There must be*
> *Moments when we see right through*
> *Although we say we can't. I knew*
> *A fisher who could lean and look*
> *Blind into dazzle on the sea*
> *And strike into that fire his hook,*
> *Far under, and lean back and laugh*
> *And let the line run out, and reel*
> *What rod could weigh nor line could feel —*
> *The heavy silver of his wish,*
> *And when the reel-spool faltered, kneel*
> *And with a fumbling hand that shook*
> *Boat, all bloody from the gaff,*
> *A shivering fish.*

Archie and Ada's visit with the Hemingways in April 1956 was something of a letdown. Ernest was about to leave for Peru, in order to catch marlin on camera for a film version of *The Old Man.* The doctors were giving Hemingway shots and taking his blood pressure for that trip, and Archie thought him not at all well. Mary Hemingway, however, struck

Archie as Ernest's "finest wife with only possible exception of Pauline."
Mary laid on a "wonderful dinner with ortolans and other rarities," and
no literary conversation whatsoever. The evening went smoothly, without any hint of rancor. But it was not possible for the two writers to
take up again "before where [they] left off." Past quarrels had worn the
bonds of friendship thin.

Hemingway may have been an impossible friend. MacLeish was a
difficult one. He did not give himself fully in relationships. He was
sometimes critical of others, and hypersensitive to criticism himself. It
was his quickness to pass judgment, apparently, that caused a rift between Archie and Gerald Murphy. Something he said hurt Gerald so
deeply that the Murphys declined an invitation to attend Archie and
Ada's fortieth wedding anniversary on June 21, 1956. Such recurring
dates were important, Archie wrote Gerald early in June, only because
they gave life a kind of structure. He was saddened that Sara and Gerald
would not be with them, keeping that structure in place. Gerald in reply
philosophized that maintaining a friendship called "for a complete emotional stability on the part of one of the friends — preferably on the part
of both." He did not himself command such stability, Gerald implied.
Very likely the trouble between Gerald and Archie stemmed from a kind
of unspoken rivalry. Both men were used to receiving a great deal of
attention, and both were skilled at exerting charm. Bill MacLeish, who
was Gerald's godson, speculated that they were often ill at ease in each
other's company because both of them were driven to play the role of
the genial host. This led to difficulty. In most gatherings, one host was
enough.

For the fortieth as for the twenty-fifth anniversary, when the Murphys
and Dos Passoses had been in attendance, a jeroboam of champagne
was uncorked. Dos had memorialized the earlier event thus:

> Gerald brought a jeroboam
> Very large and full of foam
> Went to everybody's dome
> Thank you, Gerald, glad to know 'im.

Helping them down the jeroboam this time were Bob and Adele Lovett,
Lefty and Annie Burr Lewis, and Edward and Hester Pickman. Also on
hand were sons Ken and Bill and their wives, with Bill's wife, Peg —
they had married in September 1953 — expecting her first child. Ken
and Bill piped the guests in to dinner with their bagpipes. Lefty Lewis
composed a poem in acrostic. It was "a heartwarming occasion," Ada
wrote Sara Murphy afterwards, but what she especially wanted Sara to
know was that she and Gerald had been missed.

In the spring of 1956, as in several other springs, Archie required medical treatment after his return from Antigua. The surgeons removed a polyp from his colon in May. Although it proved to be benign, the operation left him flat on his back for three weeks. He was fully recovered by June 17, four days before the anniversary, when he read to an outdoor crowd of five thousand in the Boston Public Garden as first winner of the city's Arts Festival medal. "Isn't it an encouraging thing that people are ready to listen to poetry and in such numbers?" Ada inquired rhetorically.

Archie's trials and triumphs paled in comparison to the plight of Ezra Pound. Over the years Pound had done little more than scold MacLeish by way of correspondence. Nonetheless, Archie was now determined — after visiting Ezra at Saint Elizabeths Hospital in Washington — to secure Pound's release from the hospital and from the charge of treason still pending against him. If it had not been for MacLeish's resolve and his energy, Pound might well have languished in Saint Elizabeths for the rest of his life.

It was not the first time Archie had played paladin for Pound. His services to Pound seemed to grow in ratio to the scorn that the older poet visited upon him. A case in point was the Bollingen Award of 1948, which was bestowed on Pound for his *Pisan Cantos* by the fellows in American literature MacLeish had established at the Library of Congress. A controversy broke out following news of the award in February 1949. The event attracted considerable press coverage, particularly since Pound had written the winning cantos while incarcerated by the United States Army in Pisa. Leading the attack against the award was Robert Hillyer, the former Boylston professor at Harvard, with two long articles in June issues of the *Saturday Review of Literature,* one titled "Treason's Strange Fruit." MacLeish held no brief for the *Pisan Cantos.* They were Pound's "weakest work," he thought, and should not have won the Bollingen. He also thought that the choice of Pound's book "was not only misguided but damn close to irresponsible," as he wrote Luther Evans. Nonetheless, he was outraged by Hillyer's "discovery" of a fascist conspiracy among the fellows in American literature, who included T. S. Eliot, Theodore Spencer, Carl Sandburg, Allen Tate, Katherine Anne Porter, and W. H. Auden.

The brouhaha over the Bollingen got Archie thinking about the larger issue of the relationship between morality and art. He produced a long essay, published in book form as *Poetry and Opinion* (1950), focusing on whether a poem containing bad opinions was necessarily bad. His answer was no, but his argument was undistinguished by logic, misappropriated Aristotle, and failed to differentiate adequately between the aesthetically and the ethically bad. Yet MacLeish was on solid ground in accusing those who opposed the award of doing so largely on the basis of the political opinions held by its author and expressed in the *Pisan Cantos*. That, surely, was wrong, and smacked of a HUAC-McCarthy mentality on the left.

MacLeish did not seriously contemplate working for Pound's release prior to 1954. At that time Ezra himself imposed a substantial roadblock against progress. He took the position that he was owed an apology that would, in effect, repudiate FDR's position on the war in general and Pound's case in particular. This was patently impossible. Archie with his lawyer's mind understood precisely what had to be done to secure Pound's freedom. Ezra had originally been confined in Saint Elizabeths, back in February 1946, when judged unfit to stand trial. The indictment for treason still hung over his head. In order to ensure his release, Pound would have to be found still mentally unfit for trial, yet not dangerous if given his freedom. On those grounds the government might "nol pros" (quash) the indictment, and let him go. MacLeish wrote Pound in midsummer 1955 proposing such "a medical disposition" of the problem, and seeking assurance that Ezra would not insist on a solution that involved vilification "of President Roosevelt and those who served the Republic under him."

As ever, Pound's reply was baffling. "You now have me completely buffaloed," Archie wrote him on September 7. "I don't know whether you wish I would or wish I wouldn't and, in either case, what." It was clear that they needed to talk. In December 1955 MacLeish went to see Pound at Saint Elizabeths and came away a dedicated man. "I should have done it [gone to visit Pound] years ago, but just plain lacked the stomach," he wrote Quincy Mumford. "I hate asylums and I'd only met Pound once in my life in any case and so I let my conscience sleep." But the sight of the bedraggled seventy-year-old Pound, "surrounded by the insane" with few companions to talk to or books to read, converted MacLeish into an advocate for his cause. "What I saw made me sick," he wrote Hemingway, "and I made up my mind I wouldn't rest until he got out. Not only for his sake but for the good name of the country: after ten years it was beginning to look like persecution and if he died there we'd never get the stain out."

During that same visit to Saint Elizabeths, MacLeish had a constructive talk with Dr. Winfred Overholser, a Harvard man and director of the hospital. Overholser told him that Pound could "walk out tomorrow if it weren't for the indictment," and that he couldn't stand the strain of trial but was "perfectly all right as long as things didn't close in on him." This was heartening news, but it still remained to make a case for Pound with the Department of Justice, and in a Republican administration Archie had few friends to call upon. Despite this political handicap, MacLeish started a small campaign on behalf of Pound. "I am going to begin correspondence with a few assorted Senators in the hope of building up a little quiet support," he wrote Ezra in June 1956. "My notion is three or four interested Senators and a small, *very* small group of people whose presence will impress an Attorney General and some one bird who will take the lead." If the Republicans won again in the fall, as seemed probable, the front man would have to be a Republican, and the question was who? Among the Democratic senators MacLeish was particularly desirous of enlisting Herbert H. Lehman of New York, less because of his liberal sentiments than because he was Jewish, and much of the feeling against Pound was the result of his reckless and obsessive anti-Semitism. Characteristically, Ezra vetoed Lehman as a possible ally and went so far as to compare him with Lavrenty Beria, the notorious head of the Soviet secret police, though the only conceivable point of similarity between the two men was that both were Jewish. Helping Pound was not easy, Archie wrote Alexis Léger. "One cannot leave him there [in Saint Elizabeths] to rot. But whoever offers him a hand will have his fingers broken."

Archie went ahead anyway. He talked to Senator J. William Fulbright, who said he would help line up other senators. He got in touch with the sympathetic Christian Herter, Republican undersecretary of state and a friend dating back to Harvard Law School days. Unanticipated backing came from Dag Hammarskjöld, secretary general of the United Nations, who had been contacted out of the blue by Harry Meacham, a Richmond, Virginia, businessman and president of the Virginia Poetry Society, who had made Pound's release a private project. On another front, MacLeish lined up an all-star roster of writers to join him in an appeal to the attorney general. Initially he thought of using Eliot, Frost, Hemingway, Sandburg, and Faulkner, but the list was pared to the first three. Eliot and Hemingway were old friends of Pound's, and therefore logical candidates. Frost's public reputation and his manifest conservatism — as a self-styled "Grover Cleveland Democrat," he was the closest thing to an Eisenhower Republican in sight — would make him the ideal contact man in Washington, Archie realized. But Frost had known Pound only slightly in England forty years earlier and had felt patronized by him. In fact, Frost's first inclination was to avoid involvement. As he said to Richard Wilbur, "To hell with [Pound], he's where he belongs." Yet MacLeish was able to persuade Frost to change his mind. In Eliot and Hemingway, Robert would be associated with the most eminent literary men alive, Archie pointed out. Besides, he told Frost with a twinkle, Ezra was getting entirely too much attention down there in Saint Elizabeths. Frost signed on.

In January 1957 a letter over the signatures of these three writers was ready for submission to Attorney General Herbert Brownell, Jr. MacLeish wrote the first draft, which was then modified by Eliot. And Archie wangled permission to send the appeal on the letterhead of the American Academy. "We are writing to you about Ezra Pound who has been confined in St. Elizabeths Hospital in Washington under indictment for treason," the letter began.

> Our interest in this matter is founded in part on our concern for Mr. Pound who is one of the most distinguished writers of his generation, and in part on our concern for the country of our birth. As writers ourselves we cannot but be aware of the effect on writers and lovers of literature throughout the world of Pound's continued incarceration at a time when certain Nazis tried and convicted of the most heinous crimes have been released and in many cases rehabilitated.

The letter went on to reveal the doctors' opinion that Pound was still unfit to stand trial and likely to remain so, and to ask specifically that the Department of Justice proceed "to nol pros the indictment and remit the case to the medical authorities." This appeal was being made directly to Brownell, the writers emphasized, and they had "no intention at this time of making a public statement on this matter."

Six weeks later, on February 28, 1957, Brownell acknowledged receiving the letter. He was looking into the question and would get back to them, he said. Another six weeks elapsed before Deputy Attorney General William P. Rogers, who was about to succeed Brownell, invited Frost to come to Washington and discuss the Pound case. Frost did not reply before departing on a trip to Great Britain. MacLeish, who had been planning a European trip himself for some time, caught up with Frost in London during May and persuaded Robert to see Rogers soon after his return. MacLeish also talked to Eliot during his time in England. He and Ada next journeyed to Italy, where he met Pound's daughter, Mary de Rachewiltz, at Sirmione. Beholding this gentlemanly poet-lawyer with the beautiful manners and kind voice, in the hotel gardens above Lago di Garda, Mary was visited by a "strange conviction: here is a man with a golden key in his head."

That key was not going to unlock any doors, however, until the furor over John Kasper died down. The twenty-five-year-old Kasper, a rabble-rousing segregationist, had acquired his racist theories from Pound during a series of visits to Saint Elizabeths. Among his teachings was the theory that the school integration movement was a Jewish plot. On February 2, 1957, the *New York Herald Tribune* ran a story on this master-pupil relationship under the headline "Segregationist Kasper Is Ezra Pound Disciple." Soon thereafter Kasper, who was executive secretary of the Seaboard White Citizens Council of Washington, was jailed in connection with the bombing of an integrated school in Nashville, Tennessee. Mary de Rachewiltz had warned her father against Kasper a couple of years earlier, but Ezra was not prepared to disavow him. "At least he's a man of action and don't sit around looking at his navel," Pound said of him. If the effort to release Pound was to succeed, it was going to have to be in spite of Kasper, and without Ezra's assistance.

When Frost returned from England, a letter from MacLeish was waiting with a reminder of his pledge to see the attorney general. In his reply, Frost admitted to some misgivings. "Neither you nor I would want to take [Ezra] into our family or even into our neighborhood," he wrote. Still, he would hate to see him "die ignominiously in that wretched place." So, he instructed Archie, go ahead and make an appointment with the Department of Justice. But Frost wasn't in any hurry about it. He *could* see Rogers on July 17 or July 19, but thought "the affair might better wait until the Fall."

Nonetheless Archie set up a date for Friday July 19, and accompanied Frost to Washington on that torrid summer day. Rogers, who was waiting for them, came right up to Frost and seized him with both hands. "I'm so glad to meet you," the attorney general said. "My daughters are great admirers of your poetry." Frost said, "Why aren't you?" The meeting was an encouraging one nonetheless, Archie reported to Hemingway. The Department of Justice "would apparently be willing to drop the indictment if somebody could come forward with a sound plan for taking care of Pound outside St. Elizabeths." Yet they were opposed to allowing Pound to return to Italy, which both he and his daughter wanted him to do. Such a re-expatriation might produce undesirable publicity, and in Italy Pound might be encouraged to resume the kind of traitorous talk that had landed him in Saint Elizabeths in the first place. In any case, nothing could be done until the Kasper case was disposed of. That could delay Pound's release for as long as a year.

It was at this stage that Frost was coaxed to the front. As a militant New Dealer, and a publicly visible supporter of Adlai Stevenson, in 1956 as in 1952, MacLeish could hardly play that role himself. But he could — and did — make a follow-up appointment for Frost to see Rogers again, on October 23. Frost emerged from that interview "hot for consequences — all stirred up." Evidently all that stood in the way of liberating Pound was finding the money to ensure his treatment in a private institution in the United States. The publishing firm New Directions, through James Laughlin, guaranteed a small monthly stipend. Ezra reluctantly consented to such a plan, though he still wanted to go to Italy. On December 5 Overholser wrote Archie that he too favored the remove to Italy. "I am sure he would be much happier there and would of course be no menace to any persons or any government." There the question languished while MacLeish continued to orchestrate a solution. On January 2, 1958, Rogers wrote Archie that he wasn't sure if the matter could be worked out but that he was "certainly inclined in that direction." Why didn't MacLeish come to see him when he was next in Washington? Archie interpreted that seemingly hopeful reply as a stalling tactic, and called on Chris Herter to apply whatever pressure he could. On March 16 the *Washington Sunday Star* floated a trial balloon in a story titled "Liberty Being Weighed For Poet Ezra Pound." A principal source was Overholser, who commented, "It's perfectly possible to be mentally unfit to stand trial and yet be perfectly safe to be at large."

Meanwhile, Frost was fully engaged. Invited to a White House dinner by President Eisenhower on February 27, he arranged to have lunch beforehand with White House chief of staff Sherman Adams, from New Hampshire, and with Rogers. It would be a disgrace to the United States, Frost insisted, if Pound were to die in confinement. On April 14, at MacLeish's insistence, Frost traveled to Washington one last time for an appointment with Rogers. Rogers was all agreeability. The trial balloon had sailed placidly across the sky. Releasing Pound, it seemed clear, would produce no serious adverse criticism. "Our mood is your mood, Mr. Frost," he said. Four days later, in a hearing before Bolitha J. Laws, the same judge who had committed Pound to Saint Elizabeths twelve years before, the indictment was withdrawn and he was freed. Two months later Ezra embarked for Italy on the *Cristoforo Colombo* to live with his daughter and grandchildren. There he lived for another dozen years, sometimes in dire poverty. Archie did something about that, too. As Mary de Rachewiltz recalled, when her father "worried we would not have enough to eat and not enough fuel . . . Archibald MacLeish sent a check to keep [him] warm."

It was widely believed for a long time that Robert Frost was principally responsible for securing Pound's release from Saint Elizabeths. Frost did nothing to correct this misapprehension. In effect, he claimed credit in a newspaper interview a month after Pound's release. Archie had pretty much given up the cause, Frost said, and he'd taken over. He'd lined up Hemingway and Eliot. He'd "called up a man named Rogers at the Department of Justice." And so on. Some were irritated by this self-aggrandizement. "Just as all jokes are ascribed to Dorothy Parker,"

Richard Wilbur said, "all credit in the Pound release has gone to Robert Frost." Harry Meacham knew better. "It was all Archie," he insisted in his book on Pound.

MacLeish himself raised no objections to Frost's story. The mission had been accomplished; let the credit go where it was most needed. Although Frost had initially dragged his heels, Archie wrote Meacham, "there is no question whatever that it was his intervention which persuaded the Eisenhower administration to take action." He wrote Hemingway in a similar vein. "I think Frost gets a large part of the credit. The old boy despises Ez for personal reasons but once he got started nothing could stop him and I think Rogers finally gave up out of sheer exhaustion."

J.B.: Background

In the spring of 1957, Archie and Ada spent several weeks at the American Academy in Rome, with side trips throughout Italy and to Greece. At the embassies in Rome and Athens, MacLeish lectured on the predicament of the American artist. The Greek poet and diplomat George Seferis was in the audience in Athens, and his very presence underlined what was wrong with the image of artists in the United States. Foreigners tended to see the United States as a materialistic nation, and in such a nation writers and artists were classified as impractical eggheads. The trouble was that most American artists enthusiastically embraced that image of themselves. Recently, Archie had heard one such aesthete declare that the most dangerous temptation artists faced was "the temptation of public duty." Such a position was unthinkable abroad, where men like Seferis were rightly valued for their usefulness both in "the outward world of event and the inward world of conception." If American artists felt isolated from their culture, Archie concluded, that isolation was "quite as much a matter of the turning of their own backs on the age as of the age's turning of its back on them."

Before the MacLeishes left Rome, Archie gave a reading from the first draft of J.B., the play he had just finished. With J.B., MacLeish shucked off the cloak of isolation and reached the kind of audience he had been aiming for since the 1930s. It was to become far and away MacLeish's most resounding popular success. The seeds of J.B. started germinating when MacLeish visited the bombed-out London suburb of West Ham and saw the "senseless, hit-or-miss pattern of destruction." Guernica or Dresden might have served the same purpose of powerfully illustrating the disasters that had befallen innocent people during the ten or fifteen years leading up to the end of World War II. More innocents had been hurt, maimed, or mutilated during this period, he thought, than ever before in history. Preoccupied by the incomprehensible injustice of this experience, Archie hit upon the idea of expressing it through the biblical story of Job. For five years and more, starting after *Actfive*, he struggled with the problem of dramatizing that idea. A breakthrough came with his student Ted Hoagland's novel *Cat Man*, which took place in a circus environment. That gave him the notion of using the circus ring as a setting, as he had done in his early poem "The End of the World," and at once the structure of his play fell into place.

From the beginning, MacLeish knew what message he meant to convey in his reworking of the Job story. So much was clear in the 1955 sermon he gave at the First Church of Christ in Farmington, Connecticut, where he and Ada had been married thirty-nine years earlier. His text was the story of Job and "the question of belief in life." How was it possible, he asked, to "believe in the justice of God in a world in which the innocent perish in vast meaningless massacres, and brutal and dishonest men foul all the lovely things"? Such a belief was not possible, he concluded, nor was acceptance of God's will enough. "Love — love of life, love of the world, love of God, love in spite of everything — is the answer, the only possible answer, to our ancient human cry against injustice," he said. "Man, the scientists say, is the animal that thinks. They are wrong. Man is the animal that loves. It is in man's love that God exists and triumphs: in man's love that life is beautiful: in man's love that the world's injustice is resolved." Such a humanistic interpretation of Job was to cause a considerable furor in conventional religious circles when developed in MacLeish's play.

J.B. was published as a book in March 1958. The play, according to Charles Poore in the *New York Times,* fashioned "a remarkably compelling parable for our time" out of the biblical story. John Ciardi went further in the *Saturday Review of Literature,* hailing "the birth of a classic." *J.B.,* he said, was "great poetry, great drama, and . . . great stagecraft." In fact, MacLeish had created the first great poetic drama since Shakespeare. In the Sunday *Times,* Dudley Fitts substantially agreed. *J.B.,* he wrote, "is a signal contribution to the small body of modern poetic drama, and it may very well turn out to be an enduring one."

For the skeptical and cynical, such praise smacked of literary logrolling. It remained to be seen how the drama would actually *play* on stage, after all. Early in April *J.B.* had its first public airing in six performances at the Yale University theater. Student actors were used, and the play was directed by F. Curtis Canfield, dean of the Yale School of Drama. According to Charles A. Fenton's review, the academic and intellectual members of the opening night audience arrived with "an air of expectant cannibalism." They did not expect to like *J.B.*, yet most of them went away acknowledging that the play was good theater — in Fenton's words, "a fine display of a writer of genuine intellectual substance who has nevertheless always remembered and created emotion." Brooks Atkinson, the *Times* drama reviewer, introduced himself to MacLeish afterwards. "I just wanted to tell you that's a great play," he said. The same message appeared under his byline in the next morning's newspaper. "Using the Book of Job as a story of mankind," Atkinson observed, "MacLeish has written the fable of our time in verse that has the pulse and beat of modern living. In form, it is theater. In content, it is truth on a scale far above the usual dimension of our stage."

Among those who read this rave was the producer Alfred ("Delly") de Liagre, Jr. He drove up to New Haven for the second night, and on the way back to New York told his wife he'd like to do *J.B.* on Broadway. "You must be out of your mind," she told him. "It's poetry, it's the Bible, it's heavy — on Broadway?" Delly decided to go ahead, though he had considerable trouble arranging financing. Among the investors were Clare Boothe Luce and Paul Mellon, who had met Archie in Antigua. Once that hurdle was crossed, Delly signed Elia ("Gadge") Kazan as director. MacLeish and Kazan got along extremely well from the beginning. Archie respected Kazan as, in his words, "the great director of the generation," the man who had made Tennessee Williams's plays sing on the stage. Kazan liked MacLeish for his Yankee forthrightness and his willingness, at sixty-six, to throw himself into the work required to achieve a success on Broadway.

Unquestionably Gadge Kazan was a directorial genius, with a gift for composing visibly and audibly on the stage. Kazan felt no special affinity for *J.B.*, he said, but was attracted by the challenge of presenting a verse drama on Broadway. More than anyone else, he was responsible for making *J.B.* graphic and stageworthy. The inherent drama came from the Bible by way of MacLeish.

In the opening scene, two out-of-work ham actors — Mr. Zuss (Zeus) and Nickles (Old Nick) — appear under a huge circus tent. Initially they peddle balloons and popcorn, but when they put on the masks of God and Satan from the properties trunk, they enter into those roles and re-enact the famous wager about Job. Will he, under affliction beyond bearing, curse God and die? The Job of this modern play is J.B., a New England banker-millionaire. He and his family are presented at Thanksgiving dinner. His wife, Sarah, we learn through conversation, believes that the good things of life have come to them as rewards for their

obedience to divine will. J.B. disagrees. The world is too wonderful for
deserving.

> Nobody deserves it, Sarah:
> Not the world that God has given us.

Patently, that speech signals the dramatic irony ahead. But it also
foreshadows the point that if the good things are not a reward, neither
is affliction a punishment. Once Zuss and Nickles strike their bargain,
the afflictions come thick and hard. J.B. and Sarah have five hardy
children. The eldest, a soldier, is killed as the result of a military blunder.
Another son and a daughter die in an automobile accident caused by a
drunken driver. The youngest daughter is raped and murdered by a drug
addict, and the remaining daughter perishes in an atomic bomb explosion
that destroys J.B.'s bank and his millions. J.B. himself survives, but is
in constant pain from boils all over his body. Still, he will not curse
God, and in disgust Sarah leaves him.

At this point J.B. is visited by the three false comforters. Each of them,
in his own way, tempts J.B. to escape from responsibility by adopting
a philosophy of determinism. Zophar, the fat priest, tells him that all
men are innately sinful. Eliphaz, a psychiatrist in a dirty intern's coat,
says guilt is a "Psychophenomenal situation — / An illusion, a disease,
a sickness" that all men suffer from. Bildad the Marxist contends that
history goes its own way and cannot be altered. J.B.'s timing is bad; he
was born in the "wrong class — wrong century." None of these comforters offer any solace to J.B. He rejects them outright as denying free
will and dignity to man. He also rejects Nickles's tempting suggestion
that he relieve his suffering through suicide. Zuss, it appears, has won
his bet, but the victory is not the canonical one, for MacLeish has shifted
the emphasis of his play from the splendor of God and his creation to
the splendor of man in accepting a brutally unjust and apparently meaningless creation. Finally, it is J.B. who forgives God for making such a
universe. As Zuss puts it, with wonder:

> . . . In spite of everything he'd suffered!
> In spite of all he'd lost and loved
> He understood and he forgave it! . . .

What enables J.B. to forgive God is his capacity to love. At the end,
when Sarah returns to him and they start to rebuild their shattered lives,
she speaks the coda:

> Blow on the coal of the heart.
> The candles in churches are out.
> The lights have gone out in the sky.

Blow on the coal of the heart
And we'll see by and by . . .

J.B.: Broadway

Transplanting *J.B.* from its printed form (the form in which it was played at Yale) to a drama palatable to the taste of Broadway theatergoers took some doing. With the help of Kazan and de Liagre, Archie tenderly pruned and grafted until his play came abloom on the stage. He was in on the process all the way, from the selection of the cast through rehearsals and the out-of-town tryout in Washington to an opening night that happened to fall when the New York daily newspapers were on strike.

The star of the play was Christopher Plummer as Nickles. Plummer fit the character: he had the sort of clever mind that Nickles himself did. Moreover, he was trained in Shakespeare and read his verse lines beautifully, without making the mistake of trying to convert them into prose. Not that Kazan wanted a Shakespearean sound exactly. *J.B.* is full of contemporary language and punning wit, despite its somber subject matter. Archie was trying to write poetry that could be lifted off the page and delivered onstage without demanding an audience trained in apprehending the subtleties of unrhymed verse. At the first rehearsal Kazan told Plummer to read some Jack Kerouac, whose Beat novel *On the Road* had appeared the previous year. MacLeish's voice lay somewhere between that of the bard and the Beat.

If Plummer was perfect as Nickles, in MacLeish's view Raymond Massey was nearly disastrous as Mr. Zuss. Best known for his title role in *Abe Lincoln in Illinois,* Massey was "a monument of egotism in a field where everybody is an egotist," Archie said. The actor insisted on the largest dressing room, and objected to equal billing with the two other principals. He made disparaging remarks about the play and his fellow professionals. He brought to his role a degree of pomposity that went well beyond what was written into the part. When some of his lines were cut in rehearsal, he threatened to sabotage the play. Archie learned to detest him.

To start with, de Liagre tried to get Laurence Olivier to play J.B. When Olivier proved unavailable, Kazan suggested that they audition Pat Hingle, an actor from Texas appearing in *The Dark at the Top of the Stairs,* the William Inge play Kazan was directing. At the audition, Hingle read a scene with Nan Martin, who was to play Sarah. Afterwards there was a voice from the darkness.

"Do you think you can play J.B.?" MacLeish asked.

"I *know* I can play J.B.," Hingle answered.

"That's a very J.B.-like response," MacLeish said.

Hingle got the part. Although he was not expert at speaking verse, his gruffness and "moral depth" made him ideal for the role of J.B., MacLeish thought. It was a milestone in Hingle's career, the first time he'd had star billing on Broadway. Two months into the run, however, he suffered "a very J.B.-like" accident. Coming home to his apartment after a night on the town with Plummer, he fell three flights out of a stalled elevator. The little finger of his left hand was torn off, and his left wrist and left foot were fractured. James Daly replaced him in the cast, and it was two years before Hingle could resume his career.

At the first meeting of the cast, Kazan asked MacLeish to read his play from start to finish. The director wanted his actors to hear the poetry of the play from the mouth of its sixty-six-year-old Pulitzer Prize-winning author. Some who worked on the play regarded Archie with a respect bordering on awe. MacLeish looked like "the president," thought young David Amram, who wrote the music for the play. When Archie asked Hingle to address him by his first name, the actor found he could not. "Mr. MacLeish," he said, "I was reared in a way and at a time that makes it impossible for me to call you anything but Mr. MacLeish." Still a sense of camaraderie developed during the months prior to opening. MacLeish always came to rehearsals, where he established a byplay with a man named Chink who had several tough cues in the lights far above the stage. And he turned up occasionally at the evening jam sessions featuring Amram on French horn, Hingle on harmonica, and Plummer on piano.

Necessarily, MacLeish's closest relationship was with Kazan. Their collaborative efforts peaked during the two-week tryout in Washington in late November 1958. By that time MacLeish had learned to trust Kazan's theatrical instincts. After reading over the play half a dozen times, for example, Kazan saw that Nickles was a young man and must be played that way. "Life to Nickles is disgusting, a miserable, horrible thing," Kazan said. "He hates life. That's kid's talk, not an old man's." Archie said, "My eyes are opened." When the cast arrived in Washington, it was soon clear that further eye opening was required. Specifically, the second act needed work. The published version of the play consisted of eleven scenes, but these were compressed into the usual two-act format for Broadway. Kazan felt there might be problems in the first act, with audiences benumbed by the series of catastrophes that descend upon J.B. In Washington, however, the audience was clearly moved by the first act and grew restive in the second. The basic problem was that the play was about J.B., and in the second act he too often functioned as a mere listening post.

Three specific changes, each of them involving substantial rewriting, were made to humanize J.B. First, instead of having him crawl ignominiously from one comforter to another, the priest and psychologist and communist come to him. Second, the climactic "Blow on the coal of the heart" speech was shifted from Sarah to J.B. Archie resisted this change, but bowed to Kazan's sense of stagecraft. It was wrong, Kazan argued, to let the conclusion of the play be Sarah's instead of J.B.'s. But wasn't that true of the lives of most men? Archie objected. Perhaps, Kazan said, "but in the theatre you've got to end the play you've begun, not some other play." Finally, and in MacLeish's opinion most crucially, the "recognition scene" was altered.

This scene comes late in the play, after the rejection of the comforters, when the Distant Voice of God in all his magnificence and power addresses J.B. in the form of a whirlwind. "Where wast thou when I laid the foundations?" the Distant Voice demands. Appropriately humbled, J.B. then reaches a wider recognition. Yes, he is puny in the cosmic scale of the universe, where God maintains a majestic indifference to human suffering. Yet J.B. also realizes, in MacLeish's words, "the *significance* of that insignificance. He is at least *a man*," and in his humanity will struggle "to accept life again, which means . . . to risk himself in love." As originally written, the protagonist's reaction to the Distant Voice was muted behind a philosophical discussion between Mr. Zuss and Nickles. J.B. has so little to say, in fact, that director Kazan had him turn his back to the audience.

On a cold bright morning the day before Thanksgiving, MacLeish and Kazan walked round and round the park in front of the White House puzzling over this scene. Eventually they concurred that much of the talk between Zuss and Nickles would have to be cut and that J.B. must face the audience and speak lines that signaled his growth in understanding. These changes — and still others — meant that Archie was constantly working into the night in order to have revisions ready for the next day's rehearsal and performance. And, of course, it was considerably more difficult to write these in verse than in prose. Amram recalled seeing MacLeish one morning, dapper in black turtleneck sweater and tweed coat yet uncharacteristically unshaven. "I've been up all night, working on the play," Archie explained. Things got so bad that when he ran across Kazan and de Liagre in the hallway of the Jefferson Hotel one morning, Archie spied the sheaf of notes Delly was carrying and blanched. "I hope those notes aren't for me," he said, "because if they are, I'm going to go right upstairs and cry."

The sheer effort MacLeish put into revising *J.B.* amazed Gadge Kazan. "In Washington on the way to Broadway," he said, "we were in very serious trouble. Time was running out." The whole process — writing under pressure against a deadline — might have daunted a younger man, and it was new to MacLeish, who had never been on the road with a play before. But Archie did the job by working day and night. "Those two weeks in the pressure cooker made Archie and me friends forever," Kazan said. Despite the alterations made in Washington, the company was far from confident as they took the train for New York. "Well, this is just going to be a tax loss," people were saying. "It may read beautifully and win some prizes, but Broadway audiences aren't going to like it." They could not have been more wrong.

J.B. opened at the ANTA Theater on Fifty-second Street west of Broadway on Thursday night, December 11, 1958. Although opening night was sold out, there was no advance sale to speak of for later performances, and no theater parties had been signed up. So producer de Liagre opened with nothing in the till, and then the newspapers went out on strike. It seemed to Delly that the afflictions of J.B. were being visited on him. "I might just as well go out there and play J.B. myself," he thought.

Still, de Liagre, MacLeish, and others did what they could to compensate for the lack of the newspaper reviews generally thought essential to generating ticket sales. Archie called his friend Ed Murrow and asked him to see that the play was mentioned on CBS radio. John Mason Brown, an ally of Archie's in the drive for a theater building at Harvard, was enlisted to do what he could. But the most important word would come from the regular newspaper reviewers, who during the strike delivered their notices on radio and television around midnight after the opening. The cast gathered in a Chinese restaurant to await these reviews, and cheered as one after another of New York's hard-boiled critics praised the play. MacLeish was up a few hours later to appear on Dave Garroway's *Today* show on NBC television. The night before, he hadn't quite realized how wonderful the reviews were, particularly Brooks Atkinson's for the *Times*. When announcer Frank Blair read it for the national television audience, Archie thought he was going to weep out of a mixture of fatigue and joy. Under the circumstances, it did not bother him that he was preceded by Miss Florida and followed by a trained porpoise, nor that the network broke for a commercial just as he was trying to explain J.B.'s response to the Voice of God.

"For *J.B.*, the title of Archibald's MacLeish's new play at the ANTA theater, read Everyman," Atkinson's review began. "Looking around at the wreckage and misery of the modern world, Mr. MacLeish has written a fresh and exalting morality play that has great stature. In an inspired performance on Thursday evening, it seemed to be one of the memorable works of the century as verse, as drama and as spiritual inquiry." There was no topping such praise: Atkinson had elevated the admiration he expressed for *J.B.* in New Haven to the highest possible plane. The other reviewers were also enthusiastic. John McClain of the *Journal American* wrote that if he were called on to vote "for the best play of this or, perhaps, many seasons," he would cast his ballot for *J.B.* "A brilliant production," Richard Watts of the *Post* declared. "MacLeish's dramatic parable combines theatrical effectiveness and rueful lyric brooding on good and evil in the world with impressive power." Several of the reviewers considered the play a milestone in the history of Broadway: a serious drama on an important philosophical theme, in verse, that could yet appeal to the broad tastes of ordinary theatergoers. Walter Kerr of the *Herald Tribune* sounded the sole note of reservation, writing that although the play was "enormously impressive," it was basically a masque, with the actors so generalized that they rarely displayed "the small, painful reflex that betrays private and personal feeling."

Radio, television, and word of mouth more than made up for the silence of the newspapers. By midday after the opening, people were lining up around the block to buy tickets for *J.B.* The play ran for a year on Broadway, and for another year on the road. It won both the Pulitzer Prize (MacLeish's third) and the Tony Award, with Kazan taking the Tony for best director. It was translated into dozens of languages, and produced with great success in several countries, most notably in Germany. The play became a staple of college and university repertoires for many years. Even apart from royalties for the stage production, the published version of *J.B.* earned more than the rest of MacLeish's books combined.

To bolster the audience during the early weeks of the Broadway run, MacLeish, Kazan, and de Liagre held seminars after the performance, where theatergoers — sometimes as many as one hundred of them — could stay to discuss the play they had just witnessed. *J.B.* opened up several avenues of discussion and disagreement. One phrase — the first two lines of Nickles's jingle about J.B. — stuck in almost everyone's mind:

> *If God is God He is not good,*
> *If God is good He is not God;*
> *Take the even, take the odd,*
> *I would not sleep here if I could*
> *Except for the little green leaves in the wood*
> *And the wind on the water.*

There the play's overriding question is addressed: How can the indifference of God be justified? The audacity of the challenge troubled many a religious viewer or reader. Twice before, MacLeish had taken the biblical story of the Garden of Eden and transformed it into his personal vision of the relationship between humankind and nature, and between man and woman. But these were in books of verse — *Nobodaddy* and *Songs for Eve* — which reached only the poetry-reading public. In *J.B.*, Archie took similar liberties with the Book of Job, and did so for an audience in the hundreds of thousands. Many of these were disturbed by the humanistic, extrabiblical meanings he imposed on the story of Job. In the biblical story, God feels sure that Job will resign himself to the divine will and accept his afflictions; Satan argues that he will defy God and curse him. In MacLeish's play, neither is right. J.B. does not accept and he does not defy. He simply decides to love life despite its obvious evils. Moreover, the God of the play, neither omniscient nor loving, represents a kind of life force immanent everywhere in the universe, possessed of great power yet hardly to be held accountable for the haphazard triumphs of good over evil, or vice versa.

To some extent, MacLeish attempted in advance to deflect the anticipated criticism from religious circles. He intended no trespass against sacred territory, he wrote in the December 7, 1958, *New York Times*, before the play opened.

> I have constructed a modern play inside the ancient majesty of the Book of Job much as the Bedouins, thirty years ago, used to build within the towering ruins of Palmyra their shacks of gasoline tins roofed with fallen stones.
>
> The Bedouins had the justification of necessity and I can think of nothing better for myself. When you are dealing with questions too large for you, which, nevertheless, will not leave you alone, you are obliged to house them somewhere — and an old wall helps.

J.B. aroused secular as well as theological objections. Basically, these held that the conclusion was too easily arrived at and more sentimental than convincing, that the questions the play raised could not be dismissed by J.B.'s willingness to start over again out of love, despite knowing that meaningless catastrophes might strike him at any moment. As one critic observed, "MacLeish has not been able to avoid the greatest cliché of the fifties, the conviction that love cures boils." Robert Frost — who had himself adapted the Book of Job in his *Masque of Reason* (1945) — agreed. "People think everything is solved by love, but maybe just as many things are solved by hate," he said of *J.B.* Envy may have colored Frost's judgment, as it did that of a Harvard colleague of Archie's who acknowledged that he might have liked the play better if it hadn't been such a success.

Perhaps the greatest shortcoming of the play, aesthetically, was that it failed to translate its drama into individual human terms. Thus Archie's student Elizabeth Marshall Thomas went to see it, hoping to be stirred, and came away disappointed. It was hard to identify with J.B., who begins as a generically successful businessman and becomes a similarly stylized victim. The problem lay in the conception. In *J.B.*, as in most of his poetry, MacLeish was speaking to the generalized human condition. As John Gassner perceptively noted, it was "plainly a morality play, and to require it to provide rounded characters is to ask for something that MacLeish did not intend. It is a contemporary *Everyman* that is half poem and half discussion drama." On those grounds alone, though, he regarded the production of *J.B.* as "one of the two or three truly important events in the mid-century American drama."

Farewells

The tremendous effort Archie put into *J.B.* took its toll. By February 1959 he was experiencing cardiovascular spasms in Antigua, and was commanded by his doctor to take things easy. The medical troubles were hardly surprising, he wrote de Liagre. "I worked harder last summer and fall than I ever worked in my bubbling youth and something had to give somewhere." With rest, the spasms passed, and in the spring Archie was able to speak at a retirement ceremony at Columbia honoring Mark Van Doren. It had taken them almost half a century to meet, MacLeish pointed out, but he and Mark had a great deal in common. Both had been born and raised in Illinois, and both settled in the hills "about as far from Illinois as [they] could get in a northeasterly direction." More important, they shared the profession of teaching and the art of poetry. So when they finally did "fall in together," they recognized each other at once and realized they "had been friends all their lives." Archie praised Van Doren for the distinct presence of his voice in his poems. More and more as he grew older, MacLeish said, he found himself listening for the human speaking voice in poetry. "A poem is a poet's saying and his voice is in it or it is dead." The poetry of Mark Van Doren lived, for the voice it spoke with was unmistakably his.

Mark and Dorothy Van Doren suffered a Job-like blow of their own in November 1959 when their son Charles, an assistant professor of English at Columbia, confessed that he had participated in rigging the NBC television show "Twenty-One." The younger Van Doren was a successful contestant on the quiz show, where he astounded millions of viewers by his ability to call up answers to difficult questions on the spur of the moment. Word leaked out, however, that he had been coached in advance by the show's producer, and even instructed in how to deliver his answers for maximum entertainment impact. This was devastating news for his parents, and particularly for his father, who was revered at Columbia as a benevolent, honorable, and intellectually stimulating teacher, one who had served as a role model to decades of students. Yet when Mark and Dorothy came to visit the MacLeishes in Antigua a few months later, they betrayed no bitterness. The Van Dorens "are really wonderful people," Ada wrote Sara Murphy. "They in no way condone what Charlie did but they stand by with love."

Archie himself was approaching his own retirement from Harvard, scheduled by academic fiat for 1962, when he reached seventy. In the fall of 1959, he abandoned his usual poetry course, in which the students' cards shaped much of the discussion, for a final series of half a dozen lectures. A crowd of more than nine hundred assembled on October 21 for the first of these, "Words as Sounds." The lecture was moved from the Lamont Library's Forum Room to Emerson D, but even that larger room accommodated only half of those who came to hear MacLeish. The young and nimble got in; four hundred others did not. A seat was reserved for Ada, but she gave it up. As she walked outside, she saw a student hanging from the windows. "What's going on in there?" a passer-by yelled up to him. "The second coming," the student in the window replied.

Though hardly godlike, MacLeish in Jack Bate's estimation was one of the finest lecturers he'd ever heard. He was equipped with a remarkable speaking voice, and understood the uses of the pause. Bate once saw Archie's lecture notes, marked up into long and short sentences and indicating pauses between them. The effect on his listeners could be almost hypnotic, Bate said.

In those 1959 lectures Archie was summing up what he had learned about poetry "in half a century of practicing it and a dozen years of trying to teach it." These insights were then assembled into *Poetry and Experience,* published early in 1961. Therein he worked out his theory of poetry, which did away with the traditional dichotomy between the world of art and the world of action. In MacLeish's formulation, the nature of poetry demanded that its practitioners combat the social evils they encountered. "It is true enough that a poet, an artist, serves his art and not a cause. He goes his own way with his own will beside him and his own truth to find. But on the great issue, on the issue of man, his truth and the truth of history are one." The business of poetry was to communicate such truth, not the rational scientific knowledge of science but the intuited knowledge derived from one person's particular experience, yet universally resonant.

MacLeish had left the doctrine of his 1926 "Ars poetica" behind him.

A poem should not only be, but mean. Poems could not rightly be compared to "globed fruit" or "old medallions," for Archie no longer thought of them as objects but as actions. In his 1958 talk "Poetry and Journalism," he spelled out this conviction. "Great poems are instruments of knowledge — a knowledge carried alive into the heart by passion, but knowledge nevertheless. Feeling without knowing never made a work of art and never will." But he also warned against the modern tendency toward the opposite pole of trying to acquire knowledge without feeling. "To feel emotion is at least to feel. The crime against life, the worst of all crimes, is not to feel. And there was never, perhaps, a civilization in which that crime, the crime of torpor, of lethargy, of apathy, the snake-like sin of coldness-at-the-heart, was commoner than in our technological civilization."

"There is the writer here," he observed in the opening chapter of *Poetry and Experience*. "And over there, there is 'the mystery of the universe.'" The world might seem meaningless and mute, but the poet was to "struggle . . . until he can force it to mean." Part of the meaning depended on the sound of the poem, for poetry "cannot be removed from the structure of sound without crumbling away." Change the sound, and the meaning would be altered, or lost entirely.

Designed to communicate knowledge through experience, the poem must still work by indirection. In this connection Archie recalled what Oppenheimer had said at Eliot House about the difference between science and poetry. "In science you try to say what nobody has known before in such a way that everybody will understand it, whereas in poetry . . . ," Oppie said, then "stalked out to a chorus of applauding laughter." "Precisely!" MacLeish's colleague I. A. Richards said when he heard about the story. "In poetry you *do* try to say what everybody has 'known before' in such a way that nobody will 'understand' it," at least not in the sense of rational understanding. Logic did not enter into the equation at all. In MacLeish's opinion, what replaced it in poetry was imagery, the juxtaposition of images in unexpected ways that enabled readers to "feel a knowledge which we cannot think." To illustrate his point, MacLeish called up the lovely old English song:

> O *westron wind when wilt thou blow*
> *That the small rain down can rain?*
> *Christ that my love were in my arms*
> *And I in my bed again.*

This is his interpretation, eloquent in its simplicity, of how the coupling of disparate images works in this poem: "Here the two little scenes of wind and weather and love and bed are left side by side to mean if they can. And they do mean. The poem is not a poem about one or the other. It is not a poem about weather. And neither is it a poem about making love. The emotion it holds is held between these two statements in the place where love and time cross each other."

Poetry and Experience is divided into two parts, the first summarizing Archie's theory of poetry and the second devoted to individual consideration of Dickinson, Yeats, Rimbaud, and Keats. As a work of criticism it is refreshingly available. "You can't realize as well as I do how beautifully deft, dramatic & swift it all is," Richards wrote MacLeish. Richards had reason to know, for he was teaching from Archie's book alongside the considerably more convoluted and opaque prose of the linguist Roman Jakobson. The critics, nevertheless, generally ignored *Poetry and Experience,* or regarded it as a self-justifying apologia.

Archie got considerably more attention from an NBC television play, *The Secret of Freedom,* which he put together on demand as a study of democracy in action. The play, with lead roles played by Thomas Mitchell, Tony Randall, and Kim Hunter, dramatized how the citizens of one small town (Mount Holly, New Jersey, was chosen as the site) overcame the forces of repression — specifically, as exemplified by anticommunists striving to censor books in the library and to get rid of liberal teachers in the high school. Producer Robert D. Graff claimed that MacLeish's play was "the toughest thing" he'd seen in his ten years in television. "Lots of people will agree with it; lots will hate it; lots will be deeply bothered in their bones." This overstated the case. As Archie himself said, *The Secret of Freedom* was really "a pure piece of propaganda on the side of the angels." Yet when this made-to-order drama was broadcast on Sunday evening February 28, 1960, millions of viewers watched, and thousands were moved to write letters to the network in response. "It left me feeling," Archie wrote, "that TV is too powerful a medium for the brains that are poured in at the broadcasting end. A really good play . . . might shake the country loose from its water-shed," but he was not prepared to write it.

Honors descended on MacLeish as he neared the end of his threescore years and ten. It was a quiet spring when he was not given an honorary degree or two, and several foreign governments bestowed their highest awards of recognition. (In the MacLeish collection at Greenfield Community College, there are hoods from thirty-seven different colleges and universities and dozens of medals.) With the election of John F. Kennedy to the presidency, Archie was once more a favored citizen of the government in power. He was one of four poets invited to the inaugural ceremonies in January 1961, and was on the guest list for the Kennedys' dinner in honor of André Malraux the following year.

In the spring of 1961, still other diversions awaited. In April the MacLeishes flew to Lisbon and drove through Spain to visit Rome, Florence, and southern Italy. Then they cruised around the Greek islands for two weeks with Larry and Roxanne Hammond and Jay and Lee Gould before ending their trip with a visit to Israel with Ken and Carolyn. At Harvard, Lillian Hellman occupied their quarters in Leverett Tower, a handsome flat that had been assigned to Archie and Ada when they switched allegiance — along with master John Conway — from Eliot to Leverett House. Hellman found nothing in the cupboards except a large supply of Metrecal, for Ada's diet. Later, when the Van Dorens used the MacLeish apartment during Mark's visiting appointment at Harvard, Archie left a well-stocked bar for their use. By the time the Van Dorens moved in, someone had pilfered the liquor. What remained, Dorothy Van Doren reported, were "two bourbon bottles, empty, one Dubonnet, empty, one vermouth, empty, and about an inch of Scotch in the Scotch bottle. Also six full bottles of soda water."

The MacLeishes were scarcely back from their journeys when word came of Hemingway's suicide on July 2, 1961. In a memorial piece for *Life*, Archie commented that "Hemingway's life was a strange life for a writer as we think of writers in our time. Writers with us are supposed to be watchers: 'God's spies' as John Keats put it once. . . . Hemingway was not a watcher: he was an actor in his life. He took part." Some of his greatness, MacLeish felt, derived from the intensity and courage with which he faced experience. But from the beginning of their friendship, Archie had known of Ernest's dark side, and it was the troubling chiaroscuro of his personality that MacLeish emphasized in his poem for the November 1961 *Atlantic*.

Hemingway
"In some inexplicable way an accident."
Mary Hemingway

Oh, not inexplicable. Death explains,
that kind of death: rewinds remembrance
backward like a film track till the laughing man
among the lilacs, peeling the green stem,
waits for the gunshot where the play began;

rewinds those Africas and Idahos and Spains
to find the table at the Closerie des Lilas,
sticky with syrup, where the flash of joy
flamed into blackness like that flash of steel.

The gun between the teeth explains.
The shattered mouth foretells the singing boy.

Curiously, those last two lines have the facts wrong, and have undoubtedly contributed to a widespread misapprehension. It was a shotgun blast to the forehead, not in the mouth, that killed Hemingway. Ernest's ghost lived on, nonetheless. Three years later, in *A Moveable Feast,* he spoke as from the grave about the early days in Paris. In a powerful passage near the end of that book, he expressly blames "the rich" for breaking up his idyllic marriage to Hadley. These undesignated homewreckers include not only Pauline Pfeiffer herself but Sara and Gerald Murphy and even John Dos Passos. "I don't think I've ever read anything that sickened me more," Archie wrote Carlos Baker about Ernest's attempt to absolve himself of all responsibility. "And not only because it's self-pity of the most nauseating kind but because it's self-delusion of the most degrading kind." He'd been using the phrase "sick at heart" all his life, Archie said. Never before had he understood what it meant.

Late in August, Archie survived a medical emergency of his own when his prostate was removed. There were no complications, and he recovered in time to undertake his last full semester of teaching at Harvard in September. During that fall Archie and Ada met Jill Ker, an Australian woman who was finishing her doctorate in history at Harvard and was engaged to marry John Conway. Jill had heard Archie read at Leverett House, an experience that deeply moved her. Still, she was hardly prepared for the charmed circle the MacLeishes had constructed for themselves, and their close friends, at Uphill Farm. John brought her to Conway, she recalled, "to meet the couple who were clearly his surrogate parents." Archie and Ada struck her as "exempt from age and infirmity," with more zest for living than people half their years. They seemed possessed of magical powers that enabled them to convert their life together into a work of art. For the next two decades the MacLeishes and the Conways were intimate friends who saw each other often, particularly after Jill became president of Smith College in nearby Northampton and she and John built a house in Conway.

MacLeish's departure from Harvard occasioned a series of farewells. He met his last class, the dozen students in English S, in December 1961. To them as to all his students, he declared his belief in the essential relevancy of what they were doing. " 'English' always stands with one foot in the text and one foot in the world, and what it undertakes to teach is neither the one nor the other but the relation between them."

Stephen Sandy, once his student in English S, was at the Signet Society when MacLeish made a valedictory speech there. Fifty men in evening clothes sat in a candlelit banquet room while MacLeish sang out an impassioned indictment of American selfishness. The theme moved the poet to think of his brother, who had died long ago in the service of an ideal: "My brother, my brother whom I loved, you are dead, so long dead. It is I who have stayed to fail and fail." He spoke of his old friendship with Hemingway, and read his poem about the gun between the teeth. When he was through, there was a three-minute standing ovation.

In an address to the department of English, MacLeish characterized himself as "a Michelmas swallow, a man-who-came-to-dinner, an inveterate amateur who was carried in on a Chair and out on a Statute" — the one that set seventy as mandatory retirement age. His colleague Howard Mumford Jones, who was also retiring, had been a famous scholar and teacher for half a century, and Archie for only a dozen years. In that short time, though, MacLeish had grown to love Harvard. There he found "a whole new world of friendship" in his fifties and sixties. There he had learned to take pride "in the mere fact of association" with men of intellectual passion and moral dignity.

There were those among his students who felt about MacLeish much as he did about Harvard. Walter Kaiser, his student in both English S and his poetry course, then his graduate assistant, and in due course his colleague as a young assistant professor, thought Archie one of the greatest teachers of all, not merely in the classroom but by the example of the integrity and commitment he brought to everything he did. "What he finally taught all of us, with both his life and his words," Kaiser said, "is the ultimate lesson we all thirst to learn: what it means to be a man."

Archie left the Boylston professorship with reluctance. At Harvard, as at the Library of Congress, Archie was unable to select his successor. He wanted Richard Wilbur to succeed him, but Wilbur was happily affiliated with Wesleyan and withdrew from consideration. Robert Fitzgerald was chosen the next Boylston professor.

Undoubtedly the most valuable legacy of MacLeish's Harvard years was the cadre of brilliant young writers he guided at the beginning of their careers. Retirement did not dim his interest in these young men and women; he kept in touch with many of his English S students for the rest of his life. And in the summer of 1961, he took on another writing student who presented himself for instruction outside academic channels entirely. This was Thomas H. ("Tom") Johnson, an aspiring poet who started corresponding with Archie while still in high school in northern Virginia. With his admission to West Point assured for the fall of 1961, Tom secured an appointment to see Archie in Conway before matriculating. The youth brought everything he had written with him, including a thirty-six-page poem. Archie read a seven-page segment of this opus, while Tom impatiently fumed around the music room at

Uphill Farm, wondering at Gerald Murphy's painting *The Wasp and the Pear* and reading the book titles on the shelves. At last the master was finished reading, and it seemed to Tom that his whole future depended on his verdict. Archie looked up from the script, fixed the boy with his eyes, and said, "You've certainly got a good ear for it." Tom nearly swooned with relief.

So commenced a mentor-pupil relationship that continued through Johnson's West Point years and into his distinguished career as author of poems for the nation's leading quarterlies and as professor of both English and physics at the U.S. Military Academy. After his junior year at West Point, Tom declared that he was ready to publish his poetry. Archie thought not, and made the lad promise to hold off a year then reread his poems and decide. It was a salutary delay. At the end of the waiting period, Tom scrapped most of what he had thought publishable a year before and revised the rest. From 1962 to 1968, Johnson went up to Conway once or twice a year to confer with Archie. Finally, during a lunch at New York's Century Club in the summer of 1968, MacLeish pronounced him graduated. "You have found your voice," he told Tom. When Norman Cousins stopped by their table to say hello, Archie introduced him as "the finest young poet in America." That was a day Tom Johnson did not forget.

23

POET LAUREATE

On the Road

THOUGH OFFICIALLY PASTURED OFF by Harvard, Mac-
Leish was far from ready to retire. Instead of lecturing in Cambridge,
he took his show on the road. Rarely was he so visible as a kind of
national resource as in the weeks and months immediately following his
seventieth birthday.

On July 4, 1962, *The American Bell* was presented for the first time
at Independence Hall in Philadelphia. The performance was neither play
nor pageant but an outdoor hybrid modeled after the *son et lumière*
productions in France. The city wanted such a production to commem-
orate the hanging of the Liberty Bell in Independence Hall, and enlisted
T. Edward Hambleton of the Phoenix Theater to produce it. Hambleton
in turn called on MacLeish to supply the voices and a rationale for the
show. He took the assignment, Archie said, because Independence Hall
was "holy ground" to him. It was there, the night before his inauguration
in 1861, that Abraham Lincoln made his speech articulating his interpretation of the Declaration of Independence.

Bell focused, logically enough, not on Lincoln in 1861 but on Jefferson
and John Adams and Tom Paine and Benjamin Franklin in 1776, while
they were in Philadelphia struggling toward a Declaration that would
satisfy them all. For the most part, Archie let these men speak for themselves, from their letters and the surviving documents. Julian Boyd, the
Jefferson scholar at Princeton, advised him on the selections. Then
MacLeish threaded these together with a narrative of his own that moved
the drama toward its climax with the signing of the Declaration and the

ringing of the Liberty Bell. Talented actors including Fredric March as narrator and E. G. Marshall as Jefferson taped their speeches, and these were blended into the music composed by David Amram and the colored lights exploring the facade of Independence Hall. Prices were kept low — $1.50 for adults, 75 cents for children — to encourage the largest possible audience. And the show was put on nightly until mid-October.

The *Philadelphia Inquirer* of July 5 was ecstatic about the opening of *Bell*. It was "an unforgettable experience to sit in the soft summer night" and watch and listen as history came alive. Archie himself felt that the *son et lumière* suffered from a shortage of visual effects. Unlike the magnificent chateaus along the Loire that the French used for their shows, Independence Hall was a rather small building and did not offer the same range of opportunities for the play of spotlights. Then, too, he thought Amram's music perhaps a trifle too intellectual for a drama aimed at so wide an audience. As far as MacLeish's career was concerned, *Bell* represented only the first of several attempts at dramatizing and celebrating the American past.

A month after the opening of *Bell*, CBS television showed a prime-time hour of MacLeish and Mark Van Doren in genial discussion. The project was initiated by Warren Bush, a producer at CBS News, who came to Archie and asked if he would participate in such a filmed discussion. That depended on with whom, Archie said. For two days in the middle of June, Bush's cameramen followed Archie and Mark around the house and grounds at Uphill Farm, staying as unobtrusive as possible as the two men talked of poetry and love and the American ideal, among other things. Bush then edited six hours of film down to a one-hour show, and used much of the rest in putting together a book, *The Dialogues of Archibald MacLeish and Mark Van Doren*.

Jack Gould, reviewing the television show for the *New York Times*, faulted certain aspects of the production but praised the network for its audacity in letting these two poets, scholars, Pulitzer Prize winners, and friends speak. The result "stood in refreshing contrast to the pedestrian tone of most TV dialogues," he pointed out. And he gave an example. Van Doren: "To let a day just go by, you know, it's a lovely thing . . . the day is more important than you are: sometimes you can appreciate that." MacLeish: "And you watch yourself drift down in the pool of the day." The conversation unconsciously emphasized the difference between the two men. Archie the Scotsman was all animation and nervous energy, eager to get on to the next thing. Mark the Dutchman seemed far more at peace with the world, and somehow wiser for it. To Jack Bate, it seemed that the dialogues were "all Archie." He was on his home ground, after all, so it was he who suggested when it was time to go in to lunch or to cocktails, or to tramp over to his stone work house. And it was Archie who swam in the upper pond while Mark watched, who caught a rainbow trout in his lower pond while Mark looked on.

As for the conversation, it was not quite unrehearsed. Both men had enough advance notice to establish in broad outline what they intended to talk about and to think of what they wanted to say. Yet the obvious warmth between them kept the talk from degenerating into any kind of competitive show of erudition or eloquence. The talk was "good talk, relaxed, amiable, wide-ranging, wise without being sententious, witty without seeming rigged or contrived," Carlos Baker wrote, and this was because of the obvious "shared liking and respect of the two men." In one of the most moving passages of the *Dialogues,* Archie concludes that what he really believes in "is the unspeakable, infinite, immeasurable, spiritual capacity of that thing called a man; a capacity which . . . expresses itself nowhere more perfectly than in the capacity for friendship, which is really a capacity for love." And what he meant by love was "not the love that desires something for itself, but the kind of relationship which gives itself in praise and wonder and awe."

With Van Doren as with no one else, the friendship that was love deepened and deepened. After reading the proofs of the *Dialogues,* Archie wrote Mark that it "has throughout a sweet smell. These two characters are FOR things. They believe in life and know why. They love their wives. They care seriously about poetry. And under and over it all their affection and respect for each other makes a wonderful rosy aspic." And he wrote him with tenderness when Mark was ailing. "Don't leave me, dear friend, unless they promise you better quarters elsewhere. And even then, consider that there's not apt to be . . . anything lovelier anywhere than this small earth." On his part, Van Doren saluted some of his friend's virtues. Archie, he wrote, "is quick in kindness, dexterous with wine, and a connoisseur of chicken. . . . He is funny, he is serious, he is affectionate all at once, in a fashion I have never encountered elsewhere, and I cannot doubt that it exists only in him."

At a White House dinner soon after his election, President John F. Kennedy offhandedly asked Archie, "Why don't you move down here to inspire us all?" Kennedy appointed him special ambassador from the United States for the inauguration of the Colombian president, Dr. Guillermo Leon Valencia, on August 6–9, 1962. And Archie was tapped to write a poem for the one hundredth anniversary of the Emancipation Proclamation. During the ceremony at the Lincoln Memorial, Archie read his poem, Mahalia Jackson sang, Thurgood Marshall spoke, and the Marine Band played a composition by Ulysses Kay, but all of them were drowned out by the airplanes taking off from National Airport.

During the fall months MacLeish was often on the road. He read his poems or gave speeches or accepted awards at Milwaukee and Charlotte and Hartford and Mexico City and Tulsa and Berkeley and Savannah, at Rockford, Illinois, and Fitchburg, Massachusetts, at Brockport and Geneva, New York, at the Cosmos Club and the Century Club, at Yale and the Hill School and Hobart and William Smith Colleges and the University of Pennsylvania. Everywhere he went, he drew crowds. In mid-October 1962 he gave a reading at Penn. When Professor Sculley Bradley of the English department arrived with Archie in tow, they found the auditorium jammed, with "hundreds of undergraduates filling the lobbies and storming the doors." Recognizing MacLeish, the massed undergraduates practically prostrated themselves to let him pass into the auditorium. In a letter to the campus newspaper, Bradley said that he had been officially involved in the visits of many speakers, including "statesmen and athletes, administrators and rulers of finance, evangelists and politicians." It gave him some pleasure "to realize that a poet [was] the only one of those speakers who had to break into his own lecture in order to give it."

Some of MacLeish's reputation derived from his longevity. He was reaching an age when, as one of the survivors, he was increasingly summoned to speak or write about old friends who had died. From Paris word reached Archie that Sylvia Beach, proprietor of the Shakespeare and Company bookstore, had suffered a heart attack and died alone in her apartment. No, MacLeish insisted, she was "not alone, then or ever. She had that Company around her." Eleanor Roosevelt's passing he commemorated in an article for the *Nation*. Mrs. Roosevelt was not a public figure like her husband, he wrote, and yet he supposed that she was known — recognized and remembered — by more human beings than any other woman in history. She was famous not because "what she did was useful and generous and good" but because she saw the world in human terms. "No problem was big enough to become abstract to her — not even the problem of a world full of underfed children or exploited women. . . . She felt what she thought. And she made others feel it." In praising Mrs. Roosevelt, Archie was paying homage close to home. Eleanor Roosevelt was exactly the kind of woman his mother had been.

Family Pictures

With his Harvard days at an end, MacLeish spent more time in Conway than ever before. There, Ada fashioned an almost perfectly ordered life for them. She ran the household with the aid of the domestic help the MacLeishes always managed to afford, even in the bad times. Nellie Foster, a local woman of considerable culinary talent, cooked for them from 1958 to 1976. Maids came and went, including one who used to chat with guests as she served them. As she presented dessert one evening, she began to reminisce about the day her husband died. She'd just given him a piece of pumpkin pie, she said, and he ate it and passed away.

Unlike some of Conway's summer visitors, Archie actually worked around the place, and dressed for the part. After the morning's writing in his stone house, he liked to drive down to the post office to collect his mail and chat with postmaster Sid St. Peter. After lunch, he would do whatever outdoor chores needed doing. The local residents took some time to discover they had an important person in their midst, and when they did, they were pleased to learn that, like them, he wore work clothes and hats to ward off the sun, that he worked with his hands and knew how to farm as well as how to make verses.

Tall tales sprang up about MacLeish's incessant work habits. According to one such legend, a passing car slowed down one afternoon as Archie was mowing the lawn in his jeans and work shirt. "Excuse me, my good man," the tourist inquired, "is this where Archibald MacLeish lives?" "Yup," said Archie. "Is he in the house?" "Nope." In an alternative story, the driver slowed down to compliment Archie on his lawnmowing and to try to hire him. "You do a good job on that lawn. Are you available on Thursdays?"

As always, though, MacLeish's most important work was done mornings, alone — with nature — in the stone house.

> An apple-tree, a cedar and an oak
> Grow by the stone house in the rocky field
> Where I write poems when my hand's in luck.
> The cedar I put in: the rest are wild —
>
> Wind dropped them. Apples strew the autumn ground
> With black, sweet-smelling pips. The oak strews air,
> Summers with shadow, winters with harsh sound.
> The cedar's silent with its fruit to bear.

What MacLeish did in his stone house remained a mystery to many of his fellow townspeople. A local story has it that a neighbor boy, walking across the field one morning, spied an old man in work clothes sitting inside, staring vacantly out the window while he gnawed on a crust of bread. The lad ran home to report that he'd seen a poor starving derelict.

Conway was a poor town of about one thousand citizens, most of them farmers, supplemented in the 1960s and 1970s by an influx of academics and artists associated with the growing Five Colleges in and around Amherst. In their last decade the MacLeishes saw a great deal of Conway summer residents John and Jill Conway, but otherwise most of their friends came from Boston or New York or Washington. Archie and Ada made very few friends in the Conway community, and neither did their children, growing up. To a considerable extent he repeated his own father's behavior, so that Uphill Farm resembled an eastern version of Craigie Lea, situated on a hill instead of a bluff but still a kind of manor house of the village. During the summer months they naturally saw a great deal of Ishbel and Alec Campbell, who occupied their house at Downdale whenever academic duties permitted. Archie and his sister remained close friends, and Alec's wit enlivened family gatherings.

The MacLeishes were on excellent terms with the Warren Harrises, their farming neighbors a mile down Pine Hill Road, but it was the sort of relationship in which the lord of the manor occasionally demonstrated his benevolence. When the Harrises' daughter Christine asked him to read a poem to her second-grade class, Archie did so. And he helped see to it that their son Warren Eddy was admitted to Deerfield Academy. A different relationship developed with Lydie Keith of Deerfield, who was so entranced by J.B. that she felt she had to meet its author, living only a few miles away. She called Ada, arranged a dinner party, and established a lasting friendship with the MacLeishes.

Otherwise, much of their social life, summers, was built around those who came to the hills to escape the heat. Richard and Charlee Wilbur would drive over from Cummington, or Ken and Kitty Galbraith down from Newfane, Vermont, for a long lunch with talk of politics and writing. Those were "glowing journeys," Galbraith recalled, and May Sarton used the same image for a day at Uphill Farm so perfect that she did not dare go back. It was late June, with the lilacs in bloom. She and Archie went for a swim in the pond, followed by an alfresco lunch in the garden with the bottle of Montrachet she had brought along. There were just the three of them — Archie and Ada and May — and everything seemed "aglow." When it was time to leave, the MacLeishes said, "You must come back," and May said, "Of course," but knew she would not, for it could never have been so good again.

For somewhat larger gatherings on a weekend, the MacLeishes developed the tradition of the Pond Picnic. Archie would drive the car, laden with food and drink, to the pond half a mile away, while the guests walked down. At the pond there was a small hut for utensils and a grill. The menu was invariably the same. Archie grilled the hamburgers, using half a bag of charcoal and producing meat crusty on the outside and juicy underneath. Golden Bantam corn from the vegetable garden was picked at the last moment to be served "palpitating from the stalk."

While the food was in preparation, everyone drank a concoction of grapefruit juice, Beefeaters' gin, mint, and sugar. Afterwards there was chocolate cake, and, for most, a time to lie back and gaze at the sky through the leaves.

The invariable ritual of the Pond Picnic reflected the MacLeishes' pattern for entertaining. At dinner parties a charmingly formal aspect prevailed, with Archie and Ada dressing up for the occasion. Though stout, Ada managed to look "absolutely stunning" in her clothes, Jill Conway observed, while Archie might appear in a Japanese kimono, in kilts, or in a velvet dinner jacket. If guests were invited for 7 P.M., they were expected to arrive at that hour. After dinner, Ada would choose the music for coffee and cordials. Everything proceeded smoothly, as the MacLeishes wanted it to, and yet they themselves were far from stuffy, ever ready to laugh out loud. Liquor paved the way for this conviviality. Archie invariably made stiff drinks, his son Bill said, since this was one of the tests that people of a certain station and background were supposed to be able to pass. For those who passed the test, a dinner party — or better, a weekend — at Uphill Farm could be one of the pleasantest experiences of their lives. For weekend visitors, the festivities began at cocktail hour on Friday. Saturday morning was free time, while Archie repaired to his stone house to write. In the afternoon, guests embarked on long walks or participated in croquet. After a gala Saturday night, Archie was back in the stone house the next morning, emerging in time to bid the visitors adieu shortly after noon. Archie and Ada sent everyone off with "a wonderful lift," John Conway said. "I never stayed at a house that was so lively and happy and gay."

Archie grew more uxorious, and more public in his praise of Ada, as they approached their golden wedding anniversary. "You and I have two of the only really permanent marriages in America," he said to Mark Van Doren in 1962. "They ought to be visited like holy shrines." Persistently he cautioned young writers against divorce. As he wrote Ted Hoagland, "A writer needs a wife — a good wife — a true wife. . . . Otherwise he is too naked, too exposed. When I married mine I had that sense of someone always *with* me which you lack." And it was only in the long term, he felt, that one could learn about love. "You have to *live* relationships to *know*. Which is why a lifetime marriage with a woman you love is a great gift, and five marriages in a raddled row is a disaster to everyone, including the marrier."

Twenty-six old friends assembled for the fiftieth wedding anniversary in June 1966. As a present the MacLeishes gave themselves a swimming pool adjoining the house. There were three parties in two days, and at the last of these — a dinner party at Uphill Farm — Archie fought back the tears to deliver a tribute to Ada. Many regarded the love of an old man and an old woman as laughable, or even nasty, he knew. But it seemed to him that love grew "dearer toward the dark." What happened was that "you move into a period in which the presence of the other person is not as important as the foreseeing of [her] absence . . . fear of loss can be even more poignant than longing for presence."

This theme Archie stressed in one of the several poems about love and marriage he wrote in the mid-1960s.

> *Everything they know they know together —*
> *everything, that is, but one:*
> *their lives they've learned like secrets from each other;*
> *their deaths they think of in the nights alone.*

Another of these poems, "Late Abed," he described "as an open shameless advertisement for matrimony."

> *Ah, but a good wife!*
> *To lie late in a warm bed*
> *(warm where she was) with your life*
> *suspended like a music in the head,*
> *hearing her foot in the house, her broom*
> *on the pine floor of the down-stairs room,*
> *hearing the window toward the sun go up,*
> *the tap turned on, the tap turned off,*
> *the saucer clatter to the coffee cup . . .*
>
> *To lie late in the odor of coffee*
> *thinking of nothing at all, listening . . .*
>
> *and she moves here, she moves there,*
> *and your mouth hurts still where last she kissed you:*
> *you think how she looked as she left, the bare*
> *thigh, and went to her adorning . . .*
>
> *You lie there listening and she moves —*
> *prepares her house to hold another morning,*
> *prepares another day to hold her loves . . .*
>
> *You lie there*
> *thinking of nothing*
> *watching the sky . . .*

To their friends, the MacLeish marriage seemed almost perfect. "I always thought of Archie and Ada as one word," said Dorothy de Santillana, MacLeish's editor at Houghton Mifflin for more than two decades. "It was the closest marriage I've ever seen." They made a wonderful pair because they set each other off, Hester Pickman said. "Archie was utterly dependent on Ada, and Ada thought of nothing but Archie." But Ada's incessant devotion to her husband's every slightest want had its cost. As she grew older, Ada increasingly regretted that she had given her children second place, particularly her first son, Kenneth.

Whatever deprivation of mother love Ken may have suffered, it was his father he was most eager to please and to impress. His career had taken him from science editor at *Life* to a post as editor and correspondent for *National Geographic,* two of the best magazine jobs imaginable. Despite his success in commercial magazine writing, Ken never felt sure of his work until Archie had pronounced it all right. The trouble was that sometimes — often — Archie either did not read his pieces or had no comment on them. When that happened, Ken felt himself diminished. His attitude is reflected in an August 26, 1963, letter to his father, shortly after Archie had suffered a rare writer's block. "I'm terribly sorry about your bad time," Ken wrote him. He could understand it all too well, since he'd had similar dry spells himself. Still, Archie's situation was much tougher, Ken wrote. "It doesn't make a hell of a lot of difference whether I ever write again, except for such things as salary, but it does matter enormously whether or not you do."

Bill MacLeish did not take up his writing career on a full-time basis until after Archie died. In the meantime he held a number of interesting jobs, including the executive directorship of the Center for Inter-American Relations and four years as special assistant to Yale president Kingman Brewster. Bill knew that he was a good writer, but he was cowed by his father's illustrious example. Archie was too daunting a figure to try to emulate.

Ken commanded a degree of attention by exposing himself to physical danger. In the fall of 1962, he suffered an attack of the bends while diving to the *Lusitania* off the coast of Ireland. He spent twenty hours in a decompression chamber, but his optic nerve was damaged, and his full vision did not return for some time. This did not stop him, soon after, from establishing with one other diver a record for the deepest nonoceanic dive at Lago Maggiore. In less dangerous circumstances, he loved to scuba dive at Antigua. Archie's poem "The Reef Fisher," written "for K. MacL.," revealed his ambivalence about his son's chance taking. The poem revels in the excitement and strangeness of the dive, yet warns of the peril below.

> *Plunge beneath the ledge of coral*
> *Where the silt of sunlight drifts*
> *Like dust that settles toward a floor —*

. . . .
> *Look, look down until you see*
> *Far, far beneath in the translucent*
> *Lightlessness, the huge, the fabulous*
> *Fish of fishes in his profound gulf:*

. . . .
> *But fear that weed, as though alive,*
> *That lifts and follows with the wave:*
> *The Moray lurks for all who dive*
> *Too deep within the coral cave.*
> *Once tooth of his has touched the bone*
> *Men turn among those stones to stone.*

In the spring of 1969, Archie accompanied Ken on assignment to Scotland's Outer Hebrides. The weather was wet and biting cold, with thirty-knot winds off the sea, but Archie admired the "tall, blond, warm, reserved" Gaels who lived there. He loved the way they spoke English with the respect and affection it deserved, and he wondered at the light that dissolved and deepened, so enlarging everything that a cow at a hundred yards looked "as big as a Mack truck and mountains rising naked out of that gray, wild sea are Everests clothed in forest." That joint trip probably did not diminish Ken's sense of inferiority. Ken's long and thorough article on the Outer Hebrides appeared in the May 1970 *National Geographic*, along with a short poem by his father that the magazine ran in large type across a two-page spread.

If as a father Archie gave his children less love and support than they wanted, as a grandfather he found it difficult to cope with the natural disorder of his grandchildren. For a television series, "Reading Out Loud," in 1960, he read Walter de la Mare's "Peacock Pie" to Ken and Carolyn's four youngsters, and engaged them in an unconvincing version of amiable conversation between the generations. Archie's technique was mostly interrogation. He asked the twelve-year-old Bruce a question, then had to repeat it because the lad was daydreaming. "Bruce, can't you speak when you're spoken to?" Archie asked. He also put a question to Martha, the eldest at seventeen. "I want to go to Antigua," she responded.

During summer visits to Conway, the grandchildren were expected to behave themselves in ways that went against the grain of childhood exuberance. Ada would lay down the law at breakfast. "Well, dear, how did you sleep?" she would ask, fitting her coral pink fingernails together, and then issue the program for the day. Archie's stone house was off limits, of course. Otherwise, the mothers — Ken's wife, Carolyn, Bill's wife, Peg, daughter Mimi — were in charge of ensuring as much parental restraint as possible. The grandchildren were not allowed at the dinner table until they were eight or ten years old. Karl and Mimi's daughter Mina so rebelled at being confined to the kitchen during Mimi's birthday dinner that the children's table was moved into the dining room. Still, it was not all bad for the grandchildren at Uphill Farm. There was land aplenty to explore, they got riding lessons, and in the attic there was a cache of old clothes from Paris to play with on rainy days.

As the granddaughters grew older, Archie, and especially Ada, tried to arrange their lives for the better. Were they going to the right schools? Were they making appropriate friendships? Martha, Ken and Carolyn's eldest, received more of this sort of guidance than the aftercomers, and resisted it more fiercely. When Martha was at Radcliffe in the early 1960s, Archie and Ada would invite her to lunch at the Somerset Club. There she was lectured about her table manners and the unsuitable people she was running around with. At her grandmother's urging, Martha did attend one, and only one, debutante party. Everyone was eating too much and drinking too much and yelling, she recalled. One boy burned a hole in her dress with a cigarette, and another threw up on it. "Then I knew what socialism was all about," Martha wryly observed.

A crisis arose when Martha threatened to marry, largely out of pity, what Archie called "the most dreadful specimen of the human male" he had ever seen. He wrote a poem on the subject that ended:

> Go out, my dear, too old to play,
> but never give the heart away
> for pity's sake.

Martha did not see the poem until after she'd broken up with that sorry fiancé. Her grandparents also disapproved of her next beau, a young man at Harvard named Ray Glazier. Ostensibly the argument was that they were both too young, and neither had graduated from college. But the real reason, Martha felt sure, was that they thought Ray was Jewish. (He wasn't.) Since her parents were overseas at the time, Martha went to Uphill Farm to discuss her marriage plans. "Of course we're not anti-Semitic," Ada said, "but family is so important." Moreover, Ada added, if she went ahead with the marriage, she and Ray couldn't expect any help from them. Presumably this remark was intended to discourage Ray in case he was a fortune hunter. The thought of financial support from her grandparents had never entered Martha's mind. She and Ray were married, publicly in February 1963 though actually the previous spring in secret. In 1968 Ray was badly crippled in an auto accident on the Massachusetts Turnpike; he became embittered and depressed, and the marriage did not last.

Passages

Much as they loved Conway, Archie and Ada continued to escape the New England winter in Antigua. In December 1962 they went cruising with the Cowleses and Achesons over the Christmas holidays. Betty Cowles decreed that no fuss would be made on Christmas Day. The second mate produced a Bible, Archie read the Christmas story, and when he was through, Betty announced, "Now that's over, we can all go swimming." Their route from St. Lucia to Grenada took them past Begue, the island where former British prime minister Anthony Eden had a house. Dean Acheson sent a message by taxi (there were no phones) inviting the Edens to dinner on the yacht. Yes, the answer came back, if the six travelers would come for tea at the Edens' place. Over dinner Betty Cowles advised Eden to speak a little louder. "All the men are deaf and all the women hear *everything*," she said. In fact, the three hard-of-hearing males reminded Archie of the story about the Englishmen in the railroad compartment. "1: This is Wembley. 2: I thought it was Thursday. 3: So am I: let's have a drink."

As the most famous winter resident of Antigua, MacLeish was often commandeered for educational and social functions. Cowles interested Archie in the University of the West Indies, where he became a member of the council and delivered a commencement address. In Antigua itself he was an active supporter of the Mill Reef Fund, which offered scholarships to promising Antiguan students. When notable guests arrived, the MacLeishes were called upon to help entertain them. Adlai Stevenson stayed with them on his trip in the winter of 1963. At a dinner for Princess Margaret, Archie was placed at her right. The princess, he thought, was "a poop."

Mostly, life at Antigua moved at a slow and easy pace, with occasional diversions. Ada reported the "News of the Week" in one letter home: "A cow crashed through the cover of Hester Pickman's [water] tank, while being chased from her garden. It took most of the men of Firetown Village and the better part of a day to hoist her out. The cow seemed undamaged." All of Mill Reef turned out to watch the removal operation.

Over a period of time, the character of island life gradually changed. Prices rose with the influx of new Mill Reefers "from the bad climates" — Ada thought there were entirely too many people from Grosse Pointe — and so did the cost of native labor. The MacLeishes lost the cook who had been with them for more than a decade. Ada fell and tore the ligaments in her knee on a shopping expedition. In February 1967 they decided to sell La Désirade, as it had become a real financial and domestic burden. Fortunately, Noel and Elena Macy offered to let Archie and Ada occupy their house for succeeding winters. Called Isiri, the Arawak word for "thumb," the Macys' home was situated on a point of land one hundred feet above the ocean, with a swimming pool that seemed to flow out over the edge of the precipice into the bay and the islands below. Hubert Humphrey stopped in for a swim and a drink there in December 1967. "Guess who was in your swimming pool today?" Archie wrote Elena Macy. "The Vice President of the United States. And guess what was in the Vice President of the United States. Your very best Mount Gay rum."

Archie did not entirely abandon teaching when he left Harvard. By the end of 1963, he had made a connection with Amherst College. Robert Frost died in January 1963, and to honor his memory Amherst named its new library after him. Archie spoke at the dedication in October, along with President Kennedy. During his brief remarks in the college "cage," or field house, Kennedy struck precisely the right note. "A nation reveals itself not only by the men it produces but also by the men it honors, the men it remembers," the president said. (Within the month, he was himself to die in Dallas.) MacLeish spoke eloquently of Frost, or tried to, battling a balky microphone. As the mike whined away, he shook it as though it were alive, and announced, "Either you win or I win." Even though he could not be heard clearly, that gesture won over his audience. They "were so moved . . . by my obvious anguish," Archie commented, "that they would have liked me if I had recited Mother Goose."

Two months later Calvin H. Plimpton, the president of Amherst, announced Archie's appointment as Simpson lecturer to succeed Frost. MacLeish's duties were not onerous. He was to spend two weeks in residence each fall and spring speaking to classes and meeting informally with students and faculty, and to give two public lectures each year. According to the college records, he actually taught only four one-semester half-credit courses in creative writing, from 1965 to 1967, with a total of twenty-five students enrolled.

Archie's appointment was not popular with the English department. Some professors resented the idea of MacLeish's succeeding Frost. Archie anticipated such a reaction, as he wrote Mark Van Doren on first assuming the post. "I am too old to sleep in other people's beds . . . and I won't have to. But Robert's ghost will be shuddering in the wall." Not only Robert but his supporters: as William H. Pritchard commented, "If you really liked Frost, you didn't admire Archie." They were different kinds of poets, different kinds of men. Frost liked to tease Archie, to test his conservatism against Archie's liberalism, his deviltry against Archie's probity. Besides, Frost had lived in Amherst much of the time, not an hour away in Conway, and made himself far more available to the college undergraduates than MacLeish ever did. Others were upset that the appointment had been made over their heads by a president who seemed more concerned with outside image than with good teaching. MacLeish did offer to attend others' classes and performed very well under those circumstances. Robert C. ("Kim") Townsend recalled a brilliant session on Matthew Arnold, with Archie drawing out the "talented tenth" of the best Amherst undergraduates. But he was rarely invited to such classes, for though certainly genial, MacLeish gave off an aura of eminence that annoyed some of his younger colleagues. "Archie trailed clouds of glory," as Townsend put it, "and then he trailed them off to Antigua."

MacLeish's friends among the Amherst professoriat included those of established or developing eminence, such as historian Henry Steele ("Felix") Commager and critic and novelist Benjamin DeMott. Archie also looked up Allen Guttmann, whose 1962 book *The Wound in the Heart: America and the Spanish Civil War* had mentioned him favorably. The relationship fell apart after a forum on *J.B.* at Amherst. Guttmann, one of the panelists, said he thought *J.B.* had much the same problem as the Book of Job: God seemed rather a bully. Archie responded with great pain. "You've plunged a knife into my heart," he said. At this point fellow panelist Lewis S. Mudge backtracked to reassure MacLeish. Guttmann had in his mild criticism associated Archie with the author of the Book of Job — that is, with God himself. Mudge went further. "No, no," he insisted, "*J.B.* is really much better than the Book of Job."

With the students, MacLeish got on rather better, though some of the brightest were counseled away from his writing classes by sarcastic references from English professors. None of the lads at Amherst compared, he felt, with the best of his Harvard English S writers, and Archie did not devote nearly as much time to their work as he had at Harvard. After the spring term of 1967, when only four students were in his class, Plimpton suggested to MacLeish that they "cease and desist." That was a good idea, Archie agreed. The Simpson lectureship simply hadn't worked out.

Archie moved more easily in the corridors of the great than the halls of academe. In August 1964 Adlai Stevenson, who was serving as U.S. ambassador to the United Nations, invited the MacLeishes to dinner with Richard Burton and Elizabeth Taylor. Although Stevenson was dog-tired, Liz Taylor took his fancy, and it turned out to be "about the most amusing night" of Adlai's time in New York. The following day Burton sent Archie a record of his *Hamlet,* along with a note to the effect that "Elizabeth . . . was thrilled that a great poet could be so talkable-to." In the fall of 1965, the Burtons and MacLeishes foregathered again for dinner at Uphill Farm, during the filming of Edward Albee's *Who's Afraid of Virginia Woolf?* at Smith College in nearby Northampton. Burton's brother Ifor came along, and the two Welshmen entranced the company by singing a couple of Welsh songs. For his share of the after-dinner entertainment, Archie read some of his poetry. As a professional actor, Burton thought his host's delivery embarrassingly bad. MacLeish "moan[ed] without sense or sound his own lovely verse," he recorded in his diary. "E. and Ifor and I listened in a tortured agony in a house on a hill in Massachusetts, longing to smash the book out of his hands and read it ourselves."

Archie's old friend Gerald Murphy passed away on October 17, 1964. The two managed to make up the differences between them before Gerald's death. As Archie wrote Gerald in June 1964, "The process of getting older throws one more and more, in one's deepest self, on the friends (and how few they are) with whom one has lived through this curious journey (to nowhere? somewhere? where?)." When he and Ada saw Gerald at East Hampton in the early fall, it was painfully clear that he had only a short time to live. Archie then called Alfred Barr at the Museum of Modern Art in New York, and offered to donate Murphy's painting *The Wasp and the Pear* to the museum, if a decision to accept it for the permanent collection could be made promptly. Barr cut through the red tape in short order. Gerald was too weak to read Archie's letter when it arrived early in October. His daughter, Honoria, read it to him. The museum accepted the painting "with the greatest eagerness," Archie wrote. Gerald's face lit up at the news. "How wonderful," he said. Soon after he lapsed into a coma, not to emerge.

There were yet other memorials to observe with the deaths in 1965 of Felix Frankfurter and Adlai Stevenson. The "distinction of [Frankfurter's] life," Archie said at the Supreme Court's observances, "was its happiness: not its extraordinary success, not its good fortune, its offices, its honors, but its happiness." It was a happiness born of the intellectual and emotional generosity Felix offered his friends.

After Stevenson's death in July 1965, Cass Canfield at Harper and Row tried to interest MacLeish in writing Adlai's biography. He need not be inundated in detail, Canfield assured Archie. Someone could be found to do much of the research. The answer from Uphill Farm was no. Memorial tributes Archie was happy to prepare. Otherwise, he had his own writing to do.

Myths and Legends

In the fall of 1965, two of MacLeish's dramatic works — one based on a classical myth, the other on a modern legend — were ready for public performance. For five years, ever since completing *J.B.*, Archie had been grappling with a play based on the Greek story of Herakles (Hercules). The heroic Herakles, it may be remembered, completed his twelve miraculous labors only to return and dementedly cause the murder of his sons. This myth, Archie believed, "was *the* great modern myth," and he undertook to present it in *Herakles,* his dramatic parable that opened, on the road, at the University of Michigan on October 27. As he outlined his theme to director Alan Schneider, the myth of Herakles had become "true" for contemporary audiences "in the sense that we see ourselves in that bewildered hero, struggling with the immensity of the universe, with the darkness and dread of the world, who performs impossible labors only to find that he has killed his sons, lost his humanity." Specifically, MacLeish drew a parallel with "the modern myth of science. . . . Science fights against cancer. It cures infantile paralysis. It puts an end to yellow fever. It accomplishes miracles in regard to the decency of living." Yet at the same time, science "has produced the bombs . . . produced the destruction of the young."

After five years, Archie had managed to complete only a forty-five minute play on this theme. Originally he thought that a simple re-creation of the ancient myth in modern verse would convey his message clearly enough. Then, asked to underline the point, he added a short first act in which the accomplishments and the dangerous discoveries of a contemporary scientist are depicted in obvious comparison with those of Herakles. The play went to Ann Arbor with an excellent cast, headed by the brilliant Rosemary Harris as Herakles' wife, Megara, and with strong promise of a Broadway production. But prospective producer T. Edward Hambleton of the Phoenix backed down.

From the beginning, *Herakles* had most of the commercial handicaps of *J.B.* It was written in verse, it dealt with an ancient story, and it promised an unmistakably "cultural" night at the theater. Like *J.B.* also, *Herakles* had a message, but this time the message was a dire warning rather than a celebration. *J.B.* proclaimed the victory of humankind over disaster through love. *Herakles* foreshadowed the destruction of humanity through intellect. This was not a prophecy Broadway theatergoers were eager to hear. Besides, the Ann Arbor production of *Herakles,* like most of MacLeish's plays, lacked what reviewer Tom Prideaux called "a hooker." "Despite the flow of poetic lines and provocative ideas, [MacLeish] has not . . . hooked our sympathy or intense curiosity about anything."

No such hooker was required to interest audiences in *The Eleanor Roosevelt Story,* the full-length documentary motion picture Archie wrote to accompany films and still photos of the former first lady. His concept was to emphasize the contrast in Eleanor Roosevelt's life — "the extraordinary disparity between beginning and end." At the end, she was probably the best-known and most-loved woman in the world. Yet she had grown up in the heyday of old New York society as "a child of her class and place and time who asked for nothing better than to win its approval — and who failed." She failed because she was not a belle. As a young girl she was "deeply ashamed" of her inability to become popular. Her alcoholic father neglected her. The old photographs showed a tragic, miserable child, sad around the eyes and unloved. Even her marriage to fifth cousin Franklin D. Roosevelt in 1903 did not liberate Eleanor's potential. It was not until World War I, when she worked in a canteen, that she suddenly discovered her vocation. There was something she could do about the suffering in the world — "she herself, dutiful and obedient child and girl and woman." Thereafter she accepted it as her personal responsibility to alleviate that suffering as best she could. In the endeavor she was guided by two principles: first, "what one has to do usually can be done," and second, "hope is not enough." The film reached its most poignant moment, MacLeish thought, with a snapshot of Mrs. Roosevelt as a widow, leaving Washington to move up to New York, walking along the Pennsylvania Railroad tracks in the dim early morning light, absolutely alone.

The reviews of *The Eleanor Roosevelt Story* could hardly have been more luminous: "a most moving, heartening film," "one of the finest the screen has yet offered," "a picture to be treasured by millions," "informative, dramatic, touching and often humorous." In choosing the film as one of the year's ten best, Bosley Crowther of the *New York Times* called it "a beautifully written and selectively illustrated documentary . . . which not only transmits an informative and moving tribute to one of the great women of our times, but conveys a sense of great social change in the first half of the 20th century." The film, he added, was eloquently narrated by MacLeish himself, Eric Sevareid, and Mrs. Frances Cole, a relative of Eleanor Roosevelt's. In January 1966 the National Board of Review chose *The Eleanor Roosevelt Story* as the best picture of the year, bar none. Two months later it won the Academy Award as the best documentary of 1965.

As a three-time winner of the Pulitzer Prize, MacLeish was the fifth and final speaker at the fiftieth anniversary dinner of the Pulitzers on May 10, 1966, following Aaron Copland, Arthur M. Schlesinger, Jr., James Reston, and Robert Penn Warren. A week later, Archie and Mark Van Doren were in Washington for "An Evening with Two Poets," sponsored by President Johnson's cabinet. Novelist Herman Wouk hosted a dinner for the MacLeishes and Van Dorens, along with Washington notables. Archie laughed as merrily as anyone present when Stewart Udall, the secretary of the interior, reminded the assembled guests of a jingle composed by one of his Republican enemies during his Library of Congress days: "I took my dog upon a leash / And wished each tree was A. MacLeish."

In July 1966 he attended a reception at the YMHA in New York for Chilean poet Pablo Neruda. Five different translators, including Robert Bly, read their versions of Neruda's poems, all of them — Archie reported — "hating each other's guts and competing in flattery and abrazos." His schedule for October included the requisite two weeks at Amherst, followed by appearances at the Taft School, Duquesne, Dartmouth, Princeton, and Yale.

His visit to Yale was for a meeting of the university's committee on the humanities, whose members included Van Doren, Aline Saarinen, Barbara Tuchman, Amos Wilder, and Ben Shahn. MacLeish was concerned about the drift toward vocationalism in higher education. It was lamentable, he thought, that so many people regarded the proper role of universities as that of helping students "get ahead." As Allen Tate noted in a sarcastic speech at the University of Minnesota, "It is all very well to say that some industrialists have now decided they would rather have bright English majors than graduates of the Harvard Business School, but the fact is that 'getting on in the world' leads through the Harvard Business School and not through William Shakespeare." Archie was inclined to blame the student revolts of the late 1960s less on racial and social unrest or on the Vietnam War than on a protest against higher education's surrender to material values.

About the war in Vietnam, MacLeish was of two minds. With a Democratic administration involved, he was reluctant to oppose the war wholeheartedly. As he wrote Kay Boyle in June 1965, "get out of Vietnam" was not a policy but a shout. Yet the next month he engaged his friend Mac Bundy in debate in the *Saturday Review*. Did the government's show of force in Vietnam and the Dominican Republic, MacLeish asked, "mean that we are no longer that idealistic nation of the First World War . . . ? Have our ways of thinking and of feeling altered? Are we 'realistic' now? 'Hardheaded'? Indifferent to those opinions of mankind which our progenitors put in the first sentence of their first communication to the world?" MacLeish's opposition to the war solidified as it dragged on for several years, with no apparent prospect of victory in sight. In April 1968, shortly after President Johnson announced his decision not to seek re-election, he summed up the feelings of many Americans. "It's a war we never meant to get in to and don't know how to get out of and the country has been increasingly sick of it for months." He welcomed Senator Eugene McCarthy's bid for the presidency and its promise of a politics based on principle. Humphrey he could tolerate. Nixon was anathema.

Versions of History

"All these years I have waited to praise this man," Mark Van Doren wrote in his poem "To Archie, at 75."

> He stretches so far forward
> That nobody, I think, will be there when he comes,
> And coming, still walks on, his back so straight,
> His voice so beautiful before him, sounding
> The unknown dark.

Archie's voice and mind were as active as ever. "The older I grow," he wrote naturalist Joseph Wood Krutch on June 1, 1967, three weeks after his seventy-fifth birthday, "the more interested I become (and the more conscious of my ignorance) in the literature of beasts and birds and insects." Could Krutch suggest some titles for him?

In mid-June, MacLeish's "outdoor play," *An Evening's Journey to Conway, Massachusetts,* was given three presentations on the town baseball diamond. Written for the bicentennial of Conway, the play was put on almost entirely by residents of the town. In form, *An Evening's Journey* was a loving, somewhat sentimental re-creation of the town's history, short on character development and long on nostalgia. In the opening scenes a surly Conway boy of the present who can't wait to get away from home meets a Conway youth of the 1830s who did leave it, in body though not in spirit. This is Marshall Field, who migrated westward to found a merchandising empire in Chicago. "Marsh" Field urges the present-day malcontent to go back into the town's past and really come to know it. So is set in motion a series of scenes from Conway's history, beginning with a pioneer woman and going on through the Green Mountain Boys and Civil War days. At the end, the boy realizes that he belongs to the town he thought he hated.

Despite a torrential rainstorm that delayed the second and third nights of the run, *An Evening's Journey* turned out to be, in Archie's words, "just about the most satisfactory thing I ever did in my life." (A television version in the fall on "NET Playhouse," using professional actors and "gussied up and slicked over with . . . professional charm," was much less successful.) After the final performance, Archie and Ada gave a cast party with hamburgers and hot dogs and beer and soft drinks and a bonfire against the evening chill. "We now feel very much a part of the town," Ada wrote the Macys. On July 4 she and Archie were honored guests on the reviewing stand for the Conway parade, where they stewed in the summer heat for three hours and saluted the flag a hundred times or more.

Another revisiting of the American past provided the subject matter for *Magic Prison,* a work for orchestra and the spoken word presented by the New York Philharmonic on June 12, 1967. Ezra Laderman, who had supplied the incidental music for *The Eleanor Roosevelt Story,* composed the score to accompany MacLeish's libretto based on the relationship between Emily Dickinson and Thomas Wentworth Higginson. Archie undertook the project at the insistence of conductor André Kostelanetz, who had befriended the MacLeishes during his sojourns in Antigua. For MacLeish the job was more editorial than creative. Colonel Higginson, who had commanded a black regiment in the Civil War and gone on to become an editor of the *Atlantic,* had written a fascinating article about his bewildering contact with the reclusive Amherst poet. Dickinson had chosen him as a kind of sounding board for her nearly secret practice of poetry, and launched an eighteen-year correspondence with him. Aware of her "half-cracked" genius, Higginson finally arranged a meeting, and came away from it more befuddled than ever. "I was never with anyone who drained my nerve power so much," he confessed. What Archie did was to take the most interesting parts of Higginson's account and intersperse them with some of Dickinson's most deeply emotional poems. There were only "about five words" of his own in the entire script, he said.

The month after MacLeish's musical piece on Dickinson premiered, Carl Sandburg died. During the September 1967 memorial observance at the Lincoln Memorial, Archie made the point that poets, unlike grains of wheat, were not interchangeable and that what especially distinguished Sandburg was that he "had a *subject* — and the subject was belief in man." Sandburg, was *"a credulous man,"* one who believed more than he could prove about humanity. Then he read four of his old friend's poems to illustrate the point, mimicking Sandburg's distinctive twang that could make six syllables out of "Peoria." Once again, the flight pattern from National Airport carried the roaring jets directly over the Lincoln Memorial. Only Jessye Norman managed to drown out one passing jet with the climax of "He's Got the Whole World in His Hands." "By God, she sang him down," remarked Ralph McGill, publisher of the *Atlanta Constitution*.

MacLeish published both a book of prose and one of poetry in 1968. *A Continuing Journey* contained essays and addresses written over the twenty uneasy years since the mid-1940s, tracing the reflections of "a writer who keeps up a running quarrel with his time." "Our cities are monstrous," he wrote in one essay. "Our suburbs are worse. . . . But what is also obvious, if you look closely and listen well, is the persistence of a human warmth, a human meaning that nothing has killed in almost 200 years."

In a perceptive review, Malcolm Cowley took issue not with Mac-Leish's opinions, for he almost always agreed with those, but with his old-fashioned rhetorical style. Many of the pieces in *A Continuing Journey* were originally speeches delivered to audiences, and on the page they kept their forensic tone. Cowley particularly objected to the use of anaphora, or repetition at the beginning of two or more successive clauses for rhetorical effect. He cited Archie's address on academic freedom as an example.

> [The teacher's] role — his role in this republic at least — is not to commit his students to belief. His role is to commit them to the human experience — to the experience of the human mind and the human soul — in the profound and never questioning confidence that if they truly taste of that experience, if they truly see the choices of their lives, they — they themselves — will choose. In that confidence political freedom was conceived. In that confidence the institutions of human freedom were established. In that confidence the faith of those who teach the free is founded.

The danger was that the drumbeat repetitions of "role," "experience," "if they truly," and "in that confidence" might merely lull MacLeish's listeners (or readers) into acquiescence instead of stimulating them to thought. With reason, Cowley preferred Archie's poetry to his oratorical prose.

The best things in *A Continuing Journey* were the portraits of people MacLeish admired. "He lives in a world where heroes have lived," Cowley observed. Among these were Yeats, Eliot, Hemingway, White-head, Justice Holmes, Frost, Frankfurter, Elmer Davis, Edwin Muir, Eleanor Roosevelt, Jane Addams. Some of these survived, such as Van Doren and St.-John Perse, yet there were discouraging moments when

MacLeish began to fear "that the big single animals are disappearing and that their place is being taken by something . . . that loves a herd."

Yeats, and in particular his sexually exuberant poem of old age that begins "Because I am mad about women," supplied the title and much of the inspiration for 1968's *The Wild Old Wicked Man and Other Poems.* Archie did not stop appreciating women in his old age. Tom Johnson recalled walking along Fifth Avenue with him shortly after the publication of *The Wild Old Wicked Man.* "Look at that," MacLeish said as a good-looking woman swept by. "My God, look at that." His new book included poetry both of connubial bliss, like "Late Abed," and of earlier extramarital loves, like "Hotel Breakfast." The latter poem is a powerful one in which the writer is unexpectedly overwhelmed by the memory of a long-ago affair as he drinks a cup of "tepid brew" on a miserable winter morning in a hotel dining room. Suddenly, his lover — Catherine Carr or Margaret Bishop or whoever — materializes in his imagination across the table, bringing with her

> . . . *laughter from another year,*
> *another country, Oh, another life;*
> *the cold sun crawls along the butter knife.*
>
> *I tremble, heartsick with a mortal fear —*
>
> *What brings you here?*

In the title poem MacLeish depicts the dilemma of the old man whose dwindling physical capacity to love is outmatched by continuing desire.

> *Too old for love and still to love! —*
> *Yeats's predicament and mine — all men's:*
> *the aging Adam who must strut and shove*
> *and caper his obscene pretense . . .*
>
> *And yet, within the dry thorn grove,*
> *singer to singer in the dusk, there cries*
> *(Listen! Ah, listen, the wood dove!)*
> *something conclusion never satisfies;*
>
> *and still when day ends and the wind goes down*
> *and not a tree stirs, not a leaf,*
> *some passion in the sea beats on*
> *and on . . .*
>   *(Oh, listen, the sea reef!)*
>
> *Too old for love and still to long . . .*
> *for what? For one more flattering proof*

the flesh lives and the beast is strong? —
once more upon the pulse that hammering hoof?

Or is there something the persistent dove,
the ceaseless surges and the old man's lust
all know and cannot say? Is love

what nothing concludes, nothing must,
pure certainty?

> *And does the passionate man*
most nearly know it when no passion can?
Is this the old man's triumph, to pursue
impossibility — and take it too?

As never before, MacLeish's poetry dealt directly with his own mortality — in "Survivor," for instance.

On an oak in autumn
there'll always be
one leaf left at the top of the tree
that won't let go with the rest and rot —

. . . .

> *No,*
it won't and it won't and it won't let go.
It rattles a kind of a jig tattoo,
a telegrapher's tattle that will get through . . .

. . . .

> *I can spell:*
I know what it says . . . I know too well.
I pull the pillow over my ear
but I hear.

The Wild Old Wicked Man was not widely reviewed. In a short notice in the *New York Times,* Thomas Lask commented that the poems seemed written without "a concern for temporary effect or approbation. It's as if Mr. MacLeish had thought, 'Well, these are the poems I feel like writing.' He hopes you will like them too, but he is not particularly perturbed if you don't." The independence of spirit Lask noted signified how far Archie had come from the time when he was roundly condemned by Edmund Wilson and others for kowtowing to the fashions of the day. After the long evolution of his career, in his late poetry he wrote only to please himself. In the process he discovered a last, powerful, surprisingly plainspoken voice.

Following the death of Robert Frost, Archibald MacLeish assumed unofficial status as poet laureate. Thus it was appropriate that the *New York Times,* the closest thing to a national newspaper in the United States, twice prevailed upon him to memorialize America's triumphs in space. The first of these was the *Apollo 8* mission, which circumnavigated the moon and sent back a famous photograph of the earth. That photograph moved MacLeish to reflect on human brotherhood: "To see the earth as it truly is, small and blue and beautiful in that eternal silence where it floats, is to see ourselves as riders on the earth together, brothers on the bright loveliness in the eternal cold — brothers who know now they are truly brothers." The *Times* ran the piece in its issue of Christmas Day 1968. Colonel Frank Borman, commander of *Apollo 8,* quoted from it approvingly. The evocative phrase "riders on the earth" began to make its way into the national consciousness.

With the next space mission — in July 1969 — scheduled to make an actual moon landing, James ("Scotty") Reston, executive editor of the *Times,* lined up Archie well in advance to write a poem in honor of that accomplishment. Then MacLeish had a call from William Safire, who was working for newly incumbent President Nixon. The president, Safire said, wanted Archie to do a commemorative poem on the moon landing. Archie did not know how to respond. On the one hand, he felt the honor of the proposal very deeply. "To be asked by the President of the United States to compose a poem on a great public event is to be asked, in a sense, to speak for the Republic and the burden of such a responsibility would be very heavy indeed." On the other hand, he disliked almost everything about Nixon, and had made a prior commitment to Reston. How could he say no to a president of the United States? Dean Acheson was no help when asked for advice. He chuckled when Archie told him of his dilemma. "Look, I'm really going crazy with this thing," Archie said. "It's really very serious." Dean said, "All right, if you say so." Finally Archie reached a sympathetic ear in Henry Kissinger, who presented the case to President Nixon in such a way that he was glad to release MacLeish from his request.

So it was that MacLeish's poem "Voyage to the Moon" appeared on the front page of the July 21, 1969, *Times,* beneath its historic "MEN WALK ON MOON" headline. CBS television filmed MacLeish reading the poem after the July 24 splashdown. He was, in effect, speaking for the republic, but through the *Times* and not on behalf of the Nixon administration. Scotty Reston sent him a plate of the front page.

MacLeish did not meet President Nixon until the December 1969 dinner of the National Football Foundation at the Waldorf-Astoria Hotel in New York. Archie, who received the foundation's Distinguished American Award, made the principal speech of the evening. He spoke eloquently of the sense of comradeship that football bred in young men, and of the apparent alienation of modern youth, some of whom were at that moment engaged in "headcracking, window-breaking demonstrations and police actions outside the hotel," in protest against the Vietnam War. Archie was well launched into his talk when a portly old man in a balcony box screamed, "Stop it, stop it!" Whether he meant the speech or the demonstrations was not determined, but Archie's voice lost some of its power thereafter. His talk limped to a conclusion. President Nixon, also at the dinner as another former college football player, came up to Archie afterwards and said he was sorry about the interruption; it must have been a terrible thing to have happen. MacLeish looked at Nixon as if for the first time. "My God," he thought, "he might be human."

24

QUARRELS WITH THE WORLD

Critical Murders

MACLEISH'S *SCRATCH* made it to Broadway, but was as disastrous there as *J.B.* had been triumphant. The idea for the play came from producer Stuart Ostrow, who had just achieved a hit with the musical *1776*. Ostrow wanted to do another musical, this one based on Stephen Vincent Benét's memorable 1936 story "The Devil and Daniel Webster." He sounded out two men fifty years apart in age to write the words and music — MacLeish to adapt the story into a playable script and singer-composer Bob Dylan to supply the songs. When first approached, Archie thought the idea preposterous. For one thing, the story had already been done on the stage, in the form of an opera written by his Yale classmate Douglas Moore. And he was suspicious of the collaboration Ostrow had in mind. The producer struck him as the kind "who begins with names and then tries to find things for the names to do." Then Archie's disinclination to refuse a challenge took effect. He began to immerse himself in the politics and morality of Daniel Webster. In Webster's career, and particularly in his willingness to compromise to save the Union as of 1850, he saw a distinct parallel to the rebellious and divided state of the country as of 1970. So he signed on with Ostrow and spent a year writing the script.

MacLeish took as many liberties with Benét's story as he had with the Bible in *J.B.* According to the original tale, a New Hampshire farmer named Jabez Stone, fed up with hard times, promises his soul to the devil — or Scratch, as he is familiarly known in New England — in order to enjoy seven years of prosperity. At the end of that period, when Scratch arrives to collect on the debt, Stone persuades Senator Daniel Webster, the great orator of the day, to defend him. The case is tried at midnight in the barn of Stone's farm, with a hanging jury made up of the dead and damned, and Judge John Hathorne, the ancestor of Nathaniel Hawthorne who helped preside over the Salem witch trials, in charge. Webster's eloquence wins a verdict for Stone nonetheless, "with the result" — so MacLeish put it — "that the Devil hasn't been seen in New Hampshire since. 'I'm not talking about Massachusetts or Vermont.' "

This was good Yankee folklore, but Archie decided to add a historical dimension. In his play, Webster himself is on trial even more than his client — Webster who, despite his antislavery views, agreed in March 1850 to the continued enforcement of the Fugitive Slave Law in order to keep the Union from dissolving. Webster was roundly criticized at the time for selling out his principles, as in this couplet by Ralph Waldo Emerson:

> *Why do all manly gifts in Webster fail?*
> *He wrote on nature's noblest brow, "For Sale!"*

As MacLeish portrayed him, however, Daniel Webster was a much-underestimated statesman who boldly faced up to the contradiction inherent in the promise of America. As Webster articulated it, "Liberty and Union, one and inseparable, now and forever." That statement directly addressed the Vietnam-era debate between "strident and implacable" voices as angry and as sure of their ground as any voices had been before the Civil War, MacLeish wrote. "To the left, the Union had become 'the System' and thus contemptible. To the right, liberty was 'permissiveness' — something to be derided and suppressed." Somehow these views had to be reconciled, if only in a realization of common fallibility, MacLeish suggested. Thus his Webster sums up his case by reminding the jury that they are all sinners and must forgive one another. "Liberty cannot endure without the Union. Union has no meaning without liberty. And liberty is one by one — one man — each man — however weak, however desperate."

Neither the intellectual passion MacLeish felt nor the parallel to modern unrest he intended to convey was communicated effectively in *Scratch*. The play he wrote sounded more like a historical preachment than a courtroom drama. Yet what happened to *Scratch* was no one person's fault. Perhaps the principal problem, producer Ostrow thought, was that it was conceived as a musical and brought to the stage as a straight play.

Though interested at first, Bob Dylan eventually backed out of writing songs for the musical. Ostrow did manage once to get Dylan and

MacLeish together in the same room, where the younger man had not one word to say. On the drive home, though, Dylan began to work in the back seat of Ostrow's car. "I've got it, I think I've got it," he'd say. "Go ahead," Ostrow told him. It soon emerged, however, that Dylan's new songs would not fit the purposes of *Scratch*. Two of the songs he prospectively wrote for the play, "New Morning" and "Father of Night," were included on his *New Morning* album of 1970. *Scratch* itself was performed without music.

Casting the part of Webster posed another obstacle. "It is a huge part for an actor to carry, involving considerable emotional strains," Archie explained in a November 1970 letter. "Both Edward G. Robinson and Lee J. Cobb have turned us down because their doctors would not let them accept." Karl Malden and Marlon Brando also declined. Finally, the Irish actor Patrick Magee was cast in the part of Webster, or rather miscast. His accent and somewhat pompous stage manner were all wrong. He sounded, one reviewer said, "like Upper Class Dogpatch." Will Geer as Scratch, by contrast, was wonderfully sly and likable in his villainy. The audience's sympathies were all with Scratch, and so undermined the play's ending, in which Webster was supposed to emerge victorious.

Scratch began its three-week tryout in Boston on April 7. Houghton Mifflin threw a pretheater party for Archie, which was attended by many academic and political luminaries. "It was quite an evening," Marjorie Sherman of the *Boston Globe* commented on the society page next morning. *Scratch* itself made for "a tedious evening in the theater," *Boston Globe* reviewer Kevin Kelly wrote elsewhere in the same issue. It was "hard to tell what's worse about it, the swirling patriotic rhetoric or the swollen conceits about the devil." Privately, many of Archie's friends agreed. The attempted transformation of Benét's fine story into *Scratch* resembled "a glass of ginger ale with all the fizz gone," Jack Bate thought. But MacLeish's stature was such in Boston that Kelly was chastised in the editorial columns of his own paper for failing to understand what *Scratch* had to say about American history, past and present. Reviews in the other Boston papers were mixed, and *Scratch* played to good audiences throughout its three weeks there.

Ostrow brought the play into New York for a May 6 opening with high hopes. The producer scheduled an after-theater party later that night. "He says if the reviews are bad we (he & I) can settle it all right there —" Archie wrote Mark Van Doren, "*there* being the pent-house on top of the Time-Life Bldg. with a forty-story drop." After reading Clive Barnes's review in the *New York Times*, MacLeish was almost ready to jump. Brooks Atkinson of the *Times* in 1958 had praised *J.B.*

so glowingly that it virtually assured the success of the play. Barnes of the *Times* in 1970 panned *Scratch* so mercilessly that it practically guaranteed the play's failure. *Scratch* "has little to declare except its aspirations to seriousness," Barnes wrote. "It is a ponderous piece, pedestrianly written and raising pseudo-moral issues. . . . The construction of the play is simply deplorable." *Scratch* opened, ran for four performances, and closed.

MacLeish could not resist lashing out in response. In a letter to the editor of the *Times*, he presented his case:

> The issue with which my play concerned itself was the issue which divided New England in the decade before the Civil War and which divides the country again today. On the one side the Boston Abolitionists who were ready to tear the Union apart in the name of freedom; on the other, Webster and his Whigs who were determined to preserve the Union even though it meant the preservation of slavery as well. On the one side the young protesters [against the Vietnam War] in Washington a few days ago; on the other the brutal rhetoric of the Attorney General of the United States. To Emerson — see his Journal for May 1851 — this was a great moral issue. To me and to many others it still is. Not so to Mr. Barnes: his awkward word for it was "pseudo-moral" — not up to Broadway standards.
>
> The Times is a great liberal newspaper with a deep sense of the American past. Does it relish the taste of Mr. Barnes' cynicism in its mouth?

Scotty Reston at the *Times* told Archie he thought Barnes's review "embarrassing," and publisher Adolph Ochs apologized for it, but there was no reprimand or corrective editorial forthcoming. In his hurt and anger, MacLeish overvalued his own play and blurred the essential point of his critics. *Scratch* failed not because its message was not understood — though generally it was not — but because it lacked dramatic action and was full of long, blustery speeches. Significantly, *Scratch* was a prose play, without the restraints of a verse line to hold MacLeish's rhetoric in check.

Archie came to New York on a pleasanter mission a year later when he was awarded the *skean d'hu*, a small dagger symbolic of Scottish pride, by the American-Scottish Foundation. He knew how he was supposed to respond to an honorary degree, "but what is a man to say to a dagger?" MacLeish asked. No one was going around shouting "Scottish Power," nor had Fifth Avenue been closed to cross-town traffic for Saint Andrew's Day. The real source of Scottish pride was that the Scots "were true to themselves as human beings — put their humanity first — their responsibility to the world and to the word and to each other."

Two poets who had differently devoted themselves to the word died in the fall of 1972. The life of Ezra Pound, who passed away in Venice on November 1, moved MacLeish to both admiration and exasperation. Pound thought of himself "as an old-line American Jeffersonian, a believer in the American Republic as its founders conceived it," he wrote in a memorial essay, but the founders would have been astonished that Pound was capable of attributing common views to Jefferson and Mussolini. Ezra was guilty not of treason but of "a total misreading of his own time," Archie wrote. He was not mad but deluded when he ranted on the fascist radio. It was a drastic delusion, and "his fame must suffer for it just as he suffered," MacLeish observed. Yet it should not be forgotten that Pound "was one of the inventors of modern poetry: in retrospect, one must say, the principal inventor." His Venetian grave "holds neither fool nor traitor but . . . an unhappy man . . . who was a poet also . . . a master poet for whom a mound should now be raised on the shore of the gray sea." As he expressed it in his poem "Ezry,"

> Maybe you ranted in the Grove —
> Maybe! — but you found the mark
> That measures altitude above
> Sea-level for a poet's work.

A month later Mark Van Doren died in Connecticut. In his tribute at the American Academy, Archie said that "Mark Van Doren was first and foremost and above all a good man, a man famous in his generation for his goodness, for his decency, for his rectitude." The goodness shone through in his poetry, and so too did the erudition that made him "the best-read poet of the century — at least in his own language." Van Doren was not only a poet of vision and courage but "the great teacher of his generation. . . . To have read Shakespeare with Mark Van Doren must have been something like talking of Shakespeare with John Keats."

Archie's memories of Van Doren focused on Mark at his house at Falls Village, Connecticut, sitting with a book to read or write in his room above the brook that coursed over the stones below, most seasons of the year. The two are as one in MacLeish's elegiac "Mark Van Doren and the Brook":

> The brook beneath the water mill
> is winter-bound, its stones are still,
> no word at all, no syllable.

Once there were two together there
talked in the dim, the humming air:
Mark above in his desk chair,

the brook below, Old murmurers,
they talked as twilight blinds and blurs,
he of his art, she of hers.

Words out of stones she understood:
he, words from lives — how flesh and blood
are spoken and the heart construed.

Year after year they talked there; now
the brook is mute, is winter-bound,
and Mark . . .

no winter knows, can sound,
the silence where his voice is drowned.

Mark was "dearer to me than any brother — than any man I have ever known," Archie wrote to his widow, Dorothy.

MacLeish was out with a book of poetry called *The Human Season* in the fall of 1972. Subtitled *Selected Poems, 1926–1972,* these were not new poems but his choice among the best he had published in the previous half century. For purposes of the volume, he arranged the poems topically rather than chronologically, under six headings: "Autobiography and Omens," "Actors and Scenes," "Love and Not," " 'Strange Thing . . . To Be an American,' " "The Art," and "News from Elsewhere." "At eighty you begin to look ahead," Archie wrote in his engaging foreword. "What will be left when they carry you off?" Specifically he wanted to flesh out the eight or ten poems usually anthologized with a more extensive selection from his other work, and so acquaint readers with poems they might not otherwise encounter. One critic praised the endeavor. "Acting in both his own best interests and ours, MacLeish has achieved in the inspired editing of this volume one of the many unacknowledged tasks of indispensable high criticism, a service usually rendered by a close friend or associate of the artist's years after his death." Yet another review, by John Malcolm Brinnin in the *New York Times Book Review,* was almost as devastating as Clive Barnes's assault on *Scratch.*

Brinnin, a poet and critic then teaching at Boston University, had little good to say about the organization of the book and even less about MacLeish's poetic career. The best poems remained the anthologized ones, including "You, Andrew Marvell," "The End of the World," "Ars poetica," "Epistle to Be Left in the Earth," " 'Not Marble Nor the Gilded

Monuments,' " and "L'an trentiesme de mon eage," Brinnin wrote. All
of these had been written before 1930, and Brinnin airily dismissed
almost all of Archie's poetry published since that time. When MacLeish
returned from Paris, embraced America, "and became in person, in
rhetoric, and in Washington the most 'official' of our poets, something
essential had been sacrificed," Brinnin declared. In a halfhearted concession, Brinnin acknowledged that *some* of Archie's poetry since the Paris
days was "still able to register, like a needle on a graph, those nicer
nuances that had once defined his talent."

The review was so nasty, Archie's editor Dorothy de Santillana said,
that it helped drive her out of publishing. "It would have crumpled me
but for the obvious malice," Archie himself said. This time he wrote
no letter of complaint to the *Times*. Instead he unleashed his private
resentment in a bitter notebook poem titled "Remarks to a Writing
Class."

> *You want to write?*
> *Get yourself born. Discover your name.*
> *Make your way through the birchwood of childhood.*
> *Arrive at your life behind the barn.*
> *Learn to see through a crack, through a knot-hole.*
> *Meet yourself in a gate at night.*
> *Talk to death: he's just behind you*
> *Walking slowly in your tracks.*
> *Prepare for the voyage with a copy of* Hamlet.
> *Learn to read your copy of* Hamlet.
> *Work all day and then start working.*
> *Learn to see through a spider's eye.*
> *Work all night, then start at day break.*
> *Marry the princess in the book.*
> *After seven years begin to write.*
> *After seven more burn everything.*
> *Publish the rest.*

And then, what would happen? A reviewer would belittle the work of
a lifetime in the Sunday *Times*.

Manifestly, such condescending reviews hurt Archie more than he
was willing to show in public. "Don't bother me with reviews," he
instructed Richard B. McAdoo, who succeeded de Santillana as his editor
at Houghton Mifflin. McAdoo took that to mean not to send him reviews
unless they were very good or very interesting. In a letter to the novelist
Stephen Becker, who was a neighbor in Conway from 1971 to 1979,
Archie reflected on the issue philosophically. "We all start out, such

being the nature of childhood, with the unstated assumption that there is someone somewhere (called the critics) who will give out the prizes. We then discover . . . that this is a delusion — that the people who call themselves critics can't read and don't know and wouldn't be able to say if they did because they aren't, and never have been, disinterested." The inescapable consequence was that the writer had to judge himself and to trust his own judgment.

Modern Problems

Steve and Mary Becker moved to Conway in July 1971, and bought a small farm about two miles from the MacLeishes. Steve, who had read some of MacLeish's poetry in college, was fully aware of the eminence at the other end of Pine Hill Road, but knew better than to rush out and introduce himself. It was deep into the winter before Steve, on crutches because of polio, stopped Archie coming out of the post office, said he was a novelist and translator, and would very much like to get acquainted. Archie raised a finger magisterially, said, "I'll call you," and was gone. Another six months passed before Ted Hoagland came to see the Beckers, and Archie wanted to see Ted, so a meeting was finally arranged. During the conversation Becker made a disparaging remark about the repressive Chilean dictator Augusto Pinochet. "Oh, those sons of bitches," MacLeish said, and looked at Steve for the first time as if this might be someone worth his while to talk to.

Soon thereafter Archie called to invite Steve and Mary for a drink, and so it went for the next half-dozen years. Every month or two the phone would ring, and the Beckers would drive down to Uphill Farm for cocktails and conversation from 5 to 6:30 P.M. or so. Steve was also invited to use the MacLeishes' pool for exercise, though he was warned by Archie not to arrive at 6 A.M., when he and Ada were taking their morning skinny dip. Despite the difference in their ages — Archie was a full generation older — Steve thought of him as a contemporary, totally informed, mentally sharp, and not the least superior in manner. Despite the age gap, the two men forged a friendship based on common literary and political views. "Why did you come at all," Archie said to him when the Beckers decided to move to the British Virgin Islands in 1979, "if you were going to leave so soon?"

It was people like the Beckers and John and Jill Conway that Archie had in mind when he made a talk to open Conway's Festival of the Hills on October 1, 1972. Conway, he said, was an example of a rapidly vanishing American phenomenon: "a small town which is happy to be a small town." In the Age of Affluence just past, it seemed that every community wanted to grow bigger and richer as rapidly as possible, with disastrous results. The developers took over, and the small towns of the past were lost in the sprawl of progress. "Where is Emily Dickinson's Amherst, once the prettiest village in the Connecticut Valley? . . . Could even Emily find it?" Conway, however, had stayed healthy and stayed small. Moreover, the artists and academics who did move in were not segregated in colonies but had simply become some of the people who lived there. If that were to change, Archie promised — if the artists went off by themselves or the developers took over — he would "haunt these hills and hollows till the church bell rings of itself and every flight of stairs in Conway creaks and groans."

After fifty years in residence, Archie was gradually becoming recognized as Conway's leading citizen. On his eightieth birthday in 1972, the town dedicated its annual report to him in recognition of his "good works and countless kindnesses." That meant more to him than a Pulitzer, Archie said. He took part in community activities as time and commitments permitted. He persuaded Marshall Field III to finance repairing of the roof of the Field Memorial Library, for example. He got Dean Acheson to dedicate the town swimming pool. And he made himself heard on the need to preserve the community against the inroads of modernity.

In 1974 Conway and the surrounding area were reminded of MacLeish's fame when Pat Hingle came up to play the leading role and direct a production of *J.B.* at nearby Greenfield Community College, which was about to open its MacLeish Collection. Archie himself recorded the Distant Voice of God for the play, which was cast with amateur actors from the college and performed at Deerfield Academy. As the final curtain fell on opening night, Helen Ellis recalled, there was a long pause before the clapping began. *J.B.* gave the audience more to think about than they had bargained for in the age of television, she thought.

Archie's most memorable appearance in Conway occurred on the second Sunday in August 1976, when he delivered a lay sermon at the church his grandfather had once served. In that talk he reminded his listeners of his ties to Conway, of his grandmother's feelings for the town when she and her husband, Elias Brewster Hillard, came there for his last parish. She thought Conway was Arcadia, and Archie loved the town too. It was the place he belonged to and understood, he suggested in the poem "New England Weather."

> *Hay-time when the Boston forecast*
> *calls for haying weather, hot and fair,*

Conway people stick to garden chores
and nod toward nightfall at the cemetery:

that's where Sumner Boyden's lying now
and Sumner always told the town, if Boston
promised shine you'd better count on showers
'long toward evening with your hay crop lost.

He meant, no man can tell the weather
anywhere but where he's from:
you have to have the whole of it together,
bred in your bones

. . . . .

New England weather
breeds New Englanders: that changing sky
is part of being born and drawing breath
and dying, maybe, where you're meant to die.

Like many another elder, MacLeish at eighty located the ideal in the past and inveighed against the abuses of contemporary civilization. In an April 1972 article, "Rediscovering the Simple Life," he observed that "something fairly disturbing has been happening . . . in the last few years." Experts might disagree on the proximate cause: "the meaningless war in Southeast Asia, the generation gap in the American family, the credibility gap in the American government, the permissive rearing of American infants, the permissive handling of American Vice-Presidents, crime in the streets, hair on the shoulders, drugs in the schools." But for whatever reasons "the Republic is not what it used to be," except for those like the Amish who stubbornly refused to let growth and technology interfere with the simple life. "When you ask their children why the Amish don't live in the city, they say, 'Where would we keep our horses?' "

Urbanism, MacLeish feared, was eroding Americans' sense of themselves as a people. "We rarely even say we live in the United States," he pointed out. "We live in New York, or Boston, or Chicago. We don't live together . . . with a common vision of ourselves and our destiny." In the crowded cities, there was no room for memories, for there were no attics in which to stow them away for later exploration. This was unfortunate, MacLeish thought, for we need to go back periodically to renew ourselves. "A nation no more than a man can exist without perpetual rebeginnings, a recurrent return to a recurrently recreative past."

On the national political front, MacLeish was distressed by the success of the Nixon administration in restricting civil liberties in the name of "law and order" or "national security." In particular, he criticized Attorney General John Mitchell for his attempts to suppress the news through enjoining newspapers (as in the controversial Pentagon Papers case), and to silence student dissent by mass arrests. The irony, of course, was that the administration that campaigned — and won — on a "law and order" platform was unwilling to obey the law once in power. Public revulsion against the chicanery of Watergate provided MacLeish with a flutter of optimism for the future, but it was overbalanced by his disgust with the commercialism and obsession with sex he found pervasive in American society.

Love, Archie wrote in May 1972, had been replaced by sex to such a degree that man "has become sort of an ambulatory penis." The sexual act he regarded "the healthy and rational consequence of love." As John Donne wrote,

> Whoever loves, if he do not propose
> The right, true end of love, he's one that goes
> To sea for nothing but to make him sick . . .

Yet with us, he observed in a February 1973 article, it was the other way around. "We start . . . with 'sex' and assume that what then happens is going to be love." That could happen, he supposed, but the odds were against it. In a late poem, he lamented the change:

> What have they done to you, all-conquering love? —
> you who taught the lecherous birds to preen and even
> men to walk like men for pride of love —
> what have they done to you?
>
> And who are these,
> these nudest, lewdest, noisiest, their naked buttocks
> scarcely skirted and their breasts tipped up to tease —

The whole process was dehumanizing, and so was the picture of the modern man being offered in the advertisements of Madison Avenue. This creature was reduced to a mere collection of wants, whose dominant desires were "to smell sweet, to weigh less, to own the automobile everyone else will envy, and to go on smoking cigarettes even if they kill him."

The nation was in the grip of a business mentality, with all endeavor assessed on a bottom-line basis. Even book publishing, once a domain where decisions were made on something more than merely economic grounds, had fallen victim to the commercialization of American culture. The point was forcefully brought home to MacLeish when in March 1975 he received a form letter from Houghton Mifflin advising him that

A Continuing Journey was to be remaindered and offering to sell him copies of his own book at thirty cents apiece. More in sorrow than outrage, Archie wrote Dick McAdoo that he knew it was a "business end" decision and that he was not barking at him. All the same, he wanted to be sure that the books that represented the major accomplishment of his life stayed in print, including his collected poems and volumes of prose such as *A Continuing Journey*. Otherwise, he would want to talk to some of his friends in New York or Boston about other arrangements. Houghton Mifflin beat a strategic retreat, and Archie remained in the fold.

Domestic Crises

That times had changed was forcibly brought home to Archie and Ada with the divorce of their son Kenneth. They were "heartbroken" at the news, Ada wrote in June 1972. None of it made sense, she thought; Ken and Carolyn had been married for thirty-five years, and neither of them was in love with anyone else. Before the year was out, though, Ken had gotten his divorce and married Roslyn Ker, the former wife of Jill Conway's brother Barry. That marriage did not last long. Then in March 1973 Ken was operated on for cancer, too late to stop the spread of the disease. To Ada, especially, it was a devastating blow. Her firstborn child was, Archie wrote Adele Lovett, "the center of her life." This was an exaggeration, for Archie himself was at the center of her life. In fact, Ada's distress was exacerbated by a persisting awareness that she had given too much of herself to her husband and not enough to her children.

After his second divorce, Ken found a devoted companion for the time remaining to him. His cancer was terminal; the only question was when it would carry him away. Nonetheless, Jean Groo, who had fallen half in love with Ken during his Paris years, left her husband in August 1974 to come and care for him. He had three years left, and Jean stayed with him until the end.

The proper MacLeishes did not know quite what to make of the relationship. When Ken brought Jean to Antigua, she immediately saw that Ken was much closer to his mother than to his father. Archie seemed to be trying to infuse some warmth into the relationship, though, and the holiday was going quite well. Then, after a rather bad day for Ken's illness, Ada said: "Jean, we have to have a talk. What are your plans?" Jean sputtered and said, "I don't understand." Ada said: "My dear, what do you mean? Of course you understand. We have to make our plans and therefore we have to know your plans." Jean was ready to burst into tears, when Ken spoke for them both. "Look," he said, "Jean and

I just want to be together as long as I'm alive, and that's the way it's going to be." After this rather traumatic discussion, Archie put his arm around Jean and said: "Now, we don't care at all what people think. Whatever you're doing is all right with us." Meanwhile, Ken took Ada off to the balcony. "If you ever speak that way to Jean or to me again, you won't see us any more," he told his mother. Ada raised the issue, perhaps, because she and Archie were considering changing their will, should Ken and Jean get married. But she spoke also in the unmistakable tones of social propriety.

Early in 1976 Ken visited Antigua for the last time. Terribly ill and in considerable pain, he talked over cocktails with Morley Ballantine about schemes to do away with himself so that his mother would not find out. He couldn't just jump from a cliff or shoot himself, he explained. Once the most vigorous of men, Ken was reduced to lying on the couch and taking injections against pain. Ada cared for him like a child, making up for lost time as best she could. Still, he longed to please Archie, and felt that he never had and never could. At sixty, as his cousin Rod MacLeish said, "Ken was still trying to ascertain if his father loved him."

Early in August 1977 Ken died in Jean Groo's arms. He had wanted to come to Conway for his last weeks, but Archie thought it would be more than Ada could bear. Ken's ashes were brought there for a simple memorial ceremony at the Pine Grove Cemetery on August 9. Archie wrote a few words for the Reverend Philip Steinmetz to read: "Here in this pine grove, this hollow in the pines and oaks and maples, half a mile as the crow flies from the house he knew as a child, the room he loved to sleep in as a man, Kenneth has come home." His brother, Bill, played "Amazing Grace" on the bagpipe. Archie and Ada stood erect, seemingly in complete composure. The appearance was deceptive.

On the surface, the MacLeishes' life could hardly have been more serene and smoothly organized. Nellie and Millie, eighteen and seven years on the job respectively as cook and housekeeper, left their employ in the fall of 1976, but they were able to locate Roger and Phyllis Cummings, an attractive, intelligent couple down on their luck, to serve as replacements. As Phyllis Cummings reconstructed it, a typical day began with Archie and Ada taking an early morning swim in the pool. Then Ada had breakfast in her room, while Archie took his — oatmeal, prunes, orange juice, coffee — in the library looking out on the English garden and Mount Monadnock in the distance. These days, forgoing the walk to the stone house, Archie worked mornings at his manual typewriter in Ada's music room. Toward noon he floated down to the post office in his Mercedes to collect the mail.

When the MacLeishes entertained, they did so at midday. There were flowers everywhere when Donald Hall and his wife, Jane Kenyon, came one day in the summer of 1977. Phyllis served them chicken and broccoli and carrots cooked with chunks of pineapple, and a bottle of Vougeot '72. How fortunate Archie and Ada were, Hall thought, to be healthy and alert and to have their lives so nicely regulated after sixty-two years of marriage.

After lunch, Ada and Archie napped. In the late afternoon there was another swim, sometimes with the granddaughter — Ellen Ishbel MacLeish Zale, Ken and Carolyn's third-born — who had moved to a house only a short distance away with her husband, Peter. Later Archie and Ada watched the six o'clock news, had a drink of Scotch, and ate a simple evening meal.

There was "an elegance and dignity about their lives, a sense of order in everything," Phyllis wrote. In his meticulous fashion, Archie asked the questions. "Are the doors locked?" "Do we need fuel oil?" "Has the pool been cleaned?" He worried about fire, and saw to it that Roger kept the fire extinguishers — one to nearly every room — charged up. He worried about Ellen when she was pregnant with her son Alex, and insisted she move to Uphill Farm while Peter was on the road. "What if Peter's away and there's an emergency?" Archie said. Well, said Peter, Roger and Phyllis could help. "But what if the Cummingses are gone and it's night and I couldn't drive Ellen to the hospital?" Well, said Peter, you could call the ambulance. "Of course, of course," Archie said, "why didn't I think of that?" He was "a world-class worrier," Peter thought. "Nonsense," he said when people told him he shouldn't worry so much. "It's the one thing I do really well." With Ellen, as with her firstborn son, Alexander MacLeish Zale, Archie exhibited the tenderness of a mellowing patriarch. He was too old to try to shape Alex's life, or that of his other great-grandchildren. He could make fun of himself. His grandson Bruce telephoned one Thanksgiving Day, asking if he had any message for Bruce and Patty's children. "Tell them to think of me," Archie said with a chuckle, "as little less than godlike."

To Peter Zale, it seemed that Archie and Ada were trying to live within a cocoon, to shut out the messiness and unpredictability of ordinary existence. When the town fathers were about to allow a Motocross dirt-bike race along Pine Hill Road, Archie complained and got the permit rescinded. "They created a world apart," Peter said. There were no mosquitoes at Uphill Farm, no mice. "It didn't *rain* up there, unless they wanted it to."

With the death of Ken, that perfect cocoon started to spin loose. It was not simply a question of "Overstaying," as Archie's poem called it.

We used to walk here in the woods, we two,
laughing at time the way young lovers do —
laughing and talking of our new-born son.

And when we're dead, you'd say, and gone . . .

So we go first?

                    It's not in nature to outlive
the life you've borne, the breath you've given.

Ada was emotionally exhausted at a party Kay Bundy gave for her not long after Ken's death. "I've been a terrible mother," she said then, and she said the same thing while working in her garden with Jill Conway. In time, the guilt spilled over into anger and even fury. In addition, she began to have "events" — small strokes — that made her still angrier. Most of the rancor was directed against Archie. "You think you've got problems?" he said to his son, Bill, whose own marriage was coming apart. "Your mother is trying to destroy me."

There was a certain rough justice in Ada's turning her wrath against Archie. To Rod MacLeish it seemed that she was in effect repaying her husband for having given up both her career as a singer and her vocation as a mother in order to devote herself entirely to him. Undoubtedly she felt some jealousy, too, for even in his eighties, as certainly in his earlier decades, he openly courted the admiration of women. Ada was mean to Phyllis Cummings at times, at least in part because Phyllis was an attractive younger woman Archie treated with conspicuous consideration. Then there was Jill Conway, a woman of great intellectual strength and personal attractiveness. Archie and Jill went for long walks together, or he drove her around the hill towns to show her New England at its best. "Archie fell in love with Jill," John Conway said, twice. "But since he was thirty years older than me, there was no cause for anxiety." "Dad had a way with women," his son, Bill, said. Archie flirted so outrageously with the woman Bill was seeing after his marriage broke up that if he had been younger, Bill said, he would have been tempted to "punch [his father] in the head." The last time Archie read at Harvard, Bill Alfred had a party afterwards and introduced him to Gjertrud Schnackenburg, a young poet whose work he admired. Seeing how beautiful Schnackenburg was, Archie kept their conversation brief. Ada was there and he didn't want to upset her, he told Bill.

Archie reacted to Ada's anger by becoming even more solicitous and attentive than usual. He was, Phyllis Cummings thought, the most patient man alive. After long years without a driver's license, Ada secured one and started to drive herself on errands. If she weren't home on the minute, Archie grew frantic. When she went into Northampton to the hairdresser, he followed behind. Eventually Ada gave up and let him drive her wherever she had to go. "My driving," she said, "took too much out of Archie." Ada became for him, Jill Conway thought, a sort of Ur-woman, a maternal figure who enclosed his world, and he spoke of her with reverence. Finally, toward the end, her anger abated. "I think we have come out on the other side in a way," Archie wrote Alice Acheson in April 1980. "Meaning that we love each other more than we ever did when we loved each other most."

Bicentennial and Other Observances

As the country's most visible patriot-poet, MacLeish was naturally summoned to participate in a number of events commemorating the bicentennial of the nation's birth in 1776. The first of these came a year in advance of the nationwide celebration, when he read his "Night Watch in the City of Boston" on April 16, 1975, for the Boston bicentennial observances. The poem links present with past, using the figures of two Harvard colleagues — Kenneth Murdock and Samuel Eliot Morison — as guides back to Governor John Winthrop's seventeenth-century vision of what the new England on these shores might become.

> Old colleague,
> Puritan New England's famous scholar
> half intoxicated with those heady draughts of God,
> come walk these cobble-stones John Cotton trod,
>
> and you, our Yankee Admiral of the Ocean Sea,
> come too, come walk with me.
> You know, none better, how the Bay wind blows
> fierce in the soul as in the streets its ocean snows.
>
> Lead me between you in the night, old friends,
> one living and one dead, and where the journey ends
> show me the city built as on a hill
> John Winthrop saw long since and you see still.

After Murdock's death in November, Archie spoke of how his vision of Harvard had changed over the years. "Not until a man's own generation comes to its last few survivors, not until the generations of the dead include his own contemporaries, does he see what Harvard is and who has made it what it is — that long succession of the famous dead who bear the living on their shoulders." With affection he recalled the Murdock whose "lazy-seeming wit . . . darted like a lizard's tongue," whose intellectual power never "called attention to itself . . . but simplified and clarified and cleared away." With his passing, Archie said in his eulogy, Murdock joined the illustrious company of those who made Harvard great, and became forever part of the university he loved.

In March 1976 MacLeish appeared on PBS television's "Bill Moyers Journal." Archie loved the extended interview, for when Moyers asked a question, he wasn't thinking about something else but really listened to the answer. Moyers probed for old memories, and Archie recited for the television audience his last, self-excoriating recollection of his brother's death in World War I. Two old photographs called up the memory.

> *Family Group*
> That's my younger brother with his Navy wings.
> He's twenty-three or should have been that April:
> winters aged you, flying the Dutch coast.
> I'm beside him with my brand-new Sam Brown belt.
> The town behind us is Dunkirk. We met there
> quite by accident, sheer luck.
> Someone's lengthened shadow — the photographer's? —
> falls across the road, across our feet.
>
> This other's afterward —
> after the Armistice, I mean, the floods,
> the weeks without a word. That foundered
> farmyard is in Belgium somewhere.
> The faceless figure on its back, the helmet buckled,
> wears what looks like Navy wings. A lengthened shadow
> falls across the muck about its feet.
>
> Me? I'm back in Cambridge in dry clothes,
> a bed to sleep in, my small son, my wife.

The most remarkable thing about the Moyers interview was how youthful the eighty-three-year-old MacLeish looked. His "appearance, voice, and attitude" were those of a far younger man, Hayden Carruth thought. "Poetry, if it doesn't kill you, will keep you young, and MacLeish's poetry is distinctly the kind that sustains, not the kind that destroys." At the end of March, Archie read his poems at the Library of Congress, where *Washington Post* reporter Michael Kernan noted that "his voice and skin had the smooth tension one might expect in a man of 50." Moreover, Kernan observed, MacLeish's "words rang. Not many people are making words ring these days."

The subject those words were sounding was the meaning of the bicentennial. In April, Archie delivered the gist of what he had to say in a speech before the American Philosophical Society. Many people were treating the bicentennial with hoopla, as a sort of national birthday, he said. It was nothing of the kind. Instead it was the two-hundredth anniversary of the Declaration of Independence, signed on July 4, 1776. That raised the question whether the Declaration was solely a statement of *American* independence from Great Britain, as John Adams thought, or as Thomas Jefferson thought a far broader revolutionary proclamation applicable to all mankind. MacLeish was fascinated by the correspondence between Adams and Jefferson that had begun with Adams's 1812 letter, saying, "We ought not to die before we have explained ourselves to each other." The two former presidents wrote each other 150 letters during the succeeding fourteen years before they both died, uncannily, on the same date: July 4, 1826, the fiftieth anniversary of the Declaration of Independence. Their correspondence forms the heart of the play MacLeish wrote for the bicentennial, *The Great American Fourth of July Parade*.

Commissioned by the International Poetry Forum, MacLeish's play was presented both in a radio production and live onstage in Pittsburgh. The radio production was broadcast on National Public Radio, with Will Geer, one of Archie's favorite actors, as Jefferson. For the live production, John Houseman, who had directed Archie's first play, *Panic*, in 1935, served as director, with Melvyn Douglas as Jefferson and George Grizzard as Adams. In MacLeish's play the two former presidents return to observe the shrunken, fearful, Nixonian United States of the present, with "a knave in office and a palace guard of fools." No matter how dark his perception of the country, Archie was characteristically unwilling to succumb to despair. *The Great American Fourth of July Parade* ends with the letter Jefferson wrote to the citizens of Washington on June 24, 1826, regretting that he would be unable to attend the planned Fourth of July celebration. "May [the Declaration of Independence] be to the world what I believe it will be: to some parts sooner, to others later, but finally to all, the signal of arousing men to burst the chains," Jefferson wrote. "The mass of mankind has not been born with saddles on their backs for a favored few, booted and spurred, ready to ride them by the grace of God."

On July 4, 1976, two segments from *The Great American Fourth of July Parade* were shown on CBS television, and MacLeish himself was interviewed for CBS radio. Asked about future prospects for the sort of human liberty Jefferson envisioned, Archie noted that although the young were naturally skeptical, having grown up in or near the modern police state with all its devices to restrict freedom of thought, human liberty was still very much alive. Nor was there any reason to despair because we had not achieved an ideal state where all might shake off their chains. Such freedom was beyond our reach today just as it had been in 1826. Freedom was a process rather than a fulfillment, Archie said. What was important was the will to keep striving toward it.

In his enthusiastic belief that freedom lay at the heart of American life, MacLeish was sometimes inclined to reinvent history. Only with difficulty, for example, did Perry Miller convince him that the Puritans were not libertarian in the least, that in fact they were extremely intolerant of divergent views. Similarly, Archie's admiration for the wisdom and humanity of the Founding Fathers mistakenly led him to attribute their virtues to late-eighteenth-century Americans in general. His heart was if anything overgenerous. Where he erred was in letting an idea take possession of his mind.

Early in 1977 Houghton Mifflin published MacLeish's *New and Collected Poems, 1917–1976*. Even with substantial omissions from his early work, the collection covered sixty years of poetry in over five hundred pages. It was "an honorable and exemplary accomplishment," Hayden Carruth wrote. The book revealed a poet "by turns lyrical, dramatic, elegiac, hortatory, satirical, philosophical, romantic, classical, colloquial, elegant, vague, and painstakingly lucid," Robert Siegel observed in his review for *Poetry*. And the two dozen or so new poems, like the late poems of Frost and of Yeats, partook of "the great plain lucidities."

There was a rumor that President Jimmy Carter would ask Archie to deliver a poem at his inauguration. The rumor was false: James Dickey, Carter's fellow southerner, did the honors instead. Rather unexpectedly, it was outgoing President Gerald Ford, a Republican, who honored MacLeish by awarding him the Medal of Freedom in January 1977. Archie was in Antigua at the time, and his nephew Rod MacLeish accepted in his stead. The next year, Archie was chosen as the recipient of the National Medal for Literature. In his acceptance speech at the New York Public Library on April 6, 1978, Archie deflected attention from himself to speak out against the gobbling up of publishing firms by corporate business giants. Book publishing was more than a business, he said. It was a public trust. "Imagine what this Republic would have been if Henry Thoreau had never found a publisher, as he all but didn't; if Whitman had been allowed to go out of print, as he very nearly did; if those little snippets of Emily Dickinson's in the bureau drawer in that house in Amherst had never found the covers of a book."

In 1979, for the third year in a row, Archie received a major award when the American Academy voted him its gold medal for poetry. Making the presentation on May 23, Richard Wilbur brilliantly summed up the two qualities that "are peculiar to [MacLeish's] vision." First, "he has been, of all our leading poets, the most *engagé*, the most given to the criticism celebration and exhortation of his countrymen." Second, and apparently at odds with the first, "from the beginning of his career, MacLeish's unique sensibility has reacted to the new 'immensities of time and space.' . . . Long before the astronauts looked back at us from the moon, MacLeish habitually saw us as transient riders of a small and mortal planet." In summing up, Wilbur proposed that Archie's poetry, "haunted both by cosmic and by human time, is animated throughout by an internal quarrel, an opposition between a sense of what used to be called 'the vanity of the world,' and a contrary impulse to accept and affirm the human lot . . . when this internal clash is keenest, the poems strike most fire." Many of those poems, Wilbur concluded, "are already part of our national inheritance."

Archie, at eighty-seven, was moved by this praise from a friend and fellow poet who had done him the service of understanding his poetry. It was, he told the guests at the academy celebration, "this acceptance by the others which counts." He may have let his thoughts drift back to his youth, and to a father who would not take notice of his achievements, in what came next. "How much it counts — how much it counted for each one of us at the start — we all of us remember although we do not talk of it. But what it means when it happens also toward the end is something else. . . . When the acceptance comes again, at the work's end or near it, it is like the touch of hands."

25

LAST LINES

A Voice of One's Own

ARCHIBALD MACLEISH in his eighties looked like the old man most want to become: physically vigorous, mentally alert, as full of wisdom as of years. Yet his ninth decade was not without its trials. Honorific awards to the contrary, he was fully aware of the decline in his reputation. Few things bothered him more than the way younger people tended to dismiss his work and his ideas as the products of a worn-out generation. "In natural societies like Confucian China and Homeric Greece," he pointed out, "what mattered was living — knowing how to live — and the old who had lived longest were assumed to know most." He was perfectly aware that merely surviving did not invariably produce knowledge, as his notebook poem "Correction" illustrates.

> Men improve with the years, says Yeats.
> Better loves? Better hates?
> Take the case of Joan Miró,
> painter of The Constellations.
> Where did all that passion go?
> What happened to the great equations?
>
> Joan Miró at eighty-one
> tells The Times, when all is done,
> he trusts his last and final word,
> his ultimate verdict will be merde!
> Improvement? Merde's the verdict of the young and verde.

Nonetheless, he deplored the youth worship of the United States and longed for the golden societies of the past where age was given its due.

Psychologically, what most troubled Archie about growing old was the "demeaning and dehumanizing" onset of fear. In a notebook entry for November 1976, he wrote of how he dreaded

> ... the cold — the draft on the stair — the first snow in autumn. You creep back into yourself, into bundles of clothes, into corners of time, into numbness. Coleridge discovered in *Dejection* that the beauty of all beauty is within — that you cannot feel, though you can see, the yellow green of the summer sward if your soul is sick. Which seems to mean that the *way* to beauty is inward and that the way is closed when the inward world is death. But old men cry — and should cry — to be carried "out of themselves." They are right. Wonder and delight cannot be felt when a man is turned inward on himself as the old are. One must grow old, prepare to die, facing outward toward the miracle of things. But how to turn!

In late poems, too, he summoned up the ways fear crept into his consciousness. It could come after a summer nap.

> *I fall asleep these days too easily —*
> *doze off of an afternoon*
> *in the warm sun by the humming trees —*
> *but I wake too soon:*
>
> *wake too soon and wake afraid*
> *of the blinding sun, of the blazing sky.*
> *It was dark in the dream where I was laid:*
> *It is dark in the earth where I will lie.*

All his life he had been obsessed by the fleeting passage of time. Now, he felt it as never before.

> *Only the old know time: they feel it flow*
> *like water through their fingers when the light*
> *ebbs from the pasture and they wade in night.*
> *It frightens them.*

Time, he said, was "what there [was] not a lot of."

Disquieted by such thoughts, he found that even the splendors of Antigua faded away. "This island — maybe it's more than an island — has lost its charm for me," he wrote Steve Becker in January 1976. Partly, he was disillusioned by the influx of newcomers, "a substitute layer of humanity which would be as much at home in Florida or Cal-

ifornia or anywhere else exposed to the sun." But his own capacity to
take joy in the sand and sea had dwindled too. "I used to hear the Trades
all night long," he wrote. "Now all I hear is wind." As it turned out,
Archie and Ada did not return to Antigua after 1976. With the death
of Noel Macy, Isiri was no longer available to them on an extended
basis. They tried other alternatives during the next few winters. At the
Coral Beach Club in Bermuda, they dressed for dinner each night and
sat in a half-empty dining room unrecognized and ignored. For companionship they struck up a friendship with the waiter. At Hobe Sound
in Florida, Archie got into a roaring argument with Adele Lovett about
the behavior of Ted Kennedy at Chappaquiddick. There wasn't another
Democrat within miles, Ada reported.

None of these difficulties of aging were obvious to others, which was
how Archie wanted it. His eyesight and hearing were fading, but he did
not choose to acknowledge these invasions of age by wearing glasses or
a hearing aid. He continued to drive, though more slowly in the haze.
And in conversation he cupped his ear and "hoped," as Warren Harris
said. As late as the summer of 1979, he worked with Ellen and Peter
Zale at putting in some potatoes, and "damned near killed" grandson-
in-law Peter, trying to keep up with him. "Oh, to be eighty again,"
Archie said, gaily.

The greatest depredation old age wrought was on MacLeish's creative
faculties. Through 1978 he was still entering poems into his notebooks.
Then they stopped coming. His short-term memory was slipping, he told
Donald Hall. He could remember what happened half a century earlier,
but not the poem he was working on. "When you are young you walk
in the woods and you are surrounded by the poem you are trying to
write; it flies around your head. When you are older you forget you are
working on it," he said. Each day he had to start anew, with no recollection of what he had done the day before. At the same time, his
compulsion to write did not leave him. "There are all sorts of things I
want to do that I haven't been able to do," the eighty-nine-year-old
MacLeish told an interviewer in November 1981. Still, he found some
consolation in the assurance "of *having been*." Although the haunting
sense of extinguishment was unavoidable, "something in you *does* marshall, against it, an unarguable sense of *having been*."

Before his powers grew dim, Archie wrote some of the best poems of
his life on the "terminal experience" of aging and death. It helped that
he had arrived at a final understanding of his craft. In a letter to Holly
Morgan, an aspiring young poet, he advised her that one must learn to
see, to hear, and to think in terms of life, not of words. To arrive at that
goal, the prescription was "Read! Read!" She should read Keats's letters,

Yeats, Shakespeare and Catullus and Sappho and Rimbaud and Li Tai Po and Villon and Emily Dickinson. He did not think poetry was "essentially autobiography," he told her. "I think it tries to make sense of the confusion." In Bermuda in the winter of 1978, he came across a definition of poetry that agreed with and extended that. In book 11 of Robert Fitzgerald's translation of the *Odyssey*, Alkinoös compliments Odysseus for having told his story "as a poet would — a man who knows the world." That was it, Archie thought at once. Those were the words he had needed for years. "Who *does* know the world?" he said to Donald Hall. "Not the businessman. Not the scientist. Yes — Shakespeare, Homer, Dante. This is what makes greatness in a poet: *to know the world*." It was a definition that provided full justification for MacLeish's ventures into the law and journalism, the government and the academy.

A poet not only knew the world well enough to make sense of its confusion, but was also one who had found his voice. For most, the discovery came late. "The voice isn't there at the start; it develops as the work piles up." This was true of Yeats and Pound and Frost. Keats was the exception who in his precocious genius had set down the admirable axiom that "if Poetry comes not as naturally as Leaves to a tree it had better not come at all." Archie, who in early and midcareer had been influenced by Eliot and other modernists, achieved such a natural voice in his poetry of old age.

At sixty-five MacLeish had written "The Old Gray Couple." Twenty years later he discovered that he hadn't known anything about the subject. For one thing, the completely familiar world the old looked at every day wasn't really familiar at all. "It has a different light from a different direction; there are different relations of light and dark." Few things were the same as they used to be.

Definitions of Old Age

Your eyes change.
Your handwriting changes.
You can't read what you once wrote.
Even your own thoughts sound wrong to you,
something some old idiot has misquoted.

*

When apple trees are old as you are,
over-aged and crooked grown,
something happens to their occupation.
What's the use, this late, of bearing apples?
Let the apples find a father of their own.

*

*Or put it in contemporary terms: the time
when men resign from their committees,
cancel their memberships, decline
the chairmanship of the United Fund,
buy a farm in Dorset or New Fane
and still get up at seven every morning
right on time for nothing left to do but
sit and age
and look up "dying" in the yellow pages.*

*

*old age
level light
evening in the afternoon
love without the bitterness and so
good-night*

He wrote of the comedy of trying to cope with the twistings and turnings of what passed for progress, as in this untitled poem.

*Old age — to live in your life
as a man in his home town, when Interstate
Ninety cuts through Parsons' orchard, slices
Florence's Lunch in two, demolishes
seven elms — all that was left of them —
kills the maple by the Tap and Die,
bulldozes Totman's woods — pines, birches,
coons and Tittleman Brook and the thrushes — all of it —*

*to live in your life like a man in his own town
when you can't remember where the church was, coming from
Pumpkin Hollow over the underpass west of it
or how to get down to the store from River Road
now they've rerouted it east instead of north
or how to get home again even —*

*   like the story:*

*Hey Rube! How do you get to Deerfield?
Well, I'll tell you — I wouldn't start from here.
You can't get home from here.*

*   When you're old.*

He wrote of the poignancy of outlasting one's time, with the children gone and the parents left alone like a crofter and his wife in the Hebrides.

A man and his wife, those two,
left on the ocean island:
they talk as the old will do
and they nod and they smile

but they think of their sons, how they laughed,
and she calls but it's not for them —
"she'd rather a kitten to have
than a child to remember."

You can live too long in a life
where the sons go off and the daughter
off over sea and the wife
watches the water.

He wrote of how time speeded up when it ought to go slow.

No need to race the days so — Sunday, Monday.
Yesterday was April: now it's May.
Time ought to stop a little just at sundown —
stand there — stay:

He wrote of how the words no longer came as they once had, in the sound of the sea at night.

Years ago in the night
there were words in the sound of the wind,
words in the sound of the sea.
I would wake in the night and know
that they spoke to me.

Now in the night the words
cry in the sound of the wind,
cry in the sound of the sea.
I wake and I know they speak
but not to me.

Most poignantly and privately of all, he described that sense of otherness that had visited him in the toolshed at Craigie Lea at eleven, and in his house in Cambridge at twenty-five when he looked in the mirror and saw a stranger's face. In "Epigraph" he suggests a reason for that alienation from himself, an overpowering feeling that in his inmost self he was not at all the Archibald MacLeish of vast accomplishment and international recognition, that in pursuing his goals he had shut himself off from companionship, that in adopting a public persona he had almost lost track of himself.

This old man is no one I know
even if his look is mine —
or was when he first wore it in the jacket
photograph that advertised his book.

Everyone seems to know him: I don't know him.
People stop him at the post office to talk:
they don't stop me when I go walking.
I've lived here fifty years but they don't stop me.

It's him they want to see: the writer.
What I am they've never figured out —
only that I take to wood-lots evenings
crazing all the door-yard dogs.

Must be out for honey, way they see it —
lining up the late, last homeward flights
for bearings on a bee-tree somewhere.
Maybe I am but not their kind of honey.

I wonder, when they come to dig his grave
and find me lying in it, will they guess
whose death he died of, his or mine? —
Whose life I lived? —
                    Who wrote this line?

More Than a Rider

In his eschatological awareness of the end of things, MacLeish begrudged any time spent away from poetry. It was partly for this reason that he did not respond to Houghton Mifflin's suggestion that he write his autobiography. For a time, in the summer of 1976, he considered doing a short book about the Paris years, but the project came to nothing. It kept turning into "a kind of old man's tribute to his generation . . . what Gertie [Stein] called the 'lost generation,' " he explained. And it threatened to emerge "as a poem of some considerable length — the worst kind of poem for practical uses." He resisted, too, the idea of confronting his life openly. When he consented to place some of his reminiscences on tape, first in 1976 to enable Bernard A. Drabeck and Helen E. Ellis of Greenfield Community College to put together an edited transcription of his remarks and next in 1979 for R. H. Winnick to begin work toward a biography, Archie firmly evaded any inquiries about the intimate details of his private life.

The process of reflecting on his own history and on the years in Paris, however, did lead to the "Autobiographical Information" section of

MacLeish's final book of prose, *Riders on the Earth,* published early in 1978. Therein he recounted tales of his football days at Yale, his decision to give up the law for poetry, and his grandparents' love for Conway. These essays, the best in the book, were preceded by six others celebrating the American past at the expense of a diminished present, and followed by elegiac recollections of Gerald Murphy, Carl Sandburg, and Mark Van Doren, among others. In a concluding article, Archie nicely described Frost's characteristic irony as "a way of saying so that one may see: a reflection, a refraction, of the light that makes the too familiar visible." Altogether *Riders* is MacLeish's most readable and interesting collection of essays. In 1980 Houghton Mifflin brought out *Six Plays,* a collection of his short verse plays from *Nobodaddy* through *This Music Crept by Me upon the Waters.* It was the twenty-sixth and last book published during Archie's lifetime.

In his final years, as MacLeish's health began to deteriorate, he cut down on his usual busy round of public appearances. He managed to turn up on most occasions important to him — when the Library of Congress observed the fortieth anniversary of his installation as librarian in the fall of 1979, for example, and when he was invited to read his poetry at Harvard in April 1980. He was also in the audience when his play *Panic* was performed outdoors in downtown Greenfield in July 1980, appropriately on the steps of an abandoned bank building. The opening night was something of a fiasco. "The whole sound system collapsed," Archie wrote, "so that the play was an hour late and when it did start we couldn't hear a word." In subsequent performances, apparently, that problem was corrected, and *Panic* was held over for three weekends, with Routes 5 and 10 closed to traffic during the play.

More and more, though, the exigencies of age kept Archie close to home. Travel became a burden, his heart was giving him trouble, and he hated to leave Ada alone now that she was losing her powers. When Tom Johnson came to call at Uphill Farm and proposed taking Archie off for a brisk mile walk, Ada tried to talk him out of it. "You have no idea," she told him, "how old we are." To almost everyone, it seemed likely that Ada would be the first to die. They no longer attempted to make the long trips south to escape winter weather. In January 1980 Archie was unable to go as far as Washington to attend the White House ceremony organized by Rosalynn Carter to honor American poets. And in the winter of 1982, he had to call off a long-planned visit to Dartmouth when he slipped on a patch of ice, fell, and broke his elbow.

On March 20, 1982, Archie was taken to Massachusetts General Hospital for exploratory surgery. He was operated on for obstruction of the bowel, and though the surgery relieved his pain, he never fully recovered. While in the hospital, he contracted the pneumonia — "the old person's friend" — that carried him off. He died April 20, seventeen days short of his ninetieth birthday. Like his mother before him, he was prepared to go.

In her distress, Ada made the two-hour journey from Conway to Boston to see Archie only once during his final month. Jill Conway, then associated with MIT in Cambridge, visited him several times. On her last visit, Archie's mind carried him back to the 1920s. He confused Jill with a woman he once had an assignation with in Paris, and refused to be summoned away from that world into the present. He had enchanted his nurses, Jill could see. Morellen and Meg, his youngest grandchildren, stopped in every other day. On one such visit Archie was out of bed, sitting up in a chair. Even under heavy sedation, he recognized both girls as members of the family. He was an old man and very tired, he said. He didn't "want to play the game" any longer. He wanted "to get on with it." He began to refuse food. To encourage Archie, Meg and Morellen tried to interest him in going back to Conway. "When are we going," Archie asked, "11:30 or 12:30?" To say something, Morellen said, "11:30." "That's too early," Archie said.

His son, Bill, on his last visit, thought of the directive Dylan Thomas had issued to his dying father. "Do not go gentle into that good night / ... Rage, rage against the dying of the light." It was natural that Dylan Thomas should come to mind. A few days before Archie went to the hospital, he gave Bill a copy of "Whistler in the Dark," which may have been the last poem he wrote. In it he confronted the darkness with a buoyancy born of the art that he had always though intermittently devoted himself to.

> *George Barker, British poet,*
> *writes a eulogy of Dylan Thomas,*
> *calls him whistler in the dark*
> *and great because the dark is getting darker.*
>
> *Is it? Was the dark not always darker?*
> *Have we not always had these silver whistlers?*
> *Listen! . . .*
>   *That's Chaucer like a bobolink.*
>
> *I think it's not the darkness, Mr. Barker,*
> *makes for whistling well, I think*
> *perhaps it's knowing how to whistle.*
> *Listen! . . .*
>   *That's Dylan trilling like a lark.*

Bill read the poem, he wrote in his splendid reminiscence, "The Silver Whistler," and rested his arm on his father's shoulder as he sat looking east toward Monadnock. "Do you know what I owe you?" Bill asked him. Archie looked up, put his hand to his son's face, and said, "Only your life."

Behind his oxygen mask at the hospital, Archie did not seem to be raging against the oncoming night. The last thing he said to Bill was, "You get along." Back to Uphill Farm, back to Ada, back to the life Archie was leaving behind. Bill went back, carrying with him an image of Archie as a wonderful friend who had never quite learned how to be a father.

Archie left an estate of nearly a million dollars. The holdings of Ada, who died two years later, came to about twice as much. Although these were substantial sums, Archie and Ada did not think of themselves as rich, their lawyer G. d'Andelot Belin said. They were "well off, not rich," and even in death cautious about money. Mimi and Bill, both in their fifties, got their inheritance in the form of a trust on which the income was conveyed to them, while the principal was held inviolate for their heirs.

Archie's resting place was ready for him at Pine Grove Cemetery. The grave plot was landscaped, and myrtle and jonquils were planted. A boulder from Uphill Farm, labeled simply *MacLeish,* declared the family site, and stones from the property marked the individual graves. Archie was buried alongside sons Ken and Brewster, the baby who died in 1921 and was reburied in Conway sixty years later. The funeral service for Archie, at the gravesite, was very simple. Ada, weary and tottery, saw to it that decorum ruled. The great-grandchildren, she made it clear, were not to attend the ceremony. Only the adult family and a few friends were present, including neighbors Warren and Priscilla Harris, Sara and Gerald Murphy's daughter, Honoria Donnelly, and Richard Wilbur. The Reverend Philip Steinmetz said a few words, and the company adjourned to the western terrace of Uphill Farm for drinks and a light lunch. It was a lovely New England spring day, on the brink of the "slow May" Archie loved.

With the quiet ceremony in Conway, the memorials had only begun. Two weeks later Greenfield Community College presented the Archibald MacLeish Symposium that had been scheduled to coincide with his ninetieth birthday. With Archie's death, the symposium celebrating his accomplishments took on the character of a wake as well. The observances, on Friday and Saturday, May 7–8, included a number of scholarly papers, a concert presentation of Alice Parker's setting of *Songs for Eve* for vocal quartet and string quartet, a reading of his radio play *Air Raid,* and showings of his television appearances with Mark Van Doren and with Bill Moyers. John and Jill Conway and Donald Hall spoke of their memories, and Bill read a brief section from "The Silver Whistler." Tributes came from a number of people who were not on hand and some who were. Among those who sent messages in absentia were President Ronald Reagan, Vice President George Bush, Senator Edward M. Kennedy, and Congressman Silvio O. Conte. On hand were Henry Steele Commager, John Kenneth Galbraith, Mark Kramer, Paul Mariani, Arthur M. Schlesinger, Jr., and Robert Penn Warren. A long message of praise for Archie from Governor Edward King was read just before it was Galbraith's turn to speak. He sat there impatiently, concocting in his mind an impromptu opening riposte. "My friends," he planned to say, "we have just heard a long encomium from Governor Ed King on the demise of Archibald MacLeish. How happy it would be if it were the other way around." But Galbraith lost his nerve and did not say that, except afterwards, privately, for Ada's enjoyment.

Richard Wilbur, who was obliged to be in Lake Forest, Illinois, on the weekend of the symposium, sent a letter in praise of Archie. "There are phrases, lines and poems of his which I say to myself whenever I want to remember how the iron of English should ring from a tongue," Wilbur wrote. "And let me say one thing more: Not all poets are good men, but Archie was always both." He helped and heartened his fellow writers, and "was stubbornly generous even to ungrateful rascals."

Later that month at Harvard, an array of the university's most eminent professors paid their respects to MacLeish. Douglas Bush, himself dying, slowly made his way to the pews as a Bach requiem was played. Five former colleagues and friends spoke: John Conway, Bill Alfred, Harry Levin, Jack Bate, and Walter Kaiser. They were assembled to praise "one of the great Americans of our time," Kaiser said. MacLeish represented "an imposing part of the landscape of this republic, standing there like a lofty graceful elm on the broad lawn of summer, an image of rectitude and compassion, a symbol of aspiration and poetic truth." That elm had been felled now, "yet the verdant memory of that noble landmark — where he stood and what he stood for — will remain with us for the rest of our days."

Archie's greatest gift, Levin said, was the "limpid lyricism as resonantly characteristic of him as his unforgettable tenor voice." Animating his poetry was his belief in man and in the capacity for friendship and love. MacLeish ranked as "one of the half-dozen best poets of his wonderfully talented generation," Jack Bate said. In illustration of the point, Bate read Archie's "Winter Is Another Country."

> *If the autumn would*
> *End! If the sweet season,*
> *The late light in the tall trees would*
> *End! If the fragrance, the odor of*
> *Fallen apples, dust on the road,*
> *Water somewhere near, the scent of*
> *Water touching me; if this would end*
> *I could endure the absence in the night,*
> *The hands beyond the reach of hands, the name*
> *Called out and never answered with my name:*
> *The image seen but never seen with sight.*
> *I could endure this all*
> *If autumn ended and the cold light came.*

Literary reputations flicker and dim, as Archibald MacLeish's surely has. But sometimes they blaze again. "He will be revived," Donald Hall says of his onetime mentor and friend. Not may be; will be. If so, it is likely to be because of such simple, moving, and unpretentious lyrics as "Winter Is Another Country," which evokes an unspoken sorrow at the heart. That poem, from 1948's *Actfive,* is not among those that customarily find their way into anthologies, for it was written too late. Most of Archie's poetry published after World War II has been regarded as the product of one who, having chosen public speech as his métier and public service as his profession for the previous fifteen years, had thereby sacrificed his claim for consideration in the second half of the twentieth century.

Yet surely the anthologized poems deserve to be remembered as well, none more than "You, Andrew Marvell." In his tribute to MacLeish at the American Academy meeting of December 2, 1982, Howard Nemerov spoke of how that poem reminded him of Dante's last long look back at the earth in the *Paradiso.* "Archie got the sense of the earth we live on, turning turning, in mysterious relation with the sun and shadow and the other stars."

> *And here face downward in the sun*
> *To feel how swift how secretly*
> *The shadow of the night comes on . . .*

As I. A. Richards put it, Archie had "the planetary sense," and from young manhood he was haunted by the coming of the night. As time sped past him, he hurried forward to do the next thing, and the next. John Broderick was struck by how forward-looking MacLeish was at eighty-seven, when he came to the fortieth anniversary celebration of his tenure as librarian of Congress. He "was not content to be known as the author of such anthology pieces as 'Ars poetica,' or 'You, Andrew Marvell,' or the renowned *J.B.,* or the *former* this, that, or the other. His eye was ever on what lay beyond the next horizon," Broderick said.

It is not simply as a poet that Archibald MacLeish deserves to be remembered. Again and again in his writing, Archie represented his life as a journey, a continuing journey that took him from one challenge to another. In undertaking those travels, he was always willing to set out afresh, to test himself against strong currents and rough terrain. He did not ride upon the earth. He bestrode it.

Acknowledgments ❖

Notes

Bibliography

Index

Acknowledgments ❖

THE MOST IMPORTANT SOURCES for this biography are the writings of Archibald MacLeish: first of all his published poems and plays and essays, but also his unpublished works, including notebooks and journals and poetry. Taken together with his letters, these bespeak the man as no secondary materials possibly could. For the same reason the taped interviews of MacLeish conducted by R. H. Winnick take on an extraordinary importance, as do his observations recorded and transcribed by Bernard A. Drabeck and Helen E. Ellis. I am grateful to Richard B. McAdoo, executor of MacLeish's estate, for permission to quote from all of his work.

In addition, this book is based on news accounts, articles, and reviews, most of them collected by Winnick, on books that deal directly with MacLeish or with figures important in his life, and on interviews with and letters from friends and family members.

Before beginning to list those who assisted the project during its twelve-year development, I want to acknowledge a few debts of great magnitude. First and foremost, Thursa Bakey Sanders provided indispensable information about MacLeish's years in government service from 1939 to 1945. Members of the family generously and without conditions consented to share their recollections, particularly MacLeish's son and daughter, William H. MacLeish and Mimi Grimm. Most of the photographs that illustrate this biography were supplied by MacLeish's grandson A. Bruce MacLeish.

Several written sources deserve special recognition. These include the privately printed memoirs of both of Archibald MacLeish's remarkable parents, Andrew and Martha Hillard MacLeish, Colin C. Campbell's splendid 1960 doctoral dissertation, and "The MacLeish of F. Bangs," a two-hundred-page compendium of reminiscences, correspondence, and commentary assembled by MacLeish's friend and Yale classmate Francis H. Bangs. Winnick's drafts of six early chapters toward a biography furnished important factual information and suggested lines of approach. Special issues of *Identity, Pembroke Magazine,* and *Massachusetts Review* offered insights into MacLeish's writing and glimpses of his life. The poet Stephen Sandy kindly sent me his account of MacLeish's final days at Harvard. Robert Cowley, Benjamin DeMott, Donald Hall, and Richard Meryman published excellent interviews with MacLeish. The single best article on MacLeish is by his son William, "The Silver Whistler." Ada MacLeish kept useful scrapbooks of reviews and articles about her husband; her letters to Maurice Firuski, Adele Lovett, and Sara Murphy contain essential background data on family movements and occurrences.

The interviews R. H. Winnick completed between 1978 and 1983, almost all tape-recorded, were with Alice (Mrs. Dean) Acheson, Thomas Boylston Adams, William Alfred, David Amram, Carlos Baker, Ellen (Mrs. Philip) Barry, W. Jackson Bate, Paul Brooks, John Bullitt, Kay (Mrs. Harvey H.) Bundy, McGeorge Bundy, William P. and Mary A. Bundy, Stanley Burnshaw, Ishbel MacLeish and Alexander Campbell, Jane (Mrs. Cass) Canfield, John and Jill Ker Conway, Malcolm Cowley, Robert Cowley, Lewis Andrew Day, Alfred de Liagre, Jr., Dorothy de Santillana, John Sloan Dickey, Honoria Murphy and William Donnelly, John Duke, Luther B. Evans, Elizabeth Eyre de Lanux, John H. Finley, Jr., Walter T. Fisher, Franklin L. Ford, Martha MacLeish Fuller, Ives Gammell and Daniel Sargent, Jean Groo, Allen Grover, Mason and Florence Hammond, Roxanne (Mrs. Laurens) Hammond, Ethel de Lang Hein, William Heyen, Pat Hingle, Edward Hoagland, Ralph M. Ingersoll, Tom Johnson, Elia Kazan, Eliza Howe (Mrs. William S.) Keith, Harry Levin, Mrs. Robert N. Linscott, Adele and Robert A. Lovett, Dwight Macdonald, Anne (Mrs. Ranald) Macdonald, Archibald and Ada MacLeish, Carolyn MacLeish, William H. MacLeish, Elena (Mrs. Noel) Macy, Richard B. McAdoo, David McCord, David C. Mearns, Keyes Metcalf, Elizabeth (Mrs. Perry) Miller, Kathleen J. and Theodore Morrison, Honor Moore, L. Quincy Mumford, Eleanor (Mrs. Kenneth) Murdock, Alice-Lee Myers and Frances Brennan, Stuart Ostrow, David Perkins, Hester Pickman and Daisy Oakley, Nathan M. Pusey, Philip and Mabel Reed, Austin W. Scott, Dorothy (Mrs. Mark) Van Doren, Edward Weeks, Helen Calhoun Wolfson, and Ellen Ishbel and Peter B. Zale.

My interviews during 1987–1991, some formal and some conversational, were with Alice (Mrs. Dean) Acheson, Mary Manning (Mrs. Faneuil) Adams, William Alfred, Morley Cowles Ballantine and Peggy Ferguson, W. Jackson Bate, Stephen and Mary Becker, G. d'Andelot Belin, Robert Bly, Birgit Carstensen, James Chace, John and Jill Ker Conway, Robert Cowley, Phyllis Cummings, Peter Davison, Bernard A. Drabeck, Helen E. Ellis, Barbara (Mrs. Robert L.) Foote, Martha MacLeish and Herbert Fuller, John Kenneth Galbraith, George J. W. Goodman ("Adam Smith"), Mimi and Karl Grimm, Robert F. Grose, Allan Guttmann, Donald Hall, Edward Hoagland, Edwin Honig, Frank Snowden Hopkins, Susan Howe, Michael Janeway, Tom Johnson, Ilona Karmel, John Knowlton, Jonathan Kozol, Richard B. and Mary Mc-Adoo, Robie Macauley, A. Bruce and Patty MacLeish, Morellen MacLeish, Roderick MacLeish, William H. MacLeish and Elizabeth Libbey, A. Martin Macy, Eugene J. McCarthy, Robert L. Merriam, Linda Miller, Honor Moore, George Plimpton, William H. Pritchard, Mary Virginia Rawlings, Thursa Bakey Sanders, Stephen Sandy, May Sarton, Patricia (Mrs. Ogden) Starr, Elizabeth Marshall Thomas, Robert C. (Kim) Townsend, Felicia Geffen Van Veen, Lael Wertenbaker, Richard Wilbur, R. H. Winnick, and Ellen Ishbel and Peter B. Zale.

In addition, William H. MacLeish, who had tape-recorded the reminiscences of his parents about their early days in Conway, Massachusetts, graciously made that tape available. Bernard A. Drabeck and Helen E. Ellis have deposited in the archives at Greenfield (Mass.) Community College the transcriptions of their interviews with Stephen Becker, Russell ("Rusty") Blossom, the Warren Harris family, Frances Steele Holden, Hugh Ralston, and Chaloner Spencer. Other tape-recordings were also enlightening, including those of MacLeish during a reading and talk at Williams College and at the memorial service for Maurice Firuski. Most helpful of all are the tapes that record the proceedings of the fortieth anniversary observance of MacLeish's term as librarian of Congress, and the deeply affecting memorial service for him at Harvard. MacLeish's remarks during two television appearances are preserved in written form in *The Dialogues of Archibald MacLeish and Mark Van Doren* and the transcript of his 1976 appearance on the "Bill Moyers Journal."

By far the most extensive MacLeish collection, including his notebooks and most of his correspondence, is located at the Library of Congress. The Beinecke Library at Yale University also has important MacLeish holdings, and Greenfield Community College is building a valuable archive of memorabilia and documents related to MacLeish. The Time Inc. archives contain numerous memoranda from MacLeish's years at *Fortune* and thereafter. The library of the American Academy and Institute of Arts and Letters has various letters, speeches, and nominations tracing MacLeish's involvement with that institution. Herbert Mitgang supplied the six-hundred-page FBI file on MacLeish he had obtained under the Freedom of Information Act, and materials in the National Archives helped to facilitate a proper understanding of his service with the Office of Facts and Figures and Office of War Information.

Other institutions that provided access to MacLeish letters and documents include Amherst College, Boston Public Library, Boston University, Bancroft Library of the University of California at Berkeley, University of California at Los Angeles, Regenstein Library at the University of Chicago, Columbia University (including its Oral History Research Project), Ford Foundation, Glencoe Public Library, Harvard University, Johns Hopkins University, Hotchkiss School, Houghton Mifflin Company, University of Illinois, University of Iowa, John F. Kennedy Library, University of Kentucky, University of Maryland, Newberry Library, State University of New York at Buffalo, Berg Collection at the New York Public Library, University of Pennsylvania, Pennsylvania State University, University of Pittsburgh, Princeton University, Franklin D. Roosevelt Library, Smith College, Southern Illinois University, Stanford University, University of Texas, Vassar College, University of Virginia, Virginia Commonwealth University, Wellesley College, Westover School, and University of Wyoming.

Among the people who through their correspondence and suggestions have contributed to this book are Stephen Becker, James A. Bell, John C. Broderick, Virginia L. Bruch, Robert Cowley, Alexander Campbell, Jean Groo, Haldore Hanson, Edward Hoagland, Edwin Honig, Frank Snowden Hopkins, Susan Howe, Walter Kaiser, William Katterjohn, Keneth Kinnamon, Malcolm Lester, Christopher MacGowan, Joan Mellen, Honor Moore, Holly (Mrs. Vance) Morgan, Edward Mullaly, Paul Quintanilla, Alan Powers, Michael S. Reynolds, Thursa Bakey Sanders, Gjertrud Schnackenberg, Radcliffe Squires, Sandra Whipple Spanier, Dabney Stuart, John Updike, J. H. Willis, Jr., and Teresa (Mrs. Kenelm R.) Winslow. Bernard A. Drabeck, Helen E. Ellis, and Margaret E. C. Howland, curator of the Archibald MacLeish Collection at the Greenfield Community College, have been repeatedly and cheerfully of service. The best recent criticism on MacLeish has been written by David Barber, Lauriat Lane, Jr., and John Timberman Newcomb.

Most of the photographs that illustrate this biography come from the family repository ably supervised by A. Bruce MacLeish. In addition, Frances Brennan discovered in old albums a number of pictures taken by her father, Richard Myers, in the 1920s and 1930s; Thursa Bakey Sanders furnished several photographs from the 1939–1945 period.

A John Simon Guggenheim Memorial Foundation fellowship enabled R. H. Winnick to collect much of the information on which this book is based. Later grants from the National Endowment for the Humanities and the College of William and Mary opened up blocks of time for my research and writing. Thanks are owed, too, to my research assistants for the last several years — Amy Zakrzewski, Maura Mahoney, Daniel Quentin Miller, and most of all Cristen Kimball, who worked with the skill and dedication of a professional. Donald Hall, Richard B. McAdoo, Thursa Bakey Sanders, and R. H. Winnick read the typescript in draft, and corrected errors of fact or misunderstanding. Peter Davison of Houghton Mifflin supported and encouraged me throughout the writing of the biography, and applied his fine editorial hand to the result. Finally, my beloved wife, Vivian, read each chapter as it emerged, and let me know by marginal annotation where matters could be improved. I am in debt to all of these, in ways that mere acknowledgment cannot discharge.

Notes ❖

Often these notes reflect multiple sources for the information in any given paragraph, a practice adopted on the principle that consulting a variety of sources is apt to reduce error. Where MacLeish's poems, essays, and plays have been collected, reference is made to the book rather than the periodical form.

The following abbreviations are used in the notes:

AMacL — Archibald MacLeish
RW — R. H. Winnick
SD — Scott Donaldson
FBI — MacLeish file, Federal Bureau of Investigation
FDR — Franklin D. Roosevelt Library, Hyde Park
JFK — Hemingway Collection, John F. Kennedy Library,
        Boston
LC — Library of Congress
NYPL — Berg Collection, New York Public Library

University libraries are designated by the name of the university alone.

PREFACE

ix multiplicity: SD, interview with W. Jackson Bate, October 13, 1988

ix Hemingway . . . Acheson: SD, interview with James Chace, April 6, 1990

ix "From the beginning": AMacL to Felix Frankfurter, May 15, 1939, *Letters of Archibald MacLeish, 1907–1982*, ed. R. H. Winnick (Boston:

Houghton Mifflin, 1983), p. 299 (hereafter *Letters*)

ix "Archie . . . poorly": John Conway, remarks at MacLeish memorial service, Harvard, May 26, 1982

x Santayana . . . the ideal: AMacL, reading notes, early 1923, p. A2, LC

x "a poet . . . who knows the world": AMacL to William Heyen, March 3, 1978, *Letters*, pp. 443–445

xi power . . . fortune's darling: SD, interview with Richard Wilbur, July 28, 1988

xi " 'a difficult thing' ": Quoted in Philip Gardner, " 'Rediscovery Would Have Its Fitness': Archibald MacLeish's Poetry," *Pembroke Magazine* 7 (1976), 144

xii "anthological rubble": AMacL, "Poetical Remains," in *Collected Poems, 1917–1982* (Boston: Houghton Mifflin, 1985), p. 426 (hereafter *Collected*)

xii "hard to get rid of": Benjamin DeMott, "Archibald MacLeish," in *Writers at Work* (New York: Viking, 1981), p. 47

xiii "I speak to my own time": AMacL, "Sentiments for a Dedication," in *Collected,* p. 286

xiii right place . . . right time: SD, interview with Mimi Grimm, July 24, 1988

xiii "poetic weathercock": Hyatt Waggoner, *American Poets from the Puritans to the Present* (Boston: Houghton Mifflin, 1968), p. 486

xiii Aeolian harp: RW, interview with Ives Gammell, November 15, 1979

xiii "We can set down": Quoted in Iris Origo, *Images and Shadows: Part of a Life* (New York: Harcourt Brace Jovanovich, 1971), p. 175

xiv rounded personality: RW, interviews with W. Jackson Bate, September 18, 1979, and with John H. Finley, Jr., September 21, 1979

1. BEGINNINGS

A Foreign Potentate

2 "Hello, Brownie": This incident is reconstructed from AMacL, notebooks, c. 1925, pp. G32–35, G52, LC

2 shredded wheat: RW, interview with Lewis Andrew Day, February 7, 1983

2 "Scots don't come shouting": RW, interview with AMacL, November 10–11, 1979

2 Norman developed a stammer: SD, interview with Roderick MacLeish, February 24, 1989

3 "more of a man": RW, interview with AMacL, November 10–11, 1979

3 "My father was a solid man": AMacL, untitled unpublished poem, notebooks, fall 1923, LC

3 "God was father's father": AMacL, notebooks, c. 1925, p. G33, LC

3 marched the family goat: RW, interview with Ethel de Lang Hein, January 5, 1983

3 "chop on a plate": RW, interview with Lewis Andrew Day, February 7, 1983

3 "T'ain't nothin' frizz": RW, interview with AMacL, April 21, 1979

4 "foreign potentate": RW, interview with AMacL, April 21, 1979

Andrew and Patty

4 Born in Glasgow: This account of Andrew MacLeish's life and career is drawn principally from *Life of Andrew MacLeish* (Chicago: privately printed, 1929)

6 Vassar . . . Rockford: AMacL's mother described her academic career in her reminiscences, *Martha Hillard MacLeish (1856–1947)* (Geneva, N.Y.: privately printed, 1949), pp. 23–30 (hereafter *Martha MacLeish*)

6 Rockefeller . . . train: SD, interview with John and Jill Ker Conway, May 23, 1989

7 "such a manly man": RW, interview with Ishbel MacLeish and Alexander Campbell, April 7, 1979

7 The August visit: *Martha MacLeish,* pp. 32–35

8 Lily . . . carriage ride: RW, interview with Lewis Andrew Day, February 7, 1983

Half Puritan, Half Scot

8 Moses . . . captain: AMacL, "Yankee Skipper," in *A Continuing Journey* (Boston: Houghton Mifflin, 1968), pp. 343–358 (hereafter *Journey*)

9 "a sound thrashing": Colin C. Campbell, "The Poet as Artist and Citizen: A Study of the Life and Writings of

Archibald MacLeish through 1958"
(Ph.D. diss., University of Pennsylvania, 1960), p. 5

9 Elias Brewster Hillard: Information about Elias Hillard and his wife, Julia Whittlesey, comes from *Martha MacLeish*, pp. 3–12

10 "my grandmother's letters": AMacL, introduction to *Martha MacLeish*, p. xxxi

11 *The Last Men*: AMacL, "Thirteen Candles: One for Every State," in *Journey*, pp. 359–369

12 Conway . . . Arcadia: AMacL, "A Lay Sermon for the Hill Towns," in *Riders on the Earth* (Boston: Houghton Mifflin, 1978), pp. 103–108 (hereafter *Riders*)

12 "Your grandfather married us": Richard Meryman, "Archibald MacLeish: The Enlarged Life," *Yankee* 45 (January 1981), 74

12 "Puritan . . . Scot . . . sin": RW, interview with AMacL, April 21, 1979

12 Scottish . . . "strength": Richard Phalon, "MacLeish and 3 Others Honored by Scottish Group," *New York Times*, June 6, 1972, p. 30

13 no greater tribute: AMacL, introduction, *Martha MacLeish*, p. xxxii

13 "one of the great . . . women": AMacL, *Archibald MacLeish: Reflections*, ed. Bernard A. Drabeck and Helen E. Ellis (Amherst: University of Massachusetts Press, 1986), p. 15 (hereafter *Reflections*)

2. GROWING UP

A Difficult Child

15 Froebel's philosophy . . . spanking: *Martha MacLeish*, pp. 46–47

15 Norman acted out: RW, interview with Ethel de Lang Hein, January 5–6, 1983

15 mock funeral: RW, interview with Ishbel MacLeish Campbell, April 7, 1979

15 "nasty little boy": *Reflections*, pp. 265–266

16 "near-great" . . . "stern but fair": SD, interview with Roderick MacLeish, February 24, 1989

16 "Once in a million times": AMacL to Martha Hillard MacLeish, March 12, 1924, *Letters*, p. 131

16 nightly reading: *Martha MacLeish*, pp. 51–56

16 "Literary Bibles": *Martha MacLeish*, pp. 46–47

17 influence of Dante: *Reflections*, p. 16

18 "There was a landscape": AMacL, "Autobiography," in *Collected*, p. 466

"like a leaf, a stem . . ."

18 Craigie Lea . . . building: *Martha MacLeish*, pp. 40–42, 45–46

19 Chicago Romanesque: RW, interview with Alexander Campbell, April 7, 1979

19 MacLeish estate . . . "big shore houses": RW, interview with Lewis Andrew Day, February 7, 1983; RW, interview with Walter T. Fisher, November 15, 1982

19 different winds: AMacL, "Cook County," in *Collected*, p. 282

20 "geese . . . foxes": *Reflections*, p. 266

20 "no beauty of oceans": AMacL to Martha Hillard MacLeish, July 4, 1923, *Letters*, p. 99

20 "Nothing — nothing": AMacL, notebooks, early 1924, p. B20, LC

20 "The hot summer night": AMacL, notebooks, c. 1925, p. G6, LC

20 "I was small": AMacL, "Ancestral," in *Collected*, pp. 99–100

21 childhood terror: AMacL to Martha Hillard MacLeish, September 21, 1924, p. 148

21 refuge . . . in the toolshed: AMacL, notebooks, c. 1925, p. G9, LC; AMacL, "Eleven," in *Collected*, p. 92

22 no divorce: AMacL, notebooks, c. 1925, p. G1, LC

Patty Hillard's Boy

22 Aunty Waters: *Martha MacLeish*, p. 62; AMacL, notebooks, c. 1925, p. G11, LC

22 baptism: RW, interview with AMacL, November 10, 1979; AMacL, "Photograph Album," in Collected, p. 519

23 ten to twelve boys: RW, interview with Ethel de Lang Hein, January 6, 1983

23 duties of parents: Mrs. Andrew MacLeish, "Has Not the Time Come When Education Should Prepare for Parenthood? In What Should Such Education Consist?" Kindergarten Review 14 (June 1904), 646–650

24 University of Chicago: Life of Andrew MacLeish, pp. 61–63, 84–87

24 annual payments of $50: Martha MacLeish, pp. 38–39

24 University . . . Press: Reflections, p. 56

24 check for $1 million: Reflections, p. 266

24 "turns the gas down": RW, interview with Ishbel MacLeish Campbell, April 7, 1979

25 Patty . . . friendships: Martha MacLeish, p. 39; RW, interview with AMacL, November 18–19, 1978

25 quarrel . . . Ravinia: RW, interview with AMacL, April 21, 1979

25 cross the threshold: RW, interview with Ishbel MacLeish Campbell, April 7, 1979

26 the little kingdom: RW, interview with AMacL, April 21, 1979

26 back east: Martha MacLeish, p. 64

26 Little Bighorn: Reflections, p. 96; AMacL to Tom Johnson, September 16, 1976

Breaking Away

26 Kenny . . . favorite: RW, interview with Ishbel MacLeish Campbell, April 7, 1979; RW, interview with Lewis Andrew Day, February 7, 1983; RW, interview with AMacL, April 21, 1979

26 Ishbel . . . name: Martha MacLeish, pp. 49–50

27 growth of . . . Ishbel: Mrs. Andrew MacLeish, "Observations on the Development of a Child during the First Year," Transactions of the Illinois So-

ciety for Child Study 3 (July 1898), 109–124

27 nearly opposite: RW, interview with Ishbel MacLeish Campbell, April 7, 1979

27 New Trier . . . discipline: RW, interview with AMacL, April 21, 1979; Reflections, p. 266

27 Hotchkiss . . . Archie: Martha Hillard MacLeish to Huber Gray Buehler, May 6, 1905, and May 22, 1906

28 raising chickens: Martha MacLeish, pp. 66–67

28 Andrew . . . grumbled: RW, interview with Lewis Andrew Day, February 7, 1983

28 chicken . . . ax: RW, interview with Ishbel MacLeish Campbell, April 7, 1979

29 admission . . . fall of 1907: Martha Hillard MacLeish to Huber Gray Buehler, June 18, 1907, Letters, p. 3; Huber Gray Buehler to Martha Hillard MacLeish, June 15, 1907

29 failed . . . dead loss: Huber Gray Buehler to Martha Hillard MacLeish, July 5, 1907; RW, interview with AMacL, April 21, 1979

3. PREP SCHOOL

Homesickness

30 "massacred": AMacL to Bernard De Voto, c. June 1934, Letters, p. 266

30 "God . . . Hotchkiss!": Robert Cowley, "America Was Promises: An Interview with Archibald MacLeish," American Heritage 33 (August–September 1982), 24

31 school history, student body, curriculum, motto: Catalogue, Hotchkiss School, 1915; Hotchkiss Record, June 1, 1909, p. 2; RW, interview with AMacL, April 21, 1979

32 "flowers" . . . "hillsides": AMacL, notebooks, c. 1925, p. G36, LC

32 transfer . . . note: AMacL to Huber Gray Buehler, c. October 1907, Letters, p. 5

33 Earl of Douglas: AMacL to Andrew

MacLeish, October 10, 1907, *Letters*, p. 5

33 "bullying seniors" . . . "whitefeather": AMacL to Martha Hillard MacLeish, c. October 1907; Martha Hillard MacLeish to Huber Gray Buehler, October 26, 1907, *Letters*, pp. 6–7

33 "summed up . . . 'homesickness' ": Huber Gray Buehler to Martha Hillard MacLeish, November 21, 1907

34 self-centeredness . . . varicocele: Martha Hillard MacLeish to Huber Gray Buehler, December 1, 1907

34 "good courage": Martha Hillard MacLeish to Huber Gray Buehler, January 5, 1908

Sex, God, and Snobbery

34 "guest-room mirror" . . . "gooseberry bushes": AMacL, notebooks, c. 1925, pp. G12, G16, LC

35 naked woman . . . "Do they know?" . . . "Bird Peak": AMacL, notebooks, c. 1925, pp. G17, G36, G38, LC

35 repudiated his body . . . tears streaming: AMacL, notebooks, c. 1925, pp. G36–G38, LC

35 Ethel de Lang . . . "Miss H." . . . Julia: RW, interview with Ethel de Lang Hein, January 5, 1983; AMacL, notebooks, c. 1925, pp. G16, G19, LC

36 Nan Hendrix . . . "death to women": RW, interview with Ishbel MacLeish Campbell, April 7, 1979

36 "English coachman": "The Oratorical Contest," *Hotchkiss Record*, June 21, 1910, p. 4

36 "quite loathsome": RW, interview with AMacL, April 21, 1979

37 "oh, the differences": Michael H. Ebner, *Creating Chicago's North Shore: A Suburban History* (Chicago: University of Chicago Press, 1988), pp. xxviii, 195–199

37 Fitzgerald . . . Lake Forest: Quoted in Scott Donaldson, *Fool for Love: F.*

Scott Fitzgerald (New York: Congdon and Weed, 1983), p. 50

37 Glencoe . . . distinction: RW, interview with AMacL, April 21, 1979; RW, interview with Ishbel MacLeish Campbell, April 7, 1979

37 racial and ethnic biases: Ebner, *Creating Chicago's North Shore*, p. 234; RW, interview with Ishbel MacLeish Campbell, April 7, 1979; RW, interview with Harry Levin, September 26, 1979

Triumphs, Near-Disaster

38 football . . . "I turned sharply": "Substitutes," *Hotchkiss Record*, November 17, 1908; AMacL, notebooks, c. 1925, pp. G38–G39, LC

38 "warmth above the heart": RW, interview with AMacL, April 21, 1979

39 "Storming . . . Bastille": "Literary Supplement," *Hotchkiss Record*, January 12, 1909, p. 1; "Criticism of the Lit.," *Hotchkiss Record*, February 16, 1909

39 "Lesson of Lincoln's Life": "Helen Yale Ellsworth Prize," *Hotchkiss Record*, November 10, 1908, p. 1; essay printed in *Hotchkiss Record Literary Supplement* (June 1909), 5–6; critique in Huber Gray Buehler to Martha Hillard MacLeish, February 10, 1909

39 Brazil . . . James Close: "Society Meetings," *Hotchkiss Record*, March 1, 1909; RW, interview with Ethel de Lang Hein, January 5, 1983

40 writing: "St. Luke's Topics for Fall Term," *Hotchkiss Record*, October 12, 1909, p. 6; AMacL, "A Chapter from a Man's Life," *Hotchkiss Record Literary Supplement* (January 1910), 10–13; "John Milton," *Hotchkiss Record Literary Supplement* (January 1910), 20–23

41 literary contest . . . annual debate: "The Literary Contest," *Hotchkiss Record*, December 7, 1909, p. 1; "Annual Debate," *Hotchkiss Record*, March 22, 1910, pp. 1–3

41 "feel no hesitancy": "The Incoming

Board," *Hotchkiss Record,* March 22, 1910, p. 2

41 ride . . . Great Barrington: RW, interview with AMacL, April 21, 1979

42 "perfect folly": Huber Gray Buehler to Andrew MacLeish, April 20, 1910

42 "thoroughly scared": Andrew MacLeish to Huber Gray Buehler, April 22, 1910, *Letters,* p. 8

42 prizes . . . 1910: Hotchkiss *Mischianza,* 1910, pp. 36, 38, 41

42 most notable success: "The Oratorical Contest," *Hotchkiss Record,* June 21, 1910; Hotchkiss *Mischianza,* 1911, p. 73

42 England . . . Wales . . . Scotland: *Martha MacLeish,* pp. 67, 70–78

43 souls . . . "variously wandering": AMacL to the MacLeish family, c. August 1921, *Letters,* p. 85

Stirrings: Love and Poetry

44 "quite a bungle": AMacL to Huber Gray Buehler, August 12, 1910, *Letters,* p. 9

45 public confession . . . St. Luke's: RW, interview with AMacL, April 21, 1979

45 "floated in a slim canoe": AMacL, "Impressions of an English Summer," *Hotchkiss Record Literary Supplement,* March 1911, pp. 5–9

45 debating . . . "suffrage": "Literary Activities," *Hotchkiss Record Literary Supplement* (June 1911), 19

45 "misconduct": Huber Gray Buehler to AMacL, March 7, 1911

45 shortcomings . . . "selfishness": Martha Hillard MacLeish to Huber Gray Buehler, March 13, 1911, *Letters,* p. 9

46 "smarty writing": Huber Gray Buehler to Martha Hillard MacLeish, March 16, 1911

46 Ada . . . understanding: RW, interview with AMacL, November 18–19, 1978

47 Uncle Billy . . . control your world: RW, interview with Adele and Robert A. Lovett, June 2, 1979; RW, interview with William H. MacLeish,

September 20, 1979; SD, interview with Martha MacLeish Fuller, May 21, 1989; SD, interview with Jill Ker Conway, October 10, 1988

47 Stevens . . . Swinburne: *Reflections,* p. 16; AMacL to Amy Lowell, January 31, 1924, *Letters,* p. 123

48 "The pale moon's wake": AMacL, "The Song of the Canoe," *Hotchkiss Record Literary Supplement* (March 1911), 19

48 "Leaping, laughing": AMacL, "The Brook," *Hotchkiss Record Literary Supplement* (June 1911), 7

49 "slipped our anchor": AMacL, "Class Poem — 1911," *Hotchkiss Record Literary Supplement* (December 1911), 11–12

49 wing collar . . . Windiest: Hotchkiss *Mischianza,* 1911, pp. 30, 40–41

50 Harvard . . . Yale: RW, interview with AMacL, April 21, 1979

4. BIG MAN ON CAMPUS

The Blue-Sweater Era

51 welcoming address: *Yale Daily News,* October 1, 1911, p. 1. This opening scene is derived from RW's draft of a chapter on AMacL's experience at Yale.

51 football and literature: *Yale Daily News,* October 3, 1911, p. 1, and *Yale Daily News,* October 7, 1911, p. 1

52 most outstanding . . . votes: William A. Jordan to RW, January 2, 1979; *History of the Class of Nineteen Fifteen,* ed. Albert H. Ely, Jr. (New Haven: Yale University Press, 1915), pp. 469–472 (hereafter *Nineteen Fifteen*)

52 "In the large square room": AMacL, "An Anonymous Generation," in *A Time to Speak* (Boston: Houghton Mifflin, 1941), p. 154

52 right clothes . . . "walled town": The diatribe against Yale came from Richard A. Douglas, class of 1914, quoted in George Wilson Pierson, *Yale Col-*

lege, *An Educational History, 1871–1921* (New Haven: Yale University Press, 1952), pp. 348–349; AMacL, notebooks, c. 1925, p. G40, LC.

53 "much more important": *The Dialogues of Archibald MacLeish and Mark Van Doren,* ed. Warren V. Bush (New York: Dutton, 1964), pp. 254–255 (hereafter *Dialogues*)

53 Harvard game: *Yale Daily News,* November 9, 1911, p. 1; *Yale Daily News,* November 23, 1911, p. 1

53 "dirtiest . . . sonofabitch" . . . "taste of blood": AMacL, "Moonlighting on Yale Field," in *Riders,* p. 96

53 water polo . . . catcher: RW, interview with AMacL, April 21, 1979; *Yale Daily News,* March 16, 1912, pp. 1, 5; *Yale Daily News,* February 29, 1912, p. 3

54 "The theory then": Cowley, "Promises," p. 25

54 a freshman record: Frank Wright Tuttle, "The History of Freshman Year," in *Nineteen Fifteen,* pp. 12–14

54 "Literary Renaissance": Pierson, *Yale College,* pp. 346–368

54 Yale *Review* . . . Elizabethan Club: *Yale Daily News,* October 6, 1911, p. 2; *Yale Daily News,* October 31, 1911, p. 1

54   "Yours was the last class": Quoted in Richard Somer, "The Public Man of Letters," in *The Proceedings of the Archibald MacLeish Symposium, May 7–8, 1982,* ed. Bernard Drabeck et al. (Lanham, Md.: University Press of America, 1988), p. 117 (hereafter *Symposium*)

The Fence and the "Daughters of Dink"

55 Fence . . . rules: *Yale Daily News,* February 20, 1912, p. 3

55 rush . . . letters: *Yale Daily News,* January 28, 1913, p. 2; *Yale Daily News,* January 29, 1913, p. 2; AMacL to the editor of the *Yale Daily News,* January 29, 1913, *Letters,* p. 11

56 institution . . . under attack: *Yale Daily News,* April 15, 1913, pp. 1, 2

57 Stover . . . secrecy: Owen Johnson, *Stover at Yale* (New York: Frederick A. Stokes, 1912), pp. 373–386

57 "Daughters of Dink": AMacL, "The History of Sophomore Year," in *Nineteen Fifteen,* p. 30; RW, interview with AMacL, April 21, 1979

57 Shortly after five: *Yale Daily News,* May 15, 1914, p. 1

58 "Bones was started": Cowley, "Promises," p. 25

58 Kenny . . . Bill: AMacL to Ranald Macdonald, July 5, 1949

The Young Aesthete

58 1915 German: *Yale Daily News,* October 8, 1912, p. 1; *Yale Daily News,* January 14, 1913, p. 5

58 "You'll be lucky": AMacL, "Moonlighting on Yale Field," in *Riders,* p. 95

58 Fence . . . talk: Printed in *Yale Daily News,* June 6, 1913

59 "mushroom college": AMacL, "The History of Sophomore Year," in *Nineteen Fifteen,* p. 31

59 flying tackle: William A. Jordan to RW, January 2, 1979

59 junior prom: *Yale Daily News,* February 3, 1914

59 Phi Beta Kappa: *Yale Daily News,* February 26, 1914, p. 1

59 Yeats . . . visit: *Yale Daily News,* March 18, 1914, p. 5; Francis H. Bangs, "The MacLeish of F. Bangs," p. 3, Yale (hereafter Bangs)

60 dance at Tryon Hall: Bangs, p. 8, Yale

60 *Lit* banquet: Bangs, pp. 8–9, Yale; *Yale Daily News,* March 14, 1914, p. 1

60 Phelps . . . lightweight: *Reflections,* p. 90; RW, interview with AMacL, April 21, 1979

61 Berdan's course: AMacL to F. W. Bronson, March 12, 1941

61 Mason . . . "genius": Bangs, p. 8, Yale; Pierson, *Yale College,* pp. 359–360

61 Tinker . . . "scholarshit": Bangs, p. 88, Yale; *Selected Letters of Stephen Vincent Benét,* ed. Charles A. Fenton

(New Haven: Yale University Press, 1960), p. 29, footnote 9

61 minor prose writers: Bangs, pp. 4–6, Yale

62 threw him out: RW, interview with AMacL, November 18–19, 1978

62 "And you in that small room": AMacL, "Lines to a Former Teacher at Yale: Musings of a Field Artillery Officer in France," in *The Yale Book of Student Verse, 1910–1918,* ed. John Andrews et al. (New Haven: Yale University Press, 1919), pp. 168–169

62 "We judged rightly": AMacL to Frank Bangs, July 3, 1921; Bangs, p. 181, Yale

62 first . . . Elizabethan: Bangs, p. 2, Yale

63 personal . . . immortality: Bangs, p. 12, Yale

63 "Bangs, the lean head": AMacL, notebooks, c. 1925, pp. G42–G43, LC

63 career in the ministry: RW, interview with AMacL, November 10, 1979

63 undergraduate writing: Campbell, *The Poet,* pp. 25–33, provides first-rate interpretations of AMacL's publications in the *Yale Literary Magazine.*

65 Emerson . . . faith: AMacL to Andrew MacLeish, c. fall 1916, *Letters,* pp. 28–29

"A Lad of Parts"

65 trip to England: *Martha MacLeish,* pp. 82–83

65 football career: *Yale Daily News,* October 12, 1914, October 19, 1914, November 2, 1914; Walter Camp, "Athletics," in *Nineteen Fifteen,* pp. 76, 79

66 water polo . . . Kenny: *Yale Daily News,* November 27, 1914, p. 3

66 "Nathan's strangulation": AMacL to the editor of the *Yale Daily News,* November 17, 1914, *Letters,* p. 12; Charles A. Merz to the editor of the *Yale Daily News,* November 18, 1914, p. 2

66 Mrs. Lanahan: AMacL, notebooks, c. 1925, pp. G21, G46, LC

66 Marjory: AMacL, notebooks, c. 1925, pp. G25, G47, LC

66 asphalt . . . lilacs . . . "elephant": AMacL, notebooks, c. 1925, p. G48, LC

67 Sally McGill: RW, interview with Ishbel MacLeish Campbell, April 7, 1979

67 Ada . . . engagement: *Martha MacLeish,* pp. 85–86

67 exchange of letters: Andrew MacLeish to AMacL, October 10, 1913; AMacL to Andrew MacLeish, budget for February 1915; AMacL to Andrew MacLeish, January 5, 1915; Andrew MacLeish to AMacL, January 7, 1915; AMacL to Andrew MacLeish, January 9, 1915

68 "I was dead without her": RW, interview with AMacL, April 21, 1979

69 Aunt Mary . . . authority: AMacL, "The Building and the Spirit," *Westover Newsletter* (Winter 1979), 4; RW, interview with Adele and Robert A. Lovett, June 2, 1979; Bangs, pp. 12–13, Yale

69 *Yale Review* . . . "Grief": Lawrence Mason, review of March 1915 *Lit, Yale Daily News,* March 31, 1915, p. 1; Huber Gray Buehler to AMacL, May 17, 1915

69 Cook Prize: RW, interview with AMacL, April 21, 1979

69 Class Poem: Bangs, pp. 14–16, Yale; "Class Poem," in *Nineteen Fifteen,* pp. 9–11; RW, interview with AMacL, April 21, 1979

70 "figure . . . most respected": AMacL to Andrew MacLeish, May 2, 1915, *Letters,* pp. 13–14

70 Hadley . . . "lad of parts": *Martha MacLeish,* pp. 86–87

71 academic world: Yale 1915 *Class Book,* p. 235; AMacL to Francis H. Bangs, September 16, 1916, Bangs, p. 90, Yale

71 "alternative . . . law": AMacL to Francis H. Bangs, c. July 1915, *Letters,* p. 16; AMacL to Francis H. Bangs, c. August 1915, *Letters,* pp. 17–18

71 "regular . . . job": Robert Van Gelder, interview with AMacL, 1942,

quoted in Campbell, *The Poet*, p. 23

71 "Never again shall I walk": AMacL to Francis H. Bangs, August 16, 1915, Bangs, p. 28, Yale

72 Tommy Cornell: AMacL to Ranald Macdonald, August 20, 1959

72 Acheson . . . commencement: RW, interview with AMacL, April 21, 1979; SD, interview with Alice Acheson, May 7, 1988; RW, interview with Alice Acheson, January 27, 1979

5. ADA AND THE MUSES

Law versus Poetry

73 Joey Beale: *Reflections*, p. 17; RW, interview with AMacL, April 26, 1980

73 "gateway to history" . . . "tradition": *Reflections*, p. 17; *Dialogues*, pp. 256–257

74 Bangs . . . free to dream: AMacL to Francis H. Bangs, October 7, 1915, Bangs, pp. 34–35, Yale

74 "As to life . . . fireflies": AMacL to Francis H. Bangs, December 12, 1915, Bangs, pp. 49–50, Yale

74 "perfect jungle": AMacL to Francis H. Bangs, January 25, 1916, *Letters*, p. 23

75 "Lawyers use words": AMacL, "Art and Law," in *Riders*, p. 83

75 "Adjudicated quarrels": AMacL, "A Library of Law," in *Tower of Ivory* (New Haven: Yale University Press, 1917), pp. 46–47

75 report to . . . father: AMacL to Andrew MacLeish, August 13, 1916, *Letters*, p. 26

Marriage at Last

75 wedding . . . squall: *Martha MacLeish*, pp. 87–88

76 "lifted the embargo": AMacL, "The Building and the Spirit," p. 5

76 Yale . . . ceremony: Bangs, p. 71, Yale

76 At sea . . . conflicted: AMacL to Francis H. Bangs, c. June 1916, *Letters*, p. 25

76 Bermuda . . . cockroach: RW, interview with AMacL, April 21, 1979

77 charge account: Andrew MacLeish to AMacL, April 25, 1916

77 Roxbury . . . Milton: AMacL to Francis H. Bangs, September 1916, Bangs, pp. 92–93, Yale

77 money . . . "great mass of reading": AMacL to Andrew MacLeish, August 13, 1916, *Letters*, p. 26

77 Masefield . . . drive: Bangs, pp. 55–57, Yale

77 time . . . passing him by: AMacL to Francis H. Bangs, August 27, 1916, Bangs, pp. 83–84, Yale

Muses: Peabody and Sargent

78 Grace Allen Peabody: Bangs, p. 74, Yale; AMacL, "Lilies," in *Tower of Ivory*, pp. 57–58; AMacL, "The Tomb of the Abbess of Tours," in *The Happy Marriage and Other Poems* (Boston: Houghton Mifflin, 1924), pp. 57–58

79 Margarett Sargent: AMacL to Francis H. Bangs, November 11, 1928, *Letters*, pp. 30–31; RW, interview with Daniel Sargent, November 15, 1979; AMacL to Francis H. Bangs, c. mid-February 1917, Bangs, pp. 105–106, Yale; AMacL, "The 'Chantress," in *Tower of Ivory*, pp. 50–51; Francis H. Bangs to Margarett Sargent, c. February 1917, Yale

79 little Archie: RW, interview with Kay Bundy, September 22, 1979; AMacL, "To My Son," in *Tower of Ivory*, p. 59

80 Ada . . . "muses": RW, interview with Adele Lovett, June 23, 1979; SD, interview with May Sarton, January 14, 1990

80 "damned near killed me": SD, interview with William H. MacLeish, July 26, 1988

80 loved . . . platonically: SD, interview with Honor Moore, August 30, 1989

80 "swallows" . . . "a blue brook": AMacL, "The Showman," in *Tower*

of Ivory, p. 36; AMacL to Francis H. Bangs, c. May 29, 1917, Bangs, pp. 117–118, Yale

81 "her hair . . . unfurl'd": AMacL to Francis H. Bangs, April 19, 1919, *Letters,* pp. 49–50; emphasis added

81 "She is not beautiful": AMacL, poem written in back of James Barr Ames, *Cases in Equity Jurisdiction,* vol 2, GCC, emphasis on repeated phrase added

81 "To have the hair of your nape": AMacL, untitled, unpublished poem, notebooks, spring 1935, LC

82 "The thing I remembered": AMacL, "Epitaph for a Young Man," unpublished poem, notebooks, August 10, 1951, LC

A First Book

82 Day Kimball: RW, interview with AMacL, April 21–22, 1979

82 Peabody . . . Gibson: AMacL to Francis H. Bangs, c. winter 1917, *Letters,* pp. 32–34

83 Faust . . . Helen: AMacL, *Our Lady of Troy,* in *Tower of Ivory,* pp. 1–21; Campbell, *The Poet,* pp. 36–40; AMacL to Francis H. Bangs, April 22, 1917, *Letters,* p. 37

6. THE GREAT WAR

Joining Up

85 "officer's training": AMacL to Andrew MacLeish, February 4, 1917, *Letters,* p. 34

85 Both . . . brothers: *A History of the Class of Nineteen Eighteen* (New Haven: Yale University Press, 1918), p. 13; Andrew MacLeish to AMacL, May 10, 1917

86 "Now out of this corruption": AMacL, "The Easter of Swords," in *Tower of Ivory,* p. 32; emphasis on last line is MacLeish's

86 mind . . . made up: AMacL to Andrew MacLeish, May 5, 1917, *Letters,* pp. 38–39

86 "I must serve": AMacL to Andrew MacLeish, May 9, 1917, *Letters,* pp. 39–41

87 "Our family . . . exempt": Andrew MacLeish to AMacL, May 10, 1917

87 American Ambulance: AMacL to President Hadley, May 28, 1917, Yale

87 supply officer: James L. Phillips, Intercollegiate Intelligence Bureau, to Samuel B. Hemingway, June 21, 1917, Yale

87 Mobile Hospital Unit: Marshall H. Williams, secretary, Yale class of 1916, account of the history of Yale Mobile Hospital Unit 39, Yale

88 Bangs . . . *Baltic:* Bangs, pp. 121–122, Yale

88 "Like moon-dark": AMacL, "Soul-Sight," in *Tower of Ivory,* p. 60; Bangs, p. 103, Yale

89 torpedo: Bangs, p. 121, Yale

89 Limoges: *Martha MacLeish,* p. 91; AMacL to Francis H. Bangs, December 23, 1917, *Letters,* pp. 42–43

89 Archie wangled: Bangs, p. 122, Yale; "The Americanization of Francis Hyde Bangs," "Biographies," in *Yale Class of 1915,* p. 92

Intimations of Mortality

90 "bold flouting": RW, interview with AMacL, April 21–22, 1979

90 "idealistic conception": Lawrence Mason, foreword to *Tower of Ivory,* pp. vii–viii

90 "Aweary of . . . reality": AMacL, "Imagery," in *Tower of Ivory,* p. 40

90 sense of mutability: Grover Smith, "Archibald MacLeish," in *American Writers: A Collection of Literary Biographies,* ed. Leonard Unger (New York: Scribner's, 1973), III:4

90 reviews . . . *Tower:* Catalogue, Yale University Press, May 11, 1918; Scrapbook (kept by Ada MacLeish), vol. 1, p. 103, GCC; John Masefield to AMacL, January 26, 1918, Bangs, p. 137, Yale

91 "Whatever happens to you": AMacL to Kenneth MacLeish, c. December 1917, recounted in Kenneth MacLeish to Priscilla Murdock, December 14,

1917; Kenneth MacLeish's wartime letters are collected in *The Price of Honor: The World War One Letters of Naval Aviator Kenneth MacLeish,* ed. Geoffrey Rossano (Annapolis: United States Naval Institute, 1991).

91 Ada . . . "cowardly self": Kenneth MacLeish to Priscilla Murdock, January 24, 1918

91 "disposition . . . in your will": AMacL to Andrew MacLeish, January 30, 1918, *Letters,* pp. 43–44

91 "baby . . . little sunbeam": Andrew MacLeish to AMacL, December 5, 1917, and July 23, 1918

92 French tractor school: AMacL to class of 1915 secretary, May 22, 1918

92 rumored . . . demise: AMacL to Francis H. Bangs, April 14, 1918, Bangs, pp. 147–148, Yale; see also Bangs, pp. 123, 158, Yale

93 "perfectly wonderful": Kenneth MacLeish to Priscilla Murdock, June 30, 1918

93 Marne . . . orchard: RW, interview with AMacL, April 21, 1979; Robert Cowley, "Promises," p. 25

94 German shell: Robert Cowley, "Promises," p. 26

94 operations officer: AMacL to Edwin Oviatt, November 1, 1918, *Letters,* p. 48

94 go home . . . Aunt Mary: RW, interview with AMacL, November 10, 1979; AMacL to Joseph Alsop, Jr., May 17, 1938

94 Ravinia . . . "doggie": *Martha MacLeish,* pp. 92–93; RW, interview with AMacL, November 18–19, 1978

94 Maryland . . . influenza: RW, interview with AMacL, November 18–19, 1978

Death of a Hero

95 Kenneth . . . more outgoing: RW, interview with Robert A. Lovett, June 2, 1979

95 "I could *never* be content": Quoted in Clifford Albion Tinker, "A Navy Roland and His Philosophy," *National Spectator,* April 3, 1926, p. 22

95 "rather quaked": Quoted in Tinker, "A Navy Roland," p. 21

95 "supreme sacrifice": *Martha MacLeish,* pp. 94–95

96 active duty: Artemus Lamb Gates, "Kenneth MacLeish," in *Yale Class of Nineteen Eighteen Book,* pp. 13–16

96 Lovett . . . commander: Ralph D. Paine, "Kenneth MacLeish's Path to Glory," in *The First Yale Unit: A Story of Naval Aviation 1916–1919,* vol. 2 (Cambridge, Mass.: Riverside Press, 1925), pp. 355–360

96 "just crushed": Kenneth MacLeish to Priscilla Murdock, October 8, 1918

96 Kenneth . . . shot down: Paine, "Path to Glory," pp. 360–361

97 Rouse's journey: Paine, "Path to Glory," pp. 362–366, includes AMacL, "A Belgian Letter."

97 corpse . . . gas: Lieutenant junior grade J. C. Menzies to Captain D. C. Hanrahan, USN, "Information regarding finding . . . the body . . . ," February 4, 1919; RW, interview with AMacL, November 18–19, 1978; AMacL to Frederick N. Bolles, November 14, 1934

98 "He had no dream": AMacL, "Kenneth," *Parabalou* 3 (1921), 3–4

98 "not a flaw to find": Colonel L. A. Beard to Chief of Field Artillery, December 6, 1918

98 Bruce . . . service: Bruce MacLeish to AMacL, February 3, 1919

98 "And the life . . . I lay down": Paine, "Path to Glory," p. 371

98 memorialized: AMacL to Martha Hillard MacLeish, October 23, 1919, *Letters,* pp. 54–55; *Martha MacLeish,* pp. 96–97; Paine, "Path to Glory," p. 373

7. A. MACLEISH, ESQUIRE

Young Marrieds

100 "terribly hard" . . . Fay Diploma: "Archibald MacLeish," in *Living Authors,* ed. Stanley Kunitz (New York:

H. W. Wilson, 1931), p. 246; Robert Cowley, "Promises," p. 26

100 occasional comments: Edward H. Warren, *Cases on Corporations*, AMacL's annotations on pp. 197, 305, GCC

100 Firuski . . . bookshop: *Harvard Crimson*, April 3, 1919, p. 1; AMacL, remarks for the memorial service of Maurice Firuski, Salisbury, Conn., 1978

100 Acheson . . . friendship: RW, interview with Alice Acheson, January 27, 1979; Walter Isaacson and Evan Thomas, *The Wise Men: Six Friends and the World They Made* (New York: Simon and Schuster, 1986), pp. 84–88

101 "mass salvation": Quoted in Isaacson and Thomas, *Wise Men*, p. 125

101 Lovetts . . . first to call: RW, interview with Adele and Robert A. Lovett, June 2, 1979

102 "Here's Cardinal Manning": AMacL, August 9, 1920, Adele Lovett's scrapbook, 1899–1931

102 closest . . . Bundy: Jessica D. Warren, "Family Matters: Conversations with Katharine Lawrence Putnam Bundy, 1978," unpublished manuscript, introduction; RW, interview with AMacL, April 21, 1979

102 community of talented: RW, interview with Kay Bundy, September 22, 1979

103 Curtis . . . *Cogitator*: RW, interview with Edward Weeks, December 1, 1981; RW, interview with Kay Bundy, September 22, 1979

103 Tavern Club . . . loss for words: RW, interview with Daniel Sargent, November 15, 1979; Warren, "Family Matters," pp. 49–50; AMacL, "Coming to the Tavern," in *The Tavern at Seventy-Five*, ed. Edward Weeks (Boston: privately printed, 1959), pp. 111–112

103 "Thy sons" . . . "He bites": AMacL, unpublished poem, "An Ode in Reminder of Adversity," April 3, 1919; RW, interview with William H. MacLeish, September 20, 1979

What Next?

104 "My various plans": AMacL to Martha Hillard MacLeish, May 7, 1919, *Letters*, p. 52

104 Yale . . . "teach government": AMacL to Anson Phelps Stokes, April 28, 1919, *Letters*, p. 51

104 Harvard . . . "affection": AMacL to Henry Pratt Judson, June 5, 1919, *Letters*, p. 53; AMacL to A. Lawrence Lowell, September 7, 1919, *Letters*, p. 54

104 two-part job: RW, interview with AMacL, April 21, 1979

104 "greatest fun": AMacL to Dean Acheson, October 28, 1919, Yale

105 "knees clicked together": AMacL to Dean Acheson, October 15, 1919, Yale

105 "train young men": AMacL to Dean Acheson, December 26, 1919, Yale

105 "You don't teach": RW, interview with AMacL, April 21, 1979, Yale

105 career in journalism: AMacL to Dean Acheson, December 11, 1919, Yale; AMacL to Dean Acheson, December 30, 1919, *Letters*, pp. 62–65

106 argument with Aunt Mary: AMacL to Martha Hillard MacLeish, February 5, 1920, *Letters*, pp. 67–69

106 "rigorously sacrificing": AMacL to Martha Hillard MacLeish, February 5, 1920, *Letters*, p. 68

106 "uninteresting outlook": AMacL to Martha Hillard MacLeish, April 18, 1920, *Letters*, p. 73

107 *New Republic* . . . "skittish . . . verses": AMacL to Dean Acheson, April 23, 1920, and July 6, 1920, Yale; RW, interview with AMacL, November 10, 1979; AMacL, "Senator Harding Finds an Issue," *New Republic*, September 8, 1920, p. 43, and "The Front Porch in Marion," *New Republic*, July 28, 1920, p. 256

107 poetry editor: AMacL to Hervey Allen, July 15, 1920; AMacL to Stephen Vincent Benét, July 16, 1920, *Letters*, pp. 74–75

107 "one large room": AMacL to Dean Acheson, July 6, 1920, Yale

107 "Through half a circle": AMacL to Francis H. Bangs, April 19, 1919, *Letters*, p. 49

107 disillusionment . . . Bangs: AMacL to Dean Acheson, August 22, 1920, Yale

108 concocted . . . hoax: Bangs, p. 176, Yale

108 *Parabalou* . . . poets: *Yale Alumni Weekly*, June 18, 1920

108 "It is not tragical": AMacL, "Sonnet," *Parabalou* 2 (1920), 29

Professional Duellist

109 "game" . . . "duellist": AMacL to Dean Acheson, October 24, 1920, Yale

109 "great experiences": AMacL to Dean Acheson, summer 1921, Yale

109 "mockery of . . . ambition": AMacL to the MacLeish family, c. August 1921, *Letters*, p. 85

109 "intricate . . . mechanism" . . . "Scotchmen": AMacL to Betty Choate, November 23, 1920, and July 27, 1921

109 Betty Choate . . . dance: Angelica S. Harter to George Goodspeed, July 25, 1982

110 "In the novels of": AMacL, "To B.C.," in *Songs for a Summer's Day* (New Haven: Yale University Press, 1915), unpaginated

111 great friendship: AMacL to Betty Choate, November 21, 1920

111 assumed . . . affair: RW, interview with Adele and Robert A. Lovett, June 23, 1979; RW, interview with Kay Bundy, September 22, 1979; RW, interview with Ives Gammell, November 15, 1979

111 "You I can never find": AMacL, "For E.C. with Reynard the Fox," April 11, 1920

111 "Rumor and sigh": AMacL to Betty Choate, c. 1921

111 Marcella . . . spurns: Entry on Marcella, *The Reader's Encyclopedia,* ed. William Rose Benét (New York:

Thomas Y. Crowell, 1948), pp. 687–688

111 "How shall I recall": AMacL to Betty Choate, November 28, 1921

111 "of the utmost importance": AMacL to Betty Choate, December 1, 1921

112 "I never touch your thought": AMacL to Betty Choate, December 9, 1921

112 travel piece: Elizabeth Choate, "Pilgrimage," *Atlantic Monthly* 129 (March 1921), 371–377

112 readings . . . Job: AMacL to Betty Choate, March 11, 1922, May 11, 1922, and June 13–14, 1922

112 Russian princess: Elizabeth Choate, "Holidays," *Atlantic Monthly* 132 (August 1923), 238–239

112 "slender girl" . . . "can't be said": AMacL to Betty Choate, c. 1923

113 Brewster . . . death: AMacL to Martha Hillard MacLeish and Andrew MacLeish, June 21, 1921, *Letters*, pp. 82–83; RW, interview with Adele and Robert A. Lovett, June 23, 1979

113 Ada . . . "wonderful" . . . "dead person": AMacL to the MacLeish family, c. August 1921, *Letters*, p. 85; RW, interview with Kay Bundy, September 22, 1979; RW, interview with Adele Lovett, June 23, 1979

113 "If her debut": AMacL to Francis H. Bangs, August 24, 1922, Bangs, p. 188, Yale

113 Hoover League: RW, interview with AMacL, April 26, 1980; AMacL to Dean Acheson, February 20, 1920, *Letters*, p. 70; AMacL to Dean Acheson, October 24, 1920, Yale

114 censure . . . Chafee: RW, interview with AMacL, April 21, 1979; AMacL to Arthur N. Holcombe, May 29, 1921, *Letters*, pp. 81–82

Conversations by Moonlight

114 "ancient . . . ambition": AMacL to Francis H. Bangs, February 22, 1922, *Letters*, pp. 88–89

115 "profound suspicion": AMacL to Dean Acheson, September 18, 1921, *Letters*, p. 86

115 "Lord Chancellor": AMacL, "The

Lord Chancellor Prepares His Opinion," in *The Happy Marriage and Other Poems* (Boston: Houghton Mifflin, 1924), pp. 40–45

115 "Our real trouble": AMacL to Dean Acheson, October 10, 1922, *Letters,* pp. 93–95

116 "There was a land breeze": AMacL to Dean Acheson, October 10, 1922, *Letters,* p. 94

116 get out of the law: AMacL, "Conversation with the Moon," Cosmos Club Award speech, May 17, 1977 (Washington, D.C.: privately printed, 1977), pp. 8–16; substantially the same as AMacL, "Autobiographical Information," in *Riders,* pp. 72–75

117 Ada . . . . voice: AMacL to Dean Acheson, January 8, 1923, *Letters,* p. 96

117 tell . . . Choate: *Reflections,* pp. 20–21; RW, interview with AMacL, April 21, 1979

Second Thoughts

117 most interesting case . . . "famous victory": *Warner v. Fuller,* 245 Mass. 520 (1923), 520–530; *National Reporter* 139 NE 811 (1923), 812; "Joseph E. Warner Won't Get Dollar," *Fall River Evening Herald,* June 5, 1923, p. 1; RW, interviews with AMacL, November 18–19, 1978, and November 10, 1979; AMacL to Dean Acheson, c. March 25, 1923, *Letters,* p. 97

118 Aunt Mary . . . "Thoreau": RW, interview with AMacL, April 21, 1979

119 "first-rate lawyer": SD, interview with W. Jackson Bate, October 13, 1988

119 "Next Philosophy": AMacL and Lawrence Mason, "The Next Philosophy," *North American Review* 217 (May 1923), 698–704

119 "FOR PLATOS SAKE": AMacL to Francis H. Bangs, May 22, 1923, Bangs, pp. 191–192, Yale

120 Mason . . . "lost": Bangs, p. 190, Yale

120 "Who will speak for us": AMacL, "The Class of Nineteen Seventeen," notebooks, 1974, LC

121 "Maybe four can live": *Reflections,* p. 26

121 bridges . . . burned: AMacL to Martha Hillard MacLeish, May 2, 1923, *Letters,* pp. 98–99

121 Amy Lowell . . . poem: RW, interview with Kay Bundy, September 22, 1979; AMacL, untitled poem beginning "Now, I shall put that evening by" in the possession of Kay Bundy; as revised, this became AMacL, "For Amy Lowell," *Atlantic Monthly* 137 (January 1926), 46.

122 invited . . . Bodenheim: RW, interview with Edward Weeks, December 1, 1981

122 her backing: AMacL to Martha Hillard MacLeish, September 4, 1923, *Letters,* p. 103

122 gap between ideal love: See Campbell, *The Poet,* p. 49

123 "Man is immortal": AMacL, "The Happy Marriage," in *Collected,* p. 50

123 "two nations": AMacL, "The Happy Marriage," in *Collected,* p. 49

123 "Whom do you love": AMacL, "The Happy Marriage," in *Collected,* p. 52

123 issue of infidelity: Discussion of October 14, 1920, Bangs, pp. 176–177, Yale

123 rhapsodized on her charms: AMacL to Francis H. Bangs, August 4, 1923, Bangs, p. 193, Yale

124 advice . . . "Wait": AMacL to Maurice Firuski, c. 1923, NYPL

8. FEVER OF GREATNESS

Setting In

125 tooting across . . . Banks: AMacL to Martha Hillard MacLeish, September 4, 1923, *Letters,* pp. 102–103

125 devastating effects: *Reflections,* pp. 23–24

126 expatriates . . . attack: *Paris Tribune,* September 10 and September 17, 1924; for this information, I am indebted to Michael S. Reynolds.

126 "Mr. and Mrs. Longfellow Little": AMacL, "Project for an Aesthetic

Sub-Title: Moonlight of a Man," in *Collected*, p. 504

126 "last of the great holy cities": AMacL, "Autobiographical Information," in *Riders*, pp. 78–79

127 "What lured us": Robert Cowley, "Promises," p. 26

127 Paris . . . arrangements: AMacL to Martha Hillard MacLeish, September 29, 1923, *Letters*, pp. 104–105; *Reflections*, pp. 24–25

127 "never . . . such freedom" . . . "dreadfully happy": Ada MacLeish to Maurice Firuski, c. fall 1923, NYPL

127 "Sprayed by a fire hose": AMacL to Harvey Bundy, c. December 1923, *Letters*, p. 113

127 long lunch: *Reflections*, pp. 26–27

128 winter . . . sunsets: AMacL to Andrew and Martha Hillard MacLeish, December 26, 1923, *Letters*, pp. 117–118

128 "waste time": Ada MacLeish to Maurice Firuski, c. fall 1923, NYPL

128 first Christmas: Ada MacLeish to Maurice Firuski, late December 1923, NYPL

128 thinking of . . . sister: AMacL to Martha Hillard and Andrew MacLeish, December 8, 1923, *Letters*, p. 114

University of One

128 Povla Frijsh . . . "diploma": RW, interview with AMacL, April 21–22, 1979; AMacL to Martha Hillard MacLeish, November 12, 1923, *Letters*, p. 108

129 "much too modest": AMacL to Martha Hillard and Andrew MacLeish, December 8, 1923, *Letters*, p. 114

129 program . . . Salle Pleyel: AMacL to Andrew and Martha Hillard MacLeish, February 10, 1924, *Letters*, pp. 126–127

129 suited to . . . Stravinsky: AMacL to Amy Lowell, March 3, 1924, *Letters*, p. 129

129 "*une voix blanche:*" *Reflections*, p. 28

129 "Outside of the law": AMacL to Andrew and Martha Hillard MacLeish, February 10, 1924, *Letters*, p. 127

129 "hell of a waste": AMacL to Francis H. Bangs, January 19, 1924, Bangs, p. 201, Yale

129 "I don't like what I do": AMacL to Amy Lowell, January 31, 1924, *Letters*, pp. 122–123

129 stop writing . . . and read: AMacL to Betty Choate, January 21, 1924; AMacL to Dean Acheson, February 5, 1924, *Letters*, pp. 124–125

130 "unfortunately so constructed": AMacL to Martha Hillard and Andrew MacLeish, December 8, 1923, *Letters*, p. 115

130 Sylvia Beach . . . "gates of dream": Noel Riley Fitch, *Sylvia Beach and the Lost Generation* (New York: Norton, 1983), pp. 92, 174–175

130 lending library . . . record: Shakespeare and Company borrowers' cards, 1923–1928, Princeton

130 Eliot's criticism: AMacL, reading notes, c. 1925, p. A36, LC

131 Dante . . . "compact with emotion": AMacL to Betty Choate, March 9 and 14, 1924

131 deep in *The Golden Bough:* AMacL to Charles R. Walker, Jr., January 15, 1924

131 Pound . . . "great wrecker": AMacL, "Poetry and the Public World," in *A Time to Speak*, p. 93

131 Pound . . . *Instigations:* AMacL, "Notebooks, 1924–1938," *Poetry* 73 (October 1948), 40–41; AMacL, reading notes, February 1924, p. B8, LC

131 "The work must come first": Amy Lowell to AMacL, June 25, 1924, LC

132 "door knobs and banisters": AMacL, notebooks, summer 1924, pp. B48–B53, LC

132 Bishop . . . the law: AMacL, notebooks, early 1924, p. B2, LC

132 "The Oklahoma Ligno": AMacL, "Corporate Entity," in *Collected*, p. 88

133 Cummings . . . "never a charm": Burton Rascoe, "A Harlequin Wailing against the Wind and Other Specters on the Sky," *Arts & Decoration* 22 (March 1925); AMacL, notebooks,

February 1924, p. B3, LC; AMacL, "Notebooks, 1924–1938," *Poetry* 73 (November 1948), 93; RW, interview with AMacL, November 10, 1979

Farewells

134 returning . . . cut his ties: AMacL to Charles F. Choate, Jr., February 5, 1924; AMacL to John Peale Bishop, July 30, 1924, *Letters*, p. 142

134 *Happy Marriage* . . . reviewers: D. R., "Clutching at Glory," *Independent*, April 26, 1924, p. 233; "Briefer Mention," *Dial* 77 (November 1924), 437

134 "Three hundred and": AMacL, "Chevaux de Bois," in *Happy Marriage*, p. 63. Campbell, *The Poet*, calls attention to the theme of man in space.

135 Bundys . . . Billy Hitchcock: RW, interview with Kay Bundy, September 22, 1979; RW, interview with Hester Pickman, September 21, 1979

135 South of France . . . Italy: AMacL, notebooks, early 1924, p. B20, LC; RW, interview with AMacL, November 10, 1979

135 Masefield . . . "shoved": AMacL to Francis H. Bangs, August 21, 1924, Bangs, p. 56, Yale

135 did not see . . . Eliot: AMacL to Amy Lowell, May 4, 1924, *Letters*, p. 132; RW, interview with AMacL, November 18–19, 1978

135 "a pint of port": Ada MacLeish to Maurice Firuski, May 17, 1924, NYPL

135 wooing . . . "misplaced clubwoman": RW, interviews with AMacL, November 18–19, 1978, and April 21, 1979

136 "'If we had the choice'": AMacL, "L'an trentiesme de mon age," in *Collected*, p. 81

136 "tragedy" . . . departure: Ada MacLeish to Adele Lovett, early June 1924

136 "'Margaret'" . . . "hurt her again": AMacL's sonnet, variously titled "The Flower of Silence is Withered" and "The Comforter," enclosed with his May 26, 1924, letter to John Peale Bishop, Princeton

137 "Now when you think of her":

AMacL to Margaret and John Peale Bishop, May 27, 1924, Princeton

137 "All dreams . . . End in a . . . body": W. B. Yeats, "The Phases of the Moon," in *Wild Swans of Coole* (London: Macmillan, 1919), p. 165

137 "You, you within": AMacL to John Peale Bishop, June 3, 1924, Princeton; printed posthumously as "The Lover Apostrophizes the Poets," in *Collected*, p. 500

138 "commercial war": *Reflections*, p. 232

138 outraged . . . Lodge: AMacL to Dean Acheson, February 5, 1924, *Letters*, p. 126

138 communion with . . . Kenny: AMacL to Ishbel MacLeish, May 31, 1924, *Letters*, pp. 132–138

139 "Ambassador Puser the ambassador": AMacL, "Memorial Rain," in *Collected*, pp. 102–103

A Second Year

140 songs by . . . Satie: *Reflections*, pp. 36–37

141 "Kenny . . . fatter": AMacL to Martha Hillard and Andrew MacLeish, June 24, 1924, *Letters*, pp. 138–139

141 polio . . . harshly: Thursa Bakey Sanders to SD, March 25, 1990

141 irritates me" . . . "crybaby": AMacL to Martha Hillard MacLeish, March 12, 1924, *Letters*, pp. 129–131; RW, interview with Carolyn MacLeish, September 10, 1979

141 Mimi . . . "celestial child": AMacL to Andrew MacLeish, August 3, 1924, *Letters*, p. 147; AMacL to Ishbel MacLeish, May 31, 1924, *Letters*, p. 133

141 writing routine: *Reflections*, p. 263; Donald Hall, "Archibald MacLeish," in *The Weather for Poetry* (Ann Arbor: University of Michigan Press, 1982), p. 15; AMacL calls himself "a slave to the eraser" in *Collected*, p. 524; *Reflections*, p. 185; DeMott, *Writers at Work*, p. 45; *Reflections*, pp. 38–39; AMacL to William Heyen, March 3, 1978, *Letters*, p.

444; RW, interview with Ishbel MacLeish and Alexander Campbell, April 7, 1979

142 tempest . . . circus: Ada MacLeish to Maurice Firuski, September 28, 1924, NYPL; *Reflections,* pp. 37–38

142 "Quite unexpectedly": AMacL, "The the World," in *Collected,* p. 89 Aunt Mary . . . future interference: AMacL to Betty Choate, February 12, 1925; AMacL to Martha Hillard MacLeish, August 3, 1924, *Letters,* pp. 145–146; AMacL to Martha Hillard, Andrew, and Ishbel MacLeish, November 23, 1924, *Letters,* pp. 150–151

143 mansion . . . Saint-Cloud: Ada Mac-Leish to Maurice Firuski, September 28, 1924, NYPL

143 Murphys . . . parties . . . artist: AMacL, "Gerald Murphy," in *Riders,* pp. 123–126; *Reflections,* pp. 42–43; Barnaby Conrad III, "A Legend & an Eye," *Horizon* 26 (June 1983), 20

144 "'Her room,' you'd say": AMacL, "Sketch for a Portrait of Mme. G — M—— ," in *Collected,* pp. 107–109

144 "shine to life": DeMott, *Writers at Work,* p. 38

144 migratory birds: AMacL and Samuel Hazo, "Those Paris Years," color video, Penn State University, 1987 (filmed 1977)

145 exhaust the oxygen . . . wrong side of the tracks: AMacL quoted in Patrick Hynan, "Hemingway," Canadian Broadcasting Company radio recording, May 26, 1970

145 corkscrew . . . note: Ernest Hemingway to Archibald and Ada MacLeish, c. 1924, LC

"I am a poet"

145 *Pot of Earth* . . . "vignettes": AMacL to Robert N. Linscott, October 31, 1924, *Letters,* pp. 148–150

145 epigraph . . . blossom: AMacL, *The Pot of Earth,* in *Collected,* pp. 59, 76; Grover Smith, *American Writers,* p. 7

146 influence . . . *Waste Land:* AMacL,

The Pot of Earth, in *Collected,* pp. 59–60, 66; T. S. Eliot, *The Waste Land,* in *Collected Poems, 1909–1935* (New York: Harcourt Brace, 1930), p. 74; Judson Jerome, "Archibald MacLeish: The Last of the Moderns," in *Symposium,* p. 13

147 "a net . . . to escape": Robert N. Linscott to AMacL, November 14, 1924, LC

147 "man who comes after": AMacL to John Peale Bishop, December 7, 1924, *Letters,* p. 153

147 "standing on your own feet": Amy Lowell to AMacL, March 14, 1924, LC

147 Pierre Garanger: RW, interview with AMacL, April 26, 1980; AMacL, notebooks, early 1925, p. B109, LC

147 read French . . . Caetani: Fitch, *Sylvia Beach,* p. 101; AMacL to T. S. Eliot, February 21, 1926, *Letters,* p. 177

148 career . . . Ada's: Ada MacLeish to Maurice Firuski, February 13, 1925, NYPL

148 Sinclair Lewis . . . bathtub: RW, interview with AMacL, November 10, 1979

148 bicycle trip to Beaune: *Reflections,* p. 43; AMacL, notebooks, c. 1925, p. G29, LC

148 certain of his vocation: AMacL to Betty Choate, February 12, 1925

149 "A poem should be palpable": AMacL, "Ars poetica," in *Collected,* pp. 106–107

150 gloss on the poem: AMacL to Norman H. Pearson, October 14, 1937, Yale

150 Monroe . . . McClure: Harriet Monroe, "Tone Poems," *Poetry* 28 (April 1926), 46; John McClure, *Double Dealer* review, Scrapbook, vol. 1, p. 12, GCC

150 Tate . . . *Dial* . . . Benét . . . Bates . . . *Times:* Allen Tate, "Rhetoric, Mysticism, Poetry," *New Republic,* October 14, 1925, pp. 209–210; "Briefer Mention," *Dial* 79 (September 1925), 261; Stephen Vincent Benét, "Distinctive Work," *Saturday Review of Literature,* July 17, 1926, p. 934; Ka-

tharine Lee Bates, "Young American Poet . . . ," *New York Evening Post,* June 6, 1925; "A Symbolic Poet," *New York Times,* June 7, 1925, p. 5

150 "the rest can wait": AMacL to Andrew and Martha Hillard MacLeish, July 19, 1925, *Letters,* p. 167

9. SHADOW OF THE NIGHT

Antibes and the States

151 potatoes . . . "flowers": *Reflections,* p. 46; Honoria Murphy Donnelly with Richard N. Billings, *Sara & Gerald: Villa America and After* (New York: Times Books, 1982), p. 31

151 tragic future . . . in wait: AMacL, "Gerald Murphy," in *Riders,* pp. 124–125

152 second set of parents: RW, interview with Honoria Murphy Donnelly, July 22, 1979

152 harrowing sail: Donnelly with Billings, *Sara & Gerald,* pp. 16–17; RW, interview with AMacL, April 21, 1979

152 Scott . . . Fitzgerald: F. Scott Fitzgerald to John Peale Bishop, probably September 1925, *The Letters of F. Scott Fitzgerald,* ed. Andrew Turnbull (New York: Dell, 1966), p. 383; Cowley, "Promises," p. 27; *Reflections,* pp. 60–61

152 injury to his back: RW, interview with Ishbel MacLeish Campbell, April 7, 1979; AMacL to Martha Hillard MacLeish, December 22, 1925, *Letters,* p. 175

153 decline of his father: RW, interview with Ishbel MacLeish Campbell, April 7, 1979; SD, interview with Roderick MacLeish, February 24, 1989; AMacL, notebooks, c. 1925, p. G52, LC; *Martha MacLeish,* p. 119

153 Stevens . . . Moore: AMacL to Wallace Stevens, October 20, 1925; AMacL to Marianne Moore, October 22, 1925

153 "Keep them as long": AMacL to T. S. Eliot, autumn 1925, AMacL to

Maurice Firuski, December 1, 1925, *Letters,* p. 174

153 rue du Bac: Ada MacLeish to Maurice Firuski, fall 1925, NYPL

154 Christmas . . . New Year's Eve: Ada MacLeish to Maurice Firuski, January 5, 1926, NYPL

Persia

154 Persia . . . adventure: *Reflections,* pp. 39–41; telegram, Dean Acheson to AMacL, c. January 15, 1926, and telegram, F. A. Delano to AMacL, January 16, 1926, FDR; AMacL to John Peale Bishop, February 3, 1926, *Letters,* pp. 176–177; SD, interview with Michael Janeway, May 10, 1988

155 things to buy: F. A. Delano to AMacL, January 23, 1926, FDR

155 Sphinx a god: AMacL, journal of Persia trip, LC

155 "rhymes with Lepantos": AMacL to Ezra Pound, March 29, 1926, Yale

155 "peach boughs": AMacL and Mark Van Doren, *Dialogues,* p. 193

155 fire . . . fever . . . "difficile": F. A. Delano, journal of Persia trip, pp. 37, 74, 80, FDR

155 withering comments: AMacL, journal of Persia trip, pp. 70–71, LC; RW, interview with Alice Acheson, January 21, 1979

156 report . . . railroad . . . route: RW, interviews with AMacL, November 18–19, 1978, and April 21, 1979

156 "no real life": Ada MacLeish to Maurice Firuski, March 13, 1926, Princeton

156 love for Ada . . . journal: AMacL, journal of Persia trip, entries for March 9, March 10, March 23, April 5, late April, 1926, LC

157 other men: RW, interview with AMacL, April 21–22, 1979; SD, interview with Jill Ker Conway, October 10, 1988

157 Antibes . . . Marseille . . . Geneva: Ada MacLeish to Adele Lovett, c. July 1926

157 "Not now": SD, interview with Richard McAdoo, May 10, 1988

157 "There she is. At Antibes": AMacL, "Old Photograph," in *Collected,* p. 515

158 "Saints and angels": AMacL, "The Treason," unpublished poem, c. 1926, LC

159 "The eyes are hers": AMacL, "Contemporary Portrait," in *Collected,* p. 487. In a talk at Williams College on October 7, 1968, AMacL made the dubious assertion that he hadn't "the foggiest idea" who the woman in the poem was.

Season of Divorce

159 beach . . . overcrowded: Ada MacLeish to Adele Lovett, c. summer 1926

159 Fitzgerald . . . punch: RW, interviews with AMacL, November 18–19, 1978, and April 21, 1979; RW, interview with Honoria Murphy Donnelly, July 22, 1979

159 Hamilton . . . apartment: RW, interview with AMacL, November 10, 1979; Ada MacLeish to Adele Lovett, c. summer 1926; AMacL to Ernest Hemingway, c. October 2, 1952, *Letters,* p. 361; *Reflections,* p. 54; AMacL to Martha Hillard MacLeish, October 7, 1926, *Letters,* p. 184; RW, interview with Adele and Robert A. Lovett, June 2, 1979

160 "Jake stays with me": AMacL to Ernest Hemingway, c. June 1926, *Letters,* p. 179

160 hotel in Monte Carlo: Carlos Baker, interview with Archibald and Ada MacLeish, March 9, 1965, Princeton

161 "the horrors": AMacL to Ernest Hemingway, December 1, 1948, *Letters,* p. 343

161 part of the family: AMacL to Carlos Baker, August 9, 1963, Princeton

161 fights . . . bike races: Ernest Hemingway to Ada MacLeish, October 5, 1952, LC

161 Zaragoza: RW, interviews with AMacL, April 21, 1979, and November 10–11, 1979; *Reflections,* p. 29

162 "He walks with Ernest": AMacL,

"Cinema of a Man," in *Collected,* p. 146

162 "no pretender" . . . "staccato": RW, interview with Alice-Lee Myers, March 10, 1979

162 "sweel history": AMacL to Ernest and Pauline Hemingway, June 19, 1927, *Letters,* pp. 201–202

162 "I don't love men": Denis Brian, *The True Gen* (New York: Grove, 1987), p. 49

162 "empty tomato can": Ernest Hemingway to Archibald and Ada MacLeish, c. October 1926, LC

163 Parker . . . "Gide": Donald Ogden Stewart, *By a Stroke of Luck* (New York: Paddington, 1975), p. 157; AMacL, "Ernest Hemingway," in *Journey,* pp. 309–310

163 Kenny . . . school . . . skiing: RW, interview with Jean Groo, September 13, 1980; AMacL to Martha Hillard MacLeish, October 2, 1926, *Letters,* pp. 184–185; *Reflections,* p. 27; SD, interview with Martha MacLeish Fuller, May 23, 1989; Ada MacLeish to Adele and Robert A. Lovett, c. January 1927; Caresse Crosby, *The Passionate Years* (New York: Dial, 1953), p. 160

163 Archie . . . short story: *Reflections,* p. 30; Robert N. Linscott to AMacL, October 24, 1928, LC

163 Mimi . . . "madly in love": *Reflections,* p. 67; RW, interview with Adele and Robert A. Lovett, June 2, 1979; AMacL, "White-Haired Girl," in *Collected,* pp. 22–23

164 Pauline . . . "always seemed": RW, interview with AMacL, April 26, 1980

164 "farce . . . solemnized": Ada MacLeish to Carlos Baker, n.d., Princeton

164 Harry Crosby . . . bathing suit: *Shadows of the Sun: The Diaries of Harry Crosby,* ed. Edward Germain (Santa Barbara, Calif.: Black Sparrow, 1977), pp. 14–15

164 ranked him second: Geoffrey Wolff, *Black Sun* (New York: Random House, 1976), p. 181

164 "H the realist": *Shadows of the Sun,* pp. 131–132

164 "fond of him": *Reflections*, p. 58

165 "Poets should sing": AMacL to Harry and Caresse Crosby, c. 1927, Southern Illinois

Star Ascending

165 Ada . . . Melisande: AMacL to Martha Hillard MacLeish, October 7, 1926, *Letters*, p. 185; Ada MacLeish to Adele and Robert A. Lovett, c. February 1927

165 *Nobodaddy* . . . "indifferent universe": AMacL to Maurice Firuski, October 28, 1925, and December 1, 1925, *Letters*, pp. 172–174

166 "Cain, the son of those": AMacL, *Six Plays* (Boston: Houghton Mifflin, 1980), p. 5

166 the best notice: Christian Herter, "New Books in Brief Review," *Independent*, May 29, 1926, p. 639

167 "horror of evil": AMacL to John Peale Bishop, August 8, 1925, *Letters*, p. 169

167 "I profoundly lack": AMacL, notebooks, 1926, pp. C1–C2, LC

167 "If a man writes": AMacL, "Notebooks, 1924–1938," *Poetry* 73 (October 1948), 34

167 "L. T. Carnavel": RW, interview with AMacL, November 18–19, 1978

167 "And here face down": AMacL, "You, Andrew Marvell," in *Collected*, pp. 150–151

168 came with a rush: DeMott, *Writers at Work*, p. 43; *Reflections*, p. 35

169 change the title: *Letters*, p. 182, footnote 1

169 "Hereunder Jacob Schmidt": AMacL, "Immortal Helix," in *Collected*, p. 85

169 "In the doorway": AMacL, " '*Le seul malheur est que je ne sais pas lire,*' " in *Collected*, p. 99

169 "Einstein" . . . *Nützlich ist:* Smith, *American Writers*, p. 10; David Barber, "It's All in the Name: The *Einstein* of Archibald MacLeish," *American Poetry* 8 (Fall 1990), 57–69; RW, interview with AMacL, November 18–19, 1978; Campbell, *The Poet*, p. 103

170 "He's agin' me": AMacL to Robert N. Linscott, September 1926, Harvard

170 reviews of *Streets:* Yvor Winters, "Streets in the Moon," *Poetry* 29 (February 1927), 278–281; Allen Tate, "Toward Objectivity," *Nation*, February 16, 1927, pp. 185–186; Louis Untermeyer, "MacLeish Emerges," *Saturday Review of Literature*, February 12, 1927, p. 578; Conrad Aiken, "Another Murex," *New Republic*, February 9, 1927, p. 337

171 Tate . . . anthology: AMacL to Allen Tate, October 20, 1926, January 1, 1927, and January 25, 1927, Princeton; AMacL to Robert N. Linscott, January 25, 1927, *Letters*, p. 195

171 endorsement . . . slapped: AMacL to Ezra Pound, November 16, 1926, November 22, 1926, and December 3, 1926, *Letters*, pp. 186–189

171 "As to Edmund Wilson": AMacL to Ernest Hemingway, c. December 1926, JFK

171 "Having a model" . . . "politesse": Ezra Pound to AMacL, December 5, 1926, LC

172 Archie seething: AMacL to Ezra Pound, December 29, 1926, *Letters*, pp. 191–193

172 "GODDAMN it": Ezra Pound to AMacL, c. January 1927, LC

173 "getting fed up": AMacL to Ernest Hemingway, February 14, 1927, *Letters*, p. 196

173 "That was by the door": AMacL, "Broken Promise" in *Collected*, p. 294; revision by Ezra Pound of "Poem," c. 1927, LC

An End to Paris

173 Joyce . . . dinner: Sylvia Beach, *Shakespeare and Company* (New York: Harcourt Brace, 1959), pp. 41–42, 121; *Reflections*, pp. 44, 59–60; RW, interview with AMacL, April 21, 1979; Richard Ellmann, *James Joyce* (New York: Oxford, 1982), p. 334

174 Roth . . . pirate . . . protest: Beach, *Shakespeare*, pp. 179–182; Ellmann, *James Joyce*, pp. 586–587

175 *Pomes* . . . "Plurabelle": Beach, *Shakespeare,* p. 175; Ellmann, *James Joyce,* pp. 590–591, 598

175 never found . . . warm: Ellmann, *James Joyce,* p. 598

175 soliciting . . . for *Commerce:* AMacL to Marguerite Caetani, January 1, 1927, *Letters,* pp. 193–194; AMacL to Ernest Hemingway, February 14, 1927, and February 20, 1927, *Letters,* pp. 196, 198–199; AMacL to T. S. Eliot, June 4, 1927

176 central Europe . . . Moscow: Ada MacLeish to Adele and Robert A. Lovett, winter 1927; RW, interview with AMacL, November 10, 1979

176 falling-out: AMacL to Ernest and Pauline Hemingway, June 19, 1927, and August 13, 1927, *Letters,* pp. 202, 206

176 "baby" . . . farmhouse: Ada MacLeish to Adele and Robert A. Lovett, January 1927 and February 1927; *Reflections,* p. 66

177 Aunt Mary . . . Ashfield: Mary R. Hillard to Martha Hillard MacLeish, April 11, 1927; RW, interview with William H. MacLeish, September 20, 1979

177 Paris . . . last months: Wolff, *Black Sun,* p. 183; RW, interview with AMacL, November 18–19, 1978

177 "world's worst winter": AMacL to Harry Crosby, May 20, 1928, *Letters,* p. 213

177 "death of your father": AMacL to Ernest Hemingway, December 14, 1928, *Letters,* p. 220

177 freak accident: Carlos Baker, *Ernest Hemingway: A Life Story* (New York: Scribner's, 1969), pp. 189–190; *Reflections,* pp. 44–45; Beach, *Shakespeare,* p. 121

178 Kay Boyle: Robert McAlmon and Kay Boyle, *Being Geniuses Together* (Garden City, N.Y.: Doubleday, 1968), pp. 237, 267; Kay Boyle to AMacL, October 4, 1932, LC; AMacL to Harry Crosby, March 8, 1929, and April 22, 1929, Southern Illinois

178 broke the seal: *Reflections,* p. 69

178 "at least a year": Hazo, "Those Paris Years."

178 "This land is my native": AMacL, "American Letter," in *Collected,* pp. 162, 163

178 Gerald . . . Scott . . . homesick: Donnelly with Billings, *Sara & Gerald,* p. 71; Margaret C. L. Gildea to Andrew Turnbull, January 10, 1959

179 "Before, though, Paris": AMacL, "Years of the Dog," in *Collected,* pp. 376–377

10. NEW FOUND LAND

Cricket Hill Farm

180 bought a flat: William H. MacLeish, interview with Archibald and Ada MacLeish, c. 1980; AMacL to Harry Crosby, May 20, 1928, Southern Illinois

180 "Beat that for fools": Ada MacLeish to Adele Lovett, May 11, 1928

180 poor farm . . . cages: Ada MacLeish to Adele Lovett, fall 1927; RW, interview with Ishbel MacLeish Campbell, April 7, 1979

181 old Franklin Arms place: RW, interview with Adele Lovett, June 2, 1979; William H. MacLeish, interview with Archibald and Ada MacLeish, c. 1980; Ada MacLeish to Adele Lovett, fall 1927

181 Ada's father . . . addition: SD, interview with William H. MacLeish, May 25, 1989; William H. MacLeish, interview with Archibald and Ada MacLeish, c. 1980; RW, interview with Kay Bundy, September 22, 1979

181 "old worn hills": William H. MacLeish, "The Silver Whistler," *Smithsonian Magazine* 13 (October 1982), 64

181 stone house: AMacL, "A Man's Work," in *Collected,* p. 399

182 saltbox house . . . unoccupied: Dan Pride, "A Visit with Archibald MacLeish," *Greenfield (Mass.) Recorder,* November 7, 1981, p. A8

182 "bird's nest" . . . "kick me downstairs": Pride, "A Visit," p. A8; Donald Hall, "Archibald MacLeish," in *Weather for Poetry,* p. 13

182 "a kind of uprightness": AMacL, notebooks, c. 1972, LC

182 thirty-two . . . households: RW, interview with Mason Hammond, September 18, 1979

183 "I grunt around": Ada MacLeish to Adele Lovett, spring 1928

183 she gave birth: Ada MacLeish to Maurice Firuski, October 29, 1928, NYPL

183 "The night was dark as coal": RW, interview with Alexander Campbell, April 7, 1979

183 skating by moonlight: Ada MacLeish to Adele Lovett, late December 1928

183 northwest wind . . . cool seasons: William H. MacLeish, "Silver Whistler," pp. 57–58

Hamlet to Díaz

184 "Make verses! . . . ease myself": AMacL, *The Hamlet of A. MacLeish*, in *Collected*, p. 125

184 "I'll tell the world": AMacL, *Hamlet*, in *Collected*, pp. 133–134

184 "It is time" . . . *my heart!*: AMacL, *Hamlet*, in *Collected*, p. 135

184 "It is always the same": AMacL, *Hamlet*, in *Collected*, p. 119

185 choked by "the stench": AMacL, *Hamlet*, in *Collected*, p. 116

185 "perfunctory" . . . Aiken . . . "tweed suit": AMacL to Ernest Hemingway, December 14, 1928, *Letters*, p. 220; Conrad Aiken, "Unpacking Hearts with Words," *Bookman* 68 (January 1929), 576–577; AMacL to John Peale Bishop, c. January 1930, Princeton

185 Blackmur . . . "Hamlet is all right": R. P. Blackmur, "Am Not Prince Hamlet Nor Was Meant to Be," *Hound & Horn*, 2 (Winter 1929), 167–169; AMacL to Robert N. Linscott, January 24, 1929, *Letters*, p. 222; AMacL to Lincoln Kirstein, December 17, 1928; AMacL to Ernest Hemingway, December 14, 1928, *Letters*, p. 220; Ernest Hemingway to AMacL, c. January 1929, LC; AMacL to Harry Crosby, March 8, 1929, *Letters*, p. 224

186 Ernest . . . Mimi: AMacL to Harry Crosby, November 4, 1928, *Letters*, p. 215; AMacL, "White-Haired Girl," in *Collected*, p. 23; Hynan, "Hemingway," CBC radio

187 "I know how your mind works": AMacL to Ernest Hemingway, December 14, 1928, *Letters*, p. 220

187 Key West . . . Mexico: AMacL, telegrams to Ernest Hemingway, December 26, 1928, and January 5, 1929, JFK; AMacL to Ernest Hemingway, February 4, 1929, *Letters*, p. 223

187 conquest . . . "obvious metaphor": AMacL to Maurice Firuski, June 14, 1927, *Letters*, p. 201; *Reflections*, p. 73

187 "writing in a vacuum": Lewis Galantière to John Peale Bishop, September 5, 1928, Princeton

187 retrace the steps . . . Morrow: RW, interview with AMacL, November 10–11, 1979; AMacL to Ernest Hemingway, March 11, 1929, *Letters*, pp. 225–226; *Reflections*, p. 74

188 frescoes of Diego Rivera: AMacL, notebooks, 1929, p. 1A, LC; AMacL, "Notebooks, 1924–1938," *Poetry*, 73 (November 1948), 95

Parents and Children

189 Finn McCool: RW, interview with AMacL, April 26, 1980

189 cow . . . turkeys . . . dam: Ada MacLeish to Richard and Alice-Lee Myers, c. September 28, SD, interview with Mimi and Karl Grimm, July 24, 1988; AMacL to Charles R. Walker, Jr., c. April 1929, *Letters*, p. 227; AMacL and Mark Van Doren, *Dialogues*, pp. 54–55

189 "Your book starts slow" . . . "great novelist": AMacL to Ernest Hemingway, June 24, 1929, JFK; AMacL to Ernest Hemingway, September 1, 1929, *Letters*, p. 230

189 "Cricket Hill turkeys": William H. MacLeish, interview with Archibald and Ada MacLeish, c. 1980; William H. MacLeish, "Silver Whistler," p. 57

190 home movies: Filmed by Alexander

Campbell, in possession of Martha MacLeish Fuller

190 Ada ... concerts: *Reflections,* p. 67; AMacL to Dean Acheson, November 5, 1930, Time Inc.; "Music and Musicians," *New York Times,* September 24, 1933; RW, interview with John Duke, October 26, 1980

190 "behaved outrageously" ... rumors: RW, interview with Kay Bundy, September 22, 1979; SD, interview with Peter Davison, October 11, 1989

190 "couldn't leave" ... full-time job: William H. MacLeish, "Silver Whistler," p. 62; SD, interview with Morellen MacLeish, July 12, 1990; RW, interview with Kay Bundy, September 22, 1979

191 children ... suffered: RW, interview with Elizabeth Miller, November 16, 1979; RW, interview with Alice Acheson, January 27, 1979; William H. MacLeish, "Silver Whistler," p. 58; SD, interview with Mimi and Karl Grimm, July 24, 1988

191 Cie ... "terrible harm": SD, interview with Morellen MacLeish, July 12, 1990; RW, interview with William H. MacLeish, September 20, 1979; SD, interview with Mimi Grimm, July 24, 1988; RW, interview with Ishbel MacLeish and Alexander Campbell, April 7, 1979

191 blamed her mother: SD, interview with Mimi Grimm, July 24, 1988

191 Ken ... taking risks: RW, interview with Jean Groo, September 13, 1980; SD, interview with Ellen Ishbel Zale, October 9, 1988

191 Peter ... conformed: SD, interview with William H. MacLeish, July 10, 1990; SD, interview with Morellen MacLeish, July 12, 1990

Fortune Beckons

192 phone call from ... Luce: RW, interview with AMacL, April 26, 1980; *Reflections,* p. 78; Robert T. Elson, *Time, Inc.: The Intimate History of a Publishing Enterprise, 1923–1941* (New York: Atheneum, 1968), pp. 136–137

192 first job ... "sleep on ... floor": Elson, *Intimate History,* p. 68; RW, interview with AMacL, November 18–19, 1978

193 "clay feet": RW, interview with AMacL, November 18–19, 1978

193 launching ... *Fortune:* W. A. Swanberg, *Luce and His Empire* (New York: Scribner's, 1972), pp. 82–83, 105; RW, interview with Ralph M. Ingersoll, May 19, 1979

193 economic crisis: RW, interview with AMacL, April 26, 1980

193 a star ... "throw the switch": AMacL, "The First Nine Years," in *Writing for Fortune* (New York: Time Inc., 1980), pp. 6–12; Campbell, *The Poet,* p. 119

194 "Each weighs ... three pounds": Quoted in Signi Lenea Falk, *Archibald MacLeish* (New York: Twayne, 1965), p. 50

194 "History ... Roosevelt": Quoted in *Writing for Fortune,* p. 5

194 excused from ... "corps": Robert Coughlan, "A Collection of Characters," in *Writing for Fortune,* p. 74

194 Agee ... "rich and beautiful": RW, interview with Dwight Macdonald, April 15, 1980

195 Macdonald ... U.S. Steel: Dwight Macdonald, *Memoirs of a Revolutionist* (New York: Farrar Straus and Cudahy, 1957), p. 9

195 editors ... "mixed bag": RW, interview with Ralph M. Ingersoll, May 19, 1979; *Writing for Fortune,* pp. 15, 123, 149

195 women ... researchers: John Chamberlain, "How I Really Learned about Business," in *Writing for Fortune,* p. 27; Mary Grace, "The Girls in the Backroom," in *Writing for Fortune,* pp. 66–67

11. CITY OF GLASS

Cries upon the Air

197 Gatsby ... possibilities: F. Scott Fitzgerald, *The Great Gatsby* (New York: Scribner's, 1925), p. 69, and "My

Lost City," in *The Crack-Up* (New York: New Directions, 1943), pp. 23–33

197 *Einstein* . . . encouraging words: AMacL to Harry Crosby, March 8, 1929, Southern Illinois; AMacL to Harry Crosby, April 22, 1929, *Letters*, p. 228

197 oblivion . . . only happiness: *Shadows of the Sun*, intro. Edward Germain, pp. 7–8

198 "Fire Princess" . . . opium pills: *Shadows of the Sun*, intro. Germain, p. 8; Wolff, *Black Sun*, pp. 5–7

198 shot and killed . . . "quite a friend": Wolff, *Black Sun*, pp. 4–10

198 "sat for a long time": Wolff, *Black Sun*, p. 288; AMacL to Martha Hillard MacLeish, February 12, 1930, *Letters*, p. 234

199 "side of the angels" . . . "REMOVED RING": AMacL to Henrietta Crosby, December 12, 1929, *Letters*, pp. 231–232; telegram, AMacL to Caresse Crosby, December 7, 1929, Southern Illinois

199 literary friends . . . "not be a writer": Ernest Hemingway to AMacL, December 31, 1929, LC; AMacL to John Peale Bishop, c. 1933, Princeton

199 hysterectomy . . . "in two" . . . "shit": RW, interview with AMacL, November 18–19, 1978; Ada MacLeish to Carlos Baker, n.d., Princeton; AMacL to Ernest Hemingway, February 10, 1930, *Letters*, p. 233

199 Key West . . . safari: AMacL to Ernest Hemingway, c. May 1930, *Letters*, p. 235; Ernest Hemingway to AMacL, c. May 1930, LC; AMacL to F. Scott Fitzgerald, September 15, 1930, *Letters*, p. 236

200 *New Found Land* . . . life must unfold: Smith, *American Writers*, p. 13; Campbell, *The Poet*, p. 158

200 reviews . . . excellent: Percy Hutchison, "New Books of Poetry," *New York Times Book Review*, June 22, 1930, p. 17; Eda Lou Walton, "America — The New Found Land," *Nation*, July 2, 1930, p. 21; Horace Gregory, Review of *New Found Land*, *New York Evening Post*, June

21, 1930; Babette Deutsch, "A Poet Who Can Work Magic," *New York Herald Tribune Books*, July 6, 1930

200 "most beautiful" . . . "human season": George Dangerfield, "Archibald MacLeish: An Appreciation," *Bookman* 72 (January 1931), 494; AMacL, "Immortal Autumn," in *Collected*, p. 153

201 punctuation . . . flat: Morton Dauwen Zabel, "The Compromise of A. MacLeish," *Poetry* 36 (August 1930), 270–275

201 "It is colder now": AMacL, "Epistle to Be Left in the Earth," in *Collected*, pp. 161–162

A Leaf on Her Hair

203 "Be proud City of Glass": AMacL, ". . . & Forty-Second Street," in *Collected*, p. 166

203 family living . . . New York: RW, interview with AMacL, April 26, 1980

203 "I wrote this poem": AMacL, "Unfinished History," in *Collected*, p. 292

204 marriage . . . "Regret to inform": "Archibald M'Leish Marries in Vienna," *New York Times*, September 20, 1933; RW, interview with AMacL, November 18–19, 1978; AMacL to the editor of the *New York Times*, September 20, 1933, *Letters*, pp. 262–263

204 companionship in New York: RW, interview with Malcolm Cowley, March 8, 1980; Ada MacLeish to Stephen Vincent and Rosemary Benét, c. September 1932, Yale

204 Lincoln . . . Mina Kirstein: AMacL to Lincoln Kirstein, c. September 1931; RW, interview with Harry Levin, September 26, 1979; "Mina Stein Kirstein Curtiss," in *American Woman Writers* (New York: Unger, 1979), pp. 438–449

205 Adele . . . beauty: RW, interview with AMacL, November 18–19, 1978; RW, interview with Adele and Robert A. Lovett, June 2, 1979

205 "Therefore I will not speak": AMacL, " 'Not Marble Nor the Gilded Monuments,' " in *Collected*, pp. 148–149

205 "way he felt" . . . "Adele weeping":
RW, interview with Adele Lovett,
June 2, 1979; AMacL, notebooks, c.
1929, p. D7, LC

206 Rosamond Lehmann . . . dream:
AMacL to Stephen Spender, c. Oc-
tober 1933, California; Stephen
Spender to AMacL, October 21,
1933, LC; RW, interview with
AMacL, November 18–19, 1978;
Reflections, p. 88; AMacL, "The
Night Dream," in *Collected*, pp. 290–
291

206 "She sailed at midnight": AMacL,
notebooks, c. 1932, p. H42, LC

207 "Here in this country": AMacL, notebooks, May 1932, LC

207 Nobody . . . he knew well: *Reflections*, pp. 90–91

Continuing Education

207 broke his arm . . . bedside: Ernest
Hemingway to AMacL, c. November
1930, LC; *Reflections*, p. 63; AMacL
and Mark Van Doren, *Dialogues*, p.
87; Hynan, "Hemingway," CBC
radio

207 Perkins . . . overtures: Ernest Hemingway to AMacL, December 28,
1930, LC; AMacL to Maxwell Perkins, January 4, 1931, *Letters*, p. 238;
AMacL to Robert N. Linscott, September 4, 1931, *Letters*, p. 242

208 decision . . . Houghton Mifflin: Robert N. Linscott to AMacL, October
28, 1931, LC; Robert N. Linscott to
Ferris Greenslet, November 21, 1931;
Maxwell Perkins to AMacL, November 23, 1931, LC; AMacL to Maxwell
Perkins, November 24, 1931, *Letters*,
p. 243; Ferris Greenslet to AMacL,
November 25, 1931, LC; AMacL to
Maxwell Perkins, November 27,
1931, *Letters*, p. 244; AMacL to Ferris Greenslet, November 30, 1931;
RW, interview with Dorothy de Santillana, September 19, 1979

208 Gerald . . . abject letter: Gerald Murphy to AMacL, January 22, 1931, LC

209 Lewis . . . Hemingway: AMacL to

Parker Lloyd-Smith, c. April 1931,
Time Inc.

209 "recesses of hack work": AMacL to
Robert N. Linscott, c. October 30,
1931, *Letters*, p. 243

209 hard times: *Reflections*, p. 273, note
5; Elson, *Intimate History*, p. 393;
AMacL to Ernest Hemingway, June
11, 1932, JFK

209 overburdened . . . "every weekend":
AMacL to John Peale Bishop, c. April
1933, *Letters*, p. 257; AMacL to Ernest Hemingway, May 31, 1933, *Letters*, pp. 259–260

209 bonus . . . agreement: Roy Larsen to
AMacL, July 14, 1933, Time Inc.;
Henry R. Luce to AMacL, November
6, 1933, Time Inc.

209 Frost . . . trapped: AMacL to H.
Phelps Putnam, c. June 1934, *Letters*,
p. 267

209 education of . . . lifetime: *Reflections*,
p. 83

210 individualism . . . died: AMacL, notebooks, April 20, 1931, pp. D77–D78,
LC

210 "sadder . . . lot" . . . apples: AMacL
to Harriet Monroe, June 4, 1931, *Letters*, p. 240; Stanley Koehler, "Conversation with A. MacLeish,"
Pembroke Magazine 7 (1976), 99

210 "That was the Thirties": AMacL,
"Changes in the Weather," in *Journey*, pp. 50–51

210 failure of intelligence: AMacL to Ernest Hemingway, February 2, 1932,
JFK; AMacL, "To the Young Men of
Wall Street," *Saturday Review of Literature*, January 16, 1932, p. 453–
454

211 series on housing: The Editors of *Fortune* [AMacL], *Housing America*
(New York: Harcourt Brace, 1932),
pp. 35, 72, 77

212 Hoover . . . remiss: Roy Hoopes,
Ralph Ingersoll (New York: Athe-
neum, 1965), p. 93; Elson, *Intimate
History*, pp. 173–174

212 Roosevelt . . . " 'What a man' ":
Elson, *Intimate History*, pp. 207–208

212 series on . . . Ivar Kreuger: AMacL,
"Death of an Era," in *A Time to*

Speak, pp. 159–165; Elson, *Intimate History,* pp. 210–211

Journeys Westward

213 "selling out": Carlos Baker, interview with Archibald and Ada MacLeish, March 9, 1965, Princeton

214 blurb . . . *Conquistador:* Ernest Hemingway to AMacL, December 23, 1931, LC

214 trip ended disastrously: Ernest Hemingway to AMacL, February 9, 1932, LC; AMacL to Ernest Hemingway, February 29, 1932, *Letters,* p. 246, and April 7, 1932, *Letters,* pp. 246–248; AMacL to Carlos Baker, January 31, 1965, Princeton; Brian, *The True Gen,* p. 88

214 "more than completely": Ernest Hemingway to AMacL, c. April 10, 1932, LC

214 Aunt Mary . . . died: RW, interviews with AMacL, November 18–19, 1978, and April 21–22, 1979

215 *Conquistador* . . . western land: Michael Cavanagh, "Conquistador — An American Epic," in *Symposium,* pp. 110–112; Cavanagh, "The Problems of Modern Epic: MacLeish's *Conquistador,*" *Papers on Language and Literature* 17 (1981), 298; John Griffith, "Narrative Technique and the Meaning of History in Benét and MacLeish," *Journal of Narrative Technique* 3 (1973), 16–17

215 first note: AMacL to Norman Holmes Pearson, October 14, 1937, Yale

216 "The poem is in the mouth": AMacL, notebooks, c. 1928–1930, pp. D22–D23, D52, D54, LC

216 Very little . . . communicated itself: Llewellyn Jones, "Soldier of Cortes Describes Perilous March into Mexico," *Chicago Evening Post,* May 20, 1932, p. 6; H. M. [Harriet Monroe], "The Conqueror," *Poetry* 40 (July 1932), 217–218; Herbert Gorman, "M'Leish Paints Aztec Glory," *New York Evening Post,* c. April 1932

217 applauded . . . form: Lincoln Kirstein, "Arms and Men," *Hound &*

Horn 5 (April–June 1932), 484, 487; Allen Tate, "Not Fear of God," *New Republic,* June 1, 1932, pp. 77–78

217 applicability . . . his own time: Horace Gregory, "The Futility of Conquest," *Nation,* June 8, 1932, pp. 655–656; S. F. [V. J. Jerome], "Escape to the Past," *New Masses* 8 (July 1932), 26; Isidor Schneider, "Warrior Plus Poet," *New York Herald Tribune Books,* April 3, 1932; Laurence Stallings, "The Book of the Day," *New York Sun,* April 7, 1932

218 cranky . . . Pound: AMacL, notebooks, c. 1928–1930, LC; AMacL to Ezra Pound, c. June 1932, Yale; AMacL to John Peale Bishop, c. September 1932, *Letters,* p. 255

218 "My dear Sir": Enclosed in AMacL to Stephen Spender, c. October 1933, California

218 Pulitzer . . . recognition: *Reflections,* pp. 77–78; Robert Frost to Ferris Greenslet, May 12, 1933, LC; Ernest Hemingway to AMacL, May 14, 1933, LC; AMacL, "Remarks on the Pulitzer Prize," in *Riders,* pp. 110–111

12. PUBLIC POET I

Not Man but Mankind

220 "considerable responsibility": AMacL to Carl Sandburg, c. July 1936, *Letters,* p. 282

221 "I shall never": AMacL to Francis H. Bangs, November 11, 1916, *Letters,* p. 30

221 "I am an evil person": AMacL to Martha Hillard MacLeish, February 12, 1930, *Letters,* p. 234

221 "no longer A MAN": AMacL, "Nevertheless One Debt," *Poetry* 88 (July 1931), 208–216. The issue of MacLeish's public and private obligations is admirably reviewed in John Timberman Newcomb, "Archibald MacLeish and the Poetics of Public Speech: A Critique of High Modern-

ism," *Journal of the Midwest Modern Language Association* 23 (Spring 1990), 9–26

221 "conception of Capitalism": AMacL, "To the Young Men," p. 454

221 "What this country needs": AMacL, "American Mythos," notebooks, September 13, 1932, LC

222 "Señora, it is true": AMacL, "Invocation to the Social Muse," in *Collected*, pp. 295–297

222 risk of . . . irony . . . "full editorial dinner": Newcomb, "Poetics and Public Speech," pp. 18–19; Barry Wallenstein, "Poetry and Experience: A Reevaluation," *Pembroke Magazine* 7 (1976), 57–58; AMacL to John Peale Bishop, c. November 1932, Princeton

224 "rather active nature": AMacL to Mark Van Doren, *Dialogues*, p. 109

224 "Millions starving": AMacL, "1933," in *Collected*, pp. 90–95

225 Roosevelt's "great perception": *Reflections*, pp. 87–88

226 "A conflict truly exists": Malcolm Cowley, "MacLeish and His Two Worlds," *Pembroke Magazine* 7 (1976), 49

226 "rhetoric" . . . "integrate the role": Somer, "Public Man of Letters," in *Symposium*, p. 115; Donald Barlow Stauffer, *A Short History of American Poetry* (New York: Dutton, 1974), p. 312; Newcomb, "Poetics of Public Speech," pp. 24, 25; Stanley Fish, "Guest Column: No Bias, No Merit: The Case Against Blind Submission," *PMLA* 103 (October 1988), 744; Smith, *American Writers*, p. 2

Frescoes and "Fascism"

226 bargain price . . . "art in flower": Newcomb, "Poetics of Public Speech," pp. 18, 12

227 "The material" . . . "exploiting her": AMacL, notebooks, 1933, pp. E10–E11, LC

227 Rivera . . . Rockefeller: Campbell, *The Poet*, pp. 167–169

227 "She lies on her left side" . . . "sunlight": AMacL, *Frescoes for Mr.*

Rockefeller's City, in *Collected*, pp. 263–273; *Reflections*, p. 98

230 Davidson . . . Brooks: Eugene Davidson, "The Symbol and the Poets," *Yale Review* 23 (1933), 182; Cleanth Brooks, *Modern Poetry and the Tradition* (Chapel Hill: University of North Carolina Press, 1939), p. 125

231 criticism . . . from the left: Michael Gold, "Out of the Fascist Unconscious," *New Republic*, July 26, 1933, p. 295; John Strachey, *Literature and the Dialectical Materialism* (New York: Covici-Friede, 1934), pp. 22–23, 27–28

232 Benét . . . spoke for him: William Rose Benét, "The Phoenix Nest," *Saturday Review of Literature*, July 29, 1933, p. 21

American Manifesto

232 reunion . . . bitterness: AMacL, "Lines for an Interment," in *Collected*, pp. 288–289; *Reflections*, pp. 85–87

233 Stallings . . . two views: AMacL, review of Laurence Stallings, *The First World War* (New York: Simon and Schuster, 1933), reprinted in Malcolm Cowley, *Think Back on Us — A Contemporary Chronicle of the 1930s* (Carbondale: Southern Illinois University Press, 1967), pp. 35–39

233 "reread without embarrassment": AMacL, foreword, *Poems, 1924–1933* (Boston: Houghton Mifflin, 1933)

233 impasse . . . politics and art: Eda Lou Walton, "Archibald MacLeish," *Nation*, January 10, 1934, pp. 48–49; Alfred Kreymborg, " 'The Moon is Dead,' " *Saturday Review of Literature*, January 27, 1934, p. 435; R. P. Blackmur, "Mr. MacLeish's Predicament," *American Mercury* 31 (April 1934), 507–508; Conrad Aiken, "Development of a Poet," *New Republic*, January 17, 1934, pp. 287–288

234 "termite army": AMacL to Robert N. Linscott, c. January 1934, *Letters*, pp. 264–265

234 Humphries zeroed in: Rolfe Hum-

phries, "Archibald MacLeish," *Modern Monthly* 8 (June 1934), 264–270, 274

235 "Pulitzer" . . . "affluence": AMacL to Robert N. Linscott, c. January 1934, *Letters*, p. 265

235 "It is just as silly": AMacL, "The Poetry of Karl Marx," in *A Time to Speak*, p. 43

235 "conceived . . . in negatives": AMacL, "Preface to an American Manifesto," in *A Time to Speak*, pp. 17–24

236 ballet . . . Nabokov: *Reflections*, pp. 92–94

236 de Basil . . . production: RW, interview with AMacL, November 10–11, 1979

237 hit of the season: Siegfried Wagener, "The First American Ballet," *Living Age* 348 (March 1935), 87–88; Earl Sparling, "Archibald MacLeish, Who Can't Dance, Writes Ballet," *New York World-Telegram*, April 25, 1934; W. J. Henderson, "Dancers Portray Rail History," *New York Sun*, April 26, 1934; "The Dowager," "Society and Artistic Circles Excited," *Chicago Herald-Examiner*, April 14, 1934; telegram, Eugene and Maria Jolas, Sylvia Beach, and James and Nora Joyce to AMacL, June 5, 1934, Scrapbook, vol. 1, p. 41, GCC

237 "Talk about really doing something": Charles A. Fenton, *Stephen Vincent Benét: The Life and Times of an American Man of Letters, 1898–1943* (New Haven: Yale University Press, 1958), p. 277

237 "fruit ripe for the picking": Cowley, "Promises," p. 28; Falk, *Archibald MacLeish*, p. 70; *Reflections*, pp. 98–99

238 plot of a three-act play: AMacL, notebooks, 1932, pp. D103–D105, LC

238 *Gallagher the Great:* AMacL, notebooks, 1932 or later, pp. D140–D141, LC

Panic, Prejudice, Public Speech

238 "Mr. Lambert struck me": AMacL to Henry R. Luce, c. March 1935, Time Inc.

239 houses . . . painted green: AMacL, notebooks, 1933, p. E9, LC

239 McGafferty . . . "is a man": AMacL to Edward Mullaly, August 7, 1979; AMacL, notebooks, c. 1934, pp. H11–H12, LC

240 Welles . . . mere boy: Frank Brady, *Citizen Welles: A Biography of Orson Welles* (New York: Scribner's, 1989), pp. 67–68

240 boos . . . curtain call . . . Saturdaynight: Geraldine Sartain, "News Ticker Is Theme Song," *New York World-Telegram*, February 25, 1935; RW, interview with AMacL, November 10–11, 1979; AMacL to John Houseman, c. March 18, 1935, *Letters*, pp. 274–275

240 After the curtain . . . discussion: *Reflections*, p. 103; AMacL, preface to *Panic*, in *Six Plays*, pp. 33–34; Donald Hall, "Archibald MacLeish: On Being a Poet in the Theater," *Horizon* 2 (January 1960), 54

241 Ohrbach . . . strike: Daniel Aaron, *Writers on the Left* (New York: Oxford, 1977), p. 276; Edwin Rolfe, "An Interview with Archibald MacLeish," *Daily Worker*, March 15, 1935, p. 5

241 Jerome . . . "doom of capitalism": V. J. Jerome, "Archibald MacLeish's 'Panic,'" *New Masses*, April 2, 1935, pp. 43–44

242 critical reactions: Chamberlain and Gannett, quoted in promotion flyer for book publication of *Panic* (Boston: Houghton Mifflin, 1935); Ben Ray Redman, "Drama of the Crisis," *Saturday Review of Literature*, March 16, 1935, pp. 550–551; Malcolm Cowley, "Men and Ghosts," *New Republic*, March 27, 1935, pp. 190–191

242 denigrate Jews: AMacL to Ernest Hemingway, June 11, 1932, JFK; AMacL to F. Peavey Heffelfinger, January 13, 1934; F. Peavey Heffelfinger to Henry R. Luce and Archibald MacLeish, February 3, 1934; AMacL to F. Peavey Heffelfinger, February 7, 1934, Time Inc.

243 Martha MacLeish . . . destroying prejudice: *Martha MacLeish*, pp. 136–137; RW, interview with Walter

T. Fisher, November 15, 1982; RW, interview with AMacL, April 21, 1979; *Reflections,* p. 231

243 MacLeish's article . . . "very sick donkey": The Editors of *Fortune* [AMacL], *Jews in America* (New York: Random House, 1936), pp. 9, 12–15, 34, 98

244 "offense to no one": AMacL to Henry R. Luce, November 14, 1935, and December 28, 1935, Time Inc.

244 "The brotherhood is not": AMacL, "Speech to Those Who Say Comrade," in *Collected,* p. 303

244 "There is only you": AMacL, "Speech to a Crowd," in *Collected,* p. 307

244 "Why then must this time": AMacL, "Speech to the Detractors," in *Collected,* p. 306

245 "Smellers of horse-sweat": AMacL, "The German Girls! The German Girls!" in *Collected,* p. 311

245 reviewers . . . lavish with praise: Malcolm Cowley, "Public Speakers," *New Republic,* April 1, 1936, p. 226; William Rose Benét, "The Phoenix Nest," *Saturday Review of Literature,* May 9, 1936, p. 19; Ruth Lechlitner, "MacLeish's 'Love that Hardens into Hate,'" *New York Herald Tribune,* April 5, 1936, emphasis added; C. G. Poore, "Archibald MacLeish's Salvo of New Poems," *New York Times Book Review,* March 29, 1936, p. 5, emphasis added; Schneider quoted in Geoffrey Stone, "Night Is Sick with Our Dreams," *American Review* 7 (April 1936), 99

245 "hats in their hands": Robert N. Linscott to AMacL, June 1, 1936, LC

245 "happier" . . . did not sell: AMacL to John Farrar, May 29, 1936, *Letters,* pp. 280–281

13. MIDDLE OF THE JOURNEY

On Trial with Ernest

247 Puss Moth: AMacL to Ernest Hemingway, May 31, 1933, *Letters,* pp. 258–259

248 "confidence in . . . courage": AMacL to the editor of the *New Republic,* c. June 8, 1933, *Letters,* pp. 260–261

248 Bliven declined . . . "Hereafter . . . hit": AMacL to John Peale Bishop, c. June 1933, Princeton; AMacL to Ernest Hemingway, c. June 14, 1933, JFK

248 "god damned head" . . . dedication: Ernest Hemingway to AMacL, July 31, 1933, LC; Brian, interview notes for *The True Gen*

249 Jane Mason . . . Prince of Wales: Jeffrey Meyers, *Hemingway: A Biography,* (New York: Harper and Row, 1985), pp. 242–243; Ernest Hemingway to AMacL, c. early July 1933 and July 27, 1933, LC; AMacL to Ernest Hemingway, April 15, 1935, *Letters,* p. 277

249 "sisterly feelings": AMacL to Ernest Hemingway, August 1936, JFK; Ernest Hemingway to AMacL, c. August 1936, LC

250 sailfish . . . bastards: Arnold Samuelson, *With Hemingway: A Year in Key West and Cuba* (New York: Random House, 1984), pp. 27–31; Baker, *A Life Story,* p. 262

250 "sullen resentful Scot" . . . "Shit Mac": AMacL to Ernest Hemingway, January 14, 1935, *Letters,* p. 272, and c. July 20, 1934, *Letters,* p. 270; Ernest Hemingway to AMacL, August 13, 1934, and June 2, 1935, LC; AMacL to Ernest Hemingway, June 5, 1935, JFK; RW, interview with AMacL, April 26, 1980

251 stomach muscles: RW, interview with Adele and Robert A. Lovett, June 2, 1979

251 O'Hara's first novel . . . gatherings: RW, interview with Adele and Robert A. Lovett, June 2, 1979; Frank MacShane, *The Life of John O'Hara* (New York: Dutton, 1980), pp. 71–72

251 commencement . . . Villard: AMacL to Bernard De Voto, c. June 1934, *Letters,* p. 266

Wounded Friends

252 Luce . . . divorce: Hoopes, *Ralph Ingersoll*, pp. 124–127; Swanberg, *Empire*, pp. 114–115

253 job offers . . . NRA: AMacL to W. Averell Harriman, February 11, 1935, and Henry R. Luce to W. Averell Harriman, February 20, 1935, Time Inc.

253 Harvard University Press: AMacL to James Bryant Conant, May 14, 1935, *Letters*, p. 278; AMacL to Ernest Hemingway, June 5, 1935, JFK; AMacL to James Bryant Conant, June 10, 1935, LC

253 public opinion . . . survey: Hoopes, *Ralph Ingersoll*, pp. 100–102

253 wheat season . . . Montana: RW, interview with AMacL, November 18–19, 1978; *Reflections*, p. 80

254 "One nude is a nude": Elson, *Intimate History*, pp. 284–285

254 "spiders . . . fluff": Hall, "Poet in the Theater," p. 55

254 journalism . . . poetry: AMacL, "Poetry and Journalism," in *Journey*, quoted in Ronald Weber, "Journalism, Writing, and American Literature," Occasional Paper no. 5 (April 1987), Gannett Center for Media Studies, n. p.; AMacL to Ernest Hemingway, October 14, 1936, *Letters*, p. 286

254 Last night it was dark: AMacL to Patrick Murphy, October 26, 1934

255 Baoth . . . died: AMacL to John and Katharine Dos Passos, March 20, 1935, *Letters*, p. 275; Donnelly with Billings, *Sara & Gerald*, pp. 90–92

255 Gerald . . . "dissuade him?": DeMott, *Writers at Work*, pp. 37–38

Gardens East and West

256 fought like hawks . . . "water line": RW, interview with Adele and Robert A. Lovett, June 23, 1979; Ada MacLeish to Stephen Vincent and Rosemary Benét, c. March 1936, Yale

256 Japan issue . . . letters: Elson, *Intimate History*, p. 311; AMacL to Henry R. Luce, c. April 1936, Time

Inc.; Henrietta Crosby to AMacL, January 25, 1936, LC

256 interrogation: RW, interview with Adele Lovett, June 23, 1979

257 military coup . . . "except to war": *New York Times Index, 1936* (New York: New York Times Co., 1937), pp. 1478–79; "Militarists Attempt Coup," *New York Times*, February 26, 1936, p. 1; *Reflections*, p. 80

257 differences . . . East and West: RW, interview with Adele Lovett, June 23, 1979; AMacL to Ernest and Pauline Hemingway, c. April 1936, *Letters*, pp. 278–279; AMacL, "Landscape of a People," in *A Time to Speak*, pp. 185–189

257 chrysanthemum . . . symbol: "Japanese Issue," in-house memorandum of *Fortune*, Time Inc.; Robert Cowley, "Promises," p. 28

258 admiration of . . . "MacReish": SD, interview with John Kenneth Galbraith, July 11, 1990

258 bandanna: *Writing for Fortune*, p. 87

258 Marriage . . . Campbells: Ishbel MacLeish Campbell, "Last Years (1934–1947)," *Martha MacLeish*, pp. 133–134; RW, interview with AMacL, November 18–19, 1978

258 Ken . . . Carolyn: RW, interview with Carolyn MacLeish, September 10, 1979

259 deathly afraid . . . Westover: SD, interview with Mimi Grimm, July 24, 1988; RW, interview with AMacL, August 2, 1979

259 Mina . . . lovers: RW, interview with AMacL, August 2, 1979; SD, interview with Mimi Grimm, May 20, 1989

259 Peter . . . Bill . . . "Mr. Stanley": RW, interview with William H. MacLeish, September 20, 1979; RW, interview with Ishbel MacLeish and Alexander Campbell, April 7, 1979

260 watermelon . . . seed: SD, interview with Mimi Grimm, July 24, 1988

260 "septic pool" . . . limerick: RW, interview with Adele and Robert A. Lovett, June 2, 1979; Ada MacLeish to Adele Lovett, December 29, 1937

260 Achesons . . . outdoor game: RW, interview with AMacL, April 21–22, 1979

261 bulldozer . . . crocus dance: SD, interview with Mimi and Karl Grimm, July 24, 1988; William H. MacLeish, "Silver Whistler," p. 64

261 garden . . . wall: SD, interview with William H. MacLeish, May 25, 1989; RW, interview with AMacL, September 20, 1979

14. PUBLIC POET II

The Antifascist Cause

262 "running quarrel" . . . radio: Quoted in Mary Evelyn McGann, "Voices from the Dark: A Study of the Radio Achievement of Norman Corwin, Archibald MacLeish, Louis MacNeice, Dylan Thomas, and Samuel Beckett" (Ph.D. diss., University of Indiana, 1979), p. 58; *Reflections*, p. 121

262 "direct sensuous mind": AMacL, "Gorky the Artisan," *New Masses*, August 4, 1936, pp. 12–13

263 review of *The People, Yes*: AMacL, "Mr. Sandburg and the Doctrinaires," in *A Time to Speak*, pp. 36–41

263 "a dialectic": Newcomb, "Poetics and Public Speech," p. 13

264 *Spanish Earth* . . . Ivens: AMacL to Paul H. Buck, January 1, 1953, *Letters*, p. 366; Townsend Ludington, *John Dos Passos: A Twentieth-Century Odyssey* (New York: Dutton, 1980), p. 361; AMacL, "The Cinema of Joris Ivens," *New Masses*, August 24, 1937, p. 18

264 second congress . . . opening session: RW, interviews with AMacL, April 21, 1979, and November 18–19, 1978; Stewart, *By a Stroke*, p. 238; RW, interview with Malcolm Cowley, March 8, 1980; Stanley Burnshaw, *Robert Frost Himself* (New York: Braziller, 1986), pp. 68–69

265 first speech: AMacL, "The War Is Ours," *New Masses*, June 22, 1937, pp. 5–6

264 Hemingway . . . "Why the hell": "Creators' Congress," *Time*, June 21, 1937, pp. 79–81

266 this war . . . different: AMacL, "Speech to the Scholars," *Saturday Review of Literature*, June 12, 1937, p. 12

266 Conant . . . disagreement: James Bryant Conant to AMacL, June 13, 1937, and June 25, 1937, LC; AMacL to James Bryant Conant, June 21, 1937, LC; Walter Lippmann to AMacL, June 29, 1937, LC

266 called on . . . Roosevelt: *Reflections*, p. 128

267 "real struggle": The Editors of *Fortune* [AMacL], "The Struggle in Spain," in *Background of War* (New York: Knopf, 1937), pp. 51–53

Radio and Photograph

267 *Fall of the City* . . . "empty": AMacL, *The Fall of the City*, in *Six Plays*, pp. 67–93; Campbell, *The Poet*, pp. 182–185, presents a useful summary of the play.

268 radio . . . came into its own: Brady, *Citizen Welles*, pp. 105, 197

268 Armory . . . "best thing" . . . leaflet . . . Miller: *Reflections*, pp. 107–109; Charles C. Alexander, *Here the Country Lies: Nationalism and the Arts in Twentieth-Century America* (Bloomington: Indiana University Press, 1980), p. 226; CBS promotion leaflet, spring 1937; Arthur Miller, quoted in Philip G. Gardner, "Verse Plays for Radio," in *Symposium*, p. 98. The ending of MacLeish's radio play is reminiscent of C. P. Cavafy's well-known poem "Waiting for the Barbarians."

269 *Air Raid* . . . *Guernica*: *Reflections*, p. 112; AMacL, preface, to *Air Raid*, in *Six Plays*, pp. 97–98

269 device of . . . announcer: Brady, *Citizen Welles*, p. 165. The play was broadcast four days *before* Welles's famous *War of the Worlds*.

269 dawn has come . . . no one will listen: AMacL, *Air Raid*, in *Six Plays*, pp. 99–123

270 "intolerable timeliness" . . . "straight projection": Quoted in Joan Louise Corey Semonella, "The Poetic Theater of Archibald MacLeish: A Search for Meaning" (Ph.D. diss., UCLA, 1984), pp. 57–58

270 "all air raids" . . . "fear-mongering": *Christian Century*, December 14, 1938, p. 1549; Louise Bogan to Rolfe Humphries, October 28, 1938, *What the Woman Lived: Selected Letters of Louise Bogan, 1920–1970*, ed. Ruth Limmer (New York: Harcourt Brace Jovanovich, 1973), p. 178

270 "half a year": Orrin Dunlap, Jr., "Exploring in Drama," *New York Times*, October 30, 1938, p. 12

270 *The Cradle* . . . "honest realism": Brady, *Citizen Welles*, pp. 113–115; AMacL, foreword to Marc Blitzstein, *The Cradle Will Rock* (New York: Random House, 1938), pp. 8–11

271 "book of photographs": AMacL, *Land of the Free* (New York: Harcourt Brace, 1938); Somer, "Public Man of Letters," in *Symposium*, pp. 119–120

272 reviews . . . "man, woman, and child": *Reflections*, pp. 85, 95–96; Babette Deutsch, "Meaning and Being," *Poetry* 52 (June 1938), 153–156; T. K. Whipple, "Freedom's Land," *New Republic*, April 13, 1938, pp. 311–312

Yeats, Frost, and "Public Speech"

272 six weeks at Princeton: "MacLeish on Princeton Faculty," *New York Times*, July 31, 1936; Christian Gauss to AMacL, April 18, 1936, and June 3, 1936, LC; AMacL to Harold W. Dodds, April 5, 1937, LC; RW, interview with AMacL, April 26, 1980

263 Yale . . . gift . . . lecture . . . exhibition: Item, Scrapbook, vol. 1, p. 55, GCC; "M'Leish Yale Lecturer," *New York Times*, January 7, 1938; Arthur Mizener, *A Catalogue of the First Edi-*

tions of Archibald MacLeish (New Haven: Yale University Library, 1938)

273 "teacup" poet . . . "political terms": AMacL, "Public Speech and Private Speech in Poetry," in *A Time to Speak*, pp. 59–69

273 no . . . separation: AMacL, "Poetry and the Public World," in *A Time to Speak*, pp. 81–96

274 annoying implication: Walter Prichard Eaton, "Mr. McLeish, Lecturer," *Commonweal*, March 25, 1938, pp. 602–603

274 "How can I, that girl": W. B. Yeats, "Politics," *London Mercury* 39 (January 1939). I am indebted to Richard Finneran for drawing my attention to Yeats's response to MacLeish's talk/essay.

275 Bread Loaf . . . Frost . . . "okay side": Wallace Stegner, *The Uneasy Chair: A Biography of Bernard DeVoto* (Garden City, N.Y.: Doubleday, 1974), pp. 206–207; Charles H. Foster's journal, quoted in Burnshaw, *Frost Himself*, pp. 270–272

An End of *Fortune*

276 dispute . . . money . . . "stay out of Pappy's way": AMacL to Ralph M. Ingersoll, July 9, 1938, and July 24, 1938, LC; Ernest Hemingway to Ralph M. Ingersoll, July 18, 1938, LC; Ernest Hemingway to AMacL, July 28, 1938, LC; Donnelly with Billings, *Sara & Gerald*, pp. 172–173

276 "absolutely incredible": AMacL to Ernest Hemingway, August 6, 1938, *Letters*, pp. 294–295

277 campaign against . . . suppression: AMacL to Franklin Folsom, League of American Writers, c. June 1938, and June 16, 1938, California; AMacL, Van Wyck Brooks, AMacL, and Thornton Wilder, letter to the editor of the *New York Times*, June 22, 1938, California

277 Winchell . . . *Time*'s bias: Elson, *Intimate History*, pp. 249–252

277 flagrantly obvious . . . "Reds": Elson, *Intimate History,* pp. 261–262
278 heart and mind of Harry Luce: AMacL to Henry R. Luce, January 25, 1937, Time Inc.; Swanberg, *Empire,* pp. 137–141; AMacL to Laird S. Goldsborough, January 16, 1937, *Letters,* pp. 286–287; Laird S. Goldsborough to Henry R. Luce, February 20, 1937, Time Inc.; AMacL to Henry R. Luce, October 4, 1937, Time Inc.
279 Luce . . . "rather naive": RW, interview with Allen Grover, early 1979
279 raise . . . promotion . . . climb the pyramid: SD, interview with G. d'Andelot Belin, July 27, 1988; AMacL to Henry R. Luce, May 5, 1937, *Letters,* pp. 287–289; *Reflections,* pp. 120–121
279 proposal to brighten *Fortune:* AMacL to Henry R. Luce et al., October 5, 1937, Time Inc.
280 series . . . Catherine Carr: *Martha MacLeish,* p. 134; SD, interview with Lael Wertenbaker, November 27, 1990
280 "Do I need to say" . . . "superiority for granted": Henry R. Luce to AMacL, July 18, 1938, Time Inc.; AMacL to Henry R. Luce, c. July 20, 1938, *Letters,* pp. 291–293; RW, interview with Ralph Ingersoll, May 19, 1979
281 "The Editor" . . . "what DOES cry": Henry R. Luce to AMacL, September 1, 1938, Time Inc.; AMacL to Henry R. Luce, c. September 8, 1938, *Letters,* p. 297

The Nieman Year

281 bequest . . . "guide, counselor, and friend": Louis M. Lyons, "Harvard Meets the Press," *Nieman Reports* 43 (Spring 1989), 4–6, 38; James Bryant Conant, *My Several Lives: Memoirs of a Social Inventor* (New York: Harper and Row, 1972), pp. 398–403
282 salary . . . "let more air into Harvard": *Reflections,* pp. 212–223; Jerome Aumette, "Archibald MacLeish . . . Talks About That Innovative Year," *Nieman Reports* 43 (Spring 1989), 34
283 weekly dinners: Lyons, "Harvard

Meets," p. 14; Aumette, "MacLeish . . . Talks," p. 36; SD, interview with Frank Snowden Hopkins, March 1, 1989
283 initial Nieman group . . . Byzantine history: Frank Snowden Hopkins, "Quest for Wisdom: How Nine Newspapermen Spent a Year at Harvard," *Harper's* 80 (February 1940), 278–287; Aumette, "MacLeish . . . Talks," p. 39
283 Italian city-state . . . "examinations": Lyons, "Harvard Meets," pp. 7–9
284 "Lahey . . . fresh as paint" . . . "repression": Aumette, "MacLeish . . . Talks," p. 13; "Thirty-Six-Year-Old Nieman Fellow," *Harvard Crimson,* October 4, 1938; "Aunt Agnes' Fellows," *Time,* January 9, 1939; "Nieman Fellow Sees End of Middle Class," *Harvard Crimson,* c. October 18, 1938
285 Hicks . . . "Lord have mercy on Boston": "Hicks, MacLeish Speak at Rally," *Harvard Crimson,* October 13, 1938; Lyons, "Harvard Meets," p. 10; "Council Spurns Any Action on Hicks," *Harvard Crimson,* October 17, 1938, pp. 1, 3
285 Morris Gray . . . presidential library . . . Supreme Court: "Frost, MacLeish, and Van Doren to Lecture," *Harvard Crimson,* October 19, 1938; "Morison, Harvard Historian, Aids Roosevelt," *Harvard Crimson,* December 12, 1938, p. 1; "Frankfurter Picked," *Harvard Crimson,* January 6, 1939, p. 1
285 bombardment . . . "MacSlush": Elizabeth Frank, *Louise Bogan: A Portrait* (New York: Knopf, 1985), pp. 304–305; William McGuire, *Poetry's Catbird Seat* (Washington, D.C.: Library of Congress, 1988), pp. 91–92
286 Wilson's . . . "Omelet": Edmund Wilson, "The Omelet of A. MacLeish," *New Yorker,* January 14, 1939, pp. 23–24
287 "bile bladder burst" . . . "bunny": AMacL to John Peale Bishop, c. January 20, 1939, Princeton; AMacL to Ernest Hemingway, c. January 1939

JFK. Wilson's nickname was "Bunny."
288 "draw his guns": SD, interview with Donald Hall, July 27, 1988; RW, interview with Harry Levin, September 26, 1979
289 Pound . . . awful place: "Ezra Pound . . . to Read Poems Here," *Harvard Crimson*, May 16, 1939, p. 1; "Ezra Pound Knocks Economics," *Harvard Crimson*, May 19, 1939; RW, interview with AMacL, April 26, 1980
289 admiration for Harvard: RW, interview with John H. Finley, Jr., September 21, 1979

15. MR. M. GOES TO WASHINGTON

A Call from On High

290 Frankfurter . . . friendship: RW, interview with AMacL, April 26, 1980; AMacL, foreword to *Law and Politics: Occasional Papers of Felix Frankfurter, 1913–1938*, ed. AMacL and E. F. Prichard, Jr. (New York: Harcourt Brace, 1939), p. ix; AMacL, "Mr. Justice Frankfurter," *Life*, February 12, 1940, pp. 53–56
291 memorandum . . . FDR: Quoted in Nancy L. Benco, "Archibald MacLeish: The Poet Librarian," *Quarterly Journal of the Library of Congress* 33 (1976), 234
291 imaginative energy and vision: Quoted in Benco, "Poet Librarian," p. 235
291 turn down the position: AMacL to Felix Frankfurter, May 15, 1939, *Letters*, pp. 299–301
292 "Republic . . . obligation to serve": AMacL to Felix Frankfurter, October 19, 1945, *Letters*, p. 334
292 long-term commitment . . . advice: *Reflections*, p. 142; Donnelly with Billings, *Sara & Gerald*, p. 200; Kenneth Murdock to Felix Frankfurter, May 16, 1939, LC; RW, interview with Keyes Metcalf, December 3, 1981; *Reflections*, p. 130
293 must reject . . . captive . . . forever:

AMacL to Franklin D. Roosevelt, May 28, 1939, and June 11, 1939, *Letters*, pp. 301–303; SD, interview with W. Jackson Bate, October 13, 1988; *Reflections*, p. 130
293 "Roosevelt . . . decided" . . . "serving kind": William H. MacLeish, "Silver Whistler," p. 58; *Reflections*, p. 142; RW, interview with Dwight Macdonald, April 15, 1980; Richard Wilbur, foreword, *Reflections*, p. xi
294 wonderful reply . . . "interrupt the Muse": Franklin D. Roosevelt to AMacL, early June 1939

The Opposition

295 "a P-P-POET!": David C. Mearns, "As Alcuin Was Saying," *Pembroke Magazine* 7 (1976), 109
295 "fellow travelers": "M'Leish Assailed," *New York Times*, June 8, 1939, p. 2
295 Rayburn . . . Thomas: Librarian of Congress debate, *Congressional Record*, June 7, 1939, pp. 6781, 6783, and June 15, 1939, pp. A2613–15; "Library, Librarian," *Time*, June 19, 1939, p. 18
296 "get me in on it": Christian Gauss to AMacL, June 10, 1939, LC
296 "no one . . . more shocked": "Changes Spotlight," *Pathfinder*, June 24, 1939, p. 1
296 League . . . in rebuttal: Franklin Folsom to J. Parnell Thomas, July 7, 1939, California
296 flurry of similes: "Library, Librarian," *Time*, p. 18; "Panned Poet," *Newsweek*, June 19, 1939, p. 20
296 "Shocking Nomination": *Reflections*, p. 132
296 ALA . . . calamity: *Congressional Record*, June 29, 1939, p. 11498
297 Metcalf . . . "I see your point": Keyes D. Metcalf, "Archibald MacLeish as a Librarian," *Pembroke Magazine* 7 (1976), 115; RW, interview with Keyes Metcalf, December 3, 1981; *Reflections*, p. 131
297 Lord . . . Raney: Milton C. Lord to AMacL, June 19, 1939, LC; M. Llew-

ellyn Raney, *Congressional Record,*
June 29, 1939, p. 11506

297 other champions: James Bryant Conant to AMacL, June 15, 1939, LC;
Keyes Metcalf to AMacL, June 15,
1939, LC; Keyes Metcalf to Felix
Frankfurter, June 19, 1939, LC

298 Acheson . . . "he was a leader": Dean
Acheson to George L. Radcliffe, June
13, 1939, *Among Friends: Personal
Letters of Dean Acheson,* ed. David
S. McLellan and David C. Acheson
(New York: Dodd Mead, 1980), pp.
38–39

298 Barbour . . . Austin: Dean Acheson to
Warren H. Austin, June 24, 1939;
Warren Barbour to Dean Acheson,
June 21, 1939; Dean Acheson to War-
ren Barbour, June 24, 1939; Reeve
Schley to J. Parnell Thomas, June 21,
1939; Warren Barbour to Dean Ache-
son, June 26, 1939; Warren R. Austin
to Dean Acheson, June 26, 1939, all
Yale

298 confirmation hearing: *Congressional
Record,* June 29, 1939, pp. 11497–
513

300 final tally . . . "disgraceful!": Alben
W. Barkley to AMacL, telegram, June
29, 1939, LC; Tommy Corcoran to
AMacL, July 5, 1939, LC

300 Munn . . . all work together: Ralph
Munn to AMacL, July 1, 1939, and
AMacL to Ralph Munn, July 5, 1939,
LC

300 "through the wicket": *Reflections,* p.
133

300 "Third Term myth": Tommy Corcoran to AMacL, July 5, 1939, and
July 18, 1939, LC

300 Hyde Park . . . "hot dogs": "Roosevelts Entertain MacLeish and Woollcott," *New Haven Register,* July 22,
1939; Ada MacLeish to Sara Murphy,
July 19, 1939

301 "how lovely to see you": RW, interview with AMacL, April 26, 1980

301 pay levels . . . "too low": AMacL,
notes on conversation with Franklin
D. Roosevelt, Hyde Park, July 19,
1939, LC

301 unpopular . . . "warm welcome":

Reminiscences of Luther Evans, 1966,
Oral History Research Project, Columbia University

The Librarian Profiled

302 voice . . . "wrong side": Jill Ker Conway, "Reminiscences," in *Symposium,* p. 49; RW, interview with
Mason Hammond, September 18,
1979; RW, interview with Paul
Brooks, c. October 1979

302 "cause seeker": RW, interview with
Robert A. Lovett, June 2, 1979

302 "life is a fight" . . . "panning for
gold": *Reflections,* p. 142; Thursa
Bakey Sanders to SD, March 25, 1990

302 optimism . . . affirmation: SD, interview with John Conway, October 10,
1988

302 wine by the case: AMacL to Frank
Schoonmaker, May 4, 1943, LC

302 work . . . ahead of play: Thursa
Bakey Sanders to SD, June 8, 1990;
SD, interview with Mimi and Karl
Grimm, July 24, 1988; AMacL, *The
Pot of Earth,* in *Collected,* p. 63; RW,
interview with Elizabeth Miller, No-
vember 16, 1979; SD, interview with
W. Jackson Bate, October 13, 1988;
AMacL and Mark Van Doren, *Dia-
logues,* p. 170

303 scorn . . . "Poor dear": Ada Mac-
Leish to Adele Lovett, July 16, 1935;
RW, interview with Adele and Robert
A. Lovett, June 2, 1979

303 withheld something . . . "no part of
him": SD, interview with Donald
Hall, July 27, 1988; Radcliffe Squires
to SD, September 21, 1988; SD, interview with John Conway, May 23,
1989; William H. MacLeish, "Silver
Whistler," p. 60; *Reflections,* p. 45

304 "when you are young . . . persona":
AMacL to Edward Hoagland, September 7, 1974, *Letters,* p. 435

304 made fun of himself: RW, interview
with Roxanne Hammond, September
14, 1980

304 autocratic . . . "bushel" . . . dressing
up: William Meredith, "Reminiscences," in *Symposium,* p. 71; SD, in-

terview with Alice Acheson, May 7, 1988; SD, interview with W. Jackson Bate, September 18, 1979; SD, interview with Ellen Ishbel Zale, October 9, 1988

304 "stupendous generosity": SD, interview with May Sarton, January 14, 1990

304 "never think about myself": RW, interview with William H. MacLeish, September 20, 1979

305 "a face I *did not remember*": AMacL, "Notebooks, 1924–1938," *Poetry* 73 (October 1948), 37–38

305 beset by such worries: RW, interview with William H. MacLeish, September 20, 1979; SD, interview with Ellen Ishbel and Peter B. Zale, October 9, 1988; Bernard A. Drabeck and Helen E. Ellis, interview with Warren Harris family, June 15, 1977, GCC

305 air hammer . . . trouble sleeping: *Reflections*, p. 155; AMacL, notebooks, c. 1950, p. K40, LC

305 difference . . . "shine of the world": AMacL, talk at State University of New York-Brockport, October 2, 1974; John Conway, "Reminiscences," in *Symposium*, p. 53

16. BRUSH OF THE COMET

The Best Job in Town

306 Library of Congress . . . 1800 . . . 1939: McGuire, *Poetry's Catbird Seat*, p. 25; "Book Mecca," *Pathfinder*, June 24, 1939, pp. 1–2, 20; David C. Mearns, "The Story Up to Now: The Library of Congress, 1800–1946," *Annual Report of the Librarian of Congress for . . . 1946* (Washington, D.C.: U.S. Government Printing Office, 1947), pp. 218–219

307 Putnam . . . "ceramic feet": *Reflections*, pp. 128–129; RW, interview with AMacL, April 26, 1980; McGuire, *Poetry's Catbird Seat*, pp. 27–28; Charles A. Goodrum and Helen W. Dalrymple, *The Library of Con-*

gress (Boulder: Westview Press, 1982), p. 33

307 great figure . . . neglect: *Champion of a Cause*, intro. Eva M. Goldschmidt, p. 1; Goodrum and Dalrymple, *Library of Congress*, pp. 33–34

308 Putnam's . . . schedule: RW, interview with David C. Mearns, June 19, 1978

308 "lengthened shadow": AMacL, *Champion of a Cause*, p. 102

308 office down the hall: Goodrum and Dalrymple, *Library of Congress*, pp. 41–42; *Reflections*, p. 134

309 "first the Scot": "Putnam Calls MacLeish Right Man for Library," *New York Herald Tribune*, October 19, 1939

309 "hand out the books?" . . . duties: AMacL, talk at dedication of Scott Library, York University, October 30, 1971, LC; AMacL, "The Librarian: His Name and Nature," talk at Johns Hopkins University, February 22, 1940, LC

310 "brush of the comet" . . . "best job": Benco, "The Poet Librarian," pp. 233, 248; RW, interview with AMacL, April 21, 1979

Opening Windows

310 Thursa Bakey . . . "glutton for work": Thursa Bakey Sanders to SD, November 4, 1989, and May 28, 1990; SD, interview with Thursa Bakey Sanders, October 11, 1990

311 personal secretary . . . "watch the hawks": AMacL to Thursa Bakey Sanders, undated notes; Thursa Bakey Sanders to SD, April 23, 1990

312 "I knew what was going on": Thursa Bakey Sanders to SD, May 28, 1990

312 all-purpose . . . recommendation: AMacL to Whom It May Concern, July 3, 1946

312 quiet . . . office . . . cacophony: Thursa Bakey Sanders to SD, November 4, 1989, and May 9, 1991; Jonathan Daniels, "Services That Can Never Be Measured," *Pembroke Magazine* 7 (1976), 29

313 Sandburg . . . "a darling man": *Reflections*, p. 99; "Auto Door Locks Play Off-Stage Drama," *Washington Evening Star*, December 1, 1939

313 people paid calls: Thursa Bakey Sanders to SD, November 4, 1989; SD, interview with Thursa Bakey Sanders, October 11, 1990

313 mother . . . "dipped her head": SD, interview with Thursa Bakey Sanders, October 11, 1990

313 Billy Hitchcock . . . will: AMacL to Alexander Woollcott, July 24, 1940; Thursa Bakey Sanders to SD, March 25, 1990

313 buying out Carson: AMacL to John Dern, March 27, 1940, LC

314 fresh air . . . eager to serve: RW, interview with David C. Mearns, June 19, 1978; Thursa Bakey Sanders to SD, May 3, 1990; *Champion of a Cause*, intro. Goldschmidt, p. 6

314 take time . . . petty grievances: Drew Pearson and Robert S. Allen, "Washington Merry-Go-Round," *New York Mirror*, December 25, 1939, Scrapbook, vol. 2, p. 22, GCC; Thursa Bakey Sanders to SD, November 4, 1989, and May 19, 1990; reminiscences of Luther Evans, 1966, pp. 135–136, Oral History Research Project, Columbia

Putting Out Fires

315 stench . . . "films": RW, interview with AMacL, April 26, 1980

315 squatters: Drew Pearson and Robert S. Allen, "Washington Merry-Go-Round," *Washington Times-Herald*, January 28, 1940

315 troubles . . . (LRS): Goodrum and Dalrymple, *Library of Congress*, p. 39; Thursa Bakey Sanders to SD, November 4, 1989, and May 19, 1990; Wilfred C. Gilbert to AMacL, June 7, 1939, LC; Thomas R. Amlie to AMacL, July 6, 1939, LC; Kenneth M. Allen to AMacL, January 13, 1940, LC; AMacL to Alben W. Barkley, January 3, 1940, LC

315 the flamboyant . . . Parma: Thursa Bakey Sanders to SD, November 4,

1989, April 23, 1990; Herbert Putnam to the Personnel Officer, June 3, 1939, and September 21, 1939, LC; FBI report, June 28, 1939, enclosed with Edward G. Kemp to AMacL, October 3, 1939, LC; V. Valta Parma to AMacL, September 29, 1939, LC; AMacL to V. Valta Parma, October 4, 1949, and November 3, 1939, LC; V. Valta Parma to AMacL, November 18, 1939, LC; AMacL to V. Valta Parma, November 20, 1939, and November 25, 1939, LC; AMacL to Eleanor Roosevelt, December 2, 1939, LC; V. Valta Parma to Frederic A. Delano, December 9, 1939, LC; AMacL to Missy LeHand, January 3, 1940, LC; Eleanor Roosevelt to AMacL, December 4, 1939, and December 12, 1939, LC; V. Valta Parma to AMacL, December 14, 1939, LC; AMacL to V. Valta Parma, December 19, 1939, LC; V. Valta Parma to AMacL, December 27, 1939, LC; AMacL to V. Valta Parma, January 2, 1940, LC; V. Valta Parma to AMacL, January 2, 1940, LC; AMacL to V. Valta Parma, January 3, 1940, LC; AMacL to Frederic A. Delano, January 13, 1940, LC; "Parma Quits Library Position after Dispute," *Washington Post*, January 14, 1940; Frederic William Wile, "Library of Congress May Face Investigation over Parma 'Purge,' " *Washington Star*, January 29, 1940

Reorganization and Outreach

318 did not set out: AMacL, *Champion of a Cause*, p. 101

318 two former LC employees . . . conferences: Thursa Bakey Sanders to SD, November 4, 1989, and January 25, 1991; Frederick R. Goff, panel discussion at fortieth anniversary observance of AMacL's becoming librarian of Congress, October 2, 1979

319 fiscal operations: AMacL, *Champion of a Cause*, pp. 104–105

319 backlog in processing: AMacL, *Champion of a Cause*, pp. 106–107

319 "acquisitions policy": AMacL, *Champion of a Cause*, pp. 107–109; Goodrum and Dalrymple, *The Library of Congress*, pp. 45–47

320 Carnegie . . . fellowships: AMacL, *Champion of a Cause*, pp. 138–139

320 Librarians' Committee . . . report: AMacL, *Champion of a Cause*, pp. 112–113; Benco, "The Poet Librarian," pp. 239–240; Reminiscences of Luther Evans, pp. 136–137, Columbia

321 divided . . . streamlined: AMacL, *Champion of a Cause*, pp. 116–117; "MacLeish Streamlines," *Newsweek*, March 24, 1941, p. 52

321 improved pay levels: AMacL to the editor of the *New York Times*, "Salaries Held Too Small," April 19, 1940; "The Underpaid Librarian," *New York Times* editorial, April 21, 1940; AMacL, *Champion of a Cause*, pp. 111, 194–197

322 budget increase . . . positions . . . upgraded: AMacL, *Champion of a Cause*, pp. 111–112; AMacL to the editor of the *Washington Post*, April 30, 1940; Benco, "The Poet Librarian," p. 245; Reminiscences of Luther Evans, pp. 156–157, Columbia

322 "keepers of the records" . . . "active . . . agents": Quoted in Benco, "The Poet Librarian," p. 243

322 "never . . . such leadership": Evelyn Steel Little to AMacL, June 4, 1940, LC

323 Congress . . . impressed: Joseph Alsop and Robert Kintner, "Poet-Librarian MacLeish Convinces Congress," "Capitol Parade," *Washington Evening Star*, May 1940, Scrapbook, vol. 2, p. 44, GCC

323 "minister of culture": RW, interview with David C. Mearns, June 19, 1978

323 WPA programs . . . folk music: "Library of Congress to Run Former WPA Writing Projects," *Washington Post*, November 8, 1939; "MacLeish Tells of $41,520 Carnegie Grant," *Washington Post*, April 21, 1940; Reminiscences of Harold Spivacke, 197—, Oral History Research Project, Columbia, p. 13

324 Budapest . . . Quartet . . . Office of Exhibits: Thursa Bakey Sanders to SD, November 4, 1989

324 overseas artists: Lewis Hanke, panel discussion at fortieth anniversary observance, October 2, 1979; AMacL to Henry R. Luce, June 30, 1943, and September 16, 1943, LC

324 Perse . . . *Exil*: St.-John Perse, *Letters*, trans. and ed. Arthur J. Knodel (Princeton: Princeton University Press, 1979), pp. 444–448; Thursa Bakey Sanders to SD, November 4, 1989; AMacL, remarks at fortieth anniversary observance, October 2, 1979

325 "dies in the desert": St.-John Perse, *Letters*, pp. 449–450

325 Thomas Mann's service: Kurt S. Maier, "A Fellowship in German Literature," *Quarterly Journal of the Library of Congress* 36 (1979), 385–400

326 interceded . . . Auden: McGuire, *Poetry's Catbird Seat*, p. 52

326 no honorarium . . . few books: Thursa Bakey Sanders to SD, March 25, 1990; McGuire, *Poetry's Catbird Seat*, p. 235

326 Auslander . . . "word fellow" . . . ease him out: McGuire, *Poetry's Catbird Seat*, pp. 44–46, 51–55

327 series of poetry readings: McGuire, *Poetry's Catbird Seat*, pp. 56–57; Edward Ryan, "Poetry Series Well Begun," *Washington Post*, March 1, 1941, Scrapbook, vol. 3, p. 54, GCC

328 offered the position: McGuire, *Poetry's Catbird Seat*, pp. 52–54; John Peale Bishop to AMacL, February 11, 1940, LC

17. THE DRUMS OF WAR

Promises

328 "attorney for a cause": AMacL, "Of the Librarian's Profession," in *A Time to Speak*, p. 29

328 Magna Carta: AMacL, "The Magna Carta," in *A Time to Speak*, pp. 140–143

330 change the title: AMacL to Bruce Bliven, telegram, October 21, 1939, LC;
Bruce Bliven to AMacL, October 26,
1939, LC; AMacL to Bruce Bliven,
October 27, 1939, LC

330 "from the first voyage" . . . "Oh believe this!": AMacL, "America Was
Promises," in *Collected*, pp. 323–331

331 "They must . . . come true": AMacL,
This Is My Best, ed. Whit Burnett
(New York: Dial, 1942), pp. 123–124

331 Lippmann . . . Nabokov: Walter Lippmann to AMacL, November 30,
1939, LC; Orrin E. Dunlap, Jr., "Epic
Poem in Melody," *New York Times*,
April 25, 1940

331 Critical . . . opposite view: Louise
Bogan, "Archibald MacLeish," in *A
Poet's Alphabet* (New York: Mc-
Graw-Hill, 1970), pp. 292–293;
Morton Dauwen Zabel, "The Poet on
Capitol Hill (Part 2)," *Partisan Re-
view* 8 (March 1941), 134–135; Jar-
rell, quoted in William H. Pritchard,
"Nasty Reviews," *New York Times
Book Review*, May 7, 1989, p. 37

332 Brooks's . . . zenith: Cleanth Brooks,
Modern Poetry and the Tradition
(Chapel Hill: University of North
Carolina Press, 1939), p. 119

332 "A poet of bitter enemies": Shapiro,
quoted in Gardner, " 'Rediscovery
Would Have Its Fitness,' " pp. 132–
133

Responsibilities

333 "No man who saw": AMacL, review
of Laurence Stallings, *The First World
War*, *New Republic*, September 20,
1933, p. 160

333 "everything in my power": AMacL,
"When America Goes to War," *Modern Monthly* 9 (June 1935), 201

333 chided for . . . inconsistency: Zabel,
"The Poet on Capitol Hill (Part 2),"
p. 140

333 "OPEN LETTER": *The Complete
Poems of Carl Sandburg* (New York:
Harcourt Brace Jovanovich, 1970),
pp. 622–623

333 fall of France . . . like an egg: RW, interview with David C. Mearns, June

19, 1978; Paul Mariani, *William Carlos Williams: A New World Naked*
(New York: McGraw-Hill, 1981), p.
441

334 declaration of war: Campbell, *The
Poet*, p. 135

334 Hollywood . . . "escape": AMacL,
"Propaganda vs. Hollywood," *Stage*
16 (January 1939), 11–12

334 "The Irresponsibles" . . . "practice
art": AMacL, "The Irresponsibles,"
in *A Time to Speak*, pp. 114–120

334 "Post-War Writers" . . . unmanned
the nation: AMacL, "Post-War Writers and Pre-War Readers," *New Republic*, June 10, 1940, pp. 789–790

335 generated . . . controversy: Kermit
Vanderbilt, *American Literature and
the Academy* (Philadelphia: University of Pennsylvania Press, 1986), pp.
463–464; James Hoopes, *Van Wyck
Brooks: In Search of American Culture* (Amherst: University of Massachusetts Press, 1977), pp. 209, 236–
237

335 "very bad conscience": Hemingway
quoted in "Writers' Influence," *Time*,
June 24, 1940

336 "un-belle epoque" . . . "old rows":
Ernest Hemingway to AMacL, late
December 1940, LC; Donnelly with
Billings, *Sara & Gerald*, p. 177

336 attacks . . . Wilson: Edmund Wilson,
"Archibald MacLeish and 'the
Word,' " *New Republic*, July 1, 1940,
pp. 30–32

336 echoing the doctrines: "Statement of
the L.C.F.S.," *Partisan Review* 6
(Summer 1939), 125–127

337 Rascoe . . . diatribe: Burton Rascoe,
"The Tough-Muscle Boys of Literature," *American Mercury* 51 (November 1940), 369–374

337 wrapping himself . . . flag: RW, interview with Dwight Macdonald, April
15, 1980; Stegner, *The Uneasy Chair*,
p. 252; Zabel, "The Poet on Capitol
Hill (Part 2)," p. 145

337 remonstrated with . . . Putnam:
AMacL to Phelps Putnam, February
15, 1941, and May 10, 1941, LC

337 Benét . . . evenhanded: Stephen Vincent Benét to James T. Farrell, April

10, 1942, *Selected Letters of Stephen Vincent Benét*, ed. Charles A. Fenton (New Haven: Yale University Press, 1960), pp. 394–395

338 isolationists ... CIO: *Reflections*, p. 233; "MacLeish Thrust at Fascism Brings Attack by Labor Group," *Cincinnati Post*, May 31, 1940

338 Murrow ... Faneuil Hall: Quoted in David Dimbleby and Davy Reynolds, *An Ocean Apart* (New York: Random House, 1988), p. 141; AMacL, "To Ed Murrow, Reporter," *Journal of Home Economics* 34 (June 1942), 361; "Faneuil Hall Rings to Cry for Liberty," *Christian Science Monitor*, November 21, 1940

338 patriotic messages ... songs: Evans Clark to Henry R. Luce, July 17, 1940, Time Inc.; AMacL to Roy Harris, July 25, 1941, LC; AMacL to Henry R. Luce, August 23, 1941, LC

339 radio play: AMacL, "The States Talking," in *The Free Company Presents*, ed. James Boyd (New York: Dodd Mead, 1941), pp. 219–237; Brady, *Citizen Welles*, p. 289

339 "giving great service": Martha Hillard MacLeish to AMacL, February 23, 1941

340 *Bold Venture* ... "pin drop": AMacL, *"Bold Venture,"* unpublished poem, c. October 27, 1941, LC; Claude Pepper to AMacL, October 31, 1941, LC

340 pledge of faith: AMacL to Carl Sandburg, telegram, November 8, 1941, LC

340 "Democracy ... must be doing": AMacL, *The American Cause* (New York: Duell, Sloan and Pearce, 1941)

The President's Man

341 "most attractive" ... jumped: Cowley, "Promises," p. 32; RW, interview with William H. MacLeish, September 20, 1979

341 dinner ... Ingersoll ... Luce: AMacL to Dean Acheson, May 2, 1940, LC; AMacL to Ralph Ingersoll, November 30, 1939, LC; Roy Hoopes, *Ralph Ingersoll*, pp. 158–

159; RW, interview with Alice Acheson, January 27, 1979

341 fiction ... Woollcott ... show: Alexander Woollcott to AMacL, June 27, 1940, July 24, 1940, and September 8, 1940, LC; Ada MacLeish to Thursa Bakey, telegram February 10, 1941, LC; Robert DeVore, "The Man Who Came to Dinner Likes Breakfast Better," *Washington Post*, March 1, 1941

341 role as a speechwriter: James MacGregor Burns, *Roosevelt: The Lion and the Fox* (New York: Harcourt Brace Jovanovich, 1956), p. 436; RW, interview with AMacL, August 2, 1979; Campbell, *The Poet*, pp. 197–198

342 fried chicken: Grace Tully et al. to Ada MacLeish, c. October 28, 1942, LC; AMacL to "Dave" (David C. Mearns?), c. 1945, LC

342 combined passages ... high-sounding: RW, interview with David C. Mearns, June 19, 1978; RW, interview with Malcolm Cowley, March 8, 1980; Burns, *The Lion and the Fox*, p. 35

343 destroyers ... " 'That's the boy'!": *Reflections*, pp. 151–152; RW, interview with AMacL, April 26, 1980

343 resource for Eleanor Roosevelt: Eleanor Roosevelt, "My Day," *Washington News*, January 10, 1941; Eleanor Roosevelt to Ada MacLeish, January 21, 1942, LC; Burns, *The Lion and the Fox*, pp. 254–255; RW, interview with AMacL, November 11, 1979; photograph of Mrs. Roosevelt, AMacL, and others at summer institute, *New York Times*, July 20, 1941; AMacL, "Eleanor Roosevelt," in *Journey*, pp. 277–279

344 outing on ... cutter: *Reflections*, p. 143; RW, interview with AMacL, August 2, 1979

Summer of '41

344 serious affair?: SD, interview with William H. MacLeish, July 26, 1988

344 "There was a time": AMacL, "Voyage West," in *Collected*, p. 366;

AMacL, "Voyage West," with head-note, *Yale Review* 106 (February 1941), 6

345 Ada . . . speaking voice: Thursa Bakey Sanders to SD, May 3, 1990; RW, interview with John H. Finley, Jr., September 21, 1979

346 coming-out party: SD, interview with Mimi Grimm, May 13, 1989

346 Alec drove down . . . unasked: RW, interview with AMacL, April 26, 1980

346 lost her footing: RW, interview with Ishbel MacLeish and Alexander Campbell, April 7, 1979

346 Bill . . . tractable . . . Ken . . . defiant: SD, interview with William H. MacLeish, July 10, 1990; *Reflections*, p. 260

347 "devils" . . . game warden: Drabeck and Ellis, interview with Warren Harris family, June 15, 1977, pp. 44–46, GCC

347 perilous game . . . ready for war: William H. MacLeish, "Stalking," *StoryQuarterly* 17 (1984), 85–92

18. PROPAGANDIST FOR DEMOCRACY

War of Words

348 Sandy Spring . . . picnic: SD, interview with Alice Acheson, May 7, 1988

348 calculated removal: Benco, "The Poet Librarian," pp. 243–244; reminiscences of Luther Evans, pp. 173–174, Columbia

349 *Rainfall in Burma:* RW, interview with David C. Mearns, June 19, 1978

349 "Subject to such policies": Franklin D. Roosevelt, executive order 8922, F.R. Doc. 41–8049, October 24, 1941

349 La Guardia . . . memo: F. H. La Guardia to Franklin D. Roosevelt, memorandum, July 9, 1941

350 "not use bally-hoo": Quoted in Allan M. Winkler, *The Politics of Propaganda: The Office of War Informa-tion, 1942–1945* (New Haven: Yale University Press, 1978), p. 23

350 Rosenman . . . drafted: *Reflections*, p. 148

350 alphabet soupiness: "Here's Where We Get OFF," *New York Herald Tribune*, October 9, 1941

350 powers . . . in his hands: Betty Houchin Winfield, *FDR and the News Media* (Urbana: University of Illinois Press, 1990), pp. 156–157

350 Pearl Harbor . . . silence: Winfield, *News Media*, p. 155

351 committee of . . . Censorship: Winfield, *News Media, p.* 173

351 propaganda . . . "American opinion": AMacL, "The Enemy to be Feared," *Think*, March 8, 1942, pp. 6, 45; AMacL to James Allen, October 12, 1943, *Letters*, pp. 318–319; Winkler, *Politics of Propaganda*, pp. 12–13

351 talented staff: Harold D. Smith to AMacL, November 4, 1941, LC; AMacL to Grace Tully, December 4, 1941, *Letters*, p. 306; RW, interview with AMacL, November 11, 1979; *Reflections*, pp. 149–150

352 "state the American cause": *Reflections*, p. 150

352 "Four Freedoms": Scott Elledge, *E. B. White: A Biography* (New York: Norton, 1984), pp. 232–235; Ernest Hemingway to AMacL, c. May 5, 1943, LC

Home Front Enemies

353 Cowley . . . reactions: Malcolm Cowley to Kenneth Burke, January 11, 1942, *Selected Correspondence of Kenneth Burke and Malcolm Cowley*, ed. Paul Jay (New York: Viking, 1988), pp. 247–248

353 Dies . . . cesspool: "Dies Says M'Leish Hires 'Communist,' " *New York Times*, January 16, 1942; "Miscellany," *Horns of Plenty* 1 (Spring 1988), 31; "Inopportune," *Time*, February 16, 1942, pp. 13–14; AMacL to Henry R. Luce, February 13, 1942, *Letters*, pp. 308–310

351 "not . . . a martyr": RW, interview

with Malcolm Cowley, March 8, 1980

354 exchange . . . Hoover: Herbert Mitgang, "Annals of Government: Policing America's Writers," *New Yorker,* October 5, 1987, pp. 82–86; AMacL to J. Edgar Hoover, February 3, 1942, and J. Edgar Hoover to AMacL, February 7, 1942, FBI

354 Biddle . . . grudges: Mitgang, "Policing America's Writers," p. 84; J. Edgar Hoover to Francis Biddle, March 1942, FBI; J. Edgar Hoover to Francis Biddle, memorandum, December 5, 1941, FBI

355 jibes and jabs: "Information Worse Confounded," *Time,* October 20, 1941; Winkler, *Politics of Propaganda,* p. 23; Carl Sandburg, "Poets, Too, Are Human," *Washington Post,* May 17, 1942; Samuel Grafton, "I'd Rather Be Right," *Chicago Sun,* June 17, 1942

355 "my one-man battle": *Reflections,* p. 148; Campbell, *The Poet,* p. 201

356 "The man who attempts": AMacL, "Divided We Fall," in *A Time to Act* (Boston: Houghton Mifflin, 1943), p. 126

356 press "actively engaged": AMacL, "The Responsibility of the Press," in *A Time to Act,* pp. 12, 14

356 broken . . . code . . . loyalty: Winfield, *News Media,* pp. 178–179; RW, interview with AMacL, November 10, 1979

357 "sisters . . . cousins . . . aunts": AMacL, "The Strategy of Truth," in *A Time to Act,* p. 22

357 returned . . . fire: Chesly Manly, "Writers War Board Aids Smear Campaign," *Washington Times-Herald,* June 4, 1942; William Fulton, "A Woman Editor Prints a Story about MacLeish," *Chicago Tribune,* July 8, 1942

357 "Society of . . . Immortals": Franklin D. Roosevelt to AMacL, July 13, 1942, LC

357 abuse . . . Pound: C. David Heymann, *Ezra Pound: The Last Tower* (New York: Viking, 1976), pp. 114–119

358 "end . . . countenancing": Tietjens,

quoted in Humphrey Carpenter, *A Serious Character: The Life of Ezra Pound* (Boston: Houghton Mifflin, 1988), p. 611

Getting OFF

358 "train . . . snail": AMacL to James Allen, October 12, 1943, *Letters,* p. 320

359 did not mention . . . OFF: E. P. Lilly, "Office of Facts and Figures," p. 24, National Archives

359 "aid and comfort": Robert E. Sherwood to AMacL, memorandum, June 1, 1942, LC

359 authority . . . (CWI): Lilly, "Office of Facts and Figures," pp. 21, 23, 25, National Archives; *Reflections,* p. 149

359 minimize differences . . . tens of millions: James B. Reston, "Washington Paints a Confused War Picture," *New York Times,* February 15, 1942; Lilly, "Office of Facts and Figures," pp. 27–28, 38–41, 44–45, 50, National Archives; Mearns, "As Alcuin Was Saying," p. 111

360 public opinion research: Lilly, "Office of Facts and Figures," pp. 34–35, National Archives

360 lacked the authority: Elmer Davis, "Report to the President — Office of War Information, 13 June 1942–15 September 1945," National Archives

360 frustration . . . Tully: AMacL to Grace Tully, January 16, 1942, LC; Lilly, "Office of Facts and Figures," p. 51, National Archives

360 reorganization . . . step down: AMacL to director, Bureau of the Budget, February 20, 1942, quoted in Lilly, "Office of Facts and Figures," pp. 52–54, National Archives; Winkler, *Politics of Propaganda,* p. 24

361 retreated . . . Rosenman: AMacL to Samuel L. Rosenman, March 24, 1942, *Letters,* pp. 310–311

361 dual role . . . costly: Benco, "The Poet as Librarian," p. 242; AMacL, *Champion of a Cause,* pp. 88–89

361 battle to tell . . . truth: AMacL to Felix Frankfurter, April 9, 1942, *Letters,* pp. 312–313

362 chosen ... Elmer Davis: Roger Burlingame, *Don't Let Them Scare You:
The Life and Times of Elmer Davis*
(Philadelphia: Lippincott, 1961), pp.
184–186; Winkler, *Politics of Propaganda,* pp. 31–35; Drabeck and
Ellis, interview with AMacL not used
in *Reflections,* p. 77, GCC; AMacL to
McGeorge Bundy, June 25, 1942, *Letters,* p. 314

Matters of Opinion

363 executive order ... teeth: Burlingame, *Don't Let Them Scare You,* pp.
188–189
363 London ... "bombed": Winkler, *Politics of Propaganda,* pp. 113–113;
AMacL and Mark Van Doren, *Dialogues,* p. 105
363 Rede lecture: Quoted in Winkler, *Politics of Propaganda,* pp. 40–41
363 Eisenhower opposed: Winkler, *Politics of Propaganda,* pp. 41–42
364 wanted to resign: AMacL to Elmer
Davis, August 12, 1942, LC
364 "brilliant ... individual": Davis, "Report to the President," pp. 42–43;
RW, interview with David C. Mearns,
June 19, 1978
364 McCormick-Patterson axis: John
O'Donnell, "Capitol Stuff," *Washington Times-Herald,* September 28,
1942; Paul C. Smith to John O'Donnell, September 28, 1942, LC; "Rib-
ber," *Time,* October 5, 1942, p. 56;
AMacL to Henry R. Luce, October 2,
1942, LC
365 "only solution" ... "prose writers":
AMacL to Elmer Davis, January 26,
1943, LC; *Reflections,* pp. 154–155;
"Poetic Justice," *Newsweek,* September 27, 1943, p. 95

19. MAKING THE PEACE

Poets at the Library

366 home ... Red Cross: Chain of title,
Robert E. Lee boyhood home, 607
Oronoco Street, Alexandria, Va.; RW,
interview with Jane Canfield, April

15, 1980; Ada MacLeish to Florence
L. Ingham, December 10, 1943; "Red
Cross Post to Mrs. MacLeish," *New
York Times,* February 1, 1944; RW,
interview with AMacL, August 2,
1979; SD, interview with John and Jill
Ker Conway, May 23, 1989
367 Jefferson ... "say to us?": Thursa
Bakey Sanders to SD, November 4,
1989; AMacL to Van Wyck Brooks,
February 2, 1943, and March 12,
1943, LC; John Y. Cole, *For Congress
and the Nation: A Chronological History of the Library of Congress*
(Washington, D.C.: Library of Congress, 1979), p. 115
367 Cowley ... FBI: Thursa Bakey Sanders to SD, November 4, 1989
367 Willkie ... speech: *Reflections,* pp.
156–157
367 Benét ... Meredith: Quoted in "We
Begin to Take the Long View," *New
York Post* "Magazine Digest," March
26, 1943, p. 46; AMacL to William
Meredith, November 23, 1943, *Letters,* p. 321
368 replacement for Auslander: McGuire,
Poetry's Catbird Seat, pp. 58–62
368 Tate ... Pound: McGuire, *Poetry's
Catbird Seat,* pp. 76–77; Ernest Hemingway to AMacL, April 4, 1943, LC;
AMacL to Ernest Hemingway, April
17, 1943, JFK; Ernest Hemingway to
AMacL, August 10, 1943, LC
368 did something: AMacL to Allen Tate,
memorandum, August 20, 1943, LC;
AMacL to Ernest Hemingway, July
27, 1943, *Letters,* pp. 315–316;
AMacL to Harvey Bundy, September
10, 1943, *Letters,* pp. 317–318
369 high standard ... recordings: Mc-
Guire, *Poetry's Catbird Seat,* pp. 76–
77, 81
369 Bishop ... condolence: AMacL to
John Peale Bishop, October 15, 1943,
Princeton; Margaret Bishop to
AMacL, April 9, 1944, LC
369 Porter's experience: AMacL to Katherine Anne Porter, January 24, 1944,
Maryland; Robert Penn Warren, fortieth anniversary observance, October
2, 1979
370 Fellows ... in American Letters:

Katherine Garrison Chapin et al., "Report to the Librarian of Congress on a Meeting of the Associate Fellows in American Letters," May 26–27, 1944, Maryland; Cole, *Chronological History*, p. 118

370 Warren . . . "up the steps": Robert Penn Warren and AMacL, fortieth anniversary observance, October 2, 1979

370 post for T. S. Eliot: AMacL to Thomas W. Lamont, April 27, 1943, and May 6, 1943, Harvard; McGuire, *Poetry's Catbird Seat*, pp. 83–85

371 confounded . . . Bogan: Louise Bogan to Morton Dauwen Zabel, November 1944, and Louise Bogan to May Sarton, February 18, 1954, *Selected Letters*, pp. 244, 285; *Reflections*, p. 137

Fighting for Freedom

371 history of the war: Franklin D. Roosevelt to AMacL, June 9, 1943, LC; AMacL to Franklin Delano Roosevelt, July 3, 1943, LC; Ernest Hemingway to AMacL, August 10, 1943, LC; AMacL to Ernest Hemingway, August 17, 1943, LC

372 Time . . . assignment . . . pet project: Allen Grover to Henry R. Luce, August 16, 1943, Time Inc.; AMacL to Henry R. Luce, September 8, 1943, LC; Henry R. Luce to AMacL, September 11, 1943, LC; Thursa Bakey Sanders to SD, January 10, 1990; William Preston, Jr., "The History of U.S.-UNESCO Relations," *Hope and Folly: The United States and UNESCO, 1945–1985* (Minneapolis: University of Minnesota Press, 1989), pp. 52–53

373 "We write the histories": AMacL, "A Poet Speaks from the Visitors' Gallery," *New Yorker*, September 11, 1943, p. 30

373 "The poets who can take a name": Quoted in *Appendix to the Congressional Record*, October 11, 1943, p. A4201

373 resignation . . . Boyd: AMacL to Franklin D. Roosevelt, November 12, 1943, LC

374 "The Young Dead Soldiers": RW, interview with AMacL, August 2, 1979; *Reflections*, pp. 172–173; AMacL, "The Young Dead Soldiers," in *Collected*, pp. 381–382

374 secret committee . . . proponents of reaction: RW, interview with AMacL, November 11, 1979; Campbell, *The Poet*, p. 216

375 remarks . . . Christmas: AMacL, "When We Speak to Each Other of Peace," *Journal of Home Economics* 35 (March 1944), 146

375 Blashfield . . . "sermons": AMacL, "The Power of the Spoken Word," May 1944, *Addresses on the Evangeline Wilbur Blashfield Foundation of the American Academy and Institute of Arts and Letters*, Academy Papers, vol. 2 (New York, 1951), p. 193; AMacL to Martha Hillard MacLeish, February 6, 1944, *Letters*, p. 322

376 *American Story:* "NBC University of the Air Opens," NBC newsletter, February 1944, p. 1, and "NBC University of the Air Offers," NBC newsletter, July–August 1945, p. 1; AMacL, "The Discovered," in *The American Story* (New York: Duell, Sloan and Pearce, 1944), pp. 76–77; *Reflections*, pp. 157–159

376 Conference . . . of Education: AMacL to G. Howland Shaw, March 15, 1944, LC; Campbell, *The Poet*, p. 203

377 Parsons . . . limerick: SD, interview with Stephen Becker, March 9, 1989

377 Declaration . . . "tissue": Cole, *Chronological History*, p. 119; McGuire, *Poetry's Catbird Seat*, p. 88

377 resignation . . . alternatives: AMacL to Franklin D. Roosevelt, November 8, 1944, *Letters*, pp. 324–325; AMacL to Julian Boyd, August 30, 1945, *Letters*, p. 332; AMacL to Franklin D. Roosevelt, February 13, 1945, and April 6, 1945, LC

378 Evans . . . took office: Reminiscences of Luther Evans, pp. 143–144, 148–149, Columbia; AMacL quoted in McGuire, *Poetry's Catbird Seat*, pp. 122–123; RW, interview with David C. Mearns, June 19, 1978; Cole, *Chronological History*, pp. 121–122

378 evaluating . . . performance: Mearns, "The Story Up To Now," p. 221; Herman Henkle and Frederick Goff, fortieth anniversary observance, October 2, 1979

378 extraordinary speed . . . "little to repent": Quincy Mumford, fortieth anniversary observance, October 2, 1979; Falk, *Archibald MacLeish,* p. 104; *Champion of a Cause,* intro. Goldschmidt, pp. 6–7

Mausoleum No. 2

379 "mausoleum" . . . "rolling stone": Franklin D. Roosevelt to AMacL, December 1, 1944, LC; Mearns, "The Story Up To Now," p. 227

379 confirmed . . . hearing ended: "Senate Unit Backs Grew Unanimously," *Washington Post,* December 6, 1944; "Senate Prepares for Battle," *Washington Evening Star,* December 6, 1944; reminiscences of Luther Evans, p. 167, Columbia; "Nominations — Department of State," United States Senate Committee on Foreign Relations hearing, December 10–11, 1944, pp. 29–85; *Reflections,* p. 161

381 Krock . . . "assassination": Arthur Krock, "In the Nation," *New York Times,* December 15, 1944; AMacL to Edward R. Stettinius, Jr., December, 15, 1944, *Letters,* p. 325

381 balloting . . . closest: "Ordeal of a Bard," *Time,* December 25, 1944, p. 17; "Senate Is Delayed on Stettinius Aides," *New York Times,* December 16, 1944; Campbell, *The Poet,* p. 206

382 staff . . . "wanted results": Haldore Hanson to SD, April 2, 1990; RW, interview with John Sloan Dickey, October 29, 1979

382 Stettinius . . . Stevenson: RW, interview with John Sloan Dickey, October 29, 1979; Dean Acheson, *Present at the Creation: My Years in the State Department* (New York: Norton, 1969), pp. 88–91; AMacL to Adlai Stevenson, January 16, 1945, *Letters,* pp. 326–327

383 short holiday . . . "always urgent":

AMacL to Thursa Bakey Sanders, early March 1945; AMacL to Martha Hillard MacLeish, March 7, 1945, *Letters,* p. 327

383 Koussevitzky . . . Bethune: SD, interview with Thursa Bakey Sanders, October 11, 1990; *Reflections,* pp. 162, 165–166

383 broadcasts . . . "public knowledge": AMacL to Robert Elson, February 22, 1945, LC; AMacL to Mrs. Ogden M. Reid, April 7, 1945, LC; RW, interview with John Sloan Dickey, October 29, 1979; Edwin A. Lahey, "MacLeish Speaks Out," *Chicago Daily News,* April 12, 1945

384 hookup . . . chaos . . . "homburg hats": Acheson, *Present at the Creation,* pp. 101–102; *Reflections,* p. 164; Lahey, "MacLeish Speaks Out"

384 communications . . . "altering . . . the world": AMacL, "Popular Relations and the Peace," *Department of State Bulletin,* January 14, 1945, pp. 47–51

384 open channels: AMacL to Joseph Grew, memorandum, February 19, 1945, LC

385 Yalta . . . "the facts?": Kenneth S. Davis, *The Politics of Honor: A Biography of Adlai E. Stevenson* (New York: Putnam, 1967), p. 161; Jim Berryman, cartoon, *Washington Evening Star,* April 5, 1945, p. 1, Scrapbook, vol. 3, p. 81, GCC

386 Roosevelt . . . proclamation of death: Cowley, "Promises," p. 32; Daniels, "Services," pp. 32–33; Benjamin DeMott, interview of AMacL, "The Most Compelling Acts of Love to Touch My Life," *Today's Health* 51 (February 1973), 62; Kenneth S. Davis, *Politics of Honor,* p. 162; William S. White, *Majesty and Mischief: A Mixed Tribute to F.D.R.* (New York: McGraw-Hill, 1961), pp. 32–34, includes AMacL's proclamation.

386 broke down . . . "April Elegy": "Sherwood, M'Leish Pay Tribute," *New York Times,* April 14, 1945; AMacL, "April Elegy," *Atlantic Monthly* 175 (June 1945), 1

One World

387 charter ... "necessary labor": AMacL, " 'We've Been Pretending ... ,' " *San Francisco Chronicle*, April 26, 1945, p. 5

387 briefings ... press: RW, interview with John Sloan Dickey, October 29, 1979; Thursa Bakey Sanders to SD, January 10, 1990, and May 3, 1990

387 allay fears ... Soviet Union: AMacL, "United States-Soviet Relations," *Department of State Bulletin*, May 27, 1945, pp. 950–951

388 preamble ... "pudding": AMacL to Edward R. Stettinius, Jr., memorandum, June 8, 1945, LC

389 "a great day": AMacL, Armed Forces Radio Service, July 1, 1945, LC

389 Mimi ... married ... "*Vogue*": SD, interview with Mimi and Karl Grimm, July 24, 1988; RW, interview with Ishbel MacLeish and Alexander Campbell, April 7, 1979

390 Stevenson ... "best detail": Acheson, *Present at the Creation*, pp. 110, 119; John Bartlow Martin, *Adlai Stevenson of Illinois* (New York: Doubleday, 1976), pp. 238–239; Adlai Stevenson to AMacL, July 26, 1945, LC

390 resignation ... "wonderful work": Lansing Warren, "Grew Resigns as Under-Secretary," *New York Times*, August 17, 1945; "MacLeish Quits with Holmes," *New York Herald Tribune*, August 18, 1945; "Resignation of Archibald MacLeish," *Department of State Bulletin*, August 19, 1945, p. 273

390 still smoldering ... "these birds": RW, interview with John Sloan Dickey, October 29, 1979; AMacL to Dean Acheson, August 30, 1945, *Letters*, pp. 331–332; AMacL to Alice Acheson, late August 1945

391 time well spent ... "a free man": *Reflections*, p. 173; Daniels, "Services," p. 33; Thursa Bakey Sanders to SD, June 8, 1990

391 Pound ... "opposite directions": McGuire, *Poetry's Catbird Seat*, pp. 90–91; AMacL to T. S. Eliot, May 18,

1945, *Letters*, p. 329; T. S. Eliot to AMacL, May 30, 1945, LC; AMacL to T. S. Eliot, August 13, 1945, *Letters*, p. 330; Carpenter, *A Serious Character*, pp. 682, 699–701; AMacL to Julien Cornell, December 6, 1945, *Letters*, pp. 335–336

391 process of decompression: William H. MacLeish, interview with AMacL, c. 1980; *Reflections*, p. 177

392 (UNESCO) ... "most underrated": Thursa Bakey Sanders to SD, January 10, 1990, and March 25, 1990; reminiscences of Luther Evans, pp. 228, 301–302, 323–324, Columbia; RW, interview with AMacL, November 11, 1979; Preston, *Hope and Folly*, p. 33

393 stripped ... "mass communication": AMacL to Dean Acheson, December 30, 1945, *Letters*, pp. 337–339; AMacL, "The Role of UNESCO in Our Foreign Policy," *Department of State Bulletin*, April 21, 1946, p. 629

393 nationalism ... withered away: Preston, *Hope and Folly*, pp. 35, 42–43, 48–49; "U.S. Decides to Remain Out," *Washington Post*, April 4, 1990

393 Archie plunged: "MacLeish Aids Rescue of 3 in Biscayne Bay," United Press dispatch, March 30, 1946, Scrapbook, vol. 3, p. 87, GCC

393 Paris ... "Lègion" RW, interview with AMacL, April 21, 1979; Evelyn Peyton Gordon, "Legion of Honor," *Washington Daily News*, September 13, 1946

394 backed away ... "broad generalizations": Thursa Bakey Sanders to SD, March 25, 1990; "Archibald MacLeish Resigns," *New York Herald Tribune*, April 15, 1947

394 elevated ... Academy: Nominations of June 1946 and July 1940, American Academy

394 Commission ... "accountable freedom": AMacL to Beardsley Ruml, February 15, 1946, LC; William Ernest Hocking, *Freedom of the Press: A Framework of Principle* (Chicago: University of Chicago Press, 1947), p. 99; Warren K. Agee, Phillip H. Ault,

and Edwin Emery, *Introduction to Mass Communication* (New York: Harper and Row, 1985), pp. 464–465, 469–470; "Freedom to Publish What?" *Newsweek*, March 31, 1947, p. 63

20. A NEW LIFE

Freedom Fenced In

396 "won't burn inside": RW, interview with AMacL, November 10, 1979; Stephen Sandy, memoir of AMacL, 1988

396 Death . . . Katy: RW, interview with AMacL, April 26, 1980

397 mother . . . "The surge of sea survives": AMacL to Martha Hillard MacLeish, August 6, 1946; Martha Hillard MacLeish to Harry S. Truman, March 5, 1946; *Martha Hillard MacLeish*, pp. 138–139, 142, 144; AMacL, "For the Anniversary of My Mother's Death," *Collected*, p. 425

398 freedom . . . "*activity*": AMacL to Henry R. Luce, November 26, 1948, *Letters*, p. 342; AMacL to Henry R. Luce, December 17, 1948, Yale

398 Condon . . . "wooden horse": "150 Scientists Condemn House Slur on Condon," *New York Herald-Tribune*, March 12, 1948; "Scientists Score Thomas Actions," *New York Times*, March 12, 1948

399 Nation . . . barred: "Ban on the Nation in Schools Fought," *New York Times*, July 9, 1948; "107 Leaders Fight Reading List Ban," *New York Times*, October 11, 1948; "Ban on the Nation Upheld at Albany," *New York Times*, May 28, 1949; *Daily Worker* editorial, May 31, 1949, p. 9

399 Duggan . . . "devoted his life": *Laurence Duggan, 1905–1948: In Memoriam* (Stamford, Conn.: Overbrook, 1949), pp. v, 11–12, 17–18, 69, 90; AMacL and Mark Van Doren, *Dialogues*, pp. 36–37; "Fund Is Proposed to Honor Duggan," *New York Times*, January 23, 1949; AMacL to Ernest O. Lawrence, as from "The

Lawrence Duggan Fund," March 21, 1949, California

400 "Conquest of America": AMacL, "The Conquest of America," *Atlantic Monthly* 184 (August 1949), 17–22; Campbell, *The Poet*, pp. 223–224; William Henry Chamberlain, "Archie and Mephisto," *New Leader*, October 1, 1949

401 *Actfive* . . . "glory left behind": David Barber, "In Search of an 'Image of Mankind': The Public Poetry and Prose of Archibald MacLeish," *American Studies* 29 (Fall 1988), 31–56; RW, interview with AMacL, November 10, 1979; Campbell, *The Poet*, pp. 240–243; Smith, "Archibald MacLeish," pp. 17–19; AMacL, *Actfive*, in *Collected*, pp. 341–361

402 "What's changed is freedom": AMacL, "Brave New World," in *Collected*, pp. 382–384

403 "We lay beneath": AMacL, "What Must," in *Collected*, pp. 371–373

403 "She has no more need": AMacL, "Poem in Prose," in *Collected*, p. 373

403 little . . . attention: Selden Rodman, "Twixt Pundit & Poet," *Saturday Review of Literature*, August 11, 1948, p. 29; H.C. [Hayden Carruth], "MacLeish's *Actfive*," *Poetry* 73 (February 1949), 287–289; Robert Fitzgerald, "Oracles and Things," *New Republic*, November 22, 1948, p. 23

404 silence . . . "poetry clique": AMacL to Robert N. Linscott, March 18, 1948, *Letters*, pp. 340–341, and AMacL to Robert N. Linscott, September 22, 1948, *Letters*, pp. 341–342; RW, interviews with AMacL, August 2, 1979, and November 10–11, 1979; Peter Viereck, "Indignant Sing-Song," *New York Times Book Review*, November 21, 1948, p. 35; Helen Wolfert, "Fate of a Poet," letter to the editor of the *New York Times*, February 15, 1949

English S

405 Harvard . . . happiest period: RW, interview with Harry Levin, September

26, 1979; RW, interviews with AMacL, November 10, 1979 and April 27, 1980; Felix Frankfurter to AMacL, March 25, 1949, LC; "Harvard Names MacLeish as Boylston Professor," *Washington Evening Star,* May 12, 1949

405 what to teach . . . Van Doren: AMacL to F. O. Matthiessen, June 27, 1949, *Letters,* pp. 346–347; RW, interview with AMacL, April 27, 1980; RW, interview with Dorothy Van Doren, April 29, 1980

406 "creative writing" . . . "ten or twelve": AMacL, "On the Teaching of Writing," in *Journey,* pp. 227–228; RW, interview with AMacL, November 10, 1979

406 "distrusted him": Donald Hall, "MacLeish: The First Year at Harvard," *Pembroke Magazine* 7 (1976), 37–38; SD, interview with Donald Hall, July 27, 1988

407 Bly . . . "jump": SD, interview with Robert Bly, August 11, 1988; Walter Kaiser, remarks at memorial service, Harvard, May 1982

407 restraint . . . "nobility": SD, interview with Robert Bly, August 11, 1988; Robert Bly, English S issue, *Identity* (1966), n.p.

408 Hall . . . *laziness: Reflections,* p. 186; Donald Hall, "Reminiscences," in *Symposium,* pp. 122–124; SD, interview with Donald Hall, July 27, 1988

408 Plimpton . . . Skull and Bones: SD, interview with George Plimpton, May 22, 1989

408 went to bat: SD, interview with Donald Hall, July 27, 1988; RW, interview with AMacL, April 27, 1980

409 Christmas . . . party: SD, interview with Donald Hall, July 27, 1988

410 Alfred . . . friendship: William Alfred, "Foreword," English S issue, *Identity* (1966), n.p.; SD, interview with William Alfred, October 13, 1988; William Alfred, "Tributes," in *Symposium,* p. 136; AMacL to Felicia Geffen, January 14, 1953, American Academy

411 Karmel . . . "very high": Sidney

Fields, "Only Human," *New York Sunday Mirror,* April 5, 1953, p. 35; Lewis Nichols, "Talk with Ilona Karmel," *New York Times Book Review,* March 29, 1953, p. 25; SD, interview with Ilona Karmel, October 13, 1988; AMacL to Ilona Karmel, July 29, 1953, *Letters,* p. 369

412 Goodman . . . skiing in Europe: SD, interview with George J. W. Goodman, October 22, 1989; Adam Smith, "A Literary Illusion," *Authors Guild Bulletin* (Summer 1989), 7

413 Hoagland . . . dedicated to him: Edward Hoagland to SD, December 17, 1988; SD, interview with Edward Hoagland, May 24, 1989; AMacL to Edward Hoagland, September 7, 1974, *Letters,* pp. 434–435; Edward Hoagland to AMacL, c. 1974, LC

413 mistake . . . Updike: Ada MacLeish to Gerald and Sara Murphy, October 1, 1953; John Updike to SD, September 8, 1989; RW, interview with AMacL, April 27, 1980

414 Kozol . . . something more important: SD, interview with Jonathan Kozol, January 16, 1990; Jonathan Kozol, " 'Faithfully, A. MacLeish,'" *Boston Globe,* April 22, 1982, p. 2

La Désirade

415 "Approach to Poetry" . . . personality: "MacLeish to Give Course on Poetry," *Harvard Crimson,* registration issue, 1950, p. M-2; "F. O. Matthiessen Plunges to Death," *Harvard Crimson,* April 1, 1950, p. 1; "Student Response Moves MacLeish," *Harvard Crimson,* September 29, 1950; RW, interview with AMacL, April 27, 1980

416 "art exists" . . . "possibilities": AMacL, "Education and the Work of Art," in *Journey,* p. 240; AMacL, "A Retiring View of Harvard," in *Journey,* p. 263

416 "What SHOULD I do": AMacL to Harry Levin, c. 1952, Harvard

416 cards . . . "through their eyes": *Reflections,* pp. 180–183; Kaiser, remarks at memorial service, Harvard,

May 1982; RW, interview with AMacL, April 27, 1980

417 "superb" . . . enthusiasm: Radcliffe Squires to SD, September 21, 1988; SD, interview with W. Jackson Bate, October 13, 1988

417 Mill Reef Club . . . founded: John C. Leslie, interview with Robertson ("Happy") Ward, March 24, 1973, "The Early History of the Mill Reef Club," privately printed, pp. 1–8

417 "we have found it" . . . "what could be handier?": Ada MacLeish to Gerald and Sara Murphy, January 11, 1951; Ada MacLeish to Sara Murphy, March 18, 1951

417 airstrips . . . fire engine: RW, interview with Philip and Mabel Reed, September 7, 1980

418 climate . . . donkeys: AMacL to Paul H. Buck, March 14, 1952, *Letters*, pp. 354–355; SD, interview with Birgit Carstensen, January 5, 1989

418 wealthy . . . "God damn the rich": RW, interview with Alice Acheson, January 27, 1979; RW, interview with Adele and Robert A. Lovett, June 2, 1979; RW, interview with Dorothy Van Doren, April 29, 1980

418 "literate and . . . powerful": RW, interview with John Bullitt, September 18, 1979

419 afternoon . . . Crokie: RW, interview with Philip and Mabel Reed, September 7, 1980

419 drinking . . . ulcers: RW, interview with Kay Bundy, September 22, 1979; RW, interview with Jean Groo, September 13, 1980; RW, interview with Philip and Mabel Reed, September 7, 1980; RW, interview with William H. MacLeish, September 20, 1979

419 "There isn't any time": AMacL to Elena and Harry Levin, April 1952, Harvard

420 Hester Pickman . . . "You have a watch": RW, interview with Carolyn MacLeish, September 10, 1979

420 *This Music Crept by Me*: AMacL, *This Music Crept by Me upon the Waters*, in *Six Plays*, pp. 177–179, 186–187, 206; Warren French,

" 'That Never Realized, Never Abandoned Dream,' " *Pembroke Magazine* 7 (1976), pp. 129–130

421 "defeated hero" . . . months of perfection: *Reflections*, pp. 194–195; Hall, *Weather for Poetry*, p. 15

21. THE VIEW FROM SIXTY

Harvard's Wonders

422 "At twenty, stooping": AMacL, "With Age Wisdom," in *Collected*, p. 422

422 sang the joys: AMacL to Alexander Campbell, October 9, 1949, *Letters*, pp. 350–351

423 friend . . . Murdock: RW, interview with Eleanor Murdock, November 16, 1979

423 "Things were planned": SD, interview with Richard Wilbur, July 28, 1988

423 "dazzling . . . parties": SD, interview with May Sarton, January 14, 1990

424 generosity . . . Williams: SD, interview with Edwin Honig, January 14, 1989

424 Sandburg . . . Eliot . . . navel: AMacL to Carl Sandburg, telegram, September 25, 1950; T. S. Eliot to AMacL, December 18, 1950, LC; RW, interview with AMacL, April 26, 1980

424 library committee: RW, interview with Harry Levin, September 26, 1979

424 Appointments . . . Perkins: Henry Rosovsky, *The University: An Owner's Manual* (New York: Norton, 1990); RW, interview with McGeorge Bundy, March 21, 1980; RW, interview with W. Jackson Bate, September 18, 1979; SD, interview with W. Jackson Bate, October 13, 1988

425 Norton professors . . . Shahn: RW, interview with AMacL, April 27, 1980; *Reflections*, pp. 190–191

426 Loeb . . . Center: "Students, Faculty, Alumni Make Theater Drive Plans," *Harvard Crimson*, February 9, 1954,

p. 1; "Special Performance to Mark Opening," *Harvard Crimson*, October 14, 1960, p. 1; RW, interview with Harry Levin, September 26, 1979

Taking on McCarthy

426 "You can't compete with Joe": AMacL to Dean Acheson, May 27, 1950, Yale

426 Galbraith argued: SD, interview with John Kenneth Galbraith, July 11, 1990

427 dismissal . . . McCarran Act: "Help Pledged 20 Professors Ousted in West," *Christian Science Monitor*, February 26, 1950; "Chafee, MacLeish, Schlesinger Urge Repeal," *Harvard Crimson*, October 19, 1950, p. 1

427 held no brief . . . "more freedom": AMacL, "Poetry and the Belief in Man," Peters Rushton Seminar, University of Virginia, May 1951; "MacLeish Lashes Unnamed Politician," *Harvard Crimson*, June 12, 1951, pp. 1–2; AMacL, "The Teacher's Faith," in *Journey*, p. 140

427 reviewers . . . admiring: Gerald W. Johnson, "Free Land, Free Citizen," *New York Herald Tribune Book Review*, December 16, 1951; Robert R. Brunn, "MacLeish Warns America," *Christian Science Monitor*, April 9, 1952, p. 13

428 "This nation, more powerful": AMacL, "The Blow Flies," notebooks, c. 1950, LC

428 *Trojan Horse* . . . "under every bed": William H. Pritchard, "MacLeish Revisited," *Poetry* 141 (February 1983), 291; *Reflections*, pp. 191–192; AMacL, preface to *The Trojan Horse*, in *Six Plays*, p. 127

429 "Bring that enormous image": AMacL, *The Trojan Horse*, in *Six Plays*, pp. 150–151, 164

429 Susan . . . "Light as a feather": SD, interview with Mary Manning Adams, July 12, 1990; SD, interview with Susan Howe, August 11, 1990;

AMacL to Susan Howe, July 27, 1957; Susan Howe to SD, August 14, 1990

430 attractive candidate: RW, interview with AMacL, November 11, 1979; DeMott, "Acts of Love," p. 60

430 ulcers . . . "McCarthy": Ada MacLeish to Felicia Geffen, May 30, 1952, American Academy; AMacL to Mark Van Doren, July 4, 1952, Columbia

430 drafting speeches . . . rhetoric: RW, interview with AMacL, November 11, 1979; "Stevenson's Ghost Writers," *U.S. News & World Report*, September 26, 1952, p. 57; Adlai Stevenson to AMacL, July 30, 1952, LC; AMacL to Adlai Stevenson, August 8, 1952, *Letters*, pp. 360–361; Adlai Stevenson to AMacL, August 11, 1952, LC; SD, interview with Richard Wilbur, July 28, 1988

430 "When an American says": Adlai Stevenson, speech to the American Legion convention, August 27, 1952, quoted in Martin, *Stevenson of Illinois*, p. 655

431 "Says McCarran to McCarthy": AMacL, "The Wisconsin-Nevada Axis," *New York Herald Tribune*, July 2, 1952, p. 18; Charles E. Wyzanski, Jr., to AMacL, July 3, 1952, LC

431 defended . . . Chafee: "Professor Chafee's Record," AMacL to the editor of the *New York Times*, dated July 4, 1952

432 unseating . . . "greatest menace": "Professors Start Appeal for McCarthy's Defeat," *Harvard Crimson*, October 9, 1951, p. 1; "Professors Fight M'Carthy, Jenner," *New York Times*, October 10, 1951

432 "pink boys" . . . "pattern is clear": "Another Senator Blasts Professors," *Harvard Crimson*, October 11, 1952, p. 1; "McCarthy Blasts 2 College Professors," *Harvard Crimson*, October 28, 1952, pp. 1, 6; Campbell, *The Poet*, p. 247

432 distinction . . . "Santa Claus": SD, interview with John Kenneth Galbraith, July 11, 1990; AMacL to Harry

Levin, July 4, 1953, *Letters*, pp. 367–368

432 Harvard . . . take a position: "Harvard Leaders Cited for Courage," February 1954, Scrapbook, vol. 4, p. 27, GCC; RW, interview with AMacL, April 27, 1980

Mastery

433 "407 pages of poetry": Hayden Carruth, "MacLeish's Poetry," *Nation*, January 31, 1953, p. 103

433 "highly intelligible" . . . "Renaissance man": Richard Eberhart, "The Pattern of MacLeish's Poetry," *New York Times Book Review*, November 23, 1952, pp. 5, 48; Charles Poore, "Books of the Times," *New York Times*, November 29, 1952

434 quarterlies . . . lukewarm: Frederick Morgan, "Six Poets," *Hudson Review* 6 (1953), 131; David Daiches, "Six Poets," *Yale Review* 42 (1953), 627–628; Reed Whittemore, "MacLeish and Democratic Pastoral," *Sewanee Review* 61 (October 1953), 700–709

434 "lyrics" . . . "light of day": Richard Wilbur, review of *Collected Poems, 1917–1952*, *New England Quarterly* 26 (March 1953), 121; Allen Tate to AMacL, December 30, 1952, LC

434 strong contender: I. L. Salomon, "A Peacemaker," *Saturday Review*, December 27, 1952, p. 19

435 "Beauty cannot be shown": AMacL, "10. Adam in the Evening," *Songs for Eve*, in *Collected*, 443

435 "the farthest" . . . "overpowering demands": AMacL to Ferris Greenslet, September 28, 1954, *Letters*, p. 376; Richard Eberhart, " ' 'The More I Have Traveled,' " *New York Times Book Review*, October 10, 1954, p. 14; Sara Henderson Hay, "Fall to Divinity," *Saturday Review*, December 4, 1954, p. 28; John Ciardi, "Recent Poetry," *Nation*, January 22, 1955, p. 77; Randall Jarrell, "Recent Poetry," *Yale Review* 44 (June 1955), 602–603

436 academy . . . Between 1948 and 1951:

Nominations in files, presentation of the Award of Merit Medal to Thomas Mann, May 1949, and presentation of the Howells Medal to William Faulkner, May 1950, American Academy; AMacL to Ernest Hemingway, February 17, 1954, *Letters*, p. 373

437 public positions . . . "superb . . . officer": RW, interview with AMacL, April 27, 1980; AMacL to Paul Manship, June 26, 1953, American Academy; AMacL to Malcolm Cowley, November 30, 1974, Newberry; SD, interview with Felicia Geffen Van Veen, March 30, 1989

438 Eliot House . . . students: AMacL to McGeorge Bundy, December 30, 1953, *Letters*, pp. 371–373; "Successful Men Find Eliot Congenial," *Harvard Crimson*, March 17, 1951, p. 1

438 farce . . . recover . . . bearings: "Faux Pas in Eliot House," *Harvard Crimson*, December 13, 1954; RW, interview with Malcolm Cowley, March 8, 1980

438 Conway . . . a regular: SD, interview with John Conway, October 10, 1988

438 notable people . . . Frost talked on: AMacL to J. Robert Oppenheimer, September 13, 1954, *Letters*, pp. 374–375; RW, interview with John H. Finley, Jr., September 21, 1979; John Conway, "Reminiscences," in *Symposium*, p. 54; SD, interview with W. Jackson Bate, October 13, 1988; *Reflections*, pp. 188–191

439 "hard to get rid of": AMacL, "The Gift Outright," in *Journey*, pp. 299–306

22. MEANS OF ESCAPE

Liberating Pound

440 last meeting . . . Ernest . . . friendship thin: Ernest Hemingway to AMacL, August 27, 1948; LC; Ada MacLeish

to Ernest Hemingway, September 29, 1952, JFK; Ernest Hemingway to AMacL, October 5, 1952, and February 3, 1954, LC; Brian, *True Gen*, p. 238; AMacL, "Poet," in *Collected*, p. 427; RW, interview with AMacL, April 26, 1980; AMacL to Ezra Pound, April 17, 1956, *Letters*, p. 380

442 rift . . . Murphy: AMacL to Gerald Murphy, June 3, 1956, *Letters*, pp. 381–382; Gerald Murphy to AMacL, June 1956, LC; RW, interview with Carolyn MacLeish, September 10, 1979; SD, interview with William H. MacLeish, June 29–30, 1987; RW, interview with Adele and Robert A. Lovett, June 23, 1979; Ada MacLeish to Sara Murphy, June 25, 1956

443 polyp . . . Public Garden: Ada Mac-Leish to Ezra Pound, May 19, 1956, Yale; AMacL to Thursa Bakey Sanders, October 26, 1957; AMacL, "A Poem for a Festival of Art," *Saturday Review*, July 28, 1956, p. 11; Ada MacLeish to Sara Murphy, June 25, 1956

443 Bollingen . . . controversy: McGuire, *Poetry's Catbird Seat*, pp. 110, 114–118; AMacL to Harrison Smith, May 27, 1949, *Letters*, pp. 344–346

443 *Poetry and Opinion:* Campbell, *The Poet*, pp. 233–236

444 Pound's release . . . "fingers broken": AMacL to James Laughlin, February 26, 1954, and November 30, 1954; AMacL to Ezra Pound, c. August 1955, *Letters*, p. 377, and AMacL to Ezra Pound, August 18, 1955, *Letters*, pp. 377–378; AMacL to Ezra Pound, September 7, 1955, Yale; AMacL to Ernest Hemingway, June 19, 1957, *Letters*, pp. 397–398; Carpenter, *Serious Character*, p. 818; AMacL to Ezra Pound, June 5, 1956, *Letters*, p. 382; AMacL to Ezra Pound, August 3, 1956, Yale; AMacL to Alexis Léger, June 9, 1956, *Letters*, p. 383

445 Archie went ahead . . . Frost signed on: Heymann, *Last Rower*, pp. 244–245; Carpenter, *Serious Character*, 821–823; AMacL to Ezra Pound, De-

cember 7, 1956, *Letters*, pp. 391–392; Donald Hall, *Remembering Poets* (New York: Harper and Row, 1978), p. 59; Wilbur, quoted in Hugh Kenner, *The Pound Era* (Berkeley: University of California Press, 1971), p. 535

446 "We are writing" . . . "a golden key": AMacL to Ernest Hemingway, c. January 14, 1957, *Letters*, pp. 393–394; Carpenter, *Serious Character*, pp. 825–826

446 furor . . . Kasper: Robert S. Bird, "Segregationist Kasper Is Ezra Pound Disciple," *New York Herald Tribune*, February 2, 1957; Carpenter, *Serious Character*, pp. 827–829; AMacL to Ernest Hemingway, June 19, 1957, *Letters*, p. 398

447 Frost . . . "better wait": Heymann, *Last Rower*, pp. 246–248

447 meeting . . . encouraging: Meryman, "The Enlarged Life," 118; AMacL to Ernest Hemingway, July 21, 1957, *Letters*, p. 401

447 coaxed to the front . . . "sheer exhaustion": William P. Rogers to AMacL, October 2, 1957, and January 2, 1958, LC; Heymann, *Last Rower*, p. 249; Carpenter, *Serious Character*, pp. 832–835, 838–840, 845–846; AMacL to Ezra Pound, March 16, 1958, *Letters*, pp. 406–407; Miriam Ottenberg, "Liberty Being Weighed for Poet Ezra Pound," *Washington Sunday Star*, March 16, 1958, pp. 1, 6; AMacL to Ezra Pound, March 30, 1958, *Letters*, pp. 407–408; Anthony Lewis, "U.S. Asked to End Pound Indictment," *New York Times*, April 15, 1958; de Rachewiltz, quoted in Ronald H. Bayes, "The Tenderness of Strength," *Pembroke Magazine* 7 (1976), 34; Carter Barber, "A Poet Speaks of Poets," newspaper interview with Frost, *Los Angeles Times*, May 22, 1958; SD, interview with Richard Wilbur, July 28, 1988; Harry Meacham to AMacL, September 5, 1966, and AMacL to Harry Meacham, October 14, 1966, Virginia Commonwealth;

AMacL to Ernest Hemingway, September 30, 1958, *Letters*, p. 411

J.B.: Background

449 predicament of . . . artist: AMacL, "The Isolation of the American Artist," in *Journey*, pp. 176–187

449 first draft . . . circus: RW, interview with Mason Hammond, September 18, 1979; Ada MacLeish to Sara Murphy, March 21, 1957; Gilbert Millstein, "Ten Playwrights Tell How It All Started," *New York Times Magazine*, December 6, 1959; Edward Hoagland to SD, December 17, 1988; AMacL and Mark Van Doren, *Dialogues*, p. 137

450 1955 sermon: Richard Calhoun, "Archibald MacLeish's *J.B.* — Religious Humanism in the 80's," in *Symposium*, pp. 78–80

450 book . . . "classic": Charles Poore, "Books of the Times," *New York Times*, March 8, 1958; John Ciardi, "The Birth of a Classic," *Saturday Review*, March 8, 1958, p. 11; Dudley Fitts, "Afflictions of a New Job," *New York Times Book Review*, March 23, 1958, p. 3

450 airing . . . Yale: Charles A. Fenton, "Theatre," *Nation*, May 10, 1958, pp. 425–226; Brooks Atkinson, "From 'Job' to 'J.B.,' " *New York Times*, May 4, 1958, sec. 2, p. 1

451 de Liagre . . . Kazan: RW, interview with Alfred de Liagre, Jr., November 1, 1979; RW, interview with Elia Kazan, June 19, 1979; Donald Hall, "Archibald MacLeish: On Being a Poet in the Theater," *Horizon* 2 (January 1960), 55

451 opening scene . . . coda: AMacL, *J.B.* (Boston: Houghton Mifflin, 1958)

J.B.: Broadway

453 star . . . Plummer: RW, interview with Archibald MacLeish, April 27, 1980; RW, interview with David Amram, March 15, 1979

453 Massey . . . disastrous: RW, inter-

view with Alfred de Liagre, Jr., November 1, 1979; RW, interview with AMacL, April 21, 1979

454 Hingle . . . accident: Pat Hingle, recording, May 1980, GCC; RW, interview with AMacL, April 21, 1979; "B'way Star Hurt in Tumble," *New York World-Telegram & Sun*, February 20, 1959, Scrapbook, vol. 6, GCC

454 read his play . . . jam sessions: Hall, "Poet in the Theater," p. 53; RW, interview with David Amram, March 15, 1979

454 tryout . . . Washington . . . revising: *Reflections*, pp. 198–199; Pat Hingle, recording, May 1980, GCC; RW, interview with AMacL, April 27, 1980; AMacL to Elia Kazan, December 12, 1958, *Letters*, p. 413; RW interview with David Amram, March 15, 1979; Elia Kazan, "Archie MacLeish," *Pembroke Magazine* 7 (1976), 146

456 opening night . . . *Today* show: RW, interview with Alfred de Liagre, Jr., November 1, 1979; SD, interview with Donald Hall, July 27, 1988; AMacL to Elia Kazan, December 12, 1958, *Letters*, p. 412; "NBC Apologizes for Treatment of MacLeish on Garroway's 'Today,' " *Variety*, December 31, 1958, Scrapbook, vol. 5, 42, GCC

457 *J.B.* . . . reviewers: Scrapbook, vol. 5, p. 52, GCC

457 seminars . . . overriding question: AMacL and Mark Van Doren, *Dialogues*, pp. 138–139; RW, interview with Alfred de Liagre, Jr., November 1, 1979; AMacL, "MacLeish Speaks to the Players," *Pembroke Magazine* 7 (1976), 82–83

458 "I have constructed": Quoted in Colin C. Campbell, "The Transformation of Biblical Myth: MacLeish's Use of the Adam and Job Stories," in *Myth and Symbol*, ed. Bernice Slote (Lincoln: University of Nebraska Press, 1963), p. 79

458 conclusion . . . too easily arrived: Sy Kahn, "The Games God Plays with Man: A Discussion of J.B.," *The Fifties: Fiction, Poetry, Drama*, ed. War-

ren French (DeLand, Fla.: Everett/
Edwards, 1970), p. 255; Gerald C.
Weales, *American Drama Since
World War II* (New York: Harcourt
Brace and World, 1962), p. 187;
Burnshaw, *Robert Frost Himself*, p.
110; Hall, "Poet in the Theater," p.
56

459 stylized . . . "morality play": SD, in-
terview with Elizabeth Marshall
Thomas, February 16, 1990; John
Gassner, "MacLeish's *J.B.*: Yale and
Broadway," in *Theatre at the Cross-
roads* (New York: Holt Rinehart and
Winston, 1960), pp. 298–305

Farewells

459 spasms . . . retirement . . . Van Doren:
AMacL to Alfred de Liagre, Jr., Feb-
ruary 6, 1959; AMacL, "Mark Van
Doren," in *Journey*, pp. 329–332

459 Charles . . . coached: "Van Doren
Admits All Charges," *Harvard Crimson*, November 3, 1959, p. 1; Ada
MacLeish to Sara Murphy, April 3,
1960

460 1959 . . . lectures: "MacLeish's Lecture Attracts 800," *Harvard Crimson*,
October 22, 1959, p. 1; *Reflections*,
pp. 183–184

460 Bate's estimation: RW, interview with
W. Jackson Bate, September 18, 1979

460 summing up . . . theory of poetry:
Campbell, *The Poet*, pp. 257–266,
admirably summarizes MacLeish's
views, as expressed in *Poetry and Experience* and "Poetry and Journalism."

460 "There is the writer" . . . self-justifying apologia: AMacL, *Poetry and Experience* (Boston: Houghton Mifflin,
1961), pp. 6, 9, 15, 29, 37–38, 62–
63; I. A. Richards to AMacL, c. late
1960, LC; Wallenstein, "Poetry and
Experience," pp. 59–60

462 *Secret of Freedom* . . . "TV . . . too
powerful": *Reflections*, pp. 205–206;
"MacLeish Play to Leave None Neutral," *Flint (Michigan) Journal*, February 28, 1960; AMacL to Adele
Lovett, March 27, 1960

462 Honors . . . diversions: Collection of
hoods and medals, GCC; White
House invitations, Scrapbooks, GCC;
Ada MacLeish to Sara Murphy, September 19, 1960, and June 29, 1961;
RW, interview with AMacL, April 27,
1980

463 Hellman . . . "soda water": SD, interview with William Alfred, October
13, 1988; Dorothy Van Doren to Archibald and Ada MacLeish, February
4, 1963, LC

463 Hemingway's suicide . . . "sick at
heart": AMacL, "Ernest Hemingway," in *Journey*, pp. 308, 312;
AMacL, "Hemingway," in *Collected*,
p. 482; AMacL to Carlos Baker, June
28, 1965, Princeton

464 prostate . . . removed: Ada MacLeish
to Sara and Gerald Murphy, August
31, 1961

464 Jill Ker . . . intimate friends: Jill Ker
Conway, "Reminiscences," in *Symposium*, p. 49

464 "one foot in the text": Quoted in Harvard University news release, December 20, 1961

464 Signet . . . ovation: Stephen Sandy,
"MacLeish, Cambridge, 1962," unpublished memoir, 1989

465 "Michelmas swallow": AMacL, "A
Retiring View of Harvard," in *Journey*, pp. 260–261

465 "What he finally taught": Walter Kaiser, memorial service, Harvard, May
1982

465 legacy . . . did not forget: SD, interviews with Tom Johnson, October 20,
1989, and December 1, 1989

23. POET LAUREATE

On the Road

467 *American Bell: Reflections*, pp. 206–
207; Stuart Brown, "Independence
Hall Drama Ready for July 4 Open-
ing," *Philadelphia Evening Bulletin*,
June 28, 1962; RW, interview with
AMacL, April 27, 1980; "Making

History Come Alive," *Philadelphia Inquirer*, July 5, 1962

469 Dialogues . . . "wonder and awe": *Reflections*, p. 205; Jack Gould, "TV: Dialogues of Poets," *New York Times*, August 3, 1962; SD, interview with W. Jackson Bate, October 13, 1988; Carlos Baker, "Reviews," *Journal of Higher Education* 36 (March 1965), 172–173; AMacL to Mark Van Doren, c. 1965, Columbia; AMacL and Mark Van Doren, *Dialogues*, pp. 266–267

469 friendship . . . deepened: AMacL to Mark Van Doren, February 17, 1964, August 29, 1968, August 2, 1969, and March 31, 1969, Columbia; Van Doren quoted by William Claire, introduction to AMacL, "Conversation with the Moon," Cosmos Club award speech, May 17, 1977

469 ambassador . . . Emancipation: Dean Rusk to AMacL, August 2, 1962, LC; RW, interview with David C. Mearns, June 19, 1978

470 "break into his own lecture": Sculley Bradley, "Undergraduate Decorum," *Daily Pennsylvanian*, c. October 19, 1962

470 "not alone, then or ever": Quoted in Noel Riley Fitch, *Sylvia Beach*, p. 414

470 Eleanor Roosevelt's passing: AMacL, "Eleanor Roosevelt," in *Journey*, pp. 277–279

Family Pictures

471 pumpkin pie: SD, interview with William H. MacLeish, June 29, 1987

471 Archie . . . work habits: RW, interview with Ishbel MacLeish and Alexander Campbell, April 7, 1979; SD, interview with Ellen Ishbel and Peter B. Zale, October 9, 1988

471 stone house . . . derelict: AMacL, "A Man's Work," in *Collected*, p. 399; SD, interview with Robert L. Merriam, June 12, 1991

472 neighbors . . . Harrises . . . Keith: Drabeck and Ellis, interview with Warren Harris family, June 15, 1977,

GCC; RW, interview with Eliza Howe Keith, October 26, 1980

472 "glowing journeys" . . . never . . . again: SD, interview with John Kenneth Galbraith, July 11, 1990; May Sarton, *The House by the Sea* (New York: Norton, 1977), pp. 219–220; SD, interview with May Sarton, January 14, 1990

472 Pond Picnic: John Conway, "Reminiscences," in *Symposium*, p. 52; SD, interview with Mimi and Karl Grimm, July 24, 1988; SD, interview with Ellen Ishbel Zale, October 9, 1988

473 entertaining . . . "happy and gay": SD, interview with Richard Wilbur, July 28, 1988; SD, interview with Jill Ker Conway, October 10, 1988; SD, interview with William H. MacLeish, May 25, 1989; SD, interview with John Conway, October 10, 1988

473 more uxorious . . . "five marriages": AMacL and Mark Van Doren, *Dialogues*, pp. 182–183; AMacL to Edward Hoagland, November 24, 1965; DeMott, *Writers at Work*, p. 33

473 anniversary . . . "fear of loss": Ada MacLeish to Sara Murphy, July 1, 1966; DeMott, "Acts of Love," p. 62

474 "Everything they know": AMacL, "The Old Gray Couple (1)," in *Collected*, p. 34

474 "Ah, but a good wife!": AMacL, "Late Abed," in *Collected*, pp. 491–492; AMacL, reading and talk at Williams College, October 7, 1968

474 almost perfect . . . second place: RW, interview with Dorothy de Santillana, September 19, 1979; RW, interview with Hester Pickman, September 21, 1979; SD, interview with Jill Ker Conway, October 10, 1988

475 Ken . . . father: RW, interview with Martha MacLeish Fuller, September 16, 1979; Kenneth MacLeish to AMacL, August 26, 1963, LC

475 too daunting a figure: SD, interview with William H. MacLeish, July 26, 1988

475 Ken . . . danger: Ada MacLeish to Alexander Campbell, November 2, 1962; SD, interview with Martha

MacLeish Fuller, May 23, 1989; SD, interview with Ellen Ishbel Zale, October 12, 1988; AMacL, "The Reef Fisher," in *Collected*, pp. 413–414

476 Hebrides . . . trip: Ada MacLeish to Sara Murphy, July 23, 1969; AMacL to Mark Van Doren, May 29, 1969, Columbia

476 "Reading Out Loud": Frederick H. Guidry, " 'A Live Voice in the Ear,' " *Christian Science Monitor*, January 23, 1960; SD, interview with Thursa Bakey Sanders, October 11, 1990

477 grandchildren . . . arrange their lives: SD, interview with Morellen MacLeish, July 12, 1990; RW, interview with Martha MacLeish Fuller, September 16, 1979; SD, interview with Mimi Grimm, May 13, 1989; SD, interview with Martha MacLeish Fuller, May 23, 1989; AMacL, reading and talk at Williams College, October 7, 1968; AMacL, "Pity's Sake," in *Collected*, p. 488; SD, interview with Ellen Ishbel Zale, October 9, 1988; Ada MacLeish to Sara Murphy, April 21, 1968

Passages

478 cruising . . . Christmas: SD, interview with Alice Acheson, May 7, 1988; AMacL to Ranald Macdonald, February 9, 1963

478 University . . . "a poop": Ada MacLeish to Sara Murphy, January 9, 1963; John Bartlow Martin, *Adlai Stevenson and the World* (New York: Doubleday, 1977), p. 755; Jean Groo to SD, April 10, 1989

478 "cow crashed": Ada MacLeish to Noel and Elena Macy, February 13, 1961

478 "bad climates" . . . "Mount Gay rum": RW, interview with AMacL, November 10, 1979; Ada MacLeish to Sara Murphy, February 11, 1967; RW, interview with Elena Macy, September 6, 1979; SD, interview with A. Martin Macy, January 6, 1989; AMacL to Noel and Elena Macy, December 16, 1967

479 library . . . dedication: Alan Powers to SD, October 1, 1989; Alan Powers, "After the Fall," Amherst; AMacL to J. Alfred Guest, November 4, 1963, Amherst

479 Amherst . . . duties: "MacLeish Named Simpson Lecturer," *Amherst Alumni Quarterly* (Winter 1963–64), 24; SD, interview with Robert F. Grose, August 31, 1979

479 not popular . . . hadn't worked out: AMacL to Mark Van Doren, February 17, 1964, Columbia; SD, interview with William H. Pritchard, May 25, 1989; SD, interview with Robert C. Townsend, August 30, 1989; SD, interview with Allen Guttmann, June 11, 1990; *Reflections*, p. 211

481 Burton . . . Taylor: Martin, *Stevenson and the World*, p. 812; Richard Burton to AMacL, August 10, 1964, LC; AMacL to Richard Burton, August 7, 1965, *Letters*, pp. 423–424; Melvyn Bragg, *Richard Burton: A Life* (Boston: Little, Brown, 1988), p. 298

481 Gerald's death . . . "How wonderful": AMacL to Gerald Murphy, June 26, 1964; AMacL to Gerald Murphy, September 29, 1964, *Letters*, p. 422; Donnelly with Billings, *Sara & Gerald*, p. 236

481 yet other memorials: AMacL, remarks at Frankfurter memorial observance, U.S. Supreme Court, October 25, 1965; Cass Canfield to AMacL, July 23, 1965, LC

Myths and Legends

482 *Herakles* . . . "a hooker": *Reflections*, pp. 213–214; AMacL to Alan Schneider, July 31, 1965, LC; Tom Prideaux, "A Sleeping Beauty and Hercules," *Life*, December 3, 1965, p. 10

483 *Eleanor Roosevelt Story: Reflections*, pp. 211–212; RW, interview with AMacL, April 27, 1980; "Eleanor Roosevelt," *McCall's* 92 (May 1965), 98–101, 172; reviews quoted in advertisement, *New York Times*, November 7, 1965; Bosley Crowther, "The Ten Best Films of 1965," *New*

York Times, c. December 1965; " 'Roosevelt' Film Voted Best of '65," *New York Times,* January 10, 1966

484 Pulitzer . . . "a leash": Paul L. Montgomery, "Dinner Salutes Pulitzer Prizes," *New York Times,* May 11, 1966; Ymelda Dixon, "Trio Sparkled at Poets' Dinner," *Washington Star,* c. May 20, 1966

484 Neruda . . . translators: AMacL to Donald Hall, July 18, 1966, New Hampshire

484 vocationalism . . . material values: AMacL to Mark Van Doren, November 5, 1966, and April 24, 1967, Columbia; AMacL, "The Revolt of the Diminished Man," in *Riders,* pp. 18–19

484 war in Vietnam: AMacL to Kay Boyle, June 4, 1965; AMacL, "A Decent Respect," in *Journey,* 104–107; McGeorge Bundy, "The Uses of Responsibility," *Saturday Review,* July 3, 1965, p. 13; AMacL to Dean Acheson, April 6, 1968, *Letters,* p. 425

Versions of History

485 "He stretches so far": Mark Van Doren, "To Archie, at 75," LC

485 "birds and insects": AMacL to Joseph Wood Krutch, June 1, 1967, LC

486 *An Evening's Journey* . . . parade: William H. MacLeish, "Silver Whistler," p. 64; Pauline Dubkin, "That Small Town in Mass. Society," *Quincy (Massachusetts) Patriot-Ledger,* November 4, 1967; RW, interview with Ishbel MacLeish and Alexander Campbell, April 7, 1979; Drabeck and Ellis, interview with Frances Steele Holden, October 28, 1976, GCC; Ada MacLeish to Noel and Elena Macy, July 5, 1967

486 *Magic Prison: Reflections,* pp. 216–217; Edward Downes, "Notes on the Program," New York Philharmonic "Promenades" program, 1967, p. B; RW, interview with AMacL, April 27, 1980; Andre Kostelanetz to AMacL, telegram of February 23, 1970

486 Sandburg . . . "sang him down": AMacL, "President Johnson Alive and Carl Sandburg Dead," in *Riders,*

pp. 127–131; RW, interview with David C. Mearns, June 19, 1978; McGill quoted in Edward P. Morgan, "The Shape of the News," *Newsday,* September 23–24, 1967

487 "running quarrel": Tom Yarbrough, "Reading & Writing," *St. Louis Post-Dispatch,* January 28, 1968, p. 4E

487 rhetorical style . . . portraits: Malcolm Cowley, draft of review of *A Continuing Journey,* Newberry

488 Yeats . . . Fifth Avenue: AMacL, reading-talk, Williams College, October 7, 1968; SD, interview with Tom Johnson, December 1, 1989

488 "laughter from another year": AMacL, "Hotel Breakfast," in *Collected,* p. 489

488 "Too old for love": AMacL, " 'The Wild Old Wicked Man,' " in *Collected,* pp. 492–493

489 "On an oak in autumn": AMacL, "Survivor," in *Collected,* p. 473

489 "feel like writing": Thomas Lask, review of *The Wild Old Wicked Man,* "Books of the Times," c. November 1968

490 "riders on the earth": AMacL, *New York Times,* December 25, 1968, p. 1; AMacL, foreword to *Riders,* p. ix; Borman, quoted in John Noble Wilford, "Crew of Apollo 8 Is Saluted," *New York Times,* January 10, 1970

490 moon landing . . . front page: RW, interview with AMacL, November 10, 1979; Ada MacLeish to Sara Murphy, July 23, 1969; James Reston to AMacL, c. late July 1969, LC

490 Football Foundation . . . "might be human": Robert Lipsyte, "Night at the Waldorf," "Sports of the Times" column, *New York Times,* December 12, 1969; RW, interview with AMacL, April 27, 1980

24. QUARRELS WITH THE WORLD

Critical Murders

492 collaboration . . . signed on: *Reflections,* pp. 219, 262; RW, interview

with AMacL, April 27, 1980; George Gent, "MacLeish, at 78, Talks of New Play," *New York Times,* March 2, 1971, p. 28

493 "the Devil" . . . "Liberty and Union": AMacL, "The Old Devil in a New Age," *New York Times,* April 30, 1971, p. 39

493 Dylan . . . backed out: RW, interview with Stuart Ostrow, May 7, 1980; AMacL to Dorothy de Santillana, October 7, 1970, *Letters,* p. 430, footnote 3

494 Casting . . . undermined: AMacL to Dorothy de Santillana, November 5, 1970, Houghton Mifflin; RW, interview with Stuart Ostrow, May 7, 1980; Kevin Kelly, "MacLeish's 'Scratch,' " *Boston Globe,* April 8, 1971, p. 40

494 tryout in Boston: Marjorie Sherman, "Publisher's Party a Hub Who's Who," *Boston Globe,* April 8, 1971; Kelly, "MacLeish's 'Scratch,' " p. 40; SD, interview with W. Jackson Bate, October 13, 1988

494 opening . . . panned: AMacL to Mark Van Doren, April 27, 1971, Columbia; Clive Barnes, "Theater: 'Scratch' Opens," *New York Times,* May 7, 1971; *Reflections,* p. 220

495 "The issue with which my play": AMacL to the editor of the *New York Times,* May 10, 1971, *Letters,* pp. 430–431

495 Reston . . . Ochs: *Reflections,* p. 220

495 *skean d'hu:* Richard Phalon, "MacLeish and 3 Others Honored," *New York Times,* June 6, 1972

496 Pound . . . "a poet's work": AMacL, "The Venetian Grave," *Saturday Review,* February 9, 1974, pp. 26, 28–29; AMacL, "Ezry," in *Collected,* p. 410

496 Van Doren . . . "dearer to me": AMacL, "Mark Van Doren," in *Riders,* pp. 140–141; AMacL, "Mark Van Doren and the Brook," in *Collected,* p. 33; AMacL to Dorothy Van Doren, Decemer 1972

497 "At eighty you begin" . . . "inspired editing": AMacL, foreword, to *The Human Season: Selected Poems,*

1926–1972 (Boston: Houghton Mifflin, 1972), pp. v–vii; Laurence Lieberman, "New Books in Review," *Yale Review* 62 (December 1972), 267–269

498 Brinnin . . . "nicer nuances": John Malcolm Brinnin, review of *The Human Season, New York Times,* November 19, 1972, pp. 6, 48

498 "crumpled me" . . . bitter . . . poem: AMacL to Richard Wilbur, June 30, 1976, *Letters,* p. 441; AMacL, "Remarks to a Writing Class," notebook poem, 1975, LC

498 reviews . . . "never . . . disinterested": SD, interview with Richard B. McAdoo, May 23, 1989; AMacL to Stephen Becker, July 8, 1979

Modern Problems

499 Becker . . . "leave so soon": SD, interview with Stephen and Mary Becker, March 9, 1989

499 "happy . . . small town": AMacL, "The People Who Live Here," talk at Festival of the Hills, Conway, Massachusetts, October 1, 1972

500 annual report . . . swimming pool: Anon., "Archibald MacLeish," *Nieman Reports* 36 (Summer 1982), 42; SD, interview with Ellen Ishbel and Peter B. Zale, October 9, 1988

500 1974 . . . *J.B.:* Pat Hingle, recording, May 1980, GCC; SD, interview with Helen E. Ellis, October 12, 1988

500 "Hay-time when the Boston forecast": AMacL, "New England Weather," in *Collected,* p. 28

501 inveighed against . . . abuses: AMacL, "Rediscovering the Simple Life," *McCall's* 99 (April 1972), 79–87

501 Urbanism . . . no attics: Alden Whitman, "MacLeish Mourns Lost Values," *New York Times,* May 7, 1972; AMacL, "News from the Horse and Wagon," in *Riders,* pp. 48–49

501 restricting . . . liberties: AMacL, "Cottonwoods Astir," *Saturday Review,* November 13, 1971, p. 40; AMacL to Ranald Macdonald, December 25, 1973, *Letters,* p. 433

502 sex . . . "love" . . . advertisements:

Whitman, "MacLeish Mourns"; DeMott, "Acts of Love," p. 39; AMacL, "Observations of P. Ovidius Naso on the Incidence of Sex in the Contemporary Novel," in *Collected*, p. 476; AMacL, "Who Precisely Do You Think You Are?" in *Journey*, pp. 4–5; Daniel H. Yergin, "MacLeish Endorses Man," *Yale Daily News*, November 8, 1966, pp. 1, 3

503 remaindered . . . retreat: AMacL to Richard B. McAdoo, March 6, 1975, Houghton Mifflin

Domestic Crises

503 divorce . . . cancer: Ada MacLeish to Adele and Robert A. Lovett, June 11, 1972; SD, interview with Jill Ker Conway, May 23, 1989; AMacL to Adele Lovett, May 21, 1973

503 Jean Groo . . . propriety: RW, interview with Jean Groo, September 13, 1980

504 Antigua . . . last time: SD, interview with Morley Cowles Ballantine, January 4, 1989; SD, interview with Birgit Carstensen, January 5, 1989; SD, interview with Patricia Starr, January 8, 1989; SD, interview with Roderick MacLeish, February 24, 1989

504 Ken . . . memorial: AMacL, remarks at the burial of Kenneth MacLeish, August 9, 1977, privately printed; SD, interview with Phyllis Cummings, July 26, 1988

504 typical day . . . "less than godlike": SD, interview with Phyllis Cummings, July 26, 1988; Phyllis Cummings, "Reminiscence," newsletter of the Friends of the Archibald MacLeish Collection, April 1988, GCC; Hall, *Weather for Poetry*, pp. 14–15; SD, interview with Ellen Ishbel and Peter B. Zale, October 9, 1988; SD, interview with A. Bruce and Patty Mac-Leish, May 24, 1989

505 cocoon . . . spin loose: SD, interview with Peter B. Zale, October 9, 1988; AMacL, "Overstaying," in *Collected*, p. 517

506 "terrible mother": RW, interview

with Kay Bundy, September 22, 1979; SD, interview with Jill Ker Conway, October 10, 1988; SD, interviews with William H. MacLeish, July 26, 1988, and May 25, 1989

506 justice . . . courted . . . women: SD, interview with Roderick MacLeish, February 24, 1989; SD, interview with Phyllis Cummings, July 26, 1988; SD, interview with John Conway, October 10, 1988; RW, interview with William H. MacLeish, September 20, 1979; SD, interview with William Alfred, October 13, 1988

506 Archie reacted . . . "the other side": RW, interview with Jean Groo, September 13, 1980; Drabeck and Ellis, interview with Warren Harris family, June 15, 1977, GCC; SD, interview with Ellen Ishbel and Peter B. Zale, October 9, 1988; SD, interview with Jill Ker Conway, October 10, 1988; AMacL to Alice Acheson, April 29, 1980, *Letters*, p. 447

Bicentennial and Other Observances

507 "Old colleague": AMacL, "Night Watch in the City of Boston," in *Collected*, p. 3

507 "a man's own generation": AMacL, remarks at memorial for Kenneth Murdock, November 16, 1975

508 Moyers . . . "words rang": "Bill Moyers Journal," March 7, 1976, transcript, GCC; *Reflections*, p. 8; AMacL, "Family Group," in *Collected*, p. 22; Hayden Carruth, "Homage to A. MacLeish," *Virginia Quarterly Review* 53 (Winter 1977), 150; Michael Kernan, "A Clear-Eyed, Poetic View of Politics," *Washington Post*, March 30, 1976, p. B1

509 bicentennial . . . broader: AMacL, "Bicentennial of What?" *Current* 16 (September 1976), 4–9; *Reflections*, pp. 229–230

509 *Great American* . . . "grace of God": *Reflections*, pp. 221–222, 227, 234

510 Freedom . . . a process: AMacL, interviewed on WQXR, July 4, 1976

510 reinvent history: RW, interview with Elizabeth Miller, November 16, 1979; Drabeck and Ellis, interview with Stephen Becker, September 28, 1976, GCC

510 *New and Collected:* Carruth, "Homage to A. MacLeish," pp. 146–147; Robert Siegel, "Emerson's Smile," *Poetry* 130 (May 1977), 102, 105

510 rumor . . . "covers of a book": AMacL to Richard B. McAdoo, November 4, 1976, Houghton Mifflin; AMacL to Gerald R. Ford, c. January 1, 1977, LC; Richard W. Couper to AMacL, March 20, 1978; AMacL, remarks at National Medal for Literature presentation, April 6, 1978; Herbert Mitgang, "MacLeish Decries Takeovers in Publishing," *New York Times,* April 7, 1978, p. C22

510 gold medal . . . "touch of hands": Richard Wilbur, presentation of the gold medal for poetry, and AMacL, acceptance of the gold medal for poetry, May 23, 1979, American Academy

25. LAST LINES

A Voice of One's Own

512 decline . . . age . . . its due: SD, interview with Alice Acheson, May 7, 1988; AMacL, "An Age of Adolescence," *Washington Post,* January 21, 1974; AMacL, "Correction," notebook poem, 1975, LC

513 onset of fear . . . "not a lot of": AMacL, notebook entry, November 1976, LC; AMacL, "Dozing on the Lawn," in *Collected,* p. 15; AMacL, "Conway Burying Ground," in *Collected,* p. 15; Don Pride, "A Visit with Archibald MacLeish," *Greenfield (Massachusetts) Recorder,* November 7, 1981, p. A8

513 Antigua faded: AMacL to Stephen Becker, January 9, 1976

513 eyesight and hearing . . . "eighty again": Drabeck and Ellis, interview with Warren Harris family, June 15, 1977, GCC; SD, interview with Peter B. Zale, October 9, 1988

514 poems . . . stopped coming: Hall, *Weather for Poetry,* p. 18; Pride, "A Visit," p. A8

514 final understanding . . . "know the world": Hall, *Weather for Poetry,* p. 17; AMacL to Holly Morgan, September 28, 1979; AMacL to Robert Fitzgerald, January 28, 1978, *Letters,* p. 443

515 found his voice: AMacL to William Heyen, March 11, 1975, *Letters,* p. 437; AMacL to Barbara Tuchman, July 28, 1980, *Letters,* p. 448

515 the old . . . "different light": SD, interview with Ellen Ishbel and Peter B. Zale, October 9, 1988; Alden Whitman, "MacLeish Mourns"

515 "Your eyes change": AMacL, "Definitions of Old Age," in *Collected,* p. 16

516 "Old age — to live": AMacL, untitled notebook poem, c. 1976, LC

517 "A man and his wife": AMacL, "Hebrides," in *Collected,* pp. 18–19

517 "No need to race the days": AMacL, "Across the River and under the Trees," in *Collected,* p. 518

517 "Years ago in the night": AMacL, "Return to the Island," in *Collected,* p. 521

518 "This old man is no one": AMacL, "Epigraph," in *Collected,* pp. 518–519

More Than a Rider

518 autobiography . . . evaded any inquiries: Drabeck and Ellis, introduction, *Reflections,* p. 10; Dorothy de Santillana to AMacL, August 4, 1972, Houghton Mifflin; AMacL to Richard B. McAdoo, January 15, 1977, Houghton Mifflin; SD, interview with Helen E. Ellis, October 12, 1988

519 occasions . . . *Panic:* RW, interview with Jane Canfield, April 15, 1980; SD, interview with Ellen Ishbel and Peter B. Zale, October 9, 1988;

AMacL to Stephen Becker, August 11, 1980

519 "You have no idea": SD, interview with Tom Johnson, December 1, 1989

520 confused Jill . . . "too early": SD, interview with Jill Ker Conway, October 10, 1988; RW, interview with Morellen MacLeish, May 19, 1982

520 Dylan Thomas . . . "You get along": William H. MacLeish, "Silver Whistler," pp. 54–55

521 estate . . . heirs: SD, interview with G. d'Andelot Belin, July 27, 1988; SD, interviews with Ellen Ishbel Zale, October 11, 1988, and October 12, 1988

521 funeral . . . "slow May": SD, interview with Phyllis Cummings, June 26, 1988; SD, interview with A. Bruce MacLeish, May 22, 1991; SD, interview with William H. MacLeish, May 23, 1991

522 "long encomium": SD, interview with John Kenneth Galbraith, July 11, 1990

522 "stubbornly generous": Richard Wilbur, "Tributes," in Symposium, p. 150

523 Harvard . . . "cold light came": SD, interview with Richard Wilbur, July 28, 1988; memorial service at Harvard, May 1982; AMacL, "Winter Is Another Country," in Collected, p. 371

524 reputations . . . "next horizon": SD, interview with Donald Hall, July 27, 1988; Howard Nemerov, commemorative tribute, December 3, 1982, American Academy; John Broderick, "Archibald MacLeish (1892–1982)," in American Philosophical Society Yearbook (Philadelphia: American Philosophical Society, 1983), p. 513

Bibliography ❖

Works by Archibald MacLeish

POETRY AND PLAYS

MacLeish, Archibald. *Tower of Ivory*. New Haven: Yale University Press, 1917. Foreword by Lawrence Mason.

———. *The Happy Marriage and Other Poems*. Boston: Houghton Mifflin Company, 1924.

———. *Poems, 1924–1933*. Boston: Houghton Mifflin Company, 1933.

———. *The Fall of the City*. New York: Farrar & Rinehart Inc., 1937.

———. *Air Raid*. New York: Harcourt, Brace & Co., 1938.

———. *Land of the Free*. New York: Harcourt, Brace & Co., 1938.

———. *The American Story*. New York: Sloan and Pearce, 1944.

———. *J.B.* Boston: Houghton Mifflin Company, 1958.

———. *The Eleanor Roosevelt Story*. Boston: Houghton Mifflin Company, 1965.

———. *An Evening's Journey to Conway, Massachusetts*. Northampton, Mass.: Gehenna Press, 1967.

———. *Herakles*. Boston: Houghton Mifflin Company, 1967.

———. *Scratch*. Boston: Houghton Mifflin Company, 1971.

———. *The Human Season: Selected Poems, 1926–1972*. Boston: Houghton Mifflin Company, 1972.

———. *The Great American Fourth of July Parade*. Pittsburgh: University of Pittsburgh Press, 1975.

———. *Six Plays*. Boston: Houghton Mifflin Company, 1980.

———. *Collected Poems, 1917–1982*. Boston: Houghton Mifflin Company, 1985.

PROSE

The Editors of *Fortune* [Archibald MacLeish]. *Housing America*. New York: Harcourt, Brace & Co., 1932.

The Editors of *Fortune* [Archibald MacLeish]. *Jews in America*. New York: Random House, 1936.

The Editors of *Fortune* [five of the six chapters by Archibald MacLeish]. *Background of War*. New York: Alfred A. Knopf, 1937.

MacLeish, Archibald. "Archibald MacLeish." In *Living Authors*. Edited by Dilly Tante [Stanley J. Kunitz]. New York: H. W. Wilson, 1931.

———. *The Irresponsibles*. New York: Duell, Sloan and Pearce, 1940.

———. *A Time to Speak*. Boston: Houghton Mifflin Company, 1941.

———. *The American Cause*. New York: Sloan and Pearce, 1941.

———. *The Next Harvard*. Cambridge, Mass.: Harvard University Press, 1941.

———. *A Time to Act*. Boston: Houghton Mifflin Company, 1943.

———. *Poetry and Opinion: The Pisan Cantos of Ezra Pound*. Urbana: University of Illinois Press, 1950.

———. *Freedom Is the Right to Choose*. Boston: Beacon Press, 1951.

———. *Poetry and Journalism*. Minneapolis: Minnesota Pamphlets, 1958.

———. *Poetry and Experience*. Boston: Houghton Mifflin Company, 1961.

———. *A Continuing Journey*. Boston: Houghton Mifflin Company, 1968.

———. *Champion of a Cause: Essays and Addresses on Librarianship*. Compiled and introduced by Eva M. Goldschmidt. Chicago: American Library Association, 1971.

———. *Riders on the Earth: Essays and Recollections*. Boston: Houghton Mifflin Company, 1978.

———. *Archibald MacLeish Reflections*. Edited by Bernard A. Drabeck and Helen E. Ellis. Amherst: University of Massachusetts Press, 1986. Foreword by Richard Wilbur.

———. *Letters of Archibald MacLeish, 1907–1982*. Edited by R. H. Winnick. Boston: Houghton Mifflin Company, 1983.

MacLeish, Archibald, et al. *Writing for Fortune*. New York: Time Inc., 1980.

MISCELLANEOUS SOURCES

MacLeish, Archibald, and Samuel Hazo. "Those Paris Years." Pennsylvania State University Audio-Visual Services color video, 1987 (filmed in 1977).

Works by Other Authors

BOOKS AND PAMPHLETS

Aaron, Daniel. *Writers on the Left*. New York: Oxford University Press, 1977.

Acheson, Dean. *Present at the Creation: My Years in the State Department*. New York: W. W. Norton & Company, 1969.

———. *Fragments of My Fleece*. New York: W. W. Norton & Company, 1971.

————. *Among Friends: Personal Letters of Dean Acheson*. Edited by David S. McLellan and David C. Acheson. New York: Dodd, Mead & Company, 1980.

Alexander, Charles C. *Here the Country Lies: Nationalism and the Arts in Twentieth-Century America*. Bloomington: Indiana University Press, 1980.

Amram, David. *Vibrations*. New York: Macmillan, 1968.

Baker, Carlos. *Ernest Hemingway: A Life Story*. New York: Charles Scribner's Sons, 1969.

Beach, Sylvia. *Shakespeare and Company*. New York: Harcourt, Brace & Co., 1959.

Benét, Stephen Vincent. *Selected Letters of Stephen Vincent Benét*. Edited by Charles A. Fenton. New Haven: Yale University Press, 1960.

Blitzstein, Marc. *The Cradle Will Rock*. New York: Random House, 1938. Foreword by Archibald MacLeish.

Bogan, Louise. *A Poet's Alphabet*. New York: McGraw-Hill, 1970.

————. *What the Woman Lived: Selected Letters of Louise Bogan, 1920–1970*. Edited by Ruth Limmer. New York: Harcourt Brace Jovanovich, 1973.

Boyd, James, ed. *The Free Company Presents*. New York: Dodd, Mead & Company, 1941.

Brady, Frank. *Citizen Welles: A Biography of Orson Welles*. New York: Charles Scribner's Sons, 1989.

Bragg, Melvyn. *Richard Burton: A Life*. Boston: Little, Brown and Company, 1988.

Brian, Denis. *The True Gen*. New York: Grove Press, 1987.

Brooks, Cleanth. *Modern Poetry and the Tradition*. Chapel Hill: University of North Carolina Press, 1939.

Burlingame, Roger. *Don't Let Them Scare You: The Life and Times of Elmer Davis*. Philadelphia: J. B. Lippincott Company, 1961.

Burns, James MacGregor. *Roosevelt: The Lion and the Fox*. New York: Harcourt, Brace & Co., 1956.

————. *Roosevelt: The Soldier of Freedom*. New York: Harcourt Brace Jovanovich, 1970.

Burnshaw, Stanley. *Robert Frost Himself*. New York: George Braziller, 1986.

Bush, Warren V., ed. *The Dialogues of Archibald MacLeish and Mark Van Doren*. New York: E. P. Dutton, 1964.

Campbell, Colin C. "The Poet as Artist and Citizen: A Study of the Life and Writings of Archibald MacLeish through 1958." Ph.D. dissertation, University of Pennsylvania, 1960.

Carpenter, Humphrey. *A Serious Character: The Life of Ezra Pound*. Boston: Houghton Mifflin Company, 1988.

Cole, John Y. *For Congress and the Nation: A Chronological History of the Library of Congress*. Washington, D.C.: Library of Congress, 1979.

Conant, James B. *My Several Lives: Memoirs of a Social Inventor*. New York: Harper & Row, 1972.

Cowley, Malcolm. *Think Back on Us: A Contemporary Chronicle of the 1930s*. Carbondale: Southern Illinois University Press, 1967.

Crosby, Harry. *Shadows of the Sun: The Diaries of Harry Crosby*. Edited by Edward Germain. Santa Barbara: Black Sparrow Press, 1977.

Davis, Elmer. *By Elmer Davis.* Edited by Robert L. Davis. Indianapolis: The Bobbs-Merrill Company, 1964.

Davis, Kenneth S. *The Politics of Honor: A Biography of Adlai E. Stevenson.* New York: G. P. Putnam's Sons, 1967.

Donnelly, Honoria Murphy, with Richard N. Billings. *Sara & Gerald: Villa America and After.* New York: Times Books, 1982.

Drabeck, Bernard A., Helen E. Ellis, and Seymour Rudin, eds. *Proceedings of the Archibald MacLeish Symposium, May 7–8, 1982.* Lanham, Md.: University Press of America, 1988.

Ebner, Michael H. *Creating Chicago's North Shore: A Suburban History.* Chicago: University of Chicago Press, 1988.

Ellmann, Richard. *James Joyce.* New and revised edition. New York: Oxford University Press, 1982.

Elson, Robert T. *Time, Inc.: The Intimate History of a Publishing Enterprise, 1923–1941.* New York: Atheneum, 1968.

Ely, Jr., Albert H., ed. *History of the Class of Nineteen Hundred & Fifteen.* New Haven: Yale University Press, 1915.

Falk, Signi Lenea. *Archibald MacLeish.* New York: Twayne Publishers, 1965.

Fenton, Charles A. *Stephen Vincent Benét: The Life and Times of an American Man of Letters, 1898–1943.* New Haven: Yale University Press, 1958.

Fitch, Noel Riley. *Sylvia Beach and the Lost Generation: A History of Literary Paris in the Twenties & Thirties.* New York: W. W. Norton & Company, 1983.

Frank, Elizabeth. *Louise Bogan: A Portrait.* New York: Alfred A. Knopf, 1985.

Frankfurter, Felix. *Law and Politics: Occasional Papers of Felix Frankfurter.* Edited by Archibald MacLeish and E. E. Prichard, Jr. Foreword by Archibald MacLeish. New York: Harcourt, Brace & Co., 1939.

Gassner, John. *Theatre at the Crossroads.* New York: Holt Rinehart & Winston, 1960.

Goodrum, Charles A., and Helen W. Dalrymple. *The Library of Congress.* Boulder: Westview Press, 1982.

Hall, Donald. *Remembering Poets: Reminiscences and Opinions.* New York: Harper & Row, 1978.

———. *The Weather for Poetry.* Ann Arbor: University of Michigan Press, 1982.

Hart, Henry, ed. *The Writer in a Changing World.* New York: Equinox Co-operative Press, 1937.

Heymann, C. David. *Ezra Pound: The Last Rower.* New York: The Viking Press, 1976.

Hoagland, Edward. *Walking the Dead Diamond River.* New York: Random House, 1973.

Hocking, William E. *Freedom of the Press: A Framework of Principle.* Chicago: University of Chicago Press, 1947.

Hoopes, James. *Van Wyck Brooks: In Search of American Culture.* Amherst: University of Massachusetts Press, 1977.

Hoopes, Roy. *Ralph Ingersoll.* New York: Atheneum Publishers, 1985.

Isaacson, Walter, and Evan Thomas. *The Wise Men: Six Friends and the World They Made.* New York: Simon & Schuster, 1986.

Jay, Paul, ed. *Selected Correspondence of Kenneth Burke and Malcolm Cowley.* New York: Viking Penguin, 1988.

Johnson, Owen. *Stover at Yale.* New York: McClure, 1911.

Kazan, Elia. *Elia Kazan: A Life.* New York: Alfred A. Knopf, 1988.

Ludington, Townsend. *John Dos Passos: A Twentieth-Century Odyssey.* New York: E. P. Dutton, 1980.

Lynn, Kenneth S. *Hemingway.* New York: Simon & Schuster, 1987.

Macdonald, Dwight. *Memoirs of a Revolutionist.* New York: Farrar, Straus and Cudahy, 1957.

MacLeish, Andrew. *Life of Andrew MacLeish, 1838–1928.* Chicago: privately printed, 1929.

MacLeish, Martha Hillard. *Martha Hillard MacLeish (1856–1947).* Geneva, N.Y.: privately printed, 1949. Foreword by Archibald MacLeish.

MacShane, Frank. *The Life of John O'Hara.* New York: E. P. Dutton, 1980.

Martin, John Bartlow. *Adlai Stevenson of Illinois.* New York: Doubleday, 1976.

———. *Adlai Stevenson and the World.* New York: Doubleday, 1977.

McAlmon, Robert, and Kay Boyle. *Being Geniuses Together.* Garden City, N.Y.: Doubleday, 1968.

McGann, Mary Evelyn. "Voices from the Dark: A Study of the Radio Achievement of Norman Corwin, Archibald MacLeish, Louis MacNeice, Dylan Thomas, and Samuel Beckett." Ph.D. dissertation, University of Indiana, 1979.

McGuire, William. *Poetry's Catbird Seat.* Washington, D.C.: Library of Congress, 1988.

Meacham, Harry M. *The Caged Panther: Ezra Pound at Saint Elizabeths.* New York: Twayne Publishers, 1967.

Meyers, Jeffrey. *Hemingway: A Biography.* New York: Harper & Row, 1985.

Miller, Linda Patterson, ed. *Letters from the Lost Generation: Gerald and Sara Murphy and Friends.* New Brunswick, N.J.: Rutgers University Press, 1991.

Mischianza, 1911 [yearbook of Hotchkiss School]. New York: Charles L. Willard Company, 1911.

Mitgang, Herbert. *Dangerous Dossiers: Exposing the Secret War Against America's Greatest Authors.* New York: Donald I. Fine, 1988.

Mullaly, Edward J. *Archibald MacLeish: A Checklist.* Kent, Ohio: Kent State University Press, 1973.

Nelson, Raymond. *Van Wyck Brooks: A Writer's Life.* New York: E. P. Dutton, 1981.

Origo, Iris. *Images and Shadows: Part of a Life.* New York: Harcourt Brace Jovanovich, 1971.

Paine, Ralph D. *The First Yale Unit: A Story of Naval Aviation, 1916–1919.* Vol. 2. Boston: Houghton Mifflin–Riverside Press, 1925.

Paul, Sherman. *Edmund Wilson.* Urbana: University of Illinois Press, 1965.

Pearce, Roy Harvey. *The Continuity of American Poetry.* Princeton: Princeton University Press, 1961.

Perse, St.-John. *Letters.* Translated and edited by Arthur J. Knodel. Princeton: Princeton University Press, 1979.

Pinsky, Robert. *The Situation of Poetry: Contemporary Poetry and Its Traditions.* Princeton: Princeton University Press, 1976.

Preston, William, Jr. *Hope and Folly: The United States and UNESCO, 1945–1985*. Minneapolis: University of Minnesota Press, 1989.

Rossano, Geoffrey, ed. *The Price of Honor: The World War I Letters of Naval Aviator Kenneth MacLeish*. Annapolis: Naval Institute Press, 1991.

Samuelson, Arnold. *With Hemingway: A Year in Key West and Cuba*. New York: Random House, 1984.

Sarton, May. *The House by the Sea*. New York: Norton, 1977.

Semonella, Joan Louise Corey. "The Poetic Theater of Archibald MacLeish: A Search for Meaning." Ph.D. dissertation, University of California, Los Angeles, 1984.

Smith, Grover. "Archibald MacLeish." *American Writers: A Collection of Literary Biographies*. Vol. 3. Edited by Leonard Unger (New York: Charles Scribner's Sons, 1973), pp. 1–25.

Stegner, Wallace. *The Uneasy Chair: A Biography of Bernard DeVoto*. Garden City, N.Y.: Doubleday, 1974.

Stewart, Donald Ogden. *By a Stroke of Luck*. New York: Paddington Press, 1975.

Swanberg, W. A. *Luce and His Empire*. New York: Charles Scribner's Sons, 1972.

Vanderbilt, Kermit. *American Literature and the Academy*. Philadelphia: University of Pennsylvania Press, 1986.

Van Doren, Mark. *The Selected Letters of Mark Van Doren*. Edited by George Hendrick. Baton Rouge: Louisiana State University Press, 1987.

Van Gelder, Robert. *An Interview with Archibald MacLeish*. New York: private printing for the Typofiles, 1942.

Waggoner, Hyatt H. *American Poets from the Puritans to the Present*. Boston: Houghton Mifflin Company, 1968.

Weales, Gerald C. *American Drama since World War II*. New York: Harcourt, Brace and World, 1962.

Welles, Sumner, et al. *Laurence Duggan, 1905–1948: In Memoriam*. Stamford, Conn.: The Overbrook Press, 1949.

Winfield, Betty Houchin. *FDR and the News Media*. Urbana: University of Illinois Press, 1990.

Winkler, Allan M. *The Politics of Propaganda: The Office of War Information, 1942–1945*. New Haven: Yale University Press, 1978.

Wolff, Geoffrey. *Black Sun: The Brief Transit and Violent Eclipse of Harry Crosby*. New York: Random House, 1976.

PERIODICALS AND MISCELLANEOUS SOURCES

Atkinson, Brooks, et al. *Pembroke Magazine* 7 (1976): 3–146 (special number on MacLeish).

Barber, David. "In Search of an 'Image of Mankind': The Public Poetry and Prose of Archibald MacLeish." *American Studies* 29 (Fall 1988): 31–56.

———. "It's All in the Name: The *Einstein* of Archibald MacLeish." *American Poetry* 8 (Fall 1990): 57–69.

Benco, Nancy L. "Archibald MacLeish: The Poet Librarian," *Quarterly Journal of the Library of Congress* 33 (1976): 233–249.

Broderick, John C. "Archibald MacLeish (1892–1982)." *American Philosophical Society Yearbook* (Philadelphia: American Philosophical Society, 1983): 508–513.

Carruth, Hayden. "Homage to A. MacLeish." *Virginia Quarterly Review* 53 (Winter 1977): 146–154.

Commager, Henry Steele, et al. *Massachusetts Review* 23 (Winter 1982) (special number on MacLeish).

Cowley, Robert. "America Was Promises: An Interview with Archibald MacLeish." *American Heritage* 33 (August–September 1982): 22–32.

Cummings, Phyllis. "Reminiscence." *Friends of the Archibald MacLeish Collection Newsletter* 2 (April 1988).

DeMott, Benjamin. "The Most Compelling Acts of Love to Touch My Life." *Today's Health* 51 (February 1973): 39–40, 60–62, 64 (interview with MacLeish).

———. "Archibald MacLeish." *Writers at Work*, 5th ser. (New York: The Viking Press, 1981): 21–48.

Dilliard, Irving, et al. "Archibald MacLeish." *Nieman Reports* (Summer 1982): 41–47.

Hall, Donald. "Archibald MacLeish: On Being a Poet in the Theater." *Horizon* 2 (January 1960): 48–56.

Hoagland, Edward. "Learning to Eat Soup." *Antaeus* 61 (Autumn 1988): 222–235.

Hopkins, Frank Snowden. "Quest for Wisdom: How Nine Newspapermen Spent a Year at Harvard." *Harper's* 80 (February 1940): 278–287.

Humphries, Rolfe. "Archibald MacLeish." *Modern Monthly* 8 (June 1934): 264–270, 274.

Kazan, Elia, et al. "The Staging of a Play." *Esquire* 51 (May 1959): 144–158.

Lyons, Louis M., et al. "Harvard Meets the Press." *Nieman Reports* (Spring 1989): 4–40.

MacLeish, Martha Hillard (Mrs. Andrew). "Observations on the Development of a Child during the First Year." *Transactions of the Illinois Society for Child-Study* 3 (July 1898): 109–124.

———. "Has Not the Time Come When Education Should Prepare for Parenthood? In What Should Such Education Consist?" *Kindergarten Review* 14 (June 1904): 646–650.

MacLeish, Kenneth. "Isles on the Edge of the Sea: Scotland's Outer Hebrides." *National Geographic* 137 (May 1970): 676–691, 695–711.

MacLeish, William H. "The Silver Whistler." *Smithsonian Magazine* 13 (October 1982): 54–65.

———. "Stalking." *StoryQuarterly* 17 (1984): 85–92.

Maier, Kurt S. "A Fellowship in German Literature: Thomas Mann, Agnes Meyer, and Archibald MacLeish." *Quarterly Journal of the Library of Congress* 36 (1979): 385–400.

Mearns, David C. "The Story Up to Now." *Annual Report of the Librarian of Congress for the Fiscal Year Ending June 30, 1946* (Washington, D.C.: United States Government Printing Office, 1947), pp. 13–227.

———. "The Brush of a Comet." *Atlantic* 215 (May 1965): 90–92.

Meryman, Richard. "Archibald MacLeish: The Enlarged Life." *Yankee* 45 (January 1981): 72–77, 116–118 (interview with MacLeish).

Moyers, Bill. *Bill Moyers Journal.* "A Conversation with Archibald MacLeish." PBS television, March 7, 1976.

Newcomb, John Timberman. "Archibald MacLeish and the Poetics of Public Speech: A Critique of High Modernism." *Journal of the Midwest Modern Language Association* 23 (Spring 1990): 9–26.

"Nieman Fellowships: The 40th Anniversary." *Nieman Reports* (Autumn 1978): 36–49.

Pritchard, William H. "MacLeish Revisited." *Poetry* 141 (February 1983): 291–301.

Robinson, James, ed. "A Tribute to Archibald MacLeish: Poems and Recollections by Former Students." *Identity Magazine* 22 (1966). Foreword by William Alfred.

Tinker, Clifford Albion. "A Navy Roland and His Philosophy." *National Spectator,* April 3, 1926, pp. 20–21, 28.

Weber, Ronald. "Journalism, Writing, and American Literature." Occasional Paper no. 5, Gannett Center for Media Studies (April 1987).

Whittemore, Reed. "MacLeish and Democratic Pastoral." *Sewanee Review* 61 (October 1953): 700–709.

Wilbur, Richard. "Collected Poems." *New England Quarterly* 26 (March 1953): 117–121.

Wilson, Edmund. "The Omelet of A. MacLeish." *New Yorker,* January 14, 1939, pp. 23–24.

Zabel, Morton Dauwen. "The Poet on Capitol Hill (Part 2)." *Partisan Review* 8 (March 1941): 128–145.

Index ❖